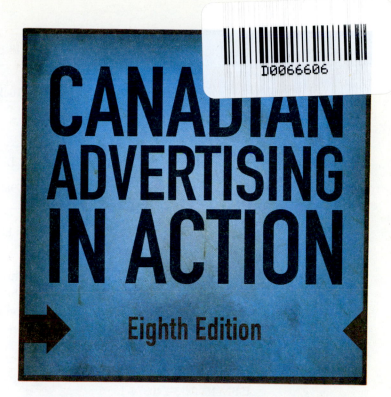

CANADIAN ADVERTISING IN ACTION

Eighth Edition

Keith J. Tuckwell

St. Lawrence College

PEARSON

Prentice Hall

Toronto

Library and Archives Canada Cataloguing in Publication

Tuckwell, Keith J. (Keith John), 1950–
  Canadian advertising in action / Keith J. Tuckwell. — 8th ed.

Includes bibliographical references and index.
ISBN 978-0-13-240574-4

1. Advertising. 2. Advertising—Canada. I. Title.

HF5823.T82 2008   659.1   C2008-900988-6

ISBN-13: 978-0-13-240574-4
ISBN-10: 0-13-240574-1

Vice President, Editorial Director: Gary Bennett
Acquisitions Editor: Don Thompson
Marketing Manager: Leigh-Anne Graham
Senior Developmental Editor: Pamela Voves
Production Editor: Cheryl Jackson
Copy Editor: Martin Tooke
Proofreaders: Audrey Dorsch, Laura Neves
Production Coordinator: Patricia Ciardullo
Compositors: Phyllis Seto/Debbie Kumpf
Photo and Permissions Researcher: Lisa Brant
Art Director: Julia Hall
Cover and Interior Designer: Geoff Agnew
Cover Image: Jack Kan

2 3 4 5   12 11 10 09

Printed and bound in the United States of America.

To Esther . . . and our children,
Marnie, Graham, and Gordon

Brief Contents

Contents

PART 3 CREATING THE MESSAGE 125

CHAPTER 5
Creative Planning Essentials 126

PART 5   COMMUNICATING THE MESSAGE: Integrated Media Choices   407

Preface

The eighth edition of *Canadian Advertising in Action* has been revised according to feedback from current and potential adopters. As part of the review process, reviewers were asked to identify the major challenges they face with students regarding textbooks. Two key challenges were identified: first, it is difficult to motivate students to read their textbooks; and second, some topics tend to be more difficult than others for students to understand.

With these challenges in mind, my objectives with the eighth edition were to

1. Present content in a clear yet engaging manner to encourage reading

2. Provide well-known examples and illustrations so that students can quickly relate theoretical marketing communications concepts to applied situations

3. Present the most up-to-date material possible, recognizing that the world of advertising and marketing communications changes at a rapid pace.

4. Retain the present balance between theory and practice and the "strategic planning" focus that was offered in previous editions.

Is This Book for Your Students?

This book is ideal for courses that focus primarily on advertising while introducing students to the broader topic of integrated marketing communications. In the context of strategic planning, the core content focuses on creating and communicating the message in all forms of media (traditional and digital). Additional content that covers sales promotion, public relations, and event marketing and sponsorships broadens the focus to integrated marketing communications.

Adopters and reviewers clearly acknowledge the **strengths and benefits** of *Canadian Advertising in Action*. The eighth edition of *Canadian Advertising in Action*

- is the only "truly Canadian" advertising textbook full of examples with which your students will readily identify.

- is written in an enjoyable and engaging reading style that students appreciate.

- presents all advertising illustrations and photographs in a vivid four-colour for-mat, with each illustration clearly demonstrating how an important marketing communications concept is applied.

- offers a strong focus on strategic planning in all creative and media chapters; the textbook is perceived as an essential resource for courses where students develop their own adverting plans.

- provides media rate card information and numerous media buying illustrations; students can apply these media buying procedures in their own media and mar-keting communications plans.

- includes a sample marketing communications plan that demonstrates the rela-tionships between various components of the marketing communications mix.

- offers three unique Canadian cases presented in the form of a "communications brief" (industry style); these cases are ideal for assignments where students must develop their own advertising or marketing communications plans.

Canadian Advertising in Action is the most up-to-date book on the subject. It includes discussion on all of the latest trends and practices and shows the important role that advertising plays in the integrated marketing communications mix. All statistical information has been updated and most of the Advertising in Action vignettes and Practice of Advertising features are new. Each case presents a different problem and will challenge your students to think creatively and analytically as they develop their own marketing communications plans.

Examine the content of this book carefully; you will find it to be a unique and con-temporary presentation of advertising and marketing communications practice. You will discover that *Canadian Advertising in Action* is clear, concise, and colourful, a potent combination that should have an impact on you and your students.

New to This Edition

This edition focuses on essential issues that are shaping contemporary communications practice. No longer can we separate traditional media from new media when develop-ing marketing communications strategies. Consumers view the media as media; they don't distinguish between one media and another. In fact, people are multi-tasking with the media when consuming it. For example, they will surf the internet while watching television or send messages on their cell phone or BlackBerry while listening to the radio. Media planners and advertising practitioners must think about the media the same way if they are to devise effective plans for their clients. Planners are concerned about how engaged people are with the media, a relatively new notion in the media world. This new way of thinking is integrated into various sections of the textbook.

The eighth edition retains its primary focus on advertising and its strong emphasis on strategic planning. The goal is to present planning strategies in the context of how plans fit together. For example, what are the connections between marketing plans, marketing communications plans, and advertising plans? What are the links between advertising plans (creative and media), sales promotion plans, and public relations plans? In keeping with past editions, all material is presented with a Canadian perspective. The concepts developed here are relevant to business, marketing, and advertising students, as well as to future managers who are embarking on a career in marketing communications.

Key Features

Among the more important and exciting changes and additions are the following:

1. There are some significant **content items** worth highlighting. Throughout the book, there is more discussion about the transition to integrated marketing communications and the need for planners of advertising and marketing communications strategies to adjust their thinking process accordingly. The rapid pace of change in the digital media arena demanded a complete overhaul of the Interactive Media chapter (Chapter 12). The new content reflects the latest trends and practices in the digital media environment.

2. Some of the **key topics** that are more prominent in the eighth edition include:
   - the use of recognizable brands and advertising campaigns to clearly demonstrate essential creative and media planning concepts
   - the need for more cooperation among agency personnel operating in different areas (old media and new media) in planning campaigns
   - the challenges of advertising planners in blending old media with new media in order to meet new client demands and expectations
   - the marketing communications strategies required for reaching unique target markets such as ethnic groups, the gay community, and individuals who are targeted directly with unique advertising messages
   - the role of marketing research in creating new advertising campaigns
   - the influence of target marketing and positioning strategies on the development of creative plans and media plans
   - enhanced discussion of digital media applications including mobile advertising opportunities, video game advertising, and the use of online social networks to deliver advertising messages
   - the concept of "engagement" as a strategic media consideration
   - demonstrating how the shift in control from companies to consumers (how and when people consume the media) has influenced media strategies and plans
   - the increasing role that public relations, branded content and product integration campaigns, and event marketing and sponsorships play in achieving organizational objectives

3. Advertising remains the primary focus of the book but, since companies are looking for **"total communications solutions,"** how advertising interacts with the various components of the integrated marketing communications mix must also remain an important area of study. The book has been restructured slightly so that Chapters 7 through 12 (all media chapters) are included in Part 4—Communicating the Message: Planning Message Placement. All forms of media are given equal consideration in resolving business problems. Integrated marketing communications alternatives are discussed in Chapter 13 (Sales Promotion) and Chapter 14 (Public Relations and Event Marketing and Sponsorships).

4. Of the 23 **Advertising in Action** vignettes, 17 are new. Those that remain from the last edition have been updated. These vignettes reflect newsworthy stories about advertisers or agencies and embrace a cross-section of companies and industries.

Among the featured organizations and brands are the United Way, Schick, A&W, Scotiabank, RBC Financial, Canadian Tire, Porsche, Nike, American Express, Harley-Davidson, Tim Hortons, and Mazda.

5. In the sections titled **The Practice of Advertising**, which follow each major section of the text, new illustrations have been added. Each of these illustrations demonstrates the application of advertising or planning concepts relevant to that part of the text. For example, the illustration at the end of **Part 1** discusses the controversy that surrounds client and agency demands and expectations when an account is in review. The illustration that follows **Part 2** shows how Wal-Mart employed marketing research to identify three core groups of customers to focus on. The illustration that follows **Part 3** profiles two successful ad campaigns, one for Volkswagen that is based on fear appeals and the other for Dove which is based on a new definition of beauty. Following **Part 4** are three illustrations of effective media campaigns, each of which employs a different medium to achieve organizational objectives.

6. **Appendix 1** includes three **new cases** that are presented to the students as "communications briefs." Each brief poses a problem and challenge that involves developing an advertising plan or marketing communications plan. The companies featured in the cases are Cadbury Schweppes Accelerade, Saturn VUE Green Line, and Mr. Lube. Each case has been designed so that a complete solution or part solution can be expected; for example, if the case calls for a complete advertising plan, but time does not permit that, then only a creative plan or media plan could be the expectation for the assignment.

7. **Appendix II** includes an updated **marketing communications plan** for the Schick Quattro razor. It neatly shows how various components of marketing communications are integrated together. Advertising plays a key role in this plan.

8. One of my personal goals is to ensure **clarity of presentation** and better flow from chapter to chapter and section to section. Therefore, wherever possible, an attempt was made to streamline material. As indicated above, locating all media chapters in on part of the textbook has resulted in five primary sections, all of which are clearly distinguishable and serve specific purposes. Refer to the "brief" table of contents for an overview of the book's structure. Finally, some chapter material was re-sequenced where necessary. Without a doubt these changes have produced a better flow to the material. Reviewers were quite satisfied with these changes and very happy with all of the new content throughout.

9. The direction for this book clearly remains on **communications processes** and **strategic planning principles** that should apply to any and all industries. The examples and plans embrace business-to-consumer situations, business-to-business situations, product situations, and service situations. The principles of advertising planning and marketing communications planning are adaptable to any business or marketing problem.

10. **New visual illustrations** give the eighth edition a colourful, fresh look. New ads from Procter & Gamble, Nestle, Cadbury Beverages, Mazda, Frito-Lay, Schick, Pfizer, Bell, Pepsi-Cola, Shell, Wrigley's, Honda, Gillette, Dove, Kraft, Ontario Dairy Farmers, Porsche, Shell Oil, Audi, and many others aptly demonstrate important advertising and marketing communications concepts. Presented in colour, all of the figures are visually striking!

The new edition retains important elements of the previous editions. The text is presented in a **practical, student-oriented style** and provides good **balance between theory and practice**. It is written from a Canadian perspective while considering the influences on communications from all over the world. All media information and data are Canadian—an important consideration for students who someday could be employed in the Canadian communications industry.

Keith Tuckwell

Pedagogy

- *Learning objectives* Each chapter starts with a list of learning objectives directly related to the key concepts presented in the chapter.

- *Advertisements, figures, charts, and graphs* Throughout each chapter, key concepts and applications are illustrated with strong visual material. Sample advertisements augment the Canadian perspective and demonstrate key aspects of communications strategy and execution.

- *Key terms* Key terms are highlighted within the text and defined in the glossary at the end of the text.

- *Weblinks* Helpful internet sites are identified throughout the text and are easily identifiable by the Weblinks icon shown here in the margin.

- *Review questions and discussion questions* Both sets of questions allow students to review material and apply concepts learned in the chapter.

- *Appendix I: Case Studies* A unique set of three case studies for some well-known companies and brands will challenge students to develop appropriate plans and solutions for specific marketing problems.

- *Appendix II: Marketing Communications Plan – Schick Quattro* An extremely useful model for reviewing the format of marketing communications plans, it shows how the various models presented in the text are adapted to a real planning situation and how various marketing communications components are integrated into one plan.

- *Appendix III: Advertising Regulations and Legislation* This section provides a useful reference tool for students.

- *Appendix IV: Glossary* A glossary of key terms and definitions appears at the end of the textbook.

Organization

This book is organized into five sections.

PART 1—ADVERTISING AND MARKETING COMMUNICATIONS TODAY

The initial section presents an overview of today's advertising industry and the organizations that comprise it. The relationships between agencies and clients are explored along with some of the controversial issues facing the industry. The relationship of advertising with other components of the integrated marketing communications mix is explored.

PART 2—MARKETING COMMUNICATIONS PLANNING

The first chapter in this section presents key topics related to consumer behaviour, market segmentation and identification of target markets, and market positioning strategies. Knowledge of these topics provides essential input for strategic planning. The second chapter examines the relationships between corporate planning, marketing planning, and marketing communications planning, illustrating how each type of plan contributes to achieving organizational objectives.

PART 3—CREATING THE MESSAGE

A detailed discussion of creative planning is presented in this section. The initial chapter focuses on the creative development process by examining the content of a creative brief. The roles of creative objectives and creative strategies are discussed in detail along with research techniques and creative evaluation processes. The next chapter focuses on creative execution and presents various alternatives regarding design, layout, and production of advertising.

PART 4—COMMUNICATING THE MESSAGE: PLANNING MESSAGE PLACEMENT

Chapter 7, the initial chapter in this section, is devoted to media planning and gives consideration to the development of media budgets, media objectives, strategies, and tactics. The next five chapters evaluate the use and effectiveness of the various media alternatives. The strengths and weaknesses of television, radio, magazines, newspaper, out-of-home media, and interactive media are presented along with media-buying practices for each medium.

PART 5—COMMUNICATING THE MESSAGE: INTEGRATED MEDIA CHOICES

This section focuses on media alternatives beyond the traditional mass media. In the quest to reach customers more efficiently and to entice them to buy, organizations are embracing integrated marketing opportunities that include sales promotion, public relations, and event marketing and sponsorships. The role and impact of these communications alternatives are examined in detail.

The format of chapters is consistent throughout the book. Chapters start with a list of learning objectives directly related to key concepts presented. Chapter summaries are located at the end of each chapter, along with review questions and discussion questions, which serve two purposes: to reinforce key concepts and to stimulate discussion on issues and problems confronting practitioners today. Following each major section of the text are detailed case illustrations entitled "The Practice of Advertising" which reinforce key principles from the section of the text it represents. The Appendices contain a sample marketing communications plan, a selection of laws and regulations that govern Canadian advertising, and an advertising lexicon that defines key terms.

Supplements

A comprehensive supplements package accompanies the eighth edition.

INSTRUCTOR'S RESOURCE CD-ROM

TestGen   Pearson TestGen is a special computerized test item file that enables instructors to view and edit the existing questions, add questions, generate tests, and print the tests in a variety of formats. Powerful search and sort functions make it easy to locate questions and arrange them in any order desired. TestGen also enables instructors to administer tests on a local area network, have the tests graded electronically, and have the results prepared in electronic or printed reports. The Pearson TestGen is compatible with IBM or Macintosh systems.

Instructor's Resource Manual The *Instructor's Resource Manual* contains learning objectives, chapter highlights, additional illustrations of key concepts, answers to end of chapter questions, discussion questions, and a video guide.

PowerPoint Slides The *PowerPoint Slides* include up to 25 slides per chapter with Weblinks and images and figures used in the text. They are also available for downloading from the Companion Website.

Image Library An *Image Library* provides selected full-colour ads published in the text.

CBC/PEARSON EDUCATION CANADA VIDEO LIBRARY (DVD AND VHS FORMAT)

A new video series that includes recent segments from *Undercurrents*, *Venture*, and *Marketplace*, all CBC shows, is available with the eighth edition. The video cases and details of how to include the videos in class discussion are included in the Instructor's Resource Manual. Each video portrays an important element of marketing communications discussed in the textbook. Each case is described briefly and a short series of questions is included to stimulate discussion.

COMPANION WEBSITE

The Companion Website at **www.pearsoned.ca/tuckwell** is a handy reference for students. The site includes practice questions, experiential exercises, weblinks to related sites, CBC videos, and more. Visit the site for a learning experience!

TELEVISION BUREAU OF CANADA BESSIES

A reel of award-winning commercials from the Bessies Awards 2006 and 2007 is available to instructors using this edition of *Canadian Advertising in Action*.

   The Television Bureau of Canada annually recognizes excellence in Canadian television advertising with the Bessies Awards program. The commercials that are included with *Canadian Advertising in Action* feature the best in recent advertising from Canadian companies for Canadian audiences. Please contact your Pearson Education Canada sales representative for details. These videos are subject to availability. For further information about The Bessies or to inquire about the Television Bureau of Canada's library of nearly 30 000 commercials, please contact The Television Bureau of Canada, 160 Bloor Street East, Suite 1005, Toronto, Ontario, M4W 1B9; telephone (416) 923-8813; or visit their website at www.tvb.ca.

Acknowledgments

Many organizations and individuals have contributed to the development of the sixth edition of this text. I would like to sincerely thank the following organizations for their special co-operation and contribution:

Absolut, V&S Vin & Spirit AB
AIM Trimark
Audi Canada
BBM Canada
Bell Canada
Brunico Communications Ltd.
Cadbury Beverages Canada Inc.
Canadian Business
Canadian Geographic
Canadian Marketing Association
Canadian Media Director's Council
 Media Digest
CBS Outdoor
Choice Hotels
CKCO Television
Coca-Cola Ltd.
Cornerstone Canada
Crain Communications, Inc.
Dairy Farmers of Canada
Delta Hotels
Diesel
eMarketer
Environics Analytics
Facebook
Frito-Lay, Inc.
General Mills
Globe and Mail
Government of Prince Edward Island
Harley Davidson
Honda Canada Inc.
Inniskillin Wines, Niagara-on-the-Lake
InterContinental Hotels
Jaguar Canada
KAO Brands Canada, Inc.
Marketing magazine
Mazda Canada
Melitta Canada
Mitsubishi Canada
Molson Canada
Moores Clothing for Men

National Post Company, a CanWest
 Partnership
Nestlé Canada
New Brunswick Department of Tourism
 and Parks
Nike Canada
Nissan Canada, Inc.
Olympus, Imaging America Inc.
Ottawa Citizen.com
Pepsi-QTG Canada
Pfizer Consumer Healthcare Division
Philips Medicals
Procter & Gamble Co.
Reebok
Remtulla Euro RSCG Advertising
Resolve Corporation
RETHINK
Rogers Media Inc.
save.ca
Sears Canada Inc.
Sony of Canada Ltd.
Statistics Canada
Suncor Energy Inc.
Television Bureau of Canada
The Clorox Company of
 Canada Ltd.
The Dial Corporation
The Glad Products Company
The Holmes Group
The Salvation Army
3M Canada
Toyota Canada Inc
TSN
Unilever Canada Inc.
United Way of Greater Toronto
VISA Canada
Volkswagen Canada Inc.
WD-40 Products (Canada) Ltd.
Welch Foods Inc.
Yahoo! Inc.

For undertaking the task of reviewing the textbook at various stages of development, and for the time and energy they put into the review process, I would like to thank

Joseph Amodeo, Sheridan College
Terri Champion, Niagara College
Christina Clements, Humber College
Bill Corcoran, Grande Prairie Regional College
Kim Donaldson, Cambrian College of Applied Arts and Technology
Dwight Dyson, Centennial College
Madeleine Hardin, University College of the Fraser Valley
Marina Jaffey, Camosun College
Judith Nash, Southern Alberta Institute of Technology
Deborah Reynor, Sir Wilfrid Laurier University
Janice Shearer, Mohawk College
Ron D. Smith, Ryerson University

From Pearson Education Canada I would like to sincerely thank Don Thompson, Acquisitions Editor; Pamela Voves, Senior Developmental Editor; Cheryl Jackson, Production Editor; Martin Tooke, Copy Editor; Audrey Dorsch and Laura Neves, Proofreaders; Lisa Brant, Photo and Permissions Researcher; Patricia Ciardullo, Senior Production Coordinator; Debbie Kumpf, Senior Composition Specialist; and Geoff Agnew, Designer. As always, I would like to thank my family for their support over the past year. Another book is complete. To Marnie, Graham, and Gord . . . thank you! As always, a very special thank you to my wife, Esther.

A Great Way to Learn and Instruct Online

The Pearson Education Canada Companion Website is easy to navigate and is organized to correspond to the chapters in this textbook. Whether you are a student in the classroom or a distance learner you will discover helpful resources for in-depth study and research that empower you in your quest for greater knowledge and maximize your potential for success in the course.

[www.pearsoned.ca/tuckwell]
Enter

PEARSON
Prentice Hall

Jump to...   http://www.pearsoned.ca/tuckwell   Home   Search   Help   Profile   Companion Website

Home >

Companion Website

Canadian Advertising in Action, Eighth Edition, by Keith J. Tuckwell

Student Resources

The modules in this section provide students with tools for learning course material. These modules include:

- Learning Objectives
- Application Exercises
- Internet Exercises
- Web Destinations
- PowerPoint Presentations
- Quizzes
- Glossary

In the quiz modules, students can send answers to the grader and receive instant feedback on their progress through the Results Reporter. Coaching comments and references to the textbook may be available to ensure that students take advantage of all available resources to enhance their learning experience.

General Resources

The modules in this section provide students with material for further research. These modules include:

- CBC video cases
- Video clips of the 2006 and 2007 Bessies
- Canadian advertising trends and strategies
- Career Resources

Instructor Resources

The modules in this section provide instructors with additional teaching tools. Downloadable PowerPoint® Presentations and an Instructor's Manual are just some of the materials that may be available in this section. Where appropriate, this section will be password protected.

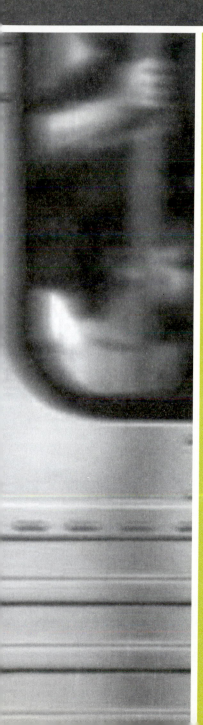

PART **1** Advertising and Marketing Communications Today

Part 1 focuses primarily on advertising and its role within the integrated marketing communications mix.

Chapter 1 examines the role of advertising and its relationship to other marketing and marketing communications activity, discussing the forms of advertising, the elements of integrated marketing communications, the factors conducive to investing in advertising, and some of the key issues that advertising planners and practitioners face today.

Chapter 2 introduces the key organizations comprising the marketing communications industry, describing the roles and responsibilities of client organizations and communications companies in planning and implementing marketing communications programs.

CHAPTER 1

Advertising in a Marketing Communications Environment

Learning Objectives

After studying this chapter, you will be able to

1. Assess the role of advertising and its relationship to marketing and other elements of marketing communications

2. Identify distinctions among the various forms of advertising

3. Identify and define the seven components of integrated marketing communications

4. Explain the conditions that are necessary for advertising to be effective

5. Identify the basic social and business issues confronting the marketing communications industry in Canada

6. Describe the role that laws and regulations play in guiding marketing communications programs in Canada

The Importance of Advertising

Advertising is undoubtedly the most visible form of marketing and marketing communications today, and it is an industry that is continuously evolving due to rapid changes in technology. It will continue to be an exciting and dynamic career field for students. The new digital media era has opened up career opportunities for young, digitally savvy people, and tradition-bound agencies now require the media insights of young people who are using the new media.

Advertising is all around us, and we as consumers underestimate the influence it has on us. Have you ever really thought about the influence that advertising has on you? Consciously or subconsciously, advertising messages reach us each day because we spend so much time with a wide variety of media. Canadians 12 years and older spend 22 percent of their time watching TV, 19 percent listening to the radio, and 16 percent surfing the internet. The balance of their media time is distributed between video games (4 percent), watching DVDs and videos (6 percent), reading (15 percent), and listening to music CDs and MP3s (19 percent).[1] These statistics indicate that media plays an important role in our lives, and, if we are exposed to the media, we are also exposed to advertising messages.

Ads also appear on outdoor posters, shopping carts, in movie theatres, and in sports stadiums. The list could go on and on, but by now you can readily see the potential influence of advertising. Advertising in Canada is big business! In fact, in 2006 the amount spent on advertising was estimated to be C\$12.6 billion, a 4.5-percent increase over 2004. Television advertising, with 24 percent of net advertising revenues (\$3.2 billion), accounts for the largest portion of advertising among the mass media in Canada. Daily newspapers follow with \$2.6 billion when all sources of revenue are included (display, local, and classified advertising).[2] Currently, online advertising is the fastest-growing medium, accounting for \$1.0 billion in revenue. Advertisers are following consumers' eyeballs and shifting their dollars away from television, newspapers, and radio, and toward the internet. For additional details refer to Figure 1.1.

The largest advertising categories in Canada include telecommunications companies and broadcasters, retail stores, packaged goods, and automotive companies. Among the largest advertisers are Procter & Gamble, General Motors, Rogers Communications, the Government of Canada, BCE Corporation, Ford Motor Company, and Telus.[3]

3

FIGURE **1.1**

Net advertising revenues by medium (Canada—millions of dollars)

Medium	2006	% of Total
Television	3240	23.7
Newspaper	2688	19.7
Radio	1388	10.1
General magazines	682	5.0
Out-of-Home	370	2.7
Catalogue/Direct Mail	1608	11.8
Internet	1010	7.4
Yellow pages	1264	9.2
Miscellaneous	1422	10.4

Medium	Sub-Division	Dollars 2006
Television	National Spot	1310
	Local Spot	392
	Network	633
	Specialty Channel	882
	Infomercial	24
Total Television		**3240**
Newspaper	National	617
	Local	1186
	Classified	885
Total Newspaper		**2688**

Source: TVB Canada, www.tvb.ca.

Advertising plays a major role in achieving brand and company business objectives by helping to attract new customers and by retaining current customers. The very nature of advertising, as seen on television or the internet, heard on radio, and read in magazines and newspapers, builds brand awareness and interest and helps form customers' opinions about a brand or company. The nature of contemporary advertising is now more targeted based on database management and interactive marketing techniques. New opportunities tend to be more micro-based (e.g., direct-response techniques, internet communications, and mobile communications) than macro-based (mass advertising on television and in newspapers and magazines), but, nonetheless, the purpose is the same—to help a brand or company grow. The challenge for advertisers is how to balance old media with new media in a rapidly changing media environment.

An Ipsos Reid research study helps substantiate the importance of advertising. The study shows that a positive corporate image is likely to help ensure that a specific brand ends up on the consumer's list of products to consider. In fact, 85 percent of adults surveyed believed that a positive corporate image affects their purchase choices.[4] This data supports the maxim, "People do business with companies they like." Essentially, a company's advertising, along with other forms of marketing communications, reflect everything that a company stands for and provides an umbrella under which all products and services carried by the company will benefit. It is designed to transform consumers' attitudes.

Ipsos Reid
www.ipsos.ca/reid

THE ROLE OF ADVERTISING

Advertising is best defined in terms of its purpose. It is a paid form of marketing communication through the media that is designed to influence the thought patterns and purchase behaviour of a target audience. While advertising can accomplish specific tasks, such as increasing the public's awareness of a product or service or inducing trial purchase through a promotion incentive, its primary role is to influence the behaviour of a target market (or target audience) in such a way that members of the target market view the product, service, or idea favourably. Once consumers develop a favourable attitude toward a specific service or brand of product, advertising attempts to motivate them to purchase that service or brand of product. Advertising can be both an informative and a persuasive form of communication.

Advertising

role: to influence the behaviour of a target market

↳ motivate the purchase

For some specific insight into the important role advertising plays in building and protecting a brand's position see the Advertising in Action vignette **Scott Paper's Big Challenge**.

ADVERTISING IN ACTION

Scott Paper's Big Challenge

Scott Paper recently faced one of the most difficult challenges in marketing. A licensing agreement with Kimberly-Clark expired, and Scott Paper lost the rights to some very popular brand names in Canada. The company had to re-brand these products under new names.

The marketing challenge for Scott Paper was to wean their customers off of one brand name and establish their loyalty to a new brand name. The brands in question were ScotTowel, renamed SpongeTowel, and Cottonelle bathroom tissue, renamed Cashmere. The deadline for the transition was June 2007. After the deadline passed, Kimberly-Clarke could reintroduce the old brands into Canada.

The SpongeTowel transition began with an advertising campaign in 2005. And what a challenge the process was, when one considers the brand equity of names like ScotTowel and Cottonelle. New ads for Cashmere used a "scorch and burn" approach. The ads stated "Cashmere is softer than cotton." Laying claim to that point would give SpongeTowels some competitive advantage in the customer's mind should Kimberly-Clark decide to re-enter the market with Cottonelle.

To enhance their softness positioning Scott made some product changes to SpongeTowels—they are now stronger and thicker. The challenge from an advertising point of view was to make consumers aware of the changes and make them believe the change in name was happening for the better, that the product was being improved and would perform better than the product they had always been buying. Scott knows that there is an emotional connection between consumers and brands and as a result not all consumers will make the leap to the new brand.

Placing the ads in the right media was another challenge. With so much fragmentation on television (consumers have access to so many channels) the intended target (primarily women) was difficult to reach. Also, with so many brands available in retail stores, consumers could turn to other brands they are more familiar with rather than the re-branded Scott paper products. Ultimately a combination of television and print ads communicated the message.

Stephen Blythe, director of marketing at Scott Paper, summed things up this way: "Our job is to make sure that through product changes, through our advertising, our marketing, and other communications, we can convince people that there is no need to be concerned about the transition. The products are better!" To achieve this task the advertising message must have a positive impact on consumers. That impact has yet to be determined.

Source: Adapted from Gigi Suhanic, "Taking on a new roll," *Financial Post*, September 16, 2005, p. FP7.

adv. success →measures by sales

not a strict relationship adv / sales

Very often a company measures the success of an advertising campaign strictly in terms of a product's sales, but such measurement can be misleading. There is no direct relationship between advertising and sales. A major problem with linking sales directly to advertising is that other variables, not just advertising, influence the consumer's decision-making process. Advertising does not operate in a vacuum; it is simply one component of the process—a subset of marketing and a complementary element of other integrated marketing communications activity.

Marketing decisions regarding matters such as product, price, distribution, sales promotion, personal selling, and event marketing all combine to have an effect on sales. As well, a host of external influences well beyond the control of the organization may influence a purchase. For example, rising fuel prices in recent years caused people to gravitate toward smaller cars. Advertising for smaller cars did not play a role in this trend. Therefore, it is neither reasonable nor practical to isolate one variable, such as advertising, and hold it responsible when sales rise or decline. It is the package of marketing and marketing communications variables that helps drive sales. Figure 1.2 reviews the position of advertising in the marketing and marketing communications process.

ADVERTISING AND INTEGRATED MARKETING COMMUNICATIONS

The nature of communications generally, and advertising specifically, continues to change. In fact, the combination of changes in consumer behaviour and new media technologies is changing the way people receive advertising messages. No longer can advertising be considered a separate entity. Instead, advertising campaigns must be designed in the context of a bigger picture, a picture that embraces all forms of marketing communications, a picture where each form of communication plays a role in achieving the overall objectives of the organization.

Today, more and more companies are approaching communications as a complete package, and that package is referred to as integrated marketing communications. **Integrated marketing communications (IMC)** involves the coordination of all forms of marketing communications into a unified program that maximizes the impact upon

FIGURE 1.2 ◀

Advertising: its position in the marketing and marketing communications process

Advertising is only one component of marketing communications activities.

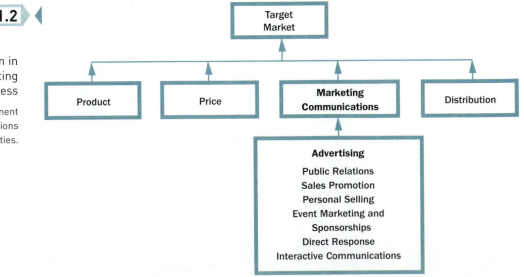

consumers and other types of customers. It embraces many unique yet complementary forms of communication: media advertising (the primary focus of this textbook), direct-response communications, interactive communications, sales promotions, public relations, event marketing and sponsorships, and personal selling. The goal of integrated marketing communications is to coordinate the various components of the marketing communications mix so that all of the components work together to achieve common objectives.

The thrust toward integrated marketing communications has forced traditional advertising agencies to rethink their roles and relationships with clients. Whereas once they were solely responsible for advertising, they are now responsible for providing input into any aspect of the marketing communications mix, or they must work more closely with communications specialists in other fields who provide the necessary expertise. Many traditional advertising agencies have been transformed into marketing communications companies.

Multi-tasking consumers and new technologies have forced marketing organizations to view communications in new ways. Reaching consumers in traditional media such as television, radio, magazines, and newspapers is no longer the only way, or the best way. Based solely on reach (some 22 million Canadians are online as of July 2006), and time spent with the medium (an average of 12.8 hours per week per person), the internet is now the number-three medium in Canada behind television and radio. In comparison, adults 18-plus spend 25 hours per week watching television and 20 hours a week listening to the radio.[5]

Changes in consumer behaviour related to media consumption dictate that a media plan must include a strong internet presence. Mobile consumers, busy consumers, and young consumers want information on demand. Consumers can now download television programming to their computers and view their favourite shows whenever they want to. Wise media planners adapt accordingly and recommend to clients that media dollars follow consumers' eyeballs. Consequently, media dollars are being shifted away from television and radio and toward digital media such as the internet and mobile communications devices. Social networking sites such as MySpace and YouTube, which contain user-generated content, are becoming new outlets for advertising as well.

The process of developing an advertising and marketing communications plan starts with a thorough analysis of the target market, market conditions, and competitors. With regard to the target market, essential information is gathered on media consumption patterns, the relevance of a company's message to customers, and contexts in which customers are most receptive to messages. The information is accumulated in a database that includes demographic and psychographic information. Armed with such information, the organization and its agency can devise a marketing communications strategy to reach customers effectively and efficiently.

One significant change in planning has occurred. Whereas the creative component (message) of the plan once dominated client–agency discussion, in the new order, the media take precedence. With so many new media alternatives available, and consumers constantly changing their media consumption patterns, media planning has moved squarely into the spotlight. As Geoffrey Roche, a partner at the advertising agency Lowe Roche, says, "In today's environment you have to flip the planning model; you figure out how to engage the consumer and then work on the media and creative."[6]

Prior to examining advertising in detail, let's briefly explain the other components of the marketing communications mix. The marketing communications mix comprises seven distinct elements: advertising, public relations, sales promotion, personal selling,

MySpace
www.myspace.com

event marketing and sponsorships, direct-response communications, and interactive communications. Refer to Figure 1.3 for an illustration of the components of the marketing communications mix.

PUBLIC RELATIONS **Public relations** includes a variety of activities that an organization undertakes to influence the attitudes, opinions, and behaviours of interest groups toward an organization. For example, a company might issue press releases announcing the launch of a new product. The release would include all of the virtues of the product and the way it will be advertised. The objective is to generate free publicity through the media (e.g., stories about the product will appear on newscasts or in newspapers). These positive news reports make the product or company credible in the eyes of the public.

SALES PROMOTION **Sales promotion** is an activity that encourages an immediate response from consumers and distributors of a product or service. On the consumer side, strategies such as coupons, cash refunds, and contests are offered by manufacturers to encourage buying activity. Among distributors, a company will offer a variety of price discounts to encourage volume buying or seasonal buying, or to encourage merchandising activity in retail stores. Such strategies are frequently implemented in conjunction with an advertising campaign. Refer to Figure 1.4 for an illustration.

PERSONAL SELLING **Personal selling** is a personalized form of communication that involves a seller presenting the features and benefits of a product or service to a buyer for the purpose of making a sale. To illustrate the importance of personal selling, consider how a new product such as Tide to Go (an instant stain remover) or Minute Maid

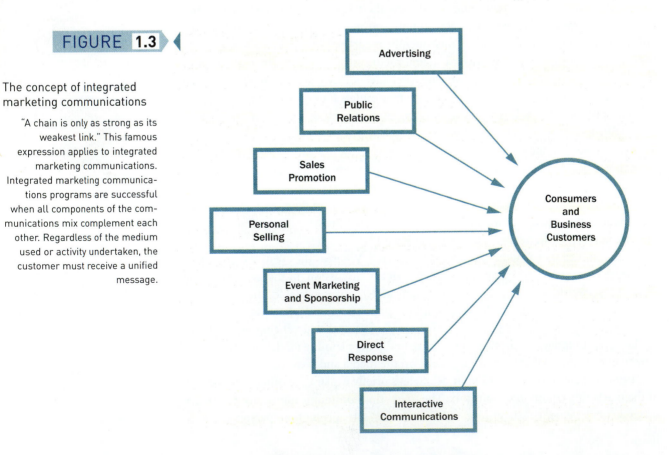

FIGURE 1.3

The concept of integrated marketing communications

"A chain is only as strong as its weakest link." This famous expression applies to integrated marketing communications. Integrated marketing communications programs are successful when all components of the communications mix complement each other. Regardless of the medium used or activity undertaken, the customer must receive a unified message.

FIGURE 1.4

Gillette combines a coupon offer and contest in one promotion to encourage immediate purchase

Simply Orange (100-percent orange juice in a carafe-shaped bottle) arrives on the shelf at your local supermarket. The sales representative for these new products would have to present the merits of these brands to a buyer at the supermarket's head office. If the buyer doesn't accept the offer that is put forth (e.g., if the quality of the sales promotion and price discounts are unacceptable), these products will not be available in the supermarket, even though they may be supported with an introductory advertising campaign that creates brand awareness. The job of personal selling is to secure widespread distribution of the product, one retail account at a time.

EVENT MARKETING AND SPONSORSHIP   **Event marketing and sponsorship**— planning, organizing, and marketing an event, or simply providing sponsorship money to support an event—is a growth area of marketing communications. Similar to public relations, participation in a major event (e.g., the Tim Hortons Men's Canadian Curling Championship) often yields favourable news coverage and publicity for the sponsor. While the direct benefits of event participation are difficult to measure, potential customers may feel better about the sponsor, knowing that it is participating in something the customer is interested in. Event marketing opportunities embrace sports, entertainment, cultural, and cause-related events.

DIRECT-RESPONSE COMMUNICATIONS   **Direct-response communications** is a form of advertising in which messages are delivered directly to potential customers on an individual basis. Direct mail is the most common means of delivering these messages, but other forms of communication such as direct-response television, direct-response print, and telemarketing now play a more significant role. Organizations that employ **database marketing** are capable of reaching customers directly through direct-response communications. Since the activity is immediate and one-on-one, as opposed to mass advertising on television, marketing and advertising organizations know immediately how effective their direct-response strategies are.

ONLINE AND INTERACTIVE COMMUNICATIONS   The future of **online and interactive communications** is the future of marketing. A bold statement, but it is very true. Given the rapid pace of advancing communications technology, the internet has the potential to become the biggest single-source generator of revenues among all communications alternatives. In fact, one research study projects internet advertising in Canada to grow by 18 percent annually between 2005 and 2010, reaching almost $1 billion by 2010.[7] The internet is direct and interactive, and consumers are spending more and more time with it—an attractive situation for advertisers. Various advertising opportunities include banner advertising, sponsorship of websites of interest to specific target audiences, rich media messages (TV-style ads), and permission-based email.

The internet has also spawned the phenomenon known as social networks or social networking. Media planners are referring to these networks as the social media. Websites such as MySpace, YouTube, and Yahoo are examples of social networks—places where people congregate to exchange ideas about topics they are interested in. The development of appropriate advertising models for these media remains a work in progress.

Mobile communications through cell phones are also interactive in nature and offer the benefit of reaching consumers at times when purchase decisions are being made. While this medium is in its infancy in terms of advertising, the cell phone is a staple tool used by younger target audiences—another attractive situation for advertisers.

For more insight into the role of advertising and how it works with other elements of marketing communications, see the Advertising in Action vignette **Human Touch Works Wonders for United Way**.

ADVERTISING IN ACTION

Human Touch Works Wonders for United Way

How does a charitable organization raise funds in a marketplace where consumers are literally inundated with requests to give? Not long ago, with so many different organizations battling for donors, marketing tactics were becoming very aggressive and in many cases these techniques began to backfire. In general terms, the level of charitable giving was dropping in Canada. At the same time, consumers were feeling helpless about poverty and homelessness—two areas in which the United Way does a lot of work.

The United Way had been using a "testimonial" campaign for three years. It was a successful campaign but there were signs that it was wearing out. A new approach was needed. Research among consumers indicated that certain desolate images had an impact. Would a harsh campaign help or hinder the image of the United Way?

Through in-depth probing it was determined that a balance could be struck by using the equity in the visual

of a hand—a helping hand. A hand is also a part of the United Way logo. The hand would capture the United Way at its best: a human touch for those in need. In terms of advertising execution, the hand represented protection. One ad showed a homeless man being sheltered from the rain. Refer to Figure 1.5 to view this image. Another ad showed the hand as a barrier between an abusive husband and wife. Yet another hand acted as a ramp to help a young woman in a wheelchair ascend a staircase. It was a series of ads with many different images that helped make the campaign work.

The new campaign helped increase donations beyond the objectives that were set for 2004—quite an accomplishment considering the donor fatigue that prevailed at the time. Overall success depended on more than just advertising, but there were clear signals it played a key role. Awareness and recall of the campaign were the highest the United Way had ever experienced. The campaign broke through the clutter and produced excellent results!

Source: Adapted from "The hand campaign," *CASSIES: Canadian Advertising Success Stories*, a publication of the Institute of Communications and Advertising, 2005, p. 26.

The Forms of Advertising

Advertising can be divided into two broad categories: consumer advertising and business-to-business advertising. Advertising can also be described as being product-oriented, corporate-oriented, and promotional-oriented.

[handwritten margin note: 2 categories]

CONSUMER ADVERTISING

Consumer advertising refers to persuasive communications designed to elicit a purchase response from consumers. Advertising directed at consumers is subdivided into categories: national advertising, retail advertising, end-product advertising, direct-response advertising, and advocacy advertising.

[handwritten margin note: make a consumer buy (through persuasion)]

National advertising is the advertising of a trademarked product or service wherever that product or service is available. In spite of its name, national advertising is non-geographic. National advertising messages communicate a brand name, the benefits offered, and the availability of the product or service. Advertising messages for branded products such as Colgate toothpaste, Honda automobiles, Michelin tires, and Dairy Queen ice cream are all classified as national advertising.

[handwritten margin note: brand names]

As the name implies, **retail advertising** is the advertising used by a retail store to communicate store image, store sales, and the like. Usually, the retailer advertises the lines of merchandise it carries, which include generic brands, private-label brands, and national brands. The framework of retail advertising can thus be expanded to include the re-advertising of national brands. Retail advertising includes advertising by large department stores such as The Bay and Wal-Mart as well as specialty chain stores such as The Gap, Tip Top, Old Navy, Bluenotes, and Sportchek.

[handwritten margin note: retail stores (show merchandise)]

End-product advertising is the advertising done by a firm that makes part of a finished product. Advertising of this nature encourages consumers to look for this particular component when buying a final product. In the computer market, Intel was very successful with its "Intel Inside" campaign. In this campaign, consumers were encouraged to look for the Intel chip in the computers they were thinking of purchasing—they were told through advertising that it was the most powerful chip available.

[handwritten margin note: final product]

Intel Corporation
www.intel.com

Direct-response advertising involves advertising directly to consumers and bypassing traditional channels of distribution (wholesalers and retailers) in the delivery of the product. Such advertising includes infomercials that are shown on television (e.g., CD and DVD offers for music and movies), direct-mail offers, and email advertising on the internet. Ads such as these include information on how customers can order goods and services directly.

[handwritten margin note: directly to cons.]

Advocacy advertising is any public communication paid for by an identified sponsor that presents information or a point of view on a publicly recognized, controversial issue. The purpose of advocacy advertising is to influence public opinion. The United Way's campaign about helping the homeless dramatically depicts the nature of the problem while encouraging the public to find a solution. See Figure 1.5 for an illustration.

[handwritten margin note: to influence public opinion]

United Way
www.unitedway.ca

BUSINESS-TO-BUSINESS ADVERTISING

Business-to-business advertising refers to advertising directed by business and industry at business and industry. Advertising to professional groups (such as doctors, lawyers, and accountants) is an example of this form of advertising. The major types of business-to-business advertising are trade advertising, industrial advertising, service-industry advertising, and corporate advertising.

An example of advocacy
advertising

When you give to United Way, you're helping homeless people overcome the obstacles in their lives by providing things like shelter, hot meals and training programs. With United Way-funded agencies helping so many in our community, making a difference is easier than you think. Visit www.unitedway.ca

WITHOUT YOU, THERE WOULD BE NO WAY

Courtesy of the United Way of Greater Toronto.

Convince intermediaries to resell the prod.

Trade advertising is advertising done by manufacturers, and it is directed at channel members. The objective of trade advertising is to communicate a convincing message that will encourage intermediaries to carry and resell the product. Messages usually stress that the product is a success (thereby suggesting that other intermediaries have accepted the product), that the manufacturer will offer promotions to help resell the product, and that profit margins are based on average selling prices. This type of advertising reaches customers by such industry-related publications as *Canadian Grocer*, *Hardware Merchandising*, and *Food in Canada*.

Industrial advertising is advertising by industrial suppliers to industrial buyers. The decision whether to purchase capital equipment, accessory equipment, fabricated parts, and raw materials may be influenced most by personal selling. However, advertising in industrial publications or direct-response advertising can stimulate initial awareness of a product and develop sales leads. Rogers Media provides numerous publications for industrial advertisers in various specialized industries (e.g., *Heavy Construction News*, *Canadian Packaging*, *Materials Management and Distribution*, and *Design Engineering*).

industrial suppliers

Rogers
www.rogers.com

Service-industry advertising raises awareness and communicates detailed information about products and services designed for companies in the service industry. Drug manufacturers, for example, address the medical profession through a number of publications including *The Medical Post* and *Canadian Family Physician*. The legal profession is reached through *Canadian Lawyer* and *The Lawyer's Weekly*. Other professions have similar publications.

Corporate advertising focuses on the broader services of a company and is designed to convey a favourable impression of the company among its various publics (e.g., shareholders, consumers, suppliers, and business customers). It may do so by showing the strength of the people employed by the firm, by showing how the company is involved with social responsibility activities, or by simply promoting goodwill. The Pfizer ad in Figure 1.6 is an example of a corporate message. Very often the organization's public relations department is responsible for this type of advertising.

Pfizer
www.pfizer.com

[handwritten margin notes: "details about prod. designed for comp."; "to give a ⊕ impression on the company"]

PRODUCT AND PROMOTIONAL ADVERTISING

Product advertising is advertising that informs customers of the benefits of a particular brand. Most of the examples described in the previous section are product advertis-

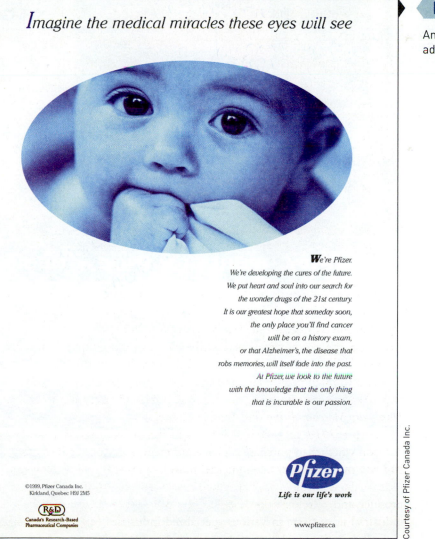

Imagine the medical miracles these eyes will see

We're Pfizer.
We're developing the cures of the future.
We put heart and soul into our search for
the wonder drugs of the 21st century.
It is our greatest hope that someday soon,
the only place you'll find cancer
will be on a history exam,
or that Alzheimer's, the disease that
robs memories, will itself fade into the past.
At Pfizer, we look to the future
with the knowledge that the only thing
that is incurable is our passion.

©1999, Pfizer Canada Inc.
Kirkland, Quebec H9J 2M5

R&D
Canada's Research-Based
Pharmaceutical Companies

www.pfizer.ca

Pfizer
Life is our life's work

Courtesy of Pfizer Canada Inc.

FIGURE 1.6

An example of corporate advertising

ing. Essentially, an advertiser communicates a feature, an attribute, and a benefit. A *feature* is something about a product (e.g., the Teflon coating on a frying pan); an *attribute* is the functional result of the feature (e.g., the pan is easy to clean); and the *benefit* clarifies how it is important to the consumer (e.g., using the new pan will give them time to spend on other things). Features, attributes, and benefits are communicated in functional or emotional terms and consumers respond to them. With reference to Figure 1.7, Sony clearly makes a promise in the headline and demonstrates that promise in the visual images.

Promotional advertising is designed to accomplish a single task—to get consumers to take action immediately. Generally, promotional advertising communicates a distinct reason why buying now is better than buying later. Automobile manufacturers, for example, are known to advertise rebate programs and low-cost financing programs. Packaged-goods companies such as Kraft and Gillette use coupons, contests, and other incentives to encourage action by consumers. Refer to Figure 1.4 for an example.

Gillette
www.gillette.com

FIGURE 1.7

A product-oriented advertisement stressing features and benefits. A strong visual reinforces the message.

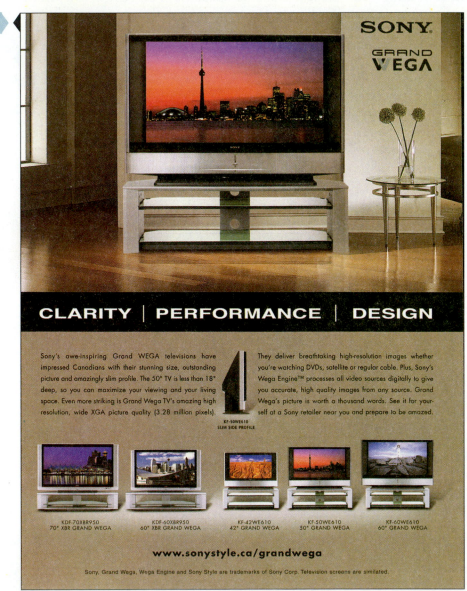

Courtesy of Sony of Canada Ltd.

Conditions Necessary for Using Advertising Effectively

For advertising and other forms of marketing communications to be effective, certain conditions must be favourable. Managers and planners must analyze certain factors and judge whether the investment in advertising will contribute to the achievement of marketing objectives. Advertising is one of the most expensive forms of marketing communications, and it is not always the right solution. Sometimes it is better to go in a different direction with communications strategies; for example, in directions that are less costly. A number of conditions are evaluated prior to making the decision to advertise.

[handwritten margin note: conditions to make the decision to advertise]

MARKET AND PRODUCT DEMAND

Assuming that customer needs have been properly identified, the first task of advertising is to stimulate demand for the product or product category. The introduction of a new product concept is quite challenging, since the marketing communications must first make customers recognize a need, then stimulate a purchase response based on that recognition. For example, when Tide to Go, an instant stain remover in a portable stick format, was launched, consumers had to be introduced to the new concept—a quick way to remove stains while you are wearing your clothes. Now there are many competing brands on the market.

If a market and product already exist, the manager will analyze the primary demand trends and selective demand trends. **Primary demand** refers to demand for the product category (product class). For example, the demand for healthier beverages such as bottled water, fruit juices, and tea, are very positive right now. Consequently, the leading brands in these product categories (e.g., Dasani, Aquafina, Ocean Spray, and Tetley) invest in advertising to help build market share.

Conversely, if primary demand is declining, investment in advertising should be reduced or even withdrawn. A company like Coca-Cola, which competes in numerous beverage market segments, faces such a situation. Coca-Cola Classic is the leading brand of soft drink in a very mature market. Consumers are drinking soft drinks less as they search for a healthier lifestyle. Coca-Cola will invest in advertising at a reduced level to protect its leadership position while concentrating more marketing resources on growing categories like bottled water (Dasani), energy drinks (Full Throttle), and fruit juices (Minute Maid).

Selective demand refers to demand for a specific product (brand) within a product category. When selective demand is positive, growing from year to year, the decision to advertise is relatively simple. For example, the iced tea segment is growing based on consumers' perceptions that tea is a healthy beverage. Brands such as Nestea Zero and Lipton Brisk are experiencing significant increases in sales (selective demand) as a result of the primary demand for the product. Both brands are investing in advertising to attract new users to their brand.

When selective demand is negative the decision to advertise is more difficult. At some point, a company must eventually decide when it will reduce or eliminate advertising support. Does a firm support brands with profit potential, or does it attempt to protect brands for which selective demand has declined? An examination of the influence of the product life cycle on advertising activity will help to resolve this question.

PRODUCT LIFE CYCLE

The stage of a brand in its product life cycle also influences decisions on advertising. A **product life cycle** is defined as the movement of a product through a series of four stages, from its introduction to its eventual withdrawal from the market. According to traditional life-cycle theory, a product starts out slowly in the introduction stage, experiences rapid sales increases in the growth stage, experiences marginal growth or decline each year as it matures, then enters the decline stage in which sales drop off at a increasing rate each year. The conditions and characteristics that are present in each stage of the life cycle are quite different. Therefore, different strategies and tactics are used in each stage.

The critical stages for advertising are the introduction and growth stages. The **introduction stage** is a period of slow sales growth as a new product idea is introduced to the market. Losses are frequently incurred due to the high initial investment required to launch a product.

Advertising objectives focus on the creation of primary demand if it is a new product category, and creating awareness for the new brand name and package in the consumer's mind. Since trial purchase is another objective, an introductory campaign will likely include promotion incentives such as the distribution of coupons or trial-size samples. Strategists believe that if these objectives are to be accomplished, the product must enter the market with a sizeable budget and a powerful message—the marketing team must do it right the first time out! A strong multimedia campaign must be implemented—at very high cost. This short-term commitment to advertising enables the brand to grow before new and competing innovations occur. Profits will be generated at a later stage of the life cycle.

The product's **growth stage** is the period of rapid consumer acceptance. It is also a period in which profits rise significantly. Several competitive brands will enter the market to get a piece of the action, which means that the original product must continue to invest aggressively in advertising to build market share. Competition is intense. A company's commitment to advertising must continue as its product strives for growth or defends its position in the marketplace. Deciding how much to spend is often difficult. It is possible that competitors with less market share but with ambitious growth plans may force another company to spend more on marketing communications than it desires to spend.

In the growth stage, marketing communications performs a dual role. There is still ample opportunity to attract new users, so creating awareness remains a priority; and, since competitors have entered the market, objectives must also focus on brand preference. A brand must clearly distinguish itself from competing brands (e.g., give customers a valid reason why they should buy their brand over another brand). By now, the target market is more clearly defined and understood, so there is an opportunity to select media that will reach the target audience more efficiently. Refer to the illustration in Figure 1.8.

In summary, the combination of awareness and preference objectives and competitive spending levels will tend to increase the size of a budget. Increased knowledge about the target market can lead to more efficient use of media and lower advertising costs. Generally speaking, however, the desire to maintain high levels of growth requires a significant investment in marketing communications. Unlike the introduction stage, however, sales are rising so rapidly that profits materialize.

The **mature stage** is characterized by a slowdown in sales growth (marginal growth and marginal decline); the product has been accepted by most of its potential buyers. Profits stabilize and begin to decline because of the expenses incurred in defending the brand's market-share position.

When a product is in the mature stage, advertising tends to give way to other forms of marketing communications. Assuming that new strategies are not implemented to

FIGURE 1.8

A print ad in a competitive product category that focuses on awareness and brand preference objectives. An incentive is offered to encourage trial purchase.

rejuvenate the product, funds formerly allocated to advertising the product may be shifted into other areas such as sales promotion and price discounting. In the mature stage, the objective is to conserve money rather than spend it. There are exceptions to every rule, however, since this is a period where the only way to grow is to steal business from the competitor(s). In Canada's soft-drink market, for example, sales are relatively flat from year to year. Consumers are switching to other beverage alternatives such as juices and bottled waters. Both Coca-Cola and Pepsi are leading brands with similar spending patterns in advertising. If one company were to reduce its investment, what might happen to its market share? With so much at risk, it is the actions of the competition that will determine how much is spent on advertising.

In maturity, a brand faces a choice. Does it adopt a defensive strategy and try to maintain market share, or does it adopt an offensive strategy and try to rejuvenate the brand? Should a defensive strategy be adopted, budgets will be established at a level that will maintain the brand's market-share position. Since maintenance of current customers is a priority, there is often greater spending on sales promotion activity than on media advertising. Promotions that encourage brand loyalty are very popular at this stage (e.g., cash refunds, contests, and premium offers) since they are designed to encourage repeat purchases and multiple purchases.

Organizations that opt to rejuvenate a brand adopt a more aggressive attitude. Strategies will be implemented to extend the product life cycle. Strategic options available include modifying or improving the product, presenting new uses for the product (and thereby increasing frequency of use), or attracting new user segments to the product. Regardless of the strategic option selected, advertising will play a key role in communicating the new direction. In the coffee market, brands such as Maxwell House and Folgers focus on package improvements to breathe new life into their mature products. Maxwell House offers the EZ-Open Fresh Seal—a sealing process that keeps unwanted air out so the product is fresher than ever before! Folgers counters with the Aroma Seal, a plastic lid that keeps coffee fresh when the product is stored. See Figure 1.9 for an illustration.

DECLINE STAGE   The **decline stage** occurs when sales begin to drop rapidly and profits erode. Products become obsolete as many consumers shift to more innovative products entering the market. Price cuts are a common marketing strategy at this stage, as competing brands attempt to protect their share in a declining market.

FIGURE 1.9

An ad campaign designed to rejuvenate a mature product: Folgers coffee

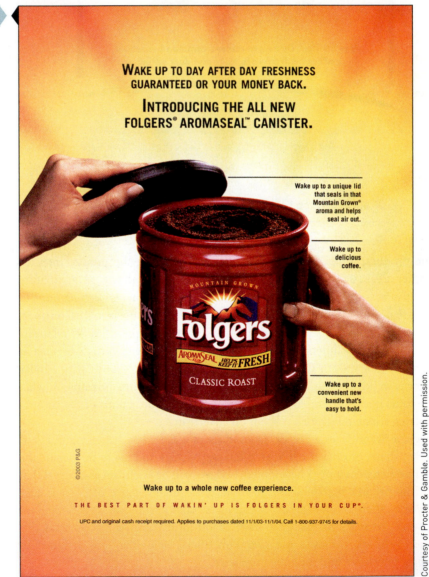

Objectives involve planning and implementing withdrawal from the market, because the costs of maintaining a product in decline are quite high. General Motors recently withdrew the Pontiac Aztek from the market after four futile years of trying to convince enough buyers to take a chance and endure the stares and taunts of fellow drivers. The radically styled, not-quite-car, not-quite-truck "crossover utility vehicle" that featured a built-in cooler and fold-out tent was heavily advertised during its life cycle but never quite caught on with the public.[8]

In the decline stage there is little sense in providing advertising support. The budget should be cut so that profit is maximized and funds are generated that can be invested in new products or growth products with greater profit potential. Some investment in advertising to help liquidate inventory may be necessary but it would only be for a short period. Car dealers, for example, would advertise to liquidate inventory in the Pontiac Aztek example described above.

COMPETITIVE ADVANTAGE

Prior to investing in marketing communications, a brand must offer something unique and desirable to a market segment—a competitive advantage. A distinctive message must be planted in the consumer's mind.

The most common way to show advantage is to demonstrate the superiority of a given product by comparing it to a similar product or by simply making significant claims about what the product will do. The claims a product makes about itself must be meaningful to consumers. Kraft Delissio frozen pizza, for example, was the first brand to market pizza with a wheat crust (an ingredient essential for healthier living). A headline in a print ad read as follows: "Introducing our new Harvest Wheat Crust. Our apologies for giving other pizzas 'crust envy.'" Refer to Figure 1.10 for an illustration. Colgate Total toothpaste implies superiority over other brands by using the phrase "Colgate Total. The #1 choice of dental professionals." The message is clear: if dentists highly recommend the brand, you should be using it!

FIGURE **1.10**

Meaningful product claims have an impact on consumers' buying intentions.

Courtesy of Dick Hemingway.

Another way of showing advantage is to communicate **product innovation**—the idea that the product is on the cutting edge of technology or research and development. Innovation is extremely important in the razor product category. When Gillette (now owned by Procter & Gamble) launched the Gillette Fusion razor, it was another step in the technology war between Gillette and Schick, maker of the four-blade Schick Quattro razor. The Fusion has five blades spaced 30 percent more closely together than Gillette's own Mach3 Turbo system. On the back of the razor is a single blade for trimming side-burns—there's breakthrough technology on the front and back! Gillette is widely known for its "best shave ever or your money back" promise.

A third opportunity to demonstrate advantage while differentiating one brand from another is to stress **hidden qualities**. A hidden quality refers to some unique feature that benefits consumers but that they cannot see, feel, or taste. It could also refer to something the product does not contain that the consumer would like to know about. A natural product like milk offers all kinds of health benefits to consumers. It makes things stronger—your bones, your teeth, and so on. Milk producers do an excellent job of communicating the hidden qualities of milk. Refer to Figure 1.11 for an illustration.

A more recent phenomenon in advertising is the progressive use of **lifestyle associations** to differentiate among products. Automobile manufacturers tend to be experts at targeting lifestyle aspirations by appealing to the emotional side of the purchase decision. Mitsubishi recently launched a campaign that resonated with young Canadian adults. Their ads show young buyers in situations they are most likely to be seen in: hanging out with their friends, listening to their music, and having a sense of community with themselves and, de facto, the car they drive in. Everyone is hip and having a blast as they drive through urban streets and well-lit tunnels. The commercials end with the phrase "Canada, meet Mitsubishi." And then, "Are you in?" The Mitsubishi marketing strategy is "spirited cars for spirited people." The advertising makes an emotional connection with potential customers and shows how the car has a role in one's life.[9] See the illustration in Figure 1.12.

COMPETITIVE ENVIRONMENT

Keeping track of what competitors are doing and how much they are investing in marketing communications is important. If, for example, a brand finds itself in a product category where competitors invest heavily in advertising (e.g., when a toothpaste brand like Arm & Hammer has to compete with Colgate and Crest), that brand may want to evaluate activities that are less costly. The size of a brand in terms of market share and the financial resources that are available based on market share would suggest that less expensive alternatives, such as sales promotion or price discounting, would make more sense. Brand leaders tend to protect their turf by maintaining significant advertising budgets. Brands that rank further down the list need to evaluate more efficient spending alternatives to protect their market share.

PRODUCT QUALITY

Simply stated, a product must live up to the promise advertising makes. Advertising messages focus on the unique selling points of the product and the benefits the customer will derive from them. Getting the customer to try a product once, at great expense, only to be disappointed in the quality or whatever the primary benefit was to be (e.g., performance or durability) is a waste of money. It is imperative that the brand meet consumer expectations (deliver as promised) so that repeat purchases occur in the longer term. Inconsistent quality, for whatever reason, is inconsistent with the customer relationship management programs that many companies are now implementing.

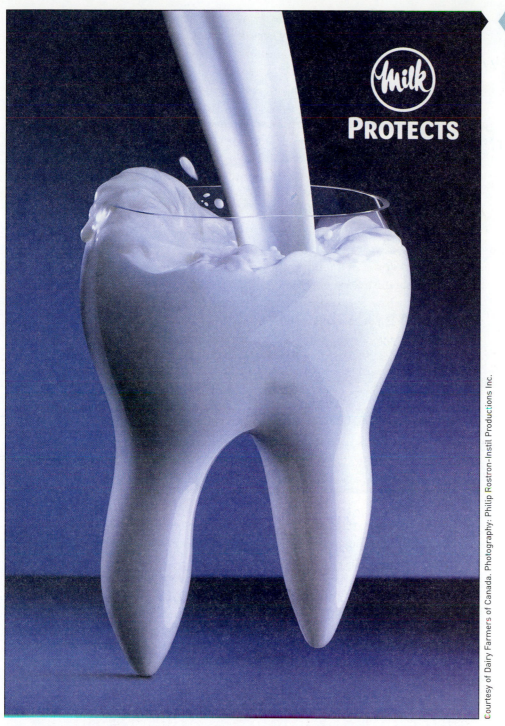

Courtesy of Dairy Farmers of Canada. Photography: Philip Rostron–Instil Productions Inc.

FIGURE 1.11

A strong visual image aptly communicates a hidden quality of milk.

MANAGEMENT COMMITMENT

How management perceives the value of advertising is also important. A management group that possesses a short-term view (e.g., advertising is an expense item on a profit-and-loss statement) of how advertising will benefit the company will not be committed to a plan that requires a long period of time to achieve the desired results. When such a view persists, budget cuts are likely to occur during the course of a year, and since advertising spending is a highly visible item on the profit-and-loss statement, it is one of the first items reviewed in a profit-squeeze situation. Such action greatly disrupts an

FIGURE 1.12

An advertising campaign that targets the lifestyle aspirations of young Canadians

Courtesy of Mitsubishi Canada.

advertising plan, since stated objectives must be reassessed in the wake of reduced financial support. In the long term, cutbacks to the advertising budget have harmful effects on brand development in the marketplace.

Conversely, senior management who view advertising and other forms of marketing communications as a long-term investment are usually more willing to commit funds to a complete campaign. Obviously, such an attitude provides a preferable operating environment for managers responsible for developing advertising plans, and to external organizations that prepare and implement various components of a marketing communications plan.

Issues in Contemporary Advertising

The advertising industry is grappling with change due to technological advancements and consumers who are now more mobile than ever. Consumers are interacting with the various media in different ways, and as a result, advertising planners must look at new and different ways of reaching people. People use different media at different times of the day and at different stages of their lives. Further, new media alternatives are not just the domain of younger generations. All age groups from youth through baby boomers are quickly migrating toward digital media usage. Advertisers and their agencies must react accordingly. This section examines some of the key issues faced by today's practitioners.

TRANSITION TO INTEGRATED MARKETING COMMUNICATIONS

Organizations today are searching for complete solutions for their communications needs. In the past it was common for various plans to be developed separately by distinct organizations that specialized in certain areas and operated independently. As indicated earlier, the environment has changed. Advertisers are looking at different ways of delivering messages, and they are experimenting with new opportunities, such as product placements and branded content (placing products in TV shows or embedding product messages into the scripts of TV shows).

Consumer behaviour has also changed. Consumers today are less reliant on television and newspapers and more reliant on computers and mobile digital technology for receiving news and commercial messages. Such switches in allegiance force advertisers to evaluate different media choices. The goal of communications now is to deliver the same message through a variety of media in order to effectively reach and influence the target audience. Familiar media such as television, newspapers, magazines, and direct mail will continue to play a key role in the media mix, while new media such as the internet, cell phones, and MP3 players will continue to make inroads. No single media delivery channel will drive the marketing industry. Truly there is a merger going on between traditional and digital media that all organizations will eventually have to adapt to. Breaking through the clutter of advertising is an increasingly more daunting prospect for advertisers.

ADAPTING TO NEW TECHNOLOGIES

Marketing and advertising managers must constantly monitor changes that influence advertising strategies. On the technology side, the increasing penetration of satellite dishes, cable television, and the availability of so many stations have changed the way people view television. Audiences will continue to be chopped into increasingly smaller sizes, a phenomenon referred to as **audience fragmentation** or simply **fragmentation**. For planners who believe in audience purity instead of audience size, this is good news. For advertisers wanting to reach a large audience efficiently, this is bad news.[10]

While extremists are forecasting the end of the 30-second television commercial, there is still a high demand for network television time. It is often the default medium for many advertisers simply because it is so visible. If the advertiser is seeking awareness, television is perceived to be the best solution! From a media perspective, the challenge is getting advertisers to continue paying as much money for ads as they have in the past, even when audience size is shrinking.

In the era of customer relationship management programs, however, such perceptions will have to change or much money will be wasted. Many advertisers have already moved to branded content, a strategy that involves placing products right in TV programs. Network hits such as *24* and *Alias* have gone as far as dedicating entire episodes to single wrap-around sponsors.[11] Other advertisers have moved portions of their budgets out of television and into more targeted media, a trend that is expected to continue.

REACTING TO AN ON-DEMAND MEDIA ENVIRONMENT

The introduction of the PVR (personal video recorder) allows programs to be recorded digitally for viewing at a later time, commercial-free. Such technology puts the value of television advertising in question. Television has been a medium in which advertisers had an assembly-line, mass-market mentality, and a one-size-fits-all strategy would work. No longer is that the case. Consumers are increasingly taking control of their television viewing by using their remote controls or PVRs.

Technological devices are transferring the balance of power from the media and the advertisers to consumers. Being able to watch television shows whenever a person likes or being able to download favourite shows (without any advertising) for a nominal fee to a computer or cell phone will force advertisers to re-evaluate how they employ television advertising. Since people no longer have to plan when and how they watch a television show, and have the capability of avoiding ad messages entirely, advertisers will have to find alternative ways of delivering their messages. Such consumer power threatens the way advertisers have done business for decades. According to Alan Rutherford, vice president of global communications for Unilever PLC, "Advertisers must now integrate advertising messages with programming content and it is the combination of content and media channels that will influence consumers."[12]

REACHING THE MOBILE AND MULTI-TASKING CONSUMER

People are now busier and more mobile than ever! They travel with their computers, Blackberries, MP3 players, and cell phones, and use these media to access information. Advertisers must take advantage of the opportunities these media offer. The rapid growth and usage of these technologies means people are viewing television less, listening to conventional radio less, and reading newspapers and magazines less. Therefore, advertising planners must resist the temptation to stay with mass-reach, mass-media campaigns and move toward selective-reach, highly targeted campaigns—a key benefit offered by the digital media.

People now surf the internet while watching television. Younger consumers send text messages to their friends while listening to music. They all talk on their cell phones and check their email while they cook or do homework. One research study showed that people somehow managed to shoehorn 31 hours of media activity into a 24-hour day because they can do two things at once. For advertisers, the challenge is getting their message across in one medium while the consumer is active at the same time in several other media. The buzzword these days is **engagement**—as in how engaged, or involved, the consumer is in a particular activity, a notion that is relatively new in the media world.[13] Placing messages at a time and place where the consumer is engaged will influence the direction of media strategy in the future.

CHANGING BUSINESS ENVIRONMENT

Other changes that must be addressed involve social and demographic trends. An aging population, smaller households, ethnic diversity, and a large and emerging "millennial" generation represent new challenges for advertisers. Advertisers have long been obsessed with attracting young targets to their products when the reality is that older age groups have much more money to spend. With both the youth market and boomer markets being so large, the target-market priorities of many companies will have to change. The new challenge is how to retain older customers while attracting new youthful customers. What lies ahead are multi-faceted message strategies aimed at multi-targeted audiences—a very difficult challenge for creative planners and media planners.

Many advertisers continue to portray Canadian households as traditional households (a white mother and father with two children) when the average household is anything but traditional. Critics of advertising claim that minority groups are not fairly represented. A sampling of recent Canadian magazines revealed the following: in *Canadian House & Home* only 2 of 37 ads with models included non-whites; in *Flare* only 10 of 86 ads featured people of colour, but in half of them they were situated among Caucasians; and in *National Post Business Magazine* only 4 of 22 ads featured minorities.[14] Such findings suggest that advertisers are not evolving with changes in Canadian society and, if they continue to follow the same path, will suffer the consequences when new groups of consumers reject them.

THE DELIVERY OF INAPPROPRIATE OR CONTROVERSIAL MESSAGES

The impact of a commercial message is always subject to review by critics of advertising. Rightly or wrongly, planned or unplanned, advertisers sometimes deliver commercial messages that spark controversy. Many advertisers tolerate the controversy as long as the campaign is delivering sales. Other advertisers bow to public pressure and remove the offending message. Key issues often focus on the use of sex, sex-role stereotyping, presenting dangerous situations in commercial messages, and misleading the public with confusing messages.

SEX IN ADVERTISING   A common complaint about advertising revolves around the use of sex to sell something. As an old saying goes, "Sex sells!" So what's the beef among members of contemporary Canadian society? Using sex appeal in an appropriate manner and for appropriate products seems natural, but gratuitous sex is something consumers shouldn't have to tolerate.

Sex Sells

An ad for the Kia Spectra was banished from the airwaves because it raised the hackles of police associations in Quebec. In the commercial, a lustful policewoman is passionately kissing a young male she has just pulled over, in the front seat of his automobile. The police cruiser is stationed behind the Kia with its lights flashing. Hearing a call from the cruiser the policewoman fixes her hair, dawns her police cap, and drives away in the cruiser. The tagline for the ad was "Life's better in a Spectra." Advertising Standards Canada agreed with the complaint and judged the ad too racy for Canadian viewing. Go figure!

An example that further dramatizes the effectiveness of using sex to market a product is Axe body spray, now the leading brand of deodorant in many countries. Axe's entire marketing strategy revolves around what's on the mind of 20-something males— sex! Visit the Axe website and see for yourself.

ex: Axe

Axe
www.axe.ca

EXTREME ADVERTISING   The strategy of depicting dangerous or disturbing situations in advertising messages has come under much scrutiny in recent years. Automakers are under the gun for showing unsafe driving practices in ads. In some cases dangerous driving practices are glamorized. A Cadillac commercial showed a male driver accelerating into a darkened tunnel (a reminder to many of how Princess Diana died). A Corvette spot clearly depicted an enraged driver racing wildly in the sports car, under the title, "A Boy's Dream." Many critics believe an ad like this helps encourage young people to get involved in risky activities such as street racing.

A television spot for Capital One (a credit card) shows a man and a woman tumbling head over heels down a rocky ski slope—without the snow. Apparently, ads like this are the ones that attract eyeballs. Such ads are designed to "turn up the volume" and basically prevent someone from fast forwarding them on the PVR. Advertisers have only a few seconds to catch the attention of today's viewers before they're gone! To many people in the advertising industry this style of ad fits with today's fads. "We have extreme sports, extreme music, extreme food and drink; ad agencies are simply trying to keep up!"[15] Is there anything wrong with that?

MISLEADING ADVERTISING   Sometimes ads can mislead the public or simply misrepresent the brand. Sometimes the public misinterprets the advertiser's message and the campaign backfires. The control of misleading advertising is the responsibility of Advertising Standards Canada. (More information about their role in the advertising industry appears later in this chapter.) The most common complaints about misleading ads concern the accuracy and clarity of the message.

To illustrate, consider a recent case. An ad for Primus Telecommunications Canada Inc. included the words "No monthly fee" in bold type to describe a long distance phone plan. At the bottom of the ad in some fine print was another statement: "A $3.95 monthly network fee applies." There was a complaint that the no-monthly-fee claim was misleading. Advertising Standards Canada agreed and stated "No monthly fee" meant there were no recurring fees or charges of any kind in connection with the advertised plan. Moreover, the disclaimer language at the bottom of the ad contradicted the more prominent aspect of the message.[16]

Primus
www.primus.ca

Laws and Regulations

The marketing communications industry in Canada is highly regulated. Regulation and control come from three primary sources: the Canadian Radio-television and Telecommunications Commission (CRTC), which governs all broadcasting laws including advertising; Advertising Standards Canada, which administers regulations based on codes of practice that are voluntarily established; and the Competition Bureau (a federal agency) through the *Competition Act*, which established laws and regulations for all marketing activity in Canada.

CANADIAN RADIO-TELEVISION AND COMMUNICATIONS COMMISSION (CRTC)

The CRTC is an independent public authority in charge of regulating and supervising Canadian broadcasting and telecommunications. It serves the public interest and is governed by the *Broadcasting Act, 1991* and the *Telecommunications Act* of 1993. The *Broadcasting Act, 1991* ensures that Canadians have access to a wide variety of high-quality Canadian programming. The *Telecommunications Act* ensures access to reliable telephone and other telecommunications services at affordable prices. Generally, the role of the CRTC is to maintain a delicate balance, in the public interest, between the cultural, social, and economic goals of the legislation on broadcasting and telecommunications.[17]

Canadian content is the cornerstone of the *Broadcasting Act*. It addresses several key issues:

- The creation and production of Canadian programs and music
- Financial support for the broadcasting system for the creation of Canadian content
- Determining how much Canadian content must be aired on radio and television
- The ratio of Canadian and non-Canadian content distributed by Canadian cable companies and satellite providers
- Canadian ownership and control of the broadcasting system

In addressing these issues, the overall mandate of the CRTC is to enforce Parliament's intent that the national broadcasting system serves a national purpose. There are numerous broadcasting and telecommunications regulations that the CRTC is also responsible for. For a complete listing of these regulations and more information about the role of the CRTC, visit the CRTC website at **www.crtc.gc.ca**.

ADVERTISING STANDARDS CANADA

Advertising Standards Canada (ASC) is the industry body committed to creating and maintaining community confidence in advertising. Its mission is to ensure the integrity and viability of advertising through industry self-regulation. ASC members include advertisers, agencies, media organizations, and suppliers to the advertising sector.

ASC operates two divisions. The Standards Division administers the industry's self-regulating code (the *Canadian Code of Advertising Standards*), handles complaints from consumers regarding advertising, and administers the industry's *Trade Dispute Procedure*. The Advertising Clearance Division previews advertisements in five categories, helping advertisers to adhere to applicable legislation, regulatory codes, and industry standards.[18]

The *Canadian Code of Advertising Standards* (the *Code*) is the principal instrument of self-regulation. The *Code* was developed to promote the professional practice of advertising and forms the basis upon which advertising is evaluated in response to consumer complaints. The *Code* is supplemented by other codes and guidelines, including gender portrayal guidelines, which are intended to help advertising practitioners develop positive images of women and men in their commercial messages. The *Code* also addresses the following concerns about advertising:

- Accuracy and clarity of messages
- Disguised advertising techniques
- Price claims
- "Bait and switch"
- Guarantees
- Comparative advertising
- Testimonials
- Professional and scientific claims
- Imitation
- Safety
- Superstitions and fears
- Advertising to children and minors
- Unacceptable depictions and portrayals

For more complete details about the role of Advertising Standards Canada, see Appendix III of this textbook and visit the ASC website at **www.adstandards.com**.

It seems that Canadian consumers are complaining more about advertising than ever before! In 2005 there were 1271 complaints about 804 different advertisements. The council upheld 58 complaints about 52 advertisements. Retail advertising attracted the most complaints by medium; television advertising attracted the most complaints (46 percent of all complaints received). Of the complaints received, more complaints were upheld under *Code* Clause 1 (Accuracy and Clarity) than under any other clause.[19]

The advertising community gets upset over such decisions. As discussed in the previous section of the chapter, advertisers are often accused of using inappropriate sexual portrayals, or showing situations that encourage people to take risks, but rarely is that their intention. Most campaigns focus on a particular target who understands more clearly the advertiser's intent. That said, a television spot that appeared during the 2007 Super Bowl showed two famished auto mechanics under the hood of a car chewing opposite ends of a Snickers bar. As they chewed towards the centre their lips ultimately met. They quickly pulled apart looking rather stunned at what had happened. It was a funny ad! Gay rights activists objected to the ad, saying Snickers went too far with the ad. Taking risks like this could lead to ill will towards Snickers. Masterfoods, maker of Snickers bars, said feedback for the ad was quite positive from their core target audience, stating, "Humour is highly subjective and though some people may [have] found the ad offensive, clearly that was not our intent."[20]

Copywriters and art directors are frustrated by such responses from the public or regulating bodies. It's no wonder there's so much dull advertising that simply blends together. Being cautioned to stay away from the creative edge is not good for the future of advertising. In the unregulated online world, user-generated content of a risky nature is quite common. The playing field doesn't seem as level as it once was.

COMPETITION BUREAU

The Competition Bureau is responsible for the administration and enforcement of the *Competition Act*, a law that governs business conduct and marketing practices in Canada. The *Competition Act* contains criminal and civil provisions to address false, misleading, and deceptive marketing practices. Among the practices that come under scrutiny are deceptive telemarketing, deceptive notices of winning prizes, and pyramid selling schemes. Other provisions prohibit representations not based on adequate and proper tests, misleading warranties and guarantees, false or misleading price representation, and untrue testimonials.

Organizations that violate these laws and regulations are subject to financial penalties and other actions. To demonstrate, Grafton-Fraser, a chain of men's clothing stores that includes George Richards Big & Tall, Grafton & Co., the Suit Exchange, and Tip Top Tailors, was recently fined $1.2 million for misquoting prices in its advertising. Apparently, how much consumers would actually save was overstated. "The importance of truth in advertising cannot be overstated," said Raymond Pierce, deputy commissioner of the Competition Bureau. "Advertisers have both a moral and legal obligation to ensure that they provide consumers with accurate information upon which to make their purchase decisions."[21] For more insight into the Competition Bureau visit their website at **www.competitionbureau.gc.ca**.

SUMMARY

Advertising is any paid form of marketing communication designed to influence the thought patterns and purchase behaviour of a target audience. The specific role of advertising is to favourably influence potential customers' responses to a product by communicating relevant information about the product, such as how the product will satisfy a need.

The nature of communications has changed. Companies now plan and implement integrated marketing communications programs that embrace strategies beyond advertising. An integrated marketing communications strategy involves the coordination of advertising with other strategies such as sales promotion, public relations, personal selling, event marketing and sponsorships, direct-response advertising, and interactive communications. All of these elements combine to achieve common objectives.

Advertising is one element of marketing communications; granted, it is the most visible and probably most costly element. Advertising is divided into two broad categories: consumer advertising and business-to-business advertising. Advertising is also described as being product-oriented, corporate-oriented, or promotional-oriented. Consumer advertising is used by companies that produce national brands and by retailers. It includes direct-response communications and advocacy advertising. Business-to-business advertising includes trade, industrial, service-industry, and corporate advertising. Corporate advertising is used to help create favourable images about a company or to promote a point of view held by a company. Product-oriented advertising communicates the unique benefits of a brand, whereas promotional advertising encourages customers to take action now (as opposed to later).

Before a company invests in advertising, a situation analysis should be conducted to determine if market conditions are favourable or unfavourable. If favourable, the investment in advertising should proceed. There must be market and product demand; the product must be at an appropriate stage in the product life cycle; the product should have a competitive advantage; the competitive environment must be conducive for investment; the product must be of adequate quality; and management must be committed to investing in communications in the long term. Finally, advertising must be integrated with other integrated marketing communications (IMC) elements to produce a coordinated and consistent message to customers.

Some of the major issues confronting the industry include the transition toward integrated marketing communications, adapting to new technologies that have created new ways to deliver messages, adapting message and media strategies to fit into an on-demand media consumption environment, figuring out ways of reaching an increasingly mobile and busy consumer, adapting to a changing business environment, and being criticized for delivering inappropriate or controversial messages.

Regulation and control of the advertising industry comes under the jurisdiction of the federal government through the Canadian Radio-television and Telecommunications Commission, the voluntary regulations administered by Advertising Standards Canada, and by laws and regulations established and enforced by the Competition Bureau.

KEY TERMS

REVIEW QUESTIONS

1. What is the primary role of advertising? How is advertising related to marketing and marketing communications decisions?

2. What is integrated marketing communications and what role does it play in solving business problems today?

3. Identify and briefly explain the various components of integrated marketing communications.

4. Identify and briefly explain the various types of consumer advertising.

5. Identify and briefly explain the various types of business-to-business advertising.

6. What is the difference between product advertising and promotional advertising?

7. What is the primary role of corporate advertising?

8. How do market demand and the product life cycle influence the decision to invest in or not invest in advertising?

9. How does a product communicate its competitive advantage? Identify the various options and provide a new example of each option.

10. How important is product quality when making the decision to invest in advertising? Briefly explain.

11. What roles do the Canadian Radio-television and Telecommunications Commission (CRTC) and Advertising Standards Canada play in the advertising industry?

DISCUSSION QUESTIONS

1. Collect some print advertisements for a product that uses sex as its central means of appealing to its target market. Analyze the advertisements for applicability and potential impact. Do you agree or disagree with this type of advertising practice? Why or why not?

2. How significant will the influence of new communications technology be in the future? Will advertisers shift their media dollars away from mainstream media such as television and newspapers and toward interactive forms of communications? What is the rationale for such a shift? Conduct some research on this issue and present a justified opinion.

3. Are some advertisers (car makers and energy drink manufacturers, for example) too extreme in terms of the messages and images they direct at their target audiences? What are the benefits and drawbacks of delivering controversial messages? Provide a few examples of campaigns that demonstrate your position on the issue.

4. Is "stretching the truth" the same thing as "misleading advertising"? Is it okay to stretch the truth a little bit? What is your opinion? Review the section in the chapter about misleading advertising before formulating your thoughts.

5. Is the use of sex and sexual innuendo in advertising acceptable, or should advertisers be more sensitive to the values of the viewing audience? Refer to the chapter for some insight. For what kinds of products are sexual appeals appropriate? Provide examples to defend your position.

NOTES

1. Patti Summerfield, "The future of TV is on demand; the question is how," *Media in Canada*, **www.mediaincanada.com**, October 10, 2006.

2. TVBCanada, **www.tvb.ca/tvbresources**.

3. "Top spenders in Canada," *Strategy*, March 2006, p. 38.

4. Jo Marney, "Image-building," *Marketing*, January 2/9, 1996, p. 15.

5. Adapted from data in Canadian Media Directors' Council, *Media Digest*, 2006–2007.

6. Geoffrey Roche, from a panel discussion, Media in Canada Forum, Toronto, October 3, 2006.

7. "PwC: Internet ad spend to reach almost $1 billion by 2010; other mediums see slower growth," *Media in Canada*, June 29, 2006, **www.mediaincanada.com**.

8. Paul Brent, "Farewell, old dog," *Financial Post*, June 7, 2003, p. FP6.

9. Lisa D'Innocenzo, "Traditional women's brands go for men," *Strategy*, August 2005, p. 24.

10. Bruce Classen, "The top media issues of 2005," *Marketing*, January 24, 2005, p. 17.

11. Anthony Crupi, "Will DVR really kill the 30-second ad?" *Cable World*, September 29, 2003, **www.cableworld.com**.

12. Alan Rutherford, "Media in Canada Forum: It's damn complicated and dangerous," *Media in Canada*, **www.mediaincanada.com**, October 4, 2006.

13. Sharon Wazman, "At an industry media lab, close views of multitasking," *The New York Times*, May 15, 2006, **www.nytimes.com**.

14. Lisa D'Innocenzo, "The colour of marketing," *Strategy*, April 6, 2001, pp. 1, 6.

15. Kelley Beaucar Vlahos, "Extreme ads aim to shock 'em and lock 'em," *Fox News*, April 16, 2005, **www.foxnews.com**.

16. Advertising Standards Canada, *Ad Complaints Report*, Quarter 1, 2006, **www.adstandards.com**.

17. "The CRTC," **www.crtc.gc.ca/eng/background**.

18. Advertising Standards Canada, **www.adstandards.com**.

19. "Advertising Standards Canada releases 2005 ad complaints report," Advertising Standards Canada, February 22, 2006, **www.adstandards.com**.

20. Thulasi Srikanthan, "Snickers bicker doesn't kiss publicity goodbye," *Toronto Star*, February 7, 2007, pp. C1, C11.

21. "Grafton-Fraser pays $1.2 million to settle misleading advertising case with Competition Bureau," Press release, Competition Bureau, July 27, 2006.

CHAPTER **2**

The Advertising Industry

Courtesy of Dick Hemingway.

Learning Objectives

After studying this chapter, you will be able to

1. Identify the organizations that comprise the advertising industry

2. Identify and describe the various advertising management systems used by clients

3. Identify the roles and responsibilities of clients in the advertising development process

4. Describe the roles and responsibilities of the agency in the advertising development process

5. Discuss the nature of relationships between clients and agencies

6. Distinguish among the various types of advertising agencies

7. Outline the organizational structure of agencies and the functions of agency personnel

8. Identify the key concepts associated with managing a client's business

9. Identify the methods of compensating advertising agencies

This chapter focuses on the relationships between advertisers (the client) and advertising agencies. Once the primary groups that comprise the industry have been identified, discussion will focus on the relationships between clients and agencies as they develop and implement advertising campaigns.

The management of advertising does vary from company to company. Depending on the size and nature of the company, responsibility for communications programs could be with the advertising manager, marketing manager, or even the owner of a small business. Or, a product manager or brand manager may be entirely responsible for communications activities for his or her brands. While recognizing these title variations, this chapter will use the term "advertising manager."

Advertising agencies exist to help companies communicate with the public and to help market a company's product. The agency is a service company that provides an essential link between the client (advertiser) and the public. An agency provides expertise that a client itself does not possess. Specifically, the client company gains access to creative and media specialists who will be responsible for planning and implementing vital components of the overall marketing plan.

Composition of the Advertising Industry

The Canadian advertising industry comprises three primary groups: advertisers, advertising agencies, and the media. All advertising revenues generated in Canada result from advertisers' print ads and broadcast commercials placed by advertising agencies in the media. Advertisers are the companies whose investment in advertising is largely responsible for keeping the other two component groups in business. Other organizations that support these primary groups include advertising production companies, audience measurement and media research companies, media support services, and regulation and control agencies.

ADVERTISERS (THE CLIENT)

Canadian advertisers include manufacturers, retailers, service firms, technology companies, governments, and non-profit organizations. Among the largest advertisers in Canada are Procter & Gamble, Rogers Communications, General Motors, BCE, and Telus Corp. See Figure 2.1 for further information. The Association of Canadian Advertisers is a national association exclusively dedicated to serving the interests of companies that market and advertise their products and services in Canada. The ACA's primary goal is to help members maximize the value of their marketing communications investments. As the voice for Canadian advertisers, the ACA safeguards advertisers' rights to free speech and represents the views of advertisers before governments and industry bodies.[1] For more information about the ACA visit their website at **www.aca-online.com**.

ADVERTISING AGENCIES

Omnicom Group
www.omnicomgroup.com

Advertising agencies are service organizations responsible for creating, planning, producing, and placing advertising messages for clients. Most of the larger advertising agencies in Canada are subsidiaries of large American agencies. As with many other industries, consolidation has occurred in the advertising industry in the past decade. Large global agencies continue to grow through the acquisition of domestic agencies (many in Canada). Essentially, four multi-national marketing communications conglomerates—Omnicom Group (American), WPP (British), Interpublic Group (American), and Publicis Groupe (French)—control the advertising agency business worldwide, accounting for approximately 58 percent of all advertising revenues.[2] Most large Canadian agencies are affiliated with these marketing communications companies. Refer to Figure 2.2 for details.

In Canada, the largest agencies include Cossette Communication Group (a Canadian-owned company) with domestic revenues of $143.4 million; MDC Partners (a global company that owns a collection of Canadian agencies) with domestic revenues of $61.6 million; and Carlson Marketing Group (a collection of Canadian agencies) with revenues of $48.0 million.[3] The different types of agencies that exist include full-service agencies that provide a complete range of services to their clients, and specialists that

FIGURE 2.1

Canada's top 10 advertisers

Rank	Advertiser	Media Spending ($ millions)
1	Procter & Gamble	172.0
2	Rogers Communications	106.0
3	General Motors	99.0
4	Telus Corp.	71.0
5	BCE	67.0
6	Wendy's International	61.0
7	L'Oreal	59.0
8	Sony Corp.	57.0
9	Toyota Motor Corp.	56.0
10	Hyundai Motor Co.	54.0

Source: Reprinted with permission from the November 20, 2006, issue of *Advertising Age*, Copyright, Crain Communications Inc. 2006.

This is a partial list of agencies owned by foreign-based multinational companies. They include many prominent agencies operating in Canada.

Omnicom Group—New York	WPP—London	Interpublic Group—New York	Publicis S.A.—Paris
BBDO Canada	Ogilvy & Mather Canada	MacLaren McCann	Saatchi & Saatchi
TBWA\Canada	JWT Canada	M2 Universal	Zenith Optimedia
DDB Canada	Young & Rubicam	Initiative Media	Taylor Tarpay Direct
Rapp Collins Canada	Wunderman Canada	FCB Canada	Starcom Mediavest
Ketchum Public Relations	Hill & Knowlton	Lowe Group	Leo Burnett
Tribal DDB	National Public Relations	Draft Canada	Bensimon-Byrne

Source: "Agency family trees," *Marketing*, 2005, www.marketingmag.ca.

FIGURE 2.2

Marketing communications services in Canada are owned by relatively few multinational holding companies.

offer limited services in certain areas of expertise. For a listing of some of Canada's larger advertising agencies and their major clients see Figure 2.3.

There are all kinds of smaller, regional advertising agencies that serve the needs of local and regional clients. In Atlantic Canada, for example, Bristol Group is an agency offering a complete range of marketing communications services. Bristol's clients include the Atlantic Lottery Corporation, NB Power, Nova Scotia Fruit Growers, and the Atlantic Toyota Dealers Association.

Agency	Gross Revenues in Canada ($ millions)	Clients
Cossette Communication Group	143.4	BMO Financial Group, Canada Post, Coca-Cola, Dairy Farmers of Canada, General Motors, General Mills, McDonald's, Nike, Shoppers Drug Mart
MDC Partners	61.6	Client list not supplied for rankings
Maritz Canada	51.9	Acura, Aeroplan, BMW, Ford, Hewlett-Packard, Honda
Carlson Marketing	48.0	Amex, Banque National, Bell Mobility, CIBC, ING Direct, Sears Canada, Via Rail
Nurun	33.2	Home Depot, Hydro-Quebec, Cingular, Danone, L'Oreal

Note: Several large American-owned agencies operating in Canada did not participate in the rankings in 2005. Maritz generates 55 percent of its revenues from promotion marketing. Carlson Marketing generates 52 percent of its revenue from direct marketing. Nurun generates all of its revenue from interactive and digital marketing. Cossette is an integrated agency but generates a majority of its revenue from advertising.

Source: "The rankings," *Marketing*, June 19, 2006, p. 29.

FIGURE 2.3

Canada's largest agencies and a selection of their clients

The Institute of Communication Agencies (ICA) is the national association representing full-service advertising agencies. The work of the ICA may be divided into two broad categories: external and internal. The external mission of the ICA is to act on behalf of the agency industry as spokesperson, negotiator, and defender of advertising. Its role is to discourage regulation, improve regulatory procedures, support self-regulation, and fight for the freedom to advertise. Its internal mission is to anticipate, serve, and promote the collective interests of ICA members with particular regard to defining, developing, and helping maintain the highest possible standards of professional practice.[4] For more insight into the ICA visit their website at **www.ica-ad.com**.

THE MEDIA

The Canadian media are divided into numerous categories: *broadcast,* which includes radio and television; *print,* which includes newspapers and magazines; *out-of-home,* which includes transit and outdoor advertising; *direct-response,* which includes direct mail and direct-response television companies; and *digital,* which includes the internet and various forms of mobile communications. We are living in an era in which new forms of electronic advertising communications are growing at a much faster rate than traditional forms of mass advertising.

According to the latest revenue data available, net advertising revenue in Canada from all sources (the amount actually spent on media) totals $12.6 billion. The traditional mass media, comprising television, daily newspapers, radio, magazines, and out-of-home advertising, generate $8.0 billion in revenue. The remaining $4.6 billion comes from direct-response advertising, online advertising, yellow pages, and a variety of miscellaneous sources. Television is the largest single medium, with advertising revenues of $3.0 billion.[5]

Much of Canada's media is controlled by a few large corporations that have acquired smaller media companies over the years, a concept referred to as **media convergence**. The two largest media companies are CTVglobemedia (CTV Network, 16 specialty channels including TSN and The Comedy Network, *The Globe and Mail*, CHUM radio and television, and numerous websites) and Rogers Communications (Rogers Sportsnet and Omni TV, 46 radio stations, a collection of consumer and trade magazines, and a host of related websites). Other large media companies include Canwest Mediaworks and Torstar.

CTVglobemedia
www.ctvglobemedia.com

ADVERTISING SUPPORT COMPANIES

This group comprises research companies that measure and evaluate the effectiveness of advertising messages. Other support firms include photographers, radio and television commercial production houses, print production specialists, music and sound production and editing companies, and media representatives who sell time and space for particular media. These support service groups operate behind the scenes, and awareness of their role and function has been low until recently.

The nature of advertising is changing; the most progressive advertising now borders on entertainment, and is increasingly viewed as content—storytelling so compelling consumers will actually want to watch it. Such advertising has many forms: half-hour TV shows, video downloads to the internet or MP3 players, live events, and word-of-mouth campaigns. Traditional agencies are seeking help to navigate these new ways to advertise, and are developing ongoing partnerships with production companies that were once considered simply vendors to the agency.[6]

MEDIA SUPPORT SERVICES

All major media in Canada have a support group whose primary mandate is to educate potential advertisers about the merits of their particular medium. Acting as a resource centre of information, each organization attempts to increase its medium's share of advertising revenue in the marketplace. Where appropriate, these organizations also liaise with governments and the public on matters of interest. This group includes the Television Bureau of Canada (TVB), the Radio Marketing Bureau, the Canadian Newspaper Association, Magazines Canada, the Outdoor Advertising Association of Canada, the Interactive Advertising Bureau (IAB), and the Canadian Marketing Association.

Radio Marketing Bureau
www.rmb.ca

RESEARCH AND AUDIENCE MEASUREMENT COMPANIES

Advertising planners working with limited budgets are constantly evaluating various media alternatives to develop the most effective and efficient media mix. To make sound media decisions requires a factual and objective information base. Media research, therefore, is concerned with quantitative measures of media exposure. In Canada, numerous independent organizations compile and publish reliable measurement data. Among these organizations are BBM Bureau of Measurement, Nielsen Media Research, Audit Bureau of Circulations, the Print Measurement Bureau, and Nielsen/Net Ratings. The services provided by these organizations are discussed in appropriate media chapters later on.

Client-Side Advertising Management

Management of the advertising function usually falls under the jurisdiction of the marketing department in an organization. Thus, it is very common for numerous managers to be directly or indirectly involved with the task of advertising. The number of managers involved depends on the size and nature of the organization and on the relative importance that advertising plays in the marketing of the products. For example, in a large organization where brand managers are employed, numerous managers may be involved in advertising. Junior-level managers are active in the day-to-day affairs of their brands, while senior-level managers are active in the approval process for advertising strategies of all company brands. In some organizations, approvals may be required from a brand manager, from all members of the marketing management ranks, and, finally, from the president of the company. Obviously, all managers are concerned about the quality and content of the messages communicated about the company and its products.

A **brand manager** (product manager) is an individual who is assigned responsibility for the development and implementation of marketing programs (including marketing communications) for a specific product or group of products. In the context of advertising and other forms of communications, the manager deals directly with the agencies on creative and media assignments, sales promotion programs, event marketing activities, direct-response and interactive communications, and public relations. Internally, this system encourages friendly competition, as managers compete for the resources of the firm (people, time, and money) to ensure that their product receives the attention it deserves. Kraft Foods, for example, would assign a brand manager to each of its key brands, which include Maxwell House, Kool-Aid, Kraft Dinner, Dream Whip, and Ritz.

Kraft Foods
www.kraft.com

A **category manager** is an individual who is assigned the responsibility of developing and implementing the marketing activity for all products grouped in the category. Category managers are common in large packaged-goods companies such as Procter & Gamble and Kraft Foods Inc. The category manager adopts a more generalized view of the business than would an individual brand manager. Consequently, trade-offs among brands are the decision of the category manager (i.e., determining which brands receive more or less advertising support). At Kraft, for example, there is a category manager for all cereal products (Post cereal) and all snack products (a variety of brand names). Brand managers in each category report directly to the category manager.

Canada is a diverse country, both geographically and culturally. Therefore, some organizations employ a **regional management system** and implement regional advertising campaigns. Molson, for example, has a three-region structure that impacts on marketing communications: Western Canada, Ontario/Atlantic, and Quebec. A national marketing team manages a group of brands referred to as "strategic national brands." Canadian and Export beers are in this group. Each region has a staff of marketing, sales, and promotion personnel who develop marketing and communications strategies and implement plans for "strategic regional brands." According to Molson, such a system allows a company to build on its strengths and chip away at its weaknesses.[7] Regional managers can respond more quickly to changes in the marketplace.

Companies operating on a global scale now view the world as one market and are switching to **international management systems** that divide the globe on a continental basis. In doing so, the management structure or hierarchy in countries like Canada is streamlined in order to accommodate the time required to approve marketing and marketing communications plans. Kraft Foods Inc. recently merged Kraft USA and Kraft Canada into a single North American structure, the goal of which is to reduce operational costs. About 80 percent of Kraft's brands are sold in both Canada and the United States, so such a move makes economic sense. Kraft hopes to implement its advertising strategies on a North American basis wherever possible.[8]

On a more grand scale, the often-used expression "Think globally and act locally" is now a common refrain among multi-national marketers. The objective of a global system is to develop a global campaign that can be tweaked where necessary to meet local market conditions. A few years ago McDonald's established a goal to capture more meal occasions among young adults and families. Advertising would play a key role. A campaign concept originating in Germany was implemented globally. The tagline for the campaign is the now very familiar, "I'm lovin' it."[9]

Since management structures can vary in organizations, we shall use the term **advertising manager** to describe the individual responsible for advertising in the client organization. The position of advertising manager is usually a mid-management position. A good advertising manager possesses analytical and planning skills, leadership skills, and knowledge and experience in the operation of the advertising industry. The advertising manager's position in the client organization is outlined in Figure 2.4. The figure also outlines the flow of communications between the advertising agency and the client at mid-management and senior management levels. For the sake of convenience, the diagram assumes the use of the brand-management system of advertising planning.

The advertising manager is responsible for coordinating advertising plans with plans for related marketing communications activity such as sales promotions, public relations, and events and sponsorships. In this capacity, the manager is responsible for developing the objectives and strategies for each plan. The following are the key areas of responsibility.

Molson
www.molson.com

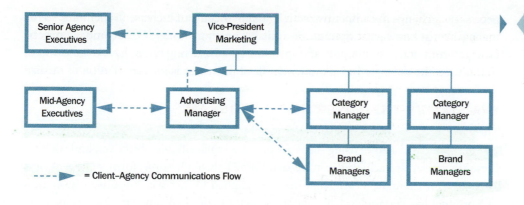

ADVERTISING PLANNING AND BUDGETING

Working with other marketing managers, the advertising manager will contribute to the marketing plan. At this stage, advertising would be recognized as one element in the marketing mix; hence, the role it will play in the achievement of objectives will be clearly identified. When the marketing plan is developed, general budget guidelines will be established that will aid in the development of a more comprehensive advertising plan at a later point. The expertise of the advertising manager will be called upon when budget requirements are being established in the marketing plan.

COORDINATING ADVERTISING WITH OTHER MARKETING COMMUNICATIONS

Other activities closely associated with advertising are sales promotion, event marketing, public relations, and marketing research. It is quite common for promotion activity to become part of the advertising communications process. Coupons and contests, for example, are often the focal point of an advertisement. As well, in today's changing marketplace, new digital campaigns that embrace the internet, cell phones, and video games must be given due consideration for inclusion in the media mix.

The advertising manager is responsible for integrating the various marketing communications activities with advertising activities and plans. Effective integration and strategic continuity across all activities and plans will produce a more effective plan, one that achieves objectives. Perhaps the expression "A chain is only as strong as its weakest link" applies here. When necessary, the advertising manager will allocate resources to **marketing research** in order to better understand target consumers and to devise better advertising concepts. For example, potential messages can be tested at various stages of development or implementation to measure the impact they are having on the target audience.

Once advertising and other communications plans are finalized, the advertising manager must distribute plan details to sales management personnel. Communicating advertising details to the sales force is vital, since the information can be used to inform customers of programs that will help them resell company products.

MONITORING THE ADVERTISING PROGRAM

In this area, the advertising manager ensures that advertising execution is in accordance with the actual plan. For example, the manager may request a post-buy media analysis to ensure that desired reach levels were achieved. Also, the manager carefully reviews budgets and planned media expenditures throughout the year, making changes when necessary. A change in competitive activity might dictate an increase in spending, so the manager must know what options are available on short notice. Or, a company may be facing a profit-squeeze situation, and spending on advertising might have to be reduced. In this case, the manager must know what flexibility there is for cancellation of media.

EVALUATING THE ADVERTISING PROGRAM

The advertising manager is accountable for the success or failure of company advertising programs. Most advertising plans are based on quantifiable objectives, and whether these objectives are achieved can be determined through some form of **advertising research**. For example, a campaign may be designed to increase consumers' awareness of a product to a certain level, to generate sales leads, or to communicate a specific message. To measure the success of a commercial or print advertisement, the manager may conduct research at various stages (pre-test and post-test research). The evaluation process is critical, as the advertising manager must make recommendations for changes in advertising direction if research information so dictates. Also, research at carefully timed intervals, for any campaign, often helps in identifying potential trouble spots before they become problems.

LIAISON WITH ADVERTISING AGENCY

Advertising managers are the direct link with the advertising agency, and hence they are in constant contact with agency personnel, checking the status of assignments and projects that the agency may be working on. As a liaison, one of the manager's key responsibilities is providing the agency with appropriate information when new assignments occur. For example, if a new advertisement or commercial is to be developed, the advertising manager will compile a creative briefing document outlining appropriate information regarding advertising background and marketing and advertising objectives. As the intermediary, the advertising manager is often in the hot seat, because individuals and their egos must be satisfied at both ends of the advertising spectrum (client side and agency side). The manager is responsible for developing advertising that will be acceptable to all company personnel, who must approve the program (based on client input). Let's examine this situation more closely.

From the viewpoint of the agency, the advertising manager is the person it must satisfy first. If the manager does not like a particular creative or media recommendation, the chances that it will be seen, let alone approved, by others on the client side are minimal. As an experienced critic, and knowing client personnel and their expectations, the manager will provide the agency with feedback so that changes to the proposal can be made before the corporate approval stage.

On the client side, once the creative or media assignment meets the specifications outlined in the marketing plan or briefing document, the advertising manager must carry the agency proposal through the corporate approval network. At this stage, the idiosyncrasies of senior executives often come to the forefront. These executives offer opinions on how the advertisement or media proposal could be improved. The advertising manager must remain objective and use the required selling skills to combat unnecessary changes to agency proposals. The ongoing requests for changes to the proposal that result from the corporate approval system (and from attempting to satisfy each individual manager) often have a negative impact on client–agency relations. Client–agency relations are discussed later in this chapter.

Advertising Agency Roles and Responsibilities

Advertising agencies perform various functions, tailoring their services to meet the specific needs of individual clients. The actual degree of the agency's involvement and responsibility may vary among clients, depending on factors such as the size and expertise of the client company. For example, large advertisers such as Procter & Gamble, Kraft Canada, or Coca-Cola are typically staffed with marketing managers whose expertise is used for devising marketing strategies. In this case, the agency's role will likely be confined to advertising and other forms of marketing communications. A key role is to develop and implement creative and media plans that are effective and efficient. For small advertisers, many of whom may lack marketing skills, agencies can provide marketing planning assistance that will complement overall client operations, not just advertising.

Since the relationship between a client and an agency is essentially a partnership, each will contribute to the planning and decision-making process. The services that the advertising agency offers are experience and expertise in communications, planning assistance, and some objectivity in the planning process.

PROVIDE EXPERIENCE AND EXPERTISE IN COMMUNICATIONS

Clients normally develop a comprehensive marketing plan that embraces all elements of the marketing mix (product, price, distribution, marketing communications, and public image). The agency will develop, in more detail, elements from the communications component of the plan. Specifically, the agency will use the guidelines and objectives established in the marketing plan to develop and execute an advertising plan that will contribute to the achievement of the client's objectives. Such a plan would include recommendations on creative (message) and media strategy that would embrace traditional print and broadcast media along with other options such as direct-response advertising, interactive media, event marketing, and sales promotion activities. The agency's responsibility is to recommend the most cost-effective solution to the client.

In some cases several agencies may work on one client's business at the same time, but in different capacities. For example, a traditional advertising agency may work on creative for television and print media, a media planning company may work on the media strategy and execution, and a digital agency may develop the online creative. Specialized expertise is often demanded by the client.

PROVIDE PLANNING ASSISTANCE

The agency, through its account group (account directors, account executives, and account supervisors), provides assistance not only in advertising but also in other areas of marketing. Depending on the internal structure of the client, the account group might be used as an external planning group. Such external planning may be used in the areas of marketing research, sales promotion, public relations, and event marketing. Account managers must look at the bigger picture, not just advertising, when it comes to solving a client's problems. If other elements of the marketing communications mix can play a vital role, then they too should be recommended as part of the solution.

PROVIDE OBJECTIVITY IN THE PLANNING PROCESS

Many advertisers tend to use advertising that suits the company's established style or image. Often, clients view a change in direction as a risk. The use of familiar-looking campaigns is a safe strategy, but it is not necessarily the most effective means of communicating with a target market. In advertising, safe usually means ineffective. The advertising agency is not directly associated with the internal environment and therefore can provide an objective perspective that might offer alternative directions and recommendations for communicating with target markets. This external position can result in the development of customer-oriented campaigns rather than company-oriented campaigns.

Taking risks in adopting new directions is becoming increasingly necessary as advertisers attempt to reach and attract mobile consumers. Advertisers must be willing to try new creative ideas and new media alternatives (cell phones, MP3 players, and video games, for example) as a means of breaking through the vast amount of messages directed at consumers. Based on recommendations from agencies, many clients have moved successfully into online communications and are seeing good returns for their investment. Coca-Cola introduced iCoke in 2005, a new consumer touch point that revolves around the **iCoke.ca** website. "The website cuts through the clutter and makes the brand feel consistent, and the online presence provides for measurability 24/7," says Pina Sciarra, vice-president of marketing at Coca-Cola.[10] Refer to the illustration in Figure 2.5.

www.icoke.ca/en. ®/TMCoca-Cola Ltd. iCoke appears courtesy of Coca-Cola Ltd.

FIGURE 2.5

The iCoke website is now a focal point for marketing communications at Coca-Cola Ltd.

Based on the advice of its agency, Pontiac's G5 coupe was launched entirely (every media dollar) by an online advertising campaign. Mark-Hans Richer, Pontiac's marketing director, conceded "It was a radical experiment but since we were only targeting young males it was a calculated risk."[11] Nonetheless, Pontiac listened to its agency and took the risk. If the campaign works, it will trigger a change in thinking for other General Motors brands.

Honda is experimenting with five-second commercials in an attempt to get more bang for their advertising dollar in a crowded, on-demand media environment. The TV ads feature the new Honda Fit hatchback, followed by a robotic voice saying, "The fit is go."[12]

PROMOTE ACTIVE LIAISON WITH CLIENTS

It is very important for agencies and clients to communicate regularly with each other. The account executive is the primary link between the agency and the client. An account executive channels vital information from the client into the agency and takes recommendations that are prepared by various agency departments back to the client for review. It is also appropriate for employees at similar management levels to be communicating with each other. For example, a director of account planning (agency) should keep in touch with the director of marketing (client), and the presidents of both organizations should meet periodically to discuss matters. Ongoing and open communications between the parties fosters an environment where both parties can prosper. It helps build a better partnership.

For a summary of the roles and responsibilities of clients and advertising agencies, refer to Figure 2.6.

Client–Agency Relationships

The quality of advertising produced is the outcome of a sound business/professional and personal relationship between a client and an agency. When the client–agency

---

CLIENTS ARE RESPONSIBLE FOR:

- Providing appropriate background information and a budget for the advertising assignment
- Coordinating advertising strategies with other marketing communications strategies
- Monitoring the implementation of advertising programs
- Evaluating the effectiveness of advertising programs

AGENCIES ARE RESPONSIBLE FOR:

- Providing experience and expertise in specialized areas: mainly creative and media strategies and executions
- Offering planning assistance to solve clients' marketing problems
- Producing objective, customer-focused advertising strategies
- Conducting research when necessary to support advertising recommendations

FIGURE 2.6

A summary of the roles and responsibilities of clients and agencies

Regardless of roles and responsibilities, if the client–agency partnership is to be a successful one, there must be effective two-way communication between the partners. The partners must share a similar vision and agree to achievable objectives.

relationship is a partnership, the relationship is long term. If the relationship is one of buyer–vendor, the association is much more likely to be short term.

The connection between client and agency is often very delicate and can be broken for various reasons. Deteriorating relationships contribute significantly to the amount of account shifting that occurs in Canada each year. **Account shifting** refers to the movement of an advertising account from one agency to another. Clients are attracted to agencies that produce good creative and to agencies that develop campaigns that achieve business objectives.

There are a variety of reasons why clients shift their business to different advertising agencies. Most of these reasons have to do with the client–agency relationship—or lack of it. Following are some of the more common reasons for account shifting:

- Clients are dissatisfied with the quality of the advertising or any of the other services provided by the agency.

- There are new communications demands from clients that cannot be adequately served by existing agencies (e.g., all aspects of integrated marketing communications).

- There are philosophical differences between client and agency in terms of management style and approach, detected only after the association has begun. For example, the two parties might disagree on the direction the advertising should take.

- There is an absence of the team concept—necessary relationships between people do not develop, whether because of poor communications, differences in needs, or negative attitudes. Sometimes, the players on the teams change during the relationship, upsetting the chemistry that had existed.

- Clients decide to consolidate their business with fewer agencies (multi-product advertisers)—often, the reorganization of client management structures leads to changes in advertising assignments.

- Conflict situations may arise owing to account realignments in the United States (shifts at the U.S. parent agency often create shifts in Canadian subsidiaries). Also, agency mergers, in Canada or internationally, can bring competing accounts under one roof, which creates a need for one account to switch to another agency.

To demonstrate how a relationship can dissolve, consider an example involving Cossette Communication Group. Since the 1970s the company had been handling McDonald's $44 million Canadian account, and the client was quite satisfied with the advertising Cossette was producing. However, a decision by McDonald's in the United States to consolidate its global media account with OMD Worldwide meant that OMD Canada automatically gained McDonald's Canadian advertising business.[13] For Cossette, this must have been a bitter pill to swallow indeed.

Here is further example to illustrate the ambivalent nature of client–agency relations. Downtown Partners of Toronto was widely considered one of Canada's hottest agencies in 2005. Its work for Forzani Group's SportChek brand was winning creative awards, one of its Budweiser ads ran on American television during the Super Bowl, and its Bud Light Institute campaign was acclaimed around the world. Forzani put the account up for review (a surprise move, according to the agency) and Downtown Partners lost out to another agency. Such a decision in the wake of good work done for the client dramatizes the cold nature of the advertising business. "Agencies ebb and flow . . . " says Tony Atilia, president of Downtown Partners.[14]

When things aren't going well for the client (e.g., sales are down or market share is down) it is quite common for the agency to take the fall. Clients, rightly or wrongly, link

OMD Worldwide
www.omd.com

their investment in advertising to sales and market-share results. Instead of dissolving the partnership, clients and agencies must look squarely at each other, acknowledge any shortcomings in the relationship, and devise strategies to correct them. Among the shortcomings that a client might ascribe to its agency are a high degree of personnel turnover, understaffing, and lack of interest. Among the problems that agencies have with their clients are poor communication of objectives and strategies, lack of senior management involvement, and indecision.

To encourage the best possible relationship between clients and agencies, and to clearly review the expectations of parties, clients must conduct agency evaluations at planned intervals. Also, since the agency invests considerable resources in its client's business, it should have the opportunity to review the client's performance. A good working relationship depends on honest, open communication between the partners, an attitude of respect for each other, and the sharing of common goals so that both partners can be successful. Dissolving a business partnership shouldn't be a quick decision.

In recent years there has been a trend toward **project assignments** and short-term relationships. Clients and agencies are not seeking commitment and nobody wants to get married. Many agencies report that it is the same kind of work, but it is handled on an "as-needed" basis. According to Terry Johnson's advertising agency, Allard Johnson Communications, "The project approach means you have to prove yourself over and over again, but that can work to your advantage. Most of our clients have been with us five or six years, even though we're working on a project basis."[15]

Project-based work offers flexibility for clients. If they don't like what the agency is doing, they can audition other agencies where the fit might be better, without going through a long review process. In these times, the pressure is squarely on the advertising agency; it must provide results or suffer the consequences.

For more insight into the dynamics between clients and agencies, see the Advertising in Action vignette **A Thing or Two about Client–Agency Relations**.

Allard Johnson Communications
www.allardjohnson.com

Types of Advertising Agencies

The type of agency a client chooses to work with can be a difficult decision. When choosing an agency, the client's goal is to find the one that will recommend and produce cost-efficient, effective advertising to achieve the desired results in a traditionally expensive area of communications. The client must consider factors such as agency size, the service mix the agency is capable of providing, and compatibility of personnel. Essentially there are four different types of agencies: full-service agencies, boutique agencies, media-buying agencies, and specialist agencies. Let's examine the various types of advertising agencies operating in Canada.

FULL-SERVICE AGENCIES

Full-service agencies appeal strongly to advertisers that need a wide variety of services, or require international connections for global advertising campaigns. Services most often provided by full-service agencies must embrace all of the possible demands a client may place on them. Therefore, the services list is diverse and may include creative planning, creative development and execution, media planning and placement, sales promotion, public relations and direct response, and interactive communications. In other words, a full-service agency must offer integrated marketing communications solutions to its clients.

→ ADVERTISING IN ACTION

A Thing or Two about Client–Agency Relations

Clients and agencies share a common goal—to get the very best results for the client's business. On paper it sounds so simple, but the reality is that client–agency relationships can be very complicated. Establishing good working relationships that prevail over the long term to the mutual benefit of both parties is challenging.

Consider the following example of how quickly relationships can dissolve. A few years ago when the Holt Renfrew account was up for grabs, Roche Macaulay & Partners Advertising Inc. went after it. To do so, Roche had to resign its high-profile Harry Rosen account because the two clothing retailers were competitors (a conflict situation). The resignation was a surprise to Rosen, but the Holt Renfrew account was worth much more in terms of revenue for Roche. Holt Renfrew spent much more on advertising. Was the resignation motivated by money?

After holding the Holt Renfrew account for 16 months, Roche Macaulay was shown the door. The agency's irreverent ads were supposed to attract younger shoppers and refashion Holt as a hip place to shop. Evidently, Holt wasn't impressed with the work. The Holt account was then given to Zig Inc., a relatively new agency that ironically enough was started by Geoffrey Roche's former partner Andy Macaulay.

The manner in which Roche was dismissed has created some resentment, but there's a saying that may apply here: "What goes around comes around." Perhaps the Roche Macaulay agency was just getting what it deserved. It might have been wiser to stay with Harry Rosen.

The reasons for dissolving a relationship are many: money and compensation disagreements, poor chemistry between the people on both sides, lack of constructive and meaningful communications, and failure to agree on creative or media direction are the reasons that lead the pack. All of these issues are within control of the two parties, however, and they can be corrected if the proper steps are taken. A framework for the relationship must be established when the partnership is in its infancy stages, and the client and agency must abide by it. The Institute of Communication Agencies offers many good suggestions for building client–agency relationships: encourage a genuine partnership; relate everything to deliverables (objectives that can be measured later on); only critique that which needs fixing; reinforce the good points of the other partner; be candid with each other about risk; and finally, don't fall out over money!

As in other kinds of relationships, good relationships in advertising usually boil down to the quality of communications. "Being able to talk openly and constructively goes a long way in building a harmonious and effective relationship," says Aldo Cundari, chairman and CEO of Cundari Integrated Advertising.

Sources: Adapted from David Rutherford, "Starting with the right attitude," *Marketing*, January 28, 2002, p. 32; John Heinzl, "Holt dumps advertising agency," *The Globe and Mail*, September 11, 2001, p. B2; and Aldo Cundari, "Over-servicing is not the problem," *Marketing*, June 25, 2001, p. 41.

Large agencies such as BBDO Canada and Cossette Communication Group are full-service agencies. BBDO's expertise is concentrated in creative planning, media planning, promotions, and interactive communications. Cossette changed its name to Cossette Communication Group partly to suggest the diversity of services it offers. Padulo Integrated Inc. is another agency whose name suggests total-solution communications services.

Alternatively, full-service advertising agencies are acquiring or affiliating with specialists in other areas of marketing communications so they have access to the services their clients want. Under the MacLaren McCann umbrella, for example, is the original agency MacLaren McCann, which offers account planning and creative services; M2 Universal, a media planning and media placement company; MacLaren McCann Direct & Interactive, a direct-response and online specialist; MacLaren Momentum, an event marketing specialist; MM Public Relations; McGill Productions (design and production); and Edge Productions (post-production and corporate videos).

From a purely traditional advertising perspective, full-service agencies such as MacLaren McCann and BBDO Canada offer three essential services to clients: **account management** (sometimes referred to as account services or client services) liaises with the client, helps develop marketing communications strategies and oversees the development of campaigns inside the agency; **creative services** develops and executes creative ideas in the form of advertisements and commercials; and **media services** develops and implements media plans that show how ads will be placed, how much the advertising will cost, and the timing of the placements.

Figure 2.7 illustrates the internal structure of a typical full-service advertising agency.

CREATIVE BOUTIQUES

Creative boutiques are smaller agencies specializing in the development of creative ideas and their execution for clients' advertising campaigns. In a world of specialization, it is now quite common for an advertiser to divide its advertising assignments among agency specialists, one of which is a creative boutique. Creative boutiques are usually formed and staffed by personnel previously employed by the creative departments of full-service agencies; due to past performance, their key personnel have excellent credentials within the industry. Full-service agencies often sub-contract work to creative boutiques to avoid the fixed costs of maintaining full-time staff, or to complete work during busy periods.

Using advertising and marketing objectives as a guideline, a creative boutique concentrates on producing the single most important component of a campaign—the sales message. Creative boutiques are quite successful in attracting clients from full-service agencies, especially if they are staffed with respected and successful creative people. Such was the case when Chris Staples, Tom Shepansky, and Ian Grais bolted from Palmer Jarvis DDB, a full-service agency based in Vancouver, to form a boutique named Rethink Communications. Their objective was to stay close to their clients and produce good

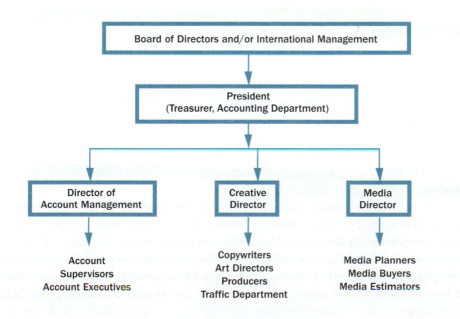

FIGURE 2.7

Organizational structure of a full-service agency

Source: Institute of Communication Agencies.

advertising for them. Like other boutiques that have experienced success, Rethink has now grown to become a mid-size agency with 50 employees. Clients include A&W, the B.C. Lions football team, Bell Solo Mobile, Future Shop, and Science World.

MEDIA-BUYING SERVICE

A **media-buying service** is a specialist agency responsible for planning and purchasing the most cost-efficient media for a client—that is to say, responsible for gaining maximum exposure to a target audience at minimum cost. In addition, a media-buying service often obtains government and other clearances for advertisements, ensures that each ad runs as scheduled, and generally takes care of administrative work associated with the media-buying transaction.

Since efficiency is important, the use of a media-buying service might generate cost savings that can be reinvested in the creative product. Very often a client will have creative matters handled by several different agencies but have the media planning coordinated and implemented by a media-buying service. Placing advertising through one media-buying service leads to bigger discounts since the agency has more leverage with the various media suppliers.

Among Canada's larger media-buying companies are M2 Universal, Zenith-Optimedia, and the Omnicom Media Group. There is a trend toward relatively few but very large media companies placing a majority of advertising in Canada. M2 Universal, for example, reports media billings of more than $750 million annually, and their clients include General Motors and Wendy's, both of whom are top-ten advertisers in Canada. **Media billings** refer to the total dollar volume of advertising in terms of time and space handled by an agency in one year.[16]

OTHER BOUTIQUES AND COMMUNICATIONS SPECIALISTS

Other options are available for clients who like to work with specialists. In today's cluttered media environment, clients are demanding efficiency and as a result are moving toward **direct-response communications** and **digital communications**, and away from the mass media. Such movement calls for a different kind of specialization. Consequently, agencies specializing in direct-response and online communications are in greater demand. As indicated earlier, some full-service agencies have diversified to offer these forms of communications or they have acquired smaller specialists who are integrated into the overall organizational structure (a subsidiary, for example).

Carlson Marketing Group Canada Inc., the country's fourth-largest marketing communications company, generates 52 percent of its revenues from direct-response advertising programs and 8 percent from interactive and digital communications.[17] Ogilvy & Mather, a large multi-national agency, operates several divisions including Ogilvy & Mather Advertising, Ogilvy & Mather One (direct-response communications), and Ogilvy Interactive. These and other agencies have reorganized to meet the changing needs and new demands of their clients.

With clients now searching for expertise in online and mobile communications, the demand for agencies offering dedicated services in these areas has exploded. Small and savvy boutique-style shops have opened to serve the needs of clients of all sizes. Eyeblaster is an example of a successful interactive agency whose technology allows advertisers to create and manage ad campaigns in rich-media formats (online video-style advertising).[18] MyThum is a leading mobile company that is helping brands and broadcasters build a direct relationship with consumers through their cell phone. As an indication of the demand for their services, MyThum's client list includes such advertisers as Rogers Media, Best Buy, Molson, Coors, Nissan, and Ford Motor Company.[19]

Other specialists focus on product categories or niche market segments that are identified as profitable opportunities. Pharmaceutical marketing, for example, is a highly specialized product category in which laws and regulations governing advertising are very different from other product categories. Consequently, it is an area that not many agencies get involved in. A few prominent agencies in this group include Euro RSCG Life, Ogilvy Healthcare, and M2 Healthcare (a division of MacLaren McCann).

In the niche market segment, there are agencies, or separate divisions of agencies, that specialize in targeting age groups such as youth and baby boomers. BOOM Communications operates as a division of Padulo Integrated Inc. BOOM focuses on the baby boomer market and helps advertisers understand that particular segment of the population. Boomers Marketing (established in 2004) serves the same market, a market that has been largely ignored by advertisers over the years. People over 50 look younger, act younger, and generally feel younger than previous generations. "The assumption that older people with disposable income are closed-minded, not susceptible to advertising, and not willing to try new things, is absolutely false," says Humphrey Taylor, chairman, Harris Poll.[20] In fact, the boomer segment of 50-plus years is the fastest-growing and wealthiest demographic in Canada. Clients and agencies recognizing this fact stand to reap the benefits.

Boomers Marketing
www.boomersmarketing.com

Clients tend to go in two different directions when selecting the type of agency they would like to work with. Some migrate to the large multi-national agencies, while others prefer to work with boutique-style shops. The trend toward project assignments and shorter relationships is beneficial to the smaller agency for which the costs of operations are lower. In contrast, larger agencies need a long-term relationship in order to operate cost-effectively. Boutiques offer clients a unique advantage. The highly experienced creative and media people who started the boutique usually work directly with the clients. Such is not the case in larger agencies. Ironically, these creative and media people generally honed their craft at much larger agencies.

Indeed, the use of creative boutiques and media-buying services together could provide the best of both worlds for advertisers. However, full-service agencies argue that they can handle both services equally well for their clients—and all under one roof, too.

For more insight into issues regarding agency size and specialization, refer to the Advertising in Action vignette **Big Agency or Small Agency: Which Direction to Take?**

Structure and Management of the Advertising Agency

We know that advertising agencies are divided into three primary functional areas: account management, creative, and media. See Figure 2.8 for more detail on functional areas. Large agencies may include additional departments, embracing functions such as marketing research, interactive communications, sales promotion, and public relations. The following sections summarize the roles and responsibilities of the primary functional areas of the agency: account planning and management, creative, and media.

ACCOUNT MANAGEMENT

As the name implies, account management staff are responsible for managing the affairs of the agency's clients. Account personnel perform a dual function: they are both

Big Agency or Small Agency: Which Direction to Take?

Should a client choose a large full-service agency that can meet all of its communications demands, or should a client spread the business around to a group of smaller agencies, each of which claims special expertise in specific areas of marketing communications? Which situation is best for the advertiser?

In recent years two trends have been noticed. The first trend is for large multi-national advertisers to consolidate their advertising globally with one agency network, typically a group of full-service agencies. This direction allows the advertiser to tap into resources all over the world and is cost-efficient for planning and buying media time and space.

The second trend sees advertisers reassigning their account to small agencies that are capable of reacting faster to changing conditions. These agencies don't get bogged down in bureaucratic corporate structures that delay decisions and action. The digital era of communications, for example, has produced a multitude of interactive agencies that literally have stolen business from traditional agencies.

Heineken has chosen to be a part of the second trend. Heineken recently moved its global account from McCann-Erickson (a large multi-national agency) to a small agency known as StrawberryFrog.

StrawberryFrog proved to Heineken that it was more nimble than larger firms, and very capable of producing advertising that will sell beer. StrawberryFrog keeps its operating costs down by hiring freelancers on short-term bases from all over the world. In the age of digital communications, geography (physical presence at an agency desk, that is) just isn't a factor.

To many employees toiling away in large agencies, this trend in the industry might come as a breath of fresh air. Advertising people don't necessarily want to be in big network agencies, and in recent years the smaller shops have begun winning awards and helping businesses grow. Among the hottest shops are Rethink, Zig, Taxi, and John Street. Taxi was founded on a very simple principle: projects could benefit from the use of small teams of key decision makers—teams comprising a similar number of people as could fit into a taxi. This idea seems to be working!

However, as Taxi has discovered, growth is inevitable in a successful company. Effective campaigns attract new clients, and more business means more employees. You simply get bigger! However, Taxi prides itself on the fact that it still produces great ads. They are independent thinkers accountable only to their clients.

Source: Adapted from Paul Brent, "Small agency leaps ahead of bigger rivals," *Financial Post*, September 9, 2005, p. FP8; and Keith MacArthur, "Hot ad shop Taxi adopts strategy to never get so big it gets bad," *The Globe and Mail*, December 12, 2005, p. B4.

consultants and coordinators. Account personnel must fully understand the client's business so that they can advise the client on a variety of strategic marketing issues, identify and motivate agency resources to build the client's business, and coordinate communications between the client and agency.

Account-management personnel must understand the major marketing issues facing the client and, using all available resources of the agency, recommend a course of action to the client. Thus, they are actively involved in the planning process and in presenting agency work to the client. They are expected to be experts on the consumer and to understand how the client's business relates to, and is perceived by, the consumer. The account-management group includes an account executive, an account supervisor, and an account director.

ACCOUNT EXECUTIVE Often viewed as occupying an entry-level position, the **account executive** is responsible for facilitating ongoing communications with the client, project planning, budget control, preparing annual advertising plans, and advising on

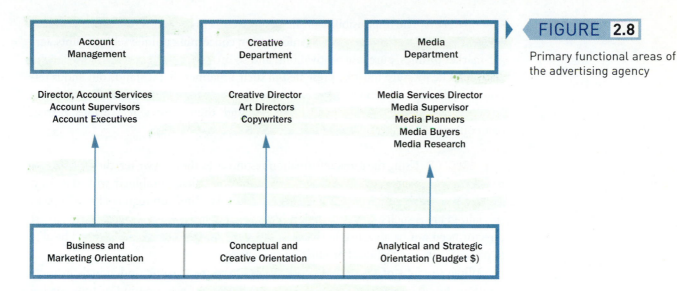

▶ FIGURE **2.8**

Primary functional areas of the advertising agency

strategic issues. The account executive liaises between the client and agency, and communicates frequently with the personnel in the client organization who are responsible for the advertising function (advertising manager, product manager). An account executive is usually responsible for one or several clients, depending on the size and resources of the agency. The working relationship between the agency account executive and the client product manager is a close one.

ACCOUNT SUPERVISOR   As a middle manager, the **account supervisor** manages a group of account executives and is therefore responsible for an expanded list of clients. Job functions include strategic planning, market analysis, competitive activity analysis, and analyzing and capitalizing on business-building opportunities. In such a position, the supervisor must look beyond the scope of current projects and assignments, and assist in developing the future direction of a product or service.

ACCOUNT DIRECTOR   The **account director** deals directly with senior members of the client organization and is responsible for how the agency handles client accounts. Specific responsibilities include long-term planning, deployment of agency personnel, and overall account profitability. Also, the account director is responsible for working with senior agency executives from other functional areas in seeking new business for the agency.

CREATIVE DEPARTMENT

The **creative department** is responsible for developing the idea or concept for communications plans. Once the nature of the message (often referred to as the *creative concept*) has been established, members of the creative team must sell it to the client; once the client approves the concept, the creative team must execute the creative. Heading the creative department is the creative director, who oversees the development of all creative developed by the agency. The creative director is ultimately responsible for maintaining a high standard of creative quality on behalf of the agency. In such a position, the creative director must motivate the copywriters and art directors who work directly on client assignments.

COPYWRITER The responsibility of the **copywriter** is to convert information provided by the client and account personnel (information concerning unique selling points, target-market profiles, purchase motivations, and so on) into an effective, persuasive sales message. The message must be presented in such a manner that it stands out and is relevant to potential customers. The copywriter develops the main idea of the advertisement in conjunction with an art director, and then creates its various textual components: the headline, sub-headlines, and body copy or text.

ART DIRECTOR Using the same information resources as the copywriter, the **art director** is responsible for developing a visual communication that, combined with the copy, elicits a favourable reaction from the target market. Art direction requires knowledge in specialized areas such as graphic design, photography, and electronic publishing. An art director need not be an artist, but must understand the production process and be able to direct artists and technical production specialists.

While the jobs of copywriters and art directors are separate, individuals in these positions usually work as a team on client assignments. Over a period of time, such a working relationship provides continuity and consistency in the creative product, something that clients are usually looking for. As clients and agencies increasingly look to creative plans that combine traditional media with digital media (two separate areas of creative expertise), the team concept has been emphasized. Further discussion of the team concept is included in the next section of the chapter.

PRINT AND BROADCAST PRODUCTION MANAGER **Production managers** are responsible for preparing print advertisements for newspaper, magazine, outdoor, and transit; and commercials for broadcast on television and radio. They are also responsible for preparing the contents of direct-mail offers, if direct-response advertising is part of the communications strategy. Since production is an activity that involves execution, it requires coordination with numerous external suppliers such as acting agencies and film production houses.

The production manager offers technical advice about matters such as production cost estimates and ensures that all activities are completed within scheduled time frames—publishers' material deadlines or television air dates, for example. Often, a **traffic manager** is responsible for ensuring that the final product (print ad or broadcast commercial) reaches the media destination on time.

MEDIA DEPARTMENT

The media department is responsible for the planning and placement of advertising time and space. The proliferation of media forms, fragmentation within specific media (e.g., the large number of television channels available to viewers), the escalating cost of media, and the uncertainty regarding the accuracy of audience measurement in the digital media, have all added to the complexity of the media responsibility. The functions of the media department are as follows:

- *Media planning* The plan that documents how the client's money will be spent to achieve advertising objectives is prepared and presented at this stage.
- *Media buying* Once approved, the elements necessary to execute the media plan are purchased. The objective when buying is to achieve the most at the least expense—that is, to achieve maximum impact and reach at the lowest possible cost to the

client. Each purchase must be checked to see that it ran correctly. Sometimes, media buys must be upgraded midstream to compensate for audience loss (actual audience versus estimated audience). Media buying is a negotiated process between agencies or media-buying services and the media. Buying time and space in volume yields preferred rates for the advertiser.

- *Media research* Larger agencies have a media research department that provides up-to-date information regarding audiences and circulation. Such data are used frequently when alternative media forms (e.g., television, magazines, newspapers) are being compared, or when the respective abilities of specific media to reach a certain target market are being compared. Media research has a strong analytical orientation. External databases containing audience measurement information are available online, or, alternatively, an agency can hire an independent research company to tap into these data banks and provide media analysis.

Position responsibilities in the media department are distributed among the media planner, media buyer, media supervisor, and media director.

MEDIA PLANNER The **media planner** assesses the strengths, weaknesses, cost efficiencies, and communications potentials of various media to develop a media plan. The ability to communicate is vital for planners, since they must sell the plan, first within the agency and then to the client. Since the client's money is on the line at this stage, planners must be prepared to address all of the client's concerns. Media plans may go through many revisions before receiving client approval. One of the major challenges of a media planner today is to develop strategies and recommendations that effectively blend the mass media with the more targeted direct-response and interactive media.

MEDIA BUYER The **media buyer** is responsible for developing an intimate knowledge of the media marketplace and being aware of all developments affecting media buying. Buyers must evaluate and make decisions on the competitive claims of the various media in order to make the most efficient and effective buys for their clients. Good negotiating skills are vital if one is to be successful in a media-buying role. The buyer's objective is to get the best possible deal for their client.

MEDIA SUPERVISOR The **media supervisor** is generally responsible for a team of media people and for coordinating the efforts of buyers and planners during the development and execution of the media plan.

MEDIA DIRECTOR The responsibility of the **media director** depends on the size of the agency. In smaller agencies, the director is involved in planning and buying media. In a larger agency, the director is more of an administrator. As a senior manager, the director is ultimately responsible for the philosophy that governs the media planning function in the agency and is accountable to the client for media planning and placement. Working with other senior executives, the media director usually plays an active role in business presentations to new clients.

As discussed earlier, many agencies have divested themselves of the media-planning role. The complex and time-consuming nature of this task is perhaps better suited to media-buying services that specialize in media planning and placement.

Managing the Client's Business

This section will explore the relationship between agencies and clients and describe how an agency manages a client's account and how a client compensates the agency for the services they provide. Several factors influence the professional relationship between the client and the agency.

AGENCY TEAMS

The amount of time an agency spends with a client and the personnel it allocates to serve the needs of the client affect the client–agency relationship. Agency management will form teams that will work together on a client's business. The employees who comprise a team vary among agencies, depending on factors such as the size of the agency and the various levels of personnel resources available. Generally, an **account group** includes the following:

- Account executive and account supervisor
- Art director and copywriter
- Media planner and media buyer

Keeping an account team together over a number of assignments benefits both the client and the agency. Familiarity with the products and the way the client operates are other obvious benefits. The agency team can draw upon past experiences with the client when considering new directions to pursue. Another benefit involves consistency in approach. The account team develops a strategy that will work over an extended period. Within that long-term strategy will be the flexibility to develop and execute new plans when needed. Clients who are subjected to changing personnel within an account group may question whether the agency values their business. Conversely, the agency may, by keeping an account team together, imply that a client's business is important and that it is trying to serve the client more effectively.

The team concept has been taken a step further now that agencies are recommending digital media as part of the communications mix—new and unique expertise is required. What has emerged is the **hybrid team**, a concept that calls for creative planners (copywriters and art directors) from both types of media (traditional and digital) to work together on a client's business. By working together in the initial planning stages, the combined team can search out and evaluate concepts that complement all forms of media. When the client briefs the agency on an assignment it is important that all of these team members participate in the discussion.

COMPETING ACCOUNTS

Agencies are exposed to extremely confidential client information when developing advertising plans. As a consequence, agencies will not, as a rule, accept assignments from an advertiser who is in direct competition with a current client. Numerous conflicts develop as an agency seeks new business. When agencies merge to form larger agencies, competing accounts are often brought together. In such a case, one of the clients (usually the smaller, in terms of media dollars) will take its business elsewhere, or the agency will resign the client's business.

AGENCY OF RECORD

Many large advertisers (companies with numerous divisions or multi-product lines) distribute their advertising assignments among several advertising agencies. Other agencies are consolidating all of their advertising under a single roof. Both options have their benefits and drawbacks. From the client's perspective, dividing the business among several agencies is advantageous in that the different products or services required will receive more attention than would be possible if all assignments were given to one agency. Since the agencies are competing with each other for new business, all of them seeking further assignments from the client, their performance on the products and services they handle will be of a high quality. Dividing the assignments, in other words, should positively affect the quality of the work. Clients that employ a one-agency approach on a national or international scale are searching for cost efficiencies—dealing with only one agency alone should reduce costs.

On the media side of things, the client often appoints an **agency of record** (**AOR**). This central agency is responsible for media negotiation and placement, and is one of the agencies (usually full-service agencies) employed by multiple-product advertisers. In today's marketplace, in which specialists such as creative boutiques and media-buying companies participate, the AOR could act as the media-buying service.

An AOR facilitates efficiency in the media-buying process, often making greater discounts available to the client by purchasing all media on a corporate (large-volume) basis. The AOR is responsible for corporate media contracts under which other agencies will issue their placement orders. Also, the AOR records all advertising placed, and is responsible for final allotment of time and space in a media schedule. The AOR usually receives a slightly higher rate of commission if a commission-based compensation system is in place.

Agency Compensation

How an advertising agency is paid, and how much money it makes, is an issue frequently on the minds of both client marketing executives and agency managers. Marketing executives often argue that their agency is asking for too much money, or they feel they are paying for unnecessary services. Agency managers, on the other hand, believe that the profit margins on some of their accounts are too low in relation to the amount of resources allocated to the client. Needless to say, compensation is a primary area where clients and agencies are at odds.

There are three basic methods of compensating an advertising agency for the services it provides: an **agency commission** based on the dollar volume of media placed; a fee that considers the resources an agency allocates to servicing a client; and payment-by-results, a reduced-rate commission with incentives based on performance standards. A summary of the advantages and disadvantages of each system appears in Figure 2.9.

THE COMMISSION SYSTEM

The commission system has been used in one form or another for more than 100 years. Until the early 1990s, the standard rate of commission was 15 percent. When this system is used, the agency receives a 15-percent rebate from the media it is buying time or space from. The media allow accredited advertising agencies to buy advertising time and space at a 15-percent discount off quoted rates. This discount is granted to the agency for its work in analyzing client research, preparing the overall strategy, creating and producing the advertising material, media planning and buying, billing the client, and research in support of recommendations and discounts for prompt payment.[21]

The 15-percent commission applies only to the purchase of time and space. To illustrate the commission principle, let's assume that a total media purchase amounted to

FIGURE 2.9

The advantages and disadvantages of agency compensation methods

Clients are moving toward the payment-by-results method and away from other methods. They are asking their agencies to be accountable for the strategies and executions being recommended. At the same time, agencies are asking their clients to take more risks instead of retreating to familiar ideas. Agencies want to prove to their clients that their ideas will work in the marketplace.

COMMISSION SYSTEM

Pros:
- Simple to implement
- All services provided at no additional cost
- Pressure on agency to keep costs down

Cons:
- Profit on some brands (larger budgets); losses on others (smaller budgets)
- Agency recommendations for higher expenditures may be self-serving
- Payment based on media cost, not the work provided

FEE SYSTEM

Pros:
- Client pays only for services provided
- Promotes efficient client–agency relationship

Cons:
- High administration costs
- Difficult for agency to forecast workload

**PAYMENT-BY-RESULTS SYSTEM
(LOWER COMMISSION AND INCENTIVES)**

Pros:
- Encourages neutral media recommendations involving a variety of media
- Additional revenue to agency for successful campaigns

Cons:
- Accountability; potential loss on account if results not achieved
- Influences beyond the control of agency could negatively impact advertising

MDC Partners
www.mdccorp.com

$1 million. The agency commission would be $150 000, or 15 percent of $1 million. The client would pay the agency $1 million; the agency would retain $150 000 and forward the remaining $850 000 to the media.

This system does not consider the quality or impact of the message. Imagine an industry where a company's main product (the creative) is given away for free, and on the occasions that it is paid for, the price is the same regardless of whether it is a winner or a flop. "We have created an industry in which we loudly undervalue that which we do," says Miles Nadal, CEO of MDC Partners.[22]

Production costs involved with print advertising or television and radio commercials are paid by the client but at a different commission rate. Typically, a profit margin of 17.65 percent is added to the production costs incurred by the agency. For example, if the cost of producing a single 30-second television commercial is $200 000, the agency would receive $35 300 (17.65 percent of $200 000) for its services. The agency would bill the client $235 300 and from these funds the external suppliers who produced the commercial would be paid.

The commission system has fallen out of favour with clients because it fuelled a perception that agencies were making too much money from easy media-buying assignments. There was also a perception that it was contributing to an inherent bias within an agency to emphasize media that are more profitable for an agency to buy—television, for example, is a very easy medium for an agency to recommend.[23]

In situations where clients use a media-buying service to perform only one basic function, lower commission rates apply. For buying media, the range is 2.5 to 3 percent of the amount billed. For planning the media campaign and buying the media, the commission rate increases to an average of around 5 percent.[24]

The industry is investigating some new alternatives for agency compensation. For the latest news on this topic read the Advertising in Action vignette **Agency Compensation: What's Fair?**

THE FEE SYSTEM

In its truest form, the fee system avoids any form of commission and rewards an agency for the labour (time, effort, and energy) it puts into servicing the client. The advertiser

ADVERTISING IN ACTION

Agency Compensation: What's Fair?

How to pay an agency, and how much to pay them, are controversial issues in contemporary advertising. The age-old commission system that called for agencies to receive 15 percent of media billings is all but dead, and for good reason—clients were paying the same amount for good ideas and bad ideas! It just doesn't add up anymore.

Agencies and marketers in Canada now seem generally content to use a fee-based system topped up with a performance bonus that is granted when business is good. According to the Institute of Communication Agencies, 40 percent of agencies in Canada are using this combination to compensate agencies. Of marketers using incentives, 68 percent said it resulted in improved agency performance. In the typical bonus system, agencies earn more when brand awareness increases, when sales or market share increases, and if the agency is satisfied with the level of service.

Many critics see flaws in the performance-based system and are offering two new proposals that are designed to win back some respect for the advertising industry. The first proposal is a **concept fee,** which is a one-time fee that covers the cost of developing the creative concept, and is based on the estimated value of the idea to the marketer's business. It is similar to a project fee except that the agency retains intellectual property rights to the concept. The marketer will pay more to the agency if its work is used outside agreed-upon parameters. Such a model will work well for marketers looking for "the big idea."

The second proposal is a **licensing fee** that would see marketers pay less during the concept development phase. Instead, they would pay licensing fees to use the work once it's approved. Such a model would work well for marketers looking for long-term campaigns and lower up-front costs.

These new proposals are controversial, and industry insiders don't see them being implemented any time soon. Tom Shepansky, a partner at Rethink, still believes that when a client pays for an idea, it becomes their idea. After all, agencies wouldn't be developing big ideas without clients.

Unilever Canada has moved entirely to a performance-based system and has experienced good results, so why change again? It ties agency compensation to top-line sales revenue and market share for each of its brands. Marketing director Mark Wakefield says, "Unilever has performance incentives for its employees, so it makes sense to link agency compensation to results. Everyone is focused on the same thing."

You be the judge. Is there a best system for compensating an agency?

Source: Adapted from Rob Gerlsbeck, "Creative compensation," *Marketing*, April 17/24, 2006, pp. 14, 16.

and agency agree on an hourly, annual, or overall fee. The fee can vary according to the department or levels of salary within a department. In other cases, a flat hourly fee for all work is determined, no matter the salary level of the person doing the work. There has been a movement toward fees in recent years because so much of the work in advertising today is not traditional advertising—it has gone well beyond simply buying space in the mass media. Agencies are now making recommendations involving all aspects of integrated marketing communications. Commissions cannot be calculated on recommendations involving activities such as sales promotion, direct mail, and online communications. Fees are established by assigning costs of agency operations to a client. The agency then determines what hourly charge will recover these costs and provide the agency with a profit.

Some of the more common options are minimum guarantees, hourly rates, and costs-plus-profits. If a *minimum guarantee* is used, the client and agency establish a minimum income figure, including a profit, by making assumptions about the level of service required for a period of time, usually a year. If an *hourly rate* system is used, the agency assigns an hourly rate to those employees who have direct contact with the client. The rate is designed to recover agency costs and includes a profit margin. If a *cost-plus-profits* system is used, the amount paid to the agency includes the agency's direct costs (employee salaries), indirect costs (heat, light, and power), and profits. The costs associated with all of the people employed in the agency—including those who do not work directly on a client's business—are taken into account, along with other costs. In effect, indirect costs are added to direct costs, along with a provision for profit.

Fee systems tend to be cumbersome and require a great deal of administration and paperwork. The main drawback of the fee system is similar to that of the commission system—it does not reflect the quality of the work by an agency or the impact it has on the client's business.

PAYMENT-BY-RESULTS (PBR)

One of the first advertisers to experiment with performance-based compensation was Procter & Gamble. Its rationale for moving away from the commission system was to encourage agencies to recommend a variety of media and to rely less on 30-second television ads, which are more expensive than other forms of media and thus garner larger commissions. Perhaps Procter & Gamble foresaw the coming of the internet and the demise of television commercials. In the **payment-by-results system**, agencies are paid a higher commission percentage for good business results and a lower percentage for poor results. The system keeps the client and the agency focused on the end goal: to increase brand sales.

Moving to performance-based compensation will eliminate media bias (e.g., recommending media that generate fat commissions) and encourage holistic, media-neutral marketing. Many other companies now use this system, but an obvious drawback has been raised by agencies: linking the performance of a brand to advertising is tricky because sales can be affected by a host of factors, many of which are beyond the control of the advertising agency.

There are three types of performance criteria used in PBR schemes to determine the remuneration paid to the agency: business performance, advertising performance, and agency performance. For more specific information about performance criteria, refer to Figure 2.10.

It is difficult to determine which of these remuneration systems is best for the client and the agency. The most effective model is the one designed to meet the needs of each

Business Performance	Advertising Performance	Agency Performance
Sales volume	Advertising awareness	Agency service delivery
Volume growth	Brand image shifts	Relationship management
Relative brand performance	Attitude ratings	Functional competencies
Composite performance	Ad enjoyment	Contribution to "branding"
Market share	Brand personality	Project management
Customer loyalty	Predisposition to buy	Administration
Brand equity	Ad scores	Cost efficiency
Brand profitability	Persuasion index	Proactivity

The ICA 2000 Study on PBR shows the weighting emphasis was balanced as follows: Agency 41%, Advertising 30%, and Business results 29%. Further, 83% of Canadian PBR programs include business performance criteria, 65% include advertising performance criteria, and 78% include agency performance criteria.

Source: "Payment by results 2, advertising agency remuneration best practices," Institute of Communication Agencies, **www.ica-ad.com**.

FIGURE 2.10

Performance criteria included in a payment-by-results compensation model

client–agency relationship. The compensation model should be designed to provide adequate professional service to the client, provide an incentive for both the client and the agency, fairly compensate the agency, and be reviewed periodically for effectiveness. "At the end of the day, clients will pay for results," says Miles Nadal.[25] His agency, Crispin Porter + Bogusky, is paid a combination of flat fees and performance incentives for all the work it performs for its clients, which range from Burger King to BMW.

Crispin Porter + Bogusky
ww.cpbgroup.com

SUMMARY

The Canadian advertising industry comprises three primary groups and numerous support groups. The primary groups include the advertisers (clients), advertising agencies, and the media. Support groups include the Institute of Canadian Advertising, the Association of Canadian Advertisers, and numerous media associations.

Advertising management usually comes under the jurisdiction of the marketing department. The size and marketing sophistication of the organization often dictate how advertising is managed. It could be the responsibility of a brand manager or category manager, or it could be the responsibility of many individuals. With marketing and communication strategy becoming more continental and global in scope (e.g., using strategies and executions that are effective for multiple audiences), managers are redefining targets and implementing campaigns on a North American or global scale.

In the advertising development process, the roles and responsibilities of the client include planning and budgeting,

coordination of advertising with other marketing and marketing communications activity, monitoring the implementation of communications activities, liaising with the advertising agency, and securing executive approval to implement advertising plans. Once plans are implemented, the manager is responsible for evaluating advertising, for which he or she is held accountable.

Advertising agencies provide a variety of services to their clients, but their primary role is to provide experience and expertise in the communications process. In this area, the agency provides planning assistance and contributes an objective viewpoint to that planning process. Agency recommendations must be cost-effective and have impact on the intended target.

The goal of a client–agency relationship is to have a long-term partnership in which both parties prosper. However, relationships between clients and agencies are often volatile, and account shifting is a common occurrence in the industry. Such shifting occurs for reasons such as client dissatisfaction with the quality of work, philosophical differences in creative and media direction, and the absence of a team concept. For a client–agency relationship to be a lasting one there must be open and honest communication among the parties, mutual respect, and agreement on common goals. In recent years there has been a trend toward project assignments and short-term relationships. The nature of client–agency relationships is changing as the business environment changes. Short-term relationships place added pressure on agencies to perform.

Advertisers must evaluate the services provided by agencies and decide whether to use a full-service agency or hire a specialist that may or may not offer all of the services required. Specialists include creative boutiques, media-buying services, direct-response companies, and interactive communications companies. In recent years, product-category specialist agencies and niche-market specialist agencies have entered the picture, opting for work that is seen as unattractive or unprofitable by traditional agencies. In contrast, such boutique-style specialists see profitable opportunities.

Traditional, full-service agencies are managed in specific functional areas: account management, creative, and the media. Account management personnel consult with clients and coordinate activity within the agency. The creative department develops communication concepts, and the media department plans and places advertising time and space. The services that an agency provides to a client are usually handled by an account team that includes an individual from each functional area.

Large multi-product advertisers often work with several agencies at the same time. In this situation the client designates one agency as their agency of record (AOR). The AOR is responsible for all media buying for all company brands regardless of which agency they are assigned to. The AOR may be a full-service agency or a media-buying service.

A major factor in client–agency relationships is the method by which the agency is paid. There are three different systems to compensate agencies: a commission system, under which the agency receives a percentage of the value of media purchased by an agency for a client; a fee system, which is based on the services requested by the client; and a payment-by-results system, in which agencies are compensated based on how well they meet predetermined performance criteria. Such a system usually involves a lower rate of commission and a bonus system.

KEY TERMS

REVIEW QUESTIONS

1. What are the three primary groups that comprise the advertising industry?

2. What are the alternative management systems used by clients to manage the advertising function? Briefly explain each system.

3. Identify and explain the roles and responsibilities of the client in the creation of advertising.

4. What are the key roles and responsibilities of advertising agencies in the advertising process?

5. What is meant by the phrase "client–agency relations"? What factors have a negative influence on the relationship? What factors have a positive influence on the relationship?

6. What does "account shifting" refer to? Why does account shifting occur?

7. How do a full-service agency, a creative boutique, and a media-buying service differ from one another?

8. What are the primary functions of the following agency departments? Who are the key people in each area?

a) Account management
b) Creative department
c) Media department

9. Explain the concept of agency teams. Why is the team concept important to clients?

10. What is an agency of record (AOR)?

11. What are the three primary methods of compensating an advertising agency? Briefly describe each method.

12. A client spends $3 million on network television advertising, $450 000 on magazine advertising, and $250 000 on outdoor posters. The cost of producing two television commercials was $400 000, and the production charges for the magazines and outdoor posters were $60 000. How much commission does the client's advertising agency earn, given that the agency is compensated using the traditional rate of commission? What does the client pay in total? How much does the media receive in total?

DISCUSSION QUESTIONS

1. Assume you were the director of marketing for Pepsi-Cola Canada or the TDL Group Limited (parent company of Tim Hortons). Would you work with a full-service advertising agency or would you divide your work among various specialists such as creative boutiques, media-buying services, and other types of specialists? Justify your position. What factors determine the use of generalists or specialists?

2. Given that the client hires an agency to develop creative strategies, how involved in the creative development process should the client be? Where do the client's responsibilities end?

3. "The client–agency relationship is a partnership." Discuss the significance of this statement in the context of today's business environment. Is the statement true? What are the ingredients of a successful relationship?

4. Read the Advertising in Action vignette **Agency Compensation: What's Fair?** Several different models for compensating an agency are presented in the chapter, and the vignette presents two new proposals. Evaluate the various alternatives and present an opinion on what system makes sense. Is there such a thing as a best way to compensate an agency?

5. This chapter referenced a global campaign for McDonald's that uses the theme and slogan "I'm lovin' it." The concept was developed by McDonald's agency in Germany. Is it possible for a company to take a concept like this and make it work on a global scale? Justify your position with an appropriate rationale and provide a few examples of other successful or unsuccessful global advertising concepts.

NOTES

1. Association of Canadian Advertisers, **www.aca-online.com**.

2. Craig Endicott and Kenneth Wylie, "Agency report," *Advertising Age*, May 2, 2005, p. S-1.

3. "The rankings," *Marketing*, June 19, 2006, p. 29.

4. Institute of Communications and Advertising, **www.ica-ad.com/factsheet**.

5. TVB Canada, **www.tvb.ca/tvbresources**.

6. Lisa Sanders, "Will production houses replace Mad Ave?" *Advertising Age*, April 3, 2006, p. 16.

7. Lara Mills, Molson overhauls marketing team," *Marketing*, September 20, 1999, p. 17.

8. Grant Robertson, "Kraft unites North American divisions," *The Globe and Mail*, October 15, 2005, p. B7.

9. Keith MacArthur, "McD's talks tough with its agencies," *Advertising Age*, February 3, 2003, pp. 1, 33.

10. Paul-Mark Rendon, "Coke's 'I' is on consumers," *Marketing*, December 12/19, 2005, p. 14.

11. Jean Halliday, "Pontiac G5 blazes trail to exclusively-internet advertising," *Advertising Age*, August 27, 2006, **www.adage.com**.

12. Lauren Patrecca, "Five-second commercials try to counter TiVo," *USA Today*, July 6, 2006, **www.usatoday.com**.

13. Chris Powell, "Family ties," *Marketing*, May 31, 2004, p. 23.

14. Keith MacArthur, "Shootout shows hot, cold nature of ad business," *The Globe and Mail*, April 11, 2006, p. B6.

15. Justin Smallbridge, "The short answer," *Financial Post*, August 12, 2002, p. FP12.

16. "Best media operations," *Strategy*, The Canadian Media Report, December 2003, pp. 57, 61.

17. "The rankings," *Marketing*, June 19, 2006, p. 29.

18. Eyeblaster, **www.eyeblaster.com/company**.

19. MyThum, **www.mythum.com**.

20. "A few facts on the 50+ market," **www.boomersmarketing.com**.

21. Institute of Communication Agencies, **www.ica-ad.com/remuneration**.

22. Paul Brent, "Ad agencies seek new ways of getting paid," *Financial Post*, May 7, 2005, p. FP7.

23. Joe Mandese, "Low margins? Agencies have created a monster," *Advertising Age*, February 22, 1999, pp. S12, S13.

24. Institute of Communication Agencies, **www.ica-ad.com/remuneration**.

25. Brent, p. FP7.

Client–Agency Relations:

ISSUES RELATED TO PITCHING NEW ACCOUNTS

When an account is up for review, interested agencies are asked to submit proposals to a client as a means of securing the account. Most clients follow a systematic procedure that fairly evaluates all submissions; after this process is complete, a select group of agencies appears on a short list. At this point the nature of the selection process often becomes controversial.

There are costs associated with pitching a new account. The client makes demands for a certain degree of creative sophistication. For example, will it be rough art, finished art, storyboard, or finished commercial? How far an agency will go in this process largely depends on the financial resources available for the pitch. In some cases the client will offer a flat amount of money to cover some of the agency costs, but in most cases there is no compensation.

The Issues

Mark Weisbarth, president of Due North Communications, Toronto, says, "Speculative pitches and spec creative are the wrong way to choose an ad agency. You are creating ads just for the sake of the pitch." Many agency peers agree. They say it devalues their product, is bad for the industry, is prohibitively expensive, and is unfair. If this is so, how did such a selection process come to be?

Well, it's all about competition—a war among agencies to land new accounts. The better the agency looks, the better the quality of the presentation, the greater the odds of being the agency selected. It's like being trapped on your own battlefield. The idea in a new business presentation is to knock their socks off, so putting a great deal of effort into the creative goes a long way in impressing the prospective client.

According to Chris Staples, a partner at Rethink, Vancouver, "What develops when marketers ask for spec work is an intractable game of one-upmanship. The arms race that goes on between agencies means you can spend half a million dollars on pitches." He says the high cost of spec creative gets passed on to existing clients.

A Real Situation

In January 2005, Rogers Communications put its account up for review. With an annual media budget of $80 million, it would be an attractive client for a lot of large advertising agencies. As part of the selection process Rogers clearly indicated that all short-listed agencies (those making the final cut) would submit spec creative, with Rogers paying fair market value for the work submitted. According to industry sources the amount was $50 000.

This raises the question: What is spec creative? Is it truly spec creative if the agency is paid for their effort? Is it only spec if it is provided to the client at no cost, or is all pitch creative considered spec, no matter what the compensation? Further, at this point in the process, who owns the creative—the agency or the prospective client?

Rogers' position on the matter was clear. They would own all ideas that were submitted by the short-listed agencies regardless of who was finally selected. The ad industry, through the Institute of Communication Agencies (ICA), felt this demand contravened intellectual rights laws.

To compete for an account the size of Rogers is very costly for an agency. In this case the required creative work needed deep pockets: as much as $200 000 for agencies making it to the final round, and as much as double that for any agency in the final three.

The View from the Institute of Communication Agencies

The ICA's preferred method for selecting an agency is to eliminate spec creative entirely and replace it with an optional workshop exercise that evaluates independent problem-solving skills. This approach prevents agencies from pouring resources into a pitch that wouldn't be part of the normal service model.

The Institute believes clients base their selection decisions too heavily on the spec work and pay less attention to other key ingredients, such as category experience, strategy, and chemistry. Issues that truly influence the quality of a client–agency relationship take a back seat to the creative.

Rogers justifies its position by saying that ownership of the creative submissions protects them in case future advertising resembles materials, concepts, or ideas that came from an agency that loses out on the business.

The ICA disagrees with Rogers' position completely, saying spec creative does not benefit either party. The client doesn't even know who really did the work. It could be someone in New York or London, not Toronto. Says Peter Elwood, former president of Lever Brothers and Lipton Canada, "To pick an agency based on speculative creative is like picking a bride off the internet—you have no idea what the future holds."

Frank Palmer, CEO of DDB Canada, believes agencies are hurting themselves by agreeing to these terms. "Turning over intellectual property even before they are chosen is like signing a prenuptial agreement before you even know who you are going to marry. I think agencies are doing a disservice to the industry by chasing a piece of business under these conditions."

The View from the Association of Canadian Advertisers

Ron Lund, president of the Association of Canadian Advertisers, says agencies should look at themselves in the mirror. He says he has never heard a client say, "Go out there and spend $150 000 of your other clients' time on our business." His point: agencies spend money by choice to get a lucrative client—the "short-term pain for long-term gain" principle.

The winning agency in Rogers' review was Publicis Toronto. Duncan Bruce, executive creative director of Publicis, had this to say about spec creative: "When a marketer has a huge account on the line, it may be well within its rights to ask for comprehensive spec. Big-stakes marketers like Rogers simply can't rely on agency credentials alone. For a client that size, how can you say we're going to hand over our business, the stewardship of our brand, based on the work you've done for other clients? To me, Rogers ran it the way they had to." Perhaps Bruce would feel differently if his agency had not won the account.

The Bottom Line

Spec creative and the issues that surround the practice have been around a long time, and there doesn't seem to be any solution to the problem on the horizon. Ron Lund of the ICA offers a good point. He says there are too many agencies chasing too few clients, so creative shootouts are impossible to avoid. He adds that if Canada's top-ranked agencies simply stopped doing it, the problem would go away. Clients won't work with inferior agencies.

Additional Information

For more insight into the agency selection process, visit the Institute of Communication Agencies website at **www.ica-ad.com**. The steps for selecting an agency recommended by the ICA are documented at the website. For more information about the Association of Canadian Advertisers, visit their website at **www.aca-online.com**.

Questions

1. What is your opinion of spec creative? Should it be part of the agency selection process?

2. If spec creative is part of the selection process, should standards be established that both clients and agencies can agree to? What should those standards be?

3. Who should own the spec creative? Is it the property of the agency (whether they win or lose the account) or the client who demanded the work as part of the pitch?

Source: Adapted from Paul-Mark Rendon, "Should spec be pitched?" *Marketing*, June 20, 2005, pp. 33, 34; "Rogers review," *Financial Post*, February 15, 2005, p. FP10.

PART **2**

Marketing Communications Planning

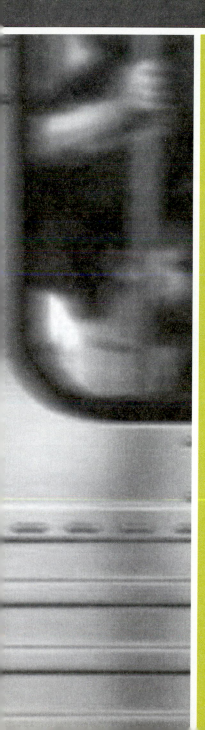

Part 2 concentrates on the central theme of the text—planning the marketing communications effort.

Chapter 3 provides the foundation for marketing communications planning, presenting the important concepts of consumer behaviour, market segmentation and target marketing, and positioning.

Chapter 4 describes the elements of strategic planning and presents the content and structure of marketing plans and marketing communications plans. It establishes the relationships among these plans and provides an appreciation of the role and importance of planning in the development of all forms of marketing communications.

CHAPTER **3**

Consumer Behaviour Concepts and Target Marketing

Courtesy of Dick Hemingway.

Learning Objectives

After studying this chapter, you will be able to

1. Explain how consumer behaviour concepts influence the development of marketing communications strategies

2. Assess the information needed to identify and select target markets

3. Distinguish between demographic, psychographic, geographic, and behaviour-response segmentation variables

4. Explain the influence of relationship marketing concepts on marketing communications strategies

5. Explain the concept of positioning and its role in developing marketing communications strategies

This chapter discusses concepts that are important to the planning of advertising and marketing communications programs. For starters, the development of an effective advertising strategy relies heavily on an understanding of basic consumer behaviour. Uncovering what makes a particular customer group tick provides direction on what appeal techniques will grab an audience's attention. It may also provide insights into what media are best suited for reaching a group of customers. Organizations must identify profitable target markets by analyzing demographic trends, psychographic characteristics, and geographic or regional differences. The end result of such an analysis is a clear description of a target market that is worth pursuing. The chapter ends with a discussion of a variety of product-positioning strategies.

Consumer Behaviour

Consumer behaviour can be defined as the acts that individuals perform in obtaining and using goods and services, including the decision-making processes that precede and determine these acts.[1] A firm understanding of how behavioural tendencies apply to purchase decisions is of significant benefit to the marketing organization. Consequently, leading marketing organizations spend a considerable amount of money on marketing research in order to learn as much as they can about their customers, and perhaps get an edge on the competition in the process. Information is power, as they say!

From a purely competitive perspective, marketers must have access to data concerning consumers' buying habits and which kinds of media they favour, in order to develop more convincing communications programs that stimulate response by the target market. The purpose of most research boils down to obtaining answers to a few key questions:

- Who makes the buying decision?
- Who influences the buying decision?
- What motivates the buyers and people of influence to take action?

Answers to the above questions will provide valuable input for developing a marketing strategy and a marketing communications strategy. To illustrate, consider the behaviour of males when shopping for clothes. Men perceive shopping as a less-than-masculine endeavour, and they are likely to bring along the opposite sex for reassurance when making decisions. Sharp men's wear retailers like Harry Rosen know this and consequently spend more time in the store selling the fashions to the females, since their approval is essential. Many retailers have found that when they encourage both sexes to shop together, sales are higher.[2] A discussion of the key influences on consumer behaviour follows.

NEEDS AND MOTIVES

Needs suggest a state of deprivation—the absence of something useful. **Motives** are the conditions that prompt the action that is taken to satisfy the need (the action elicited by marketing and advertising activity). The relationship between needs and motives is direct with respect to marketing and advertising activity. Such activity must sufficiently develop the target market's need—through an appealing presentation of appropriate benefits—so that the target is motivated to respond to by purchasing the product or service.

Maslow's *hierarchy of needs* and *theory of motivation* have had a significant impact on marketing and advertising strategies. According to Maslow, needs can be classified from lower-level to higher-level as shown in Figure 3.1. His theory is based on two prevailing assumptions:[3]

1. When lower-level needs are satisfied, a person moves up to higher-level needs.
2. Satisfied needs do not motivate. Instead, behaviour will be influenced by needs yet to be satisfied.

FIGURE 3.1

The Hierarchy of Needs

Source: Adapted from Maslow, Abraham H.; Frager, Robert D. (Editor); Fadiman, James (Editor), *Motivation and Personality*, 3rd Edition, © 1997. Adapted by permission of Pearson Education Canada Inc., Upper Saddle River, NJ.

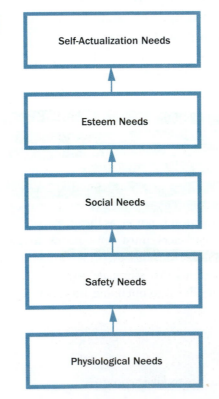

Maslow states that individuals move through five levels of needs:

- *Physiological needs* hunger, thirst, sex, shelter
- *Safety needs* security, protection, comfort
- *Social needs* sense of belonging, love from family and friends
- *Esteem needs* recognition, achievement, status, need to excel
- *Self-actualization needs* fulfillment, to realize potential (achieve what you believe you can achieve)

Numerous advertising examples can be cited to demonstrate advertising applications of Maslow's need theory. Safety needs are used to motivate people to purchase automobile tires, life insurance, and retirement savings plans. Honda delivers a message of car safety that focuses on security and protection, a need that becomes particularly important when adults become new parents. Refer to the ad in Figure 3.2 for a visual illustration.

The desire to be accepted by peers (that is, the need for social satisfaction) is commonly appealed to in the advertising for personal-care products and clothing. Advertising for products in these markets tends to appeal to one's social consciousness. For example, the images presented by brands such as Guess and Calvin Klein have impact on style-conscious youth and adults aged 20 to 29. Esteem needs are addressed

FIGURE 3.2

An ad focused on safety and security needs

Courtesy of Honda Canada Inc.

in commercials that portray people in successful business roles and occupations; for example, an executive driving an automobile symbolic of success, such as a Cadillac, BMW, or Porsche.

PERSONALITY AND SELF-CONCEPT

Personality refers to a person's distinguishing psychological characteristics, those features that lead to relatively consistent and enduring responses to the environment in which that person lives. It is influenced by self-perceptions, which in turn are influenced by psychological needs, family, culture, and reference groups. Why do people buy designer-label clothing at high prices and in upscale boutiques when low-priced items performing the same functions are available? Such purchases are based on the images we desire to have of ourselves. To appreciate this principle, one must understand the self-concept theory.

Self-concept theory states that the self has four components: real self, self-image, looking-glass self, and ideal self.[4]

- *Real self* is an objective evaluation of the individual. It is you as you really are.

- *Self-image* is how you see yourself. You might, for example, see yourself as an aspiring athlete, musician, or writer, even though you may not be any of these. It's like a role you play.

- *Looking-glass self* is how you think others see you. A person's view of how others see them can be very different from how others actually see them.

- *Ideal self* is how you would like to be. It is what you aspire to.

Marketers know that, human nature being what it is, many important decisions are based on the looking-glass self and the ideal self. In other words, many goods and services are bought on the basis of emotion; goods that help us feel better, look better, and take us to the next level of fulfillment are very attractive to us. We may not achieve what we want, but there is some psychological satisfaction in having something that represents a higher level of achievement. For example, how does a busy executive who lives in an urban area and fights daily traffic jams justify purchasing a well-equipped luxury sports car that is better suited to fast speeds and open-road driving? The answer resides somewhere in the looking-glass self and ideal self: the automobile says something positive about that person to other people—at least in the mind of the sports car owner. It also says something about his or her esteem needs. For an illustration refer to Figure 3.3.

PERCEPTIONS

Perception refers to the manner in which individuals receive and interpret messages. From a marketing perspective, how individual consumers perceive the same product can vary considerably. Perceptual images are based on influences such as advertising, packaging, and pricing. It should be noted that consumers are not aware of all that goes on around them; they are quite selective about messages they receive. The messages they select to receive depend on their level of interest and need requirements. There are three levels of selectivity:

- *Selective exposure* Our eyes and minds notice only information that interests us.

- *Selective perception* We screen out information and messages that conflict with previously learned attitudes and beliefs.

- *Selective retention* We remember only what we want to remember.

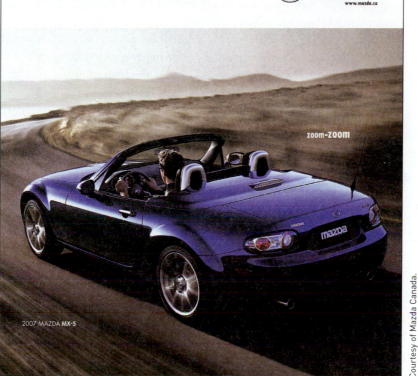

FIGURE 3.3

An ad that appeals to a person's looking-glass self or ideal self

Theories of perception help to explain why people respond differently to advertising messages. For example, as a student you may be oblivious to automobile advertising because you are not ready to buy a car. Sure, you may see some ads for smart-looking cars and say, "Someday I will own one of those." But the message is quickly discarded. Like mother always said, "In one ear and out the other!" Things change at graduation, however. Your first job may necessitate new clothes and a new car, and suddenly you begin to absorb yourself in fashion and automobile advertising at the expense of all other messages. Companies like General Motors, Ford, and Toyota know that it's all a matter of timing—sooner or later you will tune in. No doubt there are automobile ads aimed at graduates posted somewhere in your school.

General Motors
www.gmcanada.com

ATTITUDES

Attitudes are an individual's feelings, favourable or unfavourable, toward an idea or object (the advertised product). Generally speaking, organizations present their products to consumers so that they agree with the prevailing attitudes of their target audience. Product acceptance comes more quickly. They have found that it is expensive to try to change attitudes.

Sometimes, however, the public at large may take exception to the message and the way a company presents its product. Consider a situation such as this: you are a marketing manager and you see an opportunity to target the gay community. Over the past few years, society seems to have become more tolerant of gay relationships, and the gay community is now more out in the open. You conduct a cost–benefit analysis and that leaves you feeling indecisive. You see a risk in alienating your core customers—they may leave for another brand with a mainstream image. The solution here lies in media strategy. By being able to target the gay community through special-interest publications, the mainstream target market will not see the message associating the brand with the gay community. At least that's the theory behind the media strategy. See Figure 3.4 for an illustration of this approach.

Some brands have more openly targeted the gay community. A commercial for the Toyota Corolla set a new standard by showing two girls kissing in the front seat, and BMW Mini used a bisexual theme—three individuals enjoying certain activities in a very small vehicle. For more insight into how attitudes are shaping contemporary marketing communications strategies, see the Advertising in Action vignette **Advertising with Pride**.

Social changes have produced new targets: Absolut appeals to the gay community

ABSOLUT OUT.

THE SHARPE-BLACKMORE PARTNERSHIPS. ABSOLUT COUNTRY OF SWEDEN VODKA AND LOGO, ABSOLUT, ABSOLUT BOTTLE DESIGN AND ABSOLUT CALLIGRAPHY ARE TRADEMARKS OWNED BY V&S VIN AND SPRIT AB. © 1995. V&S VIN & SPRIT AB.

Courtesy of XTRA! Inhouse design. Sharpe Blackmore Inc.

Advertising with Pride

Identifying target markets that offer long-term profit potential is the responsibility of an organization's marketing department. Canada's gay market is estimated to be worth $75 billion—a market more than worthy of unique marketing and marketing communications programs. So why are so many organizations either afraid or uncomfortable in seeking out the gay community?

Many organizations resist because they are uncertain how to proceed; they simply don't understand the needs, motives, attitudes, and perceptions of gay consumers. To enter with the wrong approach could be fatal. "The gay consumer is very cynical. If you make a mistake, that's it. You should be scared," says Bruce McDonald, co-founder of the Canadian Gay and Lesbian Chamber of Commerce.

Another reason for not pursuing the gay community is the fear of alienating a brand's current customers. If there is some confusion over the brand's image in the mainstream market there could be more to lose than to gain. All risks aside, however, the gay market is well worth pursuing, based on these essential gay numbers:

- 3.2 million—the number of gay and lesbian consumers in Canada
- $75 billion—the estimated annual buying power of Canada's gay community
- 36 percent like to buy new products right away
- 57 percent are decision-makers in their business or professional roles
- 94 percent would go out of their way to buy products marketed directly to them
- $72 800 is the average gay household income in Canada; $47 600 is the national average

Many organizations have placed ads in the gay media (there are all kinds of publications available to reach this target, as well as PrideVision TV) but they have made a lot of mistakes with their message strategy. Bay-Bloor Radio, a high-end electronics store in downtown Toronto, ran an ad in *Fab* magazine featuring a heterosexual couple. A straight image in a gay publication doesn't quite cut it! "It's pretty well known that you have to show images the market is familiar and comfortable with," says McDonald.

Some markets and brands are ahead of the curve. They have done their research and decided to approach the gay community in a progressive manner. To them, a customer is a customer; their desire is to build their business; gender should not stand in the way. Leaders in this area include tourism, automotive, alcohol, and financial services companies. BMO Financial Group employs gay-positive messages in targeted publications and direct mail, and sponsors various Pride Week events.

In the automotive sector, many companies are now targeting gays, but Subaru was the trendsetter. For more than 10 years Subaru has sponsored gay film festivals, included product placements in gay and lesbian TV shows, and designed ads specifically for gay publications.

To a great extent, Canada is now a pro-gay nation. New gay marriage laws have generated a lot of publicity and exposure, so much so that Canada is a destination that gays and lesbians want to visit—a great opportunity for tourism marketing organizations. Further, it is a known fact that gay customers remain loyal (much more so than mainstream customers) to those brands that target them directly.

Should a marketing organization target the gay community? Do the benefits outweigh the drawbacks? You be the judge.

Source: Adapted from Michelle Halpern, "They're here, they're queer, and they love to shop," *Marketing*, September 20, 2004, pp. 10–13; Michelle Halpern, "Gay getaways," *Marketing*, May 22/29, 2006, p. 4.

REFERENCE GROUPS

A **reference group**, or **peer group**, is a group, class, or category of people to which individuals believe they belong, whether or not they actually do. Their relationship to their reference group may influence their buying behaviour. Reference groups could include co-workers, sports teams, hobby clubs, fraternal organizations, and schoolmates. A member of a group experiences considerable pressure to conform to the standards of the group and thereby "fit in." The desire to fit in influences the type of products a member will purchase.

Peer influence is strongest among youths. Why do teenagers start smoking or start experimenting with drugs? They are rebelling against their parents and other adults. They turn to their peers for information on what behaviour is desirable. Mothers telling their teenage sons and daughters to drink milk because it's good for them is an idea that doesn't cut it when so many beverage alternatives are available to them.

To encourage milk consumption in the Prairies, dairy farmers realized that teens had to hear the message from their peers, not their parents. Milk was repositioned based on situations the teen target actually experiences and can relate to, experiences that are physical and emotional, and relevant to the realities of teen life. Images in the milk ads illustrated various rites of passage: first love, emotional loss, wild imagination, and so on. The repositioning campaign was very successful.[5]

With the right strategy, an advertiser need only associate their brand with a certain situation and the target will become interested in it. Right Guard Xtreme, for example, gained appeal among the youth market on the basis of an ad campaign that had lots of attitude. The "Big Air" campaign was aimed directly at hip teens who enjoy alternative sports like snowboarding and mountain biking. See the illustration in Figure 3.5.

FIGURE 3.5

Lifestyle images and reference group associations have an influence on teens

FAMILY

Members of a family influence buying decisions. The actual impact each member has on the decision depends on the type of product or service under consideration. Roles and responsibilities within families have changed with the times, and the lines of responsibility are blurred between the male and female head of the household. Children seem to have more influence than ever before on what products their parents buy. Factors contributing to these role changes are the increasing numbers of two-income families, continued growth in the number of women working outside the home, as well as the growth of single-parent families.

To demonstrate how family buying patterns are changing, you need only look at the cell-phone market. Generations of children grew up without cell phones, but now it seems every kid on the block has one. Did their parents willingly go out and buy one for them? Of course not! Marketers have successfully positioned cell phones in youth markets as an essential tool for their social universe. Parents naively thought of the cell phone as a safety device, something that would be used for emergencies, but now they are paying exorbitant monthly billing fees simply to keep their kids happy. Now, that's power and influence on a purchase situation!

At the parent level, much of the decision-making is shared between partners. Consequently, many marketers are double targeting. **Double targeting** involves devising a single marketing strategy for both sexes. In its simplest form, a product would have one strategy for females and another for males—one brand with two unique messages. Considering the changes in household formations and the roles and responsibilities within households, to double target is wise. Today, there are just as many women as men trolling the aisles of Canadian Tire. Other brands in traditionally male-oriented categories, from electronics to financial services, have made a play for the fair sex. As a result, these brands have swelled their customer base and their profits.

Canadian Tire has added new brands, such as the Debbie Travis line of products, and adopted a more stylish merchandising strategy in its home decor sections, as a means of meeting the needs of female shoppers. Home Depot is another retailer executing a double-targeting strategy. Home Depot loves the guys but has shifted its emphasis to attract more females. According to Pat Wilkinson, director of marketing at Home Depot, there is a difference between men and women. "Men look at the pieces; women look at the whole project. Women start with: What's my dream?"[6] Both Canadian Tire and Home Depot have adjusted their advertising strategies successfully.

Canadian Tire
www.canadiantire.ca

Home Depot
www.homedepot.ca

Identifying and Selecting Target Markets

The ability of a company to target specific customers is based on the concept of market segmentation. **Market segmentation** involves dividing a large market into smaller homogeneous markets (segments) based on common needs or similar lifestyles. Segmentation involves three steps: identifying market segments (e.g., describing the profile of the primary user), selecting the market segments that offer the most potential (typically, targets that offer the greatest profit potential), and positioning the product so that it appeals to the target market.

When an organization identifies a target market, it develops a profile of the customer it wants to pursue. That profile becomes the first cornerstone of all marketing and marketing communications strategies for the product. The second cornerstone is a sound positioning strategy. Positioning strategy is discussed later in the chapter.

A target-market profile is the result of an organization's analysis of external variables that influence the direction of marketing strategy. These variables include demographic trends, social and lifestyle trends, and geographic (regional) trends. Behaviour-response variables also help form a target-market profile.

DEMOGRAPHIC SEGMENTATION

With **demographic segmentation**, target markets are identified and pursued on the basis of variables such as *age, gender, income, occupation, education, marital status, household formation*, and *cultural mix*. In Canada, certain demographic trends are having a direct impact on the direction of marketing strategies and all forms of marketing communications. Discussion of these trends follows.

THE POPULATION IS GETTING OLDER   Perhaps the most talked-about group in marketing circles today is the **baby boomers**, or **boomers**, as they are commonly referred to (those people born between 1946 and 1964). They are an attractive market due to their substantial numerical size and their buying power. Of course, the baby-boom generation spawned another blip in the age curve known as **Generation Y** (a group that is also referred to as millennials, the echo boom, and the iGeneration). The children of boomers embrace parts of **Generation X** (born 1961 to 1981) and parts of **Generation Y** (born 1976 to 2001). For a summary of how the population is aging, refer to Figure 3.6.

The older age segments are wealthier segments. Canadians older than 50 years are often free of financial obligations such as children and mortgages, so they should be seen as an attractive target. Many Canadians in this age group have developed a taste for the finer things in life. The sales growth of luxury items such as high-end watches and household appliances exceed the sales growth of mainstream retail goods in the same categories. Imported premium beers and craft brews are growing in popularity, while mainstream beers are stagnating. In the automobile sector, the mid-range luxury segment is booming, with a corresponding increase in the number of new models offered by brands such as Lexus, BMW, Mercedes, and Infiniti. See the illustration in Figure 3.7 for an example of an advertisement aimed at this market.

Each generation has a different outlook, different values, and different needs, so the challenge facing many products is how to retain older customers while trying to attract new customers. To simply stay with an aging population does not make economic sense in the long term. No other company knows this better than Levi Strauss. Boomers grew up with Levi's and are the customers that built the brand, but youth today see the brand as a relic from the past. Levi's has tried all kinds of advertising strategies to spark interest

Levi Strauss
www.levistrauss.com

FIGURE 3.6

The over-50 market is an attractive target

Source: Statistics Canada, "The over-50 market is an attractive market," adapted from Statistics Canada CANSIM database, http://cansim2.statcan.ca Table 052-0001.

Age Classification	MILLIONS OF PEOPLE		
	1996	2006	2016
0–9	3.968	3.941	3.125
10–19	4.024	4.384	4.301
20–34	6.896	6.837	7.402
35–49	7.217	7.977	7.610
50 plus	7.864	10.519	13.583

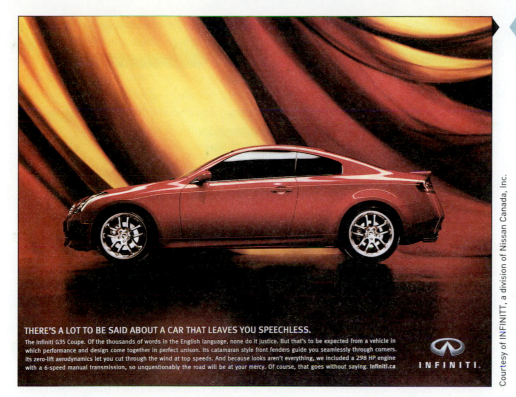

THERE'S A LOT TO BE SAID ABOUT A CAR THAT LEAVES YOU SPEECHLESS.

The Infiniti G35 Coupe. Of the thousands of words in the English language, none do it justice. But that's to be expected from a vehicle in which performance and design come together in perfect unison. Its catamaran style front fenders guide you seamlessly through corners. Its zero-lift aerodynamics let you cut through the wind at top speeds. And because looks aren't everything, we included a 298 HP engine with a 6-speed manual transmission, so unquestionably the road will be at your mercy. Of course, that goes without saying. infiniti.ca

INFINITI.

FIGURE 3.7

The Infiniti G35 Sedan and Sports Coupe appeals to the high-income baby-boom segment of the population.

among teens, but without success. As my own son says, "My dad wears them; I don't." That attitude represents an ominous challenge for Levi's. Eventually they will be out of business if they can't turn things around.

In a communications context, the boomers and the grey market represent the past while Generation X, Generation Y, and any group that follows represent the future. The younger generations will be the foundation for the success of the internet as a means of communication and commerce. As younger generations grow older, digital communications in the form of cell phones, MP3 players, and personal digital assistants will play a larger role in the media mix.

THE ECONOMIC POWER OF WOMEN Gender has always been a primary means of distinguishing product categories—personal-care products, magazines, athletic equipment, and fashion are all categorized according to the gender of the buyer. Due to the increasing presence of women in the workforce outside the home (a significant change from earlier generations) and the changing roles of men and women in Canadian households, an organization will become increasingly "unisex," as both sexes buy and use similar products. Females have been fighting off stereotypical images and portrayals in advertising for years—their goal is to be represented as they are; not as they were.

Women may earn less money than their counterparts but they make more than 80 percent of buying decisions in all homes. "Today's woman is the chief purchasing agent of the family and marketers must recognize that," says Michael Silverstein, a principal at Boston Consulting Group.[7] Further, 90 percent of women have sole or joint responsibility for their household's finances—they are actively involved with tax and estate planning and investment portfolios.[8] Companies marketing financial services, home improvement products and services, and consumer electronics are now actively and progressively targeting women with marketing and marketing communications strategies.

THE FORMATION OF HOUSEHOLDS IS CHANGING Trends such as the postponement of marriage to an older age, increased divorce rates, the desire to have fewer children, and same-sex partnerships, are producing new household formations. That traditional family personified by the Cleavers in the television show *Leave It to Beaver*, with a working father, stay-at-home mother, and a couple of children, is now more of a myth than a reality. Contemporary households are described by terms such as lone-parent families (the result of divorce), blended families (the result of remarriage or common law arrangements), and same-sex families (the result of more openness and acceptance of gay relationships).

With families evolving so dramatically, other changes are also occurring. Between 1981 and 2001, smaller households represented the fastest growth in Canadian family patterns. There are now more one-person households than there are three-, four-, or five-person households. The average size of a Canadian household today is 2.55 people.[9]

What about same-sex households? As indicated earlier in the chapter, progressive-minded companies are targeting the gay community with advertising messages. In the distilling industry, Absolut is targeting the gay community. A print ad for Absolut vodka uses the headline "Absolut Out" (aptly featuring a closet shaped like an Absolut bottle). Refer to Figure 3.4 for an image of the Absolut ad.

Given these changes in households, marketing organizations must look well beyond the traditional family and stereotypical male–female relationships if they are to successfully target and attract consumers to their brands.

ETHNIC DIVERSITY CONTINUES Canada's ethnic diversity presents new opportunities for Canadian marketers. Canadian culture comprises numerous and diverse **subcultures** (subgroups of a larger population) with distinctive lifestyles based on characteristics such as religion, race, and location (region of country). The latest data from Statistics Canada show visible minorities comprising 13.1 percent of the population (4.0 million people). The largest minority groups are Chinese (1.0 million), South Asian (941 000), Black (671 000), Filipino (315 000), and Latin American (213 000). These ethnic groups are concentrated in three key regions: Ontario, Quebec, and British Columbia. Eighty percent of Canada's ethnic minorities live in four cities: Toronto (43 percent), Vancouver (18 percent), Montreal (11 percent), and Calgary/Edmonton (8 percent). The visible minority population is expected to rise to 7.1 million by 2017.[10]

Generally speaking, advertisers have been slow to capitalize on ethnic trends, but this is changing. The Chinese and South Asian people, for example, are heavy users of computers and telecommunications devices. Members of these groups frequently switch to the newest cell phone models each year. Telus was quick to respond to this behaviour. In English-language advertising, Telus is well known for using animals in its ads. A similar strategy was employed when targeting the South Asian population. Hummingbirds and rainbow-coloured fish were employed in some Punjabi TV spots shown on multicultural channels. The hummingbird ad had a "stick with us, we know what we are doing" message. IKEA is another company targeting ethnic communities. To ensure the ads are noticed, members of the ethnic group appear in the ads and the ads are placed in ethnic media that specifically reach those groups. Refer to Figure 3.8 for an illustration.

PSYCHOGRAPHIC SEGMENTATION

Contemporary marketing organizations have added a more sophisticated variable, referred to as *psychographics*, to their marketing arsenal. The combination of demographic and

Statistics Canada
www.statcan.ca

Advertisement provided courtesy of Frito-Lay, Inc.

FIGURE 3.8

Unique messages placed in ethnic media are effective in reaching ethnic markets.

psychographic information provides the marketer with a more complete understanding of its target market. Marketers not only know who buys, but also why they buy. Therefore, the hot buttons they identify about their target are pressed when marketing communications are delivered.

Psychographic segmentation examines individual lifestyles in terms of *activities*, *interests*, and *opinions* (commonly referred to as AIOs). Therefore, when organizations target their products psychographically, advertising messages are associated with the lifestyle of the target market—the personality of the product matches the personality of the target.

Psychographic information shows how an individual's interest in a particular product depends on his or her lifestyle. Automakers produce and market a range of vehicles to satisfy the requirements of the various lifestyle groups. Trendy sports cars with European styling appeal to upscale and educated professionals who are motivated by status and prestige.

Marketers in industries such as fashion, personal-care products, beer, and automobiles frequently develop advertising campaigns based on psychographic information about consumers. Marketing research companies Environics Analytics and Millward Brown conduct annual attitudinal studies of Canadians; the results of these studies place people in various psychographic clusters. Unique labels describe the clusters. Some of the Environics cluster names include Cosmopolitan Elites, Electric Avenues, Les Chics, and Lunch at Tim's. Millward Brown's cluster names include Up and Comers, Mavericks, Contented Traditionalists, and Joiner Activists, among others. See Figure 3.9 for more information about psychographic clusters. Cluster names are often influenced

FIGURE 3.9

A sampling of lifestyle clusters in Canada

Cluster Name	Description	Estimated Households 2006	% of total
URBAN ELITE			
Cosmopolitan Elite	Very affluent middle-aged and older city dwellers	296 395	2.31
Urbane Villagers	Wealthy middle-aged urban sophisticates	315 264	2.46
Money & Brains	Upscale and educated professionals and their families	292 366	2.28
Furs & Philanthropy	High-achieving cultured urban families	333 749	2.60
SUBURBAN ELITE			
Suburban Gentry	Well-off middle-aged suburban families	161 402	1.26
Nouveaux Riches	Prosperous Quebec suburban families	178 326	1.39
Pets & PCs	Large upscale suburban families	115 832	0.90
SUBURBAN UPSCALE ETHNIC			
Asian Affluence	Established Chinese families in suburbs	205 618	1.60
South Asian Society	Young upper-middle-class South Asian families	62 344	0.49
Asian Up and Comers	Successful middle-aged Asian families	157 757	1.23
Suburban Rows	Young and comfortable immigrant families in suburbia	200 008	1.56
SUBURBAN MID-SCALE			
Upward Bound	Middle-aged families in suburban comfort	147 128	1.15
Rods & Reels	Older and outdoorsy upper-middle-class couples and families	481 462	3.75
Nearly Empty Nests	Successful suburban households starting to empty-nest	206 221	1.61
Grey Pride	Mid-scale suburban apartment-dwelling seniors	233 020	1.81
Simple Pleasures	Mature middle-income suburban homeowners	26 401	0.21

Note: The clusters and descriptions above represent a small cross-section of the segments identified in the Prizm CE segmentation system. In total there are 18 clusters and 66 descriptions. For more information visit the Environics Analytics website at www.environicsanalytics.ca.

Source: Adapted from "Canadian households, Prizm CE 2006," *The Canadian Communications Pocketbook*, 2006/7, p. 39. Courtesy of Environics Analytics.

by geography—whether the consumer is an urban dweller, suburban dweller, or rural dweller. Refer to the section on geographic segmentation for more insight.

Axe (deodorant and body sprays) is a brand that was launched entirely on the basis of psychographic profiling. Axe is a brand dedicated to the "Axe man"—a cheeky devil that has lots of sex, weekly or more frequently. Men in the Axe target audience frequent bars and are referred to as "players" and "sweethearts." Axe is dedicated to helping men compete in the mating game. Introductory ads showed women literally flinging themselves at guys. Every guy's dream!

Much more subtle in nature is a print ad for Jaguar that also uses psychographic profiling. Jaguar is an automobile suited for the urban elite (described as Cosmopolitans, Money & Brains, and Furs and Philanthropy) or suburban elite (described as Suburban Gentry or Nouveaux Riches). **Lifestyle advertising**, a form of advertising that attaches a product to a desirable lifestyle, is an effective technique to attract this target. With reference to the Inniskillin wine ad that appears in Figure 3.10, the image of the man and woman, the fine automobile, and the implicit social situation, with the bottle of Inniskillin ice wine as a point of focus, makes for a good example of lifestyle advertising.

Inniskillin
www.inniskillin.com

FIGURE 3.10

An ad appealing to upscale urban dwellers: an illustration of lifestyle advertising

Courtesy of Inniskillin Wines, Niagara-on-the-Lake.

Psychographics allows a company to position its products more effectively in the marketplace. Such intimate knowledge of consumers provides ammunition for compelling campaigns that focus on lifestyle associations. The combination of demographic and psychographic knowledge allows the marketing organization to better push the target's hot buttons. With sufficient motivation, the likelihood of purchase is stronger.

GEOGRAPHIC SEGMENTATION

Geographic segmentation refers to the division of a geographically expansive market (Canada) into smaller geographic units (Atlantic Canada, Quebec, Ontario, the Prairies, and British Columbia). The availability of psychographic information about target markets has complemented the use of geographic segmentation. Knowing more about targets in the various regions—their behaviour, attitudes, and interests—helps marketers and advertisers to develop effective marketing and advertising plans.

The region with the most obvious differences to the rest of Canada is Quebec, whose language and cultural characteristics necessitate the use of different marketing and advertising strategies. Campaigns that are designed specifically with Quebecers in mind and presented in a manner that is culturally relevant will succeed; English-language campaigns adapted to Quebec in the form of a French-language voice-over are destined to fail. Quebecers see right through it!

To demonstrate how to do it right, Telus formed a partnership with the Old Port of Montreal, a scenic and heavily travelled spot visited by six million people each year. The sponsorship provides a technical benefit: all pay phones and internet infrastructure in the area are powered by the company. However, it is from a cultural standpoint that Telus will most benefit. Telus sponsors "Fire and Ice," an annual family winter event that combines ice skating and fireworks in the Old Port. It is dedicated to families in the Montreal area. Telus, a national company, is giving back to the local community with events designed uniquely for Quebecers. Research verifies that 62 percent of Quebecers feel favourably toward sponsors of festivals and events, and 55 percent support companies that sponsor events they like. Advantage Telus![11]

More Canadians than ever before are living in urban areas. Fully 70 percent of Canada's population resides in either very highly urban or highly urban areas. The population continues to concentrate in four broad urban regions: the extended Golden Horseshoe (which includes the Greater Toronto Area) in Southern Ontario; Montreal and its adjacent region; the Lower Mainland of British Columbia and southern Vancouver Island; and the Calgary–Edmonton corridor. The latest information available indicates that these areas account for 52 percent of Canada's population.[12] It is not surprising, then, that successful marketing and advertising strategies have an urban orientation and reflect contemporary households dealing with contemporary issues.

Many Canadian organizations are moving away from national marketing strategies and "one size fits all" advertising campaigns, and toward strategies based on regional considerations and opportunities. Other companies are proceeding in the opposite direction, developing universal strategies that are appropriate for all of North America, or even the global marketplace. Which direction to take depends on the objectives of the organization and the financial resources available for marketing and marketing communications.

DIRECT SEGMENTATION

Direct segmentation simply means that companies target customers individually. In the age of sophisticated communications technology, and at a time when organizations are

The Old Port of Montreal
www.oldportofmontreal.com

using **customer relationship management (CRM)** programs to their advantage, it is now possible to design unique products and unique communications strategies for current and prospective customers. CRM programs are designed to attract, cultivate, and maximize the return on each customer the company does business with.

The backbone of a CRM program is an organization's database management system. A **database management system** involves compiling information about customers and their buying behaviour on a continuous basis. The system contains purchase history (amount bought and frequency of purchase), demographic, psychographic, and geographic information, as well as media-related information. This is such a detailed collection of information that it can be used to design campaigns to reach individual customers effectively.

What has emerged is a concept called data mining. **Data mining** analyzes and establishes relationships between pieces of information so that more effective marketing and communications strategies can be identified and implemented. Data-mining techniques attempt to locate informational patterns and nuggets within the database.[13] The goal is to identify prospects most likely to buy or buy in large volume, and to provide input on how to best communicate with that customer.

Information about consumers is readily available; it seems that every time we buy something in a store (one in which the item is scanned into a database), or do something on the internet (where we agree to cookies being placed on our computer hard drives), we leave an electronic trail. Smart marketing organizations follow the trail, determine what it means, and then use it to market products to us more effectively and efficiently.

Kraft Foods is an example of a company that has taken to relationship marketing and more direct communications with a vengeance. Seeing inefficiencies in its mass advertising programs (the costs were outweighing the benefits), Kraft shifted its focus to relationship marketing strategies and communications strategies that reached customers more directly. Kraft launched web promotions, direct-mail and database marketing programs, custom publishing programs, and experimented with television sponsorships instead of traditional TV advertising. The company and many of its brands have internet sites, and the sites are a means of collecting data about customers. Simply put, the web provides an excellent opportunity to add "stickiness" to an existing relationship between Kraft and its customers.

Kraft Canada Inc.
www.kraftcanada.com

Advanced technology is changing the nature of marketing communications. In the future there will be much greater use of direct-response, online, and mobile communications between organizations and their customers. Unique and personalized messages will be transmitted by these media at a time when consumers are making purchase decisions.

BEHAVIOUR-RESPONSE SEGMENTATION

Behaviour-response segmentation involves dividing buyers into groups according to their occasions for using a product, the benefits they require in a product, the frequency with which they use it, and their degree of brand loyalty. Marketers using the **occasion-for-use** segmentation strategy show how the product can be used on various occasions. For example, products such as milk, orange juice, and eggs are often shown being consumed at times other than their traditional breakfast meal times. Reminding consumers that a product can be enjoyed at another time has an impact on sales volume. Some brands benefit indirectly from a consumer's occasion-for-use behaviour. Red Bull and other energy drinks have enjoyed increases in sales as a result of young consumers mixing the drink with vodka. While such mixing is not recommended or condoned by the marketers, they do benefit financially from the behaviour.

Benefits-sought segmentation is based on the premise that different consumers gratify different needs when they purchase a product. If a target market is rational in nature, the communications message will stress benefits such as quality, price, and dependability; if the target is influenced by emotions, the message plays on feelings such as sexual desire, fear, love, and desire for status. Consumers can be both rational and emotional, and exhibit different shopping behaviours at the same time. For example, a recent trend shows Canadian consumers are trading down in some categories in order to trade up in other categories—they pamper themselves with the savings! Discount stores such as Wal-Mart, Payless Shoes, and Old Navy (rational behaviour) have reaped the benefits, as have brands such as Mercedes and BMW (emotional behaviour).

If **frequency of use** is considered, market research is undertaken to distinguish the characteristics of the heavy user from the average user. Very often an 80/20 rule applies (i.e., 80 percent of a brand's sales volume comes from 20 percent of its users). The profile of the heavy user, as characterized by demographic and psychographic variables, is used to determine the best way of presenting the product to attract potential users.

Loyalty-response segmentation assesses the degree of brand loyalty held by consumers. Loyalty can vary considerably: a consumer could be very loyal, moderately loyal, or not loyal at all (i.e., they have a tendency to switch brands often). The characteristics of the most loyal group are identified and that information is used to develop messages that will attract similar users. It is common for consumers to have a "short list" of brands they are loyal to in a product category, though the degree of loyalty may be stronger for one particular brand. In other words, consumers are always susceptible to some degree of brand switching. Factors such as price also enter into the brand purchase decision process.

Companies analyze and evaluate the trends and characteristics described in these sections to identify the most profitable targets to pursue. The end result of the analysis is a profile of the prototype customer, who is described in terms of demographic, psychographic, geographic, and behaviour-response characteristics. Or, the organization may target the customer directly with an individualized communications strategy. For a summary of the various characteristics that may be included in a target-market description, refer to Figure 3.11.

Market Positioning Concepts

Positioning can be defined as the selling concept that motivates purchase, or the image that marketers desire a brand or a company to have in the minds of consumers. Positioning is a strategy based on competition. It involves designing and marketing a product to meet the needs of a target market, and creating the appropriate appeals to make the product stand out from the competition in the minds of the target market. Advertising and other forms of marketing communications play a key role in positioning a product in the customer's mind.

Positioning involves an assessment of consumer needs and competitive marketing activity to determine new marketing opportunities. It involves a thorough understanding of the product in relation to competing products. The result is a clearly defined positioning strategy statement that provides guidance for all marketing and marketing communications strategies. The importance of positioning in the development of marketing strategy is presented in Figure 3.12.

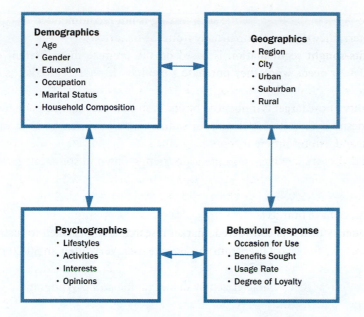

FIGURE 3.11

A summary and illustration of key target-market concepts

A clearly worded positioning strategy statement provides guidance and direction for all marketing and marketing communications activities. All forms of communication should send out the same message about a brand or company.

It is very important that the positioning statement aptly describe a primary benefit and an image that is important to the target market. The statement should be clear, concise, and uncomplicated. Here is an example of an actual positioning strategy statement for Visa (credit card):

> To reinforce our leadership position in the credit card market, and to establish it as the preferred provider of all future products.

Visa portrays its positioning strategy in its marketing and advertising by focusing on transactions and acceptance virtually everywhere in the world. In Canada, Visa ads state that Visa is "All you need." See Figure 3.13 for an illustration of Visa's advertising.

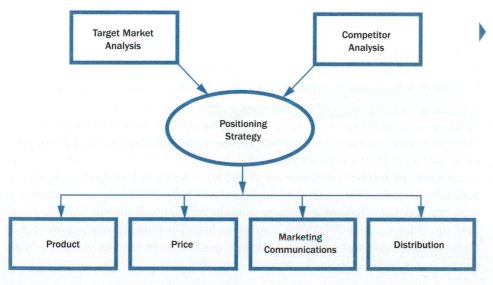

FIGURE 3.12

The importance of positioning in the development of marketing and marketing communications strategy

FIGURE 3.13

An example of brand-leadership positioning

POSITIONING AND MARKETING COMMUNICATIONS

The role of marketing communications, particularly the creative strategy (message), is to articulate the positioning strategy of a brand. Advertising will communicate the key selling point and influence the image of the product that the consumer retains. For example, Mazda has a common positioning strategy for all of its models and employs a consistent style of advertising to dramatize its positioning. Regardless of the model appearing in a television commercial, be it the Mazda 3, Mazda 5, or the new Mazda CX-7 crossover vehicle, reference will be made to the fact that "the spirit of a sports car" is built into every model. That spirit stems from the popularity of the Mazda MX-5 Miata roadster, a classic automobile in the Mazda franchise. The phrase "Zoom-Zoom" ties all of the communications together and helps position the brand in the customer's mind. Refer to the advertisement in Figure 3.14 for details.

FIGURE 3.14

A common style of advertising and the "Zoom-Zoom" theme help position the Mazda brand in the customer's mind.

Advertising can communicate the positioning strategy many different ways. Among some of the more common strategies and techniques are messages that compare one product to another, clearly differentiate one brand from competitors, portray leadership, show innovation, or present a lifestyle association.

HEAD-ON POSITIONING (COMPARATIVE POSITIONING) When a head-on positioning strategy is employed, a brand is presented as being equal to, or better than, another brand. This positioning is usually initiated by the number-two brand in a market as a means of challenging the leader. The strategy is to depict users of a competitive brand demonstrating preference for the advertised brand. Ads typically compare two brands on an attribute that is important to the target market. Which laundry detergent cleans better, which stain remover gets out the dirtiest stains, or which battery lasts longer—is it the Energizer or the Duracell? Both battery brands make the same dependability claims. Pepsi-Cola always finds unique ways to draw comparisons with Coca-Cola. Perhaps the most convincing creative execution of the comparison was an ad in which they show a Coke delivery guy secretly preferring a Pepsi.

A more subtle form of comparison involves one brand comparing itself to "other leading brands" in order to clearly point out it is better at what it does. At one time The Brick (a furniture and electronics retailer) advertised that it really offers the "best buy." That's some kind of comparison with Best Buy, another retailer in the same market.

Head-on positioning strategies can be risky and expensive since the brand leader could respond to the challenge. What could result is a war of words through advertising, an expensive proposition that neither brand will benefit from.

BRAND-LEADERSHIP POSITIONING Established brands often use icons or signatures in their consumer communications that become highly recognized and synonymous with the brand. These devices then act as a simple and lasting reminder about the essence of the brand for consumers. Coca-Cola has successfully used this approach to build the world's most recognized brand. "Coke is it," "Can't beat the real thing," "Always Coca-Cola," and, more recently, "Real" are examples of universally recognizable signatures. All of these expressions imply that other colas are just imitations. The brand name, unique bottle, and popular slogan are a winning combination for Coca-Cola—they are instantly recognizable by consumers everywhere. The Visa illustration mentioned at the start of this section and Visa's slogan "All you need" (see Figure 3.13) is another example of brand leadership positioning.

PRODUCT-DIFFERENTIATION POSITIONING Product differentiation is a strategy that focuses on the unique attribute of a product—a feature that distinguishes it from all other products. It is a strategy that sells a product strictly on its own merit. In the personal-care products market, even a subtle point of differentiation could be the difference between success and failure. Brands like Diet Coke and Diet Pepsi are popular with women, but marketers have a difficult time attracting male targets to diet soft drinks. Pepsi-Cola introduced Pepsi One (a one-calorie drink) to the market and aimed it squarely at males in their 20s and early 30s. With the stigma of the word "diet" removed, Pepsi One has enjoyed reasonable success.[14]

In the razor market the Schick Quattro razor (a 4-blade razor) differentiates itself by promising optimal contact over the contours of a man's face. The benefit for the man is a clean, comfortable, and smooth shave, allegedly better than the Gillette Mach3 razor. Refer to the image in Figure 3.15.

INNOVATION POSITIONING Innovation is sometimes more important for a company as a whole than for individual products. Companies seeking to establish their own image of continuous technical leadership will use advertising to do so, positioning themselves on the leading edge of technology. Such positioning, if firmly established in the minds of customers, will benefit new products when they are introduced to the market. At the product level, an innovation strategy stresses newness as a means of differentiation.

To illustrate, consider the impact Apple's iPod has had in the marketplace. The launch of the iPod changed the way we listen to music. Apple positions its music player, its music downloading service (iTunes), and its computers as leading-edge products that are fun to use. Apple's strategy stands in stark contrast to its competitors' strategies, which rely on technical jargon as a means of differentiating their products. A lighter style of advertising that focuses squarely on the design of Apple products helps position the Apple brand in the customer's mind. And it works! "Teens want to be cool, they want their music, and the iPod is a cool way for them to get music." In fact, teenagers don't refer to music players as "music players." They refer to them as "iPods," a clear indication of how successful Apple has been in the category.[15]

LIFESTYLE POSITIONING In crowded markets, where product attributes are perceived as similar by the target market, firms must identify alternative ways of positioning their products. The use of psychographic information has allowed advertisers to develop

Courtesy of Dick Hemingway.

FIGURE 3.15

In the razor market, Schick differentiates itself from Gillette based on the benefits offered by an additional blade

campaigns that are based on the lifestyle of the target market. Essentially, the product is positioned to "fit in" or match the lifestyle of the user. The illustrations in Figure 3.3 (Mazda) and Figure 3.10 (Inniskillin wine) are good illustrations of lifestyle positioning. In both advertisements the products are shown to be natural parts of the contemporary lifestyle of an upscale consumer.

Generally, lifestyle positioning through advertising uses emotional appeals such as love, fear, adventure, sex, and humour to elicit a response from the target. As indicated above, the automobile industry effectively uses lifestyle imagery to sell cars. It is common to see the rugged outdoors associated with sport utility vehicles, and happy family situations associated with minivans. In the beer market, mainstream brands such as Molson Canadian and Labatt Blue rely heavily on lifestyle positioning. Young guys, beautiful girls, party situations, and cottages (the desired lifestyle of the early 20-something target audience) are common backdrops for their television commercials.

For more insight into positioning strategy and how it influences the nature of advertising and other marketing communications, read the Advertising in Action vignette **Schick Repositions Brands.**

REPOSITIONING

So far, we have discussed only the initial positioning of a product in the marketplace and in the minds of consumers. But the competitive market requires positioning strategies

ADVERTISING IN ACTION

Schick Repositions Brands

A miscalculation on an advertising message sent to customers often turns out to be a costly mistake. Telling the customer what they want to hear is a much safer approach, assuming you can deliver. Schick discovered this principle first hand when it gathered together a group of women to sip coffee and share their stories. As a result of the conversation, the company had to rethink its approach to selling razors.

Instead of using the traditional focus group, which tends to be more formal and structured, Schick experimented with a new research concept called slow-sip sessions, a technique that is much more open and informal. In this case, the women gathered in a coffee shop to share their stories. The objectives were to gain insight into women's feelings about razors and to determine if the message for two women's razor brands (Intuition and Quattro) was connecting with the intended audience. New insights were discovered that led to the repositioning of both brands.

The informal research process involves three steps: in the first step the women chat about what's important in a brand; in the second step they are asked to prioritize a series of messages about the brand to decide which ones are meaningful; and in the third session they analyze actual ads to decide if they work.

In each session, 12 females openly talked about their shaving experiences. The loose structure of the session (like a get-together with girlfriends) encouraged very open and honest conversation. The women were not afraid to say what was on their minds. One woman actually hiked up her pant leg at the table to show how smooth her legs were.

Schick had been operating on the assumption that shaving wasn't that important to women, but the discussion proved otherwise. They discovered an untapped opportunity among users of disposable razors, a market segment that was based solely on cost. The women would switch to a permanent razor like Quattro or Intuition once they understood the benefits: long-term savings and a long-lasting, smoother shave.

Before the slow-sip research, Intuition was positioned as "easy to use." Women said shaving wasn't difficult but they did crave convenience. Intuition's one-step lather and shave design provides that. The positioning strategy for Intuition changed from "easy" to "convenient."

Quattro was positioned the same way as the men's version of the razor. Advertising messages talked about the four-blade technology. From the discussion it was clear that women didn't care about the engineering behind the razor, but they did want a smooth, long-

lasting shave. The positioning was shifted and new advertising messages would stress the smooth, long-lasting shave benefit. The new insights into women's shaving behaviour allowed Schick to communicate with women on an emotional level.

The informal research process produced other benefits as well. The participants felt their input was valued, and were eager to participate further if necessary. Schick believes they will become good brand ambassadors who will provide invaluable word-of-mouth for company brands.

Source: Adapted from Emily Spensieri, "A slow, soft touch," *Marketing*, June 5, 2006, pp. 15, 16.

that can be readily changed if necessary. It is unrealistic to assume that the position a brand adopts initially will remain the same throughout its life cycle. Products will be repositioned according to the prevailing environment in the marketplace. **Repositioning** is defined as changing the place that a brand occupies in the consumer's mind in relation to competitive products. There are two primary reasons for repositioning. One, the marketing activity of a direct competitor may change, and two, the preferences of the target market may change.

The process of repositioning is based on a brand's continuous monitoring of such changes. Companies that don't monitor change often lose touch with their customer and suffer in terms of lower sales and declining market share. Through some very informal discussions with consumers, Schick discovered new insights into how women perceive shaving and the razors they use for shaving. The Schick Quattro disposable razor for women had always been positioned the same as the men's version of the razor—the emphasis was on the four-blade technology. Schick discovered that women don't particularly care about all of the technology behind a razor, but they do car about a smooth, long-lasting shave. The positioning strategy was changed; the message of four-blade technology was dumped in favour of long-lasting smoothness.[16]

If a positioning strategy is working and if the advertising in use continues to perform as expected, a company should avoid the temptation to change things. Sometimes change occurs for the wrong reasons. Should a manager be in a situation where repositioning strategies are being considered, perhaps an old rule of thumb should apply: "If it ain't broke, don't fix it."

SUMMARY

Market segmentation and knowledge of consumer behaviour are important factors in marketing and advertising planning. Both have a direct impact on product positioning, creative strategy, and media strategy.

Adequate knowledge of how needs and motives, personality and self-concept theories, perceptions, attitudes, reference groups, and family influence behaviour is essential input for the development of marketing and marketing communications strategies.

In terms of market segmentation, organizations must identify their target markets as precisely as they can. Good use of information provided by demographic trends (the consumer's age, gender, income, occupation, education, marital status, household formation, and cultural mix), psychographic characteristics (the consumer's activities, interests, and opinions), and geographic variables (the consumer's location by geography or region) allows for a precise definition of the consumer and enhances the quality of marketing and advertising plans. Insights into behaviour responses such as occasion for use, benefits sought in a product, frequency of use, and loyalty also play a role in developing a profile of the consumer segment an organization may choose to target.

Database marketing and management techniques have enabled organizations to form and maintain relationships with individual customers, a concept referred to as customer relationship management. The use of database management systems and data-mining techniques allows an organization to identify customers and prospects most likely to buy or buy in large volume. Further, the system offers a means of targeting customers with unique and personalized messages that can be delivered directly, rather than through the mass media. In the future, advertisers will be moving away from the traditional media due to their inefficiencies, and toward the digital media that reach customers directly and at a critical time—the time when a buying decision is being made.

Positioning a product is an important part of pursuing target markets, and advertising plays a key role in positioning. Positioning involves designing a product or service to meet the needs of a target market, and then creating appropriate appeals to make the product stand out in the minds of the target-market members. Common positioning strategies include head-on comparisons, product differentiation, technical innovation, and brand dominance and lifestyle techniques. As a product matures, factors such as competitive activity and changing consumer preferences dictate a re-evaluation of positioning strategies.

Positioning strategies that are working should be retained for as long as possible. Often, companies adopt new strategies for the wrong reasons—companies tend to tire of things more quickly than do loyal consumers. The old expression, "If it ain't broke, don't fix it," should apply.

KEY TERMS

attitudes   71

behaviour-response segmentation   84

consumer behaviour   67

customer relationship management (CRM)   83

data mining   83

database management system   83

demographic segmentation   76

direct segmentation   83

double targeting   75

geographic segmentation   81

lifestyle advertising   80

market segmentation   75

motives   68

needs   68

perception   70

positioning   85

psychographic segmentation   80

reference group (or peer group)   73

repositioning   89

subcultures   79

REVIEW QUESTIONS

1. Explain the various levels of needs and identify the two basic principles that needs and motivation theory are based on. Provide an advertising example for each level of needs.

2. Briefly explain each of the components of the self-concept. Provide a new example of an ad campaign that uses the looking-glass self or ideal self to its advantage.

3. Briefly explain how knowledge of attitudes and reference groups influences the direction of advertising strategy.

4. What is double targeting? Provide a new example to demonstrate how it is applied.

5. What are the key elements of demographic segmentation, psychographic segmentation, geographic segmentation, and behaviour-response segmentation? Briefly explain.

6. What are the basic trends affecting demographic segmentation in Canada?

7. Explain the concept of positioning in the context of marketing and advertising practice.

8. What is the difference between head-on positioning and brand-leadership positioning? Provide a new example of each.

9. If a brand is using a product-differentiation positioning strategy, what will the advertised message focus on?

Provide two examples that show the application of this type of positioning.

10. What is repositioning and why does it occur? Briefly explain.

DISCUSSION QUESTIONS

1. Provide some additional examples to show how advertisers use the following aspects of consumer behaviour theory:
   - Social and esteem needs
   - Self-image, looking-glass self, and ideal self
   - Reference groups
   - Role and position in a family unit

2. "The economies of a national creative plan outweigh the need for numerous regional creative plans." Discuss this issue, choosing some products and ad campaigns as examples.

3. "To succeed in the future, products and services must be repositioned to appeal to older target markets." Comment on the implications of this statement.

4. "Companies are well behind in terms of recognizing the changes occurring in Canadian household formation, and this is reflected in the types of advertising they are showing." Is this statement true or false? Provide examples to support your opinion.

5. Will the influence of relationship marketing be very significant on marketing communications in the future? Will companies spend more on direct-response and online advertising and less on traditional mass-media advertising? Justify your opinion.

6. Read the Advertising in Action vignette, **Advertising with Pride**. Should Canadian advertisers fear targeting the gay community? Identify the benefits and drawbacks of taking such action and present an opinion on the issue.

NOTES

1. James F. Engel, David T. Kollatt and Roger D. Blackwell, *Consumer Behaviour*, second edition (New York: Holt Rinehart Winston, 1972), p. 5.

2. Holllie Shaw, "Retailers seek elusive key to the shopping man's heart," *Financial Post*, June 5, 2002, p. FP12.

3. A.H. Maslow, *Motivation and Personality* (New York: Harper and Row Publishers, 1954), pp. 370–396.

4. John Douglas, George Field, and Lawrence Tarpay, *Human Behaviour in Marketing* (Columbus, OH: Charles E. Merrill Publishing, 1987), p. 5.

5. Katherine Laughlin, "Peer pressure," *Marketing*, March 8, 2004, **www.marketingmag.ca**.

6. Lisa D'Innocenzo, "Is your target a man's man? Then reach out to women," *Strategy*, February 2006, pp. 30–32.

7. "I am woman, hear me shop," *Business Week*, February 14, 2005, **www.businesseek.com**.

8. Marti Barletta, "Targeting a powerhouse demographic: Older women," *Advertising Age*, October 10, 2005, **www.adage.com**.

9. "Characteristics of household population," Statistics Canada, as published in *The Canadian Communications Pocketbook 2006/7*.

10. Alain Belanger and Eric Caron Malenfant, "Ethnocultural diversity in Canada: Prospects for 2017," *Canadian Social Trends*, Winter 2005, p. 18+.

11. Natalia Williams, "How do Quebecers market to Quebecers?" *Strategy*, May 2005, p. 49+.

12. "Study: The population pattern in Canada's watersheds," *The Daily*, January 5, 2006, Statistics Canada, **www.statcan.ca**.

13. David Eggleston, "We've come along way baby," *Strategy Direct Response*, November 8, 1999, p. D13.

14. Lisa D'Innocenzo, "Traditional women's brands go for men," *Strategy*, August 2005, p. 24.

15. "Apple's Jobs taps teen iPod demand to fuel sales, stocks surge," *Bloomberg News*, October 11, 2005 **www.bloomberg.com**.

16. Emily Spensieri, "A slow, soft touch," *Marketing*, June 5, 2006, pp. 15, 16.

CHAPTER **4**

Strategic Planning Concepts for Marketing Communications

Learning Objectives

After studying this chapter, you will be able to

1. Identify the distinctions and relationships between the various types of planning

2. Describe the key variables that comprise a corporate plan

3. Outline the organization and content of a marketing plan and a marketing communications plan

4. Show how integrated marketing communications plans provide solutions to marketing problems

Business planning is an integrated process that involves planning at three levels of an organization: corporate planning, marketing planning, and marketing communications planning. Advertising is one aspect of marketing communications planning. It is important for students to understand the planning process and appreciate the interaction of plans at each level and within each level. Marketing communications plans are not created independently; they are linked to plans at other levels of the organization. The corporate plan will influence the marketing plan, and the marketing plan will influence the marketing communications plan.

There are no design norms against which marketing plans and advertising plans are measured. The design and content of plans vary considerably among organizations, and their structure depends on the needs and degree of marketing sophistication of the firm developing the plan. A well-thought-out plan should provide direction, outline key activities, and include a means of measuring its success. Students should be aware that there are no limits placed on the design, organization, and content of marketing or marketing communications plans.

Business Planning Process

Strategic business planning involves making decisions about three variables: objectives, strategies, and execution or tactics. Let's first define these planning variables:

1. **Objectives** are statements that outline what is to be accomplished in the corporate, marketing, or advertising plan.
2. **Strategies** are statements that outline how the objectives will be achieved and usually identify the resources necessary to achieve the objectives, such as funds, time, people, and types of activities.
3. **Execution (tactics)** refers to tactical action plans that outline specific details of implementation, which collectively contribute to the achievement of objectives. Tactical plans usually provide details of an activity's cost and timing.

A diagram of the business planning process as it applies to marketing and advertising is provided in Figure 4.1.

Strategic Planning

When a company embarks on a **plan** it anticipates the future business environment to determine the course of action it will take. For example, a firm will look at trends in the economy, demography, culture, and technology, and then develop a plan that will provide growth. A typical plan considers the long-term (five years) and the short-term (one year) situation. Each year the plan is evaluated and changes are made where necessary.

Strategic planning is the process of determining objectives (setting goals) and identifying strategies (ways to achieve the goals) and tactics (specific action plans) to help achieve the objectives. A corporate plan originates at the top of the organization and is largely based on input from senior executives. Such plans are usually not elaborate documents, since their purpose is to identify the corporate objectives to be achieved over a specified period. The corporate plan acts as a guideline for planning in various operational areas of the company. Marketing and advertising are two of these operational areas.

In examining Figure 4.1, we find that business planning throughout the organization begins and ends at the corporate or senior-management level. Senior management formulates the overall strategic direction for the organization and establishes the financial objectives the company should aspire to (sales, profit, return on investment). Then, in accordance with the objectives and directions passed down from senior management, the marketing department develops marketing plans that embrace objectives, strategies, and tactics for individual products, divisions, or target markets.

Marketing plans consider such matters as the marketing mix (product, price, distribution, and marketing communications), target-market characteristics, and control and evaluation mechanisms that determine the effectiveness of the strategies being

FIGURE 4.1

PLANNING MODEL EXHIBIT

Strategic planning: the links between plans at various levels of an organization

The corporate plan provides guidance for the marketing plan, and the marketing plan provides guidance for the marketing communications plan. Corporate plans are strategic in nature, while marketing plans and marketing communications plans are strategic and tactical in nature.

Corporate Plan

Marketing Plan

Marketing Communications Plan
- Advertising Plan
- Sales Promotion Plan
- Direct-Response Plan
- Online/Interactive Plan
- Public Relations Plan
- Event Marketing Plan
- Personal Selling Plan

implemented. Marketing plans are very specific, and all activities related to product, price, distribution, and marketing communications are outlined in the plan. With reference to Figure 4.1, our primary concern is marketing communications, which is subdivided into advertising, direct-response communications, online and interactive communications, sales promotion, personal selling, public relations, and event marketing. Advertising can be further subdivided into creative plans and media plans.

As this planning process indicates, each plan is related to another. The saying "A chain is only as strong as its weakest link" is an appropriate description of these relationships. Strategic planning attempts to coordinate all activity so that elements from various areas work together harmoniously. In the case of marketing, advertising, and any other form of communications, all activity must present a consistent image of the company or its product in order to create a favourable impression in the minds of consumers. One weak link in the chain can create conflict or confuse the target market. For example, a product's selling price could be set too high in relation to the customer's perception of quality. Such a situation occurred when Chrysler launched the Pacifica, an SUV crossover vehicle. The Pacifica was introduced with significant advertising but was rejected by consumers because the price was too high compared to competitive vehicles. Sales fell well short of expectations, and the entire marketing plan had to be re-evaluated. Inconsistent activity spread over numerous company products could seriously disrupt attempts to achieve marketing and corporate objectives.

Chrysler Pacifica
www.chrysler.ca/en/pacifica

The Corporate Plan

A **mission statement** is the foundation of the corporate plan; it is a statement of the organization's purpose. It reflects the operating philosophy of the organization and the direction the organization is to take. Such statements are related to the opportunities the company identifies for itself in the marketplace. Mission statements are market-oriented; they will work for the company only if its products are designed and marketed according to consumers' demands. Stemming from the marketing concept, mission statements recognize customers' needs and consider the competition, the need to build long-term customer relationships, and how to balance corporate goals with societal goals. They may be quite detailed or very brief in content.

The format of a mission statement varies among organizations. Some organizations combine their mission with a longer-term vision of the direction the organization will take. Coca-Cola's mission statement is part of the company's manifesto for growth. Refer to Figure 4.2 for details. The Coca-Cola Company is the world's largest beverage company and owner of the world's most valuable brand: Coca-Cola.

CORPORATE OBJECTIVES

Corporate objectives are statements of a company's overall goals, and they take their direction from the mission statement. They may state what return on investment is desired, or what level of sales or market share is desired of a particular market segment. Social responsibility objectives now play a more prominent role in corporate planning. Good objective statements are written in quantifiable terms so that their success can be measured. They may also be qualitative in nature, yet still provide direction, as indicated by the following examples:

- To increase total company sales from $500 000 000 in 20XX to $600 000 000 in 20XX.

- To increase market share from 25 percent in 20XX to 30 percent in 20XX.

MISSION, VISION, & VALUES

Mission

Everything we do is inspired by our enduring mission:

- **To Refresh the World** . . . in body, mind, and spirit.
- **To Inspire Moments of Optimism** . . . through our brands and our actions.
- **To Create Value and Make a Difference** . . . everywhere we engage.

Vision for Sustainable Growth

To achieve sustainable growth, we have established a vision with clear goals.

- **Profit:** Maximizing return to shareowners while being mindful of our overall responsibilities.
- **People:** Being a great place to work where people are inspired to be the best they can be.
- **Portfolio:** Bringing to the world a portfolio of beverage brands that anticipate and satisfy peoples' desires and needs.
- **Partners:** Nurturing a winning network of partners and building mutual loyalty.
- **Planet:** Being a responsible global citizen that makes a difference.

Values

We are guided by shared values that we will live by as a company and as individuals.

- **Leadership:** "The courage to shape a better future"
- **Passion:** "Committed in heart and mind"
- **Integrity:** "Be real"
- **Accountability:** "If it is to be, it's up to me"
- **Collaboration:** "Leverage collective genius"
- **Innovation:** "Seek, imagine, create, delight"
- **Quality:** "What we do, we do well"

Source: The Coca-Cola Company, www.coca-cola.com/ourcompany.

- To increase return on investment from 10 percent in 20XX to 13 percent in 20XX.
- To financially support cause-related marketing programs that will benefit society.

Objectives like these provide the framework for the development of detailed plans in the operational areas of the organization.

CORPORATE STRATEGIES

After the corporate objectives are confirmed, the organization must identify the **corporate strategies**, which are plans outlining how the objectives will be achieved. The factors considered when strategies are being developed are marketing strength; degree of competition in markets the company operates in; financial resources (e.g., the availability of investment capital or the ability to borrow required funds); research and development capabilities; and management commitment (i.e., the priority a company has placed on a particular goal).

Assuming growth (greater profits, market share, and return on investment) is the corporate objective, corporations could proceed in an endless range of strategic directions to achieve it. One option is to follow a **penetration strategy**. A company like Coca-Cola, for example, wants to build its leadership position in the world's beverage market. To do so it focuses all of its financial and marketing resources on improving the sales of its soft drink, juice, and water beverages. Coca-Cola will invest heavily in marketing in order to keep its name top-of-mind and to build its distribution network for all of its beverage products.

A second option is an **acquisition strategy** that involves one company buying another company, or parts of another company. Recently, Adidas acquired Reebok for US$3.8 billion. As separate companies they couldn't compete with Nike (with its global market share of 33.2 percent). But together they will be more of a force in the marketplace. Working from a stronger position, Adidas-Reebok will present a stronger fashion brand and will be able to secure stronger endorsement deals from celebrities and athletes. The combined company will have a global presence (with a global market share of 26.0 percent) to take on Nike.[1] Recently, Procter & Gamble paid US$57 billion to acquire the Gillette Company. With this acquisition, P&G quickly became the global leader in the razor market.

Adidas
www.adidas.com

Another common corporate strategy to achieve growth is to invest in research and development in the pursuit of **new products**. Alternatively, a company could decide to acquire new products developed by other companies. Both Coca-Cola and Pepsi-Cola have launched a variety of flavoured colas to expand their lines. In such a competitive market, new products bring in new revenue streams. Some of Coca-Cola's new additions in the soft drink category include Coca-Cola Zero, Coca-Cola Blak, and Coca-Cola Black Cherry Vanilla, and in the bottled water category, Dasani Flavours and Dasani Sensations. Kraft Foods recently began placing greater emphasis on new products. One successful Canadian introduction was Thinsations—thin versions of the popular Oreo, Chips Ahoy, and Honey Graham brands. Thinsations are individually wrapped products that contain 100 calories per pack. The new product fits with Kraft's desire to offer healthy yet tasty products.[2] Refer to the illustration in Figure 4.3.

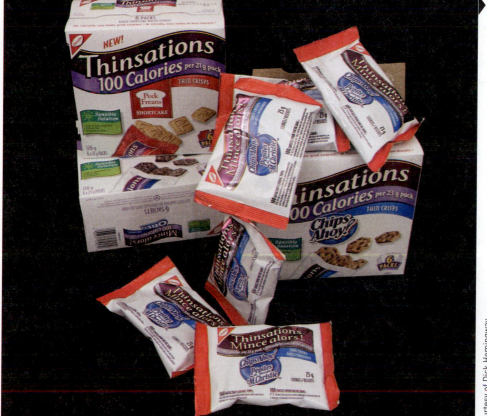

FIGURE 4.3

Innovative new products create new revenue streams for a company

Courtesy of Dick Hemingway.

Strategic alliances are now very popular among companies wanting to find ways of reducing costs or improving operating efficiencies. An alliance is a relationship between two or more companies that decide to work co-operatively to achieve common goals. Toyota and Nissan, arch-rivals in the automotive market, decided to work together on new gasoline–electric hybrid vehicles in order to speed the development of more affordable, environmentally friendly cars. They see working together as a more practical means of recovering the massive development costs of such projects.[3]

Rather than expanding, some companies are consolidating their operations by **divesting** themselves of operations that are not profitable or no longer fit with corporate goals. It seems bigger is not always better! In some cases one company's garbage becomes another company's gold. To demonstrate, Kraft Foods sold its Altoid mints and Life Savers brands because confectionary products were not one of its strengths. William Wrigley Co. was the buyer—for Wrigley it was a great opportunity to expand into product categories close to its traditional gum business.[4]

Toyota
www.toyota.ca

Wrigley
www.wrigley.com

Marketing Planning

The marketing department operates within the guidelines established by senior management. The objectives, strategies, and action plans developed by the marketing department are designed to help achieve overall company objectives. Where planning is concerned, the major areas of marketing responsibility include:

1. Identifying and selecting target markets
2. Establishing marketing objectives, strategies, and tactics
3. Evaluating and controlling marketing activities

Marketing planning is the analysis, planning, implementation, evaluation, and control of marketing initiatives to satisfy market needs and achieve organizational objectives. It involves the analysis of relevant background information and historical trend data and the development of marketing objectives, strategies, and executions for all products and services within a company. The integration of various elements of the marketing mix is outlined in the marketing plan of each product. In contrast to corporate plans, marketing plans are short-term in nature (one year), specific in scope (since they deal with one product and outline precise actions), and combine both strategy and tactics (they are action-oriented).

While there is no typical format for a marketing plan, they are usually subdivided into major sections based on background content and planning content. In terms of background, the company conducts a **situation analysis** (sometimes called environmental analysis) in which data and information about external and internal influences are compiled. It is important to examine happenings that have an impact on the performance of a brand. External factors that are considered include economic trends, social and demographic trends, and technology trends. As well, information is compiled about the market, the customers, and the competition. In the marketing plan, the objectives, strategies, and tactics for the brand or company are clearly delineated. Figure 4.4 offers a description of the various elements of a marketing plan.

MARKET BACKGROUND—SITUATION ANALYSIS

As a preliminary step to marketing planning, a variety of information is compiled and analyzed. This information includes some or all of the following:

FIGURE **4.4**

PLANNING MODEL EXHIBIT

Content of a marketing plan: a sample model

―――――――――

* Note: Including a SWOT analysis is optional. Many planners believe that you actually conduct a SWOT when the background information is compiled in the first four subsections of the background section of a plan. Other planners believe that such information must be analyzed further to determine priorities. The latter is the intention of a SWOT analysis.

MARKETING BACKGROUND

External Influences

- Economic trends
- Social and demographic trends
- Technology trends

Market Analysis

- Market size and growth
- Regional market importance and trends
- Market segment analysis
- Seasonal analysis
- Consumer date (target user)
- Consumer behaviour (loyalty)

Product Analysis

- Sales volume trends
- Market share trends
- Distribution trends
- Marketing communications activities

Competitor Analysis

- Market share trends
- Marketing activity assessment

SWOT Analysis*

- Strengths
- Weaknesses
- Opportunities
- Threats

MARKETING PLAN

Positioning Strategy

- Positioning statement

Target-Market Profile

- Demographic
- Psychographic
- Geographic

Marketing Objectives

- Sales volume
- Market share
- Profit
- Marketing communications
- Other

Marketing Strategies

- Product
- Price
- Distribution
- Marketing communications
- Marketing research
- Budget (total available for brand)

Marketing Execution

(Action plans for each component)

- Product
- Price
- Distribution
- Marketing communications
- Marketing research
- Profit improvement

Budget and Financial Summary

- Budget allocation (by activity, time, area)
- Brand profit & loss statement

Marketing Calendar

- Activity schedule by month

EXTERNAL INFLUENCES

- *Economic trends* Basic economic trends often dictate the nature of marketing activity (e.g., if the economy is healthy and growing, more resources are allocated to marketing activity; if the economy is in a recession, a more conservative approach is often adopted).

- *Social and demographic trends* Basic trends in age, income, immigration, and lifestyle influence decisions on what target markets to pursue. For example, the

Canadian population is aging, and large cities are becoming more ethnic in nature. These factors necessitate change in marketing strategy.

- *Technology trends* The rapid pace of change (e.g., in computers and telecommunications) influences the development of new products, shortens product life cycles, and influences the communications strategies used to reach customers.

MARKET ANALYSIS

- *Market size and growth* A review is made of trends in the marketplace over a period of time. Is the market growing, remaining stable, or declining?

- *Regional market importance* Market trends and sales-volume trends are analyzed by region to determine areas of strength or weakness and areas to concentrate on in the future.

- *Market-segment analysis* The sales volume of total market and segments within a market are reviewed. For example, the coffee market is segmented by regular ground coffee, instant coffee, decaffeinated coffee, and flavoured coffee. The soft drink market has been subdivided further based on the growth of bottled water and energy drinks. The marketer needs to know which segments are growing and which segments are declining.

- *Seasonal analysis* An examination is conducted of seasonal or cyclical trends during the course of a year. For example, traditions such as Christmas, Thanksgiving, and Halloween often have an impact on sales volume and affect the timing of marketing activities. The seasons of the year (spring, fall, summer, and winter) may also influence sales patterns.

- *Consumer data* Current users of a product are profiled according to factors such as age, gender, lifestyle, and location. The data may consider primary users as well as secondary users and indicate new areas of opportunity.

- *Consumer behaviour* The degree of customer loyalty to the market and individual brands within a market is assessed. Are customers loyal or do they switch brands often? Other factors considered are benefits consumers seek in the product and how frequent their purchases are. Such data indicate the need for strategies that will attract new customers or retain existing customers.

PRODUCT ANALYSIS
An assessment of a product's marketing-mix strategy is reviewed at this stage. In the assessment, relationships are drawn between the marketing activity that was implemented over the course of the year and the sales volume and market share that was achieved.

- *Sales volume* Historical sales trends are plotted to forecast future growth.

- *Market share* Market share success is the clearest indicator of how well a brand is performing. Market share results are recorded nationally and regionally, and areas of strength and weakness are identified.

- *New-product activity* The success or failure of new products introduced in recent years is highlighted (e.g., new pack sizes, flavours, product formats).

- *Distribution* The availability of a product nationally and regionally is reviewed. Distribution is also assessed based on type of customer (e.g., chains and independents).

- *Marketing communications* An assessment of current activities will determine if strategies are to be maintained or if new strategies are needed. A review of expenditures by medium, sales promotions, event marketing, and any other activity is necessary in order to assess the impact of such spending on brand performance.

COMPETITIVE ANALYSIS It is wise to know a competitor's products as well as your own. A review of marketing-mix activities for key competitors provides essential input on how to revise marketing strategies.

- *Market share trends* It is common to evaluate market share trends of all competitors from year to year, nationally and regionally. Such analysis provides insight into what brands are moving forward and what brands are moving backward.
- *Marketing strategy assessment* An attempt is made to link known marketing strategies to competitor brand performance. What is the nature of their advertising, sales promotions, and events and sponsorships? How much money do competitors invest in marketing? Have they launched any new products, and how successful are they?

The combination of market analysis, product analysis, and competitor analysis helps provide direction to those managers responsible for developing a new marketing plan and presents senior managers with an overall perspective.

SWOT ANALYSIS

After assembling the market information, the next step is appraising it. While this is not a formal part of the marketing plan itself, a manager should evaluate all information collected and then determine what the priorities are for the next year. This process is referred to as a **SWOT analysis**. The acronym SWOT stands for strengths, weaknesses, opportunities, and threats. A SWOT analysis examines the critical factors that have an impact on the nature and direction of a marketing strategy. Strengths and weaknesses are internal factors (e.g., resources available, research and development capability, and management expertise), while opportunities and threats are external factors (e.g., economic trends, competitive activity, and social and demographic trends.)

The end result of a SWOT analysis should be the matching of potential opportunities with resource capabilities. The goal is to capitalize on strengths while improving weaknesses. A SWOT analysis can be conducted at any level of an organization—product, division, or company.

The Marketing Plan

POSITIONING STATEMENT

Positioning refers to the desired image that a company wants to place in the minds of customers about the company as a whole or about individual products—it is the selling concept that helps motivate purchase. The concept of positioning was discussed in Chapter 3. Effective positioning statements are realistic, specific, and uncomplicated, and they clearly distinguish what a brand has to offer.

A **positioning-strategy statement** is a working statement. It is the focal point from which relevant marketing and marketing communications strategies are developed. To demonstrate, consider the marketing dilemma Listerine once faced. Listerine was losing ground to Scope, and consumers saw little difference between the two brands. Listerine was perceived as old-fashioned; a serious and stuffy kind of brand—a new image was needed. In the mouthwash category, all brands were promoting fresh breath, but consumers were becoming more interested in oral health issues such as preventing cavities, plaque, and gum disease. A new positioning strategy emerged:

> Listerine will be positioned as the only mouthwash that provides multiple benefits for a healthy mouth, particularly healthy gums.

A completely new advertising campaign was introduced to communicate the brand's multiple benefits and to present a new brand character. Serious was out and light-hearted was in. Listerine would be the action hero for your gums, and a character in the ads would play the role of the hero. The new positioning strategy and the action hero campaign paid dividends. Between 2000 and 2005, brand sales grew 75 percent and market share moved from 39 percent to 52 percent. With little change in other marketing strategies, this case demonstrates the correlation between positioning strategy, effective advertising, and business results.[5] See Figure 4.5 for an advertisement from this successful marketing campaign.

TARGET-MARKET PROFILE

At this stage, the manager identifies, or targets, markets that represent the greatest profit potential for the firm. A **target market** is a group of customers with certain similar needs and characteristics. As discussed in Chapter 3, a target-market description is devised based on demographic, psychographic, and geographic characteristics.

- *Demographic profile* Characteristics such as age, gender, income, education, and ethnic background are considered. Depending on the product and the extent of its appeal to the population, some characteristics will be more important than others.

Listerine
www.listerine.com

FIGURE 4.5

Listerine's action hero effectively positioned the brand as a leader in oral health care

Courtesy of Pfizer Consumer Healthcare Division.

- *Psychographic profile* The lifestyle profile includes three essential characteristics: the target's activities, interests, and opinions. Such knowledge provides clues that will influence the direction of message strategies (how to appeal to the target) and media strategies (how to best reach the target). For example, the highly sought-after 18- to 25-year-old market watches much less television than in previous generations; current members of this demographic spend much more time online and with their cell phones. This presents a challenge for marketers wanting to reach them.

- *Geographic profile* Much of Canada's population is urban, and certainly there are distinct regional differences that must be considered. Geography will influence decisions about regional versus national marketing strategies and will influence how a budget is allocated across the country.

To demonstrate, the following profile might represent a target market for an upscale automobile or someone interested in the services of a financial-planning company:

- *Age:* 25 to 49 years old

- *Gender:* Male or female

- *Income:* $75 000-plus annually

- *Occupation:* Business managers, owners, and professionals

- *Education:* College or university

- *Location:* Cities of 100 000-plus population

- *Lifestyle:* Progressive thinkers and risk takers who like to experiment with new products; they are interested in the arts, entertainment, and vacation travel

To demonstrate the importance of understanding your customer, and for more insight into how a company develops its marketing and marketing communications strategies based on that understanding, read the Advertising in Action vignette **A&W Remains True to Its Roots.**

MARKETING OBJECTIVES

Marketing objectives are statements identifying what a product will accomplish during one year. Typically, marketing objectives concentrate on sales volume, market share, and profit (net profit or return on investment), all of which are quantitative (as opposed to qualitative) in nature and measurable at the end of the period. Objectives that are qualitative in nature could include new product introductions, new additions to current product lines, product improvements, and packaging innovations. To illustrate the concept of marketing objectives, consider the following sample statements:

- *Sales volume* To achieve sales of 200 000 units, an increase of 10 percent over the current-year sales.

- *Market share* To achieve a market share of 30 percent in 12 months, an increase of 4 share points over the current position.

- *Profit* To generate an after-budget profit of $600 000 in the next 12 months.

- *Marketing communications* To launch a new advertising campaign in the second quarter that will increase brand awareness from 50 percent to 75 percent among the target audience.

ADVERTISING IN ACTION

A&W Remains True to Its Roots

A&W is the original hamburger fast food restaurant in Canada, and in the '50s and '60s it pretty well had the market to itself. The company operated *American Graffiti*–style drive-ins, complete with car hops and food trays that hung in a car's open window. The food was great and teenagers loved the place! So successful was A&W, it became a gathering place for the community. Then came McDonald's, Burger King, and Wendy's, and the days of the drive-in were over.

Over the years, A&W has survived the onslaught of competition, and today competes with Burger King and Wendy's for bragging rights to second place in the market. They all own around 12 percent of the hamburger market. McDonald's is by far the leader, with a 58-percent market share. Today, A&W has more than 600 locations, making it the second largest in terms of number of units, and produces $660 million in annual revenue.

An understanding of its primary target market and a carefully devised marketing and marketing communications strategy helps separate A&W from the rest of the pack. Their strategy is directed at a very attractive target market—baby boomers. According to Jeff Mooney, chairman and CEO of A&W Food Services, "The baby boom generation is the grand prize in the consumer sweepstakes. And it's boomers who remember A&W in its heyday."

Statistics Canada confirms Mooney's viewpoint. Boomers number 10 million people, almost one-third of Canada's population—a very attractive market to pursue. A&W acknowledges that 50 percent of their customers are baby boomers; the company introduced most Canadian boomers to fast-food culture. Such ties to the boomers give A&W an edge in this highly competitive market.

From a marketing perspective, A&W offers what boomers are looking for—a pleasant environment in which to enjoy a meal (restaurants are retro-styled and play appropriate boomer music); good food (the Burger Family: Papa, Mama, Teen, and Baby, along with Chubby Chicken); and root beer served in ice-cold frosted glass mugs. In a nutshell, A&W is positioned to appeal to older age groups based on nostalgia; it's a contemporary version of the way things used to be.

And that sparks an emotional response among people who visited A&W when they were younger. A&W is a connection to their past, whether it was sitting in the back seat when they were little kids or when they had their first car and it was a ritual to visit the "dub."

Connecting with the boomer market is the responsibility of advertising, and A&W and its advertising agency, Rethink of Vancouver, have done an excellent job. A new campaign was launched in 2004 featuring the tagline "A&W since 1956." The creative strategy was based on emotion—a technique that would bring back the memories. An early commercial in this campaign, called "Drive," starred a man with a refurbished sports car. He asks his wife to go for a drive and they wind up at A&W, where he flashes his headlights. A few seconds later, Alan, A&W's "restaurant manager" spokesperson, walks out with a tray of food. The driver admits to his wife that the situation was pre-planned, but it is an enjoyable trip down memory lane for them both.

A more recent commercial features a young married couple and the parents of the young male. Arriving at the parents' house, the young male gets the cold shoulder from his father but suggests they go out for a bite to eat. Arriving at A&W, the father takes charge and places the usual order: One Papa, One Mama, and Two Teens. The young male comments to his wife, "Just like when we were kids." With the famous song "Crystal Blue Persuasion" playing in the background, the son brings the food to the table and hands a Grandpa Burger to the father—Father's a bit slow to figure things out, but Mother gets the message right away and embraces the daughter-in-law. Father and son then embrace—truly an emotional connection!

So how has A&W stood the test of time? According to Mooney, "The key to winning in a super-competitive market is reinventing yourself without changing what you are. A&W has resisted the temptation to get into pizzas and wraps like their competitors." A&W has a solid positioning strategy ("We do things the way we always have") from which an effective marketing and marketing communications strategy has evolved to build the business.

Source: Adapted from Jason Kirby, "A&W finds the right recipe," *Financial Post*, June 12, 2006, www.canada.com; Lisa D'Innocenzo, "A&W serves up new tag with a side of nostalgia," *Strategy*, April 5, 2004, p. 5; and Zena Olijnyk, "The bear bites back," *Canadian Business*, March 18, 2002, pp. 71–73.

Objectives should be written in a manner that allows for measurement at the end of the period. Were the objectives achieved or not?

MARKETING STRATEGIES

Marketing strategies are essentially the "master plans" for achieving marketing objectives. The importance of having a sound marketing strategy must be emphasized. All elements of the marketing mix and marketing communications mix must act in unison; collaboration is necessary in order to present a consistent and meaningful proposition to new and existing customers. The goal should be to have the right strategy and then work on improving the execution of it as time goes on.

At this stage of the planning process, the role and importance of each component of the **marketing mix** is identified. Priority may be given to certain components, depending on the nature of the market, the degree of competition, and knowledge of what motivates customers to buy. For example, brands like Coca-Cola and Pepsi-Cola rely heavily on media advertising, distribution strategies, and an online presence to build sales and market share. Wal-Mart dwells on product and price—a combination that offers significant value to consumers across all income groups. Automobile marketers have focused on pricing strategies (incentives and rebate offers) in recent years at the expense of building brand image through advertising.

Pepsi
www.pepsi.ca

Financial resources (the **budget**) will be laid out in the strategy section of the plan. Typically, the corporate plan has already identified a total marketing budget for the company. That budget must be allocated across all company products based on the firm's analysis of current priorities or profit potential. Managers responsible for product planning must develop and justify a budget that allows enough funds to implement the strategies identified in their marketing plan, and to achieve the financial objectives identified for the product. The final stage of the budgeting process is the allocation of funds among the activity areas in the plan (advertising, marketing research, consumer promotion, trade promotion, events and sponsorship, interactive communications, and others).

MARKETING EXECUTION

Marketing execution (often called **marketing tactics**) focuses on specific details that stem directly from the strategy section of the plan. In general terms, a tactical plan outlines the activity, how much it will cost, what the timing will be, and who will be responsible for implementation. Detailed tactical plans for all components of the plan (advertising, sales promotion, internet communications, marketing research) are included here. It should be noted that the ad agency develops a detailed advertising plan in a separate document. If advertising is a key element in overall marketing strategy, then advertising strategy and tactics will be integrated into the marketing plan in summary form in the marketing communications section.

FINANCIAL SUMMARY AND BUDGET ALLOCATION

As a summary of the entire marketing plan, a statistical presentation of key product-performance indicators is commonly included. Variables such as sales, market share, gross profit, marketing budget, and net profit are presented historically. Past performance and trends can be compared to the latest financial estimates in the new marketing plan. A detailed budget is included that indicates all activity areas in which funds will be spent. Major areas such as media, consumer promotion, trade promotion, and marketing research are often subdivided into more specific areas.

MARKETING CONTROL AND EVALUATION

Since clearly defined and measurable objectives have been established by the organization and by the marketing department, it is important that results be evaluated against the plans and against past performance. This evaluation indicates whether current strategies need to be modified or if new strategies should be considered.

Marketing control is the process of measuring and evaluating the results of marketing strategies and plans, and taking corrective action to ensure that marketing objectives are attained. For example, if financial objectives are not being achieved, then new marketing strategies may have to be considered. This is also a good time to re-evaluate the various marketing objectives. Perhaps some objectives were too aggressive, and, considering the current dynamics of the market, should be adjusted accordingly. Any modifications to the marketing objectives will have an impact on the marketing activities as well. See Figure 4.6 for a diagram of the marketing planning and control process.

Marketing Communications Planning

Prior to discussing marketing communications planning, it is imperative that the reader understand the nature of the communications process, particularly in the context of marketing communications. (See Figure 4.7.) Organizations and their agencies work together to devise a message that is transmitted by the media (television, radio, magazines, newspapers, internet, cell phones, and video games) to a target audience. In this process the organization is offering customers some kind of value (the benefits expressed in the message). If the message resonates with the target audience, it will grab their attention (a value exchange that benefits the advertiser).

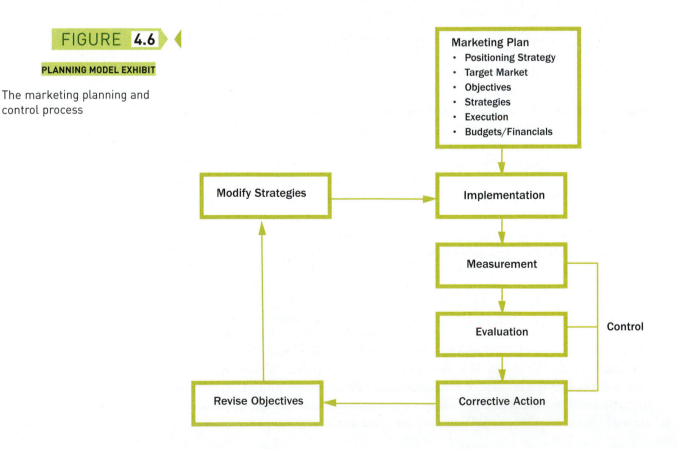

FIGURE 4.6

PLANNING MODEL EXHIBIT

The marketing planning and control process

Message and media strategies work together to offer value (benefits) to the target market.

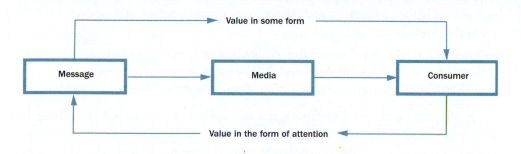

The goal of contemporary communications is to *engage* the consumer. Engagement is driven by three factors: conditions, context, and content.

Conditions include pre-existing brand interest. People are more likely to notice an ad if they have used the brand before, if they have enjoyed the brand's communications, or if they are in the market for that product.

Context includes what else the consumer is doing, where the ad is located, whether it interrupted the consumer, or whether he or she chose it.

Content is not driven by the message of the ad, but how it made the consumer feel. People notice ads that offer humour, are thought-provoking, make them feel intelligent, that are surprising, or make them feel important. Effective advertising fulfills needs. People are more likely to notice things that fulfill their needs and add value to their lives.

Source: Adapted from Jason Oke, "Op-Ed: engagement not rocket science—Leo Burnett, CanWest MediaWorks, Ideas Research Group," *Media in Canada*, October 5, 2006, www.mediaincanada.com.

How much attention a consumer gives to a message is affected by several factors: the quality of the message itself, the channel of communications employed, and the presence of competing messages. Competition for attention is referred to as **noise**. From a planning perspective, the challenge is to create a message that will break through the clutter of competing messages and instill a positive impression in the receiver's mind (a positive value exchange). Should the desired action of making a purchase occur, so much the better! If the message does not break through the clutter or it is not perceived as relevant to the individual receiving it, there is a negative value exchange. If the latter situation occurs, the very nature of the message strategy must be re-evaluated.

Many practitioners believe the quality of the message (a message that employs the proper appeal techniques) is more important than the quantity of messages delivered. An ineffective message distributed frequently is no message at all. The challenge for agency creative planners and media planners is to effectively combine the right message strategy with the right media strategy. It's a complex challenge!

When deciding what products to buy, a consumer passes through a series of behaviour stages, and marketing communications can influence each stage. One such model that refers to these various stages is AIDA. This acronym stands for *attention, interest, desire,* and *action.* Another model is ACCA—*awareness, comprehension, conviction,* and *action.* A description of the latter model follows:

- *Awareness* In the awareness stage, the customer *learns of something for the first time.* Obviously, this learning can occur only if one is exposed to a new advertisement.

- *Comprehension* By the comprehension stage, *interest* has been created. The message is perceived as relevant, and the product, judged from the information presented, is considered useful. The product becomes part of the customer's frame of reference.

- *Conviction* The customer's evaluation of the product's benefits (as presented in the advertising) leads to a decision. The product is viewed as satisfactory, and has gained *preference* in the customer's mind. The customer may be sufficiently motivated to buy the product.

- *Action* In this stage, the desired active *response* occurs. For example, a car advertisement may motivate a customer to visit a dealer's showroom or a website; a coupon may motivate a reader to clip it out for more information or for use in an initial purchase.

As discussed earlier in the textbook, it is very difficult to directly link advertising to sales (or the desired action as described above). What can be measured is how well the message communicates. For example, did the message generate the desired level of awareness? Were the desired preference scores achieved? Did the message alter the perceptions consumers' held about the product? A new ad could be tested with consumers for likeability, persuasiveness, and likelihood of purchase. Scores exceeding the norms for other products in the same category would suggest the advertiser is on to something. Therefore, advertising and other forms of communications should be measured against outcomes they can directly influence. To evaluate whether or not advertisements are communicating effectively, clients and advertising agencies engage in consumer research studies.

The Marketing Communications Plan

Similar to marketing planning, marketing communications planning involves the development of appropriate objectives, strategies, and tactics. The plan will also include objectives, strategies, and execution details for each of the marketing communications elements that are included in the plan. Students often get confused about objectives, since there is a tendency for them to overlap. For example, an objective in the marketing communications plan (an objective for the entire plan) also appears as an advertising objective in the advertising plan (an objective for a portion of the overall plan).

To explain the difference, consider that each element of the marketing communications mix—advertising, online communications, sales promotion, public relations, event marketing and sponsorships, direct-response communications, and personal selling—plays a unique role in achieving overall marketing communications objectives. For example, advertising helps achieve awareness and preference objectives, sales promotion achieves trial and repeat purchase objectives, and public relations achieves awareness and brand-mention objectives. Given this conceptual perspective, you can start to see why overall objectives in a marketing communications plan will also appear in more specific communications plans. A sound marketing communications plan will only include those marketing-mix components that contribute to achieving the overall objectives. Refer to Figure 4.8 and you will see that marketing communications objectives and the advertising objectives can be similar.

Usually a campaign is designed to resolve a specific problem or pursue an opportunity, so the primary objective of marketing communications must be stated clearly. Marketing communications objectives tend to cover a diverse range of possibilities and could involve

- Creating or building awareness for a product or company

- Differentiating a product from competitive offerings

- Encouraging more frequent use of a product

FIGURE 4.8

PLANNING MODEL EXHIBIT

Marketing communications plan: a sample model*

Marketing Communications Objectives
(A selection of possibilities)
- Awareness
- Preference
- Trial Purchase
- Alter Image
- Frequency and Variety of Use
- Promotional Incentives

Marketing Communications Strategies
- Positioning Statement
- Components of Mix
- Budget

Advertising Plan
a) Advertising Objectives
(A selection of possibilities)
- Awareness
- Product Differentiation
- Position or Reposition Product
- Trial Purchase
- Enhance Image

b) Creative Plan
- Objectives (what message)
- Strategies (how to communicate message)
- Execution

c) Media Plan
- Objectives
  Who
  What
  When
  Where
  How
- Strategies
  Target-Market Matching Strategies
  Rationale for Media Selection
  Rationale for Media Rejection

- Execution
  Cost Summaries (budget appropriation)
  Media Schedule (timing, coverage, usage)

Direct-Response Plan
- Objectives
- Strategies
- Tactics
- Budget

Online/Interactive Plan
- Objectives
- Strategies
- Tactics
- Budget

Sales Promotion Plan
- Objectives
- Strategies
- Tactics
- Budget

Public Relations Plan
- Objectives
- Strategies
- Tactics
- Budget

Events and Sponsorship Plan
- Objectives
- Strategies
- Tactics
- Budget

Personal Selling Plan
- Objectives
- Strategies
- Tactics
- Budget

*Assumes adequate input from background section of marketing plan.

Note: More detailed discussion of objectives, strategies, and tactics occurs in chapters related to each element of the marketing communications mix.

- Altering perceptions held by consumers about a product
- Offering incentives to get people to buy the product
- Fostering a strong public image of the product or company

The list could go on, but the point is that certain types of marketing communications are better than others at achieving certain objectives. Sometimes one form of communications, say, advertising, may be enough to achieve the objective while at other times a multi-discipline approach is necessary. Determining which components of the marketing communications mix will be used depends on the nature of the market, competitive activity, and the target market to be reached. As well, the funds available will influence the decision—some activities are much more expensive than others! The key to success is the integration of the various components to produce a unified approach to building the brand (or company).

A **marketing communications plan** is a document usually prepared by the company's marketing communications agency. Or it could be the result of a coordinated effort of several agencies that are doing specialized work. Agency specialists may be employed for creative and media planning, public relations, sales promotion, or event planning. To develop the plan, each agency must be informed about relevant marketing information. In the case of advertising, for example, the client will prepare a document that contains relevant information from the marketing plan. That document is commonly referred to as a **creative brief** (if message is the issue) or a **media brief** (if the issue is media-related), or it may simply be called a communications brief. The creative brief is discussed in more detail in Chapter 5 and the media brief is discussed in more detail in Chapter 7.

As discussed earlier in the textbook, it is now common for all members of a client's agency team to meet and be briefed at the same time. Agency personnel may be positioned uniquely in their own organization, based on their area of expertise (e.g., art director—print and broadcast media, and art director—digital media; or media planner—broadcast media, and media planner—digital media). However, since all could potentially be involved in solving the client's advertising challenge, they must participate in the briefing and initial planning meetings.

MARKETING COMMUNICATIONS OBJECTIVES

Marketing communications objectives define the role that advertising and other forms of communications will play in selling the client's product or service and in achieving a stated marketing objective. For example, advertising usually plays a key role in creating brand awareness, sales promotions encourage trial purchases, and public relations helps build and maintain brand image. The various plan components, therefore, work together to help achieve the marketing communications objectives.

A good statement of objectives will make it possible to quantify the success or failure of advertising by establishing the minimum levels of awareness and purchase motivation. It should also provide a description of the target market to be reached by advertising. Consider the following examples of marketing communications objectives:

1. To achieve a minimum awareness level of 75 percent among men and women, 18 to 34 years of age, in urban markets of 500 000 population.
2. To motivate at least 25 percent of the defined target market to try the product on the basis of trial incentives to be included in print advertising.
3. To improve public awareness of our company's actions in the area of social responsibility marketing.
4. To alter consumers' perceptions about brand image so that the views held about the brand are more positive.

As shown above, where possible, the objectives should be quantitative in nature (objectives 1 and 2) so that when the campaign is over, the results can be evaluated against the plan. Many firms will conduct marketing research to determine the effectiveness of their message and media strategies. For example, if the desired awareness level was not achieved, new strategies will have to be considered for the following year. These objectives also imply that marketing communications will be an integrated effort embracing activities beyond just advertising. In the case of objective 4, it could be assumed that currently held perceptions are negative; some consumer research in the post-campaign stage will reveal if perceptions have been altered favourably.

To demonstrate the relationship between objectives, communications strategy, and execution (the actual message that is delivered), consider the situation that Jergens faced in Quebec. Jergens lotion ranked fourth in market share, and sales were declining. The product was positioned as a value brand and was of little interest to Quebec women, who want their beauty products to have a prestigious image. Jergens set out to alter perceptions and create a new image for the brand (objective 4 on the list above).

Jergens
www.jergens.com

Research indicated Quebec women would spend a lot of time on clothing and makeup, but skip the step of moisturizing. Jergens would now stand for the idea that beautiful skin is just as important as any other accessory. The tagline for the campaign was "Take care of what you wear everyday." The campaign connected with the Quebec woman's view of beauty and helped increase sales by 68 percent (compared to a decrease of 4 percent the preceding year).[6] To build on the success experienced in Quebec, Jergens decided to roll the campaign out to the rest of Canada. Refer to Figure 4.9 for an illustration of the creative.

MARKETING COMMUNICATIONS STRATEGIES

A **marketing communications strategy** includes a positioning-strategy statement, identifies the various elements of the marketing communications mix that will be employed, and contains a budget for the plan. Refer to Figure 4.8 for an illustration.

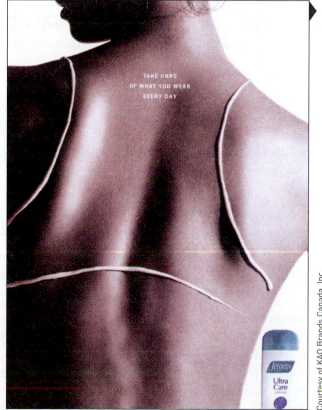

FIGURE 4.9

A new message strategy focusing on the importance of beautiful skin altered consumers' perceptions about the Jergens brand

Courtesy of KAO Brands Canada, Inc.

If the marketing communications plan is a separate document from the marketing plan, then a positioning-strategy statement should be included here even though it also appears in the marketing plan. (Positioning was discussed in the marketing planning section of this chapter and in Chapter 3.) The positioning-strategy statement acts as a guideline for the development of all communications strategies (e.g., advertising, sales promotion, and online communications).

As was illustrated by the objectives listed above, the positioning-strategy statement will identify the various **marketing communications mix** components that will be included in the plan, along with a rationale supporting their inclusion. For example, advertising would be used to generate awareness; sales promotions would generate trial purchase; public relations and event marketing could help improve brand image; and internet advertising through a website could satisfy both awareness and image objectives. Only those components of the mix that can make a contribution to achieving the objectives should be included.

This section of the plan should identify the total budget that is available for marketing communications activities. It may even allocate the money between the various components of the mix that are included in the plan. For example, what percentage of the total budget will be allocated to advertising, online communications, events and sponsorships, public relations, or other activities?

Establishing the budget and allocating amounts to each of the components of marketing communications is a major decision area. There are various methods that can be used to develop a budget. Some methods estimate sales first and then base the advertising budget on sales. Other methods develop the budget first; these methods essentially presuppose that advertising and other forms of communications are an effective means of achieving sales objectives. Regardless of the method used, the budget must be carefully calculated and rationalized by the manager responsible for it so that the plan can be implemented as recommended.

The plan is usually subdivided at this stage, with objectives, strategies, and tactics identified for each component of the marketing communications mix that is recommended.

ADVERTISING PLAN

The **advertising plan** begins with a clearly worded list of advertising objectives that specifically outlines what the advertising will achieve. For example, when Pfizer Inc. launched the Schick Quattro four-blade razor, the product was positioned as superior to Gillette's three-blade razors. Gillette is the dominant brand leader. Schick's advertising objectives may have been stated as follows:

- To create a 75-percent awareness level for the Schick Quattro razor among 16- to 29-year-old males

- To differentiate Schick from all other razors based on four-blade technology that offers the best possible shave

- To achieve a trial purchase rate of 20 percent among 16- to 29-year-old males

The advertising plan is then divided into two main areas: creative and media. The **creative plan** will document what the nature of the message will be and what strategies and techniques will be used to communicate the message. As indicated by the objectives above, the message will focus on the benefits offered by the four-blade shaving system. The message usually revolves around a key benefit statement (a brand makes a promise of something) and a support-claims statement (a statement that gives people a reason to buy the product).

In terms of how the message is communicated, advertisers have a variety of appeal techniques they call upon. Among these appeal techniques are the use of sex, humour, celebrities, product comparisons, and lifestyle associations. As well, the message usually has a central theme so that all messages (print, broadcast, and online) are focused and saying the same thing the same way.

When Viagra was first launched, a light-hearted humorous approach was used to communicate the product's benefits. Some commercials showed very happy men leaving for work. A subsequent campaign showed some happy women singing the praises of Viagra on their way to work. The ads effectively showed the effect that Viagra could have on people. Very recent executions show men trying to explain why they feel so good. Once they start talking, an image of the Viagra pill covers their mouths so the viewer doesn't actually hear what they say. This series of ads won "Best of Show" at *Marketing* magazine's 2006 Marketing Awards. See the illustration in Figure 4.10. Creative planning is discussed in more detail in chapters 5 and 6.

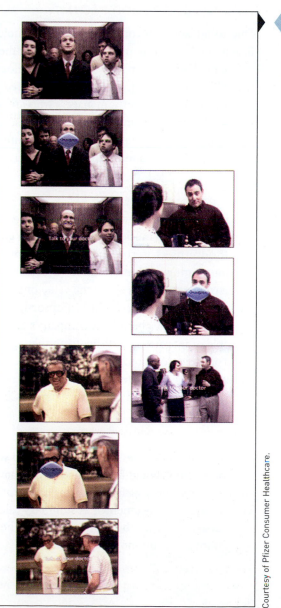

FIGURE 4.10

A humorous, light-hearted strategy communicates the key benefit of Viagra.

Courtesy of Pfizer Consumer Healthcare.

For more insight into how advertising message strategies help differentiate competing brands, read the Advertising in Action vignette **Banks Deliver Different Messages**.

The **media plan** involves decisions about which media are best suited to reaching the target audience in an effective and efficient manner. Since a lot of money is at stake, making the right decisions is crucial. The goal of the media plan is to provide maximum impact at minimum cost and to reach the target market at the right time. Therefore, numerous strategic decisions must be made. An advertiser must determine which media to use—television, radio, newspapers, magazines, direct mail, or the internet; the best time to reach the target market and how often it must be reached; which markets to advertise in (geographically) and at what weight levels; and timing and length for the media campaign. To develop the media plan, an agency must be on top of media consumption trends and be able to blend together traditional media with the new digital media. All information is summarized in a media plan. Media planning is discussed in detail in Chapter 7.

DIRECT-RESPONSE PLAN

Due to advances in communications technology, companies are now investing more heavily in direct-response techniques to get their message out. Direct response includes direct mail, direct-response television, catalogue marketing, and telemarketing activities. These types of activities can be measured for effectiveness more readily than mass advertising. Consequently, managers who are being held more accountable for producing results are investing in direct-response advertising. Appropriate objectives and strategies are incorporated into the communications plan. Direct-response communications are presented in detail in Chapter 11.

ONLINE AND INTERACTIVE PLAN

The internet and other forms of interactive communications such as cell phones, video games, and digital music players are gaining ground among the media alternatives available to advertisers. Certainly company and product websites now play an integral role in communicating vital information to customers and other publics. In terms of online advertising, companies assess the value of banner ads (ads in various sizes that viewers click on for more information), sponsorship opportunities (advertising on other websites of interest to a brand's or company's target audience), and email opportunities. An example of internet advertising from the Jaguar website is included in Figure 4.11. The rapid adoption of mobile technologies by younger people will have a significant impact on an organization's future communications strategies. Interactive communications strategies are presented in greater detail in Chapter 12.

SALES PROMOTION PLAN

If promotion incentives are to be integrated with the advertising activities, a sales promotion section should be included in the marketing communications plan. Objectives of the promotions, such as securing trial purchase, repeat purchase, or multiple purchase, should be documented. A summary calendar, outlining the activities, timing, and costs associated with the promotion, must be included. Refer to Chapter 13 for more insight into sales promotion planning.

Banks Deliver Different Messages

All banks face the same two problems when it comes to attracting new customers. First, they are offering intangible products that consumers can't see or touch. Second, consumers perceive all banks to be the same—they offer the same set of products and services. So how does a bank get new customers?

The latest round of advertising by the banks suggests that placing an emphasis on the customer is the right approach to take. The marketing decision-makers at the banks and other financial institutions believe that human interaction, and the promise of feeling comfortable and secure with your bank, is what people are looking for.

At Scotiabank the objective is to help customers to become financially better off. To meet this objective it developed an advertising campaign that differentiates itself from the others based on a "Find the money" positioning strategy. A series of humorous television commercials shows situations in which puzzled-looking employees deal with the unique quirks of various customers. In each ad the bank employee helps people find money they didn't know they had. The slogan, "You're richer than you think," tied all of the communications together. Dick White, vice-president of marketing at Scotiabank, calls this brand promise "an optimistic approach" to personal finance.

The solution at TD Canada Trust was to stress customer comfort, which was a response to the customer's need to feel appreciated. Customers don't want to feel like a number; they want to feel that people know their name and that their business is important to the bank. The result was an advertising campaign designed around the now-familiar large, comfortable green chair, and the slogan, "Banking can be comfortable."

RBC Financial has also adopted a communications strategy that is customer-focused. The "First for you" campaign uses real stories of clients to show how the bank puts clients first. The ad campaign is part of an overall marketing strategy that calls for all employees to be clear on the message and deliver the brand promise at all touch points. All print ads in the campaign have a common look and style that helps the "First for you" positioning stand out.

In such a competitive market, it seems like all of the banks have adopted a similar positioning strategy that places the focus on the customer, but have used different creative strategies and executions. With most other aspects of the marketing mix being the same for all banks, it will be the quality of the message and the impact it has on new customers that will determine which bank achieves the most from its new positioning strategy. While it is too early to evaluate the effectiveness of these campaigns, bear in mind that campaigns that are working will have a longer run than those that aren't working.

Source: Adapted from Rebecca Harris, "Connecting with consumers," *Marketing*, July 18/25, 2005, pp. 13, 14.

EVENTS AND SPONSORSHIP PLAN

Events and sponsorship are playing a more prominent role in contemporary marketing. If a company develops an event or participates in one, careful planning is required. A variety of communications elements must be built into the plan to show how the event will be supported. If sponsorship funds are required, the company offers financial support in return for advertising privileges. All of this information is documented in the communications plan. Additional details about event marketing and sponsorships are included in Chapter 14.

Courtesy of Jaguar Canada. Jaguar Canada and Ford Motor Company trademarks and Jaguar branded products are used with permission.

FIGURE 4.11

Advertising on the internet: websites play a key role in the image-building process

PUBLIC RELATIONS PLAN

Public relations can play a key role in launching a new product or generating interest about an existing product. A plan to secure media support for newsworthy information about a product should be developed. The value of such publicity can be worth much more than the value derived from paid advertising. Documentation about public relations activity should be included in the communications plan. It is now common for an organization to post all news releases, relevant photos, and video clips about the company or its products on its website. Refer to Chapter 14 for more insight into public relations.

PERSONAL SELLING PLAN

Communicating with members of the distribution channel is the job of an organization's sales force. The role of the sales representative is to communicate the benefits of the products offered for sale in terms of how they will specifically resolve a potential customer's problem. As well, the sales representative communicates to the trade any support plans that will help the distributor resell the products (e.g., price discounts and allowances, advertising programs, sponsorships). Coordination of the personal selling effort with other marketing communications activities is crucial.

For some initial insight into what a communications plan looks like and how the various elements of the plan are linked together, refer to the plan that is included in Appendix II.

SUMMARY

The quality of marketing and marketing communications planning in an organization is influenced by the business planning process itself. Business planning is a problem-solving and decision-making effort that forces management to look at the future and to set clear objectives and strategies.

In terms of marketing communications, three different but related plans are important: the corporate plan, the marketing plan, and the marketing communications plan. Each plan involves the development of appropriate objectives, strategies, and tactics, and, when one plan is complete, it provides direction for the next plan. The marketing plan, for example, directs the marketing communications plan, which in turn directs individual plans for various components of the marketing communications mix.

Corporate planning starts with the development of a mission statement followed by corporate objectives and strategies. Some of the more common corporate strategies include penetrating the market more aggressively, acquiring other companies, implementing new-product development programs, forming strategic alliances with other companies, and selling off unprofitable divisions of a company to consolidate operations.

Strategic marketing planning involves the following steps: conducting a situation analysis, which is a procedure that reviews and analyzes relevant data and information; conducting a SWOT analysis, which highlights the general direction a brand or company should be heading in; establishing appropriate marketing objectives and strategies; identifying target markets; accessing budget support; and establishing measurement and control procedures. The evaluation and control procedure attempts to draw relationships between strategic activity and results. All of this information is included in a marketing plan.

The marketing communications plan identifies the various communications objectives to be accomplished and delineates strategy in several areas. The communications plan is subdivided into specific areas depending on what components of the mix are going to be used. The advertising plan focuses on creative objectives and strategies (what message to communicate and how to communicate it). The media plan states the media objectives by answering who, what, when, where, and how. The media strategies rationalize the use of media alternatives and treat in more detail considerations of timing, market coverage, and scheduling of messages.

Finally, other elements of the integrated marketing communications mix may be included in the plan. If sales promotion, event marketing and sponsorships, public relations, and direct-response and internet communications are important, objectives, strategies, and tactics for each will be included. All plans must work together to achieve the objectives stated in the marketing communications plan.

KEY TERMS

advertising plan 114

creative brief 112

execution (tactics) 95

marketing communications plan 112

marketing control 108

marketing execution (marketing tactics) 107

marketing objectives 105

marketing planning 100

marketing plans 96

marketing strategies 107

media brief 112

mission statement 97

objectives 95

positioning 103

situation analysis 100

strategic alliance 100

strategic planning 96

strategies 95

SWOT analysis 103

target market (or target audience) 104

REVIEW QUESTIONS

1. In planning, what is the basic difference between objectives, strategies, and tactics?

2. What is the relationship between a company's mission statement and a company's marketing activity?

3. What is the relationship between a corporate plan, marketing plan, and marketing communications plan?

4. What does the term "situation analysis" refer to, and what are the key issues associated with such an analysis?

5. What role does a positioning-strategy statement play in the development of marketing strategy?

6. What are the essential components of a target-market profile?

7. Briefly describe the key elements of the marketing strategy section of a marketing plan.

8. How will a precise target-market profile affect the development of creative strategies and media strategies?

9. What is meant by "marketing control"? What are the three basic elements that constitute marketing control?

10. In the planning process, what role does a clearly worded marketing communications objective play?

11. What are the key decision areas of an advertising plan? In considering the key areas, identify the relationships between creative and media strategies.

12. What are the various components of the marketing communications mix?

120

DISCUSSION QUESTIONS

1. "Good strategy, poor execution" or "Poor strategy, good execution"—which scenario will produce better results? Support your position with an appropriate rationale.

2. Coca-Cola was used as an example in this chapter to show the relationship between a company's mission statement and its marketing communications strategies. Are there other companies that are doing the same thing? Conduct some online research for a few companies of your choosing and file a brief report on the relationships between mission (the direction a company is heading) and marketing communications.

3. Conduct some secondary research on the internet to determine the type of marketing and marketing communications strategies being implemented by the following companies. What conditions are prompting the use of these strategies?
   a) PepsiCo
   b) Nike
   c) Colgate-Palmolive
   d) United Way
   e) BMO Bank of Montreal

4. Review the Advertising in Action vignette **A&W Remains True to Its Roots**. A&W believes that targeting baby boomers with a nostalgic message is an effective strategy for achieving growth. What is your take on the situation? Is this strategy good for the long term or should A&W be looking at other options? Justify your position.

NOTES

1. Rich Thomaselli, "Deal sets stage for full-scale war with Nike," *Advertising Age*, August 8, 2005, p. 5.
2. Mary Maddever, "The new Kraft," *Strategy*, May 2006, pp. 13, 18.
3. Todd Zaun, "Toyota, Nissan cooperate," *Globe and Mail*, September 2, 2002, p. B11.
4. Mary Ellen Lloyd, "Consumer-product firms still making deals," *Financial Post*, February 2, 2006, p. FP15.
5. CASSIES 2006, *Canadian Advertising Success Stories*, Listerine, **www.cassies.ca/winners**.
6. "Skin matters: Jergens Ultra," *CASSIES Canadian Advertising Success Stories*, 2005, p. 20.

Wal-Mart Adopts New Strategy Based on New Knowledge of Shoppers:

WILL IT WORK?

When you are as big as Wal-Mart, the annual expectations for growth in sales and profit are incredible, but even the largest of companies have to reassess their situation and plot new directions, if growth is the ultimate objective.

In 2006 Wal-Mart introduced a marketing strategy that encouraged customers to "look beyond the basics" and try costlier products. Wal-Mart would offer new, more expensive goods as a means of attracting new shoppers. But, the year 2006 was a rough one for Wal-Mart. Sales growth at Wal-Mart's older stores was well below that of rivals, and for the first time in decades, Christmas holiday sales were lower than the previous year.

What Went Wrong?

In retrospect, the new lines created some confusion in the minds of customers. When your slogan's been "Low prices, always" for 44 years, telling people that products will cost more seems to go against the grain of what Wal-Mart stands for.

This was not Wal-Mart's first attempt at broadening the product line in this way. It was only a few years ago that Wal-Mart added new, more upscale product lines in an attempt to attract new shoppers: the Metro 7 urban line of clothing targeted female shoppers and the George line of clothing targeted male shoppers. The strategy was to squeeze more dollars out of every shopper by stocking higher-end products and marketing them with slick ads on television and consumer magazines. Wal-Mart was actually entering a new area of marketing, an area they weren't that familiar with.

What Now?

Wal-Mart is not giving up on this strategy. In fact, they are fine tuning the strategy based on new consumer insights that were revealed in intensive consumer research studies over the past year. With this new knowledge Wal-Mart is more confident about the direction it is taking. Most importantly, the new research uncovered not only how people shop at Wal-Mart but why they shop the way they do—that's fuel for refining or introducing new merchandising and marketing strategies.

According to John Fleming (the new chief merchandising officer) and Stephen Quinn (the new chief marketing officer) the research revealed three primary groups of Wal-Mart shoppers:

- **Brand Aspirationals** These are people with low incomes who are obsessed with brand names like Sony and KitchenAid.
- **Price-Sensitive Affluents** These are wealthier shoppers who like deals.
- **Value-Price Shoppers** These are people who like low prices and cannot afford to spend much on higher-priced goods.

These groups all currently shop at Wal-Mart. So, rather than go after new shoppers, new marketing and marketing communications strategies will focus more on current shoppers. All product decisions, for example, will revolve around the three groups: brand aspirationals, price-sensitive affluents, and value-price shoppers.

More to the point, these three groups have one thing in common—they all want deals, but not deals on cheap products. They are looking for deals on brand-name merchandise, brand names they are

FIGURE 1

Courtesy of Dick Hemingway.

familiar with. This common characteristic explains why people who have to shop at Wal-Mart do so, and why there are lots of BMWs in the parking lot.

What's Next?

Wal-Mart has created teams to rethink the lines they carry in certain power categories. In the electronics department, for example, rather than have a bunch of unknown brands, names such as Sony and Magnavox will be added. According to Stephen Quinn, "Customers really need the assurance of brands. In the past we were focused on low price, but low price on what?" Customers were reluctant to buy the unknown brands, particularly in higher-priced categories such as flat-screen TVs. Wal-Mart has little choice but to add the better-known brand names in key product categories; otherwise, shoppers will look to competitors such as Best Buy or Home Depot.

Wal-Mart has started remodeling older stores and has changed how employees' shifts are scheduled in order to offer better customer service. The biggest priority for 2007 and beyond is to fix its merchandising and marketing strategies. Now that Wal-Mart has a better handle on why shoppers shop at Wal-Mart, better marketing communications strategies can be developed to help spur sales of its upper-end clothing lines and for the proposed new brand names in other categories.

In refining the upscale strategy, Wal-Mart believes it has found some middle ground. The new positioning strategy will revolve around the concept of "Saving people money so they can live better lives." As of this writing, the new product lines and new communications strategies have not been made public, so it is difficult to comment on the appropriateness and effectiveness of the new direction Wal-Mart is taking. For certain the phrase "Saving people money so they can live better lives" will be a key element in the communications.

You Be the Judge

What do you think of the strategic direction Wal-Mart is moving in? Will it be difficult for a company that has based its success on low prices to succeed by adding more popular brand names at higher price points? Is there a chance that new forms of marketing communications will conflict with existing communications strategies?

Wal-Mart has the consumer insights that suggests it can succeed. Would you approach the situation in a different manner?

Source: Adapted from Michael Barbaro, "It's not only about price," *Financial Post*, March 3, 2007, p. FP17.

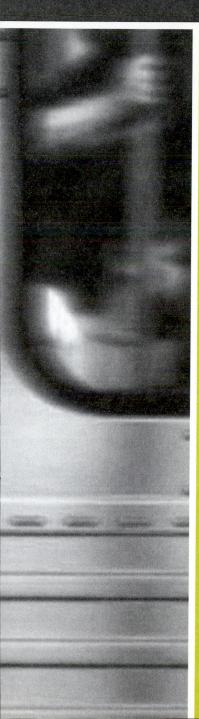

PART **3**   Creating the Message

In Part 2, the relationships between marketing and advertising were established, and a detailed review of the planning process was presented. Clearly, the content of a marketing plan or advertising plan affects the direction of creative planning.

Part 3 describes the creative planning process in detail by differentiating among creative objectives, strategies, and execution considerations.

In Chapter 5, the role of research in the creative evaluation process is examined along with the roles and responsibilities of the client and the agency in the message-development process.

Chapter 6 presents the production considerations for print, broadcast, and interactive media.

CHAPTER 5

Creative Planning Essentials

Natural attraction

George Simhoni/Westside Studios and Dairy Farmers of Canada.

After studying this chapter, you will be able to

1. Identify the basic elements of the communications process

2. Distinguish between client responsibility and agency responsibility in the creative development process

3. Explain the stages in the creative development process

4. Explain the creative briefing process and describe the content normally included in a creative brief

5. Clearly distinguish between creative objectives, creative strategies, and creative execution

6. Describe the various appeal techniques commonly used in advertising

7. Identify the various execution techniques used for presenting advertising messages

8. Explain the measurement techniques used for evaluating creative

An advertising plan is divided into two distinct yet connected sections: the creative plan and the media plan. Once the advertising objectives are clearly identified, it is the task of the agency to devise message and media strategies that will achieve the objectives.

As indicated in previous chapters, it is essential that creative planners and media planners work together in the initial stages in order to determine how best to engage consumers. Once the engagement decisions have been made (these usually involve media choices and decisions about other forms of marketing communications to be used), the creative planners can begin to develop the messages and the media planners can devise media strategies in more detail. The actual advertisements that we see, read, and listen to are simply the outcome of the planning process.

This chapter focuses on the creative planning process and the relationships between the client and the agency in that process. Initially, the creative development process is examined, and topics such as the content of a creative brief are addressed. The concepts of creative objectives, creative strategies, and creative execution are examined in detail, and numerous advertisements and campaigns are included to illustrate these concepts. Since research plays a role in the creative development process, various evaluation techniques are presented.

The Creative Development Process and Client–Agency Responsibilities

When developing creative, the roles and responsibilities of the client and agency are clearly defined. The client provides the necessary input (information) and evaluates agency recommendations; the agency takes the information and develops appropriate message strategies that will fit with other marketing communications strategies. The creative development process is subdivided into seven distinct stages. Refer to Figure 5.1 for a visual illustration of the stages.

CLIENT RESPONSIBILITY

Early in the process, the client must provide enough market, competitor, customer, and product information so that the agency understands the situation clearly. The client also plays a role in developing a list of creative objectives. The creative objectives identify the key benefits that are to be communicated to the target market.

Through consultation with the agency's creative team, the client will have some (limited) input in the development of creative-strategy statements. The agency might gain general direction by noting the client's preference for emotional or humorous appeals, but strategy is largely the domain of the agency.

The last area of client responsibility is its involvement in the creative evaluation process. Since the client's money is on the line, the client has every right to apply qualitative and quantitative research assessments at any stage of creative execution. Essentially, the client reviews creative recommendations to ensure they match the positioning strategy for the brand.

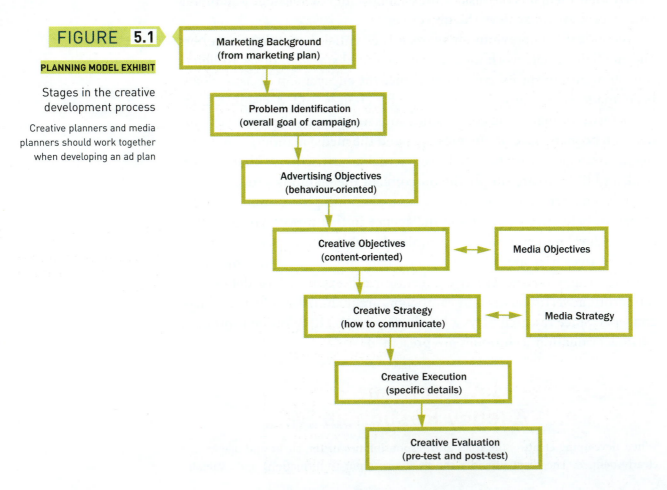

FIGURE 5.1

PLANNING MODEL EXHIBIT

Stages in the creative development process

Creative planners and media planners should work together when developing an ad plan

AGENCY RESPONSIBILITY

The agency first must familiarize itself, through consultation with the client, with the intricacies of the marketplace. Once the creative objectives have been decided, the agency must develop a more precise creative strategy. The creative team, comprising art directors and copywriters, works on numerous ideas and concepts and develops a short list of promising possibilities. The creative team also considers creative execution details to ensure the product will be presented in a convincing and believable manner. Since agencies now recommend both traditional and digital media creative solutions, it is essential that copywriters and art directors from both areas of expertise meet to discuss the project. Their goal is to find some common ground in the early thinking stages (conceptual stages) of the creative development process.

Teamwork is an important component of the creativity process as it provides consistency of thought and style to campaigns that stretch over extended periods. Therefore, it is essential that the copywriter and art director complement each other, appreciate each other's talents, and enjoy working together as a professional team.

When the creative team has completed the creative assignment in the form of rough layouts for print, storyboards and scripts for television, for example, the ideas are submitted to senior agency personnel for internal approval and then to the client for approval.

Depending on the outcome of the evaluation process, the agency either proceeds with creative execution or goes back to the drawing board to modify the concepts or develop new ideas. Very often there are several meetings between agency and client before a campaign concept is finally approved.

There isn't any magic formula for generating innovative advertising concepts. Each advertising agency has a different perspective on how the development process should be handled. Regardless of the process, a common denominator is the working relationship between the agency and the client. Figure 5.2 summarizes the key roles of clients and agencies in the creative development process. For some insight into how agencies meet the challenges posed by their clients, and how they maintain a creative edge, read the Advertising in Action vignette, **Creating the Big Idea**.

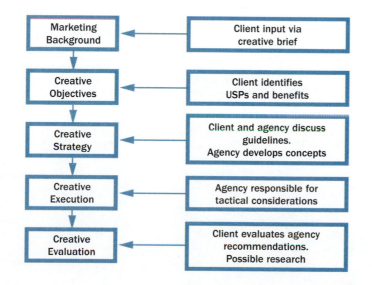

FIGURE 5.2

Client–agency responsibility in the creative development process

Creating the Big Idea

Today's advertising industry is more complicated and scientific than ever. Clients and agencies are burdened with layers of bureaucracy and endless reams of research information, both of which are factors that have a negative impact on the creative process.

In today's environment, the role of the creative team is changing. They work more closely with other disciplines in the agency and are more strategically involved with the client. In many cases, it is a collection of people from different agency backgrounds that help find that nugget that becomes the "big idea" for an advertising campaign. So, where does the creative edge come from and how is it cultivated in the agency?

Ultimately, it is the work of the creatives that is always on the line. If it's off the mark too often, the agency is history! Agencies have to produce ads that will get noticed, be remembered, and, most of all, move product—a challenging task, to say the least.

Allan Russell, chief creative officer at DDB Canada, believes the key to creativity is knocking down any barriers that are in place at the agency. "Social congregations outside the office are hot points for coming up with new ideas, and occasional retreats to do some blue-sky thinking on topics such as how to embrace the new media are good ways of getting the creative juices flowing," he says.

At BBDO, Craig Cooper, vice-president and group creative director, says, "Great advertising has to have sound, solid strategic thinking behind it. Good creative has to touch and stimulate the consumer in an emotional way." Cooper says creative product is almost always the result of "gut-feel—the skills of the writer and art director, combined with their instincts as consumers themselves.

"One of BBDO's solutions is to break down the boxes and tap into the knowledge of various disciplines within the agency—the art directors, copywriters, planners, media, PR, and others—before pencil goes to paper." A firm understanding of the problems makes selling the advertising to the client that much easier.

At Taxi Advertising, partner Paul Lavoie says, "We don't define creativity as visual or literary expression, but more as a way of thinking. Here, a small group of people—planner, writer, art director, and client—take responsibility for creative ideas rather than being caught up in the rigid hierarchy of differentiated roles, responsibilities, and job titles." The partners at Taxi believe that one small group taking a holistic approach is capable of creating one solution that can affect every dimension of a brand. Client teams at Taxi get their inspiration and direction from the company mantra, "Doubt the traditional. Create the exceptional." "We blend intuition with hard research," says Lavoie. "If we don't build our clients' business, we don't deserve to have it."

At Rethink, a smaller independent agency based in Vancouver, the key is staying close to the client in order to understand the brand completely. "What we fundamentally believe is that you need a brand with an idea. If you get the right idea, all the other parts are easy," says Tom Shepansky, account director.

Chris Staples, one of the co-founders of Rethink, believes clients that rely too much on research information have lost touch with their own instincts. Indeed, clients working with Rethink are in for a novel experience. Creative meetings happen in hallways or doorways. Concepts are scribbled down on small notepads or a huge blackboard. There's no fancy marketing jargon on the client presentations either! "Here's the idea, let's go with it!"

Source: Adapted from Laura Pratt, "Cultivating creativity," *Marketing*, November 28, 2005, www.marketingmag.ca; Eve Lazarus, "Rethink's fresh obsession," *Marketing*, November 24, 2003, pp. 11–14; and Stuart Foxman, "Canada's leading creative agencies," *Strategy*, June 2000, pp. 1, 2, 6, 11.

DDB Canada
www.ddbcanada.com

BBDO
www.bbdo.ca

Taxi Advertising
www.taxi.ca

Rethink
www.rethinkadvertising.com

The Creative Brief

The starting point for any new advertising project is the creative brief. A **creative brief** is a document developed by the client that contains vital information about the advertising task at hand. The information contained in the brief is presented and discussed with the agency personnel so that copywriters and art directors fully understand the nature of the assignment. The brief is a discussion document; therefore, its content can change based on the discussion that takes place. Sometimes sections are left blank, awaiting discussion between the two parties. For example, creative strategy is the responsibility of the agency, so the client must resist the temptation to offer its preferences in this area. Too much direction by a client sometimes has a negative influence on the creativity of copywriters and art directors.

To understand how client and agency come to agree on an advertising direction, one must first look at the information that both parties analyze and consider when determining what to say in an ad, and how to say it. The brief typically communicates essential background information, a problem statement or overall goal, a list of advertising objectives, a positioning-strategy statement, and a list of creative objectives.

Once the briefing process is complete, the creative team is in the spotlight. The team, comprising a copywriter, art director, and creative director from the traditional and digital sides of the agency, are charged with the task of developing the **creative concept** or "big idea" that will be the cornerstone of a campaign. To do so, the team considers information supplied by the client. The only way a creative team can discover ways of solving a client's advertising problems is to fully immerse itself in the product (company) so the members fully understand the current situation.

The next series of sections examine the content of a creative brief in more detail. Refer to Figure 5.3 for a summary of the information that is typically included in a creative brief. Students should understand that the content and structure of a creative brief varies from one organization to another. There is no standard or uniform way of presenting the information that is usually contained in the document.

MARKET INFORMATION

MARKET PROFILE   Initially, agency personnel are briefed on happenings in the marketplace. Key issues include the size and rate of growth in the market, identification of major competitors and their market shares, and what their strengths and weaknesses are.

PRODUCT PROFILE   The focus then shifts to the brand in question. The agency is briefed on the key benefits the brand offers, benefits that will entice consumers to buy. Typically, the benefits offered are ranked by priority. For example, the key benefit could be economy, safety, variety, durability, or reliability. Once the primary benefit is identified, it should become the focal point of the advertising message.

The Glad Products Company makes several types of bag products (garbage bags and resealable kitchen bags). Their products offer consumers strength and durability. Their garbage bags are often seen in television commercials taking a beating before they reach their destination at the curb. The "Man from Glad" makes the pitch in a rather convincing manner. A recent print campaign for Glad Kitchen Catchers focused on the tear-resistant qualities of the bag. The illustration in the ad aptly portrays the tear-resistance benefit by showing bags tied together hanging from a window. Refer to the illustration in Figure 5.4 for details.

Glad Products Company
www.glad.com

FIGURE **5.3**

PLANNING MODEL EXHIBIT

Content of a creative brief

MARKET INFORMATION

- Market profile
- Product profile
- Competitor profile
- Target-market profile
- Budget

PROBLEM IDENTIFICATION

- Clear identification of the problem advertising will resolve, or
- Overall goal of campaign

ADVERTISING OBJECTIVES

(Appropriate behavioural objectives based on problem or goal)
- Awareness
- Interest
- Preference
- Action
- New image
- New targets

POSITIONING-STRATEGY STATEMENT

- Statement of the brand's benefits, personality, or desired image

CREATIVE OBJECTIVES

- List of message content objectives
- Key benefit statement
- Support-claims statement

CREATIVE STRATEGY

- Buying motivation
- Tone and style
- Theme
- Appeal techniques

CREATIVE EXECUTION

- Tactical considerations
- Production considerations

Note: Clients and advertising agencies are unique enterprises. Therefore, the style, structure, and content of this document will vary across the industry. This is a working model to highlight content that could be contained in a brief. The creative strategy section often isn't determined until the client and agency discuss the assignment.

A brand's reputation may also influence the message. While creative direction often changes with time, quite often an important element from previous campaigns is retained in a new campaign. Such an element may have contributed positively to the image of the brand. For example, a good slogan may outlast numerous advertising campaigns, because the slogan is closely associated with the brand name and has high recall with consumers. Consider the following examples:

- Maxwell House Coffee: "Good to the last drop"

- Nike: "Just do it"

- Gillette: "The best a man can get"

- Volkswagen: "Drivers wanted"

Also, a character or spokesperson may be so closely associated with a product that their presence is expected in advertising. Here are a few examples:

- Kellogg's Frosted Flakes: Tony the Tiger

- Glad Garbage Bags: The Man from Glad

- Pillsbury: The Pillsbury Doughboy

- Michelin Tires: The Michelin Man

Elements such as these have longevity, and therefore must be considered when a new creative direction is contemplated.

COMPETITOR PROFILE   A discussion of competitive creative strategies provides a more complete perspective on what is happening in the marketplace. The creative team should know what competitor brands are saying and how they are saying it. The

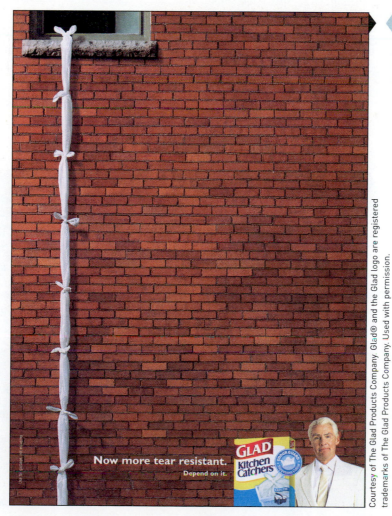

FIGURE 5.4

An ad that stresses the key benefits of strength and durability of the product

Courtesy of The Glad Products Company Glad® and the Glad logo are registered trademarks of The Glad Products Company. Used with permission.

advertiser should analyze the strengths and weaknesses of the competition, and use the analysis as a guideline for creative direction. The direction an advertiser takes may be similar to, or totally different from, that of the competition. Competitive analysis may also have an impact on the tone, style, and appeal techniques used in advertising.

To demonstrate, consider the situation Bell Canada faced when it wanted a new creative strategy for its wireless and ExpressVu satellite services. Bell started using two animated wise-cracking beavers, Frank and Gordon, in its television commercials, print ads, and outdoor posters. In the TV commercials the pair plays off of each other comically, like Abbott and Costello or Laurel and Hardy. "If one doesn't understand, the other explains," says Brett Marchand, vice-president of Cossette Toronto, the agency who developed the campaign. See an illustration of this campaign in Figure 5.5.

Bell was actually following a trend in the industry. The Fido brand (now part of Rogers Communications) has been using dog-themed ads since its inception in 1996, and Telus has used a series of nature-themed ads successfully for many years. The Telus ads incorporate reptiles, birds, insects, and flowers. It seems that in Canada's telecommunications business, creatures sell![1]

The Bell beaver campaign has done its job. Its strong performance is credited to the highly engaging creative that was perceived by consumers as something new and different from Bell. Over the period March to May 2006, the Frank and Gordon commercials ranked first in terms of consumer top-of-mind awareness and first in terms of being the most-liked commercials on air.[2]

TARGET-MARKET PROFILE   The client must provide a complete profile of the target market, which includes all relevant demographic, psychographic, and geographic information. The better the knowledge of the target market, the easier the task of developing advertising messages. If adequate resources are allocated to the collection of research information—to identifying and understanding the motivations behind consumers' purchases—such information can be used to develop convincing messages. The ability

Bell Canada
www.bell.ca

FIGURE 5.5

The unique humour of Frank and Gordon, two wise-cracking beavers, has been a hit with Canadian consumers.

Courtesy of Bell Canada.

to associate product benefits with buying motives or to present a product in a manner suited to a certain lifestyle is part of developing creative-objective and creative-strategy statements.

To illustrate the use of target profile information, consider the challenges an advertiser faces when trying to reach the youth and young adult segments. The younger generation is a more skeptical group of consumers, so the role and influence that advertising has on them is sometimes questioned. In relating to young adults, many advertisers attempt to portray a vision of "young adult cool," hoping that they'll be liked because they're cool too. But the message that young adults get is that the advertising is an attempt to fabricate a culture for them: You're telling me what cool should be. Following such a direction leads to failure. In trying to influence young consumers, there is a line in the sand that the advertiser must not cross.

As discussed in Chapter 3, target markets broken down by demographic and psychographic characteristics are then added to the profile. Descriptive expressions such as Baby Boomers, Generation X, and Generation Y have been coined to describe targets. A firm understanding of the behaviours of these and other targets provides agency creative personnel valuable insights for developing a message strategy.

BUDGET At this stage of the planning process, the client should provide a budget guideline. The amount of money available will determine whether the use of certain media is restricted or eliminated. For example, a budget judged to be small eliminates the use of television. If the budget is large, a multimedia campaign is possible. Either way, the media under consideration influence the creative direction.

Problem Identification

Typically, advertising campaigns are designed to resolve a specific problem or pursue an opportunity. In other words, all of the analysis that has occurred so far points the campaign in a certain direction. Perhaps the problem or opportunity is better described as the *overall goal* of the campaign. At this point, what the communications are expected to do is clearly identified. The following are a few generic examples of overall communications goals:

- To create or increase brand awareness
- To position or reposition a product in the customer's mind
- To present a new image (re-image the brand)
- To attract a new target market
- To introduce a line extension

These examples suggest that a campaign must have focus. Attempting to accomplish too many goals at one time only creates confusion in the customer's mind. It is preferable to focus on one primary goal and ensure that it is achieved.

Advertising Objectives

As indicated in the previous section, an advertising campaign typically has a central focus. Therefore, to facilitate the creative thinking process, the overall goal is subdivided into more specific advertising objectives. Advertising objectives usually focus on behavioural issues such as creating awareness and preference or altering the image and perceptions of a brand held by consumers, since these are the things that advertising is best at accomplishing. Objectives should be expressed in quantitative terms whenever possible, as they are used to measure the effectiveness of the campaign at a later date.

The stage a product is at in its life cycle, and the competitive environment of the marketplace, often influences the advertising objectives. For example, at the introduction and growth stages of the life cycle, the emphasis is on awareness and preference and the message deals with unique selling points. The goal is to differentiate one brand from another. In the mature stage, the message shifts to increasing frequency of use by consumers, to expand the variety of uses current customers have for the product, or to attract new users to the product.

To apply the concept of advertising objectives, consider the following examples that could apply when launching a new product:

- To achieve a brand awareness level of 60 percent among the defined target market within 12 months of launching the product
- To achieve a trial purchase rate of 25 percent among the defined target market

Since this is a new product, the objectives deal with awareness and trial purchase. As indicated above, life cycle and competitive factors influence the objectives. Let's examine a few of these challenges in more detail and see how they influence the direction of the creative.

TO INCREASE AWARENESS AND PREFERENCE   Thinking strictly in terms of consumer behaviour, advertising objectives are stated in terms of achieving certain levels of brand awareness and brand preference. Advertising that achieves the desired levels will produce a stronger likelihood of purchase among members of the target market. Achieving good levels of awareness and preference depends on a host of factors. For example, the impact of the message (how memorable it is) and the media (the impact of the medium itself) combine to influence consumer behaviour.

When Virgin Mobile was launched in Canada, creating brand awareness was crucial. To do so, Virgin immediately challenged established brands like Bell, Rogers, and Telus. Virgin knew that consumers were frustrated by the long-term contracts and hidden fees of these brands. Virgin went with short-term plans to appeal to younger audiences. An integrated campaign that included print advertising, online media, direct mail, in-store display material, and street-level marketing created an awareness of Virgin Mobile as high as 24 percent within two weeks of launch. "It was the best launch ever of a Virgin business," says Richard Branson, owner of all Virgin brands.[3]

TO INCREASE FREQUENCY OR VARIETY OF USE   When a product is firmly established in the market (mature stage of the product life cycle), the marketing objectives usually reflect an attempt to convert light or casual users into heavy users. Since users know the benefits of the product, the costs associated with increasing usage are much less than attempting to attract new users. Advertising can play a role in this process by showing alternative uses for the product. With reference to the ad for Welch's Grape Juice in Figure 5.6, the brand is positioned as a healthy beverage that should be consumed more frequently. Here, Welch's Grape Juice promises consumers the health benefits of grape juice. That promise is reinforced in the body copy, which shows the product being endorsed by the Heart and Stroke Foundation's Health Check Program. Consumers find third-party endorsements like this very convincing.

FIGURE 5.6

An ad encouraging greater frequency of use

Courtesy of Cadbury Schweppes Americas Beverages.

TO ATTRACT NEW TARGETS In the case of mature products that are experiencing marginal sales growth, or actual decline, making the product appeal to different user segments represents opportunity. Moores faced this situation in the men's fashion market. Moores' "Well Made. Well Priced. Well Dressed" campaign was well known but was attracting only a segment of the market (men who typically shopped at Sears, The Bay, and Tip Top). Another segment was identified that accounted for 35 percent of the market—the guy who's not involved with fashion at all and would prefer to do all his shopping in a hardware store. Moores attempted to reach this segment by using a humorous approach, with ads showing clothing as a problem to be fixed. A series of commercials focused on different problems. It worked! Sales increased by 6.5 percent over a 12-month period. See Figure 5.7 for an example of an ad from this campaign.[4]

TO COMMUNICATE PRODUCT IMPROVEMENTS In the late growth and early mature stage of the product's life cycle, marketing strategies often deal with product changes and improvements to keep the product competitive. This strategy is very popular in the food industry (where advertisements often focus on a product's new and improved taste) and household products industry (where messages focus on improved product performance).

FIGURE 5.7

Moore's went after a new male target with a light-hearted message

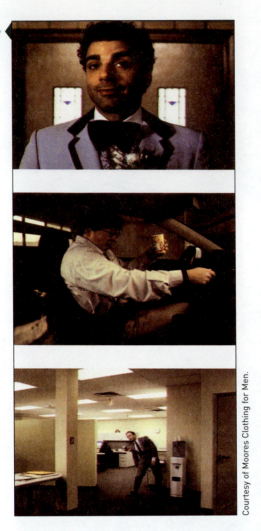

Courtesy of Moores Clothing for Men.

In this situation, advertising messages make the consumer aware of the improvement. This strategy is often used as a defensive measure to entice current users to stay with their current brand rather than switch to a newer brand that may offer trial-purchase incentives. In the advertisement in Figure 5.8, WD-40, a product that is good for loosening just about anything of a mechanical nature, improves its product by adding the "smart straw" that allows the product to be distributed in a spray or stream form, and attaches more effectively to the can.

TO ENCOURAGE TRIAL PURCHASE When a product is in the introduction and growth stages of its life cycle, achieving high levels of awareness and trial purchase are key objectives. Sometimes incentives have to be offered to give consumers an extra nudge to buy. If that is the case, the ads will carry a coupon offer, refund offer, or some other incentive. The incentive provides an additional benefit for the customer.

In other situations, the ad alone may be enough to achieve trial purchase. When Unilever launched Axe deodorant, a product aimed directly at 18- to 24-year-old males, they understood that their target preferred to discover brands, rather than being sold to. Therefore, the launch campaign bypassed traditional television ads in favour of banner ads on websites of male magazines such as *Maxim* and *FHM*. The online world is the hub of Generation Y's lifestyle. The banners clicked through to a flashy website that played short video clips. In each clip, an attractive young woman is instantly

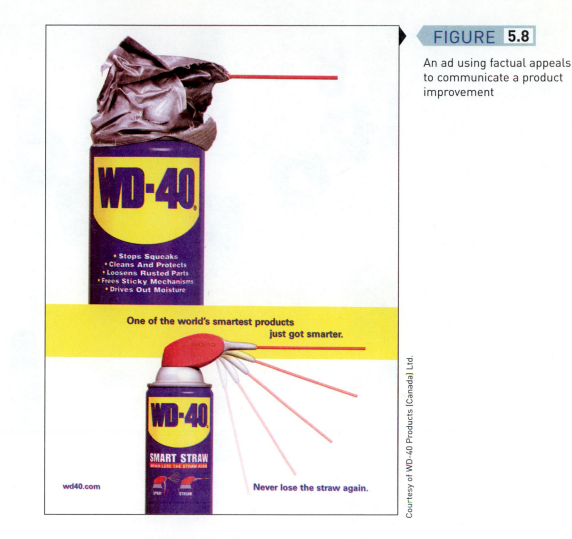

FIGURE 5.8

An ad using factual appeals to communicate a product improvement

transformed into a nymphomaniac by a whiff of Axe deodorant. One clip shows a high school cheerleader sprinting onto the football field, whereupon she starts to tear off a player's uniform. Such a response by females is referred to as "The Axe Effect."

The campaign was a huge success at getting trial purchases! By year-end Axe had captured four percent of the male deodorant market. It is now threatening Old Spice for overall leadership in the market as both brands claim to have a 12-percent market share. An illustration of Axe advertising appears in Figure 5.9.

TO COMMUNICATE PROMOTION INCENTIVES   Very often an entire campaign revolves around a special offer from a manufacturer. In the previous section some trial-oriented incentives were mentioned. Other promotional incentives include contests, premium offers, rebate offers, and loyalty programs.

In these situations, advertising may temporarily depart from communicating **unique selling points** in order to focus on the brand name and promotion. For example, the automobile industry frequently switches from image-oriented brand advertising (a long-term strategy) to promote rebates, low financing, and special option packages (sometimes involving free options) as a means of stimulating sales (a short-term strategy). Contests for packaged-goods products also require short-term investment in advertising and in-store merchandising and display activity to spark awareness and interest in the promotion.

AXE is a registered trademark owned by Unilever Canada Inc. Used with permission.

FIGURE 5.9

Axe deodorant appeals directly to the instincts of 18- to 24-year-old males

TO COMMUNICATE A POSITIVE CORPORATE IMAGE In addition to product-oriented advertising, a company can implement advertising campaigns that benefit the company as a whole. Multi-product firms may run a corporate advertising campaign as part of their "corporate responsibility" positioning.

Shell Oil, for example, ran an ad campaign about sustainable development, while being careful not to promise too much. "Solutions for global warming won't come easy," the ads say, "but you can't find solutions if you don't keep looking." Shell believes that they and other companies are an integral part of society. Says Phillip Watts, chairman of the Royal Dutch/Shell Group of Companies, "When we take a business decision, we try to strike a balance between economics, the environment, and social impacts."[5] Making the public aware of their actions improves how people perceive Shell as a corporation. A Shell ad appears in Figure 5.10.

TO ALTER A PERCEPTION OR IMAGE Sometimes a company or a product doesn't seem to be in control of its image, or, as an old saying goes, "Perception is reality." For example, a name like Frigidaire brings one product to mind—refrigerators! Sure enough, research showed that consumers thought Frigidaire was "just a fridge company." But the company also makes laundry machines, stoves, and dishwashers. In recent years advertising for appliances has changed dramatically—they are more of a home furnishing than an appliance now; they are part of the decor. Frigidaire desperately needed to join the party. To alter its image, the company launched a series of television ads showing their contemporary-looking appliances as a key part of some feel-good domestic scenes (e.g., kids helping mother bake and a couple preparing a meal together). The voiceover says, "Beautiful, practical, part of the family. Frigidaire."[6]

Frigidaire
www.frigidairecanada.ca

Courtesy of Shell.

FIGURE 5.10

An ad designed to build and improve corporate reputation with the public

Positioning-Strategy Statement

Positioning refers to the selling concept or message that motivates purchase of a particular brand of product or service. It involves the message or image of the brand (company) to be instilled in the customer's mind. Agency creative people refer to this statement when they are trying to discover the creative concept—that big idea for communicating the message effectively. The positioning statement influences the content of creative-objective and creative-strategy statements.

To illustrate the role of a positioning-strategy statement, consider what Harvey's Restaurants is doing with its creative. Harvey's positioning strategy could read:

> Harvey's is the true home of the best-tasting, freshly grilled hamburger garnished to your taste.

Prior to launching the "grilled" campaign, Harvey's was targeting a very broad demographic, much like the other chains; a kind of follow-the-leader approach. Marketing research revealed that Harvey's greatest asset was the grilled cooking of its burgers. It was a natural to go in that direction. It was also a strategy Harvey's used successfully between 1985 and 1989 when its slogan was "Harvey's makes your hamburger a beautiful thing." Essentially, Harvey's is returning to its roots by offering great-tasting grilled hamburgers served with toppings that their customers want. The new slogan that captures the essence of Harvey's positioning strategy is "It's a beautiful thing." Television commercials show people at the counter selecting the condiments that are just right for them . . . there's the Vanessa burger, the Gordon burger—a unique burger for each customer.

When creatives (art directors and copywriters) are brainstorming ideas for a campaign, the creative concept or "big idea" often arises from the positioning-strategy statement. (Ads have to fit with overall brand strategy.) The big idea must draw attention to, and effectively communicate, the key benefits. The slogan plays a key role by ingraining the essence of the positioning strategy in the customer's mind. Consider the following examples and how they relate to the brand's positioning strategy:

- FedEx: "Relax, it's FedEx" (a promise of reliable delivery)
- Tim Hortons: "Always fresh" (an obvious promise that drives the entire company)
- Lexus: "The pursuit of perfection" (Lexus is a top-quality automobile, continually striving to improve, and always better than competitors)
- Adidas: "Impossible is nothing" (an inspirational strategy to encourage people to participate or compete to the best of their ability)

Creative Objectives

Whereas advertising objectives are behavioural in nature or are written to identify a certain task that advertising will achieve, **creative objectives** are statements that clearly indicate the content of the message to be communicated to a target audience. As indicated above, positioning-strategy statements have a direct influence on what will be said about a product or company. Although the formats for writing creative objectives vary, a common practice is to consolidate what has to be said about a product in a short list of objectives.

To demonstrate how creative-objective statements are written, consider the situation Wrigley's Juicy Fruit gum once faced. Juicy Fruit was perceived by consumers as being old, stagnant, and boring, and half of its users were over 35 years of age. The brand had become irrelevant to teens. A new creative approach was needed to re-image the brand. Here are a few creative-objective statements that could have applied to the campaign:

- To reposition Juicy Fruit gum to appeal to teenagers
- To communicate in a manner (with an edge) that will resonate with the teen market
- To communicate how "sweet" the gum is (sweetness is cool with teens)

Wrigley recognized that a new creative approach could alienate its older target market but was willing to take the risk in order to start rebuilding the brand.

Sometimes objectives are written in a different format. The objectives are summarized in the form of a *key-benefit statement* and a *support-claims statement*; in other words, what the most important information to communicate is and on what basis it can be stated. Let's examine each of these elements:

- ***Key-benefit statement*** A statement of the basic selling idea, service, or benefit that the advertiser *promises* the consumer. This benefit is the primary reason for buying the product over any competitive product. Additional supplementary benefits may be described in another objective statement. With reference to the Wrigley Juicy Fruit situation described above, the primary benefit is the "sweet taste" (this will appeal to teens if presented the right way).

- *Support-claims statement* A statement describing the principal characteristics of the product or service, the characteristics that substantiate the promise made in the key-benefit statement. It provides *proof* of promise based on criteria such as technical-performance data or consumer-preference data generated from marketing research. For example, the primary benefit of Crest toothpaste is that it helps prevent cavities. Crest can make that promise because it is "clinically proven." The support-claims statement would indicate the results of various clinical studies or its endorsement by the Canadian Dental Association.

In other situations support claims may not be as black and white as they are for Crest toothpaste. People buy based on their emotions and are susceptible to lifestyle advertising that associates a brand with an image or a desirable lifestyle. The imagery presented in the advertisement may be proof enough that they should buy that product.

The new Juicy Fruit commercials were so out of character with past messages that the shock value alone attracted the attention of teens. During the course of the campaign (2001 to 2004), Juicy Fruit switched from a too-good-to-be-true image, in which bright-eyed young skiers listened to a goody two-shoes type of character named David sing the Juicy Fruit song, to a commercial where an anger-management instructor flies into a guitar-busting rage when David strolls into the room. Juicy Fruit definitely had a new, edgier image!

There were complaints about the campaign, but Wrigley's stuck with it. Market share moved from 4.3 percent to 10.8 percent by the end of 2004 and Wrigley's was the number-one brand for the first time in its history.[7]

For an additional illustration showing the relationship between positioning strategy, creative objectives, key-benefit statements, and support-claims statements, refer to Figure 5.11. This information is usually included in the creative brief.

Creative Strategy

After confirming the message content, the next stage is to develop the creative strategy. In contrast to the first two stages, the agency's creative team plays a dominant role here. In essence, the client pays the agency primarily for the strategy (i.e., the ideas and concepts used in presenting the message). Sound strategies, in accordance with the positioning strategy and the creative objectives, are the foundation of successful advertising campaigns.

The **creative strategy** is a statement of how the message is to be communicated to the target audience. It is a statement of the character, personality, and image that the agency will strive to develop for the client's product or service. Strategy is reflected in the *central theme* that is developed along with the *tone, style,* and *appeal techniques* of the advertising. Tone and style, for example, may be informative, persuasive, entertaining, or warm in nature, to suggest just a few options. The creative team must determine which approach will have the most impact on the target audience. Information gleaned from the target's demographic and psychographic profile influences this kind of decision.

The **central theme** or **"big idea"** is the glue that binds the various creative elements together. It must work in all different media forms if it is to have impact. To demonstrate the role of the big idea, consider the situation Diet Pepsi once faced. Diet Pepsi was losing ground to Diet Coke, and the brand was being overshadowed by the image of regular

FIGURE **5.11**

Relationships between positioning strategy and the writing of creative objectives

This example was created for illustration purposes only. The information in this chart is usually included in a creative brief along with market and competition information.

PRODUCT
Levi's Jeans

POSITIONING-STRATEGY STATEMENT

To position Levi's as a brand that is proactive in response to changing consumer fashion tastes and preferences. Levi's is to be thought of as a fashionable and hip brand, a brand of choice among lifestyle peers across diverse age groups.

CREATIVE OBJECTIVES

1. To communicate that Levi's offers a fashionable line of blue jeans.
2. To communicate that Levi's offers a diverse line of jeans that are suited to the needs of all consumer segments.

KEY BENEFIT(S)

1. Levi's offers in-style jeans.
2. Levi's offers an opportunity to satisfy social needs.
3. Levi's offers a wide range of styles to suit diverse consumer needs.

SUPPORT CLAIMS

1. Imagery will portray a target consumer being thought of as "trend-conscious" and "cool."
2. The product will be shown as being accepted by peer groups, implying those who wear Levi's will be accepted.
3. A variety of styles will be shown throughout the campaign to show the diversity of the product line.

Pepsi. The primary target market was 20-something adults; individuals in the throes of making their first big decisions—where to live, career choices, and relationships. Marketing research revealed they didn't want to lose their spontaneity and spirit even though they were getting older. The big idea had to consider the youthful feelings of a maturing audience.

The agency creative team recommended a "forever young" theme. The tone of the Diet Pepsi television ads was a bit wacky. The ads portrayed a temporary break from maturity by asking people what they would like to have back from their past. One guy wanted his long hair back; another wanted his tight blue jeans. Neither wish was a good fit for their current lifestyle! The ads ended with the tagline "Taste the one that's forever young."[8] The campaign is still thriving today. Refer to the illustration in Figure 5.12.

These strategic characteristics of ads usually stem from the basic appeal technique that the creative team decides upon. A brand may appeal to a potential buyer on the basis of factual information, emotion, humour, or sex, to name only a few of the alternatives available. The following is a discussion of some of the more common creative **appeal** techniques.

POSITIVE APPEALS

When positive appeals are used in advertising, the product promise and benefits (i.e., the primary reason for buying the product) are presented as the basis of a positive, enjoyable experience for the consumer. The mood, tone, and style of the advertising is upbeat, and

Reprinted by permission of Pepsi-QTG Canada.

FIGURE 5.12

The central theme of Diet Pepsi advertisements is "Forever Young." It is a drink for maturing young adults who wish to retain their youthful spontaneity.

is intended to leave the consumer with a favourable impression. Dairy Farmers of Canada often employs positive appeals when advertising milk and butter. To connect the consumption of butter with the trend toward healthier living, marketers tapped into butter's biggest advantage—it's natural! And something that is natural usually gets linked to something that is healthy. A new print campaign was launched anchored by the tagline "Natural attraction." In each print ad a vegetable was shown as a predator out to capture a rosette-shaped piece of butter. Refer to Figure 5.13 for an illustration.

NEGATIVE APPEALS

For negative appeals, the product promise and benefits presented are based on an experience the potential buyer can *avoid* by purchasing the advertised product or service. In some cases, fear may be used to really grab peoples' attention. A television commercial for the Volkswagen Jetta shows two young men discussing the best way to impress a date. Without warning, a truck backs out of a hidden driveway. In a split second the front of the car implodes, the mens' necks snap forward, making contact with exploding airbags. The message is clear: if they were in another car they would be dead.[9] Perhaps this is an overly dramatic use of the negative appeal technique, but it does stress the safety features of the car.

Something more subtle is the now famous Buckley's Cough Mixture campaign featuring the tagline "Tastes awful and it works." Since Buckley's started attacking itself with the

Natural attraction

Butter.
www.dairygoodness.ca

George Simhoni/Westside Studios and Dairy Farmers of Canada.

awful-taste message, the brand has experienced new popularity and a positive increase in sales. Their success is based solely on their negative style of advertising. More recent television ads show people wincing in a rather agonizing manner after consuming the product.

FACTUAL APPEALS

In this appeal technique, the promise and benefits are presented in a straightforward, no-nonsense manner. The benefits are stated in a factual way and any visuals that are employed usually state the obvious. Products that appeal to the rational buying motives of consumers such as proprietary medicines—cough and cold remedies, nasal sprays, and liniments (which relieve the tension of aching muscles)—tend to employ a direct, here's-what-the-product-does approach.

Products in other categories can also use this strategy successfully. For example, a headline of a print ad for the Olympus digital camera states that it "resists water, dust, snow, and imitation." Body copy goes on to explain the versatility of the camera in a very straightforward, simple manner. With only a few words and a compelling, attention-grabbing visual, Olympus effectively communicates its message. An Olympus ad appears in Figure 5.14.

Olympus Canada
www.olympuscanada.com

Resists water, dust, snow, imitation.

Take it to the beach. Take it to the ski slope. Take it anywhere. Four megapixels, 3x optical zoom lens and five easy scene programs in a compact, all-weather body. No other digital camera gives you all this. Stylus Digital. **Designed to do more.**

OLYMPUS
Your Vision, Our Future

FIGURE 5.14

A straightforward message communicates the key benefits of the Olympus camera

COMPARATIVE APPEALS

When comparative appeals are used, the benefits of the advertised product are presented through comparison of those attributes that the product shares with competitive brands—attributes that are important to the target market and are usually the primary reason why consumers buy the product. Comparative appeals can be indirect, in the form of a comparison with other unidentified leading brands, or direct, with the other brand mentioned by name.

In recent years, the use of comparative appeals has come to the foreground through campaigns dubbed as the "Cola Wars" or the "Burger Wars." In the soft drink market Pepsi-Cola will challenge Coca-Cola in taste comparisons, and in the burger market Burger King will claim that their flame-broiled hamburgers taste better than those cooked by other means by their competitors. Comparative campaigns present an element of risk for the initiator, who is usually the number-two brand in a market. To participate in a potential battle with a competitor requires long-term financial commitment by the initiator, since there is always the danger of retaliation by the market leader. This commitment factor demands that advertisers of a product analyze the competitive situation carefully before deciding to proceed with a comparative campaign.

HUMOROUS APPEALS

When an advertiser uses humorous appeals, the promise and benefits of the product are presented in a light-hearted manner. Advertisers often use humour but do so with reservation. Many advertisers feel a campaign will suffer from premature wearout after a few exposures: when the humour is familiar, it is no longer funny. Also, the use of humour allows for a great deal of creative latitude, and some advertisers argue that the humour gets more attention than the product. If brand-name recall is low after research testing, the problem is often attributed to the excess use of humour in advertising.

In spite of certain drawbacks, a humorous strategy can work. Successful campaigns tend to use a pool of commercials in order to keep the message fresh. That's exactly what Bell Canada did with its Bell Mobility campaign built around Frank and Gordon, the two animated beavers discussed earlier in this chapter. The character and personality of Frank and Gordon evolved as the campaign progressed, and their wise-cracking antics generated lots of chuckles with viewers. Refer to the illustration in Figure 5.5.

A recent campaign for Dairy Farmers of Canada used a low-key style of humour. In one of the television spots, two desperate parents give their middle-aged son's room a makeover (something he would dread) in an effort to get him out of the house. But, alas, he just loves cheese too much to leave. A nosey neighbour from outside yells out, "If you want him to leave stop cooking with cheese!"

EMOTIONAL APPEALS

Advertisers who use emotional appeals successfully do so by arousing the feelings of the audience or by showing the psychological satisfaction that can be gained by using the product. Tim Hortons effectively uses emotional appeals to demonstrate how Tim Hortons outlets and coffee are part of the Canadian experience. "Tim Hortons has become part of the fabric of the country, so it defines what being a Canadian is. Not just today, but over the generations," says Paul Wales, president and CEO of Enterprise Advertising.

The Tim Hortons "Proud Fathers" commercial that aired during the 2006 Winter Olympics featured a grandfather and his middle-aged son watching the third-generation son play hockey. The commercial is another of Tim Hortons' "true stories." In the spot we see a coffee-toting grandfather headed to the rink to watch his grandson play hockey. Through flashbacks, we see how years before he would constantly nag his own son to study more and play hockey less. But we learn, in a bittersweet twist, that despite his objections, he also would secretly watch his son play hockey.[10]

Campaigns that promote awareness of social causes also use emotional appeals. To illustrate, consider some of the images in television commercials for campaigns that discourage drinking and driving, or encourage people to stop smoking. Seeing a distraught man sitting on a curb in the dead of night after a fatal accident, wishing he had made a wiser decision earlier on, or hearing an older woman talking about the perils of second-hand smoke, does tug at the heartstrings of the viewing audience. Emotional advertising has impact!

SEXUAL APPEALS

The use of sexual appeals is popular and appropriate in certain product categories. Categories such as cosmetics, colognes, perfumes, lingerie, and alcoholic beverages use sexual appeals as an effective motivator.

Over the years, sexual appeals have played a large role in beer advertising. After all, sex is always on the mind of the 19- to 24-year-old male that the beer brands are after, or so the marketers think. Coors Light uses sexual appeals to promote the Coors Light Maxim Golf Experience. In the television ads the males will do anything to win the prize, which is a weekend of free golf at a private club accompanied by atractive, mini-skirted female caddies. Naïve males show up at the club with fake winning cans in an attempt to join the fun while we see the female caddies carrying on in the background with the real winners. Smiles all around on the guys' faces!

Diesel uses sexual imagery effectively to market its jeans to 20-something males and females. Their ads typically show lots of skin and couples enjoying each other's company; they are provocative and tend to grab one's attention. The product is always prominent in the ads. Their latest campaign includes references to global warming issues, a tactic some people find objectionable. The ads sparked controversy, and that too is good for Diesel jeans. Refer to Figure 5.15 for an illustration.

Advertising of this nature is risky, but it does reflect general trends in society. People are now more accustomed to seeing provocative imagery and language in television shows, movies, and music videos. These trends open up new doors for advertisers.

FIGURE 5.15

Sexual appeals are a popular means of attracting a younger target audience

Courtesy of Diesel.

LIFESTYLE APPEALS

Advertisers who use lifestyle-appeal techniques are attempting to associate their brand with the lifestyle (lifestyle refers to activities, interests, and opinions) of a certain target audience. The key to the success of this type of campaign is in the association. If an individual feels part of the lifestyle, then he or she is likely to view the product favourably. Lifestyle appeals are becoming increasingly popular, owing to the greater availability of psychographic information on Canadian consumers.

The automobile industry has begun to use lifestyle messages, particularly in the sport utility vehicle and luxury vehicle segments of the market. The need to experience adventure, for example, is effectively portrayed by placing a consumer and vehicle in an exciting situation. The need to experience recognition and status is portrayed by showing a young business executive behind the wheel of a luxury automobile. Images like these speak louder than words! Audi, for example, connects with executives on the way up the ladder of success with its "Never Follow" ad campaign. The combination of images and copy suggest the vehicle is for leaders, for people on the move. See the illustration in Figure 5.16.

Courtesy of Audi Canada.

Audi effectively uses lifestyle appeals to attract potential buyers

Lifestyle advertising is problematic because little attempt is made to differentiate one brand from another. Usually, the advertisements focus on the lifestyles of the target market instead of the product benefits. Therefore, if such a technique is overused in a product category, a brand can expect to benefit only marginally from its use.

Advertisers have a variety of reasons for introducing new advertising campaigns and in most cases the new creative strategies are quite different from the strategies that are being replaced. Canadian Tire made a big change in direction when it dropped "The Canadian Tire Guy" campaign. For more insight into this decision see the Advertising in Action vignette, **Canadian Tire Shakes Things Up.**

⟶ ADVERTISING IN ACTION

Canadian Tire Shakes Things Up

Canadian Tire decided to drop one of the most talked-about campaigns in Canada; a campaign that was so popular it was parodied on TV shows like *Royal Canadian Air Farce* and *This Hour Has 22 Minutes*. You may be familiar with Ted and Gloria, the know-it-all couple that solved all kinds of car and household problems with innovative products sold by Canadian Tire.

According to Tracy Fellows, vice-president of advertising at Canadian Tire, "The commercials were effective but research showed them to be wearing thin with consumers. It was time to move on and try to build more of an integrated campaign so that the brand spots and product spots work closer together." Most people would agree. Eight years is a long time for any campaign to run.

The Canadian public developed a love–hate relationship with the Canadian Tire couple, and reaction to their departure was mixed. "I always thought what a horror it'd be to live next door to those two. Everything you own is crap, and their stuff is better, newer, and faster," was one reaction. Industry veteran Gary Prouk said, "I really got tired of that couple because they were so corny." Corny, yes, but they became the personification of Canadian Tire. The actors were recognized everywhere they went.

A new campaign was conceived. "The idea behind the new campaign was to inject a little more wit, a little more personality, a little more charm—something we felt was missing," said Lance Martin, associate creative director at Taxi Advertising and Design. The new campaign features a variety of different couples each looking for a solution to a household problem. An element of humour is injected into each spot.

One of the first spots featured a couple covetously eyeing their neighbour's well-maintained backyard. As they imagined the things they could do in their own yard (which appears to be rather barren), Canadian Tire signs appear in different parts of the yard, indicating the aisle numbers where different yard-improving products can be found. Another ad showed a man duct-taping a decrepit lounge chair, as a sign naming the correct aisle for patio furniture appears overhead. His wife falls though the chair and a sign for first-aid kits appears. As he patches up another chair, a dog house sign appears to indicate how much trouble he is in.

So, TV's most annoying neighbours are gone, replaced by other types of neighbours. However, without the Canadian Tire guy to help out, the new neighbours seem clueless about what to do until the signs drop down. Did Canadian Tire make the right decision?

Source: Adapted from Keith McArthur, "That Canadian Tire couple won't be annoying you anymore," *The Globe and Mail*, March 10, 2006, p. B3, and Rebecca Harris, "Suburban appeal," *Marketing*, March 27, 2006, p. 6.

Creative Execution

The **creative execution** stage of the creative development process is concerned with two main areas: tactical considerations regarding how to present the message (and generate impact on the audience) and production considerations regarding the media to be used.

TACTICAL CONSIDERATIONS

At this stage, the agency's creative team evaluates specific ideas on presenting the client's product or service. These ideas, often referred to as "tactics," are simply more precisely defined strategies. Tactics undertake to answer questions such as the following:

- What is the best or most convincing way to present a product so that the consumer will be motivated to take the desired action of purchasing the product?
- Does the advertisement use a demonstration, a product (brand) comparison, a testimonial, or a celebrity spokesperson?

PRODUCTION CONSIDERATIONS

As indicated earlier, the media budget has probably already restricted the use of certain media. Budget considerations may also affect the production of advertising messages. Considering the media to be used, the client must communicate to the agency any production restrictions. For example, if television is being used, what is the desired commercial length (15, 30 seconds or longer)? How many commercials will be needed (one commercial, or a pool of commercials on the same theme)? Can the same message be used online and in the broadcast media or are unique online ads necessary? If print is being used, what are the size specifications (one page or less)? Are there any restrictions on the use of colour (black and white, spot colour, or four-colour process)? How often should the brand name be mentioned?

The creative team must decide how to best present the product so that the message will have maximum impact on the target market. The following are some of the more commonly used presentation tactics.

TESTIMONIALS   In a **testimonial** ad, a typical real-world user of the product presents the message. Since real people are used, as opposed to professional models or celebrities, the message is usually perceived as believable even though the presenter works from a carefully prepared script. As indicated in the creative strategy section (see the discussion about lifestyle advertising), Tim Hortons uses testimonials effectively in its "True Stories" campaign. In each television commercial, someone has a story to tell about how Tim Hortons plays an important and enjoyable role in his or her life (refer to the creative strategy—lifestyle appeals section for details).

ENDORSEMENTS   Essentially there are two types of **endorsements**: those given by associations or other organizations, and those given by celebrities. Brands like Crest and Colgate have, for years, used the endorsement of the Canadian Dental Association in their advertising. The ad for Welch's Grape Juice that appears in Figure 5.6 includes an endorsement from the Heart and Stroke Foundation—an appropriate organization to endorse the health benefits of the product.

When a celebrity is used, the advertiser attempts to capitalize on the popularity of the star. Stars from television, movies, music, and sports form the nucleus of celebrity endorsers. Gatorade Canada was quick to sign Sidney Crosby as a spokesperson. The

Canadian Dental Association
www.cda-adc.ca

hockey sensation, often described as the next Wayne Gretzky, has the right background and personality for the assignment. "The teenagers that Gatorade targets will more easily relate to a teenage rookie than a grizzled superstar," says Jeff Jacket, marketing manager for Gatorade.[11]

Reebok International sees a natural relationship with Crosby and its hockey equipment line. Crosby is seen as a great addition to Reebok's "I Am What I Am" advertising campaign. One of the television spots traces Crosby's most poignant moments growing up as a young hockey player in Nova Scotia. The "I Am What I Am" campaign celebrates authenticity and individuality.[12] Refer to the illustration in Figure 5.17.

A potential danger of celebrity endorsements is overexposure if the celebrity is associated with too many brands. Could that happen with Sidney Crosby? He is already the most active hockey player in the sponsorship game, having other endorsement deals with Telus Communications and Upper Deck Co. The more ads he appears in, the less special each occasion is.

PRODUCT DEMONSTRATION   The use of a **product demonstration** is quite common in advertising focused on product performance. Several execution options are available to the advertiser. For example, a before-and-after scenario is a common strategy for diet-related products, where the message implies usage by the presenter. Such a technique is suitable for both print and television media, although with television the technique is much more effective. A second strategy is to simply show the product at work— a technique commonly used for advertising household products such as oven cleaners, tub and tile cleaners, and floor wax. Typically, such advertisements show how easy the product is to use or how well it works. In a print ad, a Gillette Fusion shaving gel demonstration shows how the product helps produce a smother, more comfortable shave. The same demonstration appears in television commercials. See the illustration in Figure 5.18.

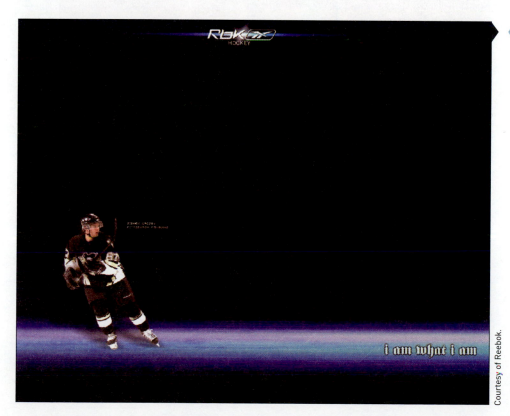

Courtesy of Reebok.

FIGURE 5.17

Advertisers benefit from an endorsement relationship with sports figures such as Sidney Crosby

FIGURE 5.18

A demonstration of the key benefits of using Gillette Fusion shaving gel

EXAGGERATED DEMONSTRATIONS—TORTURE TESTS In a **torture test**, the product is exposed to exaggerated punishment, or the situation the product finds itself in is exaggerated in order to substantiate a product claim that is known to be of interest to consumers. For example, truck brands are often presented performing stunts well beyond what the average user would do. As an example, an ad for the Toyota Tundra that debuted during the 2007 Super Bowl game involved a genuine death-defying stunt. The vehicle was shown towing a trailer-load of cement blocks up a steep ramp to dramatize payload capacity, and then shown going down the steep ramp to dramatize braking. It looked impossible but the truck stopped on a dime. If it has a good cup holder, I'm sold!

The BMW Mini is a small automobile with a "cute" reputation, not exactly the image BMW wanted for its small but high-performing vehicle. A series of TV commercials was developed to highlight safety, speed, and spaciousness. To demonstrate how much space there is in a Mini, one commercial shows a male and a female suddenly popping up in the front seat while putting their clothes back on. If that wasn't enough to make the point, a second female pops up from the back seat, also putting her clothes back on. Message delivered!

PRODUCT AS HERO   If the **product-as-hero** technique is employed, the advertiser presents a problem situation (e.g., using negative appeal strategy), which is quickly resolved when the product comes to the rescue. The advertisers of Glad Garbage Bags have used this technique effectively for many years. In many commercials, other garbage bags are shown ripping open, leaving a mess. The obvious message is that the use of Glad Bags prevents such situations. In this example, the execution effectively dramatizes the durability of the Glad product.

Household cleaning products are notorious for using the product-as-hero technique. Mr. Clean, for example, always mops up a rather messy situation. SpongeTowels really "suck things up." And no matter how much baked-on grease and grime there is on pots and pans, Cascade 2in1 ActionPacs can handle the situation.

PRODUCT COMPARISONS   For product comparisons to be used successfully, the attribute singled out for comparison must be of value or highly interesting to the target market. So as not to mislead the consumer in the message, the competitor must be identified fairly and properly, and the advertiser must be able to substantiate its claims with independent, objective research. Duracell once used the phrase "The CopperTop tops them all," a superiority claim, but was forced to change to "Nothing tops the CopperTop," a parity claim, because it could not prove the superiority claim when challenged by Energizer in court.[13] Legal and ethical considerations aside, if used properly, comparative advertising can present a convincing argument to consumers.

There are many critics of comparative advertising techniques. The most obvious drawback is the fact that one product's advertising budget is providing free exposure for another product. Comparative ads can also leave a consumer confused as to which brand is actually better. Certainly, the execution must deliver the message clearly and emphatically to the consumer in order to avoid any confusion.

PRE-PRODUCTION CREATIVE EXECUTION

With creative strategy and tactical details confirmed, attention shifts to production requirements of the campaign. Production requirements are often determined by media usage. For example, storyboards must be prepared for television, scripts for both radio and television, and layouts and designs for print advertisements.

Very often the content of the ad, if not the budget, restricts or makes necessary the use of certain media. For example, demonstrations are effective on television, while factual details are best left to magazines and newspapers. If sales promotion activity is to be part of the creative execution, a media mix may be required, with broadcast media used to build awareness and print media used to communicate details. Consideration must also be given to how traditional forms of advertising will be linked with digital communications—internet, cell phones, and portable music players. A consistent look and theme should be common to all forms of media.

In addition, the pre-production stage should review any mandatory items that must appear in an advertisement or commercial—for example, should brand and company logos appear in a certain place; how many times should the package be shown (in the case of a television commercial); or directions as to whether the execution is to be consistent across all forms of media. Specific details about design, layout, and production are presented in Chapter 6.

Refer to Figure 5.19 for a summary of the key elements and considerations for the various aspects of communications planning.

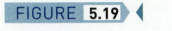

A summary of the key elements and considerations of creative planning

Planning Model Exhibit

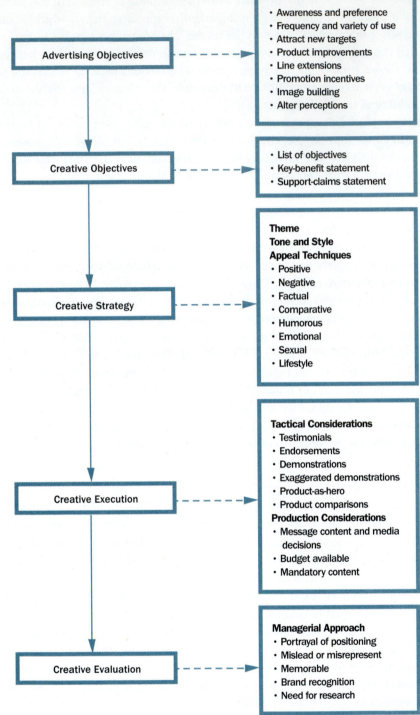

For an applied illustration of a creative brief and an illustration of the creative that was developed from the brief refer to figures 5.20 and 5.21.

For an applied illustration of advertising objectives, creative objectives, and creative strategies, refer to the marketing communications plan that is included in Appendix II.

SAMPLE CREATIVE BRIEF
CENTRE FOR ADDICTION AND MENTAL HEALTH

BACKGROUND INFORMATION

- 3 million Canadians suffer from clinical depression.
- Only one-third of sufferers seek help since there is a fear of being labelled as mentally ill.
- 80 percent of people who commit suicide are suffering from a depressive illness.
- 40 percent of cases of depression are diagnosed in people under the age of 20.
- Depression accounts for 30 percent of all disability claims in Canada.

PROBLEM

The public knows little about depression. It is a silent disease with a prevailing stigma surrounding it. Many perceive it to be a simple coping deficiency that "weak" people have and that they will, and can, snap out of it. Or they are just feeling "blue." Depression is a misunderstood illness.

OVERALL GOALS

- To create awareness about depression as a disease and to influence the public's attitudes about how to interact with people suffering from it
- To make the public aware of the Centre for Addiction and Mental Health and the services it provides

COMMUNICATIONS OBJECTIVES

- To remove the social stigma that surrounds depression and sell understanding of the disease
- To encourage those who may have the disease to seek help
- To raise awareness of the Centre for Addiction and Mental Health

CREATIVE OBJECTIVES

- To communicate the fact that depression is an illness and is the result of a chemical imbalance in the brain, and that it can be controlled with modern medication and professional counselling
- To communicate the idea that people with depression can't help themselves. Those who have it, or think they have it, need to know they are not to blame, and that there is compassionate help available to deal with it

CREATIVE STRATEGY

Dramatically portray the real suffering situations (at work, at home, etc.) that people with depression go through each day by using compelling, human, and empathetic headlines and images

CREATIVE EXECUTION

- Black and white ads of various sizes will be placed in the print media
- Similar images will be placed on the website
- Images will portray empathy and compassion

Source: Compiled with the assistance of David Sharpe, Vice-President and Creative Director, Remtulla Euro RSCG Advertising.

FIGURE 5.20

PLANNING MODEL EXHIBIT

Sample Creative Brief

This is an example of a creative brief for a public service campaign designed to increase awareness for the Centre for Addiction and Mental Health and its efforts to make the public more aware and more understanding of depression and what can be done to those who suffer from it.

FIGURE **5.21**

Creative execution from the Centre for Addiction and Mental Health creative brief

EMPLOYEE EVALUATION FORM

Associate name _CAROLYN WONG_
Department _R+D_
Position _CO-ORDINATOR_
Date of hire _6/15/90_
Date of transfer _N/A_
Review period _Q3_
Reviewed by _D. SHARPE_
Date _10/1/00_

Performance factors	Comments	Rate 1-5
Quality of work	MARKED DECREASE OVER LAST QUARTER	1
Quality of work	NOT UP TO PREVIOUS STANDARD. SEEMS VERY DISTRACTED.	2
Internal relationships	ARGUMENTATIVE, UNDECISIVE, DISTANT.	1
External relationships (where applicable)	MISSES APPOINTMENTS WITH SUPPLIERS AND CLIENTS	2
Problem-solving/decision-making ability	CAN'T HANDLE PROCEEDURAL CHANGES - LOOKS TO OTHERS FOR DECISIONS	1

Her mind isn't on her job. But maybe you're the one who's not paying attention.

It can come on suddenly or creep into everyday life – dramatically changing the way someone feels – causing uncontrollable waves of sadness, anxiety, fatigue, utter hopelessness and even shame.

It used to be called 'feeling blue'.

Today it's called Depression – an illness like Asthma or Diabetes – caused by a chemical imbalance in the part of the brain that controls mood.

Unfortunately only about a third of people with Depression actually seek treatment because of the stigma of having a mental illness. Left undiagnosed and untreated it can cripple families, friends and relationships. In the work-place it's costing over 8 billion dollars a year in lost time and productivity – more than any other health problem. Over the next 20 years, it will become the leading cause of premature death and of workdays lost to disability.

But there *is* help.

Depression is an illness. With modern advances in medication and counselling, it can be treated – just like any illness. Find out what the common signs of Depression are and what help is available by talking to your doctor, calling our 1-800 number or visiting our web site.

(All calls and e-mails will be held completely confidential).

depression
There *is* help. There *is* hope.

Toll free 1-800-463-6273
Toronto (416) 595-6111 / www.thereishelp.org

Centre for Addiction and Mental Health
Centre de toxicomanie et de santé mentale

Creative Evaluation and Research

CLIENT EVALUATION

Creative can be tested at numerous stages of the development process. The first step is usually a qualitative assessment by the client to determine if the message conforms to the strategic direction that was provided to the agency. This evaluation is conducted by means of a "managerial approach." In this evaluation, a client must resist the impulse to assess the creative on personal, subjective bases. However, if a "to proceed or not to proceed" decision must be made, the client reserves the right to conduct consumer research prior to making the decision.

Clients using the **managerial approach** for evaluating creative may apply some or all of the following criteria:

1. *In terms of content, does the advertisement communicate the creative objectives and reflect the positioning strategy of the brand (company)?* The client reviews the creative for the primary message and support claims outlined in the creative brief.

2. *In terms of how the ad is presented (strategy and execution), does it mislead or misrepresent the intent of the message? Is it presented in good taste?* The client must be concerned about the actual message and any implied message, since they are responsible for the truthfulness of the message. Legal counsel often has the final say regarding message content. Consumers also lodge complaints about ads they find offensive or that encourage risky behaviour. Consumer complaints forced the Ford Motor Company to pull an ad for the Ford Focus. There were complaints about a scene in which a female shopper pushes a male clerk into the hatchback of her car. For some reason the ad was perceived to condone violence, which certainly wasn't the intention.

3. *Is the ad memorable?* Breaking through the clutter of competitive advertising is always a challenge, and a lot of advertising that is approved doesn't quite cut it. Is there something that stands out in the ad that customers will remember? What will they take away from the ad? For example, the two beavers that now appear in Bell Mobility ads (see Figure 5.5) present the message in a humorous way. Characters like this play an integral role in providing continuity of message from one medium to another. Over an extended period of time the character becomes synonymous with the brand. So memorable are the characters that the public misses them if they are not included. The loveable A&W Root Bear is one of those characters.

4. *Is the brand recognition effective?* There must be sufficient brand registration in the ad. Some companies go as far as to stipulate how many times the package should be shown in a television commercial. The creativity of the commercial or print ad should not outweigh the product; it should complement the product. For example, people often recall funny ads and they can talk knowledgeably about the humorous situations that were presented until they are asked for the name of the product that appeared in the ad. So much for the laughs!

5. *Should the advertisement be researched?* When it comes to assessing the impact and effectiveness of the advertisement, subjective judgments by the client have the disadvantage of not being quantifiable. Prior to spending money on production, the client may decide to conduct consumer research to seek quantifiable data that will help the decision-making process. Better safe than sorry!

The evaluation process can occur at virtually any stage of the creative-execution process. A television commercial, for example, could be evaluated by consumers at the storyboard, rough-cut, or finished commercial stage. While it is not practical to test commercials at all stages, if the quality or effectiveness of the commercial is ever in question, the client should conduct research to avoid costly and embarrassing errors in judgment.

RESEARCH TECHNIQUES

Creative evaluation involves a variety of research techniques. The objective of most **creative research** is to measure the impact of a message on a target audience. Creative research is conducted based on the stage of creative development; it is either a pre-test or a post-test situation. **Pre-testing** is the process by which an advertisement, commercial, or campaign is evaluated before final production or media placement, so that the strengths and weaknesses of a strategy and execution may be determined. **Post-testing** is the process of evaluating and measuring the effectiveness of an advertisement, commercial, or campaign during or after its placement. Post-testing provides information that can be used in future advertising planning.

Among the more common techniques used to measure the effectiveness of creative are recognition and recall testing, opinion-measure testing, and physiological-response testing. Post-testing using procedures such as inquiry tests. Controlled experiments are also used to measure the effectiveness of the message.

RECOGNITION AND RECALL TESTING In **recognition tests**, respondents are tested for *awareness*. They are asked if they can recall an advertisement for a specific brand or any of the points made in the advertisement. For example, consumers who have read a publication in which an ad has appeared are asked if they remember the editorial content of the advertisement or the advertisement itself. Are they aware of the brand name that was advertised?

In **recall** tests, respondents are tested for *comprehension*, a measure of the impact of advertising. The test can be an **aided recall** situation (some information is provided to the respondent to stimulate his or her thinking) or an **unaided recall** situation (no information is provided). In either situation, respondents are asked to recall specific elements of an advertisement or commercial, such as its primary selling points, the characters used in it as presenters, or its slogan. Test scores are usually higher for tests where some aid is provided.

Two of the more common methods for collecting recognition and recall information are Starch readership tests and day-after recall tests. A **Starch readership test** is a post-test recognition procedure applied to both newspaper and magazine advertisements. The objectives of a Starch readership test are to measure how many readers have seen the ad and what percentage of those who saw it read it. In terms of procedure, a consumer is shown a magazine and, once he or she has read it, an interviewer goes through the magazine ad by ad with the respondent. For each advertisement in the magazine (the entire magazine is "Starched"), respondents are divided into three categories:

- *Noted* The percentage of readers who remember seeing the ad in this issue.
- *Associated* The percentage of readers who saw any part of the ad that clearly indicated the brand or advertiser.
- *Read Most* The percentage of readers who read half or more of the written material.

The Starch readership test offers several benefits: the client can measure the extent to which an ad is seen and read; by reviewing the results of other ads that were tested, the extent of clutter breakthrough can be determined; and by reviewing scores obtained by other products in previous tests, various layout and design options can be evaluated for effectiveness.

In the broadcast media, particularly television, the use of **day-after recall testing (DAR)** is quite common. As the name implies, research is conducted the day after an audience has been exposed to a commercial message for the first time. By means of a telephone-survey technique, a sampling of the client's target market is recruited and asked a series of questions so that their exposure to, and recall of, particular commercials may be determined. Once it has been determined that a respondent saw the commercial, they are asked what the ad actually communicated. Specific information is sought about the primary selling message: what the respondent likes and dislikes about the ad, areas of disbelief or confusion, and purchase motivation.

The actual quantified measures obtained in a DAR test are described as related recall levels. **Related recall** refers to the percentage of the test-commercial audience who claim to remember the test execution and who are also able to substantiate their claim by providing some description of the commercial. The higher the percentage is, the more intrusive the message with respect to the audience.

OPINION-MEASURE TESTING **Opinion-measure testing** exposes an audience to test-commercial messages in the context of special television programs. In terms of procedure, a group of people are seated around television monitors, or they view commercials in a theatre environment, and respond to a series of questions.

The test commercial is usually presented twice during the program, in cluster situations. Also included in the cluster is a set of control commercials, against which the test commercial or commercials (sometimes more than one commercial is being tested) can be compared. The position of the test commercial is different in each cluster. The test measures three key attributes: the audience's awareness of the commercial based on brand-name recall; the extent to which the main idea of the ad is communicated; and the effect the commercial could have on purchase motivation (e.g., the likelihood of the respondent buying the brand). This final measure is based on a comparison of pre-exposure brand purchase information and post-exposure brand preference data.

This procedure is often referred to as a **forced-exposure test**, a name that suggests its potential weakness: the artificial environment in which it occurs. However, the results for commercials are compared to results from previous tests, and since the procedure remains constant, the data should provide reasonable direction to advertisers.

PHYSIOLOGICAL TESTING Advertisers also have access to a variety of physiological testing methods that measure involuntary responses to a specific element of an advertisement. In an **eye-movement camera test**, consumers read an advertisement while a hidden camera tracks their eye movements. Such a test gauges the point of immediate contact, how a reader scans the various components of an ad, and the amount of time spent reading it. The **pupillometer test** measures a person's pupil dilation to determine the level of interest in the ad. In a **voice-pitch-analysis test**, a person's voice response is taped. It measures changes in voice pitch caused by emotional responses.

Testing procedures and the need for them are controversial issues in the industry, particularly among advertising agencies, whose work is being tested. Many creative directors argue that too much testing defeats the creative process (it stifles creativity) and that what people say in research and do in the real world can be completely different. Nevertheless, clients like to know how customers will react to their messages, preferably before they spend money on them.

INQUIRY TESTS (SPLIT-RUN TESTS) Perhaps the most meaningful tests are those that measure an ad's actual influence on a target audience: did the target actually purchase the product or take advantage of a special offer because of the ad? With an **inquiry** or **split-run test**, an advertiser can measure the effectiveness of two or more advertisements at once. For example, an advertiser can run two different ads with the same coupon offer (the coupon being pre-coded differently for each of the two ads). The number of coupons redeemed for each ad may be indicative of the relative strength of the overall ad. Small-scale tests of this nature are excellent for determining which advertisement should be more widely distributed. This procedure can be adapted for use by direct-response advertisers who use return coupons of a "send for more information" nature.

CONTROLLED EXPERIMENTS   To measure the potential impact of advertising activity on sales, an advertiser could set up a **controlled experiment** situation in which the advertising activity used in a test market differs from that used in a control market. To conduct this type of test, the advertiser would select two markets that were closely matched in terms of demographics, shopping habits, and media-consumption habits. In the control market, a given set of planned marketing activities would be implemented. In the test market, the advertising variable would be altered: different media might be used, or the expenditure level or weight of advertising might vary. Sales would be monitored closely in both markets so that test results would be obtained and conclusions about advertising effectiveness reached.

SUMMARY

The communications process begins with a sender (the advertiser) developing a message that is sent through the media to the receiver (the consumer or business user). From this fundamental understanding of communications, advertisers deliver messages to customers with the objective of prompting some kind of action (e.g., buying the product). Before such an action occurs, the consumer passes through several stages of behaviour: awareness, comprehension, conviction, and then action.

The creative development process begins with a creative brief, which is a discussion document prepared by the client. The brief includes the appropriate background information that creative personnel require prior to undertaking a new creative challenge. The content of a creative brief includes market background information, product information, competitor product and advertising information, target-market profile, budget, clear identification of the problem that advertising will resolve, the advertising objectives, positioning-strategy statement, and a list of creative objectives.

Creative objectives are statements that clearly indicate the information to be communicated to a target audience. They include a key-benefit statement and a support-claims statement. The key-benefit statement identifies the primary benefit and makes a promise to consumers about what the product will do. The support-claims statement provides details that substantiate the promise made. The client is usually responsible for developing the creative objectives.

Creative strategy is the responsibility of the agency and is concerned with theme, tone, style, and appeal techniques. Some common appeal techniques include positive and negative approaches, the use of factual information, making comparisons with competitor products, humour, emotion, and sex and lifestyle appeals.

At the creative execution stage, the primary concern is to make an impact on the target market. Considerations in this area include the use of testimonials, endorsements, product-as-hero tactics, demonstrations, or torture tests. The final stage, creative evaluation, occurs when the client appraises and indicates approval (or disapproval) of the agency's creative recommendations. It may also involve conducting consumer research to evaluate the potential impact the advertisement or campaign will have on the target market.

Should research be necessary, a variety of pre-test and post-test techniques are available. If recognition and recall of the message is of concern, a Starch readership test, a day-after recall test, and an opinion-measure test can be implemented. These tests generate data regarding brand identification and message comprehension. In post-test situations, inquiry (split-run) tests and controlled experiments are undertaken.

KEY TERMS

REVIEW QUESTIONS

1. Briefly describe the four behavioural stages that a consumer passes through prior to making the decision to buy a product.

2. Briefly describe the key responsibilities of clients and agencies in the creative development process.

3. What is a creative brief, and how is it used by an advertising agency?

4. What are the stages in the creative development process? Briefly describe each stage.

5. In the context of creative development, what is the role of the positioning-strategy statement?

6. What are the components of creative-objective statements? Briefly describe each component.

7. What is the difference between creative strategy and creative execution?

8. Identify and briefly describe the factors that influence the direction of creative objectives and creative strategies.

9. Briefly describe the various appeal techniques commonly used in advertising.

10. Explain the differences among the following types of creative execution: demonstration, exaggerated demonstration, and product-as-hero. Provide a new example of each.

11. What is meant by the "managerial approach" to evaluating creative output? Briefly describe the criteria that comprise such an evaluation.

12. What is the difference between pre-testing and post-testing of creative?

13. What is the difference between recognition testing and recall testing?

14. What does a Starch readership test measure?

DISCUSSION QUESTIONS

1. "Humorous advertising campaigns are effective in the short term, but do little to achieve long-term objectives for a product or service." Agree or disagree with this statement, citing some specific examples to substantiate your position.

2. "Comparative advertising: Is it wise to acknowledge a competitor while you pay for the ad?" What is your opinion on this style of advertising?

3. Conduct some secondary research (online or otherwise) and compare and contrast the creative strategies being used by the following brands. Are the strategies similar or different?

   a) Coca-Cola and Pepsi-Cola
   b) Guess jeans and Levi's jeans
   c) Canadian Tire and Home Depot

4. The "managerial approach" for evaluating creative was discussed in this chapter. Do you think this activity by the client impedes the creative process in the advertising agency? Discuss.

5. Review the Advertising in Action vignette **Canadian Tire Shakes Things Up**. The "Canadian Tire Guy" campaign was quite successful. Did Canadian Tire make the right decision when it retired this campaign? Is the new campaign the right replacement, considering the competitive nature of the market Canadian Tire competes in?

NOTES

1. Paul Marck, "Canadians heed call of the wild," *Financial Post*, February 24, 2006, p. FP7.

2. "Beavers versus the bank," *Marketing*, June 26, 2006, p. 6.

3. "Virgin Mobile," *Strategy*, December 2005, p. 56.

4. "Moores: Dressed for success," *CASSIES, Canadian Advertising Success Stories*, 2005, p. 11.

5. Ellen Roseman, "Most want socially responsible companies," *Toronto Star*, February 1, 2002, p. E2.

6. Rebecca Harris, "In from the cold," *Marketing*, May 1, 2006, p. 10.

7. "Juicy Fruit 2001–2004," *CASSIES, Canadian Advertising Success Stories*, 2005, p. 26.

8. Susan Heinrich, "Forever Young: Pepsi campaign wins top Cassie," *Financial Post*, November 6, 2002, p. FP7.

9. Emily Mathieu, "Fear drives it home," *Financial Post*, June 23, 2006, p. FP6.

10. Keith McArthur, "The hard sell goes to the Olympics," *The Globe and Mail*, February 21, 2006, p. B7.

11. Keith McArthur, "Crosby follows in Gretzky's footsteps," *The Globe and Mail*, April 17, 2006, p. B3.

12. "Reebok launches hard hitting 'I Am What I Am' TV ad starring Sidney Crosby," *The Globe and Mail*, November 10, 2005, **www.globeandmail.com**.

13. "Marketers move from stores to courts," *Marketing*, January 1/8, 1996, p. 5

CHAPTER 6

Design, Layout, and Production

Courtesy of Keith Tuckwell.

Learning Objectives

After studying this chapter, you will be able to

1. Explain the roles and functions of copywriters and art directors

2. Identify the design principles and creative considerations for developing print, broadcast, and electronic advertising

3. Explain the various types of print layout options

4. Characterize the functions of the various sections of a television commercial

5. Explain the production stages of television and radio commercials

This chapter examines in greater detail the design, layout, and production considerations associated with the execution stage of the creative development process. Focusing on the differences between the various print and broadcast media, it examines the copywriting and art direction function in more detail by presenting the techniques that are used to develop ads for the various media.

A significant amount of a client's advertising budget can be tied up in production expenses. The combination of production expenses and the high cost of media time and space places pressure on the agency to produce creative that sells the client's product or service. Theoretically, the various elements of an advertisement or commercial must work together effectively to present a convincing message. In essence, the message must create a favourable impression in the mind of a consumer as quickly as possible. Further, in the context of integrated marketing communications, the message delivered should be the same in each medium—one sight, one sound, one sell!

For those who make their living developing advertising messages, the challenge is to stop readers at a certain page, to keep viewers in the room and mentally alert during commercial breaks, or to attract attention to a banner ad so that visitors click on the banner to obtain more information. To achieve this requires inspired copywriting and art direction, and a desire to experiment with new approaches and techniques.

Magazine and Newspaper Advertising

In traditional print advertising, the central idea is conveyed primarily through the headline and visual illustration. The elements work together to produce a single message. As a unit, the headline and illustration must attract attention and create sufficient interest so that the reader moves on to the body copy, which, in turn, must sufficiently expand on the promise made in the headline or illustration.

THE COPYWRITING FUNCTION

The major areas of concern for the copywriter are the headline and subheadlines, the body copy, and the signature elements of an advertisement. Each element will be discussed in the context of the influence it is intended to have on the reader.

HEADLINES   The primary purpose of the headline is to command the reader's attention. According to legendary adman David Ogilvy (co-founder of Ogilvy & Mather), "Headlines get five times the readership of the body copy. If your headline doesn't sell, you have wasted your money."[1] There is no magic formula for distinguishing a good headline from a bad headline, but some research indicates that short headlines are more effective than long ones. To attract readers' attention, various types of headlines are commonly used.

Ogilvy & Mather
www.ogilvy.com

The **promise-of-benefit** headline makes an immediate promise to the reader. The promise is substantiated with other body copy and illustrations. For example, a headline for Right Guard Sport deodorant reads, "Odour, you're going down." The image of a football player in mid-tackle rising out of the deodorant stick reinforces the primary benefit. Refer to Figure 6.1 for an illustration of this ad. Note that the headline meets the "sell" criteria described above by David Ogilvy.

A **curiosity** headline makes the reader inquisitive enough to seek more information (to look for an explanation). British Airways used the headline "Upgrade from a power nap to a good night's sleep." Readers might wonder about how an airline can provide a

FIGURE 6.1

An ad with a promise-of-benefit headline

good night's sleep when, in their experience, any seat becomes uncomfortable on a long flight. British Airways has taken positive steps to provide more space on seats and the seats actually convert into beds for more complete comfort. They want their transatlantic customers to be aware of this.

A **question** headline asks a question and encourages readers to search for an answer in the body copy or illustration. This type of headline implies some kind of benefit. Volkswagen uses a clever headline: "Is it possible to go backwards and forwards at the same time?" There is no body copy to explain the headline, only a picture of the uniquely shaped Volkswagen Beetle—a car that looks like it could go both ways. See the illustration in Figure 6.2.

A **news** headline expresses a sense of urgency or announces something new to the reader. Words commonly used in news headlines are "New!" or "Introducing!" or "Finally!" When Schick launched the Schick Quattro razor, it employed a very simple headline: "New Schick Quattro. The World's First Four-Blade Razor!" A year later Gillette responded to Schick's challenge by launching a five-blade razor. The headline read: "Presenting Gillette Fusion. The Best Shave Ever!" In this game of cat and mouse it's always about being one step ahead of the competitor. In supporting body copy, both brands go on to explain how the product offers an unbelievably smooth shave.

A **command** headline politely makes a request of the reader to do something. A Campbell's Soup ad has the following headline: "Try something a little different with soup. Don't just stir, stir-fry." The ad goes on to explain the versatility of the soup in a variety of recipes.

A more subtle type of command is to simply reassure the reader that taking action is the right thing to do. The Mazda MX-5 Miata uses the headline "To stir your soul, use the proper utensil." Mazda commands drivers looking for the experience of driving a small sports roadster to make the logical choice. The company prides itself on building vehicles that evoke real passion, and the MX-5 Miata is the inspiration for all of their vehicle models.

SUBHEADLINES   A **subheadline (subhead)** is a smaller headline that amplifies the main point of a headline, making it possible to keep the headline short; it also acts as a

Volkswagen Beetle
www.vw.com/newbeetle/en/us/

FIGURE 6.2

An ad with a question headline that provokes curiosity in the reader

Is it possible to go backwards and forwards at the same time?

Drivers wanted.

breaker between the headline and the body copy. However, it more commonly takes the reader directly from the headline to the body copy and/or illustration. Subheadlines are an optional component of a print ad. Many ads run without one. If there is to be a transition it is from the headline to the body copy.

BODY COPY　The **body copy** is the informative or persuasive prose that elaborates on the central theme of the advertisement. The body copy helps create preference by providing information the consumer needs as a basis for making a purchase decision. Body copy is the substantiation—the proof of promise or product claims. It is a device that integrates headline with illustration. The headline announces something new, the subhead provokes curiosity in the reader, and the body copy and visual of the product provide proof. There are several types of body copy commonly used in print advertising:

1. *"Reason-why" copy* This straightforward copy relates the product's benefits to customers' needs. Typically, reason-why copy methodically resolves a problem the reader may encounter.
2. *Dialogue copy* Dialogue copy delivers a message from a spokesperson's point of view (e.g., in the form of a testimonial or endorsement). Dialogue copy can stand alone, but it is commonly integrated with other types of copy.
3. *Narrative copy* Narrative copy presents a message in the third-person. Using this type of copy can be problematic; it must be very good to hold the reader's attention.

How long should body copy be? Advertising practitioners have varying opinions on this subject. Generally, people read more of the copy if they are interested in the product or the idea communicated in the advertisement. Also, people will read more of an ad at a time when they are actually contemplating purchase, particularly if it is a major purchase. The body copy provides the information that helps the consumer decide.

While not discounting the value and importance of body copy, some creative experts believe the complete message should be communicated in the headline and visual. Their point is simple: the first thing people avoid is the body copy—they don't have enough time to read it!

Here are some guidelines that should be considered when working with body copy. Remember, a creative team does not have to follow guidelines to develop persuasive advertising—many believe you have to break the rules to be seen, heard, and read!

1. Short copy is most appropriate for image advertising. The illustration plays a key role in portraying a certain image, and lengthy copy would detract from it.
2. Purchase value has a bearing on copy length. The higher the cost of the product or service, the more likely that the consumer will use advertising as a source of information, and thus more copy is necessary.
3. Copy for new products may be longer than copy for established products. More copy is needed in the informative stage of advertising than in the retentive stage, where short messages are used to remind consumers of product benefits.

SIGNATURE　The final copy element in a print advertisement is the **signature**. Often referred to as a **tagline**, the signature can include a company or product logo and a brand or company slogan. A *logo* or logotype refers to the distinctive copy style that identifies the company or product. Logos are used in advertising to provide a common corporate identity to all products of a multi-product firm (e.g., a corporate logo appears in all ads for individual products). The purpose of the signature is to achieve the following:

1. ***To summarize the concept or central theme of the advertisement.*** For example, the logo and slogan can reinforce a key benefit or reinforce a company position that applies to several products.
2. ***To position the product in the customer's mind.*** For example, the logo and slogan will appear in all forms of advertising and be selling messages themselves. Recognizing that readers may pass over body copy entirely, the signature must leave an impression with the consumer. In addition, the signature provides continuity from one advertisement to another.

Here are some good examples of signatures and slogans:

- "Panasonic... Ideas for Life"
- "Canadian Tire... Let's Get Started"
- "Gillette... The Best a Man Can Get"
- "Visa... All You Need"

Slogans like these become familiar and meaningful to people the more often they appear in advertising. To demonstrate the role of the signature in relation to other copy and art components of an ad, refer to the Aquafina ad in Figure 6.3. Aquafina is a leading

FIGURE 6.3

Aquafina's tagline reinforces the brand promise and positions the brand in the mind of the consumer

Reprinted by permission of Pepsi-QTG Canada.

brand of bottled water and is positioned on the basis of purity. The headline invokes a curiosity in the mind of the consumer that is addressed in the body copy. The tagline, "Aquafina: The Taste of Purity," summarizes the entire message and reflects the positioning strategy of the brand. The tagline is a key aspect of the label design as well.

The advertisements for Jaguar in Figure 6.4 and Mazda in Figure 6.5 also demonstrates the concept of transition, and the relationships between various components of an ad. In each ad the bold, striking visual captures the attention of the reader. The gaze then moves to the headline in the middle of the page. This headline is a statement that creates some curiosity in the mind of the reader. A headline does not have to appear at the top of an ad. The body copy focuses on the key benefit that the headline alludes to. In each ad the body copy is not very long, but in each case it adequately elaborates on the key benefit.

Jaguar
www.jaguar.ca

Mazda
www.mazda.ca

THE ART DIRECTION FUNCTION

The primary responsibility of the art director is to design the layout of the advertisement. **Layout** refers to the design and orderly formation of the various elements of an advertisement within specified dimensions (size specifications). The layout combines the illustration with the copy and offers an overall impression of what the final advertisement will look like. Advancing computer technology is changing the nature of layout and design procedures. Formerly, the art director would progress through three distinct design stages: the thumbnail sketch, the rough art, and the comprehensive. **Thumbnail sketches** are small, experimental drawings of various ideas and design concepts. Their purpose is to identify a few options that can be used as a basis for more extensive design development.

Rough art refers to the drawing of an ad that is done in actual size (derived from the best of the thumbnail sketches), with the various elements of the ad included so that their size and position are shown—the location of headline, body copy, and illustration. The rough artwork and copy sheet (where precise copy is composed) are usually presented by the agency to the client for approval. Again, several options may be presented, with the preferred option progressing to the next stage of design. Refer to Figure 6.6 for an illustration of thumbnail sketches and rough artwork.

In a **comprehensive**, or **comp**, the copy and illustration appear as a highly refined facsimile of what the finished ad will look like. A comp usually includes the actual font styles and sizes and finished photographs or drawings. Given the computer technology available today, the comp is typeset on computer and positioned with the visuals. The ad is then printed in full colour or black and white (whatever the production specifications are) and shown to the client for final approval. Refer to Figure 6.7 for an illustration.

Computer technology has changed the way that ads are prepared. A copywriter's words can be instantly transferred to an art director's layout. The art director chooses a font from a library of typefaces, sets it in position, imports images and logos from a library of images, and commissions artwork as needed. The art director can play with all of the parts until satisfied with a design, and then produce a colour printout for client approval. Computer-aided design allows art directors to quickly examine "what if" experiments with raw ideas. For the client, the changes mean shorter production times, lower costs, more involvement in creative, the chance to see a more precise version of the final advertisement at an earlier stage, and the ability to make changes without hassle and expense.

XKR

JAGUAR

born with: 390 supercharged hp

lives for: permission

Shown with optional wheels and red calipers.

Two lines of cracked yellow paint, or a cage? With a 390-horsepower supercharged V8 and 20" wheels, a chance for freedom is never wasted. Of course, the race-inspired Brembo brakes may also prove quite useful, should the menacing strips of paint return.

Courtesy of Jaguar.

DESIGN PRINCIPLES AFFECTING LAYOUTS

The client and agency strive for distinctiveness in their ads in order to break through the clutter of competition. To achieve that distinctiveness, the art director considers factors such as balance, unity and flow, the use of colour, size alternatives, bleed pages, the use of artwork and photography, and the use of white space.

BALANCE   **Balance** refers to the relationship between the left side and the right side of an advertising layout.

Formal balance occurs when both sides are equal in weight. If different weights are assigned to the various elements of an ad, there is *informal* balance.

UNITY   **Unity** refers to the blending of all elements of an ad to create a complete impression. The headline, visual, and body copy must work together to create an impression.

FIGURE 6.5

An ad that demonstrates effective transition between illustration, headline, and body copy

FLOW   **Flow** refers to the movement of the reader's eye—from left to right and top to bottom—when he or she is exposed to a print advertisement. When some people scan an advertisement, their eyes move diagonally, from upper left to lower right. Others follow a "Z" pattern, with eyes moving left to right across the top, then diagonally from upper right to lower left, and then across the lower portion of the page to the right corner. See Figure 6.8 on page 175 for an illustration of these patterns.

Such reading patterns suggest the ideal locations for various elements of a print ad. For example, headlines often appear at the top to attract attention and state the key point of the ad. The illustration is used as background to the entire page, or part of the page (say, in the middle), with body copy. The signature (summary message) usually appears in the lower right-hand corner of the page, along with any purchase incentives to encourage action. Signatures are strategically located to make an impression on those who skip the body copy. The Aquafina ad that appears in Figure 6.3 and the Jaguar and Mazda ads that appear in figures 6.4 and 6.5 are good illustrations of balance, unity, and flow.

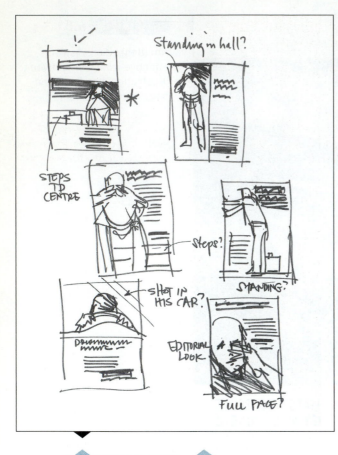

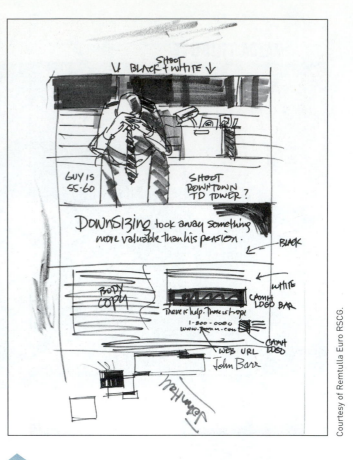

FIGURE 6.6

An Illustration of thumbnail sketches and rough artwork

Thumbnail Sketches

The creative team experiments with a variety of layouts to find the best location for the various elements of the ad: the headline, body copy, and signature.

Rough Artwork

The idea is roughed out in linear form to give the client an impression of what the final ad will look like. When approved by the client, computer art is initiated.

COLOUR AND CONTRAST   Colour, or contrast in colour and style, can be an effective attention-grabber. In a black-and-white medium, reverse printing (white letters on black background) or spot colour may attract more attention. In a colour medium that uses photography, black-and-white photos, line drawings, or spot colour can distinguish one ad from another.

Most magazines publish in full colour, so to be different and to grab the reader's attention, Audi designed a black-and-white ad that included limited but effective use of one colour (red). The stormy visual imagery (shades of grey, and black) offers contrast and places the focus squarely on the automobile. The Audi ad appears in Figure 6.9 on page 176.

Does colour increase readership? As a rule of thumb, the answer is yes, but factors such as the layout of the ad and how the various elements of an ad fit together also have an impact on readership. In a major study, one-third more respondents remembered seeing the four-colour ads than the black-and-white ads.[2]

SIZE   The decision to use a full page, a double-page spread, or a fractional page (a half-page or a quarter-page) has an impact on how effectively an advertisement draws readers. Sometimes small ads can achieve the same result as larger ones (which is a boon to

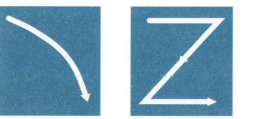

Flow of reader's eye from left to right and top to bottom

Courtesy of Remtulla Euro RSCG.

FIGURE 6.7

An illustration of comprehensive artwork

All elements of the ad are placed in their exact position. Font style and font size for headlines, body copy, and signature are precise and the illustration (photograph) is cropped to fit the specifications of the layout.

FIGURE 6.8

Reader's eye movement

the client paying the bill), but generally speaking, the full-page ad gets higher readership than a smaller ad. In fact, the degree of increased readership is surprising. Full-page ads receive 71-percent more readership than fractional-page ads, and double-page spreads get 37-percent more readership than single pages.[3] A fractional page ad appears in Figure 6.10 on page 177.

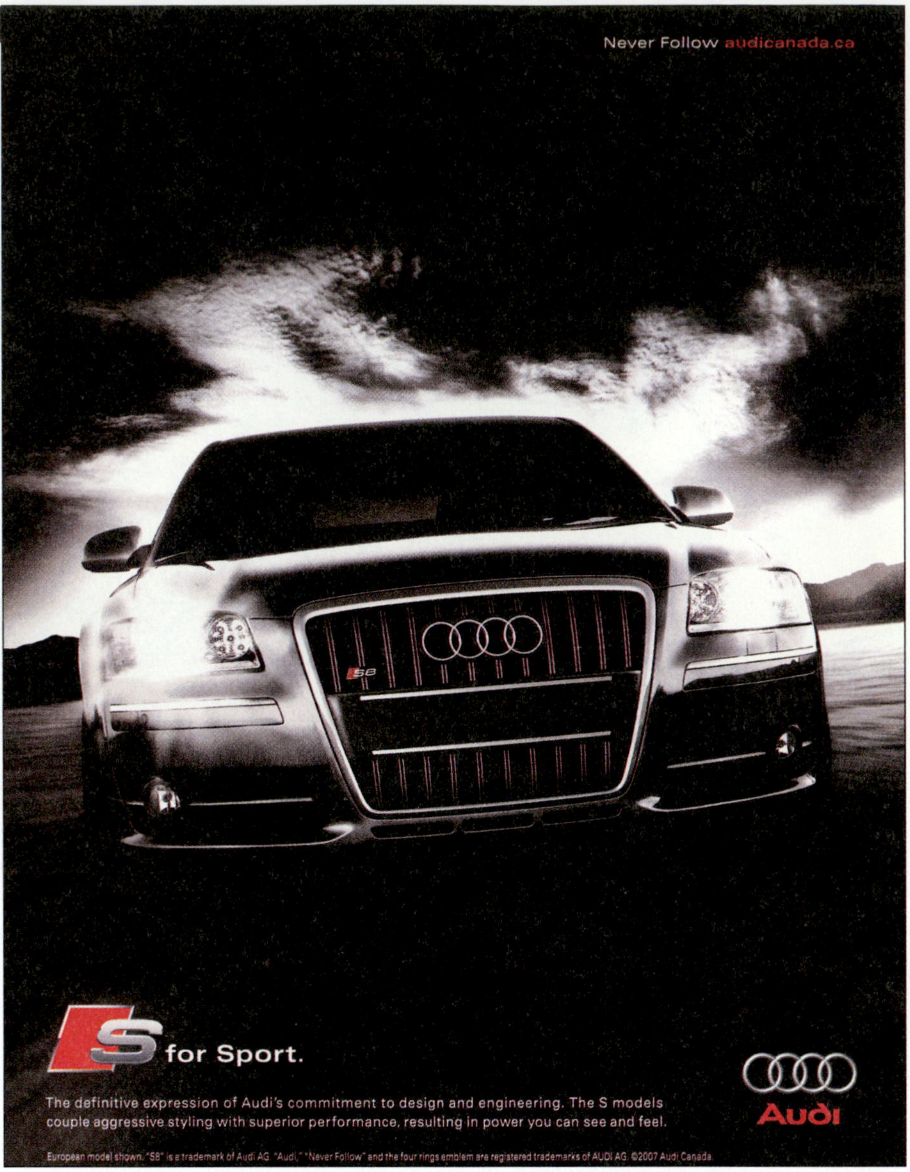

Courtesy of Audi Canada.

BLEED PAGES   In the case of a magazine, a **bleed page** is an advertisement in which the dark or coloured background extends to the edge of the page (often explained as an arrangement in which the colour appears to run off the page). The Audi ad in Figure 6.9 is an example of an ad that bleeds. Most magazines offer bleed flexibility. A bleed page attracts more attention (21-percent more) and preference (22-percent more) than a non-bleed page.[4] Typically, a majority of ads in magazines are bleeds but some advertisers distinguish their ads by including framed borders or by having white space surround the visual.

ARTWORK VERSUS PHOTOGRAPHY   The two basic illustrating devices are photography and drawn (or painted) illustrations. In the case of a four-colour medium such as magazines, logic suggests that colour photography be used, but the end product will, of course, be similar to numerous other ads in the same publication. An artist's drawing— something as simple as a black-and-white drawing—may command a higher level of attention through contrast. The opposite is true of newspapers. Generally, a good photograph will be most effective in conveying realism, emotion, or urgency. But there

FIGURE **6.10**

An ad that occupies only a fraction of a page: one-third of a page in a three-column magazine

are benefits to using drawings. Drawings allow artists to create the desired impression in their own style. The end product can exaggerate or accentuate in ways a photograph cannot often match. In Figure 6.11 a drawing is very effective in communicating the benefits of Charmin—softness: a true benefit for a sensitive area of the body.

WHITE SPAC0E   **White space** is the part of an advertisement that is not occupied by other elements. The careful use of white space can be an effective means of providing contrast and of focusing attention on an isolated element such as a beauty shot of the product. White space is also the means of achieving an uncluttered appearance. The ad for Volkswagen that appears in Figure 6.2 aptly portrays the use of white space. The ad is simple and uncluttered. The Old Spice aftershave ad in Figure 6.12 also uses white space effectively. In both cases the ad focuses on the product and the key benefit.

CLARITY AND SIMPLICITY   Any elements that do not serve a specific function should be eliminated. Too much variety in type style, too many reverses or illustrations, and any unnecessary copy should be cut. To achieve the desired impact, the ad should be pleasant to the eye and easy to read. The ads that appear in figures 6.3, 6.10, and 6.12 demonstrate clarity and simplicity.

FIGURE **6.11**

An ad using drawings as a
primary means of illustration

All of the above factors are considered in the design of an ad, but there is no magic formula for success. The effect of advertising is in the eye of the beholder. Therefore, when an ad is designed by the creative team, submitted to a focus group for its blessing, and ultimately sent to the client for final approval, everything must be kept in perspective. Relying on old evidence that colour offers more impact than black and white, and that full pages produce higher readership than fractional pages, is questionable today. The objective is to be noticed and remembered—and that may mean breaking a few rules!

TYPES OF LAYOUTS

The creative team considers the factors discussed in the preceding section when positioning the various elements in an ad for layout. With its decisions depending on the importance of an illustration and the need for explanatory copy, the creative team must blend all elements together to create an overall "look" for an advertisement. Here are some common types of layouts.

FIGURE **6.12**

An ad that effectively combines the principles of white space, clarity, and simplicity

Courtesy of Procter & Gamble.

A cooling after shave from our *Pure Sport* line.

POSTER   The **poster** layout relies almost entirely on visual impression. The advertisement is picture-dominant, with a minimum of copy. The Audi ad in Figure 6.9 is an example of a poster layout. The strong visual in the ad combined with a different type of headline that reads "Never Follow" suggests what type of consumer the Audi is trying to attract: upscale urban and suburban achievers, people that like to take risks and reflect a certain status in what they own. The ad presents a powerful image; as the old expression goes, "A picture is worth a thousand words."

VERTICAL SPLIT   In a **vertical-split** layout, the copy dominates one side of the ad and the picture dominates the other side (left side versus right side). In a single-page ad, an imaginary line down the middle can divide the page. Vertical splits are popular with a double-page spread (two pages).

HORIZONTAL SPLIT   A **horizontal split** divides the page across the middle. A common format sees the copy on one half of the ad and the visual illustration on the other half. The Honda ad that appears in Figure 6.13 demonstrates a horizontal split.

MULTIPLE ILLUSTRATIONS   In the **multiple-illustration** layout, a series of illustrations is presented, either in sequence or showing a variety of related features and benefits.

Courtesy of Honda Canada Inc.

In Figure 6.14, the versatility of WD-40 is presented using multiple illustrations. Note the element of humour in one illustration.

LONG COPY   The **long-copy** advertisement is copy-dominated, with limited or no use of illustrations. The body copy plays a key role in explaining the product's benefits. The ad for Nerds on Site in Figure 6.18 (later in this chapter) is one that effectively combines a strong visual of the product with important body copy.

INSERT LAYOUT   In the **insert layout**, a smaller, secondary visual illustration appears as an "insert" on the page. Inserts are commonly used to emphasize the product, package, or special features. The ad for the Philips neonatal monitor in Figure 6.15 contains an emotional visual image that grabs the reader's attention, and uses the insert technique to feature the product itself.

For more insight into copy and design elements that produce better advertising, see the Advertising in Action vignette **Attention, Interest, Action!**

ADVERTISING IN ACTION

Attention, Interest, Action!

What makes good copy and layout? Are there rules that great copywriters and art directors follow? These are interesting questions. Research reveals that when readers leaf through pages of a magazine, the average ad has less than half a second to grab their attention. With so little time to work with, the relationship between copy and illustration has to be readily apparent.

While there is no secret formula for success, here are some tried and true tips to ponder:

- **Successful ads have visual magnetism** An ad should be constructed so that a single component dominates the area—a picture, a headline, or text. The more pertinent the picture, the more arresting the headline, the more informative the copy, the better the ad will be.
- **Successful ads select the right target** There should be something in the ad that the reader can readily relate to. The ad should say to the reader, "Hey, this is for you."
- **Successful ads invite the reader into the scene** The art director has to visualize, illuminate, and dramatize the selling proposition.
- **Successful ads promise a reward** Readers must be given a reason to continue reading, for if they do, they will learn something of value. A promise must be specific. The headline "Less maintenance cost" is not as effective as "You can cut maintenance costs by 25 percent."
- **Successful ads back up the promise** A promise is only believable if hard evidence is provided (e.g., comparisons with the competition can be convincing, as are third-party testimonials).
- **Successful ads present the selling proposition logically** The parts of an ad must be organized so that there is an unmistakable entry point and the reader is guided through the material in a sequence consistent with the logical development of the selling proposition.
- **Successful ads talk person-to-person** Copy is more convincing when it talks to the reader as an individual. The writing style should be simple: short words and short sentences.
- **Successful ads are easy to read** Magazines and newspapers are loaded with ads in which the copy is too small to read. The typeface selected should be easy to read, and should not be printed over an illustration.

Copywriters and art directors like to present risky concepts to clients, believing that such messages stand out, make more noise, and work! Conservative-minded clients see things differently and as a result there can be conflict between the two parties. Clients who are overly critical of an ad usually get what they deserve, a teddy-bear type of ad—something cute and cuddly but not very effective. So, in terms of evaluation, here are a few unbiased fundamentals to consider:

- **Is the single most important benefit properly emphasized?** Readers pause only briefly as they flip through a publication. Make sure the ad selects the strongest benefit and presents it prominently and persuasively.
- **Is the visual a show stopper?** Get beyond the beauty shot of the product and dramatize the most important benefit either by showing the product in action or by visualizing the problem and offering the product as a solution.
- **Does the layout have a sense of balance and flow?** Is there a single large visual that catches your eye first? Does the headline work in tandem with the main visual? Are the logo and slogan given their own space as a signature?
- **Is the offer clear?** What exactly do you want the reader to do? Request a sample? Send for more information? Log on to your website?

In the end, these copy and design fundamentals are certainly food for thought. But advertising is very subjective—too many guidelines could produce boring advertising. The greatest idea in the world will lose all its power when supported by uninspired writing and art direction. You can lure a casual reader with an exciting photograph or stir their fancy with a snappy headline, but the reader must be rewarded with copy that is both entertaining and informative to read. Truly good advertising is in the eye of the beholder!

As an exercise, the reader may wish to analyze some of the ads in this chapter and evaluate them against the criteria described in this vignette.

Source: Adapted from Allan Sneath, "If you owned the firm, would you run the ad?" *Financial Post*, June 1, 2004, p. FP4; and Bob Lamons, "Guidelines for making better advertising decisions," *Business Marketing*, April 21, 1998.

FIGURE **6.14**

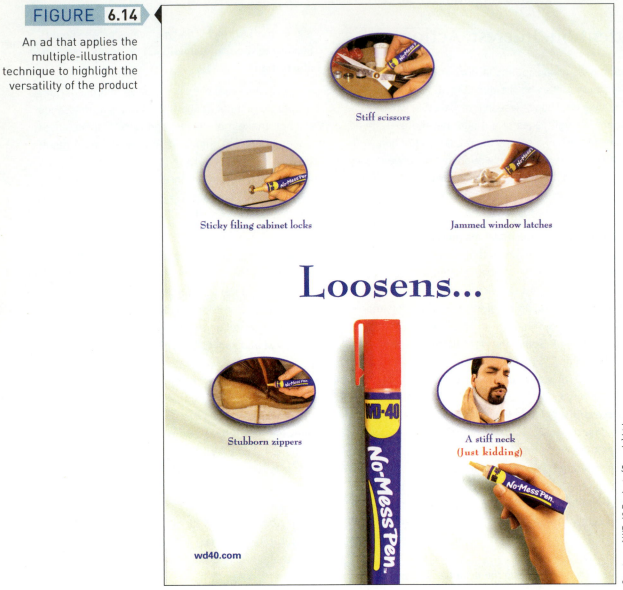

An ad that applies the multiple-illustration technique to highlight the versatility of the product

Courtesy of WD-40 Products (Canada) Ltd.

Out-of-Home Advertising

Other print media possess different characteristics and present different problems and opportunities for the creative team to explore. Out-of-home advertising is the current term for advertising in formats such as outdoor posters, transit ads, outdoor digital displays, and mural ads. These formats usually function as supplemental media and seem to work best when introducing new products, building awareness, or adding reach to a campaign.

OUTDOOR POSTERS

A research study conducted by Perception Research Services (U.S.) indicated that 75 percent of all individuals who see an outdoor board are likely to be drawn to the name of the product advertised, so bold identification of the name is important. In addition, factors such as size and the use of *cut-out extensions* affect the attention-getting ability of the board. Cut-out

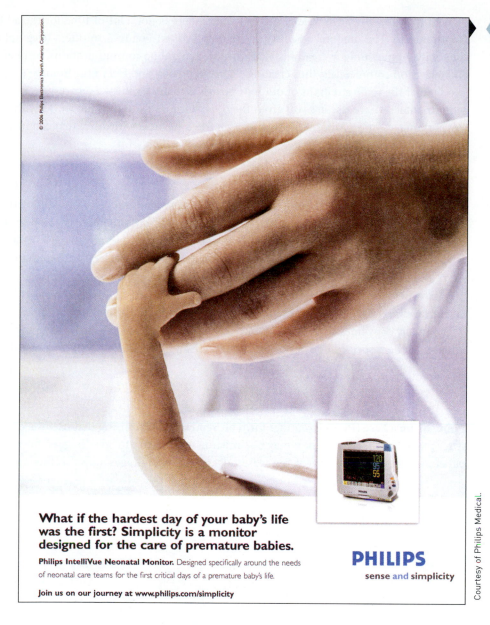

© 2006 Philips Electronics North America Corporation.

What if the hardest day of your baby's life was the first? Simplicity is a monitor designed for the care of premature babies.

Philips IntelliVue Neonatal Monitor. Designed specifically around the needs of neonatal care teams for the first critical days of a premature baby's life.

Join us on our journey at www.philips.com/simplicity

PHILIPS

sense **and** simplicity

> **FIGURE 6.15**
>
> An ad that uses an insert technique (smaller secondary pictures) to highlight key features

extensions are outdoor designs that extend beyond the perimeters of the standard space. Cut-outs lead to higher levels of readership and more repeat examination by readers.[5]

Other design factors important for **outdoor advertising** include the simplicity of the design and the use of colour. Since outdoor advertising is often used as a complementary medium (i.e., in conjunction with a primary medium such as television) the outdoor message should contain creative concepts from the other media. This method is referred to as the **integrative concept** of creative design.

Here are some basic guidelines for outdoor layout and design:

- Use bold colours and high contrast.

- Use typefaces that are simple, clear, and easy to read.

- Size the copy and place it appropriately in relation to the product.

If simplicity is a key to good advertising, then telegraphic simplicity is the key to good outdoor advertising. If you consider that people drive by a street poster at 100 km per hour or rapidly walk by it, arms loaded with packages, there is not a lot of time for the ad to communicate. The outdoor ad for Apple that appears in Figure 6.16 offers telegraphic simplicity. Apple's unique creative style is also used in online communications, print ads, and television commercials, thus creating a consistent look and feel to the brand.

One of the main strengths of outdoor boards is that they invoke our respect for the monumental. Where else are you given the opportunity to shout at the world with letters and images up to 7 metres high and 16 metres long? It is a medium that can inspire awe, so copywriters and art directors should take advantage of it.

TRANSIT ADVERTISING

Because the transit rider is sometimes moving and sometimes standing still, certain design considerations are particularly relevant to both interior and exterior transit advertising. With **interior transit**, the advertiser can use time to its advantage. The average length of a ride is 28 minutes, so copy and illustrations can be detailed. Alternatively, short and quick messages tend to be read and reread by idle passengers.

Exterior transit advertising reaches pedestrians and travellers in other vehicles. Since travelling displays on buses are often viewed from an angle and a distance, bold type, punchy copy lines, and absolute simplicity are preferable. The impact of a powerful visual must be respected in exterior transit advertising. The ad for Nike in Figure 6.17 is a good illustration of transit advertising.

POINT-OF-PURCHASE ADVERTISING

Point-of-purchase (POP) is another form of "reminder" advertising that uses the design concepts of another medium; it may be similar in appearance to ads designed for newspapers or magazines. Point-of-purchase advertising encourages impulse buying and

FIGURE 6.16

Telegraphic simplicity on an outdoor board communicates Apple's brand image

Courtesy of Keith Tuckwell.

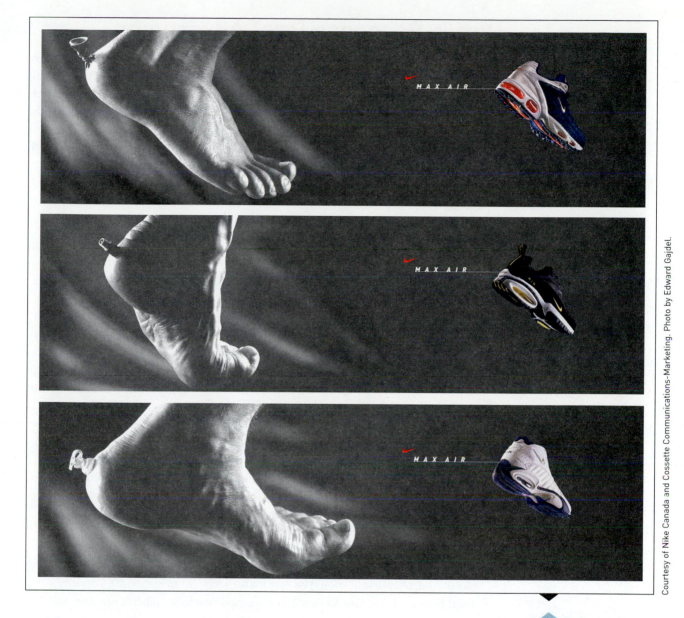

Courtesy of Nike Canada and Cossette Communications-Marketing. Photo by Edward Gajdel.

FIGURE **6.17**

A strong visual is important in exterior transit advertising

influences last-minute choices between comparable brands. When it comes to retail display materials, which include posters, shelf-talkers (small posters at shelf locations), ad pads (tear-off coupon, contest, and cash rebate offers at shelf level), and floor ads, the design must provide what the point-of-purchase industry refers to as the four *I*'s: impact, identification, information, and imagery.

- *Impact* The display must generate immediate impact. It must say "Here I am, buy me."

- *Identification* The brand or business name must be boldly displayed. Identification must link the message to the source.

- *Information* In a brief format (i.e., in the copy and the illustration), the display must provide the consumer with a reason to buy.

- *Imagery* The overall impression must be relevant to the customer. As in a print ad, the various elements of a display must blend together to make a complete message.

Direct-Response Print Advertising

Direct refers to a marketing situation in which there is no distributor between the advertiser and the customer. Instead, there is a one-on-one link between the advertiser and customer through a phone call, a letter, or a print, radio, or television ad. With **direct-response print**, the message is communicated through magazines, newspapers, or the mail. A response opportunity is provided for the customer through a toll-free telephone number, reply card, or website address. Direct-response advertising aims to solicit a call for action quickly, either in the form of a purchase or a request for more information.

Since direct mail remains the most widely used form of direct-response advertising, let's focus on some copy and design characteristics of this medium.

1. *Get the reader's attention* Since so many people discard direct mail without opening it, there has to be some relevant copy or design element that gets the mail opened. The envelope must function like a headline in a print ad. It should grab the reader's attention. Bright colours, unusual envelopes, and interesting graphics tend to generate more interest.

2. *Personalize the mailing* Direct mail is a targeted medium that relies on database marketing for success. With technology advancing rapidly, advertisers have access to accurate mailing lists. Taking the step to personalize each mailing is integral to the one-on-one sales situation referred to earlier. Also, the language in the letter and other elements of the mailing should be warm and informal and should echo the language of the consumer.

3. *Include a complete presentation* Unlike traditional forms of advertising, direct-mail advertising functions as a complete sales message. The copy must grab attention, stimulate interest and desire, provide ample proof of the promise, handle objections, and close the sale. The offer must be compelling and presented in a manner that makes it absolutely irresistible.

4. *Include multiple pieces in the mailing* A typical direct-mail piece includes several items (e.g., a letter, pamphlet, involvement device, and an offer of a free gift to encourage immediate action). Direct advertisers believe that many items working together to communicate the same message is more effective than one element alone. And, of course, it should be easy for the recipient to respond. Order cards must be easy to read and fill out. A postage-paid envelope, toll-free number, and website address should be included. A sample direct mailing is shown in Figure 6.18.

Television Advertising

The nature and content of a television commercial are derived from the same base of information as print advertising, but there are obvious differences. Print advertising uses space, whereas television advertising is concerned with the use of time; since the message is delivered within a period of time, the creative team is concerned with the flow of the commercial from beginning to end. A television commercial is typically divided into three distinct sections: an opening, middle, and closing.

OPENING

The purpose of the opening section is to grab the viewer's attention and introduce the key benefit before the audience "disappears" physically or mentally. A common means of attracting attention is to present a problem situation that subsequently must be resolved.

▶ FIGURE **6.18**

Contents of a typical direct-mail campaign

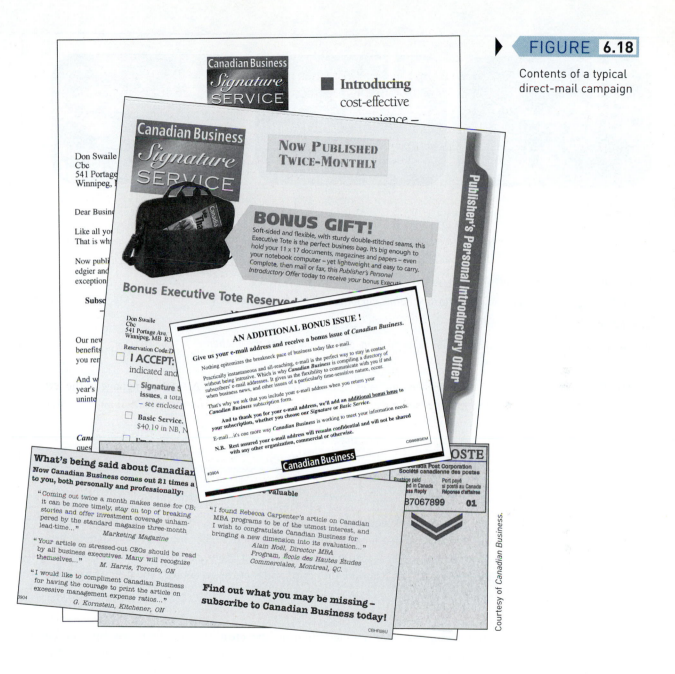

Courtesy of *Canadian Business.*

MIDDLE

This section's purpose is to communicate the bulk of the message; it must hold the viewer's interest by elaborating, in an interesting manner, on the single most important benefit of the product or service, clearly identifying the name of the product or service.

CLOSING

The closing section of a commercial, which is usually the final few seconds, will definitely resolve the problem. The focus is usually on the product's name and package, if applicable. It may repeat a promise and should suggest some course of action to the viewer (e.g., "Visit your dealer for a test drive" or "Visit our website"). A tagline usually appears at the end of a commercial.

"DOG TIRED"

Video: Open on a shot of a dog lying on a kitchen table. Camera stays on dog, still just lying on table.

Super: Pine-Sol cleans the dirt you know about.

Video: The dog then hears his owner returning home and jumps off the kitchen table.

SFX: Car pulling in, keys opening door.

Video: The dog settles into his same comfortable position, except now under the kitchen table.

Super: And the dirt you don't.

Video: Cut to a mid-shot of Pine-Sol Original bottle.

Super: The thorough clean.

FIGURE 6.19

A television spot with a well-defined opening, middle, and closing

Figure 6.19 demonstrates the concept of opening, middle, and closing. In this ad, an unattended dog in a house leaps off a table (a place he shouldn't be) when he hears his owners return. These scenes demonstrate that Pine-Sol cleans the dirt you see and the dirt you don't see. Examine the script and pictures to capture the flow of the ad.

DESIGNING TELEVISION COMMERCIALS

In designing a television commercial, the creative team first develops the **central concept** or **theme** and then creates a story around it. For example, a nudge-and-wink product such as Viagra used a central theme showing the enjoyment a man has describing the night before to his friends. The campaign included a series of commercials. One takes place in an elevator, another on the golf course, and another at a coach's press conference. The audience does not hear what the men are saying, as an image of the little blue pill covers their mouths when they are talking and prevents whatever they are saying from being heard. A theme like this is easy to extend into different scenarios to keep the campaign fresh.

In the development stage, the creative team is concerned with the sequence of events in the ad, and the team creates a storyboard for this purpose. A **storyboard** is a set of graphic renderings (an artist's rough version of a finished commercial) in a television-frame format, with appropriate copy showing what the commercial will look like. An alternative to the storyboard is a complete **script**, which details in words the audio and visual elements of the commercial. It is common to have the description of the visual on one side, and the audio on the other. Clients approve advertising campaigns on the basis of the script and storyboard, so the combination of the two items must plant a good visual impression in their minds. Once approved, the script and storyboard act as the guideline for producing the commercial.

CREATIVE CONSIDERATIONS FOR TELEVISION

The creative team must consider several factors when trying to design a television commercial that will stand out from the competition. Given the context in which commercials appear (six or more in a cluster during a station break), the need for a commercial to break through a viewer's perceptual barriers is paramount.

UNITY   **Unity** refers to the visual and aural flow of a broadcast commercial, from the customer's perspective. Viewers do not distinguish between the opening, middle, and closing sections of an advertisement as they watch. Instead, they perceive the ad as a continuum of action focused on a central idea. The commercial, therefore, must flow logically: it presents the problem or situation, and then provides an explanation and solution. In the case of the Pine-Sol commercial shown in Figure 6.19, the message flows quickly, but it clearly communicates in a humorous way how well Pine-Sol cleans the dirt you see and the dirt you *don't* see.

INTEGRATION OF AUDIO AND VIDEO   In a commercial, the voice-over and action should be focused squarely on the product; if a benefit is depicted, it should be emphasized appropriately. The product should be the main element of the commercial; the creative team will consider using sound effects and music, where appropriate, but in so doing they must recognize that their purpose is to enhance the product message, not to overwhelm it.

Music can play a special role by grabbing the viewer's attention. If rights are obtained for a popular song, the song must enhance a key benefit. For example, A&W uses hit songs from the 1960s to capture the attention of its primary target market—baby boomers. In one ad, an older couple on a first date are seen enjoying a meal while the song "Just My Imagination" plays in the background. Different hits that are appropriate for the story are used in different commercials. The music establishes a mood for the commercials.

SPECIAL EFFECTS   Special effects are such devices or techniques as animation, trick photography, or supers. A **super** is copy superimposed onto a picture in a television commercial, as is done with the final tagline in the Hall's commercial in Figure 6.20. Most video production companies use digital video effects (DVE) units that can manipulate graphics on the screen in many different ways—fades, zooms, rotations, and more. As with sound effects and music, special effects are to be used only to enhance the commercial message. No technique should captivate viewers to the point that they focus more on it than the product.

PACE   A television commercial airs for 15, 30, or 60 seconds. Using the time limit as a guideline, the creative team must produce a message that will communicate itself at a suitable **pace**. In recent years, the 15-second commercial has become popular with advertisers, as it saves money in media time. However, scaled-down versions of 30-second commercials do not have the same impact. It is preferable to use the time constraint as a guideline from the beginning and develop an original commercial designed to suit the 15-second period.

The product and product image have an effect on the pace of a commercial. For example, a commercial for a perfume product may suggest romance and use emotional situations in the communications process. In this circumstance, the pace is likely to be slow. In contrast, a commercial for a soft drink like Mountain Dew aimed at a youthful target market may use fast-paced rock music and action sequences to create the appropriate image for the product.

The penetration of personal video recorders (PVRs) is causing advertisers to rethink the length of their commercials. A PVR lets a viewer skip forward in 30-second intervals to avoid the commercials; perhaps as a result of this, there has been some movement toward shorter commercials of 5 seconds and 10 seconds. For example, one episode of *The Apprentice* included a series of 10-second spots to introduce the new Pontiac Solstice.[6] The shorter commercials aren't detected as easily by the PVR, hence they are less zappable—advantage advertiser!

LIVE ACTION OR ANIMATION   **Live action** involves using real-life situations and real people in a commercial. The real people may be amateur or professional actors. **Animation** is a technique whereby hand-drawn cartoons or stylized figures generated by design software on a computer are given movement and visual dimension. There is an animated television commercial for Charmin that uses this technique. The animation is identical to that which appears in the print ad featured in Figure 6.11. Some commercials combine live action and animation. Do you remember the commercials for Kellogg's Frosted Flakes that showed Tony the Tiger sitting at a table with real people and communicating with them? The Pillsbury Doughboy live-action commercials employ another animation technique.

There are advantages to both live-action and animated ads. A live-action commercial can generate a sense of realism and immediacy. As well, personalities can be used as persuasive presenters, and effective locations can be selected in which to shoot the commercial. The animated commercial is potentially entertaining; the advertiser can use a fantasy situation to advantage, and the commercial will no doubt be unique in its animation techniques. As well, animation is becoming more innovative as technology advances. New computer-assisted television cameras that control camera movement, complex effects from multiple exposures of the same frame, and computer-generated graphics have added to the quality of animated commercials.

FORMAT   In terms of creative execution, choosing the proper format is a key decision. **Format** refers to the best means of executing a strategy, the best means of dramatizing the benefit that has to be expressed. The most common formats are as follows:

1. *Demonstrations* In a demonstration, the objective is simply to demonstrate how the product works. There are several options: showing actual usage (e.g., the paper towel cleans up the entire spill), a comparison with a competitor (e.g., a thick ketchup compared to runny varieties), and a before-and-after scenario (e.g., a shirt with a messy spill on it is stain-free when removed from the laundry).

2. *Narratives* In a narrative, a story is told during the commercial. Some of the common options in this format include slice-of-life, vignettes, and little movies. The *slice-of-life* option usually introduces a problem situation that is remedied by using the product (e.g., the product comes to the rescue of the person in the commercial). The *vignette* shows a series of quick stories, one right after the other (e.g., many different people enjoy the use of the product). The *little movie* is one complete story with a short but strong plot, developed characters, and honest

dialogue, often emotion-tugging. The "True Stories" campaign for Tim Hortons is a good example. In these ads much time is spent developing the featured character in order to show how his or her lifestyle has a close relationship with Tim Hortons.

3. *Testimonials and endorsements* Often referred to as "talking heads," such tactics have proven to be a durable technique in convincing customers about the merits of a product. Testimonials may come from a variety of sources, such as animated characters (e.g., the Pillsbury Doughboy), the common man or woman (e.g., the charming and lovable manager who appears in all A&W commercials), or celebrity endorsers (e.g., Don Cherry for Cold FX and Sidney Crosby for Reebok or Gatorade).

TELEVISION PRODUCTION STAGES

The creative team and the account executive are responsible for presenting the storyboard and script to the client for approval. With a significant amount of money on the line at this stage (i.e., actual production costs and the cost of media time), both the agency and client want the message to be right.

Once the client has approved the concept, storyboard, and script, the commercial goes into production. The production process involves four separate stages: securing cost quotations, pre-production, production, and post-production.

COST QUOTATIONS   The task of producing the commercial is the responsibility of a production house (i.e., a specialist in commercial production). Evaluating production cost estimates from various production houses is a critical assignment, as the costs of producing a 30-second, live-action commercial—without celebrity talent—average between $100 000 and $300 000. Some beer commercials have reached as high as $500 000.[7] The inclusion of celebrity talent, popular music, or a lot of special effects increases the production costs of TV advertising. Smaller advertisers in local markets can produce commercials for much less by using the production services offered by local television stations.

The agency typically solicits estimates from two or three production houses. The busiest production houses in Canada, as measured by shooting days, are The Partners Film Company and Radke Films. The production companies submit bids, with the lowest bid being accepted. To estimate costs, the production house will use the storyboard and script as a guideline and add in other costs normally associated with commercial production. Some of the factors that add to production costs include travel to distant locations; using celebrity talent; complexity (which calls for large crews and many cameras); special effects; studio rental charges; the use of animals; the director (good ones are expensive); and additional days for production (time is money).

Production is a one-time cost, except for the talent used in the commercial. Talent can include actors, models, musicians, and others. Talent is paid union scale for an appearance in a commercial, and an additional payment, known as a **residual**, is payable to the performer each time the commercial is broadcast. Therefore, the costs of the talent increase with the frequency and coverage of the media buy. A celebrity may be employed under contractual agreement. Such agreements may call for participation in a certain number of television commercials each year.

The Partners Film Company
www.partnersfilm.com

PRE-PRODUCTION   At this stage, a meeting is held with representatives of the production house, the agency (i.e., the creative team), and the client. The storyboard and script are reviewed, and final decisions and arrangements are made. Prominent areas of discussion are casting, the use of secondary suppliers (e.g., music specialists, editors, and mixers), and finding appropriate props, costumes, and film locations. If an announcer is required, who should it be? Announcers in a commercial do not appear on screen, but are heard as a **voice-over** that communicates a key point. Agreement by all parties on all details is essential.

If music is part of the commercial, the advertiser has several options depending on the price it is willing to pay. For the highest cost, specific music, such as a current rock tune, can be requested (usually such music is under copyright by the original musician or producer). The cost depends on the popularity of the artist and the song, with a range from US\$20 000 to US\$100 000.[8] Several types of rights packages are available, including sound-alike rights, parody rights, and even original music rights. As an alternative, music writers and arrangers can prepare original music scores. The cost of original music, if produced locally, is much less than the costs of pop or rock music quoted above. Less costly alternatives include the use of pre-recorded music prepared and distributed by recording studios, and the use of public-domain music, which is music whose copyright has expired.

PRODUCTION   The actual shooting (production) of the commercial can be very long and tedious, but—since time is money—every effort is made to complete the task as quickly as possible. However, quality is also paramount. Therefore, when scenes are shot it is common to try several takes to get them right. The director may adjust the lighting, for example, a process that often requires two or three good takes of each scene. However, scenes do not have to be shot in sequence. For example, scenes without sound, which therefore do not require a full crew, can be done last. Finally, considerable time is lost between scenes as cameras are moved, actors briefed, lights reset, and so on. It is important that there be continuity from scene to scene; otherwise, the finished commercial will appear disjointed. As discussed earlier, the concepts of pace and flow are critical to the success of the message.

POST-PRODUCTION   The post-production stage involves putting the commercial together, and requires the coordinated effort of the director, film editor, and sound mixer. The normal procedure is to assemble the visuals and the sound separately, without extra effects such as dissolves, titles, or supers. Post-production activity can be described in a series of steps, which are as follows:

1. *Rough cut* A copy of the original film or video, referred to as a work print, is used in editing as a way of preventing damage to the original. The film editor reviews all footage and splices together the best takes to form a **rough cut**.
2. *Interlock* The **interlock** is the synchronization of sound and picture by means of a special editor's projector. The synchronized film and sound are projected onto a large screen to provide a feeling of what the finished commercial will be like. At this stage, scenes can be substituted and music added or deleted at the discretion of the creative team or client.
3. *Addition of optical effects* The movement from one scene to another in the rough cut and interlock is usually abrupt. Optical effects, such as dissolves, are added to make the transitions between scenes appear smooth. These dissolve effects involve **fades**, whereby one scene fades away and another gradually appears, and **wipes**, whereby one scene pushes the other away. Other options include the use of split-screen techniques or the addition of supers to the film.

4. *Mixed interlock* With the soundtrack and film edited, other audio elements and music can be added in a mixing section. Sound effects dubbed into other elements are called a **mixed interlock**.

5. *Answerprints* In the **answerprint**, film, sound, special effects, and opticals are combined and printed. The answerprint is presented to the client for approval, and duplicates (dupes) are made for distribution to television stations.

Direct-Response Television Advertising

Direct-response television (DRTV) advertising has two distinct formats: the 30-, 60-, and 120-second spot, or the 30-minute infomercial. An **infomercial** presents in more detail the benefits of a product or service and encourages immediate action through the use of toll-free telephone numbers. Some of the more common infomercials are for health-oriented products (e.g., exercise videotapes and workout equipment) and financial-planning products. The shorter direct-response commercials are commonly used to promote small kitchen appliances and music offers. The objective of a direct-response commercial is to initiate immediate action by the customer.

Mainstream advertisers are recognizing the benefits of direct-response advertising. Companies and brands including Ford, Procter & Gamble, Rogers, Bell, Apple, and Royal Bank have entered the direct-response arena. Time has proven that the consumer will no longer be swayed to a brand solely because of the image portrayed in a linear 30-second television spot. By allowing the consumer to interact with the brand through toll-free numbers and other means, a closer relationship develops. The customer is one step closer to the purchase decision.

Planning and implementing a direct-response commercial is very different from a 30-second brand awareness/image campaign. Typically, there is much more time to spend on the message. Successful direct-response commercials incorporate a strong offer that gives the viewer a reason to call. Stressing a sense of urgency, offering a discount, or providing free information or a bonus incentive such as a gift are some techniques that help create action. The following are some proven creative techniques used in infomercials.[9]

- Always focus on the product. Extol it, praise it, and sell it.

- Include a strong offer—one that is clear, compelling, and simple. The stronger the offer, the greater the response will be.

- Clearly demonstrate the product in a convincing manner, and establish and maintain credibility by using testimonials, research statistics, and judicious use of the brand name.

- Consider a magical transformation, that is, show the need and how it is easily fulfilled. This is similar to the problem-solution technique used in other forms of television advertising.

- Use an appropriate tone and style to communicate the message. The infomercial must consider the brand's image. For example, the tone and style of a Ford F-150 infomercial will be very different from one for the Bowflex Home Gym.

- Longer is better. Sixty-second spots outperform thirty-second spots, which makes them a better investment. The additional time allows for a more thorough sales presentation.

- More is better. You must convey as much information as possible to elicit a response. DRTV works by building a comprehensive and convincing case for purchase.

Cost must also be considered in the infomercial equation. Infomercials can cost between $100 000 and $500 000 to produce, when one considers the extent of involvement by producers, writers, directors, musicians, studio rental fees, travel costs, the cost of tapes and dubbing, rough-cut and final editing costs, talent fees, and contingency fees.

Radio Advertising

As in television execution, radio execution focuses on the effective use of time and on making the commercial flow from beginning to end. The creative team develops the concept or central theme in script form, which indicates the words to be spoken and provides direction regarding the use of sound effects and music.

CREATIVE CONSIDERATIONS FOR RADIO COMMERCIALS

Radio commercials must grab the listener's attention immediately and hold it until the end. This is a challenging task; listeners tend to tune out quickly if they are not interested. Radio is often listened to when a person is doing something else (e.g., reading, driving, sun-bathing). To command attention, therefore, the ad must be catchy and memorable. Some proven techniques in the creation of radio advertising include the following:

1. Mention the advertiser's name often. Many practitioners suggest that the brand or company should be mentioned three times during a 30-second commercial.
2. Be conversational, but use short words and sentences.
3. Centre the message on one significant idea. Variations of the key message should be made repeatedly.
4. Use sound effects to create a visual image. Radio advertising, to be effective, must activate listeners' imaginations.
5. Make the tone of the radio commercial positive, cheerful, and upbeat.

Figure 6.20 includes two examples of a radio script. In each script, the creative team has used a combination of humour and sound effects to catch the imagination of the listener. Read each script and visualize the situation—you may even laugh! If you do, you will know it will be an effective radio ad.

TYPES OF RADIO COMMERCIALS

Generally, radio commercials can be divided into four categories: musical commercials, slice-of-life commercials, straight announcements, and personality announcements.

MUSICAL COMMERCIALS For commercials in which music plays a major role, there are several ways of "deploying" music: a commercial may be all music, as in the case of many soft drink ads; music jingles may be interspersed with spoken words; or orchestral arrangements can be used.

SLICE-OF-LIFE COMMERCIALS Much like a television commercial, a slice-of-life situation involves the presentation of a problem and then of product benefits that will resolve the problem. Effective use of listeners' imaginations enhances slice-of-life commercials.

Advertiser: *Playland Amusement Park*
Agency: *Rethink, Vancouver*

SCRIPT 1

"Father, Son"

SFX:	Amusement park sounds.
Son:	I don't know about that ride, Dad. I'm kinda scared.
Dad:	Son, sometimes we do things in life because they scare us. That's how you grow as a person. It's not easy. But in the end, it's worth it. Now whatta you say?
Son:	(*sucking it up*) All right, Dad. I'll do it.
Dad:	Atta boy.
SFX:	Safety bar being snapped shut on the ride.
Son:	Aren't you getting on with me?
Dad:	(*laughs*) What, are you nuts? Have you seen how fast this thing goes?
SFX:	Ride starting up.
Son:	(*terrified*) Daddy?
Dad:	Don't "Daddy" me, you picked it.
Son:	(*screaming*) Daddy!
Announcer:	Playland. Now open weekends.

SCRIPT 2

"Scream"

SFX:	Rollercoaster going up incline at beginning of ride.
Man:	Whoa, this is going to be great.
Woman:	Yeah! This thing goes really high, doesn't it?
Man:	If you're scared, just hang on to me.
Woman:	Oh-h-h-h.
Man:	Here we go!
SFX:	Rollercoaster rushing down first slope. We immediately hear high-pitched, blood-curdling, girlie screaming that lasts throughout the ride. Every curve and every swoop, the scream gets louder. As we hear the ride slow down and come to an end, the hysterical screaming continues.
Woman:	Honey! Snap out of it! It's embarrassing.
Man:	(*man's screams come to an end*) Oh, sorry.
Announcer:	Playland. Now open daily. Admission includes unlimited access to 25 rides.

FIGURE 6.20

A radio script that includes conversation, sound effects, and a voice-over

These ads are part of a campaign that won the Gold Award in the Radio Campaign classification at *Marketing* magazine's 2003 Marketing Awards.

Courtesy of RETHINK.

STRAIGHT ANNOUNCEMENTS   With these commercials, the message simply states the facts. The message is relatively easy to prepare and deliver. Music may be used in the background.

PERSONALITY ANNOUNCEMENTS   This method differs from the first three alternatives in that the advertiser gives up the control of commercial delivery. In a **personality announcement**, the radio host presents the message using his or her radio personality style. The radio station is provided with a **feature sheet** that outlines the key benefits and the product slogan. The host develops the specific wording for the message. Personality announcements have increased in popularity due to the flexibility they offer. Unlike a pre-recorded commercial, the content of a personality announcement can be changed on short notice.

RADIO ADVERTISING—THE PRODUCTION PROCESS

In the case of a radio commercial, the finished product is a **mixed tape** that contains all of the spoken words, music, and special effects. For radio commercial production that involves a production house, the basic steps in the process are as follows:

1. Once the client has approved the script and the production costs, the commercial producer selects the studio and the casting director.
2. The casting director finds appropriate actors for slice-of-life commercials and the right voices for announcement-type commercials.
3. If music is required, the decision whether to hire a composer or use stock music is made. Decisions regarding the use of special effects are also finalized.
4. The director supervises rehearsals, and several commercial readings are made so that the agency and client have a selection to choose from.
5. Music and sound are recorded separately and mixed to form a *master tape*. From the master tape, *duplicates* or *dubs* are made. The dubs are sent to radio stations for broadcast.

The Internet

The **internet** is a network of computer networks linked together to act as one. It works just like a global mail system in which independent authorities collaborate in moving and delivering information. It is now very common for an organization to establish its own website to communicate with customers and to place ads on third-party sites that are visited by their target market. Internet surfers simply have to click on the ad to access more information.

The average online Canadian spends 30 hours a month surfing the web, so it is a medium to be given worthy consideration by creative planners. With today's high level of broadband penetration it is proving to be an effective medium for brand building, just like television is.[10] As indicated earlier, it is important for digital media creative planners to meet with traditional media creative planners in order to discover the "big idea" that can be used across all media.

There are differences between online communications and traditional media communications. Traditional media are passive by nature while the internet is active by nature. Traditional media target an audience; on the internet, consumers target the content they are interested in, and in the process are exposed to messages that should be of interest. From a creative design perspective, the primary options are banner ads and rich media advertising. Establishing an interactive website is another option, though that is beyond the scope of copywriters and art directors at an advertising agency.

BANNER ADS

The most common form of advertising on the internet is the banner ad. A **banner ad** stretches across the screen in a narrow band, or appears in another shape such as a rectangular box or column down the side of a webpage (this style is known as a skyscraper). The content of the ad is minimal. Its purpose is to stir interest so that the viewer clicks the ad for more information. Once clicked, the viewer sees the ad in its entirety, or accesses additional information from the advertiser's website. The design characteristics of the banner ad are critical since the goal is to encourage clicking. See Figure 6.21 for examples of this kind of ad.

Including features such as animations in a banner ad draws additional attention. Internet users perceive the internet to be a different medium than traditional mass media. When online, people expect to be entertained, and they want to receive information quickly. These behaviours suggest that advertising must also entertain. Some proven techniques in the creation of banner advertising include the following:[11]

1. *Choose words wisely* Due to the limited amount of space, simplicity should be the rule of thumb. Simple phrases such as "Click here" and "Enter here" tend to improve response rates. A call to action is never out of place.

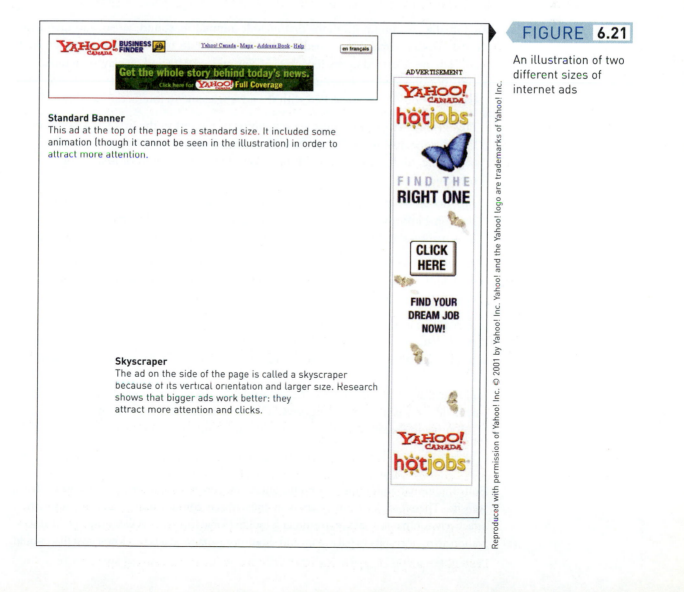

Standard Banner
This ad at the top of the page is a standard size. It included some animation (though it cannot be seen in the illustration) in order to attract more attention.

Skyscraper
The ad on the side of the page is called a skyscraper because of its vertical orientation and larger size. Research shows that bigger ads work better: they attract more attention and clicks.

FIGURE 6.21

An illustration of two different sizes of internet ads

2. *Provide an incentive* Including a free offer boosts response rates 35 percent higher than ads without such offers. If free is out of the question, offer a chance to win something in a contest, such as a car, trip, or T-shirt.

3. *Add some humour* Ads that make a real point in a very humorous way are effective. Perhaps this is an aspect of the entertainment expectations people have of the internet.

4. *Be specific* Because of the small space, conciseness and brevity are good guidelines. Be straightforward and don't make viewers guess your message. The goal should be good strong copy, a clear call to action, and an emphasis on impact over design.

5. *Use colour effectively* Colour has an impact on all forms of advertising. Using bright colours can help attract a viewer's eye, contributing to higher response rates.

6. *Consider animation* Animation (movement) can help attract a user's eye. Strategic use of movement grabs attention and generates more clicks than static banners.

7. *Size matters* Research has proven that bigger is better. The bigger ads get more attention and a higher clickthrough. Therefore, the use of rectangles and skyscrapers is preferable, even though they may cost more.

RICH MEDIA

Rich media are communications that include animation, sound, video, and interactivity. Advertisers perceive rich media ads to be similar to television commercials. Rich media ads are streamed in small packets of compressed data and displayed on the screen as full-motion video. In designing a rich media ad, the copywriter and art director must consider various layers associated with the ad: engagement, interaction, and exit.[12]

- *Engagement* The viewer must see something of interest in the first few seconds or they're gone. Just like a TV ad, the rich media ad must tell a story and include a beginning, middle, and closing. It must have the right amount of image, copy, movement, and sound.

- *Interaction* Once hooked, the viewer is ready to interact. The viewer plays with the ad, gets some information, gives you something of his or hers, and is rewarded. Information should be kept simple and the interaction should be fun and imaginative.

- *Exit* This layer is about reward. You must now fulfill the desire that has been created. Offer a "Click here" or "Submit" button so viewers can get more information or take the desired action. Thank them for doing so.

People naturally look to the internet for information about computers. Therefore, Hewlett-Packard implemented an online branding campaign that included 30- and 60-second video ads. The campaign slogan, "The Computer Is Personal Again," aimed to promote computers as expressions of users' individuality. The online video ads helped build buzz about the ads before they appeared on television. Tracy Trachta, director of worldwide consumer advertising, says, "Online is incredibly powerful in terms of word-of-mouth and is really effective for engaging with our target audience."[13]

WEBSITES

Both traditional and online communications encourage people to visit an organization's website. Therefore, it is important that the website communicate detailed information effectively, for that is what the consumer is looking for at this stage. A website gives the organization an opportunity to tell a story and show more images at a much lower cost than would be the case in other media. Websites play a role in building brand awareness and preference, and provide an opportunity for a company or brand to engage with its target audience.

Consumers like to visit websites for information, and they do so frequently when collecting information about particular products they are interested in purchasing. In general, they want a website to be easy to navigate, offer an enjoyable experience, and provide meaningful information. Preparing material for a website is much different from writing for print or filming for television. Research conducted by Sun Microsystems reveals that 80 percent of users merely scan webpages rather than read them carefully, and that it takes people 25 percent more time to read a given amount of text on a computer screen than on paper.[14] Therefore, a webpage should contain less content and be presented in a manner that can be grasped quickly by the reader.

Here are some tips to improve the design of a website.

1. *Have a focused concept* Many sites have floundered because they simply duplicated information that was available in printed form. Content must be carefully edited to suit the webpage format. Concise, well-organized, and easily read information offers much more to the viewer.

2. *Use an informal writing style* The web is an informative and immediate medium, so users appreciate a lighter style of writing combined with an element of humour. Using a simple sentence structure is very appropriate.

3. *Have a consistent look* A corporate identity is important. Therefore, keep a consistent look and feel throughout the site by using the logo, graphics, and colours of the company's corporate identity. For example, a viewer would expect to see red at the Coca-Cola website.

4. *Limit the use of graphics* People like to navigate a site quickly. Too many full-page graphics take time to download and slows the navigation process considerably. Images must support key selling points, so they should be used wisely.

5. *Keep scrolling simple* Don't force a viewer to scroll across and down a page. A default screen is not that large, so the actual display may not be visible to a large number of viewers. Introduce the site with single screens of information, allowing content to increase in length as the viewer explores deeper.

6. *Clarity of graphics is essential* Don't use small fonts in graphics. Viewers may be visually impaired, so descriptions should always be available for graphics. A site should be tested with different fonts and font sizes.

7. *Pages must be scannable* People do not read word by word; they scan the page, so key information-carrying words should be highlighted. Links to other relevant pages (called hyperlinks) should also be highlighted.

8. *Write to be read* Headings should appear at the top of the page to indicate why the page is important. Lists with simple numbering schemes to highlight points are acceptable, but the points should be listed from most important to least important. Captions should uniquely identify illustrations or visual images.

9. *Plan for expansion* A site may start at a modest 20 pages in length, but could grow into hundreds of pages. Begin with an organizational system that allows for easy updates and logical growth. The web is a fluid medium; pages must be updated often as time passes to reflect change.

Web design is a combination of design features and emotional experiences. Good content clearly presented is the most important factor that leads to repeat visits.

More specific information on the strategic implications of interactive media and internet advertising is presented in Chapter 12.

SUMMARY

Numerous tools are employed to penetrate the customer's perceptual barriers. For example, the copywriter is responsible for the headline, body copy, and signature, and the art director is responsible for the illustration; the two join forces to create a complete message—an impression on the customer. In print advertising, the impression is affected by variables such as balance, unity, flow, use of colour and size, white space, clarity and simplicity, and use of artwork or photography in illustrations. Art directors also consider layout alternatives for delivering the message. Among the layouts commonly used are the poster, vertical split, horizontal split, multiple illustration, long copy, and insert layout.

Other print media have unique creative considerations. Out-of-home messages (outdoor posters, transit ads, and point-of-purchase ads) must be simple in design and use bold colours. In these media, strong visual imagery works to the advertiser's advantage. Point-of-purchase advertising must be brief, but also convincing enough to promote impulse purchasing. Transit ads have a more captive audience (often idle), and, therefore, their messages can be more detailed. In the case of direct-response advertising, the advertiser must grab the customers' attention quickly and use specific techniques that will hold their interest and encourage them to take the desired action.

For television commercials, the element of flow is the critical creative consideration. Variables such as integration of audio and video, the use of music and special effects, and the pace of the commercial are also significant in that they, too, have an impact on the viewer. In commercial production there are four stages: obtaining cost estimates, pre-production, production, and post-production.

Radio commercials are also concerned with flow. Effective commercials tend to be positive and upbeat in tone, conversational in nature, and focused on one central idea. Radio ads that involve the listener's imagination have proven to be successful. The production process is very similar to that of television.

Online advertising presents unique challenges for creatives. The most common form of internet advertising is the banner ad. If banner ads are employed they must be clear and concise and include a call to action. Rich media ads must be engaging and interactive and tell a story much like a television commercial would. Website designs must be concise, have a consistent look, offer a simple scrolling procedure, and include fonts of an appropriate size for good readability.

KEY TERMS

REVIEW QUESTIONS

1. Identify the basic elements of a typical print advertisement, and describe the primary purpose of each.

2. Briefly describe the various types of headlines.

3. What are the stages in the design of a print layout? Briefly describe each stage.

4. What are the factors affecting the design and layout of print advertising? Briefly discuss the influence of each.

5. Distinguish between the following:

    a) balance versus unity (print advertising)
    b) vertical split versus horizontal split (print advertising)
    c) poster versus long copy (print advertising)
    d) unity versus pace (television advertising)
    e) live action versus animation (television advertising)
    f) rough cut versus interlock versus answerprint (television advertising)
    g) engagement versus interactive (online rich media)

6. What are the design characteristics of an effective outdoor ad?

7. What are the four *I*'s of point-of-purchase advertising? Briefly explain each one.

8. In direct-mail advertising, what copy and design characteristics are critical to success?

9. What are the various sections of a television commercial? Explain the role of each section.

10. In television advertising, what does "format" mean? Briefly explain.

11. Identify and briefly explain each stage in the television production process.

12. Identify and briefly explain some of the proven techniques for producing effective infomercials.

13. What are the different types of radio advertising?

14. Identify and briefly explain any two copy and design elements for creating better banner ads.

DISCUSSION QUESTIONS

1. Read the Advertising in Action vignette **Attention, Interest, Action!** Select a few of the advertisements included in the chapter and assess their potential effectiveness in light of the rules of thumb presented in the vignette.

2. Scan a magazine of your choosing and select an ad that you think is effective and one that is ineffective. Evaluate the impact of each ad based on some of the layout and design principles discussed in this chapter.

3. "Tell more, sell more." Discuss this statement in the context of print advertising (or web-based advertising).

4. Assess the role and effectiveness of the internet for advertising purposes. How important will the internet be in future advertising strategies? What is your opinion?

5. Visit a website of your choice. Analyze the site based on the design elements for websites included in this chapter.

NOTES

1. David Ogilvy, *Ogilvy on Advertising* (Toronto: John Wiley & Sons Ltd., 1983), p. 139.

2. "Design, colour & size," from *Marketing Tips*, December 15, 1997, p. 2, a *Marketing* publication.

3. *Ibid.*

4. Laboratory of Advertising Performance, reported by Jo Marney, "Sizing up ads: Bigger is better," *Marketing*, n.d.

5. Jo Marney, "Posters turn all heads," *Marketing*, September 8, 1996, p. 30.

6. Keith McArthur, "TV ads try to zip past the zap," *Globe and Mail*, June 6, 2005, pp. A1, A8.

7. James Careless, "Where's the price tag?" *Marketing*, January 31, 2000, p. 15.

8. Susan Heinrich, "Tuning up the pitch," *Financial Post*, July 30, 2001, p. C4.

9. Ian French, "Trick of the trade," *Marketing*, August 20, 2001, p. 18.

10. Mike Sharma, "If not online, where are you?" *Marketing*, June 5, 2006, p. 20.

11. Jim Sterne, *What Makes People Click: Advertising on the Web* (Que Corporation: Indianapolis, IN, 1997), pp. 283–295.

12. Dorian Sweet, "The rich media ad: A thing of beauty," *ClickZ*, March 18, 2005, **www.clickz.com**.

13. Wendy Davis, "HP breaks video ads online," *Media Post*, July 13, 2006, **www.mediapost.com**.

14. "Writing for the web," Sun Microsystems Inc., **www.sun.com**.

Creative Strategy and Execution:
FEAR WORKS FOR VOLKSWAGEN

Advertising agencies often get a request from their clients along the lines of the following: "Develop an advertising campaign that will break through the clutter and firmly position my brand in the customer's mind."

Well, some advertising does break through the clutter. And it is the brilliant work of copywriters and art directors, along with a willingness among clients to take risks, that sets advertising campaigns apart.

Various appeal techniques have been presented in Part 2 of this textbook. Very often the appeal technique is the key ingredient that makes a campaign a success. For example, in the automobile market, it is very common to show beautiful people doing wonderful things or going to great places driving a shiny new automobile. The ads are always very upbeat and positive, but they all seem to blend together after a while.

To shake things up, and to break through the clutter, Volkswagen went in a new direction, or rather an opposite direction, when launching the 2007 Jetta. The objective of the new campaign was to position the Jetta as one of the safest vehicles on the market. In the bigger picture, Volkswagen was attempting to position itself as a safe vehicle in an automotive market populated by many safe brands—Volvo and Honda rate very highly in this regard, to mention only two other brands.

In a television commercial titled "Like," things start rather harmlessly. A driver and a passenger are chatting as they travel down the road. The passenger is pointing out to the driver that he uses too many "likes" in his sentences—an annoying habit. Then, in a split second, the calm of the situation is shattered as another vehicle appears out of nowhere. There is a sickening "whack" and then dead silence. Heads mash into airbags and passengers are stunned, as the Jetta rests bent and mangled. The ad ends with the slogan "Safe happens." The intensity of the commercials is quite shocking!

While other brands promote safety, they usually don't show how the safety features actually work. In sharp contrast, the Volkswagen ads really push the envelope by using fear to position the Jetta as a premium safety product at an affordable price. Volkswagen wanted advertising that was realistic and convincing—mission accomplished! Some viewers actually inquired if anyone was hurt during the filming of the commercials.

Research seems to validate Volkswagen's move in this direction. J.D. Power and Associates finds that what people want most is to be kept free of harm on the road. Among safety features people want, side-impact airbags rank first, followed by run-flat tires and stability control. These features are hard to demonstrate in advertising, but Volkswagen found a way to do it. Volkswagen is gambling that its audience will not be turned off by the brashness of its advertising, and defends the honesty of its ads. The Jetta will protect passengers in real-world situations. Refer to the illustration in Figure 1.

Dove Changes the Definition of Beauty

One of the most talked-about campaigns in recent years is Dove's "Campaign for Real Beauty." While most personal care and grooming products promote the stereotypical image of beauty (i.e., the perfect shape and size), Dove chose to do things differently. Instead of images of long locks, longer legs, and incredibly lean bodies, Dove promoted its message of "real beauty" by encouraging women to celebrate themselves as they are—while using Dove products, of course!

When the campaign first broke in 2004, outdoor boards quickly delivered the new message in a very effective manner. Ads created by Ogilvy & Mather's Toronto, New York, and London offices got women thinking about the traditionally narrow definition of beauty. The models in the ads showed a bald fitness

FIGURE   1

Courtesy of Dick Hemingway.

trainer, a 95-year-old wrinkled woman, a freckled red-head, and asked the question: Just what is real beauty?

What's the motivation behind this campaign? Comments from Erin Iles, master brand marketing manager for Dove Canada, helps explain things. "As we look to build this beauty brand, we really want to be an agent of change in our society and in our culture. We have looked at research data and it has become startlingly obvious that women are asking for a different view of beauty." The study found that 68 percent of women around the world strongly agree that advertisers are presenting an image of beauty that is unattainable. Dove wants women to know that beauty is within reach for them and is something that they can celebrate. The new campaign reflects a long-term philosophy for all Dove brands.

From a creative perspective, the images used in the advertising reassure women who might be self-conscious about their bodies. Candid and confident images of curvy, full-bodied, real women reflect the new definition of beauty. To see real women of all shapes and sizes represented in such an honest way makes for bold and compelling advertising. It says women are attractive no matter what their weight or skin colour. See the illustration in Figure 2.

Lynn Fletcher, chief strategic officer of Arnold Worldwide Canada, likes what she sees in the Dove campaign: "It does a couple of things: it's more about marketing with people than at people. They seem to understand that what is needed is engagement more than attention."

The campaign goes well beyond advertising, and invites women to share their views with women around the world through interactive communications, a dedicated website (www.campaignforrealbeauty.ca), billboards, magazine ads, and events.

Has the campaign worked? The brand continues to excel in its role as marketer-turned–social activist, while never losing sight of its core business. The love-your-beauty attitude has worked well with new brand extensions that include facial moisturizers and hair products. The Dove Self Esteem fund was launched to provide support for organizations that aim to broaden the definition of beauty. Women now seem much more connected to the brand. They are starting to see that Dove is working toward social change. According to Mark Wakefield, marketing director for Dove Canada, "Brand recognition has never been stronger. In fact 90 percent of women respondents in a survey recognize the Dove blue bird symbol. The brand is experiencing double-digit growth in every new category it has entered. The plan is to evolve the campaign by listening to what women are asking of us."

FIGURE 2

Source: Adapted from Jeremy Cato, "Fear is a powerful motivator," *Globe and Mail*, October 19, 2006, p. G16; Rebecca Harris, "Keeping it real," *Marketing*, November 8, 2004, p. 10; Theresa Howard, "Ad campaigns to tell women to celebrate who they are," *USA Today*, July 7, 2005, www.usatoday.com; and "Brand beautiful," *Strategy*, November 2005.

PART 4

Communicating the Message:
PLANNING MESSAGE PLACEMENT

Part 2 established the relationships between marketing planning and marketing communications planning. Part 3 described the creative planning process. Part 4 describes the media planning process and discusses each of the major media alternatives in detail.

Media planning involves identifying media objectives, strategies, and execution. Decisions in each area depend largely on budgets. Chapter 7 discusses media objectives and media strategies, along with budgetary issues. In Chapter 8, the print media are examined in detail, followed by broadcast media in Chapter 9.

Chapter 10 is devoted to out-of-home media. Planning and buying media time and space varies from one medium to another. The unique considerations for the various media are presented in the appropriate chapters.

Chapter 11 examines the growing field of direct-response communications, while Chapter 12 discusses the increasing role of online and other forms of interactive communications. These media are attracting a lot of attention and media dollars, as advertisers see the benefits of technology-driven communications.

CHAPTER **7**

Media Planning Essentials

After studying this chapter, you will be able to

1. Assess the roles and responsibilities of both client and agency in media planning

2. Differentiate among media objectives, media strategies, and media execution

3. Utilize terminology used in media planning

4. Describe the steps involved in the media selection process

5. Identify the factors affecting the size of an advertising budget

6. Describe the methods of determining the size of an advertising budget

The process of developing a media plan is very complex. The task of an agency's media planners is to reach the desired target market efficiently. Efficiency in media planning can be loosely defined as "gaining maximum impact or exposure at minimum cost to the client." The assignment is complicated by variables such as media reach information, the ways in which competitors utilize the media, and consumers' media habits. Technology and on-demand media consumption patterns exercised by consumers are changing the way planners look at the various media alternatives. In addition, the agency must develop and execute a plan that meets stated expectations within certain financial parameters.

Essentially, input from the client to the agency becomes the foundation of the media plan. The direction a media plan takes is largely based on the guidelines provided by the client's marketing plan. It is important to realize that the media plan is a subset of a broader marketing communications plan. Therefore, media strategies must be coordinated with other communications and marketing activities.

Media Planning Process

Media carry a brand's selling message to a predetermined target market. The selling success of any advertising campaign, therefore, depends on the effectiveness of the media plan. **Media planning** involves developing a plan of action for communicating messages to the right people (the target market), at the right time, and with the right frequency.

The emergence of various digital media has complicated the media planning process, and for a time media planners found it difficult to integrate digital media plans with traditional media plans. Certainly, media planners felt more comfortable recommending media they and their clients were more familiar with. The situation has now changed. The internet is now a fairly standard component of a media plan, and agencies are examining how to better integrate mobile communications devices such as cell phones and personal music/video players into the mix.

How and where people use and consume media is now a very important factor driving the direction of a media plan. People are more mobile now, and they take their media devices with them (cell phones and music/video players). They are also described as "multi-taskers"—they use several different media simultaneously—so it is more difficult to determine which medium, or combination of media, is best suited to deliver the advertising message.

With media such as television, radio, magazines, newspapers, and outdoor, the strategic emphasis has always been on reach and frequency—how many people receive the message and how often they receive it. It was the advertiser who controlled the timing of people's exposure to the message. With digital media it is more about consumer involvement; it is the consumer who controls when he or she sees the message. For example, television shows, news, and sports reports are available online, for a fee (or free if the user accepts the ads accompanying the show), which means consumers receive the message whenever they want to; it's random rather than pre-determined.

The digital media (internet, cell phones, and portable music players) are part of the consumer's lifestyle—they have become essential tools that people interact with on a daily basis. Therefore, rather than stressing reach and frequency, digital media strategy focuses on timing and engagement. In the context of advertising, **engagement** refers to how involved an individual is with the media when the advertising message is delivered—the higher the degree of involvement the greater the likelihood of the message being noticed.

Both the creative plan and the media plan must flow from the marketing plan, and they are designed to work together to help achieve the overall advertising objectives. Both client and ad agency play a role in the media planning process. The client provides the agency's media personnel with background information, along with some basic direction for the media plan based on past experience and their knowledge of the target audience.

Information typically provided to the agency is carefully outlined in a document called a **media brief**. The media brief includes some or all of the following information: a market profile, a product media profile, a competitor media profile, a target-market profile (which includes media consumption habits), media objectives, and media budget. Figure 7.1 illustrates a schematic diagram of the media planning process.

As discussed in Chapter 5, it is now common for the client to brief the agency creative team and media team at the same time. Discussing the issues with all parties and inviting all people working on the project to participate in lively discussion allows the message and media strategies to evolve together. The result should be a stronger plan.

MARKET PROFILE

The market profile reviews the market size and growth trends. It also includes current and historical market-share trends, which give the media planner a perspective on what is happening in the market and the level of competition within it.

PRODUCT MEDIA PROFILE

Prior to developing a new media plan, it is wise to review and evaluate past media practices. What media have been used and how effective have they been? A qualitative and quantitative evaluation of the strengths and weaknesses of past media plans provides input for new plans. If little else, such a review should produce strong feelings about what worked and what did not. This information is particularly important if the client is briefing a new ad agency.

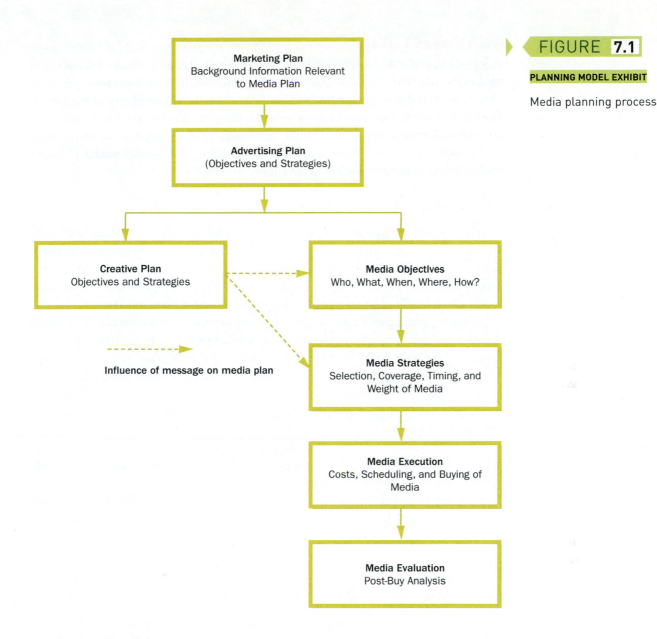

FIGURE 7.1

PLANNING MODEL EXHIBIT

Media planning process

COMPETITORS' MEDIA USAGE

A summary analysis of competitors' media usage and spending trends influences the strategic media direction chosen for the product. For example, what media do the competitors dominate? How much do they spend? Where do they spend it? How does competitive information influence the media direction an advertiser should take?

TARGET-MARKET PROFILE

The marketing plan provides the media planner with a precise definition of the target market. All relevant demographic, psychographic, and geographic information available influences media strategy and execution. Knowing the activities and interests of the target market can enable media planners to choose the best times and places in which to advertise. If information about the target's media consumption is known, it too should be communicated to the agency. For example, the medium the target refers to most, how frequently is it referred to, and how long they refer to it is valuable information. Media consumption habits are changing across all age categories. A general trend away from the mass media toward the digital media must be factored into all media plans today.

MEDIA OBJECTIVES

The provision of a precise description of the target market and a basic description of what the media plan will accomplish is the client's responsibility. Information regarding when, where, and how the message will be delivered is the responsibility of the agency. The intent is not to restrict the agency in its thinking; on the contrary, the detailed consideration of these elements will be the responsibility of the agency media planners. Media objectives set priorities and establish guidelines for agency media planners. Media objectives are discussed in detail later in the chapter.

MEDIA BUDGET

Usually, the amount allocated to the media budget has already been established by the time the client meets with the agency. At an earlier stage (the marketing communications plan), the budget is allocated among activities such as media advertising, sales promotion, and events and sponsorships. The relative size of the budget provides the framework within which media planners must develop strategies and achieve stated goals.

Once the briefing process is completed, the agency media personnel take over. **Media planners** are specialists who put together the detailed media strategies and tactics. They assess all of the input from the client and devise a media strategy and execution plan that will achieve the stated objectives. Media strategy is discussed in detail later in the chapter.

Once the media plan has been approved, **media buyers** purchase the time and space. They interpret the media plan and purchase the best deals available through the various media representatives for the different media vehicles. A media buyer's task is to deliver the maximum amount of impact (against a target audience) at a minimum of cost (client's budget). The sophistication of computers has enhanced the ability of both media planners and buyers to generate more efficient media plans. Once the media plan has been implemented, the agency is responsible for evaluating the plan through a post-buy analysis. A **post-buy analysis** is an analysis of actual audience deliveries calculated after a specific spot or schedule of advertising has run.

The Media Plan

A **media plan** is a document that outlines all relevant details about how a client's budget will be spent: objectives are clearly identified, strategies are carefully rationalized, and execution details are documented with precision.

Since a significant amount of the client's budget is at stake in an advertising campaign, communications between client and agency peak when media plans are presented. Media planners must present and defend their recommendations and be prepared to consider client input. Media plans have been known to undergo numerous revisions prior to final client approval. The structure and content of a media plan is discussed in this section. Refer to Figure 7.2 for a summary of the content.

Media Objectives

Media objectives are clearly worded statements that outline what the media plan should accomplish. Within this framework, media objectives can be subdivided, and more precisely defined statements can be developed in response to questions concerning who, what, where, when, and how. Although answers to some of the above questions are often

Media Budget

- Total Budget Available for Media Advertising

Media Objectives

- Who (target market profile)
- What (nature of message)
- When (best time to reach)
- Where (market priorities)
- How (how many, how often, how long)

Note: Media objectives are usually clear, definitive statements

Media Strategy

- Target Market Strategy (Shotgun, Profile Match, Rifle)
- Reach Considerations
- Frequency Considerations
- Continuity Considerations
- Engagement
- Market Coverage
- Timing
- Media Selection Rationale
- Media Rejection Rationale

Note: Media strategies usually expand upon the objective statements by providing details about how objectives will be achieved.

Media Execution

- Media Cost Summaries
  a. Spending by Media Classification
  b. Spending within Media Classification
  c. Spending by Time of Year
  d. Spending by Region or City
- Blocking Chart
  a. Calendar of Activities
  b. Media Used
  c. Market Coverage
  d. GRPs
  e. Timing

Note: For an applied illustration of these concepts, see the marketing communications plan for Schick Quattro in Appendix II.

FIGURE 7.2

PLANNING MODEL EXHIBIT

Content of a typical media plan

judged to be strategic elements of the media plan, they are intended to provide broad guidelines for more detailed strategic considerations. Refer to Figure 7.3 for an illustration of these questions.

The components of media objective statements are as follows:

- **Who?** Who is the target market? A precise definition of the target market provides the foundation for the media plan. A *target-market profile,* defined in terms of

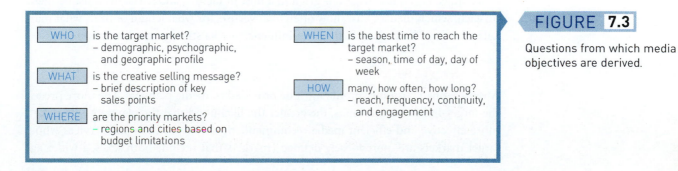

FIGURE 7.3

Questions from which media objectives are derived.

demographics, psychographics, and geographics, is collected, and media planners use it to match the target with a compatible media profile (those who read, listen to, or watch a certain medium). The behaviour of the audience when consuming the media is also a factor to consider when describing the target.

- *What?* What is the message to be communicated? A brief summary of the selling message should be included in the objective statement. Note that the creative strategy may already be complete. The message, and the manner in which it is presented, can have an influence on media selection. Conversely, if media decisions are made first, such decisions could influence the direction of creative strategy and execution. Clients may prioritize differently from one another.

- *Where?* Where are the market priorities? This question is critical, as most advertising campaigns are restricted by the size of the budget. Based on directives from the client regarding which regions or cities have priority, and the media planner's ability to work efficiently with little money, decisions must be made whether to reach a few markets more frequently or to reach more markets less frequently. The issue is how far or how many markets will be reached with the budget that is available.

- *When?* When is the best time to reach the target market? Certain product and target-market characteristics have bearing on this question. For example, the fact that a product is sold on a seasonal basis will directly influence media timing. A heavier media schedule in the pre-usage season may be recommended as a way of building awareness prior to the purchase period of the seasonal product. Knowledge of the customer can also influence the timing of advertising messages. For example, is there a best time of the day, or better days of the week, to reach the target? Information about target audience media consumption is useful when making decisions on when to advertise.

- *How?* How many? How often? How long? How involved? Several questions must be answered here. These questions are strategic considerations regarding reach, frequency, continuity, and engagement. Objective statements on these issues stem from more detailed media strategies. Strategy considerations will be discussed separately in this chapter.

Media Strategy

Similar to other types of planning, media planning deals with the best way to advertise the product or service within the budget guidelines provided. **Media strategy** focuses on how media objectives will be achieved—it results in a recommendation of what media to use, along with supporting rationale detailing why certain media were selected and others rejected. Consideration is given to a host of factors, and decisions must be made on each: which media to use, how often to advertise, for what length of time, what markets to cover. The various factors that influence media strategy are discussed below.

TARGET MARKET

A well-defined customer profile must be provided to media planners. The more precise the target-market definition is, the greater the likelihood that the planners will make a more effective and efficient media recommendation. For products and services whose target markets are more loosely defined (markets that include both sexes, a wider age range, no specific income requirements), the task of selecting the most effective and efficient media is less challenging.

Essentially, the task of the media planner is to match the advertised product's target-market profile with a compatible media profile, such as the readership profile of a magazine or newspaper or the listener profile of a radio station. Theoretically, the more compatible the match, the more efficient the media buy. For example, on the internet, people target the content they are interested in. A sports enthusiast may visit a sports site such as www.tsn.ca frequently to access scores and highlights. If that's your target audience, you place an ad there. Depending on the media planner's knowledge about the target market (such as its characteristics, attitudes, interests, and location), certain matching strategies can be considered.

SHOTGUN STRATEGY   The nature of the word shotgun suggests that the target market for which the **shotgun strategy** is best suited is more general than other target markets. For example, the target may be described as all adults 18 years of age and older. The product or service being advertised has widespread appeal. For target markets that are loosely defined, particularly in terms of demographics, the media selected to advertise the product can be more general in nature.

Members of the television audience watching a popular situation comedy or action/drama show during prime time (8:00 to 11:00 p.m.) will range in age, encompass both sexes, cover the entire range of income groups, and lead all kinds of lifestyles. For advertisers with sizeable media budgets, television is an effective means of reaching such a broad target market. The cost of placing an ad on a top-ranked weekly show like *American Idol* or *CSI* will be in the $65 000–$70 000 range, in Canada. Cable channels with smaller audiences charge much less for a 30-second spot.[1] For advertisers with more limited media budgets, daily newspapers, transit media, and outdoor media can provide good reach at a lower cost.

American Idol
www.americanidol.com

When an organization launches a new product, it may opt for a strategy called roadblocking as a way to maximize reach and frequency. **Roadblocking** involves buying commercial time on all available stations at a fixed time (or approximately the same time) so that viewers can scarcely avoid seeing the commercial. When Bell Canada launched its new branding campaign using the theme "Making it simple®" a few years ago, it aired a special two-minute commercial simultaneously on four networks in Ontario. TD Canada Trust also used a roadblock strategy to unveil its first major branding strategy since the merger of the TD Bank and Canada Trust.[2]

PROFILE-MATCHING STRATEGY   In the case of a **profile-matching strategy**, the customer target market is carefully defined by demographic, psychographic, and geographic variables. When using this strategy, the advertising message is placed in media whose readers, listeners, or viewers have a similar profile to that of the product's target market. The media planner looks for close matches.

Certain media types are characterized as general interest, while others are seen as special interest. Magazines such as *Canadian Living*, *Canadian Business*, and *Canadian Geographic* appeal to a more selective target market, and may be suitable for a profile-matching strategy. *Canadian Living*, for example, appeals to female readers between the ages of 25 and 54 who are college- or university-educated, have a household income between $50 000 and $75 000, and reside in markets of 100 000-plus population. If that is the brand's target-audience profile, then *Canadian Living* would be a wise media selection.[3]

Canadian Business
www.canadianbusiness.com

The same could be said of television programs that appeal specifically to children (e.g., the YTV specialty network offers programs for children and young teens), or sports networks like Rogers Sportsnet and TSN that appeal to a predominantly male audience. Radio is another medium suited to a profile-matching strategy. A radio station's format (e.g., adult cotemporary, rock, soft rock, news, top 40) is designed to appeal to a particular demographic group. Advertisers wanting to reach a certain demographic group will select the appropriate stations in a local market.

Examine the profile presented in Figure 7.4. *Financial Post Business* magazine reaches over one million readers with each issue, two-thirds of them male and one-third of them female. These readers possess high household incomes, and by occupation they are classified as MOPES—managers, owners, professionals, and entrepreneurs. These readers are four times more likely than average to make business purchase decisions valued at $100 000 or more. The readership profile suggests that advertisers who appeal to a target that is more affluent and upscale should consider *Financial Post Business* as an appropriate advertising medium. *Financial Post Business* competes for advertisers with *Canadian Business* and *ROB Magazine*, a publication of the *Globe and Mail*.

Globe and Mail
www.theglobeandmail.com

RIFLE STRATEGY A **rifle strategy** is a matching strategy used in situations where the target market can be precisely defined by some common characteristic, such as employment in a certain industry, having a certain occupation, or having a particular leisure-time interest or hobby. It is the common characteristic that makes this audience a target. In many situations, a specific medium can reach this target market.

An interest in recreational downhill skiing or snowboarding, for example, could be the common characteristic of a group. The demographic profile of such a group could be diverse, but the fact that all members of the group ski or snowboard is important to equipment manufacturers. A specific medium can be used to reach each target group. *Ski Canada* or *Le Ski* would be an appropriate medium to select for a rifle strategy to reach skiers and *Snowboard Canada* could be used to reach snowboarders. To reach business decision-makers employed in the hospitality and tourism business, advertising in a publication such as *Foodservice & Hospitality* would be an option; if the target is trucking industry decision-makers, *Today's Trucking* would be a good option.

A summary of the various target-market matching strategies appears in Figure 7.5.

NATURE OF ADVERTISING MESSAGE

Creative strategy and media strategy should be developed simultaneously for a coordinated effect in the marketplace. However, the nature of the message, determined by the advertiser's needs, often influences the media selection process. If factual details such as technical data and performance ratings must be communicated, print media is a practical option, along with a website on the internet. If an emotional connection between product and target is the objective, then broadcast advertising through television and radio are preferred choices. Online video ads and extended video presentations at a corporate website also generate an emotional response. If a promotion, such as a contest, is part of the advertising campaign, a combination of media could be recommended as the means of achieving a variety of objectives (e.g., television to create awareness, and print, point-of-purchase materials, and a branded website to communicate details on how to enter). If the objective is brand-name awareness among a general cross-section of a population, then outdoor advertising and transit media are good choices.

Each issue of Financial Post Business magazine reaches 1.25 million readers. These readers are highly motivated and receptive to goods and services that help them achieve their goals quickly. The key demographics are:

- 1.25 million adult readers monthly
- Male skew
- Average age 45
- University+ education
- Upper-income households
- Business executives

Total Readers: 1 250 000
Male: 856 000
Female: 349 000

Demographics	Readers	Index
Average Age	45	98
Age 18–24	104 000	67
Age 25–34	222 000	102
Age 35–49	452 000	119
Age 50–64	344 000	119
Age 65+	127 000	61
Own Dwelling	995 000	107
Married	878 000	117
University+	812 000	157
Self-employed—Professional	140 000	229
Owner/Manager/Professional	584 000	212
Executive/Senior Manager	284 000	254
Average Household Income	$94 544	143
Household Income $75 000+	751 000	169
Household Income $100 000	551 000	213
Personal Income $50 000	595 000	229
Personal Income $75 000	288 000	309

Source: Material reprinted with the express permission of "National Post Company, "a CanWest Partnership. *Financial Post Business*, www.financialpostbusiness.com.

FIGURE 7.4

Readership profile of *Financial Post Business* magazine

REACH/FREQUENCY/CONTINUITY

These strategic factors are grouped together because of their interaction in the media planning process.

REACH **Reach** is the total unduplicated audience (individuals or households) potentially exposed one or more times to an advertiser's schedule of messages during a given period (perhaps a week). It is expressed as a percentage of the target population in a geographically defined area (e.g., a television station might reach 30 percent of a metropolitan market). To explain the principle of reach, assume that a message on a particular station was seen by 40 000 households in a geographic area of 100 000 households.

FIGURE 7.5

Key aspects of target-market matching strategies

Shotgun Strategy

Target market covers a wide cross-section of the population; therefore, media options that have a diverse reach are appropriate (e.g., conventional television networks, daily newspapers, outdoor advertising, and transit advertising).

Profile-Matching Strategy

Target market is described by certain demographic, psychographic, and geographic variables. Media options with audience profiles that are a close match are selected (e.g., magazines, radio, business newspapers and journals, and special interest television networks).

Rifle Strategy

Target market precisely defined by a special characteristic such as a hobby, sport, or occupation. Media options that specifically reach the target are selected (e.g., special-interest consumer and business magazines, special-interest cable channels, direct mail, online and interactive communications).

Reach is calculated by the formula

$$\text{Reach} = \frac{\text{Number of households tuned in}}{\text{Number of households in area}}$$

To complete the example,

$$\text{Reach} = \frac{40\ 000 \text{ (tuned in)}}{100\ 000 \text{ (in area)}}$$

$$= 40\%$$

The dynamics of reach apply to all media forms. The only variation is the time frame for which reach is expressed. It may be weekly on television and radio, and monthly in magazines and out-of-home media (outdoor and transit).

FREQUENCY **Frequency** is the average number of times an advertising message has been exposed to a target audience (an individual or a household) over a period of time, usually a week. Reach and frequency variables are considered together in media planning. The media planner must delicately balance reach and frequency objectives within budget guidelines.

In any given market, households receive different numbers of exposures due to their different viewing habits. As a result, media planners think of frequency in terms of average frequency. The terms *frequency* and *average frequency* mean the same thing. Frequency is calculated by dividing the total possible audience by the audience that has been exposed to the message at least once (reach).

Therefore, average frequency is based on the formula

$$\text{Average frequency} = \frac{\text{Total exposures of all households}}{\text{Reach (households)}}$$

To illustrate this formula, let us assume that the total exposure of all households is 180 000, and the total number of households reached in one week is 50 000. The average frequency is as follows:

$$\frac{180\ 000}{50\ 000} = 3.6$$

A common dilemma faced by the media planner is whether to recommend more reach at the expense of frequency, or more frequency with less overall reach. The stage of the product life cycle a brand is in plus the size of the media budget often dictates which variable gets more attention. For example, a new product that has a high awareness objective may place greater emphasis on reach (and frequency, if the budget will accommodate it). A mature product that is trying to defend its position may opt for more frequency directed at a defined target audience.

IMPRESSIONS **Impressions**, or **total exposures**, refers to the total number of commercial occasions or advertisements scheduled, multiplied by the total target audience (households or people) potentially exposed to each occasion. A media plan's impressions are usually referred to as *gross impressions*. You calculate it by multiplying the actual number of people who receive a message (reach) by the number of times they receive it (frequency). To illustrate the concept of impressions, let's assume that a message on a television station reached 100 000 people, and that the message was broadcast three times a week for eight weeks. The calculation for the number of impressions would be

$$\text{Impressions} = \text{Reach} \times \text{Frequency}$$
$$= 100\ 000 \times 3$$
$$= 300\ 000$$

Therefore, over the eight-week schedule, the gross impressions or exposures would be 2 400 000 (300 000 × 8).

GROSS RATING POINTS In television advertising the weight (amount) of advertising in a market is determined by a rating system. Media weight is expressed in terms of gross rating points. **Gross rating points (GRPs)** are an aggregate of total ratings in a schedule, usually in a weekly period, against a predetermined target audience. It is a description of audience delivery without regard to duplication or repeat exposure to the media vehicles, thus the word *gross*. Reach multiplied by frequency results in GRPs.

To explain the principle of GRPs, let us assume that an advertiser buys media time in Toronto at weight level of 200 GRPs. When calculating GRPs, a percentage figure for reach is used. The desired GRP level is achieved by manipulating both variables: reach and frequency. Therefore, if reach is 20 percent, the frequency would have to be 10 to achieve the 200 GRPs (10 × 20). If reach is 25 percent, the frequency would be 8 to achieve 200 GRPs (25 × 8).

To further illustrate this concept (GRPs = Reach × Frequency), let us assume that a message reaches 50 percent of the target households three times in one week. The GRP level would be 150 (50 × 3). If the message reaches 40 percent of the target households with an average frequency of 4.6 per week, the GRP level would be 184 (40 × 4.6).

The reach of a television program is also referred to as a rating. If, for example, *CSI* reaches 30 percent of households with televisions in its weekly time slot, the show has a 30 rating. Therefore, another way calculating GRPs is to multiply a show's rating by the frequency of messages on that show. Here is an illustration:

Audience	Rating	Number of Spots	GRPs
18–49 years	30	2	60
18–49 years	25	3	75
18–49 years	20	2	40
Total		**7**	**175**

In this example, the advertiser scheduled seven spots over the period of a week on shows with various ratings. This resulted in a weight level of 175 GRPs for the week. Typically, an advertiser will vary the weight levels over the duration of the schedule and by geographic market. Markets that are given priority, for whatever marketing reason, will receive higher GRPs than less important markets.

Decisions about reach and frequency are difficult. Traditional wisdom suggests frequency is the more important variable—you have to drive the message home before consumers will take action! But what is the reaction of consumers if they are exposed to the same message too many times? Will it hurt or help the brand? Some media traditionalists believe three ads get awareness, six ads get interest, and nine ads lead to possible action. At 12 ads, the consumer is tuning out the message.[4] Rather than go overboard with unnecessary spending on television, it is more efficient to add a new medium (say newspapers or magazines) to an existing medium if the goal is to maximize reach.

Traditional buying models in the mass media are based on reaching as many "eyeballs" as possible, or the weight of advertising (some combination of reach and frequency). But there is a threshold at which an advertiser starts to turn the consumer off. Some media planners now give more credence to timing and have adopted a media concept referred to as recency. **Recency** is a model that suggests advertising works best by reminding consumers of a product when they are ready to buy.[5] For more insight into the concept of recency, refer to the Advertising in Action vignette **Shattering the Paradigm: How Does Advertising Work?**

CONTINUITY   **Continuity** is the length of time required to ensure that a particular medium affects a target market. A single theme or selling proposition is delivered over that time period. For example, will the schedule be four weeks long, six weeks long, or eight weeks long? Media planners must juggle the reach, frequency, and continuity factors to obtain maximum benefit for the dollars invested in media. Quite often the continuity is the first of these variables to "give way" when budget (that is, lack of budget) becomes a key factor.

Only an exceptional advertiser would purchase media time on an annual basis (52-week schedule). More moderate advertisers tend to stretch dollars over a one-year period by purchasing media time in "flights." **Flighting** refers to the purchase of media time in periodic waves (usually expressed in weeks) separated by periods of inactivity, a tactic that stretches media dollars over an extended period of time. Refer to Figure 7.6 for an illustration of continuous spending versus flighting. A **hiatus** is an inactive period between flights.

ENGAGEMENT   **Engagement** as described earlier refers to the degree of involvement a person has with the media when they are using it. It is a response driven by emotion and is something that happens inside the consumer's mind. The message itself plays a key role in encouraging engagement. The media can also play a role.

ADVERTISING IN ACTION

Shattering the Paradigm: How Does Advertising Work?

The traditional thinking is that advertising does not begin working until perhaps the third exposure. It takes time for the message to penetrate the mind. One model that describes how advertising works is called "AIDA," which stands for *awareness*, *interest*, *desire*, and *action*. Another is the "funnel" model, with the sequence being *awareness*, *knowledge*, *attitudes*, and then *behaviour*.

There is a growing body of evidence suggesting that advertising can first influence behaviour, with attitudinal changes following, not the other way around. The traditional view of how advertising works is that media planning assumes there is no value to the initial two exposures. The emphasis is on ensuring a certain minimum frequency, namely three or more exposures, within a given time frame.

Research conducted by John Philip Jones of Syracuse University (U.S.) and Colin McDonald of McDonald Research (U.K.) indicates that the initial exposure is more powerful in influencing behaviour than subsequent ones. If so, the implications to strategic media planning are profound, with the emphasis shifting to reach, while minimizing excessive frequency.

This new approach has come to be known as recency. Canadian media expert Lowell Lunden of LLunden & Associates Limited, Strategic Media Explorers, defines recency as "the delivery of media messages in a way that maximizes the likelihood of reaching the most people at a time close to when a purchase decision will be made." Recency might be described as "Just-In-Time Communications™."

Success is based on the finding that if recency is properly executed with creative that works, a single impression can influence behaviour if it is delivered at the right time. Lunden has done in-field Test vs. Control experiments in Canada, demonstrating the success of different ways of implementing recency.

While the goal of advertising should be to build a brand's power in the long term, Lunden believes it is irresponsible for advertisers to accept a continued lack of measured success in the short term and to simply continue spending behind the same creative. Powerful creative tends to be memorable, linked to the brand, relevant, fresh/current/unpredictable, and likeable. The problem is that too often advertising does not work. "Half of my advertising is wasted," it is said, "I just don't know which half." There is more truth to this than people realize.

Misinterpretations of how recency can be effectively implemented are common. The biggest risk is spreading advertising too thinly, running more duration but below some threshold level. Another risk that advertisers must minimize is wearout of creative. Executing recency can help minimize commercial wearout. The challenge is to cost-effectively produce different executions of creative, including multimedia, to help maintain high attention levels.

When implemented and measured properly, recency can help in building more powerful advertising. But the success of any advertising effort is dependent on having creative that works, and on media executed with individual brand objectives and the competitive environment in mind.

Source: This vignette was prepared by Lowell Lunden, president and chief learning officer, LLunden & Associates Limited, Strategic Media Explorers™, www.recency.ca or www.jitcommunications.com.

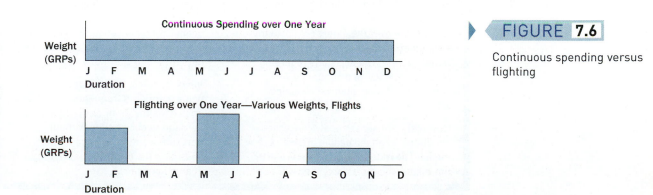

> FIGURE **7.6**

Continuous spending versus flighting

In a fragmented media universe (so much choice for consumers) media planners struggle to find ways of engaging consumers with advertising messages. People get distracted easily, or they multi-task while viewing a particular medium. For example, a television viewer may avoid commercials by channel surfing during commercial breaks. In contrast, an internet user, intent on what he or she is doing, could be more involved, and consequently will take more notice of advertising messages. A magazine reader may spend 30 minutes of uninterrupted time with their favourite magazine—that's engagement! The level of potential engagement does vary from one medium to another.

From a strategic viewpoint, creative planners and media planners know online and mobile communications must be entertaining, otherwise consumers will reject the message. The goal, therefore, is to get the consumer to interact with the message. Pepsi-Cola encouraged engagement in a recent promotion campaign that offered consumers customized ring tones for cell phones, which could be downloaded from the internet with codes found under soft drink bottle caps. Pepsi believes that whenever the phone rings, the consumer will link the tone to Pepsi-Cola. "That engagement with Pepsi and that depth of brand experience is far superior to a quick passing message like a TV commercial," says Dawn Hudson, president and CEO of Pepsi-Cola North America.[6]

Engagement is another strategic factor to consider. By selecting media that engage consumers with advertising messages, the advertiser is starting to develop a relationship with the consumer, a relationship that can thrive if planned properly. For this reason many advertisers are directing their advertising dollars toward the internet. These advertisers perceive the internet to be more engaging than the media they are more accustomed to using.

For a summary of issues relating to engagement, reach, frequency, and continuity, refer to Figure 7.7.

FIGURE 7.7

Some key issues related to engagement, reach, frequency, and continuity

Engagement	The degree of involvement an individual has with a medium when consuming it
Reach	The total audience exposed one or more times to a message in a given period
Frequency	The average number of times a message has been exposed to a target audience over a period of time, usually a week
Continuity	The length of time required to ensure a particular medium affects a target market

Are these strategic variables equally important or does any one variable take precedence over the others? Prior to the advent of the internet, media planners would wrestle with decisions regarding reach, frequency, and continuity. Any plan that included all three variables would be a costly plan.

Now planners are seriously concerned about how engaged people are with the media. The more engaged they are with the media, the more likely they will be engaged with advertising messages. Therefore, planners must find the right media to engage consumers and then focus on strategic issues such as reach, frequency, and continuity.

One of the most difficult decisions for a media planner is frequency. How many times does the planner schedule a message to elicit action without overexposing the audience to the message? Too much exposure can turn off an audience.

FLEXIBILITY **Flexibility** is the ability to modify media spending plans throughout the period that advertising is scheduled. Flexibility is not a variable that influences the media selection process. It is, however, important from the client's viewpoint, since rapidly changing conditions in the marketplace or within the company may require that media tactics be changed on short notice. For example, what happens when a client is forced to cut the budget in the midst of a media campaign? Can they cancel some of the media time or space? Cancellation policies must be known prior to committing to a plan.

The various media stipulate lead times required for notification of cancellation. For example, local television stations allow cancellations on four weeks' written notice. However, the booking must run a minimum of four consecutive weeks. A media plan is, after all, exactly that: a "plan." During the year, reality sets in; that is, profit objectives of a short-term nature begin to look better than advertising objectives of a long-term nature.

Conversely, an advertiser may decide to purchase additional media. Competitive activity might dictate heavier-than-planned spending in a certain market. Often media time is sold well in advance of either air date or publication date, but the advertiser should be aware of the options that are available on short notice.

MARKET COVERAGE

Market coverage or **coverage** refers to the identity and number of markets in which advertising occurs over the course of the media plan's execution. Several coverage options are available to the advertiser. Market selection is often based on factors such as the level of distribution in a market (i.e., the availability of the product or service) and the importance of an area in terms of the sales volume generated there. An additional factor affecting market choice comes into play when an advertiser decides either to correct a problem or to pursue an opportunity through advertising. In either situation, the result is a disproportionate increase in media spending in the area of concern. Assuming there is an overall ceiling on spending, such a move involves a decrease of advertising in another region. Several market coverage plans are available to an advertiser.

NATIONAL COVERAGE National coverage requires media coverage wherever the product is available. Assuming that a product is widely distributed, the advertiser can select media that have national scope. Network television and national magazines are obvious choices. If urgency is a criterion in the decision-making process (as it usually is when launching a new product or reacting to competitive activity), newspapers in major metropolitan areas, which provide national coverage, are excellent vehicles to use. As well, online communications reach people anywhere, anytime—a kind of 24/7 medium.

REGIONAL COVERAGE If an advertiser chooses to advertise regionally there must be an equitable system of allocation so that all regions benefit from advertising. All regions do not require the same level of advertising weight; competitive advertising and promotion factors vary among regions, and this variance affects regional allocations and causes either upward or downward adjustments.

Assuming that Canada is divided geographically into five regions and that the regional sales volume importance (the contribution to total volume) as shown on the next page is accurate, an advertiser would allocate $1 million in media dollars according to the chart below. Each region is treated fairly.

Geographic Regions	Regional Volume Importance (%)	Media Budget ($)
Atlantic	8	80 000
Quebec	28	280 000
Ontario	40	400 000
Prairies	12	120 000
British Columbia	12	120 000
Canada	100	1 000 000

Another way of allocating a budget to various regions is based on a brand development index. A **brand development index (BDI)** is a percentage of a brand's sales in a region in relation to the population of the region. For example, if a brand's sales in Ontario represent 34 percent of total sales but Ontario accounts for 39 percent of the total population, the BDI for the region would be 87.2 (34 divided by 39, multiplied by 100). This indicates that the brand is underdeveloped in Ontario. Therefore, if media advertising is a key influencer on purchase behaviour, additional media dollars may be needed there to correct the situation. Conversely, an overdeveloped region may require less advertising dollars.

When funds are being allocated and media are being purchased on a regional basis, media such as regional television networks, selective spot television, radio, regional editions of magazines, and newspapers are attractive alternatives.

KEY MARKET PLAN   A **key market plan** is a media plan according to which time and space are purchased in urban markets that have been identified as priorities. Providing coverage only in key markets is often considered an option when budget constraints do not allow for much flexibility. In this situation, the advertiser uses a predetermined system to prioritize its key markets.

To illustrate, let us assume that a product had reasonably good national distribution, but only enough funds to advertise in a selective list of markets. We know that Canada's population is largely urban (close to 80 percent of people live in or near an urban area). Therefore, urban areas could be ranked based on population. The top 10 cities in Canada, ranked by population, account for 51 percent of the total population (see table on next page).[7] Advertising in those cities alone could have positive impact on a brand's sales nationally.

The media planner would plan for adequate levels of reach, frequency, and continuity in all cities in which media advertising is recommended. Media time and space would be purchased from local-market television stations, daily newspapers, radio stations, and outdoor and transit advertising suppliers.

While this system appears equitable, at least in the example, some cities and areas may never receive advertising support. Such decisions often create conflict between marketing/advertising managers and regional sales managers, who argue that they are short-changed in the media allocation process. The illustration, for example, does not include any city in the Atlantic region or several larger cities in Southern Ontario.

SELECTIVE COVERAGE PLAN   In contrast to other market coverage plans, a selective plan does not consider factors such as level of distribution, population by area, or geographic product development. Instead, it attempts to reach a desired target market regardless of geographic location. Advertisers use a **selective coverage plan** with a *rifle* media strategy when a target market can be narrowly defined by a common characteristic.

Markets	Population (000)	Canadian Total (%)
Toronto	5 203	16.1
Montreal	3 607	11.2
Vancouver	2 160	6.7
Ottawa-Hull	1 142	3.5
Calgary	1 037	3.2
Edmonton	1 001	3.1
Quebec City	711	2.2
Hamilton	710	2.2
Winnipeg	702	2.2
London	445	1.4
Total	16 734	51.8

Source: Population data contained in the *Canadian Communications Pocket Book*, 2006/07, pp. 25, 27.

A selective coverage plan works because of the nature of the advertised product, the common characteristic of the target market, and the availability of a specialized medium. For example, *Photo Life* magazine would be an advertising vehicle appropriate for reaching a photography enthusiast, and *Golf Canada* would effectively reach people interested in golf. Direct-mail advertising remains a popular medium since organizations can develop unique offers for unique customers based on information contained in database management systems. Since customers chase after content they are interested in on the internet, the advertiser must follow the interests of its target audience and place ads on appropriate sites. Almost certainly, the photography buff mentioned above visits websites dedicated to photography.

Golf Canada
www.golfcanada.com

BEST TIME TO REACH TARGET

Media strategy must consider the best time to reach the intended target market. The best time could refer to the best time of year, the best season, the best time of day, or the best day of the week. As mentioned earlier, placing an ad at the right time with the right message (the concept of recency) is a combination recommended by many media planners. But there are other considerations.

If a new product is to be launched into the market, should the advertiser intensify reach and frequency initially, or gradually build intensity over a longer period? These questions are addressed when decisions about scheduling media are being made. In most cases, the advertiser works within budget restrictions, so the money available must be allocated at optimal time periods during the media plan cycle. For example, there may be periods of the year when advertising is heavy, light, or non-existent. Several scheduling options are available to advertisers. Refer to Figure 7.8 for a diagrammatic representation of each.

EVEN SCHEDULE According to the **even schedule**, media time and space are purchased in a uniform manner over a designated period. This schedule is usually a practical option for the largest of advertisers, which need to advertise on a steady basis, perhaps due to competitive factors. However, advertisers should be cautious about such a spending approach. Consistent levels of advertising for extended periods can be wasteful. The goal is to spend at a level necessary to achieve the desired action. An even

FIGURE 7.8

Media scheduling options

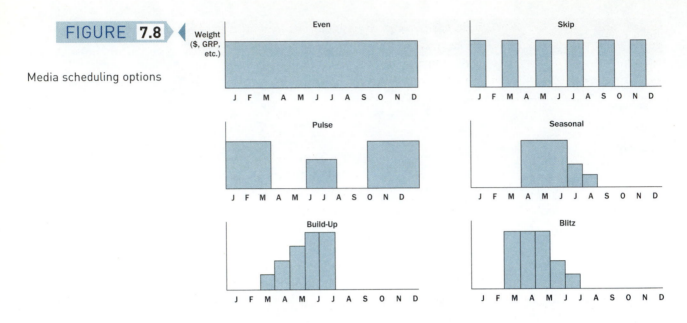

spending pattern is not very common, but it does serve as a basis for comparison with the other alternatives.

SKIP SCHEDULE   In a **skip schedule**, media time and space are purchased on an alternating basis—every other week or month. In terms of media usage, skip can refer to alternating media—magazines one month, television another month. A skip schedule stretches media dollars over an extended period while maintaining the effect of advertising in the marketplace.

PULSE SCHEDULE   **Pulsing** refers to the grouping of advertisements (spending of media dollars) in flights over a predetermined length of time. Flights, as mentioned earlier, are the periodic waves of time in which the product or service is advertised. In this case, a flight would be followed by a hiatus in a continuous cycle throughout the year. The grouping of advertisements in flights contributes to the synergistic effect desired. In any particular flight, the weight of the advertising (reach and frequency) and the duration of the advertising (continuity) can be different. The result resembles a pulsing action when shown on a schedule.

SEASONAL SCHEDULE   A **seasonal schedule** is used for products that are sold and purchased at traditional times of the year. Media advertising is usually heavy in the pre-season and then tapers off in the purchase season. Sun-related products such as lotions and sun blocks start advertising in late May and June (the pre-season) to create the necessary awareness levels for July and August (the peak buying season). Retirement savings plans are advertised heavily in January and February—the deadline for contributions is usually the end of February.

BUILD-UP SCHEDULE   A **build-up schedule** is characterized by low initial media weight, often due to selective use of media, which gradually builds to an intensive campaign in subsequent time periods, with an increase in media weight and the use of additional media. The build-up strategy is often associated with new product launches (e.g., new movies being released by Hollywood studios). Such a strategy is often called a *teaser campaign*.

BLITZ SCHEDULE   The **blitz schedule** is often associated with the introduction of a new product, an event for which multimedia campaigns are implemented. To create high levels of awareness during the introductory period, advertising saturates the market and then gradually tapers off. Another feature of this schedule is that certain media will be used less frequently, or eliminated, as time goes on.

COMPETITIVE MEDIA STRATEGIES

Prior to committing to a plan, media planners should analyze competitors' media usage and expenditure patterns. What the competition does can help planners recommend a media direction for their own product. Should the media recommendation follow a similar pattern, or should a unique strategic direction be recommended?

Assume that a product has a large media budget and dominates other products because it is extensively advertised on television. Does a competitor attempt to compete at the same level in television (assuming adequate funds are available) or should its media planners choose another medium or media combination so that, by dominating the different media, the product can reach a similar target market? The media budget that is available influences such a decision.

MEDIA ALTERNATIVES

Advertisers must choose among television, radio, newspapers, magazines, out-of-home, direct-response, and various forms of digital media (online and mobile). Each medium has its own advantages and disadvantages, so selection is largely based on the nature of the product, the description of the target market and the media they refer to most often, and the budget available. Typically, an advertiser will not rely solely on one medium but will select a combination of media to achieve the stated objectives of the campaign. They may identify a primary medium and support it with secondary media. As explained earlier, television may be ideal for creating awareness and for emotionally connecting with consumers, while print may be ideal for communicating details and appealing to consumers on a rational basis. Combinations of media, therefore, may be the best bet!

Currently, television and newspapers attract the lion's share of advertising investment in Canada. However, advertisers are slowly moving away from conventional media forms aimed at the mass market and toward media forms that offer greater targeting potential. As a general trend, people are spending less time with television and newspapers (hard copy) and increasing the time they spend with the internet. This trend has to affect the decisions of media planners—old rules don't apply any longer.

Detailed discussion of the advantages and disadvantages of each medium is included in chapters 8 through 12.

BUDGET   Essentially, all media strategy decisions are affected by the budget. For example, a small budget can restrict the use of media, extent of coverage, and reach and frequency levels; a sizeable budget can provide considerable flexibility with respect to the same factors. A large budget allows flexibility in the media selection process, since a multimedia campaign can be considered. Media planners who face restrictions or smaller media budgets must be more selective in the evaluation process. The size of the budget (small or large) means that media planners face different challenges when trying to allocate funds efficiently.

To maximize the potential of scarce media dollars, media planners often recommend a primary medium that provides an effective and efficient means of reaching a target market. Such a plan is referred to as a **concentrated media strategy**, since most media dollars are allocated to a primary medium. The advantage of a concentrated strategy is potential media cost savings, since the purchase of one medium in larger quantities creates higher discounts. Then, after considering additional factors such as reach, frequency, and market coverage, media planners will recommend secondary media. Secondary media are often used selectively, and serve to complement the primary medium. The result is a **media mix** that maximizes the use of scarce media dollars.

Alternatively, a media planner could recommend an **assortment media strategy** in which the media dollars are distributed more equitably among several media types. Such a strategy allows the advertiser to reach the same target market in different environments—if members of the target market are not watching television in their leisure time, they may be surfing the internet or reading their favourite magazine. Figure 7.9 summarizes the effect of budget size on media strategy.

Media Execution

The final stage in the media planning process is media execution. Essentially, **media execution** is the process of fine tuning the strategy and translating it into specific action plans. These action plans, or tactics, can be divided into the following areas: evaluating cost comparisons so that a particular medium may be chosen over another; scheduling specific media in a planning format (calendar or blocking chart); developing budget summaries that outline media spending details; and buying the media time when the client approves the plan.

MEDIA SELECTION PROCESS

Media selection can be viewed as a "funnelling" process, since the focus of the process is moving from the general types of media to a specific medium. The process is based on a three-stage decision system that involves selecting the general type of media to use (media strategy), selecting the class of media within the type, and selecting the particular medium. See Figure 7.10 for an illustration of the media selection process.

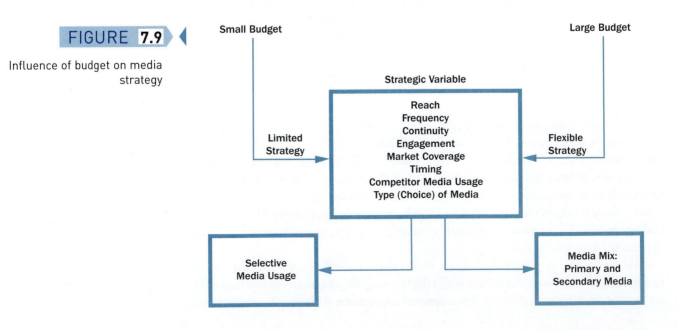

FIGURE **7.9**

Influence of budget on media strategy

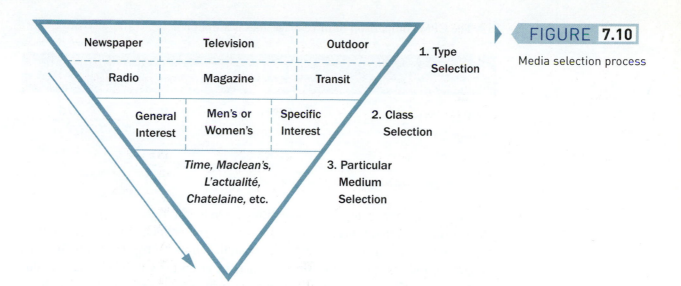

FIGURE **7.10**

Media selection process

The *first* decision is selecting the *type of media* that will best allow the advertisers to meet the objectives for the product and to execute the advertising strategies devised for the product. In the selection process, the various media types are evaluated and compared on the basis of how effectively and efficiently they reach the target market.

The *second* decision involves comparing the *class options within the type of media* recommended. Such a decision often depends on the overall target-market matching strategy being employed: *shotgun, profile matching,* or *rifle.* For example, if magazines are recommended, what class of magazine should be used? Will it be general interest, specific interest, or a magazine tailored specifically to the needs of men or women? If television is recommended, will it be a conventional network such as the CBC or CTV, a specialty cable channel that has a specific theme (such as the Outdoor Life Network or Star!), or a selective spot at a local-market television station?

CBC
www.cbc.ca

The *third* decision of the media planner is recommending which *particular medium* within a class provides the most cost-efficient means of delivering the advertiser's message. For example, if the female or male head of the household is the intended target market, and magazines have been recommended, which publications are most cost-efficient? The recommendation would have to consider magazines that have a readership across both genders. Some options include *Canadian Geographic, Cottage Life,* and *Harrowsmith Country Life.* Depending on funds available, one publication or all three might be recommended. If television is recommended for a key market plan, which network, or which station or stations (to be purchased locally) should be part of a key media buy? The decision is largely based on how cost-efficient the medium is at reaching the intended target.

Harrowsmith
www.harrowsmithcountrylife.ca

Cost **efficiency** is based on a mathematical model called CPM (cost per thousand). **CPM** is defined as the cost incurred in delivering a message to 1000 individuals. In the case of magazines, the data required for the calculation are the cost of a comparable advertisement in each publication and the circulation figures. The CPM calculation allows for easy comparison of magazines that have different rate structures and circulations. The formula for calculating CPM is as follows:

$$CPM = \frac{\text{Unit Cost of Message}}{\text{Circulation (in thousands)}}$$

The CPM comparison of three magazines is as follows:

Magazine (National Edition)	Cost ($) (1P, 4-colour)	English Circulation (in thousands)	CPM
Canadian Geographic	14 990	222.7	67.31
Cottage Life	9 940	70.3	141.39
Harrowsmith Country Life	8 100	125.5	64.54

Source: Canadian Media Directors' Council, *Media Digest*, 2005–2006, p. 47.

These magazines compete for advertising revenue in the general interest category. The figures reveal that *Canadian Geographic* and *Harrowsmith Country Life* reach their respective audiences at a lower cost per thousand than does *Cottage Life*. Both *Canadian Geographic* and *Harrowsmith Country Life* may be given priority in a media buy due their efficiency (the lower cost per thousand) at reaching the target audience. Note, however, that the same calculation can be made based on actual readership (instead of circulation) of the magazine. This may result in different CPMs and different decisions. Readership is discussed in more detail in Chapter 9.

The sample decisions outlined above are based solely on cost efficiency. Other, more qualitative factors are often considered in the decision-making process. Factors such as editorial content, quality of reproduction, and demographic selectivity can lead the media planner to prefer one magazine over another, even if the preferred magazine's CPM is greater than the other magazine's. For example, readers of *Cottage Life* tend to own cottages. Their household incomes may be much higher than the readers of the other two magazines.

Another factor that could enter into the selection process is the method by which the magazine is distributed. Some magazines are given away or use a combination of paid and unpaid circulation. If magazines are to be compared, the common factors should be the cost of the ad and paid circulation. The inclusion of unpaid circulation could make a magazine look better than one that relies solely on paid circulation. There are those who believe that readership is higher in a magazine a consumer pays for.

Similar calculations can be made for other media. In television, for example, the cost of the commercial divided by the size of the viewing audience (in thousands) produces a CPM figure. This calculation helps determine which show to advertise on. Generally, high demand shows such as *Survivor*, *CSI*, and *Canadian Idol* have high CPMs because television rates are determined based on the demand for time slots. To demonstrate, CTV may charge as much as $65 000 for a 30-second spot on *CSI* but the show reaches an average national audience of about 2.8 million each week. The CPM is 23.21 ($65 000 divided by 2800), a reasonable CPM compared to other media.

In deciding on the best media strategy and execution, there are a lot of variables that must be considered. Companies and brands face unique situations, so the strategies they employ will certainly differ from one another. Certain media consumption trends also affect the decisions on what media to employ and how much money should be invested in them.

To broaden the perspective on tactical considerations, refer to Figure 7.11 for a list of some critical factors affecting decisions about broadcast, print, and outdoor media decisions.

For some insight into how various media are integrated into a successful plan, read the Advertising in Action vignette **Good Strategy + Good Execution = Good Results!**

\When a media planner evaluates various media alternatives, certain decisions must be made to ensure that the media objectives are achieved within budget guidelines. Here is a selection of some of those decisions.

BROADCAST MEDIA (TELEVISION AND RADIO)

- What levels of reach and frequency are required?
- Which is more important—reach or frequency?
- Is seasonality a factor (some seasons are less costly than others)?
- How important is placement of commercials in prime time?

PRINT MEDIA (NEWSPAPER AND MAGAZINES)

- Is run of press okay or should preferred positions be requested?
- Are there special creative considerations to be addressed (gatefolds, flexform layouts, or colour in newspapers)?
- What are the reach and frequency objectives?
- Which is more important—reach or frequency?

OUT-OF-HOME MEDIA (OUTDOOR AND TRANSIT)

- What geographic markets are most important?
- Is location of ads within geographic markets important?
- What kind of outdoor ad will be used (poster-style or something more elaborate like a video board)?
- Are interior and exterior transit ads equally important?

FIGURE 7.11

Some tactical considerations for various mass media options

MEDIA SCHEDULING AND BUDGETING

With the media selection process complete, planners proceed to the final stage in developing the media plan: formulating a media schedule and related budget summaries. This portion of the planning document outlines for the advertisers how, where, and when the media expenditures will occur. The media schedule is normally presented in a calendar format, often referred to as a blocking chart. A **blocking chart** outlines in one or two pages all of the details of the media execution (e.g., media usage, market coverage, weight levels, GRPs, reach, frequency, and the timing of the campaign).

Accompanying the blocking chart are budget allocation documents. Typically, the media budget classifies spending allocations according to product (for multi-product advertisers), medium, region, and time of year (months and quarters).

Detailed expenditure plans are important to the client for budget control purposes. As indicated in the strategy section of this chapter, flexibility in media planning is important, due to the possibility of rapidly changing conditions throughout a planning cycle. Budget control documents are referred to often, particularly when cancellations are being considered.

For an applied illustration of the content of a media plan (media objectives, strategies, and execution), refer to the sample advertising plan that appears in Appendix II.

MEDIA BUYING

The media buyer purchases the time and space according to the media plan, requiring the buyer to interpret the work of the media planners and to make decisions regarding actual buys. Buyers are also charged with the responsibility of making replacement buys if the original choice is unavailable.

ADVERTISING IN ACTION

Good Strategy + Good Execution = Good Results!

What media strategy would you recommend to reach urban-dwelling managers and professionals interested in the BMW 525i? That was the challenge that John Ware (The Media Company) faced a short time ago.

The BMW 525i is an expensive automobile with a starting price of about $60 000. The brand and model appeal to men who like to drive. The goal of the campaign was two-fold: to highlight the X Drive (all-wheel drive) capability of the new model, and to increase sales from the previous year.

The target market is described as an "urban-dwelling middle manager or professional with relatively high income." Age is not a factor since owning a BMW is more of an income and "mind" thing—the status of owning the car!

The key to developing the media campaign came from new consumer insights provided by BMW. "These guys love to drive and because they love to drive, they are driving to work. So, when you are looking for touch points, we thought we could build a lot of frequency by placing messages on the routes that they take to work," says Ware. The strategy also addressed the target's emotional needs in a rational manner so that the buying decision was easy to justify. The messages suggested there was no need to settle for anything less.

The campaign was implemented in Toronto, Montreal, and Vancouver (a key-market plan). The media mix included online communications (banner ads and a brand website); outdoor boards that were located on routes leading to major commercial areas and on the way to the airport; a print ad in *enRoute*, Air Canada's in-flight magazine, along with 15-second spots on Air Canada's in-flight television programs; radio spots on business-oriented stations; and advertising in parking garages, elevators, and Esso gas stations. The execution literally hit the customer wherever the customer was!

Where possible the message was tied to the medium. For example, ads in elevators would read: "A better way to elevate yourself" or "You'll be tempted again tomorrow." If reading the online version of the *Globe and Mail*, the target would see advertising banners that directed consumers to the brand website for a video presentation. When parking the car in a downtown garage, there was a beauty shot of the car placed on the wall.

The campaign worked! BMW exceeded their sales goals by 27 percent. This campaign offers good insight into how a media plan may be strategically developed. Factors such as the target-market profile, the message, reach and frequency, timing, and market coverage were all addressed when the plan was is the development stage. A combination of good strategy and good execution yielded great results!

Source: Adapted from Natalie Williams, "It's all about the insight," *Strategy*, April 2006, p. 41.

Time is often a critical factor in the buying process. For example, in broadcast television, the CBC, CTV, and Global networks are booked in late June to cover a 52-week period, starting in September, with bookings being non-cancellable. This buying pattern is referred to as **upfront buying**, or simply **upfront**. In a rather competitive situation, media agencies bid for time slots on popular shows, with the cost of any particular spot being dictated by the demand for the spot. Spots on popular weekly shows fetch high prices! While Canadian statistics are unavailable, upfront buying for the 2006–07 season in the U.S. generated $9.05 billion for the four major networks (CBS, ABC, NBC, and Fox).[8]

It is anticipated that upfront buying will change for the 2007–08 season. By then research data will be available that shows how many people watch the commercials, instead of the show. It will be commercial ratings that determines the price of a spot instead of the show's ratings. The fact that people are recording shows and watching them later (the DVR phenomenon) or they are downloading shows to iPods and other digital devices, has forced the American networks to change the way they do business with advertisers. Canadian media outlets will no doubt follow suit.

The media buyer acts as a negotiator with media representatives. He or she must maximize the efficiency of the media budget by seeking favourable positions and negotiating

230

the best rates possible in light of the guidelines in the media plan. In essence, the buyer fulfills the schedule by implementing the plan.

The media-buying process is a complicated process involving numerous companies. The industry now uses an electronic data interchange (EDI) system in all four stages of a media buy: the purchase order, order acknowledgement and request for changes, invoice, and payment. EDI helps reduce costs and speeds up the payment process.

THE ROLE OF COMPUTERS IN MEDIA PLANNING

The process of media planning and buying has always been a complicated task, so it is not surprising that computers play a prominent role. User-friendly software developed by organizations such as BBM Bureau of Measurement, Nielsen Media Research, and Telmar-Harris Media Systems lets media planners and buyers alike make reasoned, detailed decisions. Nielsen Media Research offers a software tool called Media Advisor to assist with media planning. The software allows planners to extract top-ranked shows, hours of tuning, station share, program profile information, and comparative grids for standard demographics by program and time period.[9] To demonstrate, Media Advisor lets a planner create custom demographics, such as women between the ages of 35 and 49 who are professionals and who have a household income of $70 000. The software identifies television programs that reach these women.[10]

Telmar-Harris provides advertisers and agencies with a host of computer media planning and analysis services for most major media. Their software allows a media planner to analyze and use data in databanks provided by organizations such as the BBM Bureau of Measurement (television and radio), NADbank Inc. (newspapers), and the Print Measurement Bureau (magazines). The software provided by Telmar-Harris allows for quantitative assessments for reach, frequency, GRPs, and CPMs—many of the concepts discussed in this chapter. In the context of media planning, software allows planners to maximize reach at the least cost.

Nielsen Media Research Canada
www.nielsenmedia.ca

The Media Budget

Determining the amount of money to spend on marketing communications generally, and advertising specifically, is a problematic process the manager must face each year. How much does each component of the marketing communications mix deserve?

Senior executives like to know what their return on investment will be from their marketing communications expenditures, but the payback from advertising remains rather vague—a direct link to sales or profit just isn't there. Organizations must realize that investment in advertising requires a long-term commitment if a plan is to have a chance at success. To think otherwise is foolish, but chopping advertising budgets in midstream is a common phenomenon when advertisers try to protect short-term profit margins. Such decisions are questionable as they conflict with the long-term expectations of the brand, and they can accentuate a rough financial situation by reducing revenues further. Regardless of the size of a business, managers should resist the temptation to cut budgets without just cause.

FACTORS AFFECTING BUDGET SIZE

To develop an advertising budget, the manager analyzes a host of factors that will influence the size of the budget. When these factors are examined collectively, they provide insight into the amount of money required for advertising. A discussion of each factor follows.

SIZE OF CUSTOMER BASE   Organizations directing consumer products at mass target markets tend to rely more heavily on advertising, while organizations directing products at industrial markets, which represent a more selective and geographically centred audience, rely more on personal selling. If viewed from a budgeting perspective, a competitive advertising budget is essential for the long-term success of any product in a consumer-oriented market. For industrial products, the money available for promotion will be wisely spent if less is allocated to conventional advertising than to personal selling and sales-promotion budgets. Direct-response and internet communications are useful for reaching both consumer and industrial targets.

DEGREE OF COMPETITION   The amount of money spent on advertising by competitors may be the single most important influence on the size of a product's advertising budget. If nothing else, it is a useful indicator of how much money the company will have to spend to remain competitive. Information on competitors' advertising spending is available to consumer-goods advertisers through marketing research firms such as Nielsen Marketing Research. While past expenditures are well known, the advertising manager must also predict with reasonable accuracy what the main competitors will spend next year, for these projected expenditures can help him or her develop and justify a budget.

A decision must be made regarding how competitive the brand will be with respect to advertising expenditures. In many markets, the competition is so intense and the media spending so high that an advertiser might be forced to spend more than it would like. In the battle for soft-drink supremacy between Coca-Cola and Pepsi, is it realistic for either brand to reduce its investment in advertising? Both brands compete in a segment of the beverage industry that is experiencing flat growth year to year, so to protect market share, advertising spending has to remain competitive. In the process, profits may have to be sacrificed.

STAGE IN THE PRODUCT LIFE CYCLE   Advertising is more important in the introductory and growth stages of the product life cycle than in the mature and decline stages.

In the **introduction stage**, the advertiser is mainly concerned with creating a high level of awareness for the new product. In relation to sales (which are low in this stage), the investment in advertising will be extremely high. Since the objective is brand development, it is quite common to have an advertising expenditure that exceeds the projected return in sales. Initial losses are offset by profits made in the longer term.

In the **growth stage,** competition is present, so the competitors' advertising budgets enter the picture. A manager is concerned about two objectives: continuing to build awareness, and creating brand preference in the customer's mind. Accomplishing both objectives costs money. Securing growth and improving market share in a competitive environment is a challenge and requires a budget that will attract users of competitive brands. Consequently, a brand may wind up spending much more on advertising in this stage than it would like to.

When the brand enters the **mature stage**, most advertisers shift the strategic focus from brand development to profit maximization. Rather than spending money on advertising, there is a conscious effort to preserve money wherever possible. Being in a maintenance position, the budget should just be enough to sustain market share position while increasing bottom-line profitability. If life-cycle extension strategies such as product modifications, new packaging, and new varieties occur, there may be a temporary need to invest in advertising to make consumers aware of new things.

In the **decline stage**, profit motives take priority. Advertising budgets are generally cut significantly or withdrawn entirely. Profits that are generated from brands in this stage are allocated to brands that are in their developmental stages.

PRODUCT CHARACTERISTICS   The nature of the product (the degree of its uniqueness) and its perceived value to potential customers can have an influence on the amount of money that is spent on advertising the product.

Assuming a **high-interest unique selling point** exists, an advertiser must invest heavily in advertising to establish in consumers' minds the perceived value of the unique selling point.

The Gillette division of Procter & Gamble understands this principle well. The razor category is unique as it is one of only a few product categories where the most expensive product is the market leader. Apparently, male consumers will pay handsomely for a clean, smooth shave! And that is the brand promise. Gillette owns about 75 percent of the market, and every time it launches a new generation of razors it makes a significant investment in advertising, both to generate awareness, and to get current users to switch to Gillette's latest razor technology. Gillette's media buys are heavy enough to come as close as possible to forced viewing.[11] Once the brand is established, or when adequate levels of brand loyalty have been achieved, the investment in advertising can be reduced.

For product categories in which brands have only **marginal unique selling points** (i.e., its unique selling points are easily duplicated), the amount spent on advertising is determined by the overall objectives for the brand and the degree of competition. For example, if a brand like Wisk laundry detergent wants to be competitive with leaders such as Tide and Sunlight, which are brands that traditionally spend heavily on advertising, then Wisk will have to spend at similar levels. Conversely, Wisk may choose a different strategic approach and focus on other areas of marketing or marketing communications where the competition is less intense. For example, Wisk may focus on price incentives such as coupons and cash refunds, or simply market the product at a lower price.

MANAGEMENT PHILOSOPHY ABOUT ADVERTISING   The size of a company and the attitude and perceptions of senior executives about the value of advertising often determine the financial resources available for marketing communications. For example, expense-oriented managers who consider only the short term may be reluctant to spend scarce dollars on advertising; investment-minded managers, however, are more willing to take budget risks to encourage long-term brand development. They will see a plan through to the finish before passing judgment on the investment. For a summary of the factors influencing the budget and budgeting methods, refer to Figure 7.12.

BUDGETING METHODS

Annual sales and profit projections are normally established at the corporate level of an organization. These projections often become guidelines for developing potential advertising budgets. An advertising budget can be developed in a variety of ways, each with its own pros and cons. Since no one method is ideal for all situations, it may be wise to compare a variety of methods so that the budget is realistic, given the competitive situation in the marketplace. Discussion of the various methods follows.

PERCENTAGE OF SALES   If a company uses the **percentage-of-sales** method it usually forecasts the sales-dollar volume for the forthcoming year and allocates a predetermined percentage amount of those sales to advertising. Management determines the percentage

FIGURE 7.12

Factors influencing size of budget and budget methods

Factors Influencing Budget Size	
Customer Base	Consumer goods require larger budgets than industrial goods, due to size and location of customers
Degree of Competition	Assuming growth is the objective, a brand must be at or above competitor advertising spending levels
Stage in Product Life Cycle	Introduction and growth require significant budgets (awareness and trial); spending is reduced in maturity (retention), and non-existent in decline
Product Characteristics	High-interest USPs require high investment to promote benefits; marginal USPs should look at less costly alternatives
Management	The perception of the value of advertising is questioned (short-term expense orientation versus long-term investment orientation)

Budgeting Methods	
Percentage of Sales	A predetermined percentage of forecast sales is allocated to advertising
Fixed Sum/Unit	A predetermined dollar amount per unit sold is allocated to advertising
Industry Average	The average amount spent on advertising by competitors (historical or forecast) is allocated to advertising
Advertising Share/ Market Share	Invest at a level to retain share (ad share equals market share); invest at a level to build market share (ad share is greater than market share)
Task (Objective)	Define the task; determine the activities to achieve the task; associate a cost with the activities

to be used. Percentages often used are past industry averages or simply the percentage the company has used in the past. This method of developing a budget has an obvious shortcoming. The philosophy underlying the method is that advertising results *from* sales, whereas the wiser manager prefers to believe that advertising results *in* sales.

This method is popular largely due to its simplicity, and because it relates advertising expenditures directly to sales. If used, the budget implications are very predictable. If sales decrease, so does the budget, and vice versa. The percentage-of-sales method may be appropriate for companies and products that face very similar market conditions year after year. However, if conditions are volatile, the advertising expenditure should change with the market.

Note: Depending on the competitive situation, on the stage the product has reached in the life cycle, and on other factors, the actual percentage allocated to advertising may vary as time passes. For example, a company may allocate to a new brand a very high percentage of the sales, perhaps 200 percent (two dollars in advertising for one dollar in sales), in order to establish the brand's position (thus sacrificing short-term profit). Conversely, a mature brand with a high level of annual sales will be allocated a reduced percentage (perhaps 5 to 10 percent) since maximizing profit is the motivation at this stage.

FIXED SUM PER UNIT SOLD The **fixed-sum-per-unit-sold** method of budgeting is very similar to percentage of sales in that the volume of product sold has a direct influence on the size of the brand's advertising budget. According to this method, the company allocates a predetermined amount to advertising for each unit sold. For example, Toyota Motor Company spends an average of $475 on media advertising for every car it sells, and its cars are selling well. General Motors spends $675 per car but is not seeing similar sales results. This might suggest that the quality of the creative (message) and consumer's perceptions of product quality are more important than the actual amount spent on advertising. The Toyota Camry, the number-one selling car in North America, only spends $152 per vehicle on advertising.[12]

This method is suitable for products with a high unit price (appliances, automobiles). Similar to the percentage-of-sales method, the major weakness of this method is that the budget fluctuates with changes in sales volume.

INDUSTRY AVERAGE (COMPETITOR SPENDING) Advertisers using the **industry average** approach base their advertising budgets on what competitors are spending. Depending on the performance objectives established for a product, the advertiser could choose to lag behind, to be equal to, or to exceed the spending of the competition. Using competitors' past expenditures as a starting point, advertisers attempt to forecast competitive advertising expenditures for the next year, and then position their own budgets accordingly.

An advertiser may also review historical industry averages as a starting point. For example, if a cosmetics company knows that the cosmetic industry historically spends 15 to 20 percent of revenues on advertising, then this range would provide a "safe" starting-point figure for a particular brand's budget. Industry averages provide a good preliminary guideline. However, the influence of other variables may force the advertiser to modify this "starting-point budget." An alternative approach simply examines the average spending patterns of your closest competitors. For example,

Brand A	$400 000
Brand B	200 000
Brand C	300 000
Industry Average	**$300 000**

Using this method, we see that Brand B falls behind its competitors. Assuming advertising is equally important to all brands, the company that produces Brand B would not anticipate much in the way of improved brand performance if the budget remains at $200 000.

TASK (OBJECTIVE) METHOD Which comes first, the chicken or the egg? In contrast to other methods, the **task,** or **objective,** method shows how advertising can influence sales instead of being dependent upon sales. The task method involves a few basic steps: defining the task, determining the type and quantity of advertising needed, and determining the cost of the advertising recommendation.

- *Defining the task* The task of advertising is often expressed in communications terms; usually, it is described as the task of achieving a specified level of brand awareness (e.g., "to increase brand awareness for Brand X from 60 to 75 percent in the next year").

- *Determining the type and quantity of advertising* The difficult part of the task method is determining the most efficient and effective ways of achieving the desired objectives. The myriad media options available suggest that knowledge and experience in media planning are essential for determining reasonable and reliable budget estimates. A detailed understanding of the strategic variables discussed earlier in the chapter—reach, frequency, continuity, impressions, and GRPs—is essential.

- *Determining the cost of the advertising recommendation* This last step in the process is more mechanical. Presuming there is agreement as to objectives and the type and quantity of advertising required (i.e., the first two stages), the costs are calculated arithmetically according to media. Production costs are estimated, and the sum of all media and production variables becomes the advertising budget.

Since many variables are considered in the task method, it is often viewed as the most scientific of the various methods. It is also argued that if the input variables (media-planning variables such as reach, frequency, and continuity) are incorrect, serious miscalculations for a budget will follow. Further, this method does not consider the profit objective of the brand or company. Once a budget figure is arrived at, the company must decide if it can afford to spend that much on advertising. If it can't, the objectives of the plan must be re-evaluated and the plan altered accordingly.

SHARE OF ADVERTISING/SHARE OF MARKET   Share of advertising, or **advertising share**, refers to the amount invested in advertising by one brand expressed as a percentage of the total category investment in advertising (e.g., Tide's investment in advertising may be 20 percent of the total invested by all laundry detergents).

This method is based on the premise that advertising plays a key role in motivating consumers. A brand that spends at a level where advertising share equals market share can reasonably expect to retain its market-share position. Brands that want to grow in a market and increase market share will have to increase spending so that advertising share is greater than market share. Consider the example in the table below and the consequences it presents:

Brand	Market Share (%)	Projected Advertising Budget ($)	Advertising Share (%)	Consequences
A	40	5 000 000	50	Share increase
B	30	2 500 000	25	Decrease
C	20	1 500 000	15	Decrease
D	10	1 000 000	10	Maintenance
	100	10 000 000	100	

If the projected budgets came close to equalling actual spending that year, advertising expenditures for Brand A would have been at a level greater than Brand A's market share, while those for brands B and C would have been below market share. As a consequence, we would expect Brand A to achieve market-share increases while B and C would suffer share declines.

The use of this method requires an advertiser to review competitors' media spending. It produces a good starting point (guideline) for developing a budget. However, it does not consider profit objectives. A preoccupation with what competitors are spending may force a company to spend more than it can afford.

This chapter has presented the various components of a media plan and demonstrated how the budget influences the nature and direction of a plan. For an applied illustration of how the budget and the media objectives influence media strategy and the selection of specific media, refer to the advertising plan that appears in Appendix II.

SUMMARY

In the media planning process, the client is responsible for providing the agency with adequate background information, which is usually contained in the marketing plan. Using this information, the agency develops a detailed media plan and assumes responsibility for selecting, scheduling, and buying media time and space.

The media plan flows logically from the overall marketing strategy and marketing communications strategy. The media plan is divided into three basic sections: media objectives, media strategies, and media execution.

Media objectives are statements that outline who (i.e., what the target market is), what (i.e., what the selling message is), where (i.e., where the markets to advertise in are located), when (i.e., when is the best time to reach the target market), and how (i.e., how often and for how long one should need to reach the target market). These objectives act as the framework for more detailed strategies and tactics.

Media strategy deals with the selection of appropriate media to accomplish media objectives. Strategies are affected by variables such as the characteristics of the target market; the nature of the message; reach, frequency, and continuity; the degree of engagement; flexibility of the plan; the degree of market coverage desired; the best time to reach the target; competitive influences; the pros and cons of the various media alternatives; and the budget.

Media execution is the section of the media plan that outlines the specific tactics for achieving the media objectives. Within these detailed action plans are the specific media usage recommendations and summaries of how media funds will be allocated. Once the client approves the media plan, the agency media buyers negotiate the best possible prices with media representatives.

Whether the budget devised is appropriate for a media plan depends largely on the marketing sophistication of the organization. A variety of factors influences the potential size of an advertising budget, including the size of the customer base, the degree of competition the product will face, the stage the product has reached in the product life cycle, the product's characteristics, and management's commitment to advertising.

Advertisers can select from a variety of methods when determining the size of an advertising budget. Commonly used methods include percentage of sales, fixed sum per unit of sales, industry average, and the task (or objective) method. Since each method offers benefits and drawbacks, it is recommended that a company use several methods and compare the results of each before committing to a final budget.

KEY TERMS

advertising share   236

assortment media strategy   226

brand development index (BDI)   222

blitz schedule   225

blocking chart   229

build-up schedule   224

concentrated media strategy   225

continuity   218

coverage (market coverage)   221

CPM   227

efficiency   227

engagement   208, 218

even schedule   223

flexibility   221

flighting   218

frequency   216

gross rating points (GRPs)   217

hiatus   218

impressions (total exposures)   217

key market plan   222

media brief   208

media buyer   210

REVIEW QUESTIONS

1. Identify and briefly explain the basic roles and responsibilities of the client and agency in the media planning process.

2. What are the basic differences between media objectives, strategies, and tactics?

3. Identify and briefly describe the components of media objective statements.

4. Describe the differences between

    a) profile-matching strategy
    b) shotgun strategy
    c) rifle strategy

5. Briefly explain the impact that reach, frequency, and continuity have on strategic media planning.

6. What are gross rating points (GRPs), and how are they calculated?

7. Briefly explain how the degree of engagement affects decisions regarding which media to recommend.

8. What is the difference between a key-market media plan and a selective market plan?

9. What is a pulse media schedule? What strategic variables combine to create the pulsing effect?

10. Briefly explain the difference between a build-up media schedule and a blitz media schedule.

11. What is the difference between a concentrated media strategy and an assortment media strategy?

12. What are the stages in the media selection process?

13. What is CPM? How is it calculated? What purpose does it serve?

14. Identify and briefly describe the factors that influence the size of an advertising budget.

15. Contrast the strengths and weaknesses of the percentage-of-sales budgeting method with those of the task (objective) budgeting method.

16. How does the product life cycle influence the amount of money a company or brand invests in advertising?

DISCUSSION QUESTIONS

1. "Media planning is an activity that should be in the hands of specialists." Discuss, in the context of clients doing their own media planning, the use of a full-service agency and a media-buying service (a specialist).

2. "The client is at the mercy of the agency's media recommendations." Is this a problem? Discuss.

3. "The budget should be based on the media plan, not the media plan based on the budget." Discuss from the perspectives of both the client and the agency.

4. Read the Advertising in Action vignette **Shattering the Paradigm: How Does Advertising Work?** Conduct some secondary research on the issue of recency. Is it suitable for all products, or should it be used selectively? What is your opinion of this media strategy? What are the advantages and disadvantages of such a strategy?

5. Review the Advertising in Action vignette **Good Strategy + Good Execution = Good Results**! In this media plan the agency did not recommend television advertising. Put yourself in the media planner's position and provide your rationale for rejecting television. In hindsight, should television be included in the mix?

NOTES

1. Estimated costs based on the 2005–06 Advertising Age Network Rate Card.

2. John Heinzl, "Viewers get caught in ad roadblocks," *Globe and Mail*, October 19, 2002, p. M1.

3. *Canadian Living*, **www.canadianliving.com**.

4. Tom Hespos, "Reach and the law of diminishing returns," *Media Post*, January 6, 2004, **www.mediapost.com**.

5. Chris Daniels, "Media buying gets scientific," *Marketing*, July 31, 2000, pp. 11–12.

6. Stuart Elliott, "New rules of engagement," *New York Times*, March 21, 2006, **www.nytimes.com**.

7. Calculation based on data included in *Canadian Communications Pocket Book*, 2006/07, pp. 25, 27, published by *Marketing* magazine.

8. Claire Atkinson, "TV ad market primed for pay-by-pod," *Advertising Age*, July 9, 2006, **www.adage.com**.

9. Nielsen Media Research, **www.nielsenmedia.ca**.

10. John Bell, "Be a brand surgeon," *Marketing*, January 22, 2001, pp. 11–12.

11. Jack Neff, "Bad ads, big sales: How fusion went nuclear," *Advertising Age*, March 27, 2006, pp. 3, 48.

12. Advertising Spending in Measured Media, "Top 10 auto brands and top 6 auto companies," *Advertising Age*, **www.adage.com/datacentre**.

CHAPTER 8

Print Media: Newspapers and Magazines

Courtesy of Dick Hemingway.

Learning Objectives

After studying this chapter, you will be able to

1. Identify the classifications of newspapers and magazines available to Canadian advertisers

2. Explain the advantages and disadvantages of newspapers and magazines as advertising media

3. Assess the considerations and procedures involved in buying newspaper and magazine space

4. Understand the basic terminology used in newspaper and magazine advertising

5. Assess the influence of technology on print media

Newspapers in Canada

In Canada, there are currently 134 *daily newspapers* with a total average daily circulation of 6.4 million copies. The largest daily is the *Toronto Star*, which has an average Monday to Friday circulation of 452 500 per day. Of the 134 dailies in Canada, 120 are published in English and 14 in French.[1] Included in these figures are two free daily tabloids that are distributed in Toronto: *Metro* and *24 Hours*.

The term "circulation" in print media refers to the number of issues sold. **Circulation** is defined as the average number of copies per issue of a publication that are sold by subscription, distributed free to predetermined recipients, carried within other publications, or made available through retail distributors.

Newspapers rank second to television in Canada, controlling 15 percent of net advertising revenues.[2] That revenue is generated from four advertising sources: retail advertising, classified advertising, general (national advertising), and inserts (e.g., retail flyer advertising).

Community newspapers are generally smaller-circulation newspapers published once a week (sometimes more often in larger markets) and directed at a local target audience. There are just over 1100 English and French community newspapers in Canada. Penetration of community newspapers is quite high, as 69 percent of English Canadians (18-plus years of age) and 63 percent of French Canadians (18-plus years of age) read a community newspaper each week.[3]

From an advertising viewpoint, the demographic profile of community newspaper readers closely matches that of the entire population. Among adults they have a fairly even reach among all age, education, income, and gender brackets. There is a modest skew in the direction of older readers.[4] Therefore, community newspapers are truly an advertising medium for the local market, appealing more to independent advertisers. A weekly newspaper stays in the home longer than a daily, owing to its weekly distribution cycle.

NEWSPAPER FORMATS

Canadian newspapers are published in two formats: tabloids and broadsheets. **Tabloids** are flat, with only a vertical centrefold, and resemble an unbound magazine. They are usually produced in one section. In terms of size, the tabloid page is 8 to $10\frac{3}{4}$ inches wide by 11 to 15 inches in depth. The highest-circulation tabloids in Canada are *Le Journal de Montréal* (265 600), the *Toronto Sun* (199 400), and the *Vancouver Province* (154 900).

Toronto Sun
www.torontosun.com

241

Broadsheets are much larger newspapers. A broadsheet page is 11 ½ to 13 inches wide by 21 to 22 ½ inches deep. The majority (84) of Canadian daily newspapers are published in broadsheet format, the largest being the *Toronto Star*, with an average daily circulation of 452 500, the *Globe and Mail* (335 000), the *National Post* (244 000), and the *Vancouver Sun* (165 900). Canada's largest daily newspapers and their circulations are listed in Figure 8.1.

Toronto Star
www.thestar.com

Newspaper Readership Highlights

Readership data about newspapers is compiled by an industry-sponsored measurement organization called NADbank Inc. This organization provides advertisers, advertising agencies, and daily newspapers with accurate and credible information on newspaper readership, retail data, and consumer behaviour. NADbank updates its data annually by conducting a detailed survey among Canadian adults. The nature of information produced by NADbank includes weekday and weekend readership, demographic profiles of readers, product ownership and purchase intentions, and media habits (e.g., other media referred to).

NADbank Inc.
www.nadbank.com

The circulation of newspapers is declining everywhere, but readership remains relatively steady. NADbank research indicates that local news is the most regularly read content in daily newspapers and that newspapers are the medium adults refer to first for information. Newspapers continue to draw a mass audience, which makes them attractive to advertisers.

By the numbers, daily newspapers reach 51 percent of Canadian adults. Readership tends to increase marginally on weekends, a time when people have more time to read. By region (Atlantic Canada, Quebec, Ontario, Prairies, and British Columbia), and by

FIGURE 8.1

Canada's top 10 daily newspapers

Market	Newspaper	Circulation (000s)
Toronto	*Toronto Star*	452.5
Toronto	*Globe and Mail*	335.0
Montreal	*Le Journal de Montreal*	322.6
Montreal	*La Presse*	270.9
Toronto	*National Post*	240.0
Toronto	*Toronto Sun*	199.4
Vancouver	*Vancouver Sun*	165.9
Vancouver	*Vancouver Province*	150.8
Montreal	*Gazette*	136.8
Ottawa	*Ottawa Citizen*	128.6

A few daily newspapers that are distributed for free also have high circulation figures. There are plans in place to expand these newspapers to other large Canadian cities.

Market	Newspaper	Circulation (000s)
Toronto	*24 Hours*	249.3
Toronto	*Toronto Metro*	233.7

Source: Adapted from Canadian Media Directors' Council, *Media Digest*, 2006–2007, p. 40.

age in each region, readership does not vary significantly. There is, however, a tendency for readership to increase as a person's level of income and education increases, and there is an ongoing migration to online editions of newspapers. In the top ten markets, online readership is at the 15-percent level, and growing each year.[5] The transfer of eyeballs to online editions of newspapers has implications for the newspapers and their advertisers. For a summary of newspaper readership by key demographic variables, refer to Figure 8.2.

Types of Newspaper Advertising

The revenues generated by advertising significantly offset the production and overhead costs of publishing a newspaper. Advertising accounts for roughly 60 percent of newspaper space. The advertising layouts are put into position first; the editorial content is then arranged around the advertising. A larger newspaper results from an increase in advertising revenues. For example, the Wednesday edition of many daily newspapers is often much thicker than the other days' editions, in part because of the addition of

FIGURE 8.2

Readership of daily newspapers by demographic characteristic

This type of information is compiled by NADbank Inc. each year. NADbank data cover 77 newspapers in 54 Canadian markets.

Demographic Characteristic	% Canadian Adults (18+)
AGE	
All Adults 18+	51
18–24	45
25–34	41
35–49	49
50–64	59
65+	61
GENDER	
Men	49
Women	51
INCOME	
$75 000+	55
$50 000–$75 000	52
$30 000–$50 000	49
Under $30 000	41
EDUCATION	
College or University Grad	56
Some Post-Secondary	50
High School Grad	49
Some High School	44

Source: Adapted from NADbank 2006 Study, www.nadbank.com. Reprinted by permission of NADbank.

preprinted inserts by supermarket and department-store chains. The same could be said of Friday or Saturday editions, when television guides and other inserts are included.

There are two broad forms of advertising: *display* and *classified*. **Display advertising** is defined as any advertisement appearing in any part of the publication, excluding the section of classified ads. Display advertising can be subdivided into two types: *general* or *national advertising* and *retail advertising*. Preprinted inserts are another form of advertising that produces revenues for a newspaper. Let's examine the various types of advertising in greater detail.

GENERAL ADVERTISING (NATIONAL ADVERTISING)

General advertising, or **national advertising**, is sold to advertisers and advertising agencies by a national sales department or a media representative firm. Advertisements of this kind normally feature products or services marketed on a national or regional basis, through a network of local retailers. Included in this category are advertisements for brand-name food and beverages, automobiles, airlines, banks and other financial institutions, computers, and telecommunications products and services. Ads placed by national advertisers very often include a **hooker** (also called a **tag**), which identifies local retailers where the product can be purchased; a hooker is usually placed at the bottom of the advertisement. General advertising is usually placed by advertising agencies on behalf of the advertiser (the client).

RETAIL ADVERTISING

As the name suggests, **retail advertising** is used by such businesses as department stores, supermarkets, drug stores, restaurants, and shopping malls. Retail ads usually stress sale items and specials, or they re-advertise national brands that are carried by the retailer at special prices. Another important function of retail ads is the communication of store location and hours of operation. Most daily newspapers have a sales department that is responsible for selling retail ad space. Retail advertising generates about two-thirds of a newspaper's revenues.

CLASSIFIED ADVERTISING

Classified advertising appears in a much-read section of the newspaper, and in many of the larger dailies it has a full section to itself. It produces a considerable amount of revenue for a newspaper. Classified ads provide readers with opportunities to buy, sell, lease, rent, or obtain a variety of products and services such as jobs, houses, apartments, cars, recreational vehicles, and furniture.

PREPRINTED INSERTS

Preprinted inserts, often referred to as **free-standing inserts** or **flyers**, are inserted into the fold of the newspaper and look like a separate, smaller section. On any given day, it is not uncommon for a newspaper to include several different inserts. Large users of inserts include supermarkets, department-store chains, and automotive and hardware chains, to name a few. See Figure 8.3 for some examples of flyers. While many advertisers do not perceive flyers to be a glamorous medium, 70 percent of Canadians rate flyers as their top source of local shopping information. Canadian retailers spend $2 billion annually advertising in flyers.[6]

For more insight into the newspaper industry's fastest-growing revenue stream, see the Advertising in Action vignette **Flyer Ads: Sexy? No! Effective? Yes!**

FIGURE 8.3

Flyers are an important medium to some advertisers

Newspapers as an Advertising Medium

An advertiser must assess the use of newspapers in the context of the problem that advertising has to resolve and the objectives of a campaign. This section presents the case for selecting or rejecting newspapers for advertising purposes.

ADVANTAGES OF NEWSPAPERS

GEOGRAPHIC SELECTIVITY   Newspapers serve a well-defined geographic area (town, city, trading zone), so they are attractive to local merchants. For the national advertiser, newspapers offer placement on a market-by-market basis. The advertiser can select specific newspaper markets or all the markets in a region. Therefore, newspaper advertising is useful for national advertisers following a key-market media strategy.

Although predominantly local in nature, Canada's largest daily illustrates how newspapers can expand coverage into regional markets. The *Toronto Star* has excellent penetration in trading zones surrounding Metropolitan Toronto. The Greater Toronto Area (GTA) accounts for 75 percent of the *Star*'s circulation, with the remainder distributed throughout southern Ontario.[7]

COVERAGE AND REACH   As indicated in the readership highlights section, newspapers effectively reach a broad cross-section of the adult population. Current readership statistics show that newspapers effectively reach 51 percent of adults 18 years of age and over. The medium also offers high reach among all household income, occupation, and

Flyer Ads: Sexy? No! Effective? Yes!

Look in any blue recycling box and you'll see lots of advertising flyers. They seem to get tossed out as quickly as they come in. But that doesn't mean they aren't effective. Retailers just love them!

Flyers are big business in Canada. On average, every household in Canada receives about 20 each week, and those flyers represents more than $2 billion in advertising expenditures by major retailers.

Flyers do have an image problem, and because of that they are perceived as the black sheep of marketing communications by many managers. For certain, advertising agencies do not routinely recommend their use to clients. For retailers, however, the flyer is very important. In fact, they may account for the largest portion of the advertising budget. Think about it—major supermarkets issue multiple-page weekly flyers; Canadian Tire issues a bi-weekly flyer right across Canada.

So what's the catch? Flyers allow marketers to communicate with their best customers and provide detailed information about products. M&M Meat Shops firmly believes in flyers. "We use television, radio and direct mail, but nothing stands up to our flyers," says Chris Styan, director of marketing at M&M.

Research confirms M&M's belief in flyers. Apparently, 70 percent of Canadians rate flyers as their top source of local shopping information. In other words, it's only junk mail if you don't want it.

The home electronics store Radio Shack and many of its competitors are heavy users of flyers. In this industry, flyers are the starting point for consumers to compare different retailers and prices. They are the preferred choice for home electronics information. "Flyers are by far our largest single investment in advertising," says Duncan Hunter, manager of relationship marketing at Radio Shack.

M&M Meat Shops sends flyers to five million households every two weeks. M&M's Max card, a CRM program with four million members, allows the company to know where its best customers live, and as a result can pinpoint specific households to receive the flyers—an example of true efficiency in the way it spends advertising dollars. M&M has an entirely novel view of how to use flyers. Most organizations still see them as nothing more than wasteful mass-marketing tools. M&M sees them as an essential piece of a comprehensive customer relationship management program.

The future looks good for flyers. With the fragmentation of broadcast media, and declining circulations of newspapers and magazines, flyers look like a viable alternative. Other companies had better join in!

Source: Adapted from Rebecca Harris, "High flyers," *Marketing*, March 7, 2005, pp. 15, 16.

Canadian Tire
www.canadiantire.ca

education groups. For all of these demographic variables, readership increases proportionately with income, education, and occupational status. For advertisers with loosely defined target-market profiles, newspapers represent significant reach opportunity.

ENGAGEMENT   Newspapers are an engaging medium—people devote a considerable amount of time to reading the paper, and tend to consume it more carefully than other media such as radio or television. (It's more like a date than a chance meeting.) A study conducted by the Canadian Newspaper Association reveals that readers are distracted less while reading the newspaper. Although readership patterns (how a newspaper is read) vary among individuals, readers do tend to go through the entire paper. Such reading tendencies suggest a high possibility of exposure for products and services advertised in newspapers. In comparison, viewers of television and listeners of radio tend to be easily distracted by other activities while watching or listening.[8]

Canadian Newspaper Association
www.cna-acj.ca

FLEXIBILITY   Newspapers provide several forms of flexibility. It is a medium where ads can be placed with short lead times, say, two to three days. Therefore, it is a useful medium for reacting to unforeseen competitive activity. In terms of creative execution, an advertiser can take advantage of flexform advertising. **Flexform** refers to an advertisement that does not conform to normal shapes. Editorial may intertwine with the ad in a variety of ways. Oddly shaped advertisements stand out from the clutter surrounding them.

CREATIVE AND MERCHANDISING CONSIDERATIONS   Since newspapers are a closely read medium, and since there are many size options for ads, advertisers are able to present messages that include long copy or factual information (as is not the case with broadcast media). Also, newspapers offer merchandise tie-in opportunities, such as cooperative advertising with local distributors, or ads containing coupons or other promotional incentives geared toward trial purchase or building loyalty. Newspapers are often referred to as the "sales action" medium since many ads carry incentive-oriented promotions that encourage purchase. See the ad in Figure 8.4 for an illustration.

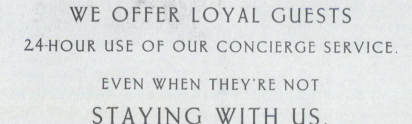

WE OFFER LOYAL GUESTS
24-HOUR USE OF OUR CONCIERGE SERVICE.

EVEN WHEN THEY'RE NOT
STAYING WITH US.

(WE KNOW SOME OF YOU TAKE WORK HOME WITH YOU.)

At Delta Hotels, we understand that as a business traveller, you need a different kind of service. A service that's not limited to the hours of 9a.m. to 5p.m. Which is why we created Delta Privilege – a recognition program specifically designed for business travellers. As a Privilege member, you'll get guaranteed one-minute check-in, free local calls, and exclusive use of our 24-hour concierge. So you never have to stop working. (Sorry.)

DELTA
HOTELS

Your room is ready.

AFTER 3 STAYS*	AFTER 7 STAYS*
EARN	ENJOY
5,000	**2** nights free
AEROPLAN MILES	AT ANY DELTA HOTEL OR RESORT

To take advantage of this promotion, and all the great benefits of Delta Privilege from your very first stay at any of our hotels or resorts, sign up at www.deltaprivilege.com today. There's never been a better time to join.

*Stays must be between February 1 and May 31, 2004. You must be a Delta Privilege member and register for this promotion in order to participate. Only stays at qualifying rates are eligible for Aeroplan miles. Visit www.deltaprivilege.com for full terms and conditions.

Aeroplan ✦ | DELTA privilege

*Aeroplan is a registered trademark.

FIGURE 8.4

A newspaper ad that includes a sales incentive to generate action

Courtesy of Delta Hotels.

EDITORIAL SUPPORT   Newspaper content can offer positive benefits to advertisers. For example, a luxury automobile ad that is targeted at business executives can be placed in an appropriate section of the newspaper—the business section. Similarly, an ad for a sports and recreation product would be seen by readers of the sports section. It should be noted, however, that requests for specific positions in the newspaper add to the costs of advertising. For specific page or location requests, an advertiser must pay a position charge. Position charges are discussed in the media-buying section of this chapter.

SUITABILITY FOR SMALL ADVERTISERS   To retail advertisers, particularly local-market independents, newspapers offer high reach and flexibility at relatively low cost, compared to other media. Also, retailers lacking advertising expertise can draw upon the creative services of the newspaper, usually at no extra cost. Retailers and automobile manufacturers and dealers are among the largest investors in newspaper advertising across Canada.

DISADVANTAGES OF NEWSPAPERS

SHORT LIFESPAN   "There is nothing as stale as yesterday's news." This phrase sums up any newspaper's biggest drawback—a short lifespan. A daily newspaper is around for only one day or less, so the likelihood for an advertisement to receive exposure is drastically reduced if the newspaper is not read on the day of distribution. To reach the audience an ad may have to be placed several times during the week.

LACK OF TARGET-MARKET ORIENTATION   Excluding newspapers like the *Globe and Mail* and the *National Post*, which have a more selective target-market reach (a reach determined by demographics), newspapers in general reach a very broad cross-section of the population. For advertisers using a shotgun strategy (mass reach), newspapers serve a purpose. But advertisers wishing to reach a target market that is upscale in terms of income, occupation, or education must recognize that newspaper advertising will reach many who are not in the target market, resulting in a wasteful spending of an advertising budget. Therefore, advertisers with well-defined targets may find other media more appropriate and efficient.

CLUTTER   Clutter is the extent to which a publication's pages are fragmented into small blocks of advertising and/or editorial. Generally, 60 percent of a newspaper's space is devoted to advertising. Therefore, making an ad stand out and make an impression on the reader is a challenging creative task. The inclusion of advertising inserts on certain days compounds the clutter problem, as does the hasty manner in which people read newspapers. The inclusion of colour will increase an ad's attention-grabbing ability, but colour is an added cost.

POOR REPRODUCTION QUALITY   Advertisers may compare newspapers to magazines on any number of bases. With respect to quality of print reproduction, newspapers compare very poorly. Detracting from the quality of the print production in newspapers are the quality and speed of the printing presses and the poor quality of newsprint used. Newer, technically advanced offset presses are improving the quality of reproduction, particularly for colour ads, but it is not magazine-standard quality.

HIGH COST   The high cost of newspaper advertising is a problem faced by national advertisers. As an advertiser adds markets to its list in order to reach regional or national market coverage objectives, the cost of newspaper advertising suddenly becomes quite high. For example, the cost of running a full-page black-and-white ad in six key markets (1MM-plus population) involves 23 daily newspapers. The cost of the space would be $360 200. The same ad in colour would cost $418 900.[9] This example demonstrates that advertisers must consider alternative media if they wish to increase regional or national coverage for a product, or if the product's target market is precisely defined. Fractional-size ads cost much less but they are usually clustered with other ads.

Buying Newspaper Space

Newspaper space is sold on the basis of agate lines or modular agate lines. An **agate line** is a non-standardized unit of space measurement, equal to one column wide and $\frac{1}{14}$-inch deep. For **broadsheets**, standard pages are $11\frac{1}{2}$ inches wide with column widths of $1\frac{1}{16}$ inches. The number of columns ranges from 7 to 10, so full-page lineage ranges from 1800 to 3150 agate lines. In **tabloids**, the number of columns ranges from 5 to 10, and full-page lineage ranges from 875 to 1050 agate lines. A majority of broadsheets and tabloids use agate lines to determine the size of an advertisement.

A **modular agate line** is a standardized unit of measurement equal to one column wide and $\frac{1}{14}$-inch deep. Standard column widths are $2\frac{1}{16}$ inches in broadsheets. A modular agate line is wider than an agate line.

Readers should note that the lines and columns referred to here are not physical lines and columns. They are invisible lines and columns that the newspaper industry refers to for the purposes of measuring the size of an ad.

The basic procedure for buying newspaper space is to determine the size of the ad either in agate lines or modular agate lines. In either case, the cost is calculated by multiplying the width of the ad (number of columns) by the depth of the ad (inches of depth). *One column inch* of depth equals *14 agate lines*. Other factors that influence costs include the number of insertions, creative considerations such as the use of colour, and position charges, if applicable. The following section includes some examples of how to calculate the costs of newspaper advertising.

To simplify matters, newspapers like the *Globe and Mail* (see Figure 8.5) and *Toronto Star* have moved to standard-sized ads with sizes that are easier for advertisers to understand. Some popular sizes are $\frac{1}{2}$ page, $\frac{1}{4}$ page, and $\frac{1}{8}$ page. The Toronto Star has dropped line rates and quotes advertising rates based on the size of the ad and the section in which it appears.

DETERMINE SPACE SIZE

For the sake of example, let's assume that space is being purchased in agate lines. The size of the ad is 4 columns wide by 12 column inches deep. Considering that each column inch of depth equals 14 agate lines, the size of the ad would be calculated by the following formula:

$$\text{Number of columns wide} \times \text{inches of depth} \times 14$$
$$4 \times 12 \times 14 = 672 \text{ agate lines}$$

If the size of the advertisement were 6 columns wide by 8 inches deep, the size of the ad in agate lines would be:

$$6 \times 8 \times 14 = 672 \text{ lines}$$

These two examples illustrate that different configurations of ads (combinations of width and depth) may produce the same size of ad in terms of space occupied and rates charged for the space.

FIGURE 8.5

Some standard size options in newspapers

SAMPLES OF ADVERTISING SPACE SIZES
(ASK ABOUT YOUR SPECIFIC AD SIZE)

Full Page
1,800 agate lines
13"w x 21 7/16"d
(6 cols x 300 mals)

2/3 Page
1,200 agate lines
10 3/4"w x 17 1/8"d
(5 cols x 240 mals)

1/2 Page
900 agate lines
13"w x 10 11/16"d
(6 cols x 150 mals)

1/2 Page
900 agate lines
6 3/8"w x
21 7/16"d
(3 cols x
300 mals)

Magazine Page
616 agate lines
8 9/16" w x 11"d
(4 cols x
154 mals)

1/4 Page
450 agate lines
6 3/8"w x
10 11/16"d
(3 cols x
150 mals)

1/4 Page
452 agate lines
8 9/16"w x
8 1/16"d
(4 cols x 113 mals)

1/12 Page
150 agate lines
4 1/4"w x 5 3/8"d
(2 cols x 75 mals)

1/8 Page
225 agate lines
6 3/8"w x 5 3/8"d
(3 cols x 75 mals)

Full mechanical details are available at www.globeandmail.com.

THE GLOBE AND MAIL
CANADA'S NATIONAL NEWSPAPER • FOUNDED 1844

Reprinted with permission from the *Globe and Mail.*

The calculations above would be the same for modular agate lines. The only difference is that the modular agate line is slightly wider than the agate line. Before calculating the costs of an ad, the planner must be aware of which system the newspaper is using: agate lines or modular agate lines.

Newspaper space can be sold on the basis of **modular units**, though only a few daily newspapers use this system. If this system is used, the size of the ad is expressed in terms of units of width and units of depth (e.g., 2 units wide by 5 units deep). In effect, the page is sectioned off into equal-sized units, with each unit being 30 modular agate lines deep. Therefore, to calculate the actual size of an ad that is 2 units wide by 5 units deep, the calculation would be as follows:

Number of units wide $\times$ units deep $\times$ 30 = Modular agate lines (MAL)

$$2 \times 5 \times 30 = 300 \text{ MAL}$$

RATE SCHEDULES

Line rate is defined as the advertising rate charged by newspapers for one agate line or one modular agate line. With regard to rate schedules, several factors must be noted. First, rates charged by line go down as the volume of the lineage increases over a specified period. Second, costs for the addition of colour or preferred positions are quoted separately. Third, the line rates may vary from one section of the paper to another. For example, the casual rate (the highest rate paid by an advertiser) for advertisers in *The Globe and Mail*'s News and Report on Business sections is higher than for other sections of the newspaper. More highly read sections command a higher price for advertising.

In the chart in Figure 8.6, the rates quoted start with a **casual rate** (or **transient rate**), which is defined as a one-time rate or base rate that applies to casual advertisers. Discounts are offered to advertisers purchasing volume lineage over a more extended period of time, usually one year.

To illustrate how costs are calculated in newspapers, let's develop a hypothetical plan and consider the use of agate lines and modular agate lines and the line rates for the *Globe and Mail* included in Figure 8.6.

Newspaper	*Globe and Mail*—News Section
Size of Ad/Edition	4 columns wide 10 column inches deep, Metro Edition
Rate	Casual Rate—Transient Rate
Frequency	Once (Monday)

The first calculation would determine, as follows, the total number of agate lines:

$$4 \text{ columns wide} \times 10 \text{ column inches deep} \times 14 = 560 \text{ lines}$$

The next step would be to multiply the number of agate lines by the line rate by the frequency to determine the cost of the insertion. In this case, the casual rate would apply because there are not enough lines to earn a discount.

$$560 \times \$33.14 \times 1 = \$18\ 558.40$$

Advertisers earn discounted line rates when they commit to an annual dollar volume with the newspaper. To demonstrate, assume an advertiser commits to $100 000. At that level, the line rate for the Metro Edition of the Globe and Mail drops to $26.51 if the ads are placed in the News, Business, or Toronto sections. Therefore, if the dollar commitment is divided by the line rate ($100 00/$26.51), the advertiser can place ads in various sizes totalling approximately 3780 lines. From the previous example, the total line space was 560 lines for one ad, which means that the ad could run seven times for a total of 3920 lines. This lineage earns the discounted line rate and on a dollar basis is just over the $100 000 discount plateau. The revised calculation would be:

$$560 \times 7 \times \$26.51 = \$103\ 919.20$$

If the advertiser only has $100 000 to spend, one option would be to marginally reduce the size of the ad so there are fewer total lines. For additional illustrations of how to calculate costs, refer to Figure 8.7.

The next example will consider modular agate lines and modular units. Each unit of space contains 30 modular agate lines.

FIGURE 8.6

Globe and Mail Rate Card

Newspaper	*Globe and Mail*, National Edition, News Section
Units of width	4 columns wide
Units of depth	4 units deep
Frequency	4 times

The calculation for the number of modular agate lines is as follows:

4 units wide × 4 units deep × 30 × 4 insertions = 1920 MAL

Assuming the ad is placed in the Metro edition, the cost calculation for this number of lines would be:

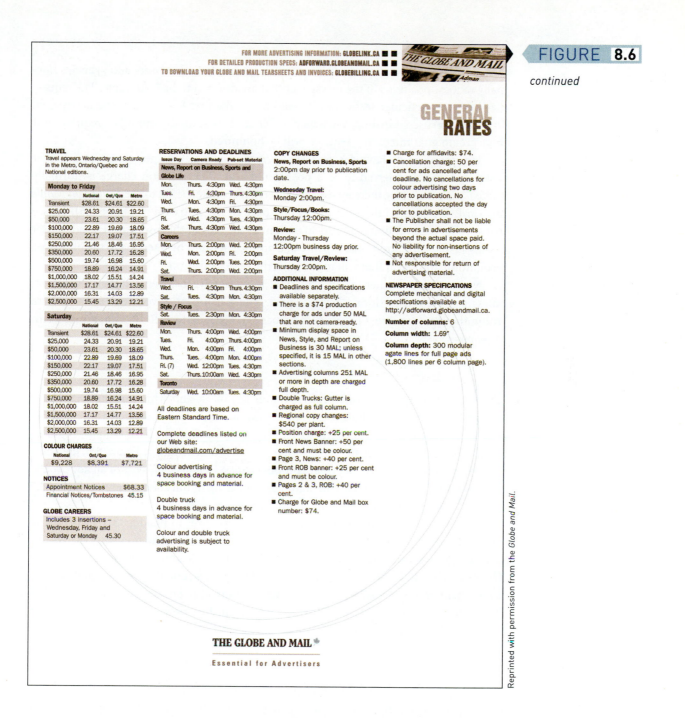

FIGURE **8.6**

continued

Total lines purchased × the line rate

$$1920 \times \$33.14 = \$63\ 628.80$$

This example assumes that the advertiser was transient and did not commit to a set investment that would earn discounts. The amount invested was $80 544. Therefore, had the advertiser committed to spend $50 000, the line rate would be $27.34 and the advertiser would have saved money. The revised calculation would be:

$$1920\ \text{lines} \times \$27.34 = \$52\ 492.80$$

Advertisers who commit to a certain dollar figure are billed at the corresponding line rate during the year. If the advertiser does not meet that dollar volume by the end of the contract period, the line rates would be adjusted appropriately. The advertiser would actually owe the newspaper some money.

POSITION CHARGES

Since a disadvantage of newspaper advertising is clutter, advertisers and agencies normally request positions in the newspaper that are deemed to be favourable. The request may be for a particular section, or it could be for the first few pages of the newspaper. To keep advertisers satisfied, a newspaper will do its best to accommodate requests, but there are no guarantees that requests will be honoured.

The privilege of having a preferred position in a newspaper comes at a higher cost—that cost is referred to as a **position charge**. The position charge is normally quoted as a percentage increase over the insertion cost. Referring to the *Globe and Mail*'s rate card (see column three on the second page of the rate card in Figure 8.6), we see that specific page requests can add 40 percent to the cost of the insertion. The advertiser usually justifies the additional expense of a position request by referring to the improved recognition and recall that will result from the better position.

Newspaper publishers reserve the right to place advertisements at their discretion, unless a preferred position charge is paid. The placing of advertisements anywhere within the regular printed pages of a newspaper is referred to as **ROP (run of press, run of paper)**.

COLOUR CHARGES

Although newspapers are often referred to as the black-and-white medium, colour is available to advertisers willing to pay for it. Additional costs are incurred as the number of colours increases. Colour charges are normally quoted on the basis of spot colour or full colour. With reference to the *Globe and Mail*'s rate schedule in Figure 8.6, the addition of full colour (Sunday to Friday editions) adds $13 800 to the cost of an ad. Usually there is a minimum size requirement for ads appearing in full colour. Refer to Figure 8.7 for cost examples that include colour and position charges.

Does the use of colour justify the additional expense? In making this decision, the advertiser must weigh the potential impact of colour on the reader against the cost of colour. Much research has been done on the impact of colour in newspaper advertising. The research finds that full colour draws readers to ads (noted scores are higher) and keeps them more involved in the message. Colour also boosts in-depth reading by 60 percent compared to black-and-white ads. Colour has more of an impact on readers than does the size of the ad.[10]

MULTIPLE-PAGE CHARGES

Multiple-page charges apply to advertisers that use multiple pages in a single issue of a newspaper. For example, supermarkets, department stores, and shopping malls often use double-page spreads, referred to as a **double truck**, or multiple pages to advertise weekly specials. In this situation, reduced line rates apply based on the number of pages purchased. Double-truck and multiple-page rates may or may not be quoted on a newspaper's rate card but are available by contacting the newspaper.

PREPRINTED INSERTS

Preprinted **inserts**, such as advertising **supplements** for supermarkets and department stores, are inserted into and distributed by most newspapers. Costs are usually quoted on a CPM (cost per thousand) basis, with rates increasing as pages are added. For example, an 8-page insert in the *Toronto Star* has a CPM of $50.50 while a 24-page insert has a CPM of $61.00.[11] The CPM is multiplied by the circulation (in thousands) to arrive at

FIGURE **8.7**

Illustrations of calculating newspaper advertising rates

Refer to the rate card in Figure 8.6. The transient line rate was used in each calculation. The following illustrations consider two aspects of newspaper buying: the addition of colour and requesting specific locations.

ILLUSTRATION 1—ADDITION OF COLOUR

Newspaper:	*Globe and Mail* Metro Edition
Size of Ad:	6 columns wide by 8 column inches deep
Colour:	all ads are full colour
Frequency:	2 insertions

The cost calculation would be as follows:

Total Number of Lines
$$(6 \times 8 \times 14) \times 8 = 1344 \text{ lines}$$

Cost of the Ad (in black and white)
$$1344 \times \$33.14 = \$44\,540.16$$

Additional Colour Cost
$$\$7721 \times 2 = \$15\,442$$

Total Cost
$$\$44\,540.16 + \$15\,442 = \$59\,982.16$$

ILLUSTRATION 2—POSITION REQUEST

Newspaper:	*Globe and Mail* National Edition
Size of Ad:	3 columns wide by 8 column inches deep
Colour:	black and white
Frequency:	6
Location Request:	page 3, News Section

The cost calculation would be as follows:

Total Number of Lines
$$(3 \times 8 \times 14) \times 6 = 2016 \text{ lines}$$

Cost of Ad
$$2016 \times \$41.95 = \$84\,571.20$$

Position Charge (add 40%)
$$\$84\,571.20 \times 1.40 = \$118\,399.68$$

total cost. Assuming the circulation of the *Toronto Star* is 450 000, the cost of an 8-page insert would be $22 725.00 ($50.50 × 450).

SPLIT RUNS

A **split run** occurs when an advertiser uses the full circulation of the publication but has different material appearing in two or more regions. Split runs can be used for testing the effectiveness of various advertisements that are under consideration. For example, an advertiser may want to test some variations in layout and design. To do so, the various ads are placed in the same newspaper but they are distributed to different areas. The action generated in each region is compared to determine which ad was more effective. If the ads contained coupons of the same value, redemption rates would determine which ad was most effective in stimulating action.

INSERTION ORDERS

Details of a newspaper ad are communicated via an insertion order. The **insertion order** specifies pertinent details including the size of the ad, the dates of its insertion, use of colour, position requests, and the line rate to be charged. Closing dates and cancellation dates may also be included.

To verify that an advertisement actually ran, the agency or the advertiser receives a tear sheet from the newspaper. As the name implies, a **tear sheet** is an ad that the newspaper personnel extract from the newspaper to illustrate to the advertiser how it actually appeared. Should there be any problems with the ad, such as poor production quality, the advertiser or agency might request a **make good**, a rerun of an ad at the publisher's expense.

COMPARING NEWSPAPERS FOR EFFICIENCY

In larger metropolitan markets, where several newspapers compete for advertising revenue, advertisers must decide which papers to place advertising with. If using a shotgun strategy, the advertiser may use all newspapers. Conversely, if budgets are limited and target markets are more precisely defined, the advertiser may be more selective in the decision-making process.

Since the circulations and the costs of advertising (line rates) vary among newspapers, the advertiser must have a way of comparing the alternatives. To make this comparison, the advertiser may use a standard figure called the CPM. **CPM** is the actual cost of reaching 1000 readers in a market. The formula for calculating CPM is as follows:

$$\text{CPM} = \frac{\text{Unit Cost of Message}}{\text{Circulation (in thousands)}}$$

To illustrate the concept of CPM, advertisers wanting to reach adults in the Toronto market would choose among three daily newspapers. See Figure 8.8 for specific details of how the newspapers are compared.

As shown by Figure 8.8, the newspaper CPM is strictly a quantitative figure and the results vary considerably. If the advertiser's decision regarding what newspaper to use were based solely on this principle, the decision would be an easy one—the *Toronto Star* and *Toronto Sun* have the lowest CPM of the four newspapers sampled. Not shown in a CPM calculation is the demographic profile of the readers of the various newspapers. The *Toronto Star* and *Toronto Sun* offer mass appeal to a broad cross-section of the Toronto population at very reasonable costs compared with those of the *Globe and Mail*. However, if the target market is more upscale in terms of income, occupation, and educational background, the *Globe and Mail* might be selected, despite the higher CPM.

In summary, CPM is a quantitative figure that fluctuates with changes in the line rate or circulation: the higher the circulation, the lower the CPM. Advertisers can use it as a base guideline for comparing the varying cost efficiencies of specific newspapers that reach a mass target market.

Magazines in Canada

Currently, 1700 magazines are published and distributed in Canada, 800 of which are classified as consumer magazines. Magazines are classified in many ways—by content and audience reached, by circulation, by frequency of publication, and by size and format.

Specifications	Toronto Star	Globe and Mail	Toronto Sun	National Post
Ad Size (lines)	900	900	900	900
Line Cost	$19.94	$30.88	$8.31	$16.20
Ad Cost (rate x lines)	$17 946	$27 793	$7479	$14 580
Circulation	433 090	414 940	179 540	237 800
CPM	$41.43	$88.25	$41.66	$61.31

Analysis: The CPM for the Toronto Star *and* Toronto Sun *are close. Both papers reach a general cross-section of adult readers. The* Globe and Mail *reaches an audience characterized by higher education, higher income, and professional occupations. The cost of reaching a more upscale reader is much more. The CPM for the* National Post *is lower than the* Globe and Mail *even though the readership profile is similar. The* National Post *is a newer paper trying to establish a circulation base. To attract advertisers its rates are lower than the* Globe and Mail.

Source: Adapted from *Canadian Advertising Rates and Data*, January 2006. Published with permission of Rogers Media Inc.

> **FIGURE 8.8**
>
> Comparison of newspapers based on CPM: Cost of reaching 1000 people

CONTENT AND AUDIENCE REACHED

In terms of content and audience reached, publications fall into two major categories: consumer magazines and business magazines. Both categories include general interest and special interest publications. In both consumer and business magazines, the content is such that it has high interest among a precisely defined target market.

CONSUMER MAGAZINES   *Canadian Advertising Rates and Data* indexes 50 sub-classifications of consumer magazines, with the classification based on the publication's content and audience. There is a strong base of general interest magazines, as well as a host of specialized classifications such as art and antiques, children, entertainment, hobbies, sports and recreation, and women's. Popular, high-circulation magazines in their respective categories include *Reader's Digest* (general interest), *Maclean's* (news), *Chatelaine* (women's), *Flare* (fashion), and *Canadian House & Home* (homes).

Canadian House & Home
www.canadianhouseandhome.com

BUSINESS MAGAZINES   Business magazines can be broadly subdivided into subject areas such as trade, industry, professional, and institutional. Sub-classifications of these general areas would include broadcasting, engineering construction, food and food processing, hardware trade, hotels and restaurants, photography, and telecommunications. Business publications tend to be very specialized, their content appealing to a particular industry, trade, or professional group. With a very well-defined target audience, such specialized publications allow an efficient use of media dollars by advertisers.

Business magazines can also be classified as horizontal or vertical. A **horizontal publication** appeals to people who occupy the same level of responsibility in a business—the senior management level, for example. Horizontal publications tend to be more general in content, dealing with subjects such as business issues and trends, management information systems, and effective business management principles. Examples of horizontal business publications are *Canadian Business*, *National Post Business*, *ROB Magazine*, and *Profit*. Also classified as horizontal are those publications aimed at people who have functions in their companies similar to those discussed in the magazine. A magazine such as *Modern Purchasing* would be directed at the purchasing managers and agents in any number of different industries.

Vertical publications appeal to all levels of people in the same industry. All specialized classifications and corresponding magazines fall into this category. *Canadian Grocer*, for example, appeals to those people employed in the food processing and food distribution business in Canada, while *Foodservice & Hospitality* appeals to those employed in the restaurant, hotel, or food service industry.

CIRCULATION BASE (DISTRIBUTION)

Canadian magazines are distributed on the basis of **paid circulation**, which refers to subscriptions and newsstand sales. Magazines such as *Maclean's, Time, Chatelaine, Flare,* and *Canadian Business* are paid-circulation magazines and rely on subscriptions, newsstand sales, and advertising space to generate revenue.

Some magazines are distributed on the basis of **controlled circulation**. In this case the magazine is distributed free to a predetermined target market (e.g., a target defined by demographic segment, geographic area, or job function). A controlled-circulation magazine generates revenue from advertising space only. Typically, receivers of the magazine are in a unique position to influence sales, so they are attractive to advertisers. *CAA* magazine is an example of a controlled-circulation magazine. It is mailed to 1.5 million members of the Canadian Automobile Association (CAA) four times a year. *CAA* contains stories geared to the lifestyle and travel interests of CAA members.

FREQUENCY OF PUBLICATION AND REGIONAL EDITIONS

The frequency of publication varies considerably from one magazine to another. The more common frequencies are monthly and weekly; more limited frequencies are biweekly, bimonthly, or quarterly. Numerous magazines offer regional editions. Popular consumer magazines such as *Canadian Living/Coup de Pouce, Chatelaine* (English and French editions), and *Maclean's* offer advertisers regional flexibility in reaching geographic targets. The following is a sampling of magazines, their respective publication frequencies, and regional flexibilities:

Magazine	Frequency of Publications	Regional Editions
Canadian Business	24 bimonthly	2
Reader's Digest	12 monthly	9
Maclean's	52 weekly	15
Chatelaine (Eng. & Fr.)	12 monthly	7
Flare	12 monthly	5

SIZE AND FORMAT

Canadian magazines are published in three distinct sizes: digest, standard, and larger size. Owing to the rising costs of production, mailing, and distribution, there is currently a trend toward smaller publications.

A **digest-size magazine**'s approximate dimensions are $5\frac{1}{2}$ inches $\times$ $7\frac{1}{4}$ inches (14 cm $\times$ 18.4 cm), with a two-column printing format. *Reader's Digest/Sélection du Reader's Digest* is a good example of this type of format. The dimensions of a **standard-size magazine** are 8 inches 11 inches (20.3 cm $\times$ 27.9 cm), with a three-column format. Among the popular magazines that appear in this size and format are *Maclean's, Chatelaine, Canadian Business*, and *Equinox*.

Some magazines are produced in a **large-size format**. The dimensions of larger magazines vary from one publication to another. *Marketing* is a large-size business publication, with dimensions of 11¼ inches × 16¼ inches (28.6 cm × 41.3 cm).

Marketing
www.marketingmag.ca

MAGAZINE CIRCULATION AND READERSHIP HIGHLIGHTS

Generally, magazine circulation is declining in Canada, largely due to the growth and influence of digital media alternatives driven by the internet. However, although circulation is declining, readership levels remain relatively high. Research studies show that 87 percent of Canadians read at least one magazine every three months, with that figure rising to 94 percent for managers, owners, and professionals.[12] Magazines are sold to advertisers on the basis of circulation and readership. Circulation and readership figures are verified by independent data collection organizations: Audit Bureau of Circulations and the Print Measurement Bureau.

The Audit Bureau of Circulations (ABC) issues standardized statements, referred to as publisher's statements, verifying circulation statistics for paid-circulation magazines and most daily newspapers in Canada. A **publisher's statement** includes the average paid circulation for the past six months, paid circulation for each issue in the last six months, new and renewal subscriptions, and a geographic analysis of **total paid circulation**. BPA Worldwide (formerly Canadian Circulations Audit Board—CCAB) provides similar information, but its focus is primarily on business, trade, and professional publications.

The Print Measurement Bureau (PMB) implements an annual research study to track the readership of all magazines. The readership data that is collected is cross-referenced with other data of interest to advertisers. That data includes product and brand usage data, retail shopping habits, and lifestyle information. When analyzing what magazines to select for advertising, circulation and readership comparisons are made among a selection of prospective magazines. Wise managers will look at both statistics when making decisions. It is possible that a magazine with a lower circulation has more readers per copy than a magazine with higher circulation, resulting in a higher readership level. **Readers per copy** is the average number of people who read a single issue of a publication. For example, *Outdoor Canada* has a circulation of 87 000 (relatively low) but has 20.4 readers per copy (very high), for a total monthly readership of 1.77 million.[13]

For a summary of circulation and readership data for a selection of magazines, refer to Figure 8.9. In each of the classifications in Figure 8.9, the magazines listed compete with each other for advertisers. How efficient they are at reaching the target is an important influence on what magazines an advertiser chooses.

Magazines as an Advertising Medium

Magazines offer advertisers a unique set of advantages and disadvantages. This section presents some of the strategic considerations for using or rejecting magazines for advertising purposes.

ADVANTAGES OF MAGAZINES

TARGET-MARKET SELECTIVITY   Magazines are often referred to as being a "class" medium rather than a "mass" medium. Both consumer magazines and business magazines have target audiences that are well defined by some combination of demographic and psychographic variables. Therefore, advertisers with well-defined target markets can select specific magazines by using a profile-matching strategy (i.e., by selecting

FIGURE 8.9

Circulation and readership of selected magazines

In their respective classifications, each of these magazines competes for advertisers. Advertisers use circulation and readership data to determine which magazines to select and with what frequency. Readers-per-copy data is compiled from an annual research study conducted by the Print Measurement Bureau.

Classification/ Magazine	Average Circulation	Readers Per Copy	Total Readership
BUSINESS			
Canadian Business	83 000	11.8	979 400
Profit	103 000	3.6	370 800
ROB Magazine	296 000	5.0	1 480 000
WOMEN'S			
Canadian Living	519 000	8.2	4 255 800
Chatelaine	586 100	6.4	3 751 000
Chatelaine (Fr.)	200 000	6.2	1 240 000
Homemakers	512 200	4.9	2 509 700

Analysis: Although the circulation of Canadian Business is much lower than the other two business magazines, its readers per copy are much higher. Canadian Business compares favourably to ROB Magazine in terms of readers reached. Canadian Living's circulation is only 90 percent of Chatelaine's circulation, but it has many more readers per copy. Despite the lower circulation, Canadian Living reaches more readers than Chatelaine. Both magazines are a good advertising buy for advertisers wanting to reach women. Similar comparisons can be made in other classifications of magazines.

Source: Adapted from data contained in Canadian Media Director's Council, Media Digest, 2006–2007.

magazines whose audience closely matches the product's target market). The profile-matching strategy becomes a little more complicated when a group of comparable magazines competes for the same target audience. Nevertheless, target-market selectivity is the primary advantage of magazines.

GEOGRAPHIC FLEXIBILITY   Numerous high-circulation consumer magazines offer regional editions. An advertiser wishing to advertise in a certain area, such as the Prairies or the Atlantic provinces, may make use of the flexibility offered by regional editions—provided, of course, that the regional readership is similar to the advertiser's target market. Regional editions also provide advertisers with the opportunity to increase spending in certain geographic areas on an as-needed basis. Canada's more popular magazines offer regional flexibility: Maclean's (15 editions), Canadian Living (11 editions), and Reader's Digest (9 editions).

LIFESPAN   Because of the relative infrequency (in comparison to newspapers) of magazine publication (weekly, biweekly, monthly), the advertiser gets the benefit of longevity. Magazines remain in the home and are read intermittently over a period of time; hence, readers may be exposed to an advertisement several times during the lifespan of the magazine (which means that the product gets repeat exposure at no extra cost). Some magazines, such as Canadian Geographic, may be retained in the home permanently as part of a collection.

ENGAGEMENT Magazines are purchased and read because the editorial content interests the reader. Some research studies show an overwhelming percentage of readers pay full or complete attention when reading magazines. Magazine readers demonstrate the lowest level of multi-tasking when compared to multi-tasking rates for other media. An advertiser will benefit from the prestige of the magazine and the quality it represents, and from the attention shown by readers while reading.

QUALITY OF REPRODUCTION Magazines are printed on high-quality paper, by means of a four-colour process that creates a high-quality, attractive presentation of both editorial and advertising content. Recent innovations, such as bright metallic inks that create a striking visual effect, have added to the quality of reproduction. Ads always look good in a magazine!

CREATIVE CONSIDERATIONS In terms of creative strategy and execution, magazines offer some flexibility. For example, most magazines offer gatefolds (multiple-page fold-outs), double-page spreads, and bleeds. They can also accommodate special features such as scent strips, **pop-up coupons** (coupons with a perforated edge appearing on top of an advertisement for a product), and even product samples. Although the use of such options may increase the cost of advertising, the resulting distinction and potential impact on the reader may justify the additional expense. See Figure 8.10 for an illustration.

PASS-ALONG READERSHIP Magazine space is sold to advertisers at costs that are based not only on the magazine's circulation but on the number of readers it reaches. As well

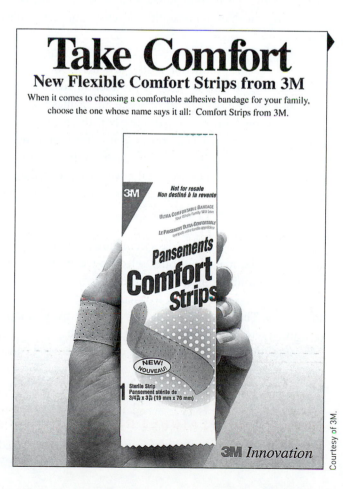

FIGURE 8.10

An insert (tip-in) in a magazine that includes a sample of the product

Courtesy of 3M.

as being exposed to its primary readers, a magazine may be exposed to other readers. The actual readership of the magazine will be much greater than the circulation. A **primary reader** is a person who qualifies as a reader because he or she lives (works) in the household (office) where the publication is initially received. Additional readers, called **pass-along readers**, are those that do not live (work) in the household (office) where the publication is originally received. The combination of primary readers and pass-along readers equals **total readership**.

Porsche spends a considerable amount of money on magazine advertising, and for good reason. To find out why magazines play such an important role in Porsche's media mix, read the Advertising in Action vignette **Involved Readers Important to Porsche**.

DISADVANTAGES OF MAGAZINES

LEAD TIME   The layout of a monthly magazine is planned well in advance of the issue date so an advertiser must likewise be prepared early (usually six to eight weeks or so) with the advertisement. For a weekly magazine, an average of four weeks is required. Long lead times do not allow advertisers the flexibility of changing advertising content should market conditions so warrant; nor can they increase advertising weight on short notice.

CLUTTER   **Clutter** in magazine advertising refers to the clustering of ads near the front and back of the magazine. Advertisers can partially overcome the problem by ordering preferred positions (covers), assuming such positions are available. Although covers are available at higher cost, the resulting impact may justify the additional expense. Other position requests, such as being on the right side (as opposed to the left side), are available at no additional cost, but the publisher will not guarantee the position.

COST   Magazine production costs, particularly for four-colour advertisements, are significantly higher than newspaper production costs. Because of these high production costs and because of the cost of space, magazines may not be an efficient buy for the local or regional advertiser, particularly if the regional target is small. Although many magazines offer regional editions, the absolute cost of advertising does not decline proportionately with the decline in circulation. In fact, the cost of reaching the regional reader is actually higher. National advertisers, with their larger budgets, can consider regional editions and the higher costs associated with them when market conditions warrant such activity.

FREQUENCY   Although mass-circulation magazines offer high reach to the advertiser, and specialized magazines offer selective reach, magazines do not offer the advertiser much opportunity to reach the audience *frequently*, because the distribution frequency of magazines is low. Building frequency using one publication is extremely difficult for advertisers. They can overcome this problem by adding magazines that reach similar target markets, but such a solution is expensive.

Magazines are often a medium of choice among consumer-goods advertisers that want to reach fairly specific targets with a message. Generally speaking, magazines are useful when a profile-matching media strategy or a rifle media strategy is in place.

ADVERTISING FEATURES OFFERED BY MAGAZINES

Magazines have some special features that make the medium attractive to potential advertisers. The use of these features adds to the cost of advertising, however, so

Involved Readers Important to Porsche

The Porsche brand is no longer exclusively geared toward expensive sports cars. The company now offers models that meet other consumer needs, such as the Porsche Cayenne SUV, a family-oriented vehicle. Consequently, the target-market profile of the Porsche customer continues to broaden, and this has led to changes in the brand's media mix.

Porsche uses television on a very selective basis and also does a substantial amount of online advertising. The company recognizes that people spend a lot of time researching information about automobiles online—especially when they are in the mood to buy! Yet, for Porsche, magazines form the foundation of the entire media plan.

Magazines have played a huge role in bringing the "experience of driving" a Porsche to life. "It's about the thrill you can get in a Porsche that you can't get anywhere else." The headline of an ad for the new Cayman S model reads, "The black t-shirt under the white lab coat." Body copy talks about "calculated engineering meeting pure muscle," tempting the reader to defy the ordinary. Style and elegant photography are part of every ad, as is the closing line in the body copy: "Porsche. There is no substitute."

Magazines get top billing at Porsche because they target the audience efficiently and they can tap into the magazine's strong relationship with its readers. "We are trying to hit people when they are deeply involved in the media they are consuming," says John Colasanti, president of Carmichael Lynch,

an agency working closely with Porsche. Porsche sees magazines as an on-demand medium. It's not attached to anything. It's cordless. It's not forced upon you. It's the reader who decides when they are going to spend time with it, and usually it's quality time.

For a brand like Porsche, the message has to be communicated in way that lives up to the righteousness of the brand. Print makes it happen. The photos in the ads look like works of art—just like the real car!

Ad placements in popular automotive magazines like *Car and Driver*, *Motor Trend*, and *Road & Track* are a certainty. But given the expanded profile of the target, and the varied lifestyles it represents, lead ads now appear in news, business, and lifestyle magazines such as *Maclean's*, *Canadian Business*, *Report on Business*, and *Score Golf*.

Porsche doesn't dismiss the merits of other media; they simply like the efficiency of magazines and the deep interaction the reader has with the medium.

Source: Adapted from "Porsche finds magazines provide firm foundation," *Advertising Age*, April 26, 2004, p. M5.

---

advertisers must carefully weigh the additional cost of these features against the potential impact their use will have on readers. These features include bleeds, gatefolds, preferred positions, inserts and reply cards, and split-run availability.

BLEEDS   The term **bleed** refers to a situation in which the coloured background of an ad extends to the edge of the page. An ad can bleed on some or all sides of the page, depending on creative strategy and execution. Most magazines offer bleeds, and either build bleed charges into published four-colour rates or quote the additional costs separately. An example of a bleed ad is shown in Figure 8.11.

GATEFOLDS   A **gatefold** is an advertisement that folds out of a magazine, spanning two, three, or four pages. Gatefolds are usually used on special occasions. For example,

FIGURE 8.11

An example of a bleed ad

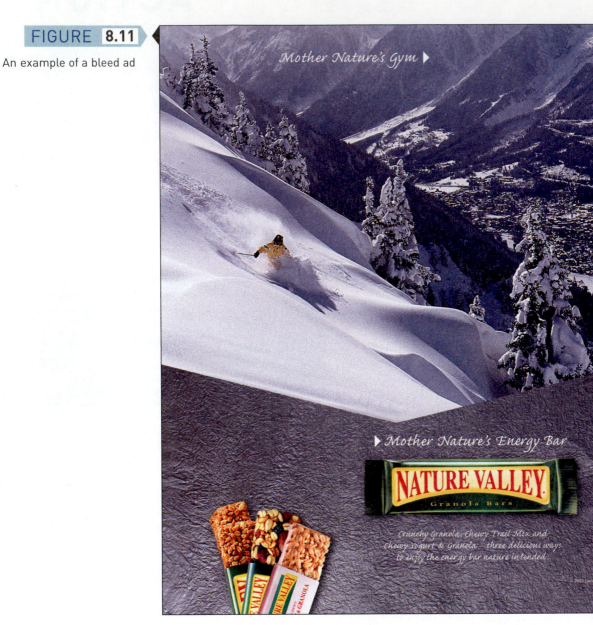

a car manufacturer may use gatefolds when launching a new line. The most common position for a gatefold is the inside front cover. Magazines are now experimenting with gatefolds as part of the front cover (e.g., a one-page foldout from the side of the cover or a window-style foldout from the middle of the cover). Since gatefolds are not used very frequently and require significant lead times, most magazine rate cards state that rates are available on request. See the illustration of a front-page gatefold in Figure 8.12.

PREFERRED POSITIONS   Obtaining a **preferred position** in a magazine involves requesting a specific position for an ad to be placed within the magazine. Since the potential for an advertisement to be seen is very great if it is positioned on the inside front or back covers, such positions command a higher price than others. While the cost of cover positions varies from one magazine to another, an increase of 15 to 20 percent above a normal page is common. Position charges are discussed in the magazine media-buying section of this chapter.

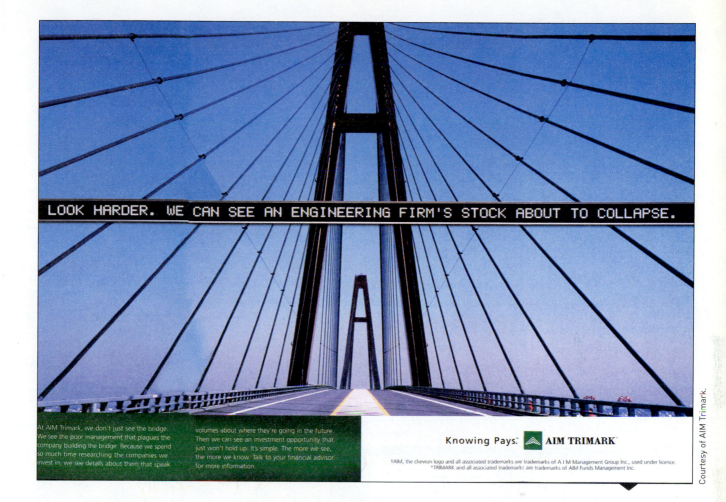

LOOK HARDER. WE CAN SEE AN ENGINEERING FIRM'S STOCK ABOUT TO COLLAPSE.

At AIM Trimark, we don't just see the bridge. We see the poor management that plagues the company building the bridge. Because we spend so much time researching the companies we invest in, we see details about them that speak volumes about where they're going in the future. Then we can see an investment opportunity that just won't hold up. It's simple. The more we see, the more we know. Talk to your financial advisor for more information.

Knowing Pays.  **AIM TRIMARK**

†AIM, the chevron logo and all associated trademarks are trademarks of A I M Management Group Inc., used under licence.
*TRIMARK and all associated trademarks are trademarks of AIM Funds Management Inc.

FIGURE 8.12

An ad that folds out from the front cover of a magazine: a real attention-grabber

INSERTS AND REPLY CARDS   Practically any size of business reply card, small multiple-page insert, or booklet can be bound into a magazine. Business reply cards are common in business publications, as are pop-up coupons and small recipe booklets in consumer publications. **Tipping** (gluing) items such as recipe booklets or small product catalogues into magazines is now very popular. The brochure or catalogue is easily removed once the magazine is purchased. The illustration in Figure 8.10 is an example of a tip-in. Advertisers usually must contact the publisher for rates and availability information.

SPLIT-RUN AVAILABILITY   As with some newspapers, certain consumer magazines offer split-run availability. In this case, different ads may appear in different regional editions. Assuming that all conditions are constant and that each of the two or more ads contains a coupon, split-run availability can help advertisers determine which ad is more effective; they can compare actual customer responses to the coupon.

Buying Magazine Space

The procedure for buying magazine space begins with deciding on the size of the ad, which involves choosing from among the variety of page options sold by the magazines under consideration. The rates quoted are based on the size of page requested. Other factors that could influence the cost of advertising in magazines include the frequency of insertions and appropriate discounts, the use of colour, guaranteed-position charges, and the use of regional editions.

SIZE OF AN ADVERTISEMENT AND RATE SCHEDULES

Canadian Geographic
www.canadiangeographic.ca

Magazines offer a variety of page options or page combinations. For example, *Canadian Geographic* sells space in the following formats: double-page spread, double half-page spread, one page, two-thirds page, half-page digest, half-page horizontal, and one-third page. See Figure 8.13 for illustrations of various magazine ad sizes.

The size selected for the advertisement determines the rate to be charged. Magazine rates are typically quoted for all page combinations sold on the basis of full colour. Rates may also be quoted for black-and-white ads and black-and-white ads with one colour added.

To illustrate how costs are calculated, let's consider a simple example. Assume an advertiser would like to purchase a one-page, four-colour ad in *Canadian Geographic* for the January/February and March issues (see Figure 8.14). Since the frequency of the advertising does not reach the first discount level (three insertions), the advertiser would pay the one-time rate. The cost calculation would be as follows:

One-page rate × number of insertions = Total cost

$16 615 × 2 = $33 230

FIGURE 8.13

Various sizes of magazine ads

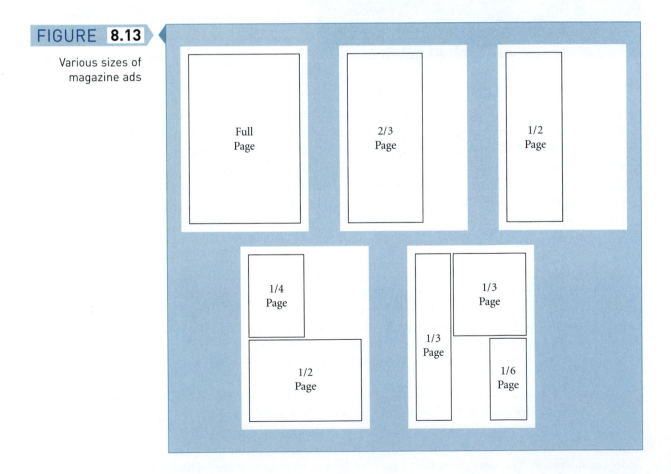

FIGURE 8.14

Canadian Geographic rate card

CANADIAN Geographic NOW 10X PER YEAR! NATIONAL RATES AND DATA

www.canadiangeographic.ca

PUBLISHING SCHEDULE 2008

ISSUE	EDITORIAL FEATURES	CLOSING DATES (insertion orders & material)	ON NEWSSTAND (subs. arrive earlier)
Sept/Oct 2007	Regional Canadian Feature w/Poster Map	July 25, 2007	August 21, 2007
November 2007	**TRAVEL — WINTER**	September 19, 2007	October 16, 2007
December 2007	Wildlife Stories of the Year	October 24, 2007	November 13, 2007
Jan/Feb 2008	Annual Photo Contest Winner	November 28, 2007	December 25, 2007
March 2008	**NEW! TRAVEL — SPRING**	January 30, 2008	March 3, 2008
April 2008	TBD	February 27, 2008	March 31, 2008
May 2008	**TRAVEL — SUMMER**	March 26, 2008	April 28, 2008
June 2008	Annual Report on the Environment	April 23, 2008	May 26, 2008
	Canadian Environment Awards	N/A	N/A
July/Aug 2008	Annual Photo Contest Launch	May 21, 2008	June 23, 2008
September 2008	**NEW! TRAVEL — AUTUMN**	July 16, 2008	August 18, 2008
October 2008	Regional Canadian Feature w/Poster Map	August 20, 2008	September 22, 2008
November 2008	**TRAVEL — WINTER**	September 17, 2008	October 20, 2008
December 2008	Wildlife Stories of the Year	October 22, 2008	November 24, 2008

NATIONAL ADVERTISING RATES 2008*

NATIONAL	1X	3X	6X	9X	12X
IFC spread	$34,030	$32,995	$31,015	$31,045	$31,115
OBC	$19,830	$19,235	$18,660	$18,105	$17,555
IBC	$19,015	$17,985	$17,445	$16,920	$16,405
Double-page spread	$29,585	$28,695	$27,835	$27,005	$26,195
Full page	$16,615	$16,160	$15,665	$15,190	$14,740
1/2-page spread	$19,465	$18,875	$18,135	$17,760	$17,230
2/3 page	$13,215	$12,810	$12,430	$12,050	$11,695
1/2-page digest	$12,075	$11,710	$11,355	$11,010	$10,675
1/2-page horizontal	$11,800	$10,270	$9,960	$9,660	$9,355
1/3 page	$7,920	$7,695	$7,450	$7,215	$7,005
EAST/WEST SPLIT RUNS	**1X**	**3X**	**6X**	**9X**	**12X**
Double-page spread	$22,190	$21,520	$20,885	$20,260	$19,655
Full page	$12,495	$12,120	$11,750	$11,400	$11,065

*GROSS CANADIAN DOLLARS

DISCOUNTS

Advertisers that purchase space in specific magazines with greater frequency will qualify for a variety of discounts. The nature of these discounts may vary from one publication to another. Some of the more common discounts offered by magazines include frequency, continuity, and corporate discounts.

In magazines, a frequency discount refers to a discounted page rate, with the discount based on the number of times an advertisement is run. The more often the ad is run, the lower the unit cost for each ad. In the *Canadian Geographic* rate card, the unit rate is reduced when the ad is run 3 times, 6 times, 9 times, and 12 times.

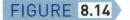

FIGURE **8.14**

Canadian Geographic
rate card *continued*

Canadian Geographic — NOW 10X PER YEAR!   NATIONAL RATES AND DATA
www.canadiangeographic.ca

MECHANICAL SPECIFICATIONS

GENERIC BOOK SPECIFICATIONS

Trim Size	7 3/4" x 10 7/8"
Bleed	Minimum 1/8" bleed
Colour	CMYK throughout
Printing	Web offset, coated stock, Staccato
Binding	Perfect-bound

STANDARD UNIT SIZES

	Non-Bleed Ad	Bleed-Ad Trim Size*
Full page	6 3/4" x 9 9/16"	7 3/4" x 10 7/8" + bleed
Double-page spread	14 1/2" x 9 9/16"	15 1/2" x 10 7/8" + bleed
Double 1/2-page spread	14 1/2" x 4 11/16"	15 1/2" x 5 1/4" + bleed
1/2-page horizontal	6 3/4" x 4 11/16"	7 3/4" x 5 1/4" + bleed
1/2-page digest	4 3/8" x 6 1/2"	4 7/8" x 7 1/4" + bleed
2/3-page (two-column)	4 3/8" x 9 9/16"	4 7/8" x 10 7/8" + bleed
1/3-page vertical	2" x 9 9/16"	2 1/2" x 10 7/8" + bleed
1/3-page square	4 3/8" x 4 11/16"	4 7/8" x 5 1/4" + bleed

*Any image or background colour intended to bleed
must extend a minimum of 1/8" past the trim on all four sides

Non-Bleed Ads
Ads that are not intended to bleed must be sized to fit within the non-bleed sizes listed.

Bleed Ads
- Ads that are intended to bleed must be sized to be trimmed to the bleed sizes listed.
- All live matter (text, images not to be trimmed) must be kept within the non-bleed measurements. Any matter that extends past the non-bleed safe area may be trimmed due to folding and bindery variations.
- Any image or background colour intended to bleed must extend a minimum of 1/8" past the trim dimensions on all four sides of the ad. Right- or left-hand positioning is not guaranteed.
- Be aware of common crossover limitations in "double-page-spread" configurations (adjoining pages can shift up to 1/8" in the binding process on certain copies).

Author's Alterations and Late Fees
Changes to supplied material will be made only when accompanied by written instructions from the client. Changes will be made only if received before the ad submission date, and clients may be charged an AA fee of $80/hour, depending on the production stage. *Canadian Geographic* endeavours to comply with all advertisers' changes but assumes no responsibility for errors or omissions resulting from requested changes. Requested changes are assumed to be final. A courtesy proof will be sent to the client upon request. Any material supplied after the published submission date will be subject to a charge of $150.

Production Requirements
Canadian Geographic does not accept film. Electronic files must be supplied.
- Electronic files must be supplied as PDF/X-1a:2001 compliant or Mac QuarkXPress 6.5 (or earlier), with all support files and fonts included. Extra charges may be applied to convert PC files.
- Acceptable removable media include CDs and DVDs.
- Compressed files must be saved as self-extracting archives (.sea).
- Type should be converted to outline when possible (Adobe Illustrator, Macromedia Freehand, CorelDraw).
- Contract colour proof must be supplied to guarantee accurate colour reproduction.
- *Canadian Geographic* will not assume responsibility for type reflow or accurate colour reproduction if all necessary fonts, support files or press-ready proofs are not included.

General Information
Acceptability: The content and design of all advertisements are subject to the publisher's approval.
Commissions: 15% of charges for space, position and colour allowed to recognized agencies.
Cash Discount: 1% on net if paid within 15 days of date of invoice.
Terms: Net 30 days; 2% interest charged per month on overdue accounts; 24% per annum.
GST: Rates do not include Goods and Services Tax. Where applicable, a 6% GST (effective July 1, 2006) will be added to the price of all advertising and services in *Canadian Geographic*.

Shipping
1. All insertion orders and contracts are to be sent to:
Canadian Geographic Enterprises
Advertising Sales Office
495 King Street W., Suite 301
Toronto, ON M5V 1K4
Telephone: (416) 360-4151
Fax: (416) 360-1526

2. All creative should be shipped to:
Canadian Geographic Enterprises
Mike Elston
Production Manager
39 McArthur Avenue
Ottawa, ON K1L 8L7
Telephone: (613) 745-4629
Fax: (613) 744-0947
E-mail: elston@canadiangeographic.ca

For FTP information, contact your Advertising Coordinator
Telephone: (416) 360-4151
E-mail: adsales@canadiangeographic.ca

Courtesy of Canadian Geographic.

A continuity discount is an additional discount offered to advertisers that agree to purchase space in consecutive issues of a magazine (such as buying space in 12 issues of a monthly magazine). When continuity discounts are combined with frequency discounts, lower unit costs per page of advertising result.

Large advertisers that use the same magazine to advertise a variety of products may qualify for corporate discounts. Procter & Gamble, for example, will buy a sizeable number of pages in *Canadian Living* each month since many of its products target the same consumer. A **corporate discount** involves consideration of the total number of pages purchased by the company (all product lines combined), resulting in a lower page rate for each product. As an alternative to using pages as the means of calculating volume discounts, magazines may use dollar volume purchased as the guideline, and offer a percentage discount on total advertising dollar volume.

COLOUR AND POSITION CHARGES

Additional costs for the inclusion of colour, or for a **guaranteed position**, are quoted separately on the rate card. For a guaranteed position, such as the back cover or the inside front or inside back covers, the additional costs are usually in the 15- to 20-percent range when compared to the cost of a regular page. Rates for guaranteed positions are usually quoted as a percentage or a dollar amount increase over the normal four-colour page rate. As for any regular page, the unit rate for a cover decreases as the frequency increases.

MAGAZINE BUYING ILLUSTRATIONS

To illustrate the cost calculations of buying magazine space, let's develop a few examples based on the *Canadian Geographic* rate card (Figure 8.14) and on the following information:

Example 1:

Size of ad: One-page, four-colour ad
Number of insertions: Ad to run in four consecutive issues

The calculation for this buying plan will be as follows:

Costs for one-page, four-colour:

Base rate   = the 3–5 times rate
$16 160 × 4 = $64 640

Example 2:

Size of ad: Double-page spread, four-colour ad
Number of insertions: six issues

The calculation for this buying plan will be as follows:

Costs for DPS, four-colour:

Base rate   = the 6–8 times rate
$27 835 × 6 = $167 010

SPACE CONTRACTS AND THE MAGAZINE SHORT RATE   To facilitate the use of discount scales offered by magazines, larger advertisers usually enter into a space contract with magazines they use frequently. The space contract provides an estimate of the advertising space required for a one-year period. At the end of the year, adjustments are made (whether positive or negative) when actual usage of space is known. Should advertisers not meet their estimates, a short rate would be due the publisher. To illustrate, let's assume the advertiser estimated that 12 ad pages would be purchased in *Canadian Geographic*, but by the end of the contract period only 8 pages had been purchased. The advertiser would be billed as follows:

Ran 8 times but paid the 12-times rate:
8 × $14 740 = $117 920

Earned only the 8 times rate of $15 285:
8 × $15 665 = $125 320
Short rate due publisher = $7400

In this example, the advertiser owes the magazine $7400, according to the terms of the space contract. Conversely, if the advertiser purchased more than the estimated amount, to the point where another frequency discount plateau was reached, the magazine would rebate the difference to the advertiser.

MAGAZINE INSERTION ORDERS   Depending on the extent of an advertising campaign with any particular magazine, the advertiser may decide to enter into a space contract with the magazine or place an insertion order on an as-needed basis. To obtain the best possible rate, large advertisers will opt for the space contract. The space contract is not an order for a specific amount of space; rather, it protects the advertiser's right to buy space at a certain rate. Publishers retain the right to announce increases in rates at predetermined levels.

When the advertiser is ready to run an ad, an insertion order is sent to the magazine. The insertion order specifies the date of issue, the size of the ad, any applicable position requests, and the contracted rate. The advertiser must be aware of the closing date for placing ads. The **closing date** usually refers to the deadline for the insertion order and material due at the publication. In some cases, however, the insertion order date is a few weeks in advance of the material date. The **insertion order date** is the last date for ordering space and the **material date** is the last date for having production material at the publication.

COMPARING MAGAZINES FOR EFFICIENCY

Assuming that a decision has been made to use magazines, with the understanding that magazines usually have a well-defined target audience based on demographic variables, advertisers must choose particular magazines in which to advertise. Since costs and circulation figures vary, the advertiser must have a way of comparing alternatives. As with newspapers, **CPM** is an effective quantitative means of comparing competing magazines.

In most magazine classifications, there is usually a group of publications competing for the same market. For example, *Chatelaine*, *Homemakers*, and *Canadian Living* compete against each other in the women's classification. Although the editorial content varies from one magazine to another, they do reach a similar target, so advertisers must look at the efficiencies of each.

Figure 8.15 contains the comparative calculations for three of the magazines in the women's classification. In terms of a purely quantitative measure, *Homemakers* offers the best efficiency in reaching the target market. The CPM of *Homemakers* is considerably lower than that of *Canadian Living* and *Chatelaine*. However, *Chatelaine* and *Canadian Living* rely solely on subscriptions and newsstand sales for readers, while a portion of *Homemakers* readers get the magazine free. This could affect readership. Large advertisers are likely to select a combination of these three magazines. By doing so they are expanding their reach. The question is, how much weight does each magazine receive?

FIGURE 8.15

Comparative statistics used for making magazine buying decisions

	Chatelaine	Canadian Living	Homemakers
1 page, 4-colour	$46 505	$35 500	$23 230
Circulation	586 136	519 045	512 200
CPM	$79.34	$68.40	$45.35

CPM is calculated by dividing the cost of the ad by the circulation in thousands. For *Chatelaine* the calculation would be $46 505 divided by 586.14. That results in a CPM of $79.35. On a purely quantitative basis, *Homemakers* appears to be the most efficient magazine for reaching the target audience these magazines reach. *Homemakers* has the lowest CPM.

Source: Adapted from Canadian Media Directors' Council, *Media Digest*, 2005–2007, p. 526.

Technology and the Print Media

The information age and the electronic revolution together have changed the very nature of newspaper and magazine publishing. While the printed format remains the dominant form, major daily newspapers and national magazines have launched websites containing online versions. Some magazines have even launched their own television shows on specialty networks.

The major newspapers and magazines referred to in this chapter (the *Globe and Mail*, *National Post*, *Toronto Star*, *Chatelaine*, *Canadian Geographic*, and *Canadian Living*) offer a portion of their content online, as do many others. For advertisers using newspapers or magazines, the addition of a website means they can reach the same audience profile but in a different way. Ads in the form of banners (rectangular or square ads) and sponsorship opportunities are available on these websites. If readers are migrating to online editions of newspapers and magazines, advertisers will be less inclined to advertise in hard copy editions. Newspapers and magazines will have to convince their advertisers to shift their investment from hard copy to the online edition or they will incur lost revenues. More details about online advertising opportunities are included in Chapter 12. For an illustration of a magazine's website, see Figure 8.16.

Newspapers and magazines are also expanding into television. *Canadian House & Home* magazine produces a television show called *House & Home with Lynda Reeves*, which reaches an audience of 768 000. The hard-copy magazine has a circulation of 250 000 and readership of 2.7 million monthly.[14] The two media are a good combination for an advertiser seeking reach and frequency. *Cottage Life* magazine operates a television show by the same name, and the *Globe and Mail* operates a cable channel called *ROBtv*. They represent integrated marketing communications opportunities for advertisers wanting to reach the same target market but in different ways.

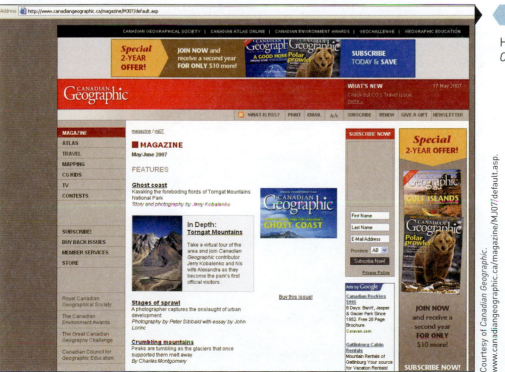

FIGURE 8.16

Homepage for *Canadian Geographic*

Courtesy of *Canadian Geographic*.
www.canadiangeographic.ca/magazine/MJ07/default.asp.

This trend of extending brands into other media is in its infancy—there is lots of room for growth for other newspapers and magazines. However, there is acknowledgement within the industry that the revenue model for newspapers and magazines may have to change over time. People are accustomed to viewing online information for free.[15] To sustain the online content, the publishers must find a way of getting people to pay for it. For their part, television cable channels are keenly interested in the idea of magazines expanding into television shows. In fact, they are constantly looking for new partnerships with other media suppliers, because content produced by others lowers their production costs.

SUMMARY

With respect to print media, the primary options for an advertiser are newspapers and magazines.

Newspaper advertising is divided between daily and weekly publications. Dailies and community newspapers attract both national and local advertisers, though they are more suited to local-market advertisers. A newspaper is published in one of two formats: the broadsheet, which is the larger, folded newspaper; and the tabloid, which is the smaller, flat newspaper. All newspapers receive revenues from four different types of advertising: national or general advertising, retail advertising, classified advertising, and preprinted inserts (flyers distributed via a newspaper).

As an advertising medium, newspapers offer the advertiser geographic selectivity, local-market coverage, and flexibility. Major disadvantages include the short lifespan, the lack of target-market orientation (demographic distinctions), and clutter. The rates charged an advertiser decrease as the volume of lines purchased increases, and rates are increased by position requests and requests for the use of colour.

Magazines are classified according to factors such as size and format, frequency of publication, circulation base, content, and audience reached. As an advertising medium, magazines offer target-market selectivity, quality in reproduction and editorial environment, and a longer lifespan than other media. On the negative side, significant lead times are required for materials, the use of colour raises costs, and clutter remains a problem.

Additional features of magazines that make them an attractive advertising medium include the use of bleeds, gatefolds, inserts, and reply cards. Magazine advertising rates depend on the size of the ad, the frequency of insertion, and the use of colour. A variety of discounts are available to advertisers that choose magazine advertising, with frequency and continuity being the most important factors reducing the cost of advertising.

Newspapers and magazines are now expanding their content on websites and television shows. The goal of such offerings is to provide synergies among print publishing, the internet, and television and to present new advertising opportunities for their advertisers.

KEY TERMS

REVIEW QUESTIONS

1. What is the difference between a tabloid and a broadsheet?

2. What are the differences among general advertising, retail advertising, and classified advertising?

3. What are the advantages and disadvantages of using newspapers as an advertising medium?

4. In a city where more than one daily newspaper dominates the market, how would you determine which newspaper to advertise in, assuming you could select only one? What factors would enter into your decision?

5. Provide an explanation for the following newspaper terms:

   a) hooker

   b) MAL

   c) transient rate

   d) make good

   e) split run

   f) ROP

   g) tear sheet

   h) make good

   i) flexform

   j) position charge

6. Calculate the total cost of the following newspaper campaigns based on the information provided. Use the transient rates for each calculation.

Campaign 1

Newspaper: *Globe and Mail* Sports Section

Size of Ad: 4 columns wide by 8 column inches deep

Colour: Black and white

Frequency: 10 ads (2 ads each week—Tuesday and Thursday)

Campaign 2

Newspaper: *Globe and Mail* National Edition

Size of Ad: 6 columns wide by 6 column inches deep

Colour: Black and white

Position Request: page A2 ROB Section

Frequency: 8 ads (2 ads each week—Wednesday and Friday)

7. What are the advantages and disadvantages of using magazines as an advertising medium?

8. What is the difference between the following pairs of magazine terms:

   a) Paid-circulation magazine versus controlled-circulation magazine

   b) Vertical publication versus horizontal publication

   c) Primary reader versus pass-along reader

9. Provide a brief explanation of the following magazine terms:

   a) digest ad

   b) bleed ad

   c) gatefold

   d) tipping (tip-in)

   e) reply cards

   f) insertion order date

   g) material date

   h) space contract

   i) split run

   j) preferred position

10. Calculate the cost of the following magazine campaigns using the information provided:

Campaign 1
Magazine: *Canadian Geographic*
Size: 1/2-page spread
Frequency: 4 ads
Colour: Full colour
Edition: National

Campaign 2
Magazine: *Canadian Geographic*
Size: 1/3 page
Frequency: 8 ads
Colour: Full colour
Edition: National

11. Identify and briefly describe the various discounts frequently offered by magazines.

12. How does the magazine short rate work?

13. Explain the CPM concept as it applies to the purchase of advertising space in magazines.

DISCUSSION QUESTIONS

1. Newspapers like the *Toronto Star*, the *Vancouver Sun*, and the *Globe and Mail* charge higher rates to advertisers requesting specific sections and specific pages for their ads. In some cases, the additional charge is as much as 40 to 50 percent more. Do the benefits gained outweigh the costs involved? What is your opinion?

2. "Paying a premium price for a cover position (inside front, inside back, or outside back) in a magazine is always a wise investment." Discuss this statement.

3. "The location of an advertisement in a newspaper is the key factor in determining the success of the ad."

Discuss this statement in the context of other variables you judge to be important.

4. Read the Advertising in Action vignette **Involved Readers Important to Porsche**. Porsche's media mix includes magazines, selective television, and online communications. Are there any other media that are suitable for reaching Porsche's target market? Consider the brand image and integrity of message that is so important to Porsche. Justify your media recommendation.

NOTES

1. Canadian Media Directors' Council, *Media Digest*, 2006–2007, p. 36.

2. *Ibid.*, p. 12.

3. *Ibid.*, pp. 43, 44.

4. Jim McElgunn, "Community press demographics," *Marketing*, June 26, 1995, p. 14.

5. Canadian Media Directors' Council, *Media Digest*, 2005–2006, p. 10.

6. Rebecca Harris, "High flyers," *Marketing*, March 7, 2005, p. 15.

7. Based on data from *Canadian Advertising Rates and Data*, Rogers Media, January 2006, p. 27.

8. "Demonstrating newspaper engagement," *A Study of Media in Canada*, Canadian Newspaper Association, 2006.

9. Canadian Media Directors' Council, *Media Digest*, 2006–2007, p. 38.

10. *Outstanding Newspaper Advertising—Thirteen Creative Principles*, Canadian Newspaper Association, n.d., p. 12.

11. Advertising rates obtained from the *Toronto Star*, **www.thestar.com**.

12. Hasting Withers, "Magazine readership stable," *Marketing*, April 9, 2005, p. 20.

13. Richard Blackwell, "Niche titles help boost magazine readership," *The Globe and Mail*, March 31, 2004, p. B6.

14. Danny Kucharsky, "Magazines to watch," *Marketing*, November 7, 2005, p. 15.

15. Barbara Shecter, "Newspapers still reach 77% of the population," *Financial Post*, April 11, 2006, p. FP3.

CHAPTER 9

Broadcast Media:
Television and Radio

Courtesy of Dick Hemingway.

Learning Objectives

After studying this chapter, you will be able to

1. Identify the organizations involved in the Canadian broadcasting industry

2. Assess the advantages and disadvantages of television and radio as advertising media

3. Explain the factors considered in, and procedures used for, buying television and radio time

4. Identify recent technologies affecting commercial television and radio in Canada

The latest statistics available reveal that 99 percent of Canadian households are reached by both television and radio. Further, 65 percent of Canadians live in multi-set households and 85 percent of Canadians live in households equipped with cable or satellite. On an average day, 86 percent of Canadians view television at least once, and over the period of a week, adults over the age of 18 spend 24 hours watching television and 22 hours listening to the radio.[1] Such spectacular penetration and reach suggests that the potential impact of broadcast media on their audience is enormous. From an advertising point of view, the placement of messages in broadcast media offers the same high reach/high impact potential.

While these facts are impressive, the television and radio industries are in a state of transition because new technologies are affecting the way people watch television and listen to the radio. People can now watch a selection of shows on the internet or they can download them to their cell phones. On the radio side, people can listen to digital radio stations that are free of advertising, and new satellite options are available. Radio listeners can also download music from radio stations to their iPods or other portable music players. Perhaps the biggest change of all is that consumers now control when, where, and how they receive broadcast shows and advertising messages. Consumers have more control over their consumption of media than ever before, and both the broadcast industry and the advertising industry have to respond to it. Placing 30-second spots on prime time television shows is no longer the answer—just part of the answer. The competition for eyeballs is intense!

The Canadian Television Market

The television market is divided between conventional national networks and stations, specialty cable channels, and pay-TV. The conventional networks include CBC Television, CTV, Radio-Canada, and TVA. Both the CBC and CTV serve English Canada, reaching 99 percent of English-language households, while Radio-Canada and TVA serve French Canada, reaching 99 percent of French-language households.

CTV
www.ctv.ca

277

Both the CBC and CTV operate regional networks; the CBC, for example, has Atlantic, Central, Western, Pacific, and North networks. CTV operates regional networks in Ontario, Atlantic Canada, and Saskatchewan. Global TV is a prominent network in Ontario and Atlantic Canada, reaching 90 percent of households.

A multitude of specialty networks is available to viewers. Some of the more popular specialty networks are TSN, Space, Rogers Sportsnet, Showcase, Discovery, MuchMusic, CBC Newsworld, HGTV, and The Weather Network. Recently added to the television mix are a group of digital specialty channels available for additional fees through cable suppliers. This group includes The Biography Channel, ESPN Classic Canada, Leafs TV, MenTV, NHL Network, SexTV, and many more. Pay-per-view options are also available to cable subscribers.

MuchMusic
www.muchmusic.com

The Biography Channel
www.thebiographychannel.ca

Trends Affecting Television and Television Advertising

The landscape of the Canadian television industry is changing. Several trends are converging on the industry: consumers' fascination with the internet has created opportunities for alternative forms of broadcasting shows (a circumstance referred to as video-on-demand or VOD); emerging technologies in the form of personal video recorders allow viewers to record shows and edit out commercials automatically (a phenomenon referred to as commercial avoidance); mobile technologies such as cell phones, iPods, and other portable music/video players are extremely popular with younger targets—the more time they spend with these gadgets the less time they spend watching television.

Conventional television networks such as the CBC and CTV are concerned about the time viewers spend watching television. Generally speaking, viewers are spending less time each week with television. Reasons for their departure stem from a dissatisfaction with the programming that is offered and a fascination with new entertainment technologies such as the internet and cell phones. A study by Decima Research revealed half of the respondents were dissatisfied with the quality of shows available; their view: "TV has been dumbed down by so much reality programming."[2] Young males 18 to 34 years old have strayed from television, preferring to play DVDs or video games (including online video games).[3] Generally, time spent online takes away from time spent watching television.

Similar patterns are also being detected in younger age groups. Teens, for example, are the tuned-in generation, but they are tuned in to the internet, cell phones, and portable music players. Teenage females use their phones to text message friends more often than call them. If they aren't text messaging, they are surfing iTunes or exchanging rapid-fire instant messages online.[4] In other words, there is much less time for television viewing among today's youth.

AUDIENCE FRAGMENTATION

In Canada there are 47 specialty channels and 51 digital channels. These channels, combined with traditional broadcasters such as the CBC, CTV, Global, and TVA, provide so much choice for viewers that audiences have become fragmented. From purely an advertising perspective, television is viewed as the optimal mass medium—it delivers a large audience quickly. But the size of the audience is diminishing. The true irony is that the costs of television advertising are increasing while the audience size is decreasing. How long will advertisers pay more for less?

In more positive terms, the specialty channels do offer some targeting capability, though the audience that the advertiser reaches is usually smaller than on conventional networks. Advertising rates are lower on cable channels, and because of the targeting capability advertisers are moving their dollars in that direction. Stations such as TSN (sports) and HGTV (home and garden) are examples of channels that are attractive to advertisers wanting to reach specific demographic and lifestyle targets.

ALTERNATIVE VIEWING: VIDEO-ON-DEMAND

Internet access has seen steady growth, with 78 percent of all Canadians now online. The 18- to 24-year-old age group is by far the most highly connected segment, using multiple connection devices (computers, cell phones, and personal digital assistants) to hook up to the internet. They have grown up with the internet as part of their lifestyle.[5]

A recent survey reveals that television is the biggest casualty of internet usage, with 27 percent of respondents saying their television watching has fallen as a consequence of being online.[6] Popular online activities include playing video games, downloading music, and instant messaging. Broadcasters and advertisers are now following this online audience by offering content downloads of television shows. CTV, for example, through the CTV broadband network, offers shows such as *Corner Gas, Degrassi: The Next Generation, Smith,* and *Canadian Idol.* Each episode included five to six minutes of advertising.[7] In the United States, networks are experimenting with a fee-paying model for online shows: $1.99 per episode; no advertising. However, new research suggests that consumers, by a margin of almost three to one, would rather see commercials than pay a fee.[8] That information is good news for advertisers wanting to be more involved with video-on-demand content. Similar to television, networks offering shows online must compete for viewers. To attract viewers, the ABC network is offering a selection of shows online for free that have been previously broadcast on television.

"The future is definitely about an on-demand audience. So if you want to hit the broadest audience, you need to provide content in a non-linear (digital) as well as linear (television spot) fashion," says Maria Hale, vice-president, content business development, at CHUM.[9] This observation coincides with a research study conducted by IBM in the United States. The study predicts that by 2012 the "massive passives" who only watch network television will be outnumbered by people watching shows on their own timetable online.[10]

CHUM
www.chumlimited.com

MOBILE MEDIA

The emergence of mobile devices such as cell phones, portable music/video players, and personal digital assistants presents another challenge for television networks. It is now possible and even enjoyable to watch television shows on something other than a TV. The highly sought-after 18- to 34-year-old age group is the mobile, multi-tasking generation that has an affinity for media devices such as iPods and cell phones.[11] Broadcasters and advertisers must find a way to follow this audience. CTV is offering made-for-mobile video news, business news, and sports news that is updated hourly for distribution to Bell Mobility users. Short advertising messages will accompany the content. The consumers' acceptance of small-screen viewing has yet to be determined.

COMMERCIAL AVOIDANCE AND PERSONAL VIDEO RECORDERS

The personal video recorder (PVR) will revolutionize television programming and television advertising. A PVR allows consumers to digitally record and store their favourite shows for later viewing. Commercials can be skipped in the recording process—a frightening thought for the networks and advertisers. In the United States, two companies, TiVo and Replay, offer machines that can store between 8 and 28 hours of programming.

Research studies from the United States reveal that early adopters of PVRs watch 60 percent of their television from their computer, and they skip 90 percent of the ads in these programs. PVR penetration in the United States is at the 15-percent level, but still only at 5 percent in Canada.[12] The TiVo technology was recently made available to Rogers and Videotron customers in Canada, a situation that will add fuel to the commercial-avoidance issue. Bell ExpressVu (a satellite provider in Canada) offers a similar device as an option to its subscribers. Conventional networks have no alternative but to offer their programming (with commercials) in the digital media.

From an advertiser's perspective, commercial avoidance is a major issue. To compensate, advertisers are looking at options such as product placement in shows and branded content strategies. These strategies are discussed later in the chapter.

MEDIA CONVERGENCE

Media convergence refers to a concentration of ownership of a variety of media outlets by one company. For example, CTVglobemedia is a multimedia company with ownership interests in CTV Inc. and The *Globe and Mail*. The CTV portfolio includes the CTV Network (a conventional network) and 15 specialty channels including TSN, MTV, CTV Newsnet, The Comedy Network, Report on Business Television, RDS, Discovery Channel, and OLN, along with several digital channels. All of these channels have complementary websites. The *Globe and Mail* publishes *Report on Business* magazine and owns many interactive properties including **www.globeandmail.com**, **www. globeadvisor.com**, and **www.globetechnoology.com**.

With convergence the premise is simple: If the advertiser doesn't generate sufficient reach in one medium (e.g., television), additional reach is possible by advertising on other media outlets controlled by the media company. Packaged deals embracing a number of different media outlets produce economies of scale when buying the media time and space.

All of these trends point to a more complex television market in Canada. Advertisers will have to look beyond the 30-second spot if they are to reach their target audience. The new combination might include a 30-second commercial on a conventional network or cable channel, product placement in a show, sponsorship of a show downloaded from the internet, and an ad on a mobile newscast. As an indication of how quickly broadcasters and advertisers must act, Alan Sawyer, a media and entertainment consultant with IBM says, "The magnitude of change we saw over 50 years of the traditional TV industry will be repeated or exceeded in the next five years."[13]

Television Viewing Highlights

Media-viewing data is collected by two prominent and competing organizations in Canada: BBM Bureau of Measurement and Nielsen Media Research. The BBM is divided into two divisions: BBM TV and BBM Radio. BBM TV collects viewing data through a combination of electronic observation and diaries.

Electronic observation is achieved through PMT meters (picture-matching technology). PMT meters identify the on-screen video image of what people are watching (a kind of time-stamped video fingerprint). It measures minute-by-minute viewing behaviour of more than 5000 individuals in Canada. Each week the BBM publishes the top 30 programs nationally and by selected key markets. This information is a valuable resource for advertisers and agencies in terms of assessing the value of their advertising expenditure, and for networks in terms of identifying what programs are popular or unpopular. An illustration of basic BBM data appears in Figure 9.1.

The diary is issued three times a year to a panel of viewers in the top 40 markets across Canada. The data is compiled on the basis of time period, program, and trend, and is used to determine the rating of a program. **Ratings** are audience estimates expressed as a percentage of a population in a defined geographic area. For example, if a show has a rating of 20, it reaches 20 percent of that market's population.

Nielsen Media Research also employs electronic technology to collect viewing data. The Nielsen Television Ratings are an ongoing count of television audience size and composition. From a nationwide sampling of 3500 households, the company produces viewing data for all national and regional networks and for four local markets (Toronto, Vancouver, Montreal French, and Calgary). The top 20 programs are published weekly. The report provides viewing information 24 hours a day for the entire year. Data are organized on the basis of age, education, income, and occupation of members.

Generally speaking, Canadians spend more time with television than they do with any other medium. All people aged two years and older watch 24 hours of television each week, and the number of hours escalates with age. People over the age of 60 spend more than 30 hours a week watching television. Refer to Figure 9.2 for some specific data about television viewing by age and gender.

The data collected by BBM Bureau of Measurement and Nielsen Media Research reveal other key trends. By **daypart**, a block of time in a programming schedule (e.g., a

Ratings

24 hrs/week

English, February 5–11, 2007			
Rank	**Program**	**Broadcast Outlet**	**Total 2+ AMA (000)**
1	C.S.I	CTV	3557
2	C.S.I New York	CTV	3308
3	American Idol 6 AP	CTV	3153
4	C.S.I. Miami	CTV	2937
5	American Idol 6 AR	CTV	2749
6	Survivor: Fiji	Global	2643
7	House	Global	2449
8	Grey's Anatomy	CTV	2216
9	Deal or No Deal Can.	Global	2193
10	ER	CTV	2094
11	Law and Order: SVU	CTV	2082
12	Desperate Housewives	CTV	1918
13	CTV Evening News	CTV	1869
14	Grammy Awards	Global	1826
15	Law and Order Fri.	CTV	1703
16	H.N.I.C. Game #1	CBC	1667
17	Prison Break	Global	1650
18	Corner Gas	CTV	1628
19	Ghost Whisperer	CTV	1623
20	Lost	CTV	1592

FIGURE 9.1

The top 20 English and French shows on Canadian television by audience size

FIGURE 9.1

continued

French, February 5–11, 2007

Rank	Program	Broadcast Outlet	Total 2+ AMA (000)
1	Banquier, Le Wed.	TVA	1997
2	Banquier, Le Thurs.	TVA	1952
3	Tout le monde en...	SRC	1670
4	Poupées russes, Les	TVA	1250
5	Taxi 0-22	TVA	1219
6	Nos étés	TVA	1195
7	Annie et ses hommes	TVA	1189
8	On n'a pas toute la soirée	TVA	1112
9	Poule aux oeufs d'or, La	TVA	1064
10	Petit monde de Laura Cadieux, Le	TVA	1037
11	Bob Gratton ma vie/my life	TQS	1015
12	Auberge chien noir	SRC	926
13	TVA 18 heures, Le	TVA	839
14	Promesse, La	TVA	836
15	Cercle, Le	TVA	830
16	Km/h	TVA	827
17	J.E.	TVA	780
18	Providence	SRC	775
19	Caméra café	TVA	767
20	Rumeurs	SRC	766

Understanding this report: These charts show the top 20 programs for all home market stations for the week indicated. Programs are ranked based on their AMA (000). AMA (000) is the average minute audience in thousands.

Used with permission of BBM Canada.

FIGURE 9.2

Time spent with television and various media

Weekly hours of television viewing in Canada by age group

Age	Hours and Minutes of Viewing
All Persons 2+	24:11
Men 18+	25:11
Women 18+	27:26
Teens (12–17)	15:20
Children (2–11)	15:54

Source: Adapted from TVB Canada, *TV Basics 2006–2007*, pp. 8, 17.

Daily time spent with various media

Adults 18+	Hours and Minutes Spent with Medium
Television	3:24
Radio	2:24
Internet	:36
Newspaper	:30
Magazine	:18

Source: Adapted from TVB Canada, *TV Basics 2006–2007*, pp. 8, 17.

half-hour or one-hour period), prime time (7 to 11 p.m. Monday to Sunday) attracts the most viewers. While accounting for only 20 percent of viewing hours, prime time generates 40 percent of total viewing time.

On a seasonal basis, there is a drop-off in viewing in the summer, a reflection of consumers changing their patterns when the weather is warmer. After all, why watch reruns on television when you can enjoy the outdoors? Generally speaking, viewing drops by about 25 percent in the summer. Advertising rates charged for summer shows reflect the viewer drop-off.

[handwritten margin note: Drops by 25% because of the summer weather]

Television as an Advertising Medium

As an advertising medium, television offers numerous benefits—but there are also some drawbacks. The advertiser must assess the merits of using television in the context of the problem that advertising is trying to resolve.

ADVANTAGES OF TELEVISION

IMPACT AND EFFECTIVENESS OF MESSAGES   Compared to all other media, television stands out as a multi-sense medium. Advertisers can use the combination of sight and sound that television offers to create maximum impact on the viewing audience. It is a medium that is ideally suited for delivering an exciting and emotional message. Television viewing requires only passive involvement; viewers can do something else as they receive messages from the television.

[handwritten margin note: multi-sense medium (sight + sound) → emotional attachement (ex: African kids winter olympics)]

HIGH REACH   Television's reach is astounding, particularly in prime time. As Figure 9.1 indicates, a commercial shown on any of the top 20 shows in Canada has the potential to reach more than one million viewers. Further, television reaches a broad range of demographics and in many cases mirrors the Canadian population on specific demographics, making it an extremely attractive medium for advertisers targeting fairly general audiences. The variety of programming in prime time (comedy, reality, and drama shows) is equally attractive to adult males and females.

[handwritten margin note: reach a broad range of demog. (thanks to all the options) + variety of prog.]

Consumer-packaged-goods advertisers, financial institutions, telecommunications companies, and producers of high-priced consumer durables such as automobiles and computers all value the high reach available from television.

FREQUENCY POTENTIAL   Television is an expensive medium in absolute-dollar terms, but advertisers with large budgets can use television effectively to build frequency. For example, an advertiser may purchase more than one spot within a certain program or during a certain time of day. Alternatively, an advertiser could build frequency by purchasing the same time slot in a program over a continuous period—perhaps 13, 26, or 52 weeks. In either case, owing to viewers' loyalty to a certain program or to the appeal a certain time period has for a particular target market, the target audience will be exposed to the same commercial message over an extended period. Strategically, the advertiser wants just enough frequency to prompt action—too much repetition could have a negative impact on the viewer.

[handwritten margin note: frequency]

SOME DEMOGRAPHIC SELECTIVITY   Television is primarily a mass-reach medium but it can target demographic groups based on the nature of the programming. Programs such as *Hockey Night in Canada* and *Blue Jays Baseball* are sold to advertisers on the strength of their potential to reach males of all ages. Specialty networks offer demographic targeting potential as well. TSN reaches 8.6 million people weekly (a predominantly male audience), HGTV reaches 4.8 million people (predominantly female), and MuchMusic reaches 5.5 million people (mostly teens and young adults).[14] Viewers of specialty channels like those just mentioned migrate to these channels because they offer the program content they like.

COVERAGE FLEXIBILITY   Network advertisers receive good national coverage on both of the national networks (CBC and CTV). However, advertisers with smaller budgets that want to use television can purchase commercial time from individual stations rather than from a national network. Thus, advertisers can be selective regarding markets they advertise in. Consideration of variables such as competition and opportunity markets helps advertisers determine which markets to purchase. For network advertisers, additional advertising on selected stations can be used to increase the weight of advertising in a particular market when needed, perhaps to counter competitive spending. As Figure 9.3 illustrates, an advertiser placing commercials on Kitchener's CKCO-TV would effectively cover southwest and south central Ontario.

FIGURE 9.3

Sample coverage map of a local television station

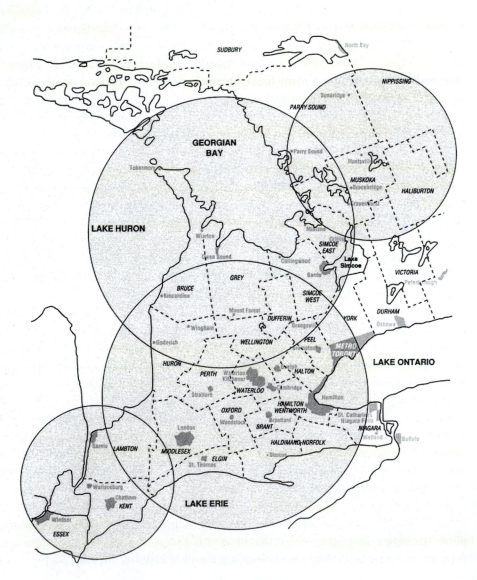

Courtesy of CKCO Television.

DEMONSTRATION CAPABILITY   Television offers creative flexibility. It is the appropriate medium for verifying a product's claims because it can show the product being used, which provides proof. Convincing demonstrations provide potential customers with a reason to buy the product. In addition, television is an effective medium for building consumers' awareness of and ability to identify the packages of products, particularly the packages of new products.

DISADVANTAGES OF TELEVISION

HIGH COST   Television offers high reach potential and relatively low CPMs, but in real spending terms it is very expensive. The cost of a prime-time 30-second commercial on CBC can be as high as $52 000 (e.g., during a Stanley Cup playoff game); on the CTV network it can be as high as $80 000 (e.g., during a leading show such as *CSI: Crime Scene Investigation*), though the average costs are not nearly that high.[15] In addition to the cost of media time, television advertising involves high production costs; the cost for a finished 30-second commercial range between $150 000 and $250 000. To counter the high costs of television advertising, many advertisers are choosing 10-second and 15-second commercials that deliver quick brand messages. The use of shorter commercials adds to the clutter problem on television, but, all things being equal, if the creative impact of those commercials is as effective as a 30-second commercial, the advertiser will save money.

CLUTTER   Television **clutter** refers to the clustering of too many commercials during a program break or taking too many breaks during a program. The level of clutter has a direct bearing on both viewing patterns and message recall. Viewers are likely to reach for the remote control when a program pauses for a commercial in a cluttered environment or they are apt to leave the room temporarily. Network promos at every break that plug upcoming shows add to the clutter. Too much clutter negates much of the reach potential of television.

Since this clustering occurs at planned intervals, and since a certain percentage of the audience may leave the viewing area during the break, many feel that particular placement within a **cluster** is important. Generally, the first and last positions in the cluster are preferable.

LACK OF TARGET-MARKET SELECTIVITY   As indicated by the list of advantages, television offers high reach to mass audiences, with some potential for reaching target markets that are defined in terms of age and sex. However, for advertisers with target markets precisely defined in terms of a combination of demographic, psychographic, and geographic variables, the use of television advertising is wasteful, since the message reaches many people outside the target definition. If there is wasted reach, there is a reduction in cost efficiency. Consequently, advertisers should consider other media that reach their target markets more efficiently.

AUDIENCE FRAGMENTATION   While the number of channels has increased dramatically over the past decade, the total number of viewers hasn't grown. The viewing audience is fragmented in such a manner that the size of the potential audience reached is lower, while the cost of placing the ads is higher. The efficiency of television is becoming an issue. Audience **fragmentation** is the result of several factors: the availability of so many specialty networks from cable and satellite suppliers; the introduction of new digital channels; and the time people spend watching pre-recorded shows on VCRs and DVDs or on the internet. For some homes, television is a 600-channel universe!

COMMERCIAL AVOIDANCE   Viewers watch the shows, but do they watch the commercials? If viewers leave the room, fast-forward through commercials, or simply pay less attention during commercial breaks, then the size of the audience is reduced. New technologies are making it easier for people to record shows while editing out commercials—an absolute nightmare for broadcasters and advertisers. New technologies are also available to track the number of people watching commercials. Once that is fully implemented, the model for buying television ads, along with the cost structure, will have to change. Rates will have to be pegged to the lower number of people watching the commercials.

Remote control devices make it easy for viewers to avoid commercials. The phenomenon of surfing through channels during commercial breaks is referred to as **zapping**. If viewers record shows for later viewing, and fast-forward through the commercials, it is referred to as **zipping**. As indicated earlier, the PVR (personal video recorder), allows the viewer to record shows digitally with the commercials eliminated. Advertisers are searching for alternative television advertising strategies to counter these behaviours.

LACK OF PLANNING FLEXIBILITY   To plan and buy television advertising space requires significant lead time. For example, network buys are negotiated in June for a complete broadcasting year that commences with the new fall program schedule in mid-September. Network contracts are usually non-cancellable, and spot advertising can be cancelled only on the basis of a minimum run and a specified notice period (e.g., advertising must run for four weeks, and four weeks' notice must be given prior to cancellation). Facing this contract, advertisers must be prepared to make an investment in television advertising.

CREATIVE LIMITATIONS   Television is a multi-sense medium offering significant impact capabilities, but a television commercial is very short—the normal length is 30 seconds. Considering the behaviours of viewers discussed earlier in this section, advertisers are using even shorter commercials in an attempt to break through the clutter. From a creative perspective it is questionable whether a 15-second spot can achieve the same communications results as a 30-second spot. Simply editing a 30-second spot down to a 15-second spot may not work! Some research evidence from the United States indicates shorter spots are less effective than 30-second spots among advertisers in packaged-goods product categories.[16] Other experts argue that shorter commercials that grab one's attention are more likely to be viewed in their entirety.

Products and services whose selling points need to be communicated via long copy are better suited to print media. Television advertisements must focus on one major benefit of a product if communications are to be effective. Alternatively, a television commercial should direct viewers to a website where more detailed information is available.

Television is frequently the medium of choice when an advertiser wants to reach a large audience quickly, say, in the case of a new product launch. For an applied illustration of recommending television as part of a media plan, refer to the advertising plan in Appendix II.

For additional insight into the present state of affairs with television and television advertising, refer to the Advertising in Action vignette **Is the King of the Hill over the Hill?**

Television Advertising Alternatives

When buying television time, advertisers choose between network advertising (either national or regional), selective-spot advertising, sponsorship opportunities, and local-

ADVERTISING IN ACTION

Is the King of the Hill over the Hill?

Many advertisers are taking a closer look at the media habits of their customers and are reallocating media budgets in accordance with the latest trends. Television, specifically network television, seems to be the medium that has been hit the hardest as advertisers move in the direction of magazines, outdoor advertising, cable TV, online, direct mail, and event marketing.

Mitsubishi Motors North America has perhaps taken the boldest step by totally abandoning network television and newspaper advertising. According to Ian Beavis, senior vice-president, marketing, at Mitsubishi, "We are targeting consumer segments based on psychographic rather than demographic information, and it's leading to more integrated communications programs." He says he must fish where the fish are, and since they are leaving network television in big numbers, he has no choice but to reallocate his budget.

Even traditional TV advertisers such as Procter & Gamble and Unilever have reduced their presence on conventional television in favour of specialty cable channels. As with Mitsubishi, it's a media strategy based on targeting consumers based more on psychographics than demographics. Procter & Gamble has instructed its agencies to adopt an approach that calls for media-neutral planning so that each brand uses the best channel to reach consumers. At P&G there is no such thing as one size fits all—each brand requires a unique marketing mix.

Sherry O'Neil, managing director of OMD Canada, says, "Some clients have moved as much as 20 percent of their TV budget to other ad media while an increasing number of advertisers are now using only specialty TV to promote certain brands."

If they aren't shifting dollars out of television they are experimenting with new alternatives within television. P&G leveraged the popularity of reality TV with a product placement deal that embedded brands such as Crest, Ivory, and Pantene as rewards on the program *Survivor All-Stars*. Coca-Cola is heavily into *American Idol*, and *The Apprentice* builds an entire show around a featured product—Burger King being one example.

When Mazda launched the new Mazda 5, a sporty-looking family vehicle aimed at 25- to 35-year-olds who didn't want to give up the "zoom-zoom," television was excluded from the mix. Convinced that this age group didn't sit in front of the television, the media plan went in a new direction. The media mix included an aggressive magazine push, online ads, direct mail, and cinema-screen advertising. Other Mazda models continue to use television advertising, and television still receives the largest portion of the company's media budget.

So, is the king of the hill over the hill? Are these companies making the right decisions or could they be making a huge mistake? You be the judge by investigating the situation further.

Source: Adapted from Jean Halliday, "Mazda switches off TV, stays out of out-of-home for new-model launch," *Advertising Age*, June 20, 2005, p. 4; Patti Summerfield, "Casting for a better net," *Strategy*, August 2004, pp. 24, 28; and Chris Powell, "The buy's the thing," *Marketing*, September 8, 2003, p. 20.

Unilever Canada
www.unilever.ca

market spot advertising. In addition, advertisers are now looking at product placement and branded content opportunities. Branded content involves integrating the product right into the television show.

NETWORK ADVERTISING

Network advertising is suitable for advertisers whose products and services are widely distributed and who have relatively large media budgets. All stations within a network carry a set of programs at a certain time—usually prime time, with some daytime. The network sells the commercial time. The advertiser must supply one commercial to a central source, and the message is broadcast across the entire network. Network advertising offers an advertiser substantial reach at relatively low cost. *CSI: Crime Scene Investigation*, for example, reaches an average audience of about 3.2 million Canadian viewers each week on the CTV network at a cost of $85 000 per spot—a CPM of $26.56. A spot on the 2007 Super Bowl broadcast on Global reached 3.4 million viewers at a cost of $100 000, for a CPM of $29.41.[17]

NATIONAL-SPOT OR SELECTIVE-SPOT ADVERTISING

At a regional level or local station level, stations fill in the balance of programming time with non-network programs and sell commercial time directly to clients wanting to advertise in that market. Alternatively, the local station that carries network programs may have the opportunity to sell some advertising time directly to advertisers during the network program. For example, in network shows such as *Marketplace*, *The Fifth Estate*, or *Hockey Night in Canada*, a certain portion of the commercial time available is allocated to local stations for **selective-spot sales**. In either case, advertisers would purchase time from the individual station, be it CBLT Toronto, CBOT Ottawa, or CBUT Vancouver. Each station from which time is purchased would require a copy of the commercial.

Selective-spot advertising offers several advantages to advertisers. First, it provides a network advertiser the opportunity for incremental coverage in key markets where more frequency is desired. Second, advertisers with smaller budgets or advertisers following a key-market media strategy can choose only markets that are important to their situation (e.g., markets where they have good distribution).

SPONSORSHIP OPPORTUNITIES

In response to changing client needs, the major networks actively market sponsorship opportunities that will integrate television advertising with other marketing and promotion efforts. Television **sponsorship** allows advertisers to take "ownership" of television properties that are targeted at their consumer audience. If the fit is right, the advertiser can leverage the sponsorship by extending the package to include consumer and trade promotions, and alternative media exposure.

The most prominent and ongoing sponsorship in Canada is *Hockey Night in Canada*, a Saturday-night institution. Both major beer companies in Canada, Molson and Labatt, have taken turns holding the primary sponsorship position on *HNIC*. At the end of the contract period, the rights for *HNIC* are up for renewal and various sponsors bid for the lead sponsorship position.

Sponsorships are also available within the *HNIC* broadcast segment. Gillette, for example, sponsors the *Gillette Game File*. The feature consists of statistical information such as goals and assists during the game, shots on goal, and player ice time. The *Gillette Game File* segment complements Gillette's ad spots that appear during the broadcast.

Large national advertisers are also attracted to Olympic broadcasts. For the 2006 Turin Olympics, the RBC Financial Group sponsored *The Olympians* during the CBC broadcasts. *The Olympians* featured profiles of Canadian athletes participating in the games.[18]

PRODUCT PLACEMENT AND BRANDED CONTENT

Product placement refers to the visible placement of branded merchandise in television shows, films, and video games. In any given show, numerous products are given exposure; such exposure has more credibility with the audience than regular advertising.

Coca-Cola is a prominent brand on *American Idol*, one of the most watched programs every year. Visa utilizes product placement on the Canadian hit show *Corner Gas*, appearing on the gas station's door and at the cash register.

Branded content (sometimes called product integration) takes placement a step further and integrates the brand into the script of the show. Visa hit a home run on *Corner Gas* when, in one episode, the feisty father and son argue about the origin of the Visa brand name—that's priceless! *Corner Gas* is watched by an average of 1.5 million viewers each week.[19]

Kia Canada joined forces with the CBC in a prime time series called *The Tournament*. The brand and selected products were integrated into the story, with real characters, real Kia dealerships, as a central part of the story. To promote the sponsorship, a five-week national contest invited viewers to win a Kia Killer Sports Weekend with Doug Gilmour. The Kia brand was also featured on rink board advertising that was visible during the show.[20]

Programs that teach, demonstrate, or offer advice, such as the do-it-yourself home and decorating shows, are proving to be good opportunities for products to be integrated in a natural and positive way. Home Depot, for example, has already formed partnerships with shows such as *Designer Guys*, *Home to Go*, and *Trading Spaces*. And let's not forget the brand name tools used in *Holmes on Homes*.

LOCAL ADVERTISING

Local advertising is similar to selective-spot sales. The local television station sells the time to local-market advertisers (such as retailers, restaurants, and entertainment facilities). In contrast to network and selective-spot advertising, local advertising is non-commissionable. Since local-market advertisers do not usually work with an advertising agency, the individual television stations provide assistance in the development and production of commercials for local clients.

Television Advertising Rates and Buying Procedures

INFLUENCES ON TELEVISION ADVERTISING RATES

The convergence of numerous factors influences advertising rates on networks and individual stations. Generally speaking, popular programs with large audiences command higher advertising rates. What follows is a discussion of the major factors that influence advertising rates.

SUPPLY AND DEMAND For the CBC, CTV, and Global, advertising costs are based on fundamental economic principles, mainly the availability of supply and the demand exerted on that supply by competing advertisers. Under such conditions, prospective advertisers outline their advertising needs in terms of desired reach levels, frequencies, seasonal implications, the ratio of prime time to fringe time, and the budget available. The network assembles a package and then the price of the advertising is negotiated between the agency's media buyer and the network sales representative. This system places added pressure on media buyers, since the rate that their clients pay depends largely on their ability to negotiate.

NATURE OF THE ADVERTISING PURCHASE   The negotiation process described above occurs well in advance of a media schedule, usually in late spring for the following broadcast year. Major networks such as the CBC, CTV, and Global operate in a similar manner. They book time in mid to late June to cover a 52-week period starting in September. Once the new season's program schedules are announced, the networks establish a *declaration date* (referred to as D-Day), at which time most advertisers place their orders for the coming broadcast year.

D-day

Every effort is made to accommodate each order as placed. If overbooking should occur as a result of the volume of orders, preference is allocated according to the following priorities: (1) incumbency position, (2) length of contract, (3) volume of contract, and (4) start date. Large-budget advertisers that have advertised on network programs in the past (incumbents) are given priority in this system. Approximately 70 percent of available commercial time on the networks is sold on or near the declaration date. This procedure of selling so much space at one time is referred to as **upfront buying**. Part of the current buying process involves gambling on what new shows will be popular. As indicated earlier in the chapter, there is a possibility that commercial ratings (instead of a show's ratings) will be more of a factor in establishing the cost of TV advertising in the future.

TYPES OF PROGRAMS   Network and selective-spot advertising is sold on the basis of a regular program schedule that is established for the entire year. However, certain programs within a schedule may be designated as special buys and are sold separately to potential advertisers. Examples of such programs include drama specials, miniseries, and programs such as the annual Academy Awards (the Oscars) broadcast, *Hockey Night in Canada*, and the World Figure Skating Championships.

In the case of sports programs, hockey and baseball broadcasts appeal largely to a particular viewing audience (that is, males aged 18 to 49) and, as a result, are attractive to a particular type of advertiser. Since the network is seeking sponsors willing to make long-term commitments over the entire season, separate rates and discount schedules apply to those that make such commitments.

DAYPARTS (TIME OF DAY)   Television can be divided into three broad time categories: *prime time*, *fringe time*, and *daytime*. Since the type of audience and size of audience vary according to **daypart**, so then must the rates for commercials within the dayparts. **Prime time** is usually designated as the viewing hours between 7 and 11 p.m. Most network shows are scheduled during prime time, and the shows with the largest audiences are usually scheduled between 8 and 10 p.m. (shows such as *Grey's Anatomy*, *American Idol*, *CSI*, and *Corner Gas*). Advertising rates in prime time vary from show to show based on popularity and reach potential. As discussed in Chapter 7, each show has a rating and the rating places advertising rates within a certain dollar range. As mentioned above, estimating the ratings for new shows is difficult. For advertising purposes, it is safer to buy time on established shows where audience estimates are based on past experience.

Fringe time is usually defined as the time preceding or following prime time. For example, early fringe would be 4 to 7 p.m., and late fringe would be 11 p.m. to 1 a.m. In early fringe time, viewing is somewhat lower among the adult population but is high among kids returning home from school. As a result, early fringe rates are lower than prime time rates. Program content in this time period usually consists of comedy reruns, music videos, and talk shows. Late fringe includes talk shows and movies. Viewing is lower in the late fringe period, so advertising rates are adjusted accordingly.

Daytime television runs from early morning (sign-on) to 4 p.m. The reach potential of television is relatively low in the morning, except for the potential to reach young children. Television rates are lowest during the day. However, audiences increase during the day and the rates are increased accordingly. The types of programs scheduled during the daytime range from news and information in the early morning, to kids' shows in the morning, to soap operas and talk shows in the afternoon. For specific details about viewing by time of day refer to Figure 9.4.

For a complete illustration of a weekly program schedule refer to Figure 9.5.

LENGTH OF COMMERCIAL Most advertising rate schedules are based on the purchase of 30-second units. Commercials that are longer in length—60, 90, and 120 seconds— are usually sold at two, three, and four times the 30-second rate.

Recently, 15-second commercials have become popular, as have **split 30s** (two 15-second commercials for the same product, one appearing at the start and one at the end of a commercial cluster). A split commercial may also involve different products of the same advertiser. Such a commercial strategy is sometimes referred to as "piggybacking." Fifteen-second commercials pose scheduling problems for networks and stations, and their policies for acceptance vary. The rates for 15-second commercials range from 65 to 70 percent of the 30-second rate. Split 30s may be accepted at the 30-second rate or range as high as 120 percent of the 30-second rate, depending on the network. Some experimentation is now occurring with 5-second and 10-second commercials.

BUYING TELEVISION TIME

In recent years, dramatic changes have occurred in television advertising. Factors such as audience fragmentation, the introduction of optimizers, and demographic and lifestyle influences have created a need for new approaches to buying and selling television time.

As discussed earlier, media buying in television is a very complicated process that requires a high level of expertise on both sides of the negotiating table (i.e., among the media buyers who represent clients and among sales representatives who represent the networks and individual stations). In a textbook of this nature it is not possible to illustrate the negotiation process, as there is so much variation among the networks. Instead, a brief overview of some of the key points for the major networks is presented below. Also, a few illustrations of specific media buys are included in this section. The concept of media optimizers will be discussed in more detail in the technology section of this chapter.

NATIONAL AND REGIONAL NETWORK RATES The supply and demand system is based on a standard **grid card** with varying price levels. The highest level on the CBC is

The figures in the chart represent the percentage distribution of weekly hours spent with various dayparts.

Daypart	All 2+	Women 18+	Men 18+	Teens (12–17)	Children (2–11)
M–F 6a–4:30p	21.5	23.7	17.6	17.5	30.9
M–F 4:30p–7p	12.9	13.2	11.8	14.5	15.9
M–Su 7p–11p	39.8	39.7	42.3	41.4	27.1
M–Su 11p–2a	10.0	9.5	12.3	8.4	2.5
Sa 6a–7p	7.4	6.4	7.2	9.2	12.0
Su 6a–7p	8.4	7.5	8.8	9.1	11.5

Source: BBM Fall 2005, Canadian Media Directors' Council, *Media Digest*, 2006–2007, p. 21. Used with permission.

FIGURE 9.4

Television viewing by age and daypart in Canada

FIGURE 9.5

Sample program schedule—
CKCO Television

CTV SCHEDULE
(last revised March 30th, 2006)

Time	Monday	Tuesday	Wednesday	Thursday	Friday	Saturday	Sunday
06:00	CTV NEWS					OWL TV (CDN)	ACORN: THE NATURE NUT (CDN)
06:30						KINGDOM ADVENTURE (CDN)	KIDS @ DISCOVERY (CDN)
07:00	CANADA AM (CDN)					WATERVILLE GANG (CDN)	GOOD MORNING CANADA (CDN)
07:30						LITTLEST HOBO (CDN)	
08:00							
08:30						GOOD MORNING CANADA (CDN)	
09:00	LIVE WITH REGIS & KELLY (S ABC)						
09:30							
10:00	ETALK DAILY (CDN)					PAID PROGRAMMING	PAID PROGRAMMING
10:30	DAILY PLANET (CDN)						
11:00	THE VIEW (S ABC)						
11:30						DAILY PLANET	
12:00	CTV NEWS					CTV TRAVEL	QUESTION PERIOD (CDN)
12:30							
01:00	BALANCE - TELEVISION FOR LIVING WELL (CDN)					PAID PROGRAMMING	W-FIVE (REPEAT) (CDN)
01:30	THE BOLD & THE BEAUTIFUL (S CBS)					PAID PROGRAMMING	
02:00	VICKI GABEREAU (CDN)					CAR/BUSINESS	
02:30	VICKI GABEREAU (CDN)					FIRST STORY	SUNDAY AFTERNOON MOVIE
03:00	GENERAL HOSPITAL (S ABC)						
03:30						MTV LIVE	
04:00	OPRAH (S CBS)					MTV HACKED	INVASION
04:30							
05:00	DR. PHIL					ACCORDING TO JIM	ALIAS
05:30						ACCORDING TO JIM	
06:00	CTV NEWS						
06:30							
07:00	ETALK DAILY (CDN)					W-FIVE (CDN)	LAW & ORDER: CI (PRE NBC)
07:30	JEOPARDY (S ABC)						
08:00	WHAT ABOUT BRIAN (PRE ABC)	AMERICAN IDOL (S FOX)	LOST (PRE ABC)	THE O.C. (PRE-FOX)	GHOST WHISPERER (S CBS)	CTV MOVIE	COLD CASE (S CBS)
08:30							
09:00	MEDIUM (PRE NBC)	LAW & ORDER: SVU (PRE NBC)	AMERICAN IDOL (S FOX) / JEFF LTD (CDN)	C.S.I. (S CBS)	CLOSE TO HOME (S CBS)		DESPERATE HOUSEWIVES (S ABC)
09:30							
10:00	CSI: MIAMI (S CBS)	THE AMAZING RACE (S CBS)	CSI: NEW YORK (S CBS)	ER (S NBC)	LAW & ORDER (CTV)	CRIMETIME SATURDAY (CTV)	GREY'S ANATOMY (S ABC)
10:30							
11:00	CTV NATIONAL NEWS						
11:30	CTV NEWS						
12:00	THE DAILY SHOW WITH JON STEWART (12:05AM)			CSI (12:05AM)		TBA	CSI (12:05AM)
12:30	THE COLBERT REPORT (12:38AM)						
01:00	TBA (1:07AM)					TBA	EBERT & ROEPER (1:07AM)
01:30	ETALK DAILY (1:37AM)						LOCAL INFOMERCIALS (1:37AM)
02:00	LOCAL INFORMERCIALS (2:06AM)			CTV LATE MOVIE (2:06AM)	CTV LATE MOVIE (2:06AM)	CTV LATE MOVIE (2:06AM)	

CTV/NETWORK SALES	STATION SALES ONLY	PAID PROGRAMMING	KIDS PROGRAMMING

Courtesy of CKCO-TV.

in the $52 000 range and at CTV as high as $110 000 for the highest-demand 30-second spot in prime time.[21] Average rates in prime time are much lower. In this type of system, rates are adjusted periodically and are affected by factors such as inventory of time available, projected audiences, continuity, and seasonality. When the agency and the network negotiate the rates, client-oriented factors come into play, such as competition for time, budget available, the ratio of prime time to fringe time required, and the program mix desired. Canadian media directors have estimated the average rates of buying 30-second spots on all Canadian networks based on these factors. For a summary of these rates, refer to Figure 9.6.

Both the CBC and CTV networks offer advertisers regional packages. The CBC offers advertisers four regional alternatives: Atlantic (New Brunswick, P.E.I., Nova Scotia, and Newfoundland), Central (Ontario and Montreal English), Western (Manitoba, Saskatchewan, and Alberta), and Pacific (British Columbia).

In the case of **spot sales**, advertisers purchase time from any of the 17 CBC-owned stations that constitute the CBC network or the 18 stations that form the CTV network. Agencies can negotiate rates with member stations individually. Commercial material must be supplied to each station where time is purchased.

LOCAL-MARKET TELEVISION RATES Spot announcement rates established by local stations also depend on the daypart (time classification) in which the commercial is scheduled to appear, projected audience size, and the time of year. As is shown in Figure 9.7, the highest rate charged for advertising was $4940 for a spot on *CSI* (Thursday

FIGURE 9.6

Estimated costs of network commercials (30 seconds) in prime time, 2005

Network	Number of Stations	Basic Range	Basic Average
CBC Full	34	100–52 000	6500
CTV	22	2500–110 000	20 000
Radio Canada	13	200–25 000	2500
REGIONAL			
ATV	3	450–2000	700
CBC Regional			
Atlantic	6	100–4000	N/A
Central	12	100–32 000	N/A
Western	12	100–11 400	N/A
Pacific	6	100–5900	N/A
CTV Ontario	5	100–39 000	3500
SPECIALTY			
Comedy	1	60–2000	400
HGTV	1	800–7000	N/A
MuchMusic	1	1200–7500	N/A
TSN	1	1000–20 000	N/A
YTV	1	425–2600	1200

Source: Adapted from Canadian Media Directors' Council, *Media Digest* 2005–2006, p. 30.

9–10 p.m.). Other popular shows in prime time include *Desperate Housewives* ($4010), *The Amazing Race* ($4010), and *American Idol* ($3700). Reduced rates are offered in fringe and daytime periods. Note there is some fluctuation in rates based on season.

Similar to the networks, the local-market station offers a continuity discount to advertisers booking a 52-week contract. In addition, some television stations may offer a seven-day reach plan. The **reach plan** is an interesting concept for television; it is more commonly used in radio as a way of selling off non-peak time. Commercials are rotated vertically throughout the day and horizontally during the week. Since the demographics of the audience change throughout the day, the number of people reached in a particular target group will vary with the schedule. However, with respect to the entire viewing audience, reach will be maximized and the plan is purchased at a discounted rate, a trade-off that must be considered against daypart scheduling.

GROSS RATING POINTS   The concept of gross rating points (GRPs) was introduced in Chapter 7. When purchasing commercial time in specific television markets, media buyers request a certain level of GRPs, basing their request on the reach and frequency objectives of the advertiser. The GRP concept offers a way of measuring the advertising weight levels in a market in terms of reach and frequency variables; it is based on the formula

$$\text{GRPs} = \text{Reach} \times \text{Frequency}$$

Assume, for example, that a commercial message reaches 20 percent of target households in a market, and the commercial is scheduled 5 times in a week. The GRPs (weight) would be 100 [Reach (20) Frequency (5) = 100]. In another week, the reach may be 25 percent and the frequency 4; in that case, the GRP level would remain at 100. Consequently, from week to week in a television advertising flight, the actual number of commercials varies depending on the estimated reach of the programs the ads appear on.

FIGURE **9.7**

CKCO-TV rate card

2005-2006 RATE CARD

REVISED EFFECTIVE: June 6/05
30 SECOND - PUBLISHED RATE (GROSS)
FOR INTERNAL USE ONLY
RATES ARE PROTECTED FOR 5 WORKING DAYS

PRIME					FALL	WINTER	SPRING	SUMMER	52 WEEK
				GROUP #	SEP 12/05- DEC 11/05	DEC 12/05- FEB 19/06	FEB 20/06- JUN 4/06	JUN 5/06- SEP 17/06	SEP 12/05 - SEP 17/06
DAY	TIME	PROGRAM							
M-F	557-7P	CTV NEWS AT 6PM	O	015	$1,140	$970	$1,140	$970	$1,010
SA-SU	558-7P	CTV NEWS AT 6PM	O	162	$690	$590	$690	$590	$610
M-F	7-730P	ETALK DAILY	O	153	$600	$510	$600	$510	$530
M-F	730-8P	JEOPARDY	SIM	001	$820	$690	$820	$690	$720
MO	8-830P	CORNER GAS	O	198	$930	$790	$930	$790	$820
MO	9-10P	MEDIUM	PRE	157	$1,600	$1,360	$1,600	$1,360	$1,420
MO	10-11P	CSI MIAMI	SIM	192	$3,400	$2,890	$3,400	$2,890	$3,020
TU	8-9P	AMERICAN IDOL	SIM	057		$3,150	$3,700		
TU	8-9P	CLOSE TO HOME	PRE	071	$1,140	$970	$1,140	$970	$1,010
TU	9-10P	THE AMAZING RACE	SIM	073	$4,010	$3,410	$4,010		
TU	10-11P	LAW & ORDER SVU	SIM	092	$1,880	$1,600	$1,880	$1,600	$1,670
WE	8-9P	LOST	PRE	096		$1,070	$1,260		
WE	8-9P	INVASION	PRE	075	$910	$770	$910	$770	$810
WE	9-10P	LOST	SIM	146	$1,890			$1,610	
WE	9-10P	AMERICAN IDOL	SIM	084		$2,690	$3,160		
WE	10-11P	CSI NEW YORK	SIM	052	$2,160	$1,840	$2,160	$1,840	$1,920
TH	8-9P	THE O.C.	SIM	167	$1,580	$1,340	$1,580	$1,340	$1,400
TH	9-10P	C.S.I.	SIM	068	$4,940	$4,200	$4,940	$4,200	$4,380
TH	10-11P	ER	SIM	049	$3,700	$3,150	$3,700	$3,150	$3,280
FR	8-9P	GHOST WHISPERER	SIM	185	$690	$590	$690	$590	$610
FR	9-10P	NIP/TUCK	O	137	$1,220	$1,030	$1,220	$1,030	$1,080
FR	10-11P	INCONCEIVABLE	SIM	061	$910	$770	$910	$770	$810
SA	7-8P	W-FIVE	O	039	$420	$350	$420	$350	$370
SA	8-9P	COLD CASE	PRE	128	$690	$590	$690	$590	$610
SA	9-10P	CRIME TIME SATURDAY	SIM	035	$690	$590	$690	$590	$610
SA	10-11P	SOPRANOS	O	104	$690				
SA	10-11P	SUE THOMAS F.B.EYE	O	172		$660	$780	$660	
SU	7-8P	LAW & ORDER CI	PRE	103	$1,010	$860	$1,010	$860	$900
SU	8-9P	THE WEST WING	SIM	042	$1,540	$1,310	$1,540	$1,310	$1,370
SU	9-10P	DESPERATE HOUSEWIVES	SIM	025	$4,010	$3,410	$4,010	$3,410	$3,560
SU	10-11P	GREYS ANATOMY	SIM	066	$2,240	$1,900	$2,240	$1,900	$1,990

Courtesy of CKCO-TV.

Since reach figures and GRPs are discussed in the media negotiation process, it is impossible to illustrate the concept in a buying plan in this book. However, to illustrate the basic use of a television rate card, and to illustrate the fact that rates fluctuate according to daypart, a few examples will be developed.

If we use the CKCO-TV Kitchener rate card (Figure 9.7) in conjunction with the buying-plan examples below, we come up with the media cost calculations listed here.

TELEVISION BUYING ILLUSTRATIONS

Plan 1 Information	
ETalk Daily:	2 spots per week
CSI Miami:	1 spot per week
Medium:	1 spot per week
(all spots run 52 weeks per year)	

Cost Calculations

On the basis of the above information, the advertiser qualifies for a continuity discount, which will be considered in the following cost calculations. (The costs are taken from Figure 9.7.)

ETalk Daily	$530 × 2 × 52 = $ 55 120
CSI Miami	$3020 × 52 = $157 040
Medium	$1420 × 52 = $ 73 840
Gross Cost	**= $286 000**

Assuming an advertising agency purchased the advertising time for the advertiser, a further calculation would be as follows:

Client is billed by agency	$286 000
Agency retains 15-percent commission	$ 42 900
Media CKCO-TV receives	$243 100

Plan 2 Information

The rates in this example are also based on the CKCO-TV rate card (Figure 9.7).

Corner Gas	1 spot (8 weeks; February 23 to April 10)
Lost	2 spots (8 weeks; February 23 to April 10)
CSI	1 spot (10 weeks; February 23 to April 24)

Cost Calculations

In this example, the continuity discount does not apply. The calculations would be as follows:

Corner Gas	$930 × 8 = $ 7440
Lost	$1260 × 2 × 8 = $20 160
CSI	$4940 × 1 × 10 = $49 400
Total Cost	**= $77 000**

Assuming the time was purchased by an advertising agency, a further calculation would be as follows:

Client is billed by agency	$77 000
Agency retains 15-percent commission	$11 550
Media CKCO-TV receives	$65 450

The buying and selling of television time evolves with changing market conditions. Many networks in the United States (Canada will soon follow) are rethinking the upfront buying process. The networks are contemplating launching new shows throughout the entire year rather than at one time (usually September and October). Such a change will definitely have an impact on media planning and media buying. In the existing system, advertising agencies have a vested interest in getting all bookings committed up front in order to reduce the cost of buying. The long-term commitment by the advertisers ensures a steady cash flow for the networks.

The American networks now find that shows launched in late spring and even the summer are garnering larger audiences than shows in the traditional heavier viewing months. It proves that good programming will attract an audience regardless of season. In Canada, *Canadian Idol* is broadcast in the summer, and it ranks as a top-three show each week, garnering an average audience of 1.8 million.[22] Advertisers who properly execute **recency** (a media strategy that emphasizes the timing of advertising instead of weight of advertising) have a negotiating advantage in this new media-buying environment. These advertisers require fewer top-rated shows and as a result need not commit so much of their television budget up front.

DISCOUNTS OFFERED BY TELEVISION

A variety of discounts are available to television advertisers, depending on the extent of their advertising commitment. In general terms, discounts are based on the amount of advertising time purchased, on seasonal factors, and on other factors important to the network or station.

FREQUENCY, VOLUME, AND CONTINUITY DISCOUNTS

A **frequency discount** is usually earned through the purchase of a minimum number of spots over a specified period of time. Offered on a percentage basis, the discount increases with the number of spots purchased in the stated period of time. For example, the purchase of 5 to 10 spots per week may earn a 5-percent discount, 11 to 15 spots per week a 10-percent discount, and so on.

A **volume discount** is linked to the dollar volume purchased by the advertiser over a 52-week period. The greater the volume purchased, the greater the discount. A network such as the CBC or CTV would typically offer a volume discount range from 2 percent to 10 percent.

A **continuity discount** is earned when advertisers purchase a minimum number of designated spots over an extended period (usually 52 weeks, but the period may be shorter). The value of the continuity discount may increase with the number of spots purchased. For example, purchasing a minimum number of prime time spots, perhaps two per week over 52 weeks, may earn the advertiser a four-percent discount. If the number increases to three spots, the discount may move to six percent, and so on.

SEASONAL DISCOUNTS

The time of year has an effect on potential reach and the size of the television viewing audience. Television viewing drops off in the summer season. Consequently, **seasonal discounts** are available to advertisers wishing to purchase commercial time in non-peak seasons. The peak television season is mid-September to mid-February (the new television season each year). Viewing is lighter in the spring (mid-February to mid-June) and lightest in the summer (mid-June to mid-September). Reruns are shown in non-peak seasons.

Networks and stations usually offer summer discounts in the 15- to 20-percent range because of the decline in television viewing (see the variation in rates in Figure 9.7). Viewing drops off by a similar percentage for all age groups except teens.

PACKAGE PLANS

Networks and stations offer **package plans** to sell off fringe or daytime spots at a discount, sometimes in combination with the purchase of prime time. The nature of such plans varies considerably. For example, an advertiser that purchases two prime-time spots per week in a popular American series may be required to purchase equivalent time in a prime-time Canadian series and/or equivalent time in daytime periods. Essentially, advertisers that demand the premium time spots must be prepared to make sacrifices through the purchase of less desirable time as well.

ROS (RUN OF SCHEDULE) **Run of schedule** refers to a discount offered by a station to an advertiser that allows the station to schedule a commercial at its discretion during any time in the programming day.

PRE-EMPTION RATES **Pre-emption** is a situation in which a special program, such as a miniseries, an entertainment special, or a hockey playoff game, replaces a regularly scheduled program. Advertisers are usually determined well in advance, and they pay premium prices for the right to sponsor such shows. Advertisers of the originally scheduled show are credited with equivalent commercial time at a later date.

MEDIA OPTIMIZERS: A PLANNING TOOL

Buying advertising time on television more efficiently is always the objective, and new software technology is playing a much bigger role in achieving that objective. TV optimizers are the highest expression of technology in media. An **optimizer** is a software program that searches the immense Nielsen TV ratings database for daypart or program combinations that increase target reach (or reduce the cost of buying it).

Procter & Gamble is one company that is advancing the use of optimizers. P&G's objective was to buy time more cheaply by negotiating around high-cost dayparts. With optimizers, agency media planners can investigate complex viewing targets and consider variables such as co-viewing and circumstance of viewing. They can study the viewer and duplication patterns of programs, dayparts, and networks, and determine how many targeted rating points in a venue is enough for a brand.[23]

The Canadian Radio Market

As of 2006, there were 602 commercial radio stations in Canada, 195 of which were AM and 407 of which were FM. FM stations reach 81 percent of persons 12-plus years of age while AM reaches 35 percent. AM radio has slightly higher reach among males, largely due to AM stations offering "all sports" or "all news" programming. The average adult listener spends about 20 hours a week listening to the radio when all locations for listening are included (e.g., home, work, and automobile).[24]

Radio broadcasting in Canada is divided between the Canadian Broadcasting Corporation, which is funded by the government (or, more precisely, by the taxpayers of Canada), and independently owned and operated stations that survive on advertising revenues. All AM and FM stations are self-regulating, with no restrictions on the number of commercial minutes or on the placement of these minutes. The radio airwaves in Canada are controlled by several large media companies that include Rogers Media, Corus Entertainment, Telemedia, and Astral Communications.

Corus Entertainment
www.corusent.com

Trends Influencing the Radio Industry

Much like television, the radio industry is in transition. New technologies are bringing radio signals to people in different ways, resulting in a gradual migration of listeners away from traditional stations. New listening options include digital radio, internet radio, iPods, cell phone radio, and satellite radio.

DIGITAL RADIO

Digital radio is a new form of broadcasting by conventional radio stations. Unlike AM and FM stations in which there is some interference in the transmission, digital broadcasting always selects the strongest regional transmitter automatically, guaranteeing the quality of the sound.

Digital audio broadcasting (DAB) offers several advantages: CD sound quality, perfect sound reception within a station's coverage area, and the ability to compress 15 signals into the transmitter space now used by one. Digital broadcasting has been designed for the multimedia age. It not only carries audio, but also text, pictures, data, and video. Due to the investment required to switch to digital broadcasting, only a small number of stations in Canada have done so. Automobile companies such as General Motors and Ford began installing digital receivers in cars in 2003. As more companies do the same, demand for digital content will grow.

INTERNET RADIO

Online radio offers listeners sound quality that is better than CD quality. Currently, the online radio stations are commercial-free, but on-air advertising revenue is certainly the objective in the future. Music content is available from a variety of streaming services. Yahoo's free LAUNCHcast service, for example, allows users to rate songs that then influence music recommendations; it even lets you ban an artist or song from your own customized station.

Traditional radio stations and the advertising industry have mixed feelings about online radio. They concede that an online presence is essential, and most stations have developed accompanying websites as a means of forming a stronger relationship with their listeners. According to a study by the Radio Marketing Bureau, 38 percent of Canadians over the age of 18 have visited a radio station website. Websites offer another revenue stream for radio stations, assuming they can show advertisers the benefit of adverting in both media.

With regard to broadcasting online, the conventional stations that make the move first will have competitive advantage. As the old saying goes, "He who hesitates is lost." While firm information about internet listening is not yet available, some industry experts estimate 30 percent of consumers with an internet connection now listen to online stations. At the same time, however, a problem with going online is cost. Local radio stations have discovered that a web presence is expensive, and cost is a deterrent.

SATELLITE RADIO

Satellite radio offers commercial-free programming and is available through two suppliers: XM Canada and Sirius Canada. Both services require a special receiver that costs between $70 and $90. Monthly subscription fees start at $12.99. Despite its name, satellite radio does not offer a selection of stations from around the world. The stations available are only those offered by the service provider. XM Canada, for example, offers a range of stations in a variety of categories: hits from across the decades; country; pop & hits; rock; hip-hop and urban; jazz and blues; lifestyle; classical; news; and sports, among many others. It's a channel guide much like satellite television. Satellite radio is very new. The question remains: Will Canadians be willing to pay for commercial-free radio?

In a bid to expand its subscriber base, XM Canada formed a partnership with Telus Corp. Satellite radio will be available on the cell phones of Telus subscribers. Bell Canada and Rogers Communications are pursuing similar satellite radio strategies.[25] In

February 2006, Sirius and XM announced they would be merging operations in the Unites States. It is expected that similar mergers will occur in Canada.

IPODS AND OTHER PORTABLE DEVICES

Younger age groups are tuning out radio altogether in favour of iPods, MP3 players, and computers, where they control the content. A **podcast** is an audio recording posted online, much like a short radio show. "Podcasting" is a pun on broadcasting, implying, of course, that you listen to it on an iPod or another music player. A podcast is generally free, and a person can listen to it whenever they like.[26] The ability for digital receivers to accept video content has lead to "vodcasting," as in the downloading of music videos.

Anyone (i.e., amateurs) can create a podcast, so the quality can be suspect. Radio stations have entered the pod world, as have content aggregators such as Apple (through iTunes) and Yahoo. Apple and Yahoo collect thousands of podcasts in one place, laying the foundation for selling shows and ads. Some advertising models have emerged. A sponsorship of a podcast may involve a 15- or 30-second audio ad at the beginning of the podcast. Popular podcasts that are available on a predetermined frequency (once a week or month) search for advertisers who will commit to a long-term sponsorship agreement.[27]

Radio Listening Highlights

The BBM Bureau of Measurement compiles listening data in a survey (diary) format three times a year in over 130 radio markets in Canada. The diary also collects data about product usage and consumer lifestyles. Market reports are published for nine key urban markets and six regions (Atlantic, Quebec, Ontario, Manitoba/Saskatchewan, Alberta, and British Columbia) three times a year. Tuning data covers 22 demographics for over 30 dayparts. Other standard data include market share, audience profiles, and listening locations.

AM VERSUS FM

Conventional radio signals are transmitted two ways: **AM (amplitude modulation)** and **FM (frequency modulation)**. AM refers to the height at which radio waves are transmitted. AM stations transmit waves by varying amplitude. Frequency refers to how fast waves travel in thousands of cycles per second (kilohertz). FM transmits waves by varying frequency. FM frequencies are above the static and noise level of AM. This results in clearer reception and better sound on FM stations. FM radio is more effective than AM in reaching all age categories and accounts for 81 percent of all tuning. Refer to Figure 9.8 for AM and FM audience-share data by age classification.

Canada	Reach		Share	
	AM %	**FM%**	**AM%**	**FM%**
12+	35	81	24	75
Women 18+	35	81	24	75
Men 18+	40	81	25	73
Teens 12–17	14	81	6	93

Source: BBM, Survey 1 2006, Canadian Media Directors' Council, *Media Digest*, 2006–2007, p. 32. Used with permission.

FIGURE **9.8**

AM and FM share of tuning by age classification

TUNING HOURS: HOW MUCH, WHEN, AND WHERE

The average listener spends anywhere from 20 to 22 hours a week with radio, depending on age category. Teens spend much less time with radio, averaging only about eight hours a week. Other entertainment options such as the internet, iPods, and cell phones are more attractive to teens. Refer to Figure 9.9 for details.

By time of day, radio is the inverse of television: radio is much more popular in the morning, but as the day progresses listening tapers off. The use of radio during the day is high because people tune in when they wake up, while they travel to work, and when they are at work. Refer to Figure 9.10 for details.

FIGURE **9.9**

Weekly reach and hours tuned by age in Canada

Source: BBM Survey 1 2006, National, Mo–Su, 5a–1a.

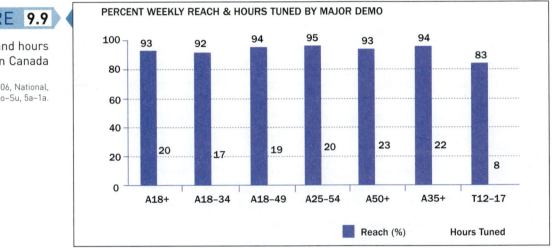

FIGURE **9.10**

Radio listening by time of day

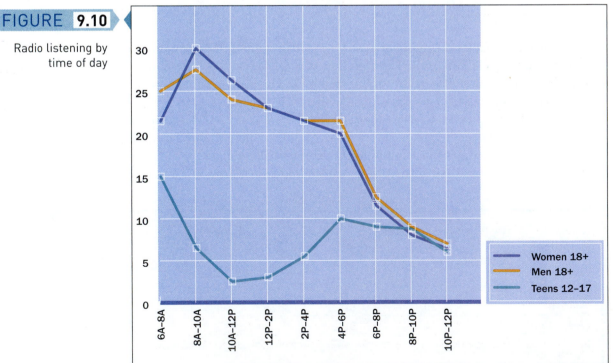

One of radio's advantages is its mobility. Listeners can be reached in a variety of contexts. Listening from the home accounts for 48 percent of listening time; automobiles account for 27 percent, and listening from work accounts for 23 percent of listening time.[28] Refer to Figure 9.11 for details.

Radio Station Formats

One of the major advantages of radio is its ability to reach selective target audiences. The audience reached depends on the format of the station. **Format** refers to the type and nature of the programming offered by an individual station. Basically, the content is designed to appeal to a particular target group, usually defined by age and interests. The most popular station formats in Canada are adult contemporary; the combination of gold, oldies, and rock; talk; country; and contemporary hit radio. Refer to Figure 9.12 for details.

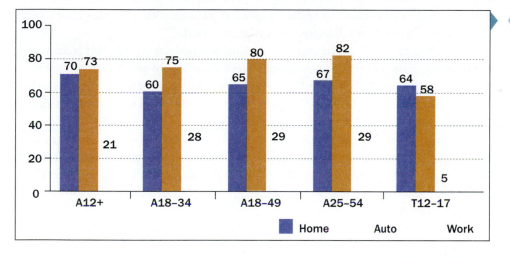

FIGURE 9.11

Weekly reach of radio by age and location

Source: BBM Survey 1 2006, Mo–Su, 5a–1a. Used with permission.

FIGURE 9.12

Radio format and listening share trends

Format	Market Share 2004	Market Share 2005
Adult Contemporary	24.6	24.0
Gold/Oldies/Rock	15.3	14.9
News/Talk/Sports	11.4	11.3
Country	10.0	10.1
Contemporary Hits	8.5	9.5
Album-Oriented Rock	5.6	5.8
Middle of the Road (MOR)	3.1	2.7
Easy Listening	2.3	3.0
Other	4.6	6.3
CBC (non-commercial)	11.1	8.8
U.S. Stations	3.5	3.6
Total	100.0	100.0

Source: Adapted from Statistics Canada publication, "Radio Listening," *The Daily*, July 21, 2006 and July 8, 2005, www.statcan.ca/daily.

Adult contemporary (AC) stations play popular and easy-listening music, current and past, and generally appeal to an audience in the 25- to 49-year-old range. **Gold and oldies** has stronger appeal among 35- to 54-year-olds, and rock appeals to 16- to 29-year-olds. **Country** music appeals to a cross-section of ages and varies in popularity by region (very popular in Atlantic Canada and the Prairies and not very popular in Quebec and Ontario). **News/talk** stations focus on frequent news reporting and listener call-ins to discuss current newsworthy issues. Some stations focus specifically on news niches such as sports. The Fan 590 in Toronto, for example, is a popular sports station with males 25 to 54 years old. The popularity of news/talk is helping to revitalize AM radio. **Contemporary hit radio (CHR)** stations play the latest hits (mainly rock), and appeal to teens and 18- to 34-year-old adults. Top-40 stations are popular in urban markets.

The variety of radio formats in urban markets reflects each individual station's desire to be successful. Finding the right niche (a niche that is underserved in a market) makes a station attractive to a particular group of advertisers. The main considerations are the age demographics of the local market and the number of competitive stations appealing to similar target audiences. Based on the degree of competition for a listening audience (e.g., competition to reach a particular demographic group), stations often change their format to reach a target that is underserved.

Canadian radio is credited with the creation of a new format labelled **train-wreck** or **whatever** radio. The philosophy of train wreck stations is to play hits from the 1970s, 1980s, 1990s—whatever the djs feel like. Whatever radio is a good fit for people who like to listen to music on their iPods. This trend started in 2003 and is primarily known as "Jack" after the moniker of the station that first popularized the format.[29]

From an advertising perspective, most stations are narrow in scope; they offer music that appeals to specific age groups. Train-wreck stations go in the opposite direction; they offer a wider variety of music that appeals to a cross-section of age groups. These stations tell listeners "We play what we want" or "We play anything." This format presents new opportunities for advertisers.

Radio as an Advertising Medium

Radio offers advertisers several advantages and disadvantages. The decision to select radio as an advertising medium depends on the problem that the advertiser is trying to resolve.

ADVANTAGES OF RADIO

TARGET-MARKET SELECTIVITY Because they tend to adopt a specific music format (e.g., adult contemporary, contemporary hit radio, country, gold), radio stations appeal to more precisely defined demographic groups than television stations do. Consequently, advertisers can use a profile-matching strategy, and select stations with audience profiles that closely match their target market. Even in smaller markets, where music formats change within a single station and the **audience flow** varies by daypart, the advertiser can schedule radio commercials at the appropriate time of day so that dollars will not be wasted reaching people outside the target. For example, advertisers for beverages and snack foods aimed at a youthful target would concentrate their advertisements in the evening time block, when the youthful target market is most likely to be listening.

REACH POTENTIAL Since radios are almost everywhere—with multiple receivers in the home, carried around by teens with portable stereos, in the car, and at the beach—radio has the potential to reach large audiences, particularly if advertisers place ads on several stations in an urban market.

The morning is the most popular listening time. Since the reach is highest in this time period, it is the most expensive time of day to advertise. The mobility of radio has a positive influence on reach potential. As indicated earlier in the chapter, tuning into the radio when travelling in an automobile accounts for 27 percent of all listening time. Another factor affecting reach potential is portability. Radio is a popular medium outdoors in the summer, when people are away from competing media. Many stations charge higher rates in the summer because of this higher reach potential.

FREQUENCY Radio is usually referred to as a **frequency medium**, a name that suggests radio's probable foremost advantage. If target-market selectivity is used, an audience can be reached on several occasions throughout the day or week (vertical and horizontal rotation plans) at a relatively low cost. For local advertisers wanting to advertise sales, radio is a preferable medium; numerous announcements can be scheduled before and during the sale to stimulate immediate response from consumers. For national advertisers, the radio can boost frequency in key markets as needed. Because radio offers frequency at a reasonable cost, advertisers can use it to supplement the reach of other media in a campaign.

COST The low cost of radio advertising attracts local clients for whom advertising otherwise would not be affordable. Radio advertising is cost-favourable in two areas. First, production costs are much less than they are for television, and changes to copy can be made on short notice. Second, in terms of time, the basic cost for each spot is relatively low (making radio an efficient means of reaching selective audiences), and numerous discounts are available for larger-volume advertisers. The combination of reasonable cost and frequency potential makes radio a good medium to supplement other media in a total campaign.

FLEXIBILITY Radio offers flexibility in three areas: creative, time scheduling, and market scheduling. In terms of creative, copy changes can be made on short notice to meet the needs of changing competitive situations as well as the needs of local markets. With respect to scheduling, the lead time required is short (two weeks or less); however, demand for popular stations in urban markets is quite high. Nonetheless, schedules can be "heavied-up" (i.e., advertising can be increased) on short notice if the competitive situation so dictates.

Radio is an ideal medium for advertisers who are following a key-market strategy. Since stations are local in nature and reach a specific demographic, an advertiser can select popular stations in each urban market it has designated as a priority. Consequently, the advertiser is not paying for any wasted reach. Several leading national advertisers allocate significant budgets to radio advertising. Among them are Goodyear, Labatt, Molson, and Dairy Farmers of Canada.

For more insight into the benefits of radio advertising, read the Advertising in Action vignette **Radio Helps Build Brands**.

DISADVANTAGES OF RADIO

AUDIENCE FRAGMENTATION While reach potential is high, the radio audience is fragmented due to station format and to the demographic groups that competing stations appeal to. An advertiser wishing to reach the teen audience in urban markets may have

ADVERTISING IN ACTION

Radio Helps Build Brands

Media planners often view radio as a supplementary medium; it plays a supporting role so it can't be recommended for building brand awareness. Recent marketing research conducted by the Radio Marketing Bureau, however, along with some real case studies, strongly suggests that radio can definitely help create awareness and build a brand.

The objectives of the Radio Marketing Bureau's research were to challenge the perception of radio as simply a tactical medium, and to show national advertisers that radio is effective in establishing a brand and for reaching specific target groups. "If your campaign can increase perception of your brand as more valuable and increase top-of-mind awareness, then there's a better chance the consumer will actually purchase."

The case studies were based on pre- and post-test data for brands in the packaged goods, automobile, and alcohol beverage categories. The research revealed that radio did improve brand perceptions and it did encourage greater levels of consumption.

In one test for a mature packaged-goods brand, multiple-use radio messaging aired in tandem with national television brand advertising. The pre-wave survey found purchase intent similar in both the radio and TV markets, but, post-wave, the consumers in the radio market were 19-percent more likely to consider purchasing the brand than those in the TV-only market. In the automotive category, a similar test produced a 12-percent increase in purchase intention.

Bill Ratcliffe, president of Millward Brown Goldfarb, the company that conducted the research, observed that, in markets where radio was used, the level of awareness didn't necessarily increase, but for more important measures such as purchase intention it did. He cautions, "When approaching a multimedia effects model, you have to make sure you are looking at a variety of brand health measures and not just awareness, because you could be totally misled."

Goodyear is a firm believer in the power of radio. In fact, the company is contemplating investing more in radio advertising and less in television advertising in the future. It currently uses both—it's simply a matter of reallocation to potentially save a lot of money.

Goodyear's consistent use of the vulnerable Goodyear guy (actor Thom Sharp) on both radio and television over the past decade means radio listeners actually visualize the character when they hear the commercials. When consumers are asked questions about advertising they often attribute awareness to television when there are no spots running at the time. Such data confirms the power of radio! Goodyear believes that radio is ideal for the automotive product category. Consumers listen to the radio when they drive. If their car has a problem, there is no better time to reach the customer.

Source: Adapted from Patti Summerfield, "A cheaper way to build brands," *Strategy Media*, July 26, 2003, p. 4.

to purchase several rock stations to achieve adequate reach levels. Listener loyalty to a certain station contributes to the fragmentation problem. The net effect of fragmentation is that radio is recognized as a low-reach/high-frequency medium.

MESSAGE RETENTION Several factors restrict the retention ability of radio messages. First, radio messages are short; there is limited opportunity for the communication of details in 30 seconds. Sixty-second commercials offer more creative flexibility, but they are less popular because of costs. Second, radio is a background medium; therefore, attention levels of listeners are potentially lower. Third, clutter is a problem, particularly on AM stations. Finally, radio is only a sound medium; as a result, there is no chance for the customer's mind to register the way a package looks (an important consideration for a new product), and there can be no product demonstration. The introduction of digital radio and online radio on a fee-paying basis (see the technology section earlier in this chapter) is eliminating some of these weaknesses.

MEDIA-PLANNING CONSIDERATIONS For local-market advertisers, the advantages of radio outweigh the disadvantages. For national advertisers purchasing a large number of radio markets, other media factors must be considered. Generally speaking, radio time is in high demand, particularly among leading stations in urban markets. This demand makes it difficult for media buyers to purchase the specific times desired by their clients. In fact, the high demand for time has precipitated a demand-driven rate card at top-ranked stations in major markets. Lead time is an important issue for advertisers wanting to maintain costs and access preferred inventory.[30]

The industry has consolidated in recent years and various radio networks have become much larger. The CHUM Radio Network, Corus Radio Network, and Telemedia Radio Network, for example, offer packaged media buys in all of their stations coast to coast. This helps alleviate some of the problems associated with planning and buying media time.

Radio Advertising Rates and Buying Procedures

The rates paid by radio advertisers are affected by several factors: the season or time of year in which commercials are placed; the daypart or time of day for which the commercials are scheduled; the utilization of reach plans; and the availability of discounts offered by individual stations. The type of advertiser (national or local) also has an impact on the basic rate charged to advertisers.

INFLUENCES ON RADIO ADVERTISING RATES

SEASONAL RATE STRUCTURES The rates charged by radio stations are often influenced by seasonal fluctuations in listening. Generally, radio rates fluctuate with the seasons, as follows:

Time Period	Rate
May–August (summer) and December	Higher
September–October	Mid-range
March–April	Mid-range
January–February	Lower

DAYPARTS Since the size and nature of the audience varies according to the daypart, different rates are charged for each. Generally, the dayparts are classified as follows:

Classification	Time
Breakfast	6 to 10 a.m.
Midday	10 a.m. to 4 p.m.
Drive	4 to 7 p.m.
Evening	7 p.m. to midnight
Nighttime	Midnight to 6 a.m.

Dayparts vary from one station to another, with some stations having more or fewer classifications than those listed above. In addition, weekend classifications are often different from weekday ones, as the listening patterns of the audience change on weekends.

REACH PLANS   Radio advertisers can purchase specific time slots and schedule a particular rotation plan during the length of the media buy, or they can purchase a reach plan. For the first option, a **rotation plan**, the advertiser specifies the time slots and pays the corresponding rate associated with it. Two types of rotation plans are available:

- **Vertical rotation:** the placement of commercials based on the time of day (within various dayparts)
- **Horizontal rotation:** the placement of commercials based on the day of the week (same daypart on different days)

Earlier in the chapter, potential reach was identified as an advantage of radio. However, since listening levels and the type of audience vary with the daypart, radio stations have developed reach plans in order to maximize reach. In a **reach plan** (or a **total audience plan**, as it is often called), commercials are rotated through the various dayparts in accordance with a predetermined frequency, in order to reach different people with the same message.

With reference to Figure 9.13 on page 308, reach-plan spots are equally divided among breakfast, daytime, drive time, and evening/Sunday dayparts. For the advertiser, the benefit of the reach plan is twofold. First, the reach potential is extended, and second, the rates charged for the reach plan collectively are lower (because of the discounts) than those that would result from the individual purchase of similar time slots. Reach plans do require a minimum spot purchase on a weekly basis.

TYPE OF ADVERTISER   Radio advertising rates vary with the nature of the advertiser. National advertisers are charged the general (national) rate that is generally higher than rates charged to local advertisers (such as retail establishments or restaurants). Rates for national advertisers are commissionable to recognized advertising agencies at the rate of 15 percent. Retail rates, being lower, are non-commissionable, but owing to their importance in the local radio station's revenue mix, stations offer production assistance either at no cost or at reasonable cost to encourage retailers to advertise. On average, local advertisers contribute 75 percent of a radio station's revenue.

DISCOUNTS OFFERED BY RADIO

Advertisers that purchase frequently from specific stations qualify for a variety of discounts. While the criteria for earning discounts vary, the discounts are similar in nature.

A **frequency discount** is a discounted rate earned through the purchase of a minimum number of spots over a specified period of time, usually a week. Having earned such a discount, advertisers are referred to a lower-rate grid schedule, or they could be quoted a percentage discount, such as 5 percent for 15 to 20 spots per week, 8 percent for 21 to 30 per week, 10 percent for over 31 spots, and so forth.

With a **volume discount**, the advertiser is charged a lower rate for buying a large number of spots; the discount might be 5 percent for 260 spots, for example, or 10 percent for 520 spots.

With a **continuity discount**, the advertiser is charged a lower rate for making a contract buy that covers a specified period of time. At intervals of 26, 39, and 52 weeks, advertisers are charged according to a discounted grid schedule, or the percentage discount offered increases with the length of the contract.

As discussed earlier in the chapter, radio can increase advertising reach; it can gain access to a different audience by rotating commercials through the various dayparts. To increase reach, stations offer **reach plans** or **total audience plans** that require advertisers to purchase a minimum weekly number of spots in return for a packaged discount rate, such as 16 spots per week divided equally among 4 dayparts.

It is quite common for independent radio stations to be controlled by one owner (e.g., two AM stations in different markets, or an AM/FM combination in the same market). Advertisers receive a discounted rate called a **combination rate** if they air commercials on more than one station. A station may offer additional discounts to advertisers if allowed to vertically and horizontally rotate commercials through a schedule at its own discretion. This is referred to as a **run-of-schedule** rate.

BUYING RADIO TIME

Without a doubt, a strategic plan will guide the buying of radio commercial time. In order to get the best possible rate from a station or network of stations, all details of the plan must be known by the radio station. Factors such as volume and frequency (the total number of spots in the buy), the timing of the schedule in terms of time of day or season in which the plan is scheduled, and continuity (the length of the plan) collectively have an impact on the spot rate that is charged the advertiser. It places an advertiser on a particular grid with the station. Refer to Figure 9.13 for a listing of grid rates and how an advertiser arrives at a certain grid. For advertisers that purchase large amounts of time, the discounts just described usually apply.

To illustrate some basic cost calculations used in buying radio time, let's develop some examples based on the rate card shown in Figure 9.13.

EXAMPLE ONE—BUYING INFORMATION

30-second spots	15 drive spots per week
10 breakfast spots per week	12-week schedule

Based on the length of the schedule (12 weeks), the advertiser does not qualify for a continuity discount. Therefore, the first calculation is to determine the total number of spots in the buy, to see if the advertiser qualifies for a volume discount.

Total number of spots	= spots per week × number of weeks
Breakfast	= 10 per week × 12 weeks = 120
Drive	= 15 per week × 12 weeks = 180
Total spots	**= 300**

Based on the total number of spots (300), the rate charged will be from grid 3. In this case, the 30-second rate is $88 for breakfast and $79 for drive time. The cost calculations are as follows:

Total Costs	= number of spots × earned rate
Breakfast	= 120 spots × $88 = 10 560
Drive	= 180 spots × $79 = 14 220
Total cost	**= $24 780**

EXAMPLE TWO The advertiser would like to evaluate a reach plan, involving 16 commercials per week, against a specific buying plan. Details of each plan are as follows:

FIGURE 9.13

CHET Radio
rate card

This rate card has been created to demonstrate to the reader the key factors that influence a radio media buy: spot rates, reach plan rates, volume discounts, and continuity discounts. Discounts are not usually published in *Canadian Advertising Rates and Data*.

CHETRadio

640 AM

All Talk! 24/7

NEWS ON THE HOUR EVERY HOUR

30-sec spot rates

Daypart / Grid	1	2	3	4	5
Breakfast 6:00 to 10:00 am	109.00	98.00	88.00	79.00	72.00
Daytime 10:00 am to 3:00 pm	92.00	82.00	73.00	64.00	58.00
Drive 3:00 to 7:00 pm	98.00	88.00	79.00	70.00	63.00
Evening and Sunday	76.00	68.00	65.00	57.00	49.00

Reach Plan – 30-sec. spots					
Breakfast 25% Daytime 25% Drive 25% Evening and Sunday 25%	88.00	79.00	71.00	62.00	54.00

Discount Schedule

Contract Buy (Continuity)		Volume (Spots)	
14 to 26 weeks	Grid 3	250	Grid 3
27 to 39 weeks	Grid 4	450	Grid 4
40 to 52 weeks	Grid 5	700	Grid 5

Plan A—Reach Plan (30-second spots) Information

Involves 16 spots per week

Rotated between breakfast, drive, day, and evening/Sunday

Runs for 16 weeks, June through September

Plan B—Specific Plan (30-second spots) Information
8 breakfast spots per week
8 drive spots per week
16-week schedule

COST CALCULATIONS FOR PLAN A   In this case, the advertiser qualifies for a continuity discount because of the 16-week schedule. Based on the rate card, the earned rate would be under grid 3 in the reach plan. The earned rate is $71 per spot. Therefore, the cost of the reach plan is

Total cost	= total number of spots × earned rate
	= (16 weeks × 16 spots/wk) × $71
	= $18 176

COST CALCULATIONS FOR PLAN B   The total number of spots in the buy are

Breakfast	= 8 spots per week × 16 weeks = 128 spots
Drive	= 8 spots per week × 16 weeks = 128 spots
Total spots	= 256

Based on this calculation, the advertiser does not qualify for a volume discount, but since the contract runs for 16 weeks, a continuity discount does apply. The advertiser is charged the rate from grid 3. Therefore, the total costs for Plan B are as follows:

Breakfast	= 128 spots × $88 = $11 264
Drive	= 128 spots × $79 = $10 112
Total cost	**= $21 376**

In conducting a comparative evaluation of Plan A and Plan B, the advertiser must weigh the more selective reach potential of Plan B against the savings of Plan A. Perhaps the advertiser wants to reach business commuters in drive time to and from work. With Plan A, the advertiser can reach a somewhat different audience by means of a daypart rotation of spots. The net result is a cost difference of $3200 in favour of Plan A. Should the advertiser decide to go with the cost savings of Plan A, or with the more selective reach of Plan B at greater cost? Would you like to make the decision?

SUMMARY

The Canadian television market comprises public networks, private networks, cable television networks, pay-TV networks, and direct-to-home broadcasting (satellite television). How people view television varies according to the time of day and the season. Television viewing tends to be lowest in the morning, somewhat higher in the afternoon, and highest in the evening. In terms of seasonal changes, viewership is much lower in the summer.

A trend in the industry is the gradual movement away from conventional mass-market television toward specialty channels that appeal to niche targets (e.g., YTV, HGTV, and TSN). Of great concern are issues such as audience fragmentation, video-on-demand, mobile media alternatives, technologies contributing to commercial avoidance, and the impact of media convergence on advertising strategies and rates.

As an advertising medium, television's primary advantages include high reach, message impact and effectiveness, frequency (for large advertisers), some demographic selectivity, demonstration capability, and coverage flexibility. Disadvantages include high cost, audience fragmentation, clutter, commercial avoidance, and the lead time required to plan and implement a media buy.

Depending on the degree of coverage they desire, advertisers can purchase television time from the national networks for national or selective spots, or from local stations. To compensate for clutter and commercial avoidance, advertisers are taking advantage of sponsorship opportunities, product placement, and branded-content opportunities. These strategies offer product exposure during the programs. The rates an advertiser pays are affected by supply and demand, type of program purchased, daypart, and the length of the commercial. The cost of television time is highest in prime time (7–11 p.m.). Discounts are generally offered on the basis of frequency, volume, continuity, and season.

In terms of planning and buying television commercial time, computer software is playing a key role. Referred to as optimizers, the software allows planners to search Nielsen databases for the best program combinations to increase target reach.

As in the television industry, the radio industry is in transition as radio tuning levels are being influenced by new technologies such as digital radio, internet radio, satellite radio, and portable listening devices such as iPods and cell phones. Traditional stations must react to these influences.

In contrast to television viewing, radio listening peaks in the morning (6–10 a.m.) and tapers off as the day progresses. Radio signals are transmitted in three ways: AM, FM, and by several digital options. FM is currently the most popular form of transmission, but digital audio broadcasting will grow in the next decade, stealing market share from traditional stations.

As an advertising medium, radio offers target-market selectivity, reach and frequency potential (based on its relatively low cost), and coverage flexibility. Radio's ability to reach selective targets is based on the format of the station. Currently, adult contemporary, the combination of oldies and rock, and news/talk are the most popular station formats. Disadvantages of radio as an advertising medium include audience fragmentation, problems associated with message retention, and clutter.

Radio rates are affected by several factors: season, daypart, reach plans, and the type of advertiser (local advertisers pay lower rates). Advertisers are offered discounts based on frequency, volume, continuity, and the use of package plans (reach plans).

KEY TERMS

REVIEW QUESTIONS

1. What is the purpose of the various time classifications in television and radio?

2. Identify and briefly explain the key issues confronting the television industry (and TV advertisers) today.

3. What are the primary advantages and disadvantages of television advertising for the national advertiser? For the local advertiser?

4. Explain the difference between network advertising and national or selective-spot advertising.

5. Identify and briefly explain any three factors that influence the cost of television advertising.

6. Identify and briefly explain the television discounts that are based on the amount of time purchased by advertisers.

7. Explain the following television terms:

   a) branded content
   b) fragmentation
   c) sponsorship
   d) daypart
   e) zipping
   f) zapping
   g) clutter
   h) upfront buying
   i) prime time versus fringe time
   j) package plans
   k) ROP
   l) pre-emption rates
   m) GRPs

8. Calculate the cost of the following television campaign on CKCO-TV. Assume an agency commission of 15 percent. What amount does CKCO-TV actually receive? Use the rate card in Figure 9.7 to do your calculations.

   Information: CKCO-TV
   Medium; 1 spot per week for 13 weeks (starting September 12)
   Close to Home; 1 spot per week for 13 weeks (starting December 12)
   CTV News at 6PM; 3 spots per week for 52 weeks

9. Identify and briefly discuss the key issues confronting the radio industry (and radio advertisers) today.

10. What does "station format" refer to in radio broadcasting?

11. What are the major advantages and disadvantages of radio advertising for the national advertiser? For the local advertiser?

12. Identify and briefly explain any three factors that influence the cost of radio advertising.

13. What is a reach plan, and what benefits does it provide the advertiser?

14. Calculate the cost of the following radio campaign. Use the rate card in Figure 9.13 to do your calculations.

    CHET Radio
    30-second spots as follows:
    Breakfast; 4 spots per week; Mon–Fri; 28 weeks
    Drive; 4 spots per week; Mon–Fri; 28 weeks
    Daytime; 8 spots per week; Mon–Fri; 28 weeks

    Now calculate the cost of a 16-spot reach plan for 28 weeks. How much money is saved compared to the original calculation? Is the reach plan a better deal?

15. If you made the decision to use radio in a city such as Toronto, Ottawa, or Vancouver, on what basis would you select specific stations? Discuss your reasons.

16. Briefly explain the following radio terms:

    a) audience flow
    b) combination rate
    c) vertical rotation
    d) horizontal rotation
    e) reach plan
    f) frequency discount
    g) volume discount
    h) continuity discount

DISCUSSION QUESTIONS

1. "Influences such as video-on-demand and commercial avoidance will be the demise of television advertising as we know it." Is this statement true or false? Conduct some secondary research on the issues and present a viewpoint.

2. What impact will the internet and cell phones have on the future of television viewing and television advertising? Will people be satisfied watching television shows on small screens? Discuss.

3. The television industry is moving in the direction of channel specialization (i.e., niche channels to reach selective targets). Will this trend continue? If so, is this trend a benefit or drawback for companies using television to deliver advertising messages? Justify your position.

4. Identify some additional strategies advertisers should be taking to counter the problem of commercial avoidance (either viewers leaving the viewing area or viewers using PVRs to avoid messages). Should funds be reallocated to other media? Present a position on this issue.

5. Is product placement and branded content a viable means of advertising? Will too much placement and branded content harm the credibility of television programs and the advertiser's reputation? Evaluate the issues surrounding this form of advertising and present a point of view.

6. Target-market selectivity is the key benefit of radio advertising. On what basis can the radio industry exploit this advantage? Discuss appropriate strategies the industry might use to attract advertisers.

7. Read the Advertising in Action vignette **Radio Helps Build Brands**. Is the potential of radio advertising underestimated? Should more advertising dollars be allocated to radio? Conduct some secondary research on the issue and present a point of view.

8. Are internet radio and satellite radio a threat to conventional radio broadcasters? If so, what strategies should conventional broadcasters be implementing now or in the near future to protect their position? Discuss.

NOTES

1. Television Bureau of Canada, *TV Basics 2005–2006*, p.8.
2. Patrick Allossery, "TV is getting worse, say majority of Canadians," *Strategy*, June 14, 2004, pp. 1, 6.
3. Seana Mulcahy, "Unnerved by young men," *Media Post*, **www.mediapost.com**, January 5, 2004.
4. Gina Piccalo, "Girls just want to be plugged in—to everything," *Los Angeles Times*, August 11, 2006, **www.latimes.com**.
5. Canadian Media Directors' Council, *Media Digest*, 2005–2006, p. 58.
6. Patrick Brethour, "Women narrow Internet gender gap," *Globe and Mail*, March 27, 2001, pp. B1, B2.
7. Barbara Shecter, "CTV adds web broadcasts to boost lineup," *Financial Post*, June 6, 2006, p. FP5.
8. Wayne Friedman, "On demand: Consumers prefer ads to VOD fees," *Media Post*, January 11, 2006, **www.publications.mediapost.com**.
9. "The future of viewership," *Strategy*, July 2006, p. 44.
10. Barbara Shecter, "Who will provide content," *Financial Post*, March 25, 2006, **www.canada.com**.
11. Frank Ahrens, "TV commercials move beyond the box," *Washington Post*, May 20, 2006, **www.washingtonpost.com**.
12. Pierre Delagrave, "Dawn of the ad zapper," *Marketing*, February 20, 2006, pp. 20, 21.
13. Barbara Shecter, "Televolution: No longer just sitting there," *Financial Post*, March 25, 2006, **www.canada.com**.
14. Television Bureau of Canada, *TV Basics 2005–2006*, p. 13.
15. Canadian Media Directors' Council, *Media Digest*, 2005–2006, p. 30.
16. Chuck Ross, "Study: Shorter spots less effective," *Advertising Age*, October 4, 1999, pp. 3, 65.
17. CPM calculated based on rates charged by Global TV and actual BBM audience data.
18. Chris Powell, "Tuned in to Turin," *Marketing*, January 30, 2006, p. 5.
19. Annette Boudreau, "Visa's double whammy on *Corner Gas*," *Strategy*, July 2005, p. 8.
20. Pia Musngi, "Kia and Subway sit rink-side for season two of *The Tournament*," **www.mediaincanada.com**, November 24, 2005.
21. Canadian Media Directors' Council, *Media Digest*, 2005–2006, p. 30.
22. Based on BBM Bureau of Measurement data, 2006.
23. Erwin Ephron, "Where's robobuyer?", *Advertising Age*, May 1, 2000, p. 45.
24. Canadian Media Directors' Council, *Media Digest*, 2006–2007, p. 32.
25. Grant Robertson and Catherine McLean, "XM Canada finds product platform with Telus deal," *The Globe and Mail*, July 7, 2006, p. B4.
26. "In one stroke, podcasting hits mainstream," *New York Times*, July 28, 2005, **www.nytimes.com**.
27. Heather Green, "Searching for the pod of gold," *Business Week Online*, November 14, 2005, **www.businessweek.com**.
28. Canadian Media Directors' Council, *Media Digest*, 2005–2006, p. 34.
29. "Random format comes to radio," *San Francisco Chronicle*, May 31, 2005, p.33.
30. *Ibid.*, p. 33.

CHAPTER **10**

Out-of-Home Media

Courtesy of Keith Tuckwell.

Out-of-home media includes various forms of outdoor advertising, transit advertising, and in-store and point-of-purchase (also known as at-retail) advertising. This chapter presents the basic types of out-of-home advertising alternatives, the advantages and disadvantages of each alternative, and the procedures for buying media space for each.

Out-of-home advertising and the variety of alternatives included in its domain represent a highly visible and effective alternative for advertisers. Think about it. If you drive a car, travel by transit, or stroll through shopping malls, you are constantly exposed to out-of-home advertising messages. Out-of-home advertising messages reach a massive cross-section of a city's population 24 hours a day, 7 days a week. In 2005, the combination of outdoor and transit advertising generated net revenues of $344 million, which accounted for three percent of net advertising revenues in Canada. On an annualized basis outdoor advertising is growing at a faster pace (over six percent) than other traditional media.[1]

There are several factors contributing to the popularity of outdoor advertising. The specialization and fragmentation that has occurred in other media, especially television and magazines, has caused advertisers to shift dollars toward outdoor. Another factor affecting growth stems from a shift in the thinking behind media planning. Many planners now pay more attention to when and why consumers come in contact with media and advertising messages. These planners believe that the proximity and timing of an advertising exposure, and the consumer's mindset at the time of that exposure, are emerging as critical factors in the communications planning process.[2] Many forms of out-of-home advertising actually reach the consumer when they are in a position to make a buying decision! Finally, new technologies have created new and innovative formats that have transformed outdoor boards from a static medium to a dynamic and interactive medium—the boards can actually entertain people who pass by! New forms of outdoor advertising are popping up every day.

Outdoor Media Research

The Canadian Outdoor Measurement Bureau (COMB) is responsible for compiling reliable data and information about outdoor advertising. COMB audits the circulations of outdoor posters, superboards, mall posters, backlit posters, and transit shelters. Circulation data for all media except mall posters are based on municipal and provincial traffic counts and are converted into circulation based on an established traffic-variation factor. COMB uses an average occupancy factor of 1.75 people per vehicle. Mall counts are based on head counts conducted by an independent organization in each market location. COMB maintains a national database of all media products and publishes the data in *Market Data Report*, a semi-annual publication.

Canadian Outdoor Measurement Bureau
www.comb.org

Sellers of outdoor media also rely on research data that is integrated with sophisticated software programs to help plan campaigns. For example, CBS Outdoor uses a system called SMART—Strategic Mapping and Response Tool. This database is based on Statistics Canada data; traffic flow and traffic volume information that is continually being added to the system. Referred to as geodemographic mapping, it has helped outdoor advertisers implement campaigns that target specific ethnic neighbourhoods with advertising in the appropriate language.[3] Outdoor has never been considered a targeted medium, but the combination of information and technology is changing things.

CBS Outdoor
www.cbsoutdoor.ca

Outdoor Advertising

POSTERS

The **poster** is the most commonly used form of outdoor advertising. Posters are either horizontal or vertical and are commonly referred to as **billboards**. The poster is composed of 10 or 12 sheets of special paper designed to withstand the wear and tear of outdoor conditions. To maximize reach potential, posters are strategically located on major routes within, or leading to, the business and shopping districts of a community. To maximize the frequency of the message, and to extend the daily viewing by consumers, posters are often illuminated. Advertisers can purchase poster space either in single panels or as a "showing." A **showing** refers to the buying of multiple panels to achieve a desired level of reach and frequency in a market. See Figure 10.1 for an illustration of an outdoor poster.

FIGURE 10.1

An outdoor poster

Courtesy of Dick Hemingway.

BACKLIT POSTERS

A **backlit poster** (often called a **backlight**) is a luminous sign containing advertising graphics printed on translucent polyvinyl material. Colour reproduction and impact are among the advantages offered by a backlit poster. At night, the lighted display takes on a three-dimensional effect. Backlit posters are strategically located at major intersections and high-volume traffic routes. The primary advantage of backlit posters is the image enhancement they offer; there is strong visual impact in the day and night. The cost of producing backlit posters is quite high, but the opportunities for exposure are estimated to be twice that of a standard poster.

Scrolling backlights are a recent innovation for high-traffic areas. The messages are timed to change with the flow of traffic so that everyone gets a chance to see the message from three different advertisers.

SUPERBOARD (BIGBOARD) AND SPECTACULARS

A **superboard** or **spectacular** is an oversized display unit positioned at high-volume traffic locations. Typically, it extends from a rectangular format to include space extensions (i.e., the product itself may extend beyond the frame of the board), and electronic messages that can change quickly to meet an advertiser's specifications. Essentially, a superboard is created to meet a specific advertiser's needs. They are typically located in high traffic areas, and generate low to moderate reach with heavy frequency.

Some recent innovations include the "superflex" board, a hand-printed or screen-printed flexible vinyl sheet that is stretched over the standard superboard frame, and a computer-designed 3-D billboard that produces a product replica as large as 16 metres high. An example of a 3-D board appears in Figure 10.2. The new "trivision" board is a three-sided board that rotates. Each rotation has louvres that rotate to change the ads. Boards of this nature are ideal for prime locations where no new billboard space is available.

Since spectaculars are usually one-of-a-kind structures fabricated at great expense, they require a long-term commitment from the advertiser. Spectaculars are beyond the budgets of most advertisers.

FIGURE **10.2**

An example of 3-D billboard advertising

Courtesy of Keith Tuckwell.

MALL POSTERS

Unlike all other forms of outdoor advertising, **mall posters** do not rely on vehicular traffic. Typically located inside shopping malls, these backlit posters are seen at eye level by passing pedestrians as they walk through the mall. These posters reach consumers at a crucial time, a time when they are making buying decisions, so they are a good outlet for retailers and branded products available right in the mall. The very presence of a message on a mall poster may encourage impulse buying. As a medium, mall posters are a good secondary vehicle in a multimedia campaign. They are ideal for reinforcing a brand's primary selling message.

The quality and impact of mall posters is advancing. Some malls hang oversized wall murals from various structures so that the advertising message is clearly visible to passersby. Refer to Figure 10.3 for an illustration of an indoor mall wall mural.

TRANSIT SHELTERS

A **transit-shelter unit** consists of two street-level backlit posters that are incorporated into the design of glass-and-steel transit shelters. Each shelter has two faces that are backlit from dusk until dawn. Transit-shelter units are located on busy public-transit routes and offer advertisers high levels of potential exposure to motorists, pedestrians, and transit riders. Transit-shelter advertising offers the advertiser strong visual impact, as the colour reproduction is of superior quality. These units are sold to advertisers on the basis of site-selection flexibility. That is, advertisers can select sites that reach certain age, income, or ethnic groups or they can concentrate on a geographic trading zone, depending on the target they would like to reach. Transit shelters offer high reach and heavy frequency. Refer to Figure 10.4 for an illustration of transit-shelter advertising.

DIGITAL SIGNS

Digital sign units display advertising messages electronically, with ads from numerous advertisers displayed on a rotating basis around the clock. Ads are typically 10 to 15 seconds in length. These signs offer tremendous flexibility, as an advertiser can change the message

FIGURE **10.3**

An example of a wall mural advertisement in an indoor mall

Courtesy of Keith Tuckwell.

FIGURE **10.4**

Examples of transit-shelter advertising

very quickly if necessary. They are generally located in high-traffic areas within large urban centres across Canada. Prime location means heavy weekly frequency can be achieved.

FULL-MOTION VIDEO DISPLAYS

In key urban markets, large-format **full-motion video screens** are available. The high-resolution screens are remotely programmable, which, as with digital signs, provides advertisers with the flexibility to change creative quickly. Outdoor video is a relatively new medium, but it is now on the media planner's radar. Clients and agency planners are starting to appreciate the medium's reach capabilities and content flexibility.

Research data from Toronto indicates an awareness level of 82 percent for the medium, while 77 percent claimed they had seen a video board in the past week.[4]

STREET-LEVEL ADVERTISING

Street-level units are rear-illuminated and are positioned adjacent to high-traffic streets in the downtown cores of major markets. Many of these signs are now popping up along sidewalks and in public squares. Their presence gives advertisers an opportunity to reach people in hard-to-target urban areas where there is a good deal of pedestrian foot traffic in the daytime. The signs are visible to vehicle traffic as well. The ads appear much like they do on a transit shelter except the street-level unit is a stand-alone structure that contains only the advertising message.

A recent innovation in this category is the mega-column. The mega-column is a tall structure; some examples are constructed using three-sided pillars that feature advertising on two sides and municipal information on the third. An example of this form of advertising appears in Figure 10.5.

WALL BANNERS AND MURALS

Banners are large PVC vinyl banners framed and mounted on the outside of a building. They can be moved and reused. **Mural banner** advertisements are hand-painted outdoor extravaganzas on the sides of buildings. They are very large, often the entire height of the building. They can be three-dimensional, which adds to their attention-grabbing capability. See Figure 10.6 for an example of a mural advertisement.

FIGURE 10.5

An innovative street-level medium—the mega-column

Courtesy of Keith Tuckwell.

FIGURE 10.6

An example of
wall-mural advertising

Outdoor as an Advertising Medium

Many advertisers overlook or ignore the benefits of outdoor advertising, yet it is a medium that is excellent at reinforcing a message communicated in another medium, such as television or magazines. This section presents the benefits and drawbacks of outdoor advertising.

ADVANTAGES OF OUTDOOR ADVERTISING

TARGET REACH AND FREQUENCY Outdoor advertising provides advertisers with the opportunity to reach a very large cross-section of a market's population in a short period of time. Depending on the weight level purchased (GRPs) and on the strategic location of outdoor boards on busy thoroughfares, outdoor advertising has the potential for multiple exposures. According to CBS Outdoor data (CBS is one of Canada's largest sellers of outdoor space), up to 90 percent of a city's traffic is concentrated on 10 percent of the streets (streets where outdoor boards are located), and significant exposure levels are achieved during the first two weeks of a campaign.[5] From that point on, reach potential is marginal.

TARGETING FLEXIBILITY Advertisers that want to advertise only in certain areas have the flexibility to do so with outdoor advertising. Outdoor units can be purchased on a regional basis (perhaps for an entire province or for an area within a province) or on a market-by-market basis. Within major metropolitan markets, advertisers can use outdoor posters to target neighbourhoods based on a combination of demographic and geographic characteristics. Other advertisers may choose transit shelters that are close to high schools if the goal is to reach teenagers. Advertisers that want to increase weight levels in selected markets can use outdoor advertising to supplement a national campaign in another medium.

SIZE AND QUALITY OF MESSAGE Backlit posters, spectaculars, and transit-shelter advertising units all offer advertisers high reproduction quality. Although the messages communicated by outdoor advertising must be short, a strong visual impression can attract the attention of people passing by. As the old saying goes, "A picture is worth a thousand words." If the goal is to create a monumental impression on consumers, outdoor boards have the capability. See the illustration in Figure 10.7.

COMPATIBILITY WITH OTHER MEDIA   Outdoor advertising can reinforce the message of other media in two ways. First, it can extend the total reach and frequency of a campaign beyond what a single medium can do. Therefore, it is a good complementary medium—a good means of reinforcing important sales messages. Second, outdoor advertising can increase the total number of impressions made on a target market that may only be light consumers of other media. For example, a light viewer of television, who is hard to reach regardless of the weight level purchased, may be easier to reach via outdoor advertising.

CREATING PRODUCT AWARENESS   Traditionally regarded as a complementary medium, outdoor advertising can also be effective in generating product awareness when used as a primary medium, particularly if a shotgun media strategy is used (e.g., if an advertiser wanted to reach all adults aged 18 to 49 in specified markets). As an example, watchmaker TAG Heuer uses outdoor posters to make a quick impression on upscale consumers in key urban markets. The outdoor ad that appears in Figure 10.8 reaches busy executives and professionals who commute to downtown Toronto each day. The outdoor component of TAG Heuer's advertising campaign complements its more targeted magazine campaign. In magazines, more product information is communicated.

TAG Heuer

www.tagheuer.com

COST   When the absolute cost of outdoor advertising is evaluated in terms of reach potential—the opportunities for exposing consumers to outdoor messages—the medium begins to seem a fairly efficient media buy. Using Toronto as an example, and assuming an advertiser purchased standard outdoor backlit posters sold by CBS Outdoor for a four-week period at a 75 GRP level (see Figure 10.10), we would calculate the CPM (cost of reaching a thousand people) as follows:[6]

FIGURE 10.7

Outdoor advertising can make a strong visual impression

Courtesy of Keith Tuckwell.

Courtesy of Keith Tuckwell.

Outdoor boards in high-traffic locations reach a diverse audience at a low CPM (cost per thousand)

$$\text{CPM} = \frac{\text{Cost}}{\text{Population (000)}}$$

$$= \frac{63\,000}{4871.7}$$

$$= \$12.93$$

This represents the cost of reaching a thousand people once. Therefore, when the daily travel patterns of people are considered (and thus the potential for multiple exposure), the cost efficiencies of outdoor advertising improve.

CONTENT FLEXIBILITY   Due to advancing technology, an additional advantage of outdoor media is content flexibility. Unique to digital signs and full-motion video displays is the fact that content can be changed quickly, based on market conditions, competitive activity, or the advertiser's desire to simply display a different message. It is the advertiser's space to use as it sees fit. Digital signs and full-motion video screens are now part of the urban advertising landscape. A fast-food restaurant, for example, could deliver a breakfast or lunch message in the morning and a dinner message in the afternoon and evening. A television network could advertise upcoming shows or specials, a situation in which the content would be constantly changing.

DISADVANTAGES OF OUTDOOR ADVERTISING

CREATIVE LIMITATIONS   The nature of the outdoor advertising medium (that is, people passing by outdoor ads either in a vehicle or on foot) is such that it must rely on instant visual impact to get attention. The message itself must be short and simple to read, and it must quickly draw attention to the brand name. Creative limitations are a bit of a myth to Brian Harrod, a former creative director at several prominent Canadian ad agencies. According to Harrod, "If you can't present an advertising idea on an outdoor board, it isn't simple and focused enough to be an effective advertising idea."[7] Examine the ad in Figure 10.9—I'm certain you will agree it is a creative piece of outdoor advertising.

LACK OF TARGET-MARKET SELECTIVITY   The broad reach potential of outdoor advertising (it reaches all adults and children) makes it impossible for an advertiser to focus on a target market. Therefore, due to wasted circulation, the cost-per-thousand figures that show efficiency may be deceptively low (since the medium reaches many people who would never purchase the product).

COSTS   Costs of outdoor advertising are high in two areas. First, the costs of producing finished materials for vehicles such as backlit posters, mall posters, and transit shelters are high (printing on a plastic vinyl material is expensive). Second, the absolute cost of buying media space is high. A 4-week showing of horizontal outdoor posters in Canada's top 3 markets (Toronto/Oshawa/Hamilton, Montreal, and Vancouver) at a 25-GRP level would cost between $210 000 (for 91 panels) and $316 000 (for 159 panels) depending on the minimum and maximum number of panels desired. At 50 GRPs, the range is $363 000 (for 214 panels) to $446 000 (for 308 panels).[8] Expanding to the top 10 urban markets increases the cost again.

FIGURE 10.9

A classic example of creativity in outdoor advertising

LACK OF PRESTIGE Outdoor advertising does not always enhance the image of the product, whereas advertising in a quality magazine can rely on the surrounding editorial content to aid in image development. Also, the association of the product with a medium that clutters the landscape may have a negative impact. Many critics of outdoor advertising refer to it as "pollution on a stick." With due respect to these critics, digital outdoor advertising in the form of full-motion video, along with new and more extravagant outdoor alternatives, have added an element of quality to the medium.

UNOBTRUSIVE MEDIUM Despite the reach and frequency potential of the medium, people who pass by may not notice outdoor ads. Unless the message catches the attention of passersby, the outdoor board will blend into the background and not break through the consumer's perceptual barriers. In urban downtown locations, the clustering of outdoor advertising may prevent any single message from being noticed.

For more insight into the effectiveness of outdoor advertising, and why Nike uses this medium, see the Advertising in Action vignette **Nike's Outdoor Innovation Builds Buzz**.

Buying Outdoor Media Space

Regardless of the outdoor advertising format under consideration, there are similarities in the media-buying process. Outdoor space is sold in four-week periods and is available on a market-by-market basis. Advertisers can purchase a single market, a group of markets (composing a regional buy), or a national buy if strategy demands it and budget permits it.

Media space is purchased on the basis of the advertising weight level desired by the advertiser, expressed in terms of GRPs (gross rating points). As indicated in the Media Strategy section of Chapter 7, GRP is a weighting factor that combines reach and frequency variables. In the case of outdoor advertising, GRP is defined as the total circulation of a specific outdoor advertisement expressed as a percentage of the market's population. With reference to Figure 10.10, on a weekly basis a weight level of 100 GRPs delivers exposure opportunities equal to the population of a market. A weight level of 50 GRPs offers one-half the exposure opportunities, and so on for the various weight levels.

OUTDOOR ADVERTISING—RATES AND DISCOUNTS

Outdoor advertising rates are quoted on a four-week basis. To illustrate Outdoor cost calculations, let's consider a few media-buying examples. Rates and data from Figures 10.10 and 10.11 are used to calculate costs.

OUTDOOR BUYING PLAN: EXAMPLE 1

Medium:	Transit Shelters (CBS Outdoor)
Markets:	Toronto/Hamilton (CMA), Montreal (CMA), Calgary (CMA), and Halifax (CMA)
Weight:	50 GRPs weekly
Contract Length:	16 weeks

ADVERTISING IN ACTION

Nike's Outdoor Innovation Builds Buzz

Boys 14 to 17 years old are hard to reach. Their allegiance to the internet means they are watching television less and listening to the radio less. So how does an advertiser reach them? You reach them on the street! And when you reach them you drive them to your website.

Working together on a key outdoor assignment for Nike Canada, Taxi Advertising (a creative agency) and Cossette Media (a media agency) developed an innovative campaign that created incredible buzz for Nike. The campaign, called the "Nike 45" campaign, was designed to drive the intended target to the nikehockey.ca website. Nike used two well-known hockey stars in the campaign: Marcus Naslund of the Vancouver Canucks and Jarome Iginla of the Calgary Flames. Both stars were seen in larger-than-life situations that garnered instant attention from the public and the media.

Vancouverites were treated to the spectacle of a 40-foot-tall Markus Naslund appearing to be engaged in a tug of war with a tugboat while straining against a set of Nike resistance bands. The super-sized image sailed past the city's main beaches for a month. In Toronto, an image of Iginla was suspended from a crane—he appeared to be doing chin-ups 75 feet above the busy Don Valley Parkway. The ads used the line "Ready for your :45"—a phrase that would only make sense to those with enough knowledge about hockey to know that 45 seconds is the typical length of an NHL player's shift on the ice. According to creative director Lance Martin, "We wanted to have statement pieces that would get kids talking. We wanted to make training fun and exciting, not a chore."

Nike likes to say it is innovative by choice, and it is. You have to be innovative if you want to make an impression on youth targets. From the very beginning, Taxi and Cossette worked closely together to "marry our imaginations with reality," explains Martin, adding that such thinking is typical of Nike work. "Nike is always striving to have new media [applications]." The campaign also included a 45-second TV spot showing Iginla racing around the city dodging pucks being shot from rooftops by Naslund. The television campaign was national, but the outdoor stunt pieces were only displayed in Vancouver, Calgary, and Toronto.

Doug Checkeris, chief executive of The Media Company, says, "Nike is a larger-than-life brand where expectations are very high. What they are doing suits their brand." Ricardo Gaitan, Nike Canada's director of marketing, says out-of-home is a significant part of their marketing mix, "It's a powerful way to get customers into the stores. The hockey campaign created real buzz. You hear people talking about those big-impact units because they are unique, because they are things they have never seen before. That's good for business!"

Source: Adapted from Paul Brent, "Blowing up the brand," *Marketing*, May 15, 2006, p. 13, 14; and Annette Boudreau, "Just do it big," *Strategy*, September 2005, p. 24.

According to Figure 10.10, the costs for a four-week period for each market would be as follows:

Toronto/Hamilton	$131 016
Montreal	75 311
Calgary	26 194
Halifax	9 558
Total	**242 079**

Since the length of the contract is 16 weeks, the cost of the markets above would be multiplied by a factor of 4 (16 weeks divided by 4-week rates). The gross cost would be calculated as follows:

$$\$242\,079 \times 4 = \$968\,316$$

325

FIGURE **10.10**

Outdoor rate card for
transit shelters

CBS Outdoor - Street Level

TRANSIT SHELTERS

	Pop.	25 Daily GRPs min. panels	max. panels	4 wk. rate	50 Daily GRPs min. panels	max. panels	4 wk. rate	75 Daily GRPs min. panels	max. panels	4 wk. rate
St. John's CMA	163,100	—	6	3,180	—	11	5,214	—	17	8,058
Mount Pearl, C (NL)	23,900	—	1	530	—	2	1,060	—	3	1,590
Halifax CMA	355,400	9	10	5,018	19	21	9,558	28	32	14,336
Cape Breton CA (Sydney)	97,600	—	3	1,847	4	5	3,519	6	7	5,278
Annapolis Valley ESA	95,000	—	3	1,168	—	6	2,238	—	9	3,310
Saint John CMA	112,700	—	3	1,486	5	6	2,830	7	8	4,245
Quebec City CMA	655,600	15	17	10,879	29	33	20,721	44	48	31,082
Chicoutimi-Jonquiere (Saguenay) CMA	147,300	4	5	2,172	8	9	4,138	13	15	6,206
Trois Rivieres CMA	129,200	4	5	1,723	8	9	3,281	13	15	4,922
Sherbrooke CMA	149,100	—	3	2,080	5	6	3,963	8	9	5,944
Montreal CMA	3,336,100	53	59	39,538	107	117	75,311	163	173	112,967
Hull C & District	196,100	—	7	2,740	—	14	5,220	—	19	7,828
Shawinigan CA & District	53,100	—	3	2,100						
Toronto CMA/Hamilton CMA	5,521,000	81	89	68,784	164	174	131,016	248	258	196,524
Toronto CMA	4,871,700	70	76	70,160	143	153	133,639	217	227	200,458
Hamilton CMA	649,300	15	17	10,287	30	34	19,595	45	49	29,393
London CMA	419,800	7	8	5,422	14	16	10,328	22	24	15,491
Windsor CMA	310,100	7	8	4,518	15	17	8,606	23	25	12,909
Leamington CA	47,300	2	3	1,129						
Sarnia CA	80,600	—	3	2,364	5	6	4,503	7	8	6,754
Barrie CA	180,700	6	7	1,736	12	14	3,306	19	21	4,959
Sault Ste. Marie CA	70,200	—	2	876	—	4	1,752	—	5	2,190
Timmins CA	39,400	—	2	1,090	—	4	2,016	—	6	2,622
Sudbury CMA	137,900	—	3	1,875	—	6	3,600	—	9	5,130
Winnipeg CMA	626,700	8	9	6,740	16	18	12,839	24	26	19,258
Calgary CMA	1,007,500	20	22	13,752	40	44	26,194	59	65	39,291
Grande Prairie C	152,500	—	—	240						
Edmonton CMA	915,900	18	20	13,752	36	40	26,194	53	59	39,291
Vancouver CMA	2,106,500	29	33	30,798	58	64	58,663	87	95	87,994

	100 Daily GRPs min. panels	max. panels	4 wk. rate
St. John's CMA	—	23	10,534
Mount Pearl, C (NL)	—		
Halifax CMA	38	42	19,115
Cape Breton CA (Sydney)	8	9	7,038
Annapolis Valley ESA	—	11	3,990
Saint John CMA	10	12	5,660
Quebec City CMA	58	64	41,443
Chicoutimi-Jonquiere (Saguenay) CMA	17	19	8,275
Trois Rivieres CMA	17	19	6,563
Sherbrooke CMA	10	12	7,925
Montreal CMA	219	229	150,623
Hull C & District	—	25	10,867
Shawinigan CA & District	—		
Toronto CMA/Hamilton CMA	332	342	262,033
Toronto CMA	291	301	267,278
Hamilton CMA	60	66	39,190
London CMA	28	32	20,655
Windsor CMA	29	33	17,213
Leamington CA	—		
Sarnia CA	10	12	9,005
Barrie CA	—		
Sault Ste. Marie CA	—	7	3,066
Timmins CA	—	7	2,961
Sudbury CMA	—	12	6,420
Winnipeg CMA	31	35	25,678
Calgary CMA	79	87	52,388
Grande Prairie C	—		
Edmonton CMA	72	78	52,388
Vancouver CMA	116	126	117,325

MECHANICAL SPECIFICATIONS:
TRANSIT SHELTERS - ALL MARKETS
Live Area: 3' 6-1/2" x 5' 4-11/16"
Visible Area: 3' 9" x 5' 6-1/4"
Trim Size: 3' 11-1/4" x 5' 8-1/4"
Prod. costs extra. Replacement/renewal material required. CBS Outdoor has full production facilities. Contact rep or see web site for product and art specs.
Data confirmed 10/13/2006

Courtesy of CBS Outdoor.

While not shown in this particular illustration and rate card, outdoor media usually offer advertisers volume discounts (e.g., a reduced rate based on dollar volume purchased) and continuity discounts (e.g., a reduced rate for extended buys such as 12 weeks, 16 weeks, etc.).

OUTDOOR BUYING PLAN: EXAMPLE 2

Medium:	Outdoor Horizontal Backlights (CBS Outdoor)
Markets:	Toronto (CMA), Montreal (CMA), Edmonton (CMA), Vancouver (CMA)
Weight:	Toronto and Montreal at 75 GRPs; Edmonton and Vancouver at 50 GRPs
Contract Length:	12 weeks

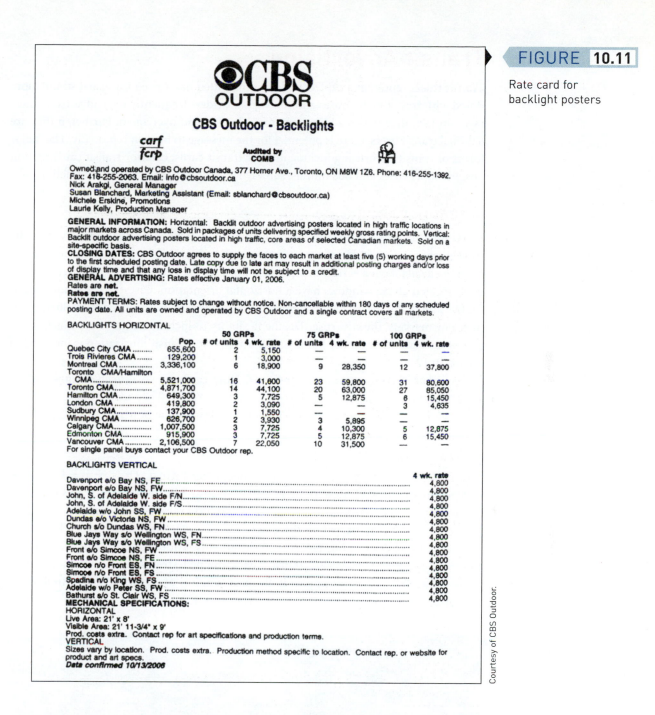

FIGURE 10.11

Rate card for backlight posters

Using the data from Figure 10.11, we would calculate the appropriate costs for each market over a four-week period as follows:

Toronto	$63 000 × 3 = $189 000
Montreal	28 350 × 3 = 85 050
Edmonton	7725 × 3 = 23 175
Vancouver	22 050 × 3 = 66 150
Total Cost	**= $363 375**

The length of the contract is 12 weeks. Therefore, the cost for each market is multiplied by a factor of three (12 weeks divided by a 4-week rate). Should volume and continuity discounts apply, they would be deducted from the gross amount shown in this illustration.

Transit Advertising

Transit riders represent a captive audience that often has a need for visual stimulation. Bored with travelling on buses and subway cars, riders frequently read advertising messages. In fact, they may read the same message over and over again. Further, if they are habitual transit users, there is potential for the message to be seen repeatedly. The major forms of transit advertising include interior transit cards, exterior transit cards, station posters, superbuses and bus murals, subway LCD screens, and station domination.

INTERIOR CARDS

Interior cards are print advertisements contained in racks above the windows of public transit vehicles (i.e., in buses, streetcars, subway cars, and light rapid transit cars). The cards are available in a variety of sizes depending on the needs of the advertiser. Interior cards located above windows have a horizontal orientation. Given that the audience is captive and that the average travel time in a transit vehicle is estimated to be 30 minutes in major markets, the advertiser has the flexibility to include longer copy, which is not an option with other out-of-home media. An interior transit illustration is included in Figure 10.12.

Another interior option is the door card. **Door cards** are positioned on either side of the doors on subways, LRTs, and many commuter trains. They tend to have a vertical orientation. Passengers are exposed to these ads while in transit or when exiting the vehicle.

EXTERIOR BUS POSTERS

Two options are available in the **exterior bus poster** format. The first is a *king poster* (larger format) located on the side of surface transit vehicles only. It is 139 inches × 30 inches (353 cm × 76 cm) in size. The second option is called a *seventy poster* (smaller format) that is either located on the side or tail of surface transit vehicles. The unique characteristic of exterior bus posters is their mobility. They move through every area of a city and are seen by motorists, transit riders, and pedestrians. A relatively new option is the tail poster. *Tail posters* appear in the back window of surface vehicles. An illustration of an exterior bus poster is shown in Figure 10.13.

FIGURE 10.12

Interior transit card advertising

Courtesy of Dick Hemingway.

FIGURE 10.13

An exterior transit ad

SUPERBUSES AND BUS MURALS

The **superbus** allows an advertiser to "own" a whole bus. The advertising is printed onto a vinyl product that is applied to all sides of the bus except the front. The advertiser has access to all interior advertising space as well. See Figure 10.14 for an illustration.

Unlike other transit advertising, the superbus option is contracted for an extended period, usually 26 or 52 weeks. Rates vary considerably from market to market. In a market the size of Toronto, the 52-week rate for one street car is $108 800; in Winnipeg, the rate is $34 500. **Bus murals** are also available in selected markets. Murals appear on the driver's side and/or the tails of buses. These are applied using vinyl products and are sold for commitments of 12 weeks or more. In Toronto, the cost of a mural for 52 weeks is $83 430 (about 75 percent of the cost of a superbus for a comparable period of time).[9]

STATION POSTERS AND BACKLITS

Station posters are advertisements located on platforms and at the entrances and exits of the subway and light rail transit systems in Canada. They are available in a variety of

FIGURE 10.14

An example of superbus advertising—on a streetcar

sizes, and the most common of these is called the station poster. The station poster is the same size as a transit-shelter or mall poster. Standard size specifications encourage cross-usage of various out-of-home media. Station posters fall into two broad categories: platform posters and subway backlits. **Platform posters** are located on the subway wall opposite the rider waiting on the platform. In the Toronto subway system, posters are also attached to steel pillars in the area between rail lines. Passengers waiting on both platforms are exposed to these messages. See Figure 10.15 for an example of this type of advertisement.

The second option is the subway backlit. The **backlit poster** is a vinyl poster with rear illumination. Backlits are usually located along station walls and above and below escalator stairwells throughout the Toronto and Montreal subway systems and the GO Transit system in southern Ontario. Light rail transit systems in Vancouver, Edmonton, and Calgary also offer a variety of backlit and poster options.

A recent innovation in subway backlits is "triples." **Triples** are three transit shelter ads placed side by side, an execution technique that gives advertisers greater impact capability. The same ad may appear on all three boards, or each panel may be used for a different part of a message.

SUBWAY—ONESTOP NETWORK

These are digital communications centres that employ 40-inch LCD screens. The screens are mounted above subway platforms for easy viewing by waiting passengers. Smaller screens will eventually be installed in subway cars. The screens feature news, sports, business news, and weather, along with video advertisements and sponsorship opportunities.

STATION DOMINATION

The Toronto and Montreal transit systems are testing various new concepts and exploring new opportunities to maximize the effectiveness of an advertiser's message. One of these concepts is station domination, an opportunity that gives a single advertiser control of every advertising space in a subway station. For advertisers looking for innovative ways of breaking through the clutter, station domination will certainly do it. Included in the mix are innovative concepts such as ceiling decals, extended wall ads, and super-sized floor ads. Refer to the illustration in Figure 10.16.

FIGURE 10.15

Subway poster advertising

Courtesy of Dick Hemingway.

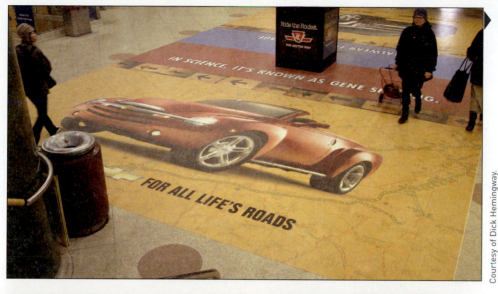

FIGURE 10.16

Two innovative advertising concepts in subway stations

Transit as an Advertising Medium

ADVANTAGES OF TRANSIT

CONTINUOUS EXPOSURE AND CREATIVITY Commuters tend to be creatures of routine, so they are exposed to the same messages on a daily basis. With the average transit ride in major markets over 30 minutes in length, passengers can relieve their boredom by reading the ads. This provides some creative opportunity, as longer copy can be used and riders can be more involved. In this regard, transit advertisements are a good vehicle for reinforcing the messages of in-home media.

REACH AND FREQUENCY Like outdoor advertising, transit advertising reaches a mass audience quickly. Transit riders cut across all demographics, with the heaviest concentration in the adult category. Consumers generally encounter the message more than once because of daily riding patterns, and the combination of high reach and frequency translates into an extremely high number of impressions on the target market. Factors such as the rising costs of running a car and the increasing numbers of commuters travelling to and from a city each day for work have had a positive effect on the reach potential of transit.

FLEXIBILITY   Certain transit media are flexible because the message can be changed easily. For example, a portion of a poster can display a permanent message and another portion can display a short-term message that can be changed periodically. Should creative direction change, new execution can replace the old execution quickly. In terms of geography, transit markets can be purchased on an individual basis, so it is a good complementary medium to add reach and frequency in a total advertising campaign.

MARKET COVERAGE   In any given market, transit advertising covers all sections of the community—residential urban and suburban, industrial, and commercial—where other forms of out-of-home media may not be available.

COST   On a market-by-market basis, the dollar outlay for transit media space is relatively low, and considering the number of consumers reached, the cost per thousand is low. Essentially, transit is a cost-efficient medium that reaches a mass audience. As a result, it is attractive to smaller-budget advertisers and to larger-budget advertisers needing a complementary medium to reach urban customers.

DISADVANTAGES OF TRANSIT

LACK OF TARGET-MARKET SELECTIVITY   In large urban markets, transit use reflects the general, non-specific demographic and socio-economic characteristics of those markets. Therefore, for an advertiser attempting to reach a precisely defined target, the use of transit results in wasted circulation. Consequently, the cost-per-thousand efficiencies, which are based on high reach of a mass audience, may be artificially low.

MEDIA ENVIRONMENT   The environment in which transit advertising operates is often a hectic one—people coming and going quickly, particularly in morning and evening rush hours. In such an environment, advertising messages are easy to avoid. In the case of interior transit, the environment is often cluttered and crowded (particularly during peak-usage periods such as rush hour), a circumstance that makes the messages both less visible and less attractive. This environment may detract from the prestige of the product.

CREATIVE LIMITATIONS   While transit advertising offers good colour reproduction, the actual amount of space it provides advertisers to work with is quite small. In the case of exterior bus posters and platform posters, there is a bit more creative flexibility. However, as indicated in the previous section, some new and innovative concepts such as station domination are being tested. This option and the opportunities it presents offer greater creative potential.

Both outdoor advertising and transit advertising are often the choice of media planners when the target-market description is fairly broad in scope (e.g., age, income, occupation, and lifestyle) or if specific geographic markets (e.g., cities) are important. As mentioned earlier in the chapter, planners now perceive outdoor and transit as a timely medium. That also factors into media recommendations.

Buying Transit Advertising

Transit advertising rates are affected by variables such as the number of markets being covered, the length of the showing (which affects discounts), the desired weight level in any given market, and the size of the space required. Transit space is generally sold on the basis of four-week minimums and is available on a market-by-market basis. Advertisers can purchase space in a group of cities in a region to qualify for greater discounts; major Canadian cities might constitute a group; cities within a geographic region might also constitute a group. CBS Outdoor and Pattison Outdoor are among the largest sellers of transit advertising space in Canada.

The first thing to consider when purchasing transit space is the weight level desired in each market. As in outdoor advertising, transit weight is expressed in terms of GRPs (gross rating points), with GRP referring to the total circulation of a showing expressed as a percentage of a market's population. For an illustration of the GRP concept and its effect on costs, refer to Figure 10.17.

As indicated earlier, all rates are based on the purchase of a four-week period, starting with a base rate for each market purchased. Usually, a **continuity discount** is available to advertisers that meet predetermined time commitments (e.g., 12-, 24-, and 52-week periods), with the percentage of the discount increasing with the time commitment.

MEDIA-BUYING ILLUSTRATIONS

Let's consider a few media-buying examples, using the rates and data in Figure 10.17 as a basis for calculating the costs. Please note that all rates are quoted for a *four-week period*.

TRANSIT BUYING PLAN: EXAMPLE 1

Medium:	Exterior King Bus Posters (Pattison Transit)
Markets:	Edmonton, Ottawa, and Halifax
Weight:	75 GRPs in Edmonton; 50 GRPs in Ottawa and Halifax
Contract Length:	20 weeks

According to Figure 10.17, the costs for specified markets for four weeks at the specified GRP levels would be

Edmonton	$30 800
Ottawa	$16 250
Halifax	$ 5 760
Total Cost (4 weeks)	**$52 810**

Therefore, the total cost for the 20-week contract would be

$$\$52\ 810 \times 5 = \$264\ 050$$

In this example, the length of the contract is 20 weeks, so the rate for 4 weeks is multiplied by a factor of 5 (20 weeks divided by the 4-week rates).

TRANSIT BUYING PLAN: EXAMPLE 2

Medium:	Standard Interior Cards (Pattison Transit)
Markets:	Halifax, Ottawa, Winnipeg, and Calgary
Weight:	Full-showing in Ottawa and Calgary; half-showing in Winnipeg and Halifax
Contract Length:	Ottawa and Calgary 16 weeks; Winnipeg and Halifax 24 weeks

According to Figure 10.17, the costs for the specified markets are

FIGURE 10.17

Exterior and interior
transit rate card

Pattison Transit Advertising

GENERAL INFORMATION: King posters are located on the sides. Seventy posters are located on the rear and interior cards are displayed on the interior of transit vehicles.
CLOSING DATES: Individual market requirements available on request.
GENERAL ADVERTISING: Rates effective January 01, 2006.
Rates are **net**.

PAYMENT TERMS: Invoices due & payable when rendered. Rates subject to change without notice.

KING POSTERS	25 Daily GRP's Approx. faces	4 wk. cost	50 Daily GRP's Approx. faces	4 wk. cost	75 Daily GRP's Approx. faces	4 wk. cost	100 Daily GRP's Approx. faces	4 wk. cost
Halifax	8	2,960	16	5,760	24	8,400	32	10,880
Moncton	4	1,360	8	2,640	12	3,840	16	4,960
St. John's	7	2,730	15	5,700	22	8,140	30	10,880
Corner Brook	2	620	4	1,200	6	1,740	8	2,240
Ottawa	25	8,750	50	16,250	76	23,180	101	29,290
North Bay	3	840	5	1,360	8	2,080	10	2,520
Sudbury	7	1,890	14	3,500	21	4,935	28	6,300
Thunder Bay	5	1,240	10	2,355	15	3,340	20	4,330
Brandon	2	635	4	1,210	5	1,445	7	2,070
Winnipeg	23	7,350	47	14,560	70	21,245	94	25,380
Moose Jaw	2	635	3	910	5	1,445	6	1,705
Calgary	29	11,310	59	21,240	88	29,040	118	34,220
Edmonton (EMA*)	37	11,950	72	22,320	110	30,800	147	35,280
Lethbridge	3	1,015	5	1,600	7	2,180	10	3,065
Medicine Hat	2	675	4	1,280	6	1,855	8	2,465

SEVENTY POSTERS	25 Daily GRP's Approx. faces	4 wk. cost	50 Daily GRP's Approx. faces	4 wk. cost	75 Daily GRP's Approx. faces	4 wk. cost	100 Daily GRP's Approx. faces	4 wk. cost
Halifax	10	2,800	20	5,400	30	7,800	40	10,000
Moncton	5	1,300	10	2,500	15	3,600	20	4,600
Charlottetown	2	460	4	880	6	1,260	8	1,600
St. John's	7	2,030	15	4,200	22	5,940	30	7,800
Corner Brook	2	460	4	880	6	1,260	8	1,600
Ottawa	29	7,250	59	13,865	89	20,025	119	26,180
North Bay	3	672	5	1,060	8	1,632	10	1,960
Sudbury	7	1,610	14	3,010	21	4,305	28	5,460
Thunder Bay	6	1,300	12	2,450	12	3,450	18	4,455
Brandon	2	525	4	1,000	6	1,445	8	1,900
Winnipeg	29	6,840	59	13,505	88	17,600	117	21,060
Moose Jaw	1	285	3	820	5	1,310	7	1,805
Calgary	35	11,200	69	21,045	104	34,750	139	34,750
Edmonton (EMA*)	39	9,750	80	20,400	121	27,225	160	37,000
Lethbridge	3	780	6	1,500	9	2,115	11	2,595
Medicine Hat	2	520	4	1,000	7	1,645	10	2,355

*Includes St. Albert & Sherwood Park garages. Decal ext. on Seventy posters are subject to a min. 25% premium of the rate card unit cost. Ultra Tails avail. at 3x the rate card unit cost of a Seventy poster.

INTERIOR POSTERS	Standard Card faces	4 wk. cost	Super Card faces	4 wk. cost
Halifax: 1/4 Showing	50	950	50	1,900
Halifax: 1/2 Showing	100	1,880	100	3,600
Halifax: Full Showing	200	3,200	200	6,400
Moncton: Full Showing	26	520	26	1,040
Charlottetown: Full Showing	4	80	4	160
St. John's: 1/4 Showing	15	285	15	570
St. John's: 1/2 Showing	29	522	29	1,044
St. John's: Full Showing	58	928	58	1,856
Ottawa: 1/4 Showing	213	3,460	213	5,880
Ottawa: 1/2 Showing	425	6,590	425	11,200
Ottawa: Full Showing	850	11,050	850	18,785
North Bay: 1/4 Showing	7	120	7	225
North Bay: 1/2 Showing	14	220	14	425
North Bay: Full Showing	28	415	28	805
Sudbury: 1/4 Showing	12	180	12	320
Sudbury: 1/2 Showing	25	340	25	615
Sudbury: Full Showing	50	590	50	1,100
Thunder Bay: 1/2 Showing	25	250	25	375
Thunder Bay: Full Showing	49	490	49	735
Moose Jaw: Full Showing	8	225	8	375
Brandon: Full Showing	15	375	15	525
Winnipeg: 1/4 Showing	134	2,680	134	4,020
Winnipeg: 1/2 Showing	268	4,690	268	7,270
Winnipeg: Full Showing	536	8,040	536	13,400
Calgary: 1/4 Showing	200	3,000	200	4,800
Calgary: 1/2 Showing.	400	5,760	400	9,200
Calgary: Full Showing	800	10,200	800	16,320
Edmonton EMA*: 1/4 Showing	215	3,225	215	4,360
Edmonton EMA*: 1/2 Showing	449	6,285	449	8,695
Edmonton EMA*: Full Showing	898	11,675	898	15,840
Lethbridge: Full Showing	36	600	36	1,015
Medicine Hat: Full Showing	25	450	25	765

Includes St. Albert & Sherwood Park Garages. Take One Pads are subjected to a 10% premium of each 4 week rates card cost.

Ottawa	$11 050
Calgary	$10 200
Winnipeg	$ 4 690
Halifax	$ 1 880
Total	**$27 820**

Therefore, the total costs for the contract would be

Ottawa and Calgary (16 weeks):	$11 050 + 10 200 × 4 = $ 85 000
Winnipeg and Halifax (24 weeks):	$ 4690 + 1880 × 6 = $ 39 420
Total cost:	**$124 420**

The multipliers (4 and 6) are used in the above example because the length of the contract is different in each market; Ottawa and Calgary (16 weeks) and Winnipeg and Halifax (24 weeks). Any continuity discount that is available would be deducted from the total cost above.

Other Forms of Out-of-Home Advertising

Outdoor advertising is everywhere! There always seems to be a unique means of reaching consumers when they least expect it. Some of the more unique and innovative vehicles for sending messages include elevator advertising, arena and stadium advertising, food court video advertising, taxicab advertising, and theatre-screen advertising. The stream of new advertising vehicles continues to grow. Here are some of them.

AIRPORT DISPLAY ADVERTISING

Essentially, this is outdoor advertising located at major airports. Included in the range of options are outdoor posters and spectaculars on roads leading to and from the airport, and backlits inside the terminals. Backlits are offered in a variety of shapes and sizes, and a scrolling option is available (i.e., the poster scrolls to reveal a new advertising message). Clear Channel Communications is a major supplier of airport advertising in North America. Airport advertising presents a good opportunity to reach business travellers.

WASHROOM ADVERTISING

Mini-posters (30 × 40 cm) are available in washrooms at universities, colleges, fitness facilities, golf clubs, resto-bars, hospitals, and health-care facilities. Such venues for advertising give an advertiser an opportunity to reach targeted lifestyles based on demographic and psychographic characteristics. Ads in washrooms are inescapable and can be gender-specific. Zoom Media and New Ad Media are major suppliers of advertising space in this medium.

Zoom Media
www.zoom-media.com

ELEVATOR ADVERTISING

This sort of advertising uses glass display cases on side panels adjacent to the control panels in high-rise elevators. The Captivate Network has taken elevator advertising a step further. Slim-line televisions installed in elevators in major office towers deliver up-to-date news and information along with ads. Ads of this nature will reach business decision-makers in all kinds of industries. Full-colour print ads placed in glass display cases on side walls of elevators are also available. Clorets gum has used elevator ads to advantage. The elevator is an environment where people are close together—there is a definite need for fresh breath![10]

MOBILE SIGNAGE

Either using a car or a truck, mobile signage vehicles display outdoor ads on the move. Go Mobile Media is one such company offering this type of advertising. Go Mobile's trucks can be seen driving around Toronto—a tiny cab pulling a glass box behind it with eight scrolling billboards. After dark, the posters on the three sides of the truck disappear, and video ads begin playing. It is a moving television set that can be dispatched to any part of the city.[11] Anything that moves, it seems, is now fair game for advertising!

FOOD COURT VIDEO SCREENS

The Digital Advertising Network (DAN) offers large-format full-motion video screens in mall food courts across the country. The screens show 15-minute video loops that combine program content from CTVglobemedia with advertisements. The content includes world events, business news, sports and entertainment news, as well as 15-, 30-, and 60-second ads from various advertisers, such as MasterCard, Nike, Telus, and Sony Music. Food court screens reach 8.7 million consumers weekly—consumers who are in buying mode and right at the point of purchase![12] Advertising in malls allows an advertiser to effectively reach a good cross-section of a market's population. See Figure 10.18 for an illustration of video screen advertising.

SPORTS AND ARENA ADVERTISING

Advertising in a sports environment can reach a more targeted audience. Some alternatives include tee-off sign boards on golf courses, signs affixed to arena boards, backboard signs placed on backstops and outfield fences, and poster advertising on ski-lift towers. Where sporting events occur, an ad is not far behind.

Within arenas and stadiums, there are numerous advertising opportunities. For example, in Toronto's Rogers Centre (formerly known as the SkyDome), advertisers can take advantage of backlit signs on concourses, fixed signs in the bowl or seating area,

FIGURE 10.18

An example of video screen advertising in mall food courts

product displays in concourses, on-deck circle signs, commercial time on a giant video screen, and temporary signs during special events. One of the more recent innovations is the rotating sign (usually three different messages) that is seen behind home plate in many major league ballparks and on the sidelines of NBA basketball games.

In hockey arenas such as the Toronto's Air Canada Centre and Vancouver's GM Place there is on-ice advertising, where an ad is painted right into the ice in the neutral zone (between the blue lines). Signs can also be located behind the players' benches and penalty box. Advertising at a sports venue starts right at the front door, with companies paying megabucks to have a facility adorned with their names. The Bell Centre in Montreal and Pengrowth Saddledome in Calgary are two examples of such arenas.

Bell Centre
www.bellcentre.ca

CINEMA ADVERTISING

Cineplex theatres have recently introduced a fast-paced 20-minute pre-show package that blends ads with entertainment. Cinema advertising is becoming a big hit with companies seeking to reach younger consumers, and new digital technologies make it cheaper to produce commercials for the big screen. "You can't underestimate the impression that the larger-than-life visual makes on the viewer," says Shelley Smit, director of marketing services at Labatt Breweries of Canada. Good sound and good visuals get attention! The new package places commercials between interviews with Hollywood stars and music videos. Separate on-screen commercials may also precede the movie trailers and feature presentation.

The benefits of cinema advertising must be weighed against the costs. The cost of a national campaign on the Cineplex Galaxy Network, all shows on all screens over a four- or five-week period, ranges from $212 000 to $435 000. The audience ranges from 2.5 million to 5.7 million, depending on the month purchased.[13] There is a clear benefit to cinema advertising: unlike most other media in which ads can be avoided, there is a captive audience in a theatre that cannot avoid the ads.

WILD POSTINGS

Wild postings are ads that are slapped on the hoarding at construction sites. Once the domain of concert promoters and sports promoters, they are now a strategic element of many mainstream advertisers' media plans. Mercedes-Benz (an upscale brand) used wild postings to launch their entry-level C-coupe hatchback. According to Joanne Caza, director of marketing at Mercedes, "People noticed them. They thought they were fun."[14]

Wild postings are cheaper than traditional billboards and they can be targeted to specific neighbourhoods. They give a brand a hip, urban feel that appeals to the hard-to-reach youth market. Unfortunately, they can be torn down easily and to date there is no means of measuring their effectiveness. In most cases the owners of the construction site are paid by the advertisers for the privilege of putting up the signs. More permanent versions of wild postings are starting to appear at construction sites. Much like an over-sized outdoor poster, the advertising message is painted on the boards that surround the construction site. See Figure 10.19 for an example of wild posting.

Students are advised to check the out-of-home section of *Canadian Advertising Rates and Data* for more information about the diverse range of out-of-home media alternatives. It seems that out-of-home advertising is everywhere, and quite frankly, it is! Entrepreneurs keep pushing the boundaries. For more insight into the latest innovations in out-of-home advertising, see the Advertising in Action vignette **Mobile Media.**

An example of wild posting advertising: permanent printed ads at construction sites

Courtesy of Keith Tuckwell.

ADVERTISING IN ACTION

Mobile Media

It's everywhere! It's everywhere! Just when you thought you had seen everything, a new media concept pops up out of nowhere. When it comes to outdoor advertising, the sky is literally the limit.

Is it possible to mount an advertising message on the hubcaps of taxis? Wheels rotate, so you would think it is impossible. E-Caps are a new mobile media product that places ads over the wheels of taxis. The hubcap-like discs don't rotate, which attracts attention because the car appears to glide along the road.

Buses and subways have carried ads for years, so why not taxis, trucking fleets, and tourist rickshaws? Mexx Canada cruised the streets of Montreal with an 18-foot illuminated shop window. The window included 10 mannequins wearing fashions from the fall/winter Mexx City collection for young men and women. The roving window was seen as a very urban way of presenting fashion to a very urban clientele. It grabbed the attention of onlookers! According to Julie Brisson, marketing director for Mexx Canada, "Marketing is like fashion—you've got to innovate. If you don't it's boring."

Mobile advertising is becoming popular due to the fragmentation factor affecting television and print media. Marketers are looking for new ways of reaching mass audiences, and outdoor ads in general are one of the few ways of reaching a mass audience. In the old days cars used to go down the main streets using a loudspeaker to announce an event that was about to happen. Today we have a company called Motomedia that operates a fleet of trucks in Toronto, Ottawa, Calgary, and Vancouver that are equipped with illuminated advertising signs. They travel through neighbourhoods of interest to the advertiser.

Put your mind to work. Can you come up with another brilliant advertising medium? Remember, these concepts were nothing more than ideas only a few years ago. Follow through. You might just hit the jackpot!

Sources: Adapted from John Heinzl, "Anything that moves," *Globe and Mail*, May 11, 2001, p. M1; and Larry Harding, "Taking it to the streets," *Marketing*, November 19, 2001, p. 18.

Mexx
www.mexx.com
Motomedia
motomedia.ca

At-Retail Media (Point-of-Purchase Advertising)

When a prominent marketing executive such as Procter & Gamble's global marketing officer Jim Stengel pronounces the in-store experience "the first moment of truth," it's no shock that other marketers are devoting more time and effort to their in-store media strategy. The term at-retail media is suggestive of retail communications that go well beyond traditional point-of-purchase activities, with much of the new forms of communications being fuelled by digital technology.

At-retail media embraces everything from shelf-talkers, to store windows, to smart shopping carts, to giant digital screens. Setting up displays and erecting signs to draw attention to sale items is one thing, but planning and implementing a coordinated marketing communications campaign to make the shopping experience more delightful is quite another.

A good marketing communications strategy at point-of-purchase will achieve several objectives. For example, it can remind consumers of a product just before they make a purchase decision. Studies conducted by the Point-of-Purchase Advertising Institute (POPAI) in the United States reveal that 74 percent of all purchase decisions at mass merchandisers are made in-store.[15] Therefore, a compelling advertising message at just right the time could lead to an immediate purchase. New digital technologies can be used to help drive consumers into purchasing categories they weren't going to consider, like higher-margin private-label products.

Some of the more common types of at-retail media include in-store video displays, exterior signs, modular display racks, display shippers, display cards, and vending machines.

VIDEO DISPLAYS

Digital point-of-purchase advertising has moved well beyond universal VHS presentations. "Today, messages can be tailored for individual stores, even individual monitors within stores," says Graeme Spicer, a digital signage expert with retail consultancy DW + Partners. Spicer firmly believes that good video presentations drive purchases. He cites Tim Hortons' use of 42-inch plasma screens to promote coffee and donut combos in the morning and lunch specials at noon as a classic example.[16] Good visuals make the combos look very tempting! See the illustration in Figure 10.20.

Large department stores and national chain stores such as Future Shop, Best Buy, Canadian Tire, and Home Depot are integrating video communications into their in-store media strategies. These and other stores find that a convincing demonstration is often a clincher in the decision-making process. Home Hardware has implemented an in-store advertising program that combines a product demonstration and commercial in a 30-second message. Referred to as a *demomercial*, it shows a simple yet effective demonstration of how a featured product works. Typically, the spot shows a flaw in an existing product and then introduces a solution in the form of a nifty Home Hardware item. Viewers can find the item only in a Home Hardware store.[17]

EXTERIOR SIGNS

The primary function of a store sign is to identify the business. The style and lettering of the sign (i.e., the store logo) becomes familiar to customers in the market area and helps to draw them to the business. The logo style of the business sign is integrated with other forms of store advertising. The McDonald's golden arches is an example of a

FIGURE 10.20

Tempting in-store video presentations stimulate purchases

familiar sign that can be seen and identified from a great distance by motorists or pedestrian traffic. The same logo appears on menu boards and promotional signs inside stores and in drive-through lanes. For most retailers, store signs and logos play a prominent role in message strategy and execution.

MODULAR DISPLAY RACKS

A **modular display rack** is a permanent display unit provided by a manufacturer to display a certain line of merchandise. These types of units are usually made of wire and metal (e.g., candy and gum counter displays, potato-chip racks in variety stores) or plastic materials. The primary advantage of a display rack is that, for as long as the display rack remains, the merchandise is located outside its normal environment, by itself, away from the competition. Signage can be appended to the display unit to help draw attention to it. Depending on the size of the unit, a poster, shelf poster, or tear-off ad pad can be integrated into modular displays to communicate special sales or promotions.

DISPLAY SHIPPERS

A **display shipper** is a cardboard shipping carton that converts into a temporary in-store display when opened and assembled. Designed to encourage impulse purchases, display shippers are often used to merchandise seasonal products. Display shippers for Halloween candies and for the summer barbecue season (exhibiting barbecue-related products such as spices and sauces) are quite common. The displays are used at the discretion of store management, and can be assembled by store personnel or the manufacturer's field sales representative. A display shipper appears in Figure 10.21.

DISPLAY CARDS

Display cards include paper or paperboard posters, shelf talkers (small-size posters that hang from the store shelves where the product is located), and tear-off ad pads that often include coupons or other purchase incentives. Designed to encourage impulse purchases, these forms of advertising can be used with display shippers or on displays that are set up at the ends of aisles or other store locations. Their primary role is to draw the customer's

Courtesy of Dick Hemingway.

FIGURE 10.21

An example of a display shipper: a shipping carton unfolds to form a temporary display

attention to something special and prompt a decision to buy. Manufacturers commonly use tear-off ad pads to promote contests, refunds, and other sales promotion activity.

VENDING MACHINES

Vending machines are a traditional component of soft-drink merchandising programs. Now available are vending machines with vivid and colourful faces (plastic front panels illuminated by interior lights) that quickly grab the attention of passersby. Their design has advanced considerably to the point where the face panels resemble a backlit poster. Soft drink and snack food brands sell significant volumes through vending machines, so it is not uncommon to see backlit-style machines for Coca-Cola, Pepsi-Cola, and Nestlé candy bars.

OTHER AT-RETAIL MEDIA

Supermarket chains and convenience store chains have been particularly innovative regarding new forms of in-store advertising and merchandising concepts. Often developed by independent media advertising companies, the merits of these concepts are sold to potential advertisers.

Among the options are grocery cart advertising, shelf ads, and floor ads. **Grocery cart advertising** uses full-colour posters that are attached to the front of shopping carts. Shoppers facing an approaching shopping cart are exposed to the message, while the shopper pushing the cart also sees a message from inside the cart. **Shelf ads** include shelf pads, recipe cards, and promotional materials that are appended to store shelves and temporary displays. A relatively new innovation is floor ads. **Floor ads** offered by Gallop+Gallop Floormedia are portable floor decals (often called **ad-tiles**) that will not scuff or peel and that carry advertising messages. These ads appear in convenience stores and help stimulate impulse purchases. Floor ads cut through the clutter of other forms of in-store advertising. All of these options provide advertisers with last-minute exposure right at the point of purchase.

At-Retail Media as an Advertising Medium

There are numerous pros and cons to the various at-retail media alternatives. Advertisers who use this medium do so because it is the last opportunity to reach a target audience before an actual purchase decision is made. In this section, some of the benefits and drawbacks are presented.

ADVANTAGES OF AT-RETAIL MEDIA

IMPULSE PURCHASING   In the case of frequently purchased product categories such as candies, snack foods, toiletries, and beverages, at-retail media advertising stimulates impulse purchasing. Furthermore, research studies indicate that more than two-thirds of all purchase decisions are made right in the store. Such unplanned behaviour creates ample opportunity for point-of-purchase advertising to influence last-minute decisions. It is often referred to as the "last chance" medium.

MESSAGE REINFORCEMENT   While the display or presentation itself stimulates action, the incidence of consumer action increases when the display visuals are used to supplement the advertising done in other media (e.g., in-home media). Point-of-purchase reinforces prior messages, finalizing sales to consumers who have been preconditioned by other forms of advertising.

MESSAGE RECEPTIVENESS   The message is communicated when consumers are shopping (i.e., it appeals to the right audience, in the right place, at the right time). Since consumers generally shop in stores whose merchandise they can afford, the selling message is visible to the desired target audience.

LAST CHANCE (DECIDING FACTOR) IN SALE   For product categories in which impulse buying is not a factor (such as expensive durable goods), point-of-purchase material can be used to inform and educate consumers. Automobile dealers rely heavily on the colour brochures in their showrooms to communicate essential details about their various product lines. These types of advertisements go home with the customer, are consulted in detail, and play a major role in bringing the customer back to the showroom. As indicated earlier in the chapter, many retailers now integrate high-quality TV-style video presentations to advertise their own products or products of branded manufacturers. Such information presented at just the right time could produce a sale.

MERCHANDISE TIE-INS   In-store communications promote the trial of new products, new packaging, and new sizes and flavours. It draws attention to warranties, rebate programs, contests, and other forms of promotional activity. It is also an effective vehicle for developing cross-promotions with related products sold in the same store (soup and crackers, potato chips and dips, bandages and antiseptics, for example, are product lines that could be displayed together to encourage additional purchases).

DISADVANTAGES OF AT-RETAIL MEDIA

PLACEMENT   The most eye-catching display will be ineffective if it is not located in the appropriate position in the store. The problem facing the retailer is the limited area in which to place the abundant display material available from manufacturers. If good placements are not found, the displays will not achieve sales objectives.

CLUTTER   Consider the number of displays you are exposed to while walking through a drug, grocery, or hardware store. Assuming a retailer grants a manufacturer permission to erect a display or poster material, the manufacturer's display will face considerable competition from other products in commanding consumers' attention. Due to clutter, some displays will be relegated to poor locations (and then they may as well not be there at all). The same principle applies to video presentations. New research about in-store consumer behaviour indicates that the location of a video presentation is important and that too many presentations will reduce the potential impact.

WASTE   Some displays and other point-of-purchase materials never get erected in the store. Manufacturers generally require permission from the retail store's head office to erect display units in corporate-owned retail stores such as Loblaws, Safeway, A&P, and Shoppers Drug Mart. Even if permission is granted, if and how the display units will be utilized is often left to the discretion of store managers. Securing co-operation from retail managers is the responsibility of the field sales force. This task can be difficult at times.

SUMMARY

Out-of-home media is the second-fastest-growing medium in Canada. New technologies and new formats have attracted new advertisers—advertisers that have shifted dollars away from television and print.

Out-of-home media are composed of a variety of outdoor poster options, transit advertising, and point-of-purchase advertising. The various forms of outdoor advertising are posters, backlit posters, superboards and spectaculars, mall posters, transit shelters, digital signs, street-level advertising, full-motion video screens, wall banners, and murals.

Outdoor advertising offers high target reach and frequency and geographic flexibility. It is an effective medium because it can reinforce a message that appears in other media, and, in the case of digital signs and video screens, the message can be changed quickly if need be. Among the weaknesses of outdoor advertising are the lack of target-market selectivity and the creative limitations related to the speed at which people pass by.

There are various forms of transit advertising, including interior and exterior cards, interior door cards, superbuses and bus murals, a variety of station posters, and station domination. Digital screens mounted on station platforms that feature content and advertising are a more engaging way to communicate with people. Other relatively new media vehicles include stair risers, ceiling decals, and floor ads. Transit advertising offers continuous exposure (a result of transit users' consistent travel patterns) and high reach and frequency against a general target market. The major weaknesses of the medium are the lack of target-market selectivity and the creative limitations owing to space restrictions.

Some new and unique forms of advertising media include airport display advertising, washroom advertising, elevator advertising, mobile signs, food court video screens, sports and arena advertising, taxicab advertising, cinema advertising, and wild postings.

At-retail media (point-of-purchase) advertising is effective in stimulating impulse purchases and reinforcing a message delivered by another medium. Advertising on digital screens is now a popular option used by retailers. A drawback of point-of-purchase is the lack of use by retailers because of the abundance of display material they receive from suppliers. As well, too many displays in a store reduce the impact of any individual display. POP advertising is often referred to as "last chance" advertising. It reaches consumers at a critical moment, that point in time when brand decisions are made and wallets are about to be opened.

KEY TERMS

REVIEW QUESTIONS

1. Briefly explain the difference between an outdoor poster, a backlit poster, a spectacular, and a full-motion video screen.

2. Identify and explain two advantages and two disadvantages of outdoor advertising.

3. Using the rate card in Figure 10.11, calculate the cost of the following advertising campaign:

   Medium: Horizontal backlits
   Markets: Hamilton, London, Quebec City, and Calgary
   Weight: Hamilton and London 75 GRPs; Quebec City and Calgary 50 GRPs
   Time: 16 weeks

4. What is the difference between an exterior king poster, an exterior seventy poster, and a tail poster?

5. Explain briefly the nature of the following transit advertising vehicles: interior cards, station posters, triples, and station domination.

6. What are the major types of transit advertising?

7. What types of products or services are suitable for transit advertising?

8. Identify and briefly explain two advantages and two disadvantages of transit as an advertising medium.

9. Using the rate card in Figure 10.17, calculate the cost of the following campaign:

   Medium: Seventy bus posters
   Markets: Moncton, Halifax, Calgary, and Edmonton

   Weight: Moncton and Halifax 50 GRPs; Calgary and Edmonton 75 GRPs
   Time: 12 weeks

10. Using the rate card in Figure 10.10, calculate the cost of the following street-level advertising campaign:

    Medium: Transit shelters
    Markets: Quebec City, Montreal, Toronto, and Vancouver
    Weight: Quebec City and Montreal 50 GRPs; Toronto and Vancouver 25 GRPs
    Time: 12 weeks in Montreal and Quebec City; 16 weeks in Toronto and Vancouver

11. Identify and briefly describe the major types of at-retail media.

12. Explain the following terms in the context of the term in parentheses:

    a) superboard (outdoor)
    b) mural ads (outdoor)
    c) 75 GRPs (outdoor)
    d) backlit poster (outdoor)
    e) superbus and bus murals (transit)
    f) continuity discount (transit)
    g) full-motion video screen (outdoor)
    h) display shipper (at-retail media)
    i) floor ads (at-retail media)

13. Identify and briefly explain two advantages and two disadvantages of at-retail media (point-of-purchase) advertising.

DISCUSSION QUESTIONS

1. "Out-of-home media are primarily recognized as a means of complementing other media forms." Is this statement true or false? Discuss this statement, assuming the role of marketing manager—first for a television station, and then for an outdoor advertising company.

2. Read the Advertising in Action vignette **Nike's Outdoor Innovation Builds Buzz**. The vignette states that outdoor advertising is a prominent part of Nike's marketing mix. If Nike places such high value in outdoor advertising, shouldn't other advertisers be doing the same? Perhaps outdoor advertising does not offer the same value to all advertisers. What is your opinion?

3. There is statistical evidence showing point-of-purchase advertising to be effective in prompting purchase response, at least in the short term. Should advertisers be spending more or less on this form of advertising in the future? Should investment in this form of advertising come at the expense of traditional brand advertising in the mass media? Discuss these issues, using examples of your choice.

4. Naming rights to arenas and advertising inside arenas such as the Air Canada Centre and GM Place are suddenly popular. What potential benefits do you see for advertisers that pursue this media strategy? Do you think arena advertising is effective? Explain your position.

5. Read the Advertising in Action vignette **Mobile Media**. Based on the examples cited in the vignette, do you think that delivering messages by moving the medium around the city is effective at reaching a target market, or will the message simply get lost in the urban landscape? Assess this medium and explain your position.

NOTES

1. Canadian Media Directors' Council, *Media Digest*, 2006–2007, p. 12.

2. Joe Mandese, "New outdoor media options challenge conventional media planning wisdom," *Media Post*, August 14, 2003, **www.mediapost.com**.

3. Patti Summerfield, "The last mass medium goes niche," *Strategy*, September 24, 2001, p. 25.

4. "OBN expands national video board network," Advertising supplement in *Marketing*, June 2006, p. 14.

5. CBS Outdoor Media, **www.cbsoutdoor.ca**.

6. Based on rate card for outdoor posters, *Canadian Advertising Rates and Data*, May 2005.

7. Brian Harrod, "The true test of a great idea," *Marketing*, April 12, 1999, p. 42.

8. Canadian Media Directors' Council, *Media Digest*, 2006–2007, p. 66.

9. *Canadian Advertising Rates and Data*, January 2006, p. 533.

10. Mary Klonizalis, "The view on the way to the top," *Marketing*, April 12, 1999, p. 36.

11. Kate Barrette, "Ads with traction," *Globe and Mail*, April 18, 2006, p. B9.

12. "DAN Media gives new meaning to dinner theatre," outdoor resource supplement in *Marketing*, June 2006, p. 8.

13. Based on data from *Canadian Advertising Rates and Data*, January 2006, p. 558.

14. John Heinzl, "Mainstream advertisers go wild for wild postings," *Globe and Mail*, n.d.

15. Patti Summerfield, "The action's at retail," *Strategy*, October 2005, p. 24.

16. "Signs of the times," *Canadian Business*, May 22–June 4, 2006, p. 12.

17. Chris Powell, "Show & Tell," *Marketing*, February, 24, 2003, p. 13.

CHAPTER 11

Direct-Response Media

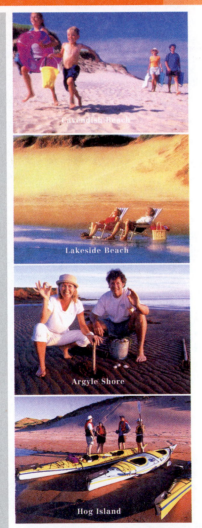

Courtesy of the Government of Prince Edward Island.

Learning Objectives

After studying this chapter, you will be able to

1. Describe the various types of direct-response advertising

2. Explain the advantages and disadvantages of various forms of direct-response advertising

3. Assess the factors considered in, and procedures used for, buying direct mail

4. Assess the strategies for delivering effective messages via direct-response techniques

Direct-response advertising is a form of media advertising that communicates messages directly to prospective customers. Among the options available, direct mail is the most common means of delivering these messages, but other forms of direct communication such as direct-response television, direct-response print, and telemarketing now play a more significant role. These forms of communication are discussed in this chapter.

Direct-Response Advertising

Direct-response advertising is one segment of the direct-marketing industry, and it now plays a major role in influencing consumer purchase patterns. Gone are the days of brand managers relying on television commercials. In today's competitive environment, a manager must deliver bottom-line results, and direct-response advertising does just that. Thanks to a convergence of trends, including the diverting of ad dollars from traditional TV and the rise of video sites like YouTube, direct-response techniques such as long-form commercials (infomercials) are in vogue among advertisers. These techniques allow marketers to more effectively engage the consumer and to market products with more in-depth sales messages.[1] Marketers today are attracted to direct-response advertising because of its targeting capabilities, its sophisticated measurement devices, and its ability to account for all dollars spent.

Direct-response advertising is big business! The latest revenue figures available indicate that direct mail generates $1.55 billion in net advertising revenues in Canada, or about 13 percent of all advertising revenues.[2] Direct-response television in the form of infomercials (or long-form commercials) accounts for an additional $20.8 million in revenues, or about one percent of all television advertising revenues.[3] As an advertising medium, direct mail ranks third, just behind newspapers (15 percent of net advertising revenue) and television (26 percent of net advertising revenue).

The trend toward direct-response advertising has been gaining momentum. Banks were the first of the major marketers to enter the direct-response arena, but have been recently joined by packaged-goods companies, automobile manufacturers, and prominent national retailers such as Shoppers Drug Mart and HBC. These companies are allocating greater portions of their marketing and marketing communications budgets to direct-response techniques.

HBC
www.hbc.com

347

The shift to direct-response advertising follows on the heels of companies adopting software technology that encourages database-management techniques and the implementation of customer-relationship management programs. Firms can now design and develop programs that reach customers individually and efficiently. Such capability offers significant competitive advantage. And the ability to reach customers directly with a message is a lot cheaper than delivering messages through the traditional mass media.

Direct-response advertising is advertising through any medium designed to generate a response by any means that is measurable (such as mail, television, a print ad, telephone, and the internet). If traditional mass media are used, the message will include a toll-free telephone number, mailing address, or website address where more information can be secured. Trish Wheaton, president of Wunderman Direct, a large direct-marketing agency, feels that a relationship with the internet is helping direct-response advertising grow. "We typically use direct mail as a door opener and then drive consumers online to tell more of the story. Consumers are very savvy about doing research online and will spend more time that way than reading something you mailed them. Direct mail today only has to catch the attention of recipients."[4]

Wunderman Direct
www.wunderman.com

The major forms of direct-response advertising are direct mail, direct-response television (DRTV), telemarketing, and the internet. The role of the internet in direct-response communications is discussed in Chapter 12.

- **Direct mail** is a form of advertising communicated to prospects via the postal service.
- **Direct-response print** is a response-oriented message delivered to prospects by magazine or newspaper advertisements.
- **Direct-response television (DRTV)** is a form of advertising communicated to prospects via television commercials (e.g., 30-minute infomercials or messages seen on cable channels, or 60-second commercials on conventional television stations that encourage people to buy something immediately).
- **Telemarketing** involves the use of telecommunications to promote the products and services of a business.

As indicated earlier, direct mail is the primary medium for delivering direct-response advertising messages; however, due to advancing technology, it is expected that direct-response television will play a much stronger role in the communications mix in the future and the role of direct mail will diminish. Advertisers will be using online techniques such as permission-based email and online newsletters to deliver marketing messages.

Direct Mail

The use of direct mail is widespread due to the ability to personalize the message with the prospect's name, the ability to send lengthy messages (e.g., copy-oriented sales messages along with reply cards and contracts that are returned by prospects), and the ability to provide a high degree of geographic coverage economically (the mailing can be distributed to designated postal codes anywhere in Canada). There are numerous options available to companies wishing to use direct mail, and these can be combined to form a compelling package of information.

SALES LETTERS

The most common form of direct mail, the **letter**, is typeset, printed, and delivered to household occupants or to specific individuals at personal or business addresses. Letters

→ mailing pack: letter brochure, reply card + env.

are usually the primary communication in a mailing package, which typically includes a brochure, reply card, and postage-paid return envelope. Refer to Figure 11.1 for an illustration.

LEAFLETS AND FLYERS

Leaflets and **flyers** are usually standard letter-sized pages (8½ by 11 inches) that offer relevant information and accompany a letter. Leaflets expand on the information contained in the letter and attempt to generate a response (i.e., convince the recipient to take action).

FOLDERS

Folders are sales messages printed on heavier paper and often include photographs or illustrations. They are usually folded and are often designed in such a way that they can be mailed without an envelope, if immediate action is requested. Folders may take the form of a postage-paid reply card or they may simply communicate information the respondent can act upon at a later date. Refer to Figure 11.2 for an illustration.

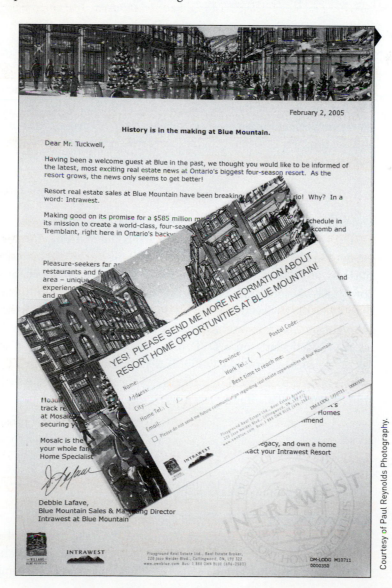

FIGURE 11.1

A personalized direct-response sales letter

FIGURE 11.2

An example of a folder mailed to past customers

STATEMENT STUFFERS

Statement stuffers, or **bounce backs** as they are often called, are advertisements distributed via monthly charge-account statements (such as those one receives from Sears, The Bay, or Visa). Capitalizing on the ease of purchasing by credit, such mailings make it very convenient for the prospect to take action. In this case, one order leads to another, and the prospect is reached at very low cost. Usually, the credit card number is the only information the seller requires.

DVDS, VIDEOCASSETTES, AND CD-ROMS

Organizations now send serious prospects information by more sophisticated means. DVDs, videocassettes, and **CD-ROMs** are popular means for demonstrating how a product works, how nice a vacation resort is, or how well an automobile performs. In business-to-business markets, these media are useful for presentation purposes (when combined with personal selling practices) and for letting customers review things on their own time. They are excellent vehicles for product demonstrations, and technical information about a product that is hard to communicate in hard copy is easily accessed, particularly on a DVD or CD-ROM. These are but a few applications for DVDs, videocassettes, and CD-ROMs. They can be part of a direct-mail campaign or a follow-up to a direct-mail campaign (e.g., for those who requested more information from the original mailing).

Direct-Mail Strategy

Essentially, an organization has the option of delivering a mail piece by itself or delivering an offer as part of a package that includes offers from other companies. This is the difference between solo direct mail and co-operative direct mail.

Solo direct mail, or **selective direct mail**, refers to specialized or individually prepared direct-mail offers sent directly to prospects. With this strategy, the marketing organization absorbs all of the costs. Solo direct-mail pieces are commonly employed in business-to-business communications, supplementing the messages frequently communicated via traditional business publications. The growth of database marketing by consumer goods organizations has led to greater usage of solo direct mail by these organizations. Due to the degree of personalization, response rates to this type of mailing tend to be much higher than for a co-operative mailing. Refer to Figure 11.3 for an illustration of a solo direct-mail piece.

Co-operative direct mail refers to envelopes containing special offers from non-competing products. Since many companies may be involved in the mailing, the costs are shared among participants. Consumer-goods marketers commonly employ this method. A typical mailing contains coupons for a variety of grocery, drug, and household products, magazine subscription offers, or discount coupons for more expensive goods such as eyewear. The illustration in Figure 11.4 is representative of a typical co-operative direct-mail piece. Co-operative direct mailing has proven to be one of the most effective forms of print media for generating trial purchase.

FIGURE 11.3

Sample content of a solo direct-mail offer

FIGURE **11.3**

continued

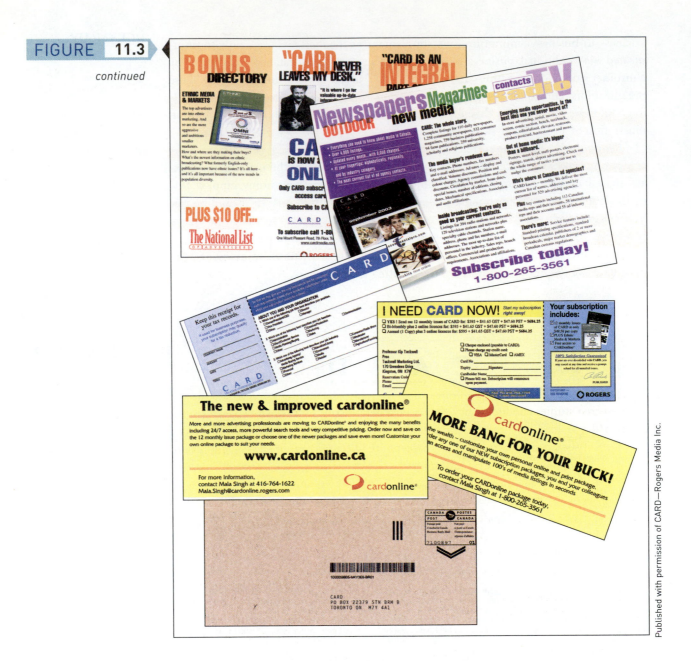

In comparing solo direct mail to co-operative direct mail, solo direct mail generates better results for coupon offers. The median response rate for all products delivering coupons via co-operative direct mail is 1.2 percent, whereas with solo direct mail the median response rate is 6.5 percent.[5]

Solo-direct mail = more effective

Direct Mail as an Advertising Medium

Direct-mail marketing has been around for a long time, but it was an activity that traditional advertisers such as packaged-goods companies, banks and financial institutions, and automobile manufacturers avoided for a long time. These industries were turned off by the negative images associated with direct-marketing techniques. Now, these very industries and the leading companies within them are among the largest users of direct mail.

FIGURE 11.4

Open & Save co-operative direct-mail envelope

Research studies conducted by Canada Post help justify a marketer's investment in direct mail. Canada Post's research indicates that 84 percent of people will open a direct-mail piece if their name is on it, and 77 percent are likely to read direct mail addressed to them.[6] It is the perfect call-to-action medium within an integrated campaign, and an ideal medium for building a relationship with current customers. Clearly, the advantages of direct mail are an attraction to companies that want to deliver messages to customers one-on-one.

Canada Post
www.canadapost.ca

personalized

ADVANTAGES OF DIRECT MAIL

AUDIENCE SELECTIVITY   Using direct mail, advertisers can pinpoint and reach targets that are precisely defined in terms of demographics—assuming that the organization acquires lists identifying the primary prospects. A good list results in minimal circulation waste. As well, a company's own customer list is a good starting point for any direct-mail campaign. Additional discussion of lists appears in the media-buying section of this chapter.

HIGH REACH   Solo direct mailings reach everyone the advertiser would like to reach—unlike other media, which reach only a portion of the target. For example, a life insurance or credit card organization that wants to reach all university graduates may be able to obtain access to such a list of students. For co-operative direct mailings (i.e., mass distribution to selected Canadian households), the national reach potential is very high. In this case, there is much circulation waste but the response rates are usually adequate to cover the costs of mass mailings.

GEOGRAPHIC FLEXIBILITY   A proper mailing list offers an advertiser not only demographic selectivity but also the opportunity to deliver direct-mail messages to specific geographic locations. This advantage appeals to retailers and other local businesses that want to confine mailings to certain areas. National advertisers can also use direct mail to isolate geographic areas they would like to concentrate on; say, for example, an area where sales are lower than average.

CREATIVE FLEXIBILITY   Like advertising in business publications, direct mail offers the flexibility to include long copy in advertisements (the longer the better, according to some practitioners). Since various pieces are often included in a single mailing, there is also flexibility in terms of style, length, and format. Generally speaking, a combination of formats in a single medium is effective. In this area, only imagination, budget, and applicable postal regulations limit the advertiser.

DISTRIBUTION OF INCENTIVES   Direct mail provides the opportunity to include items that will reach desired targets. It is a good medium for distributing coupons, free samples, and trial offers. Figure 11.5 offers an illustration of a multi-faceted trial promotion offer that was distributed by direct mail.

FIGURE 11.5

A direct-mail offer that includes trial coupon, money-back guarantee, and contest entry form

Courtesy of Dick Hemingway.

ADVERTISER CONTROL   In using solo direct mail, the advertiser retains control over such variables as the circulation and the quality of the message. The message is printed by one source, which results in a consistent quality of reproduction. This consistency contrasts with the situation that advertisers encounter when they run an advertisement in a variety of different newspapers, as the quality of reproduction may vary from one newspaper to another.

EXCLUSIVITY   Another advantage of direct mail is that mailings delivered to the household do not compete with other media at the time they are received, although they do compete for attention with other mail. This exclusivity contrasts with the clutter of newspaper and magazine advertising, in which ads compete with each other and with editorial content. Television advertising may also suffer from clutter, which can give rise to much channel surfing.

MEASURABILITY   The success of a direct-mail campaign is measured in one way—the sales generated by the mailing. As a general rule, business-oriented direct mail receives 15 percent of the responses within the first week of the mailing. Early responses, used in conjunction with historical conversion patterns, can be used to project sales for a longer period of time. In this regard, the success of a direct-mail campaign can be determined in a short space of time. Similar calculations cannot be made when using traditional forms of mass advertising. For co-operative direct mailings, coupon redemption rates are higher than for coupons distributed in newspapers or magazines.

DISADVANTAGES OF DIRECT MAIL

HIGH COST PER EXPOSURE   When the absolute costs of production, renting or purchasing lists, fulfillment (stuffing and sealing envelopes), and mailing are tallied, the total can be higher than it is for other print alternatives. Remember, though, that the selectivity of the medium reduces waste circulation.

ABSENCE OF EDITORIAL SUPPORT   In comparison to magazines, where there is editorial support that encourages people to read, direct mail stands alone. It must grab attention without assistance; therefore, it is imperative that the message be designed in a format that combines verbal and illustrative elements attractively. In other words, the envelope itself must be attractive or the message may be quickly discarded. Refer to Figure 11.6 on the next page.

IMAGE AND LIFESPAN   Direct mail is not a prestigious medium. Many consumers perceive direct mailings to be "junk mail," and pieces are promptly discarded when they reach the household. Many consumers do not perceive the special offers to be all that special. Direct mailings to businesses may suffer the same fate (i.e., they may be discarded), particularly if several mailings from different suppliers are received at the same time. However, the physical form of direct mail enables consumers to retain it for future reference.

POTENTIAL DELIVERY DELAYS   Other print media have specific issue dates, so the time of message exposure is precisely controlled. Since direct mail relies on the postal service, and since it is delivered third-class, there are no delivery guarantees. It is possible that a mailing will arrive at a destination after the offer has expired or the advertised event has occurred.

For more insight into the benefits of direct-mail communications, see the Advertising in Action vignette **Direct Mail Works for Amex.**

ADVERTISING IN ACTION

Direct Mail Works for Amex

Just a few years ago, American Express launched a new advertising campaign that focused on its brand name and all of its product offerings rather than just the specific card products. The campaign was a multimedia effort that embraced television, print media, and direct mail. By now you may be familiar with the campaign slogan: "My life. My card." In the United States, famous people such as Robert De Niro, Ellen DeGeneres, and Tiger Woods have been featured in the ads. In Canada, Mike Lazaridis, co-founder of Research in Motion and co-inventor of the famous Blackberry device, has been featured prominently.

The campaign boosted awareness of the Amex brand significantly. While television and print media created awareness and helped build image, the role of direct mail was to convert awareness into new business—to get potential customers to apply for a card. Amex boosted its investment in direct mail to the point where it became an equal partner in the media mix. According to Trish Wheaton, president of Wunderman Direct, Amex is seeing the new reality of effective marketing communications and where direct mail fits in. "It boils down to the medium's unparalleled measurability."

Wheaton is right. Broad-based television advertising plays a role, but it is measured in terms of brand favourability and intent to purchase. Direct-mail advertising is accompanied by a call to action through a phone number or a website, so that the advertiser can track how recipients responded. "The point is, direct works," says Wheaton. "Consumers are influenced by it and respond to it, especially when it is relevant and meaningful to their lives."

Amex is now a veteran of direct mail. The company has developed what is called a "control pack"— a direct-mail format that has proven to generate the best return on investment, given its combination of copy, visuals, promotional offer, and other elements. Each time Amex does a mailing, it changes one component in search of the offer that will do better than the control pack. Once found, Amex can boost its ROI further by incorporating the specific change into future material.

According to Donna English, director of acquisitions, Amex Canada, "This kind of experimentation and measurability is not possible in other media. It would simply take too long and the costs would be prohibitive. In one direct-mail campaign, we can test different offers and creative. We learn more quickly from our experiences and can roll out offers or creative that is actually working."

Source: Adapted from "Why direct advertising is increasingly part of the marketing mix," *Sorted*, a Canada Post publication, 2006, pp. 10–13.

Research in Motion
www.rim.net

FIGURE 11.6

To grab a reader's attention, a direct mail piece must effectively combine copy and visual images. Direct mail is a stand-alone medium.

Courtesy of Dick Hemingway.

Buying Direct Mail

Three basic steps are involved in buying direct mail: obtaining a proper prospect list, conceiving and producing the mailing piece, and distributing the final version.

OBTAINING DIRECT-MAIL LISTS

The **direct-mail list** is the backbone of the entire campaign. Both the accuracy and definition of the list can have a significant bearing on the success or failure of a campaign. It is estimated that as much as 60 percent of the success or failure of any mail campaign hinges upon the database that is used.[7] Companies recognize that it costs much more to acquire a new customer than it does to keep an existing one. As a result, companies are compiling databases to keep track of existing customers and are forming relationships with them through the mail and through electronic means. Lists are secured from internal and external sources.

INTERNAL SOURCES   There is no better prospect than a current customer. Therefore, a company's internal database must be monitored and updated routinely. For example, Canadian Tire accumulates considerable data on customers through its own credit card. HBC (encompassing The Bay, Zellers, and Home Outfitters) accumulates considerable data about its customers through its HBC Rewards program. Data-mining techniques allow these companies to determine who their heavy customers are, what they buy, how much they buy, and how often they buy. For companies placing value on repeat business, this information can be used to develop new offers that will be of interest to current customers. Getting current customers to buy more is a much easier challenge than trying to attract new customers. In direct-mail terms, an internal customer list is referred to as a **house list**.

As an alternative, companies can take steps to form lists of potential customers. Such customers are referred to as **prospects**. As Figure 11.7 illustrates, Jaguar Canada collects valuable information about customers that it can use in the future. Specifically, Jaguar will be able to mail directly to customers information about new car models they are interested in. This information-oriented postcard appeared in a national magazine with a full-page ad for a Jaguar automobile.

EXTERNAL SOURCES   People who have a history of responding to mail offers tend to be attractive prospects for new offers; buying by mail is part of their behaviour. Therefore, the challenge is to find prospects that have a demographic profile—and perhaps a psychographic profile—that mirrors the profile of current customers. A **list broker** can assist in finding these prospects. The buyer provides the broker with the profile of the target customer, and the broker supplies a list of possible prospects on a cost-per-name basis. Generally, a high-quality list is developed through a **merge/purge** process on a computer, whereby numerous lists are purchased, combined, and stripped of duplicate names.

TargetSource, a database-management company, is an example of a list broker that classifies names by behaviours and interests. Some of their list classifications include proven mail-order buyers, hobbies, donors to causes, owners of home electronics, travel, and outdoor enthusiasts. They also provide lists based on demographic characteristics such as income, employment, marital status, presence of children, and type of dwelling. The base rate for names is $115/M ($115 per thousand). As the quality of the list requested becomes more sophisticated or specialized, the rate per thousand increases. For example, for each demographic characteristic requested, add an extra $15/M.[8]

A reply card that collects valuable information about potential customers

If a Jaguar seems somehow more spirited than other luxury cars, it is not by chance. It is by design. It is a belief, first expressed by Jaguar's visionary founder Sir William Lyons: "The car is the closest thing we will ever create to something that is alive." This provocative idea remains at the core of what makes a Jaguar connect on a deeper level, with car and driver seeming as one.

Discover Jaguar in all its forms: the all-new XJ, the X-TYPE with permanent all-wheel drive—now available in a wagon, the S-TYPE sports sedans, XK sports cars and the supercharged R Performance Jaguars. Each offers its own interpretation of Jaguar performance and of Jaguar luxury. Yet across the Jaguar model range, you will find a singular set of characteristics: Smooth power from its state-of-the-art engines and its electronically controlled transmissions. Handling reflexes so precise they seem instinctive. And intelligent systems designed to safeguard you while in transit.

For more information, and to locate your nearest Jaguar retailer, please visit jaguar.ca or call 1-800-4JAGUAR.

TO TAKE A TEST DRIVE CALL 1-877-4-UNLEASH

JAGUAR
Born to perform

Jaguar Canada sends literature, email and special offers to individuals who are on our mailing list. If you would like to be included, please fill out the information below and drop it in the mail. It is postage paid, so there is no cost to you.

Title: Mr. ☐   Mrs. ☐   Ms. ☐   Dr. ☐
Suffix: II ☐   III ☐   IV ☐   Jr. ☐   Sr. ☐

First Name _____ Middle Initial ___

Last Name _____

Address _____

City _____ Province _____

(___) _____
Postal Code   Telephone

Email Address _____

I would prefer to receive all communications in:
☐ English   ☐ French
My first language (if other than French or English) is:
_____

1. I currently own:
Make _____ (e.g. Jaguar)
Model _____ Year ___ (e.g. XJ)
Make _____ (e.g. Jaguar)
Model _____ Year ___ (e.g. S-TYPE)

2. I intend to acquire my next vehicle in:
☐ January   ☐ February   ☐ March
☐ April   ☐ May   ☐ June
☐ July   ☐ August   ☐ September
☐ October   ☐ November   ☐ December
☐ 2004   ☐ 2005   ☐ 2006

3. I am considering the following vehicles:
1st choice: Make _____ Model _____
(e.g. Jaguar)   (e.g. XJ)
2nd choice: Make _____ Model _____
(e.g. Jaguar)   (e.g. XK)
3rd choice: Make _____ Model _____
(e.g. Jaguar)   (e.g. S-TYPE)

4a. How likely are you to consider a Jaguar for your next vehicle purchase?
☐ Very likely   ☐ Somewhat likely
☐ Not very likely   ☐ Unlikely

4b. I would like information about the following vehicles:
☐ X-TYPE   ☐ X-TYPE Wagon   ☐ S-TYPE
☐ XJ   ☐ XK
☐ Select Edition (Certified Pre-Owned)

Jaguar Canada collects information that you provide (i.e. contact and vehicle information, demographics, purchase and service experiences and preferences). We also collect information about your vehicle and your transaction from your retailer and information about your finance or lease contract from Jaguar Credit. This information is used to administer your purchase or lease, improve our products and services, and provide you with services, surveys or marketing material, which may be of interest to you. For these purposes, we share your information with your selected retailer and Jaguar Credit. If you do not want to receive marketing material from us, or to obtain our Privacy Policy or access your personal information, please call 1-800-668-6257 x 242.

Transcontinental, a publishing and database-management company, uses a technique called geomapping to assist its clients with direct-mail campaigns. **Geomapping** targets an audience based on demographic, psychographic, and behavioural data. All the target information is overlaid on a special map to home in on a very specific group of potential customers. It can target specific neighbourhoods and distribute mail pieces tailored specifically to groups as small as 200 people.[9]

Canada Post also supplies information that is vital to the accurate targeting of messages. For example, a postal code can isolate a small geographic area—say, a city block—and can then be combined with census data to provide relevant statistics regarding the ages and incomes of homeowners in the area, and whether children are present in the households.

A few types of lists are available: response lists, circulation lists, and compiled lists.

RESPONSE LISTS   A **response list** is a list of proven mail-order buyers. Such lists include book-of-the-month-club buyers, tape and CD music buyers, or people who order from co-operative direct-mailing firms. Because these lists include proven mail-order buyers, they tend to cost more. For example, TargetSource, the list broker referred to earlier, charges an additional $20/M for proven mail-order buyers in Canada.

mail-order buyers

CIRCULATION LISTS Circulation lists are magazine subscription lists that target potential customers by an interest or activity. A publishing company, for example, sells its list of subscribers to any other business that is interested in a similar target. On behalf of Rogers Media, a company called Cornerstone Group of Companies offers a consumer database comprising unduplicated active subscribers to a host of publications including *Maclean's* and *Chatelaine*. Names of *Maclean's* readers can be rented for $135/M and *Chatelaine* names are available for $125/M. The *Maclean's* list would be of interest to organizations wanting to reach well-educated middle-aged Canadians who are interested in news and current affairs. The *Chatelaine* list would be of interest to organizations wanting to reach women, 25 to 49 years old, who carefully balance a career with family responsibilities.[10] Refer to the illustration in Figure 11.8.

magazines

COMPILED LISTS Compiled lists are prepared from government, census, telephone, warranty, and other publication information. These are the least expensive of the lists and are not always personalized. For example, a business firm may be identified on the

gvmt/census info

> **MACLEAN'S MAGAZINE**
>
> This weekly newsmagazine reports on news from Canada and the world, including political, business, science, travel, entertainment, and sports. *Maclean's* readers are thoughtful, well-educated, upscale, and concerned with today's issues and trends. Readership is equally divided between males and females. Geographically, 54 percent of *Maclean's* readers are in Ontario; BC accounts for 15 percent of readership, and Alberta 13 percent.
>
> **RENTED LIST INFORMATION**
>
> | Characteristic | Cost |
> | --- | --- |
> | List size | 211 200 |
> | Minimum order | 5000 |
> | Base Cost/Thousand | $135.00/M |
>
> **SELECTS (ADDITIONAL COSTS)**
>
> | | |
> | --- | --- |
> | Male | $ 10.00/M |
> | Female | $ 10.00/M |
> | Home | $ 10.00/M |
> | Business | $ 10.00/M |
> | Province | $ 10.00/M |
> | Key Records | $ 5.00/M |
> | FSA | $ 5.00/M |
>
> *There are also costs associated with the format of the list required, for example, tape, disk, CD-ROM, and email.*
>
> Source: Adapted from information at Cornerstone Canada, www.cstonecanada.com/datacards.

FIGURE 11.8

Target information and cost information for a direct-response mail list

The data herein includes a selection of target and cost information associated with a direct-mail list for *Maclean's* subscribers.

list, but not the appropriate contact person within the firm. Names of business prospects are compiled from print sources such as the Standard Industrial Classification (SIC), Fraser's Canadian Trade Directory, or Scott's Industrial Index. Provincial and national associations commonly provide mailing lists of their members. The Canadian Medical Association, for example, will provide mailing lists of member physicians. A list broker could compile a list of a cross-section of professionals from various occupations, if that is what a client required.

Canadian Medical Association
www.cma.ca

PRODUCTION

When designing a direct-mail package, the advertiser usually engages the services of a specialist organization. In Canada, numerous full-service direct-marketing and direct-response agencies meet the needs of clients. Among them are Wunderman Direct, Carlson Marketing Group, and Grey Direct. Many of the larger traditional agencies, recognizing the growth and opportunity in direct-response communications, have formed direct-response subsidiaries. Grey Direct, for example, is a subsidiary of Grey Advertising Worldwide.

Once the mailing package is designed, it is ready for printing. Various factors such as size, shape, number of pieces to be included, use of colour, and other variables influence the cost. Costs are usually quoted on a per-thousand basis, with larger runs incurring lower unit costs. Once printed, the mailing pieces are turned over to a letter shop that specializes in stuffing and sealing envelopes, affixing labels, and sorting, binding, and stacking the mailers. Once this task is complete, the mailing units are sent to the post office or a private carrier for distribution.

DISTRIBUTION

The most common means of delivery is Canada Post. A number of options are available through the postal system: first-class mail, third-class mail, and business reply mail.

FIRST-CLASS MAIL Although it is more costly, some direct mail is delivered using first-class mail. The advantages of first-class mail are quicker delivery (if time is important), the return of undeliverable mail, and mail forwarding if the addressee has moved.

THIRD-CLASS MAIL Most direct-mail pieces—whether single pieces, bulk items, catalogues, or co-operative mailings—are delivered using third-class mail. The advantage over first-class mail is the cost savings.

BUSINESS-REPLY MAIL For the benefit of the recipient, an individual can respond at the expense of the advertiser. A preprinted reply card or envelope is included in the direct-mail package. Postage-paid return envelopes are an incentive aimed at improving the rate of response. Refer to Figure 11.9 for an illustration.

Media Buying:
Co-operative Direct Mail—An Example

The procedures for estimating the costs of solo direct mail and co-operative direct mail are similar. Taken into consideration are factors such as the distribution costs, printing

FIGURE 11.9

A postage-paid reply card makes it easier for consumers to respond

costs, mailing costs, and costs associated with fulfillment. As indicated previously, an advertiser can either undertake all of these costs or share the costs with others in a co-operative mailing program. For this example, we will assume a co-operative direct-mail program will be undertaken in the Valassis Co-operative Mailings package. The distribution costs for Valassis Co-operative Mailings are included in Figure 11.10.

INFORMATION: VALASSIS CO-OPERATIVE MAILINGS

The offer:	1 page folded ad (3¾ × 8½ inches) that includes a $1.50 coupon
Redemption rate:	3 percent
Distribution:	2 million households

FIGURE **11.10**

Rate card for
direct-mail packages

Valassis
Canada

Valassis Canada

Owned and operated by Valassis Canada Inc., 5925 Airport Rd., Ste. 615, Mississauga, ON L4V 1W1. Phone: 905-677-0499. Fax: 905-677-8021.
Frank T. Turner, Vice President, Sales (Email: turnerf@valassis.ca)
GENERAL INFORMATION: SHOP & SAVE FREE STANDING INSERTS: Delivers advtg. messages & coupons through home delivered newspapers. Printed on high quality, coated stock, Shop & Save offers product exclusively & verified distribution. Customized trade mailing to key buyers at retail head office included with each national program.
CLOSING DATES: SHOP & SAVE FSI 2006-2007:

Issue	Space	Mat'l	Live
Jan. 13	11/17/2006	12/01/2006	01/13/2007
Feb. 10	12/15/2006	12/29/2006	02/10/2007
Mar. 3	01/05/2007	01/19/2007	03/03/2007
Mar. 31	02/02/2007	02/16/2007	03/31/2007
May 5	03/09/2007	03/23/2007	05/05/2007
June 9	04/13/2007	04/27/2007	06/09/2007
July 7	05/11/2007	05/25/2007	07/07/2007
Aug. 18	06/22/2007	07/06/2007	08/18/2007
Sept. 8	07/13/2007	07/27/2007	09/08/2007
Sept. 29	08/03/2007	08/17/2007	09/29/2007
Nov. 3	09/07/2007	09/21/2007	11/03/2007
Nov. 24	09/28/2007	10/12/2007	11/24/2007

GENERAL ADVERTISING: Confirmed October 20, 2004.
Rates are **net.**
Rates are **net.**
PAYMENT TERMS: Rates based on 1 side of page & exclusivity for 1 product category only. Additional categories extra. Multiple page, volume or frequency discounts avail. on request. Regional buys subject to 10% surcharge with min. $500 in each market purchased.
GENERAL: Other promotion media rates on request. Coupons.com. Targeted Print and Media Solutions. Various Sales Promotion Services for the U.S.A.

	Per M
1 p.	9.50
1/2 p.	6.25
Outside cover cover, extra	2
Page lip.	1.50

MECHANICAL SPECIFICATIONS:
SHOP & SAVE FSI
Front Covers: 7-3/8" x 9-1/4"; Back Covers: 7-3/8" x 10-1/4"; 1 page: 7-3/8" x 10-1/4"; D.p.s: 14-7/8" x 10-1/4"; 1/2p.: 7-3/8" x 5-1/16"; LIP Copy: 5/8" x 10-1/4" Coupon: 2-1/2" x 5-1/16". Accepted hi-res file formats: PDF, TIFF-IT, Rampage DCS files & original desktop publishing files. Software used: QuarkXPress, Page Maker, Illustrator, Freehand, Photoshop, INdesign. Must be accompanied with a col. proof for each 4/C version. Contact Production Department for exact specs. 1-800-437-0497. Supplied film should be final negatives, right reading with emulsion down to correct size to MAC stds. & accompanied by a set of prog. proofs or a match print. Art work & supplied film should be suitable for reproduction on a heat-set web press with 133 screen. Prod. costs extra. Transfer protocols: FTP: ftp.valassis.com, id: prodresponse, pw: direct
Data confirmed 9/12/2006

Courtesy of Canadian Advertising Rates and Data.

COST CALCULATIONS

Distribution cost (cost to insert an offer into an envelope)

2 000 000 × $9.50/M	= $19 000

Printing cost (estimated cost)

2 000 000 × $6/M	= $12 000

Redemption cost (estimated at 3 percent of total coupons distributed)

2 000 000 × 03 × $1.50	= $90 000

Total cost	**= $121 000**

Depending on how the coupon offer is returned, there could be additional costs for the advertiser. For example, there is a handling fee provided to the retailer for conducting the coupon transaction. As well, coupons are usually sent from the retailer to a clearing house for processing. The clearing house pays the retailer and provides periodic reports to the advertiser about how many coupons are being redeemed. The advertiser pays a fee for this service.

Direct-Response Television

The forms of direct-response television include 60-second (or longer) commercials that typically appear on cable channels, and infomercials. In each case, the use of toll-free telephone numbers, websites, and credit cards makes the purchase more convenient for the viewer.

There are two types of direct-response television advertising: short form and long form. **Short-form** commercials vary in length and may be 15, 30, 60, 90, or 120 seconds long. **Long-form** commercials, commonly referred to as **infomercials**, may last 30 or 60 minutes.[11] Infomercials tend to be much like a television program. They include characters and follow a script. The benefits of the product are presented in great detail. These commercials encourage consumers to move closer to a buying decision or to actually make the buying decision. As opposed to a brand commercial on television that generates an impression, an infomercial generates a response. The effectiveness of direct-response ads is measured by responses such as cost per order, cost per lead, cost per call, or some other criteria.

The nature of direct-response television advertising has changed over time. It was once regarded as schlock, and long associated with "o-matic" types of products. But that is not the case anymore. DRTV has redefined itself, and the range of products using this technique includes anything from exercise equipment to financial investment opportunities. Infomercials no longer exclusively revolve around get-rich-quick concepts; in fact, highly informative, well-produced commercials have been created for many blue-chip companies.

The spectrum of direct-response advertisers now includes pharmaceutical companies, banks and financial institutions, automobile manufacturers, technology companies, and not-for-profit organizations. In Canada some of our mightiest mainstream marketing organizations, such as Ford, Bell, and TD Bank, have embraced direct-response television. This diversity is self-perpetuating, so it is likely that advertisers and their agencies will continue to test innovative approaches, thereby broadening the discipline.

Direct-response television commercials are classified into two categories:

- *Traditional* A commercial or infomercial that stresses the "buy now, limited-time offer" approach; it tries to sell as much as possible at the lowest cost per order.

- *Corporate/Brand* A commercial or infomercial that establishes leads, drives retail traffic, launches new products, creates awareness, and protects and enhances the brand image. It is common for these commercials to encourage consumers to visit a website where even more information is available and where the desired action (a buying decision) can occur.

One good reason why short and long direct-response commercials are popular is that they elicit measurable audience response. This is traditionally done through 1-800 telephone numbers or website addresses. The activity (response) that occurs via telephone or the website immediately following the commercial allows an advertiser to measure the success of the offer immediately. The advertiser can quickly assess the revenues generated from the offer against the cost of the infomercial—in effect, the return on investment (ROI) is measurable. In an age where managers are more accountable for their marketing investments, this benefit is very attractive!

To keep the cost of commercial placement as low as possible, the shorter commercials (up to 60 seconds) usually use run-of-schedule (ROS) time blocks rather than program-specific purchases. The ROS strategy provides the advertiser flexibility by time of day. As well, the spots will cost less, allowing more spots to be scheduled. They may also buy remnant time, which is unsold inventory that is available on short notice at a lower cost. Refer to Figure 11.11 for a summary of some advantages and disadvantages of direct-response television advertising.

Advertisers of all kinds are seeing the benefits of direct-response television. Just recently, Procter & Gamble, a company that had been spending a great deal of its media

FIGURE 11.11

Advantages and disadvantages of direct-response television advertising

ADVANTAGES

- *Message Content*—numerous benefits can be communicated in detail
- *Demonstration*—added time allows for lengthier and more dramatic demonstrations
- *Cost*—production and media costs of short commercials are less than traditional TV
- *Flexibility*—message can be altered if necessary

DISADVANTAGES

- *Time*—even a 60-second commercial faces time constraints
- *Lifespan*—commercials are fleeting; frequency is necessary
- *Image*—consumers often skeptical about message; are claims believable?

budget on conventional television, announced it would begin diverting emphasis from television to direct communications. P&G has appointed its first DRTV media-buying agency of record and has quietly broadened its use of DRTV from small efforts on low-priority brands to bigger efforts on key brands such as Cover Girl, Iams, Old Spice, and Olay.[12]

For more insight into infomercials and their potential impact on viewers, refer to the Advertising in Action vignette **Ford Goes a Step Further**.

Direct home shopping is a service provided by cable television channel TSC (The Shopping Channel). Messages to prospects are shown in the form of close-up shots of the product, or, in the case of clothing and accessories, by models wearing the goods. Athletic equipment is often demonstrated on this channel. Details about how to order are broadcast frequently and a 1-800 number is usually shown on the screen along with a description of the product. Home shopping offers the shopper a great deal of convenience.

Direct-Response Print Media

It is common for advertisers to communicate direct-response offers through newspapers and magazines. Both options are good for fielding leads for future marketing programs, for channelling prospects to a website, and for getting prospects to take action immediately. Since newspapers are a local-market medium, an organization that has adopted a key-market media strategy can target prospects geographically. Local-market retailers that want to employ direct-response strategies may do so through their local daily or weekly newspaper.

Magazines are a good alternative for advertisers targeting specific audiences based on demographic or geographic characteristics. For example, a company such as Intrawest that markets year-round travel destinations (their destinations include Whistler Blackcomb, Mont Tremblant, and Blue Mountain) will place direct-response ads in travel magazines or in general-interest magazines that reach higher-income households. Their ads always include a 1-800 telephone number and a website address so that prospects can obtain more information or book a vacation. Provincial governments follow a similar strategy. The print media is ideal for showing colourful pictures of local tourist attractions. Inquiring minds will get in touch for more specific information. See the ad for Prince Edward Island in Figure 11.12 for an illustration.

Another print-media alternative is the insert. An **insert** is a single- or multiple-page document inserted loosely or stitched directly into a publication. Sometimes an insert is

Ford Goes a Step Further

In a relatively short period of time, DRTV has gone from being the poor cousin of the advertising world to becoming one of the fastest-growing segments of the direct-marketing industry. This rapid rise is the result of an incredible number of brand advertisers who have embraced the medium. These advertisers have discovered that a careful and disciplined approach to DRTV can produce impressive results.

In a first for the automotive industry, Ford of Canada used infomercials to sell F-150-series trucks. "We're challenging the status quo of what truck advertising should be," says Dean Tesser, Ford's director of marketing. "Our national campaign for the F-series truck incorporates mass media, including TV, print, outdoor, radio, online marketing, and consumer events, in addition to our first-ever infomercial. We wanted to go one step further than any of our competition."

The infomercial does make Ford stand out, since it places emphasis on response mechanisms while competitors rely heavily on mass television ads. With traditional television advertising losing some of its lustre due to audience fragmentation and the clustering of so many ads during commercial breaks, it is inevitable that other companies will follow Ford's lead.

TV is primarily used to establish brand image, while media such as newspapers are used to present immediate offers that encourage purchase activity. Direct-response communications can be very beneficial in maintaining communication with existing customers, and automakers are becoming aware of that fact. The Ford F-series campaign was the largest and most integrated ever undertaken by the company, and it began by targeting 100 000 existing customers with a direct-mail information piece and poster announcing the launch of the F-150.

Uniquely Canadian creative positioned the new F-150 as the quietest, most luxurious "Ford-tough" truck yet, a strategy that was in keeping with Ford's overall ad message of "Built for life in Canada."

The 30-minute infomercial, loosely based on the reality TV show *Fear Factor*, was created to communicate all of the truck's benefits. The infomercial showed four participants competing in driving exercises that would be daunting if not impossible in their current trucks, but effortless in the F-150. "The message was embedded in the infomercial and that is why people tuned in," says Tesser. "It was like watching a television program." Results indicate that Ford exceeded its objectives five-fold. The most interesting result was that 50 percent of consumers who responded to the infomercial have never owned a Ford product. The creative was reaching a new consumer.

Source: Adapted from Bernadette Johnson, "Automakers rev up DM," *Strategy Direct + Interactive*, November 17, 2003, pp. 11, 12.

strip-glued (a gum-like glue) directly onto a page. In these cases an advertiser usually places an ad and then attaches the insert on top of the ad. This type of insert is referred to as a **tip-in.** See Figure 11.13 for an illustration of an insert. This Prince Edward Island insert was stitched into the magazine so that it appeared on top of the print ad that is included in Figure 11.12. Note that the government of Prince Edward Island is collecting valuable database information that can be used in future marketing efforts.

Ford Canada
www.ford.ca

Telemarketing

Telemarketing is a booming business in North America. Much telemarketing activity is conducted through call centres. A **call centre** is a central operation from which a company operates its inbound and outbound telemarketing programs. Canadian-based call centres are the focal point of North American operations for many companies.

According to the Canadian Marketing Association (CMA), there is more money spent on telemarketing in Canada in a one-year period than there is on conventional television advertising. That may be difficult to comprehend, but you must consider that

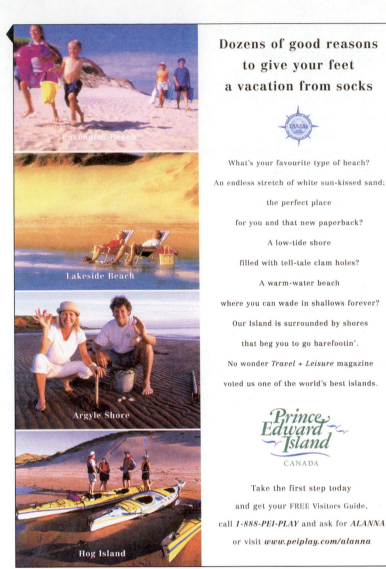

Dozens of good reasons to give your feet a vacation from socks

What's your favourite type of beach?

An endless stretch of white sun-kissed sand;

the perfect place

for you and that new paperback?

A low-tide shore

filled with tell-tale clam holes?

A warm-water beach

where you can wade in shallows forever?

Our Island is surrounded by shores

that beg you to go barefootin'.

No wonder *Travel + Leisure* magazine

voted us one of the world's best islands.

Prince Edward Island
CANADA

Take the first step today

and get your FREE Visitors Guide,

call *1-888-PEI-PLAY* and ask for *ALANNA*

or visit *www.peiplay.com/alanna*

Vacations to Prince Edward Island, Canada

I would like to receive a FREE 2004 Vacation Planning Guide to Prince Edward Island.

Name
Unit #   Street #
Street Name
City   Province
Postal Code   Phone
Email

☐ Yes, I would like to receive future information about *Prince Edward Island*, including the e-newsletter.

I plan to visit *Prince Edward Island* in 2004/2005:

☐ Definitely   ☐ Probably
☐ Uncertain   ☐ Definitely Not

Preferred month of travel: _____

My interests are in:

☐ Accommodations   ☐ History/Culture
☐ Anne of Green Gables ☐ Outdoor Activities/Trails
☐ Beaches   ☐ RV's/Parks/Camping
☐ Crafts/Shopping   ☐ Scenic Touring
☐ Dining/Seafood   ☐ Golf
☐ Festivals/Theatre

Call *1-888-PEI-PLAY*
and ask for *ALANNA* or visit
www.peiplay.com/alanna

you do not see telemarketing in practice (so we don't think about it) whereas we do see a considerable amount of television advertising. In Canada, telemarketing generated $16 billion in sales revenues in 2004 alone.[13]

There are two types of telemarketing: inbound and outbound. **Inbound telemarketing** refers to the reception of calls by the order desk, customer inquiry, and direct-response calls often generated through the use of toll-free 1-800 or 1-888 numbers. **Outbound telemarketing**, on the other hand, refers to calls that a company makes to customers to develop new accounts, generate sales leads, and even close a sale. Effective telemarketing programs often involve a two-or-more call process: the first call (or series of calls) determines the prospect's or existing customer's needs. The final call (or series of calls) motivates the prospect or existing customer to make a purchase.

Many consumers voice displeasure with outbound telemarketing practices, citing aggressive and sometimes abusive behaviour by callers. They also object to the timing of such calls that frequently occur between 5:30 and 7:30 p.m. Such an attitude exists even though legitimate organizations are trying to contact consumers in a highly professional manner. From the marketer's perspective, the timing of the call is critical and those hours that consumers object to are the hours when a majority of consumers are at home.

Marketing organizations do recognize the consumer's right to privacy and are taking steps to ensure that all government-legislated guidelines and policies are followed. In 2005, the federal government passed "do-not-call" legislation to further protect consumers from unwanted phone calls. The Canadian Marketing Association (CMA) endorses the legislation, stating that "without reasonable laws regulating organizations that use the telephone to market their goods and services, the industry risks losing its rights to use this valuable marketing channel to acquire new customers."[14] As well, the CMA has self-regulating policies that organizations follow in all forms of direct-marketing practice. Refer to Figure 11.14 for more details about the CMA's privacy code.

Given that the practice of telemarketing is not well liked by consumers, perhaps the future success of telemarketing lies in inbound telemarketing. Organizations will have to integrate 1-800 telephone numbers into their other forms of advertising, thus encouraging consumers to make an inbound call. Alternatively, as many companies are now doing, the creation and implementation of customer-relationship management programs allow for communications with customers in a variety of formats. In communicating through a mixture of telephone, mail, and the internet, there is less reliance on the telephone alone.

The use of call centres is expected to grow because of the cost efficiencies of telemarketing. The cost of contacting a customer by phone is so much lower than other

---

The Canadian Marketing Association has been at the forefront of Canadian privacy issues for over a decade and has been actively involved in various national and international forums discussing privacy issues and the protection of personal information.

The CMA's Privacy Code gives every Canadian the right to:

- Consent before your personal information is transferred to a third party
- Access information held about you
- Obtain the source of your name on marketing lists
- Correct erroneous information
- Have your name removed from telephone and direct-mail marketing lists

Each year members of the CMA sign a commitment to follow the code.

Source: Adapted from the Canadian Marketing Association, www.the-cma.org.com.

FIGURE 11.14

Members of the Canadian Marketing Association are committed to ethical guidelines governing marketing practice

forms of communications that marketers are willing to tolerate the negative reactions of consumers. Much like a game in which the law of averages kicks in, the marketer knows that for every so many calls made, someone will respond in a favourable way. As well, if a particular offer is not being well received by consumers, the marketer can change the offer on the spot in order to make it more appealing. Such flexibility is not possible in any form of mass communications.

Distinctions must also be made between business-to-consumer telemarketing and business-to-business telemarketing. Business-to-business telemarketing is firmly grounded in customer-relationship marketing practices, and the marketing strategies follow a very professional approach. In many business organizations, telemarketing is often referred to as inside sales. Highly trained inside salespeople contact or receive calls from customers and then process sales orders accordingly.

Delta Hotels
www.deltahotels.com

The development of database software and phone-system technology makes it cost-effective for companies to link their database to the phone. Delta Hotels, for example, has a very busy call centre in New Brunswick that services its North American operations. It receives an average of 2000 calls a day. In addition to taking reservations, the call centre provides services such as servicing its Privilege Card members, handling consumer complaints, and supporting the sales efforts of its business accounts.[15] For Delta Hotels, telemarketing plays a key role in managing customer relationships. For a list of telemarketing applications, see Figure 11.15.

As indicated above, the primary advantage of telemarketing is its ability to complete a sale for less cost than is needed to complete a sale using such techniques as face-to-face sales calls or mass advertising. However, to be effective, the training and preparation of telemarketing representatives needs to be just as comprehensive as for representatives involved in personal selling. Planning the message is as important as the medium itself. For additional details, see the strategic planning discussion that follows.

The primary drawback to telemarketing is the fact that consumers react negatively to it. A survey conducted by Ernst & Young concluded that 75 percent of Canadians consider marketing calls unwelcome and intrusive; they are ranked as one of the least desirable sales techniques. Further, 51 percent of people think there are too many calls, and they react to them by hanging up.[16] Consumers also have some technology on their side. Through call display services offered by telephone companies, consumers can simply avoid unwanted calls by not answering. Despite this behaviour, organizations see the advantages, such as call reach and frequency, cost efficiency, and measurability as outweighing the disadvantages.

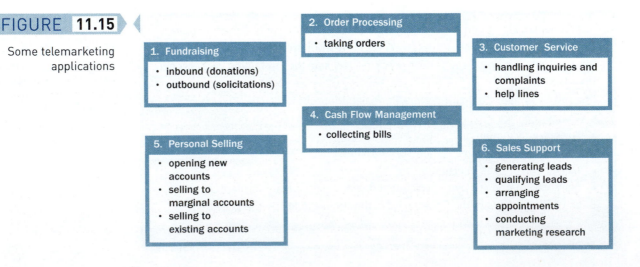

FIGURE 11.15

Some telemarketing applications

1. **Fundraising**
   - inbound (donations)
   - outbound (solicitations)

2. **Order Processing**
   - taking orders

3. **Customer Service**
   - handling inquiries and complaints
   - help lines

4. **Cash Flow Management**
   - collecting bills

5. **Personal Selling**
   - opening new accounts
   - selling to marginal accounts
   - selling to existing accounts

6. **Sales Support**
   - generating leads
   - qualifying leads
   - arranging appointments
   - conducting marketing research

STRATEGIC CONSIDERATIONS FOR TELEMARKETING

For telemarketing to be effective, the nature and quality of the message must be considered in the context of the medium that will deliver the message. How important is a carefully prepared yet flexible script for a telemarketing campaign? Organizations that want to move into the telemarketing arena must take steps to ensure that they do it right. In this regard, some tried and true principles of telemarketing communications should be considered.

Telemarketers face a common problem that is largely due to poor telemarketing practices: consumers view telemarketing as an intrusion or invasion of their privacy and they are reluctant to accept and listen to such calls. Technology, combined with an over-simplified approach at an inappropriate time, leaves people with these kinds of feelings. Successful telemarketing is a process that requires knowledge, skill, and care. Here are some of the elements of successful scripting.

- *Focus on the relationship* Selecting people with whom you have a relationship will produce higher campaign results. Telemarketing is good for securing repeat business from current customers. It is far less costly to generate sales from existing customers than it is to attract new customers.

- *Adjust the script approach to your audience* A well-tested verbatim script works well for marketing a simple or low-cost product. A guided or outline script is more suited to a business-product environment, where numerous unplanned objections occur.

- *Empathize with the receivers* Approach each prospect as an individual with unique needs.

- *Establish rapport and gain attention quickly* Clear identification of the caller, the company, the relationship, and the reason for the call should occur in the first sentence. Every phrase should reflect honesty and sincerity, and so place the recipient at ease.

- *Keep it short and simple* There is power in simplicity. Use short words and sentences. Write the script in the same way as you speak.

- *Be prepared* Practice and role-play are important before making a call. Receive feedback to fine-tune the presentation.

- *Make it easy to say yes* Structure the offer to reduce risk. Offer a free trial, discount, or return option. Show the savings and easy payment terms. Test various offers to make sure that the one selected produces the best results.

SUMMARY

Direct-response advertising is one of the largest advertising media in Canada. Its purpose is to generate a response by any means (through any medium) that is measurable. The major forms of direct-response advertising are direct mail, direct-response television, and telemarketing.

Direct mail is the most prominent form of direct-response advertising. A direct mailing usually includes a sales letter, leaflet or flyer, folder, and statement stuffer. Advertisers choose between solo direct mail and co-operative direct mail. Solo distribution is much more expensive than co-operative

distribution. With co-operative direct mail, the costs are shared among participating organizations.

The primary advantages of direct mail for advertisers are its audience selectivity (which makes it an excellent medium for the business advertiser), high reach potential, and geographic flexibility. Disadvantages include the absence of editorial support and poor image. The success of any direct-mail campaign largely depends on the quality of the list the advertiser uses. The best list is an internal list of customers that should be readily available in the organization's database.

Lists are also available externally from list suppliers and other secondary sources such as directories and trade indexes. Lists provided by list brokers are rented on a cost-per-thousand basis. Canada Post is also a large supplier of information for direct-mail advertising and is the largest distributor of direct mail.

Advancing technology has spurred growth in direct-response television and telemarketing. There are two forms of direct-response television: short form and long form. Short-form commercials are 30-second or longer commercials on cable channels. Long-form commercials, or infomercials, are 30- or 60-minute commercials that look much like a television show. Infomercials are becoming more popular with traditional advertisers and are used to establish leads, build image, and launch new products. They are effective in communicating information that involves a lot of detail, or in situations where the advertiser wants to expose an audience to a lengthy list of product benefits.

Advertisers that are targeting customers based on demographic, psychographic, and geographic characteristics often place direct-response ads in newspapers and magazines. The ads include a call to action, and customers can easily respond through the 1-800 telephone number or website address included in the ad. Direct-response inserts are another print-media alternative. Inserts are placed loosely in the newspaper or magazine or stitched directly into the

magazine, much like a normal page. It is also common for an advertiser to place an ad and an insert in a publication at the same time. The ad creates awareness and interest while the insert stimulates action.

There are two types of telemarketing. Inbound telemarketing refers to the reception of calls by an order desk, usually through a toll-free number. Outbound telemarketing refers to calls made by a company to customers to generate leads and even close a sale. Companies are attracted to telemarketing because of the relatively low cost. Quite simply, telemarketing is far less expensive than face-to-face communications or mass advertising. A drawback is the negative perceptions people have about this communication technique. Consumers tend to dislike the persistence of telemarketers and the timing of their calls, usually in and around the dinner hour.

The primary advantages of all forms of direct-response advertising are targeting capability and measurability. From a marketing planning perspective the impact of any direct-response offer can be measured while the communication is in progress or shortly thereafter. No form of traditional mass media has such capability. The advance of computer and communications technology will continue to encourage much greater use of direct-response communications. Direct-response advertising will play a more prominent role in the communications mix in the future.

KEY TERMS

REVIEW QUESTIONS

1. What are the major forms of direct-response advertising?

2. Identify and briefly explain the components of a direct-mail package.

3. What is the difference between a solo direct-mail campaign and a co-operative direct-mail campaign?

4. What are the advantages and disadvantages of direct-mail advertising for a business-product advertiser (e.g., a manufacturer of business equipment)?

5. How important is the mailing list in a direct-mail campaign? Briefly explain.

6. Explain the differences between a response list, a circulation list, and a compiled list.

7. What is a list broker, and what functions does a list broker perform?

8. Explain the following terms as they relate to direct-response advertising:

   a) bounce backs
   b) house list
   c) insert
   d) merge/purge
   e) infomercial
   f) inbound telemarketing versus outbound telemarketing
   g) call centre

9. What are some of the advantages and disadvantages of telemarketing for selling products and services?

DISCUSSION QUESTIONS

1. "The dollars an advertiser invests in direct-mail advertising are wasted, owing to the poor image of the medium." Discuss.

2. "Persistent invasion of consumer privacy will be the undoing of the direct-response advertising industry." Is this statement true or false, and does it depend on the type of direct response an advertiser uses? Discuss.

3. "Direct-response television will play a more prominent role in future television advertising campaigns for traditional advertisers such as banks, automobile manufacturers, and insurance companies." Is this statement true or false? Discuss.

4. Conduct some secondary research on the DRTV business. Has the image of DRTV really changed? What companies are using this technique, and how successful have they been with it?

NOTES

1. Laura Blum, "The return of the infomercial," **www.adweek.com**, August 26, 2006.
2. Canadian Media Directors' Council, *Media Digest*, 2006–2007, p. 12.
3. "Broadcasting and telecommunications," Service Bulletin, Statistics Canada, July 2006, p. 8.
4. "A winning combination," *Sorted*, Spring 2006, p. 13.
5. NCH Promotional Services, 2003.
6. "Why mail?" *Direct Mail: What Works?* supplement to *Strategy*, 2006, p. S48.
7. "Target your audience," *Direct Mail: What Works?* supplement to *Strategy*, 2006, p. S48.
8. ICOM Information and Communications Inc., **www.i-com.com**, 2006.
9. "Target your audience," *Direct Mail: What Works?* supplement to *Strategy*, 2006, p. S49.
10. Cornerstone Group of Companies, **www.cstonecanada.com**.
11. Canadian Media Directors' Council, *Media Digest*, 2006–2007, p. 90.
12. Jack Neff, "What P&G learned from Veg-O-Matic," *Advertising Age*, April 10, 2006, pp. 1, 65.
13. Sarah Dobson, "Wake-up call," *Marketing*, November 14, 2005, p. 20.
14. "Canada's largest marketing association welcomes national do-not-call service," press release, Canadian Marketing Association, November 28, 2005.
15. "Comprehensive efforts for Delta," *Strategy*, February 19, 1996, p. 18.
16. Mary Gooderham, "Level of antipathy a wake-up call for telemarketers," *Globe and Mail*, May 7, 1997, p. C11.

CHAPTER 12

Interactive Media

AXE is a registered trademark owned by Unilever Canada Inc. Used with permission.

Learning Objectives

After studying this chapter, you will be able to

1. Describe the various elements of internet communications

2. Identify the key organization members that constitute the online advertising industry

3. Evaluate the various advertising models available to marketing organizations

4. Identify key aspects of online audience measurement systems

5. Assess the potential of the internet as an advertising medium

6. Describe and apply various models for pricing and buying online advertising

Wireless technology, exemplified by the internet, cell phones, portable music players, and personal digital assistants, represents a new advertising environment that is challenging the best of marketers. This technology is advancing rapidly, but marketers have been slow to respond, partly because there is a generation gap between aging marketing decision-makers and younger, tech-savvy target markets. In the digitally altered media landscape, marketing organizations must find a way to adapt, or suffer the business consequences of standing aside while others embrace this new environment.

In the digital universe, marketers must contend with a lot of new terminology: video-on-demand, rich media, broadband video, text messaging, consumer-generated content, podcasting, and blogs are but a few of these terms. They must also contend with a key fact: in the realm of traditional advertising, organizations target customers, but in the world of interactive communications, customers target information that is of interest to them. Control has shifted from the advertiser to the customer. Viewers now have unprecedented choice; the internet and mobile phones allow viewers to choose not only when they watch but where they watch. Will it be the TV screen, the computer screen, or the cell phone screen?

These trends, along with the growing popularity of social network sites such as MySpace and Facebook, where users can create and change content, are forcing marketing organizations to re-evaluate how they employ the media. In fact, marketers fear that they are losing control of their brands (at least their brand messages) as consumers create their own content. The world of marketing communications isn't what it used to be! This chapter will look at a host of new and exciting interactive marketing communications opportunities.

Interactive Advertising

In the 1950s, media planners faced the problem of determining how television would fit into the advertising world. Television was a brand new medium that would upset the status quo for radio, newspapers, and magazines. Existing media survived the onslaught, but their share of the advertising pie would change forever. Now, the internet is revolutionizing how companies look at advertising, and certainly how they allocate money among the various media. Organizations are reallocating their budgets to ensure a better mix between mass media such as television, newspaper, and radio, and the digital media.

The digital revolution is being led by Canadians—we are the world leaders in internet usage per capita and we now consume 20 percent of our media online. Revenues generated by online advertising are growing each year and in 2006 reached $1.01 billion, an 80-percent increase over 2005.[1] Such a staggering increase suggests more and more advertisers are going online with their dollars.

Companies are exploring new forms of advertising made available by the internet and in many cases are adding an interactive component to their traditional media advertising. These new media are providing progressive companies with a means of reaching what was once thought to be an unattainable goal: a personal, one-to-one relationship with customers. Devices that offer interactive communications seem to offer unlimited communications potential.

Currently, advertisers and advertising agencies are struggling with the question of how to integrate internet communications with the traditional media mix. For many it is the "unknown benefit" factor that creates a kind of a wait-and-see attitude. Others have jumped in and are enjoying the ride. For example, Doritos launched an online branding contest in which the company invited visitors to create a 30-second online video celebrating the snack chip. The winners would receive $10 000 for their effort, and the ad would be broadcast during the 2007 Super Bowl. Two teenagers created an ad for $12, and the buzz the ad created via post–Super Bowl views on YouTube benefited the brand. There's an expression that sums up the impetus behind this kind of outside-the-box thinking: "If you don't like change, you'll like irrelevance even less." Marketers have little choice but to embrace the new media.

Toyota seems to get it. When Toyota launched the Yaris in Canada, it was targeted at 18- to 34-year-olds. The media strategy included several interactive techniques: 10-second ads preceding cell phone "mobisodes" (programs that are downloadable to a cell phone); a contest on Current TV's website (www.currentTV.com) that allowed consumers to create their own Yaris commercial; a Yaris profile page on MySpace; sponsorship of the Evolution Fighting Championships video game; and product placement on the comedy show *MadTV*.[2] Note the absence of traditional media techniques in this plan.

THE INTERNET AND INTERNET USAGE

The **internet** is a network of computer networks linked together to act as one. It works just like a global mail system in which independent authorities collaborate in moving and delivering information. The **World Wide Web** is the collection of **websites** on the internet. Most websites on the internet are commercial in nature. For example, a company website delivers important information about the company and/or its products to visitors. Unlike any other type of medium, the consumer controls whether he or she will see the information. The website also provides a means of collecting information about visitors (e.g., through contests and surveys). If managed properly, the internet is one component of a complete database-management system. The information collected at a website can be used to identify prospects and market products more effectively in the future.

Canadians are very active online, as more than 80 percent of Canadians have internet access at home. Factors such as income and education affect internet usage, but with the price of computers dropping, there is more widespread access by all Canadians. By age, younger Canadians in the 18- to 44-year-old range are much more likely to use the internet than those 45 years of age and older. For further information about internet usage refer to Figure 12.1.

INTERNET CULTURE AND BEHAVIOUR

The primary activities of internet users vary by gender and age. In general terms however, the top five reasons for going online are to access email, browse, obtain weather and road conditions, seek travel information, and view news and sports information. The internet has also become an important way to conduct financial affairs. Almost 60 percent of Canadians do their banking online, and 55 percent pay bills online. More important to marketers is the fact that 43 percent of Canadians have ordered and paid for goods online.[3]

Canadians are also using the internet as a research tool for buying products. They do their research online and then make either an online or offline purchase once the research is complete. Therefore, well-designed, well-targeted, and properly placed advertisements are useful resources for consumers as they engage in product research. As well, independent websites and blogs that spread positive news about a brand (news that the brand cannot control) can have considerable influence on buying intentions.

Marketers and advertisers must view the internet as a complementary medium that supports communications strategies implemented using traditional media. Refer to Figure 12.2 for more insight into internet user behaviour.

According to a Statistics Canada survey (2005), 16.8 million Canadians regularly surf the internet. In general, larger cities have younger populations and more residents with higher levels of income and education, all of which are related to higher rates of internet use.

Other key findings of the survey are as follows:

- About 88 percent of adults with household incomes of $86 000 or more use the internet, compared to 61 percent of adults in households with incomes below $86 000.
- Eighty percent of adults with post-secondary education access the internet, compared to 49 percent of adults with less education.
- The presence of children under the age of 18 is associated with a higher rate of internet use.
- The home is the most popular access point for going online (90 percent of respondents). Access from work is the second most popular access point (39 percent of respondents).
- The internet is becoming important for conducting financial affairs, as 60 percent of respondents now bank online and 55 percent pay their bills online.

Source: Adapted from "Canadian internet use survey," *The Daily*, August 15, 2006, Statistics Canada, www.statcan.ca.

FIGURE 12.1

Canadians are actively involved online

FIGURE 12.2

How Canadians
use the internet

Sending and receiving email is the most important activity among Canadian adults when online, but the internet presents a host of information and entertainment activities. Canadians go online for the following reasons:

Activity	Engaged in Activity (%)
Email	91
General browsing	84
Weather or road conditions	67
Travel information	63
View news or sports	62
Search medical or health information	58
Electronic banking	58
Window shopping	57
Pay bills	55
Search government information	52
Order goods and services	43
Education, training, or school work	43
Research community events	42
Play games	39
Chat or use a messenger	38

Source: Adapted from "Canadian internet use survey," *The Daily*, August 15, 2005, Statistics Canada, www.statcan.ca.

Currently, internet users are skeptical about commercialization. They tend to be information-oriented and have a strong sense of community. The internet represents a medium that offers users up-to-date information instantaneously and allows for interaction with the content (for example, in designing your dream car at a website). Mass advertising through media such as television, radio, and magazines is interruptive in nature. In contrast, advertising online should be more participative in nature if it is to be noticed and taken seriously by the viewer. Therefore, using the same type of communications online that is used offline will not work. Advertisers must recognize that the internet is a different type of medium, a medium in which the viewer is in control.

The remainder of the chapter discusses the potential of online advertising and social media communications, and the various tools and techniques used to reach connected consumers.

The Online Advertising Industry

The online advertising industry consists of sellers, buyers, advertising agencies, web design companies, and measurement companies. On the selling side there are website publishers that provide the content, and advertising networks that sell the media to advertisers and agencies. An **ad network** is a specialist company that represents a host of websites and serves as a sales force for participating publishers. Among the largest networks in Canada are Yahoo!, Canada.com, and 24/7 Real Media. These networks offer various advertising opportunities that include banner ads, rich media, sponsorships, permission-based email, and content integration.

Other popular sites for placing ads are portal sites that offer web searches, news, directories, email, discussion, and links to other sites. These sites include Yahoo.ca and Google.ca, among others. Portals such as these currently receive the bulk of advertising revenues generated on the internet.

On the buying side, there are advertisers, traditional advertising agencies, and interactive agencies. Traditional advertising agencies initially took a cautious approach to the internet's potential. Consequently, boutique shops popped up and helped pioneer online advertising. Among these boutique shops are Proximity Canada, Rare Method, Eyeblaster, and Rebellium (notice how different the names are from those of traditional ad agencies). Eyeblaster has developed innovative online advertising campaigns for clients that include BMW, Virgin, Ikea, Honda, Sony Pictures, Microsoft, and Unilever.

Eyeblaster
www.eyeblaster.com

Recently, traditional agencies have become much more aggressive in online advertising. Some traditional agencies have acquired digital-media agencies and integrated them into their organizational structure. On the grandest of scales, Paris-based Publicis, one of the largest agency networks in the world, acquired online and direct-marketing agency Digitas for US$1.3 billion. In explaining the acquisition, CEO Maurice Levy said, "The massive shift from old media to new media is leading to a new world, and we don't want to be on the sidewalk. We want to be in the forefront of all that is new and bring these new technologies to our clients."[4] Others are hiring digital communications expertise (human resources) or forming an alliance with a digital agency to access their expertise on an as-needed basis.

The web is more accurate at capturing measurement information than any other medium, largely due to the technology that is built into it. At portal sites such as Yahoo!, Sympatico, or Google, information is captured through an internet protocol address. Every computer has an internet protocol (IP) address in numeric code that uniquely identifies a particular computer on the internet. The codes are dynamically assigned by the portal each time a computer logs on. The information that is captured can be accumulated and then used to compile data about usage: page views, number of unique visitors, number of visits, and how long each visit lasted. Many companies have their own servers and can determine the effectiveness of their communications efforts by analyzing the data in their web server's log files.

Independent third-party measurement companies such as Nielsen/NetRatings and comScore Media Metrix also provide information about web usage. Being independent, these parties legitimize the internet as an advertising medium by providing reasonably accurate estimates of traffic at a website. Accuracy has been an issue with advertisers. Companies like Procter & Gamble, Kimberly-Clark, and Ford are demanding that web publishers hire independent auditors to verify their advertising and viewer counts. There is also a concern about click fraud (comprising a variety of fraudulent ad-clicking schemes) that can drive online advertising costs up.[5] The online ad industry must address these issues since there is a need among clients for more accountability in their advertising spending decisions.

Interactive Communications Strategies

When devising an interactive communications plan, decisions about which medium to use are based on the communications objectives and the budget. Once the objectives are established, the next step is to evaluate the various interactive media options from a strategic viewpoint. Among the options are various forms of internet advertising, advertising through mobile communications devices, advertising in video games, and advertising on social media networks.

From a strategic planning perspective, the primary benefit of using any of these forms of communication is the ability to target a specific audience—advertisers can target customers based on their behaviour. **Behavioural targeting** involves the delivery of ads based on a consumer's previous surfing behaviour. An individual's surfing behaviour is tracked by placing a **cookie**, which is a small text file, on a consumer's web browser or hard drive. The cookie can be used to remember a user's preferences.

WestJet
www.westjet.com

WestJet Airlines incorporates behavioural ads to increase bookings at its website. The site attracts some 1.7 million unique visitors each month but only a fraction of the visitors buy tickets in the ecommerce-enabled ticketing section. Now AOL Canada tracks users who leave the WestJet site without booking, and serves them additional WestJet deals, encouraging them to return and complete a booking. Online ticket bookings have increased considerably as a result of this initiative.[6]

Today's media planners must be technologically savvy; they must recognize the value of interactive communications and make appropriate recommendations when necessary. Their recommendations are based on an understanding of some fundamental advertising measurement terms. The terms defined below relate to how internet ads are measured for effectiveness.

- *Impressions* Also called *ad views*, these are the number of times a banner image is downloaded onto a user's computer. Impressions are the standard way of determining exposure for an ad on the web.

- *Clicks (clickthroughs)* Refers to the number of times that users click on a banner ad. Such a measurement allows an advertiser to judge the response to an ad. When viewers click the ad they are transferred to the advertiser's website or to a special page where they are encouraged to respond in some way to the ad.

- *Clickthrough rate* The percentage of ad views that result in an ad click. The percentage indicates the success of an advertiser in attracting visitors to click on their ad. For example, if during one million impressions there are 20 000 clicks on the banner, the clickthrough rate is two percent. The formula is clicks divided by ad impressions.

- *Visitor* A unique user of a website.

- *Visit* A sequence of page requests made by a visitor at a website. A visit is also referred to as a *session* or *browsing period*.

A site's activity is described in terms of visits and visitors, the former always being larger than the latter because of repeat visitors. A site that can report, for example, that it had eight million page views, 100 000 visitors, and 800 000 visits last month would be doing very well. It means that the average visitor returns to the site eight times each month, and views 10 pages on each visit. That's incredible **stickiness**—most sites don't do that well!

Online Advertising

As indicated earlier in the chapter, online advertising has surpassed $1 billion (2006). It is now bigger than outdoor, transit, and magazine media in terms of revenue. It is a medium that all media planners must now give due consideration.

While all media are experiencing growth in advertising revenue, the time people spend with each medium is changing, and that has implications for advertisers. Canadians now spend 88 minutes per day, or about 10 hours a week, online.[7] That leaves less time to spend with other media. Conventional wisdom suggests that advertising dollars be reallocated appropriately.

Recent BBM data confirms that Canadians are becoming more responsive to online advertising—good news for marketers! The data shows that those who click on an internet ad are 40 percent more likely to be in the 25- to 34-year-old range, a highly sought-after target market. Further, the vast majority of internet users list the internet as their most favourite medium, followed by television, and then radio. Sounds like a good media mix!

Online advertising is defined as the placement of electronic communication on a website, in email, or over personal communications devices connected to the internet. While the ultimate goal of most forms of advertising is to motivate the consumer to purchase a brand, online advertising is also useful for:

- Creating brand awareness

- Stimulating interest and preference

- Distributing incentives and contest information

- Providing a means to make a purchase

- Providing a means to contact an advertiser

- Acquiring data about real/potential consumers

online adv. goals.

Based on these objectives, the essential role of the internet is to communicate vital information about a company and its products. When a company quotes a website address in other forms of communications, it finds that interested buyers start to visit its site for new information. Such action could trigger an online or offline purchase. Therefore, organizations shouldn't neglect traditional forms of advertising. Advertising in the traditional media should always provide a website address and encourage customers to visit the site for additional information.

With reference to Figure 12.3, the homepage and a subsequent page for Holiday Inn, it can be seen how the hotel chain uses the internet to communicate with current and prospective customers in more complete detail than is possible in other media. From the homepage, a traveller need only click on an icon of interest, for example, "special offers" or "specific destinations," for more information. A customer wishing to reserve a room can do so online. If such a transaction occurs, then the loop, from creating awareness and interest to making a sale, is complete—and all done online!

For more insight into the blending of interactive media with traditional media, read the Advertising in Action vignette **Integrated Campaign Works for Mazda**.

Online Advertising Alternatives

Marketing organizations now have an abundance of advertising alternatives available on the internet. This section examines these opportunities. Bear in mind while reading through this section that, of the $1.01 billion invested in online advertising in 2006, display advertising and search advertising account for a majority of spending. See Figure 12.4 for details.

DISPLAY ADVERTISING

Display advertising includes banner ads in a variety of sizes and rich media ads.

A **banner ad** usually refers to third-party advertising on a website. In terms of design, banner ads stretch across a page in a narrow band; or they may have other standard shapes such as those referred to below. The industry, through the Interactive Advertising Bureau (IAB), has established standard ad sizes based on International

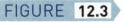

FIGURE 12.3

Selected pages from the
Holiday Inn website

ADVERTISING IN ACTION

Integrated Campaign Works for Mazda

In the spring of 2006, Mazda teamed up with CanWest MediaWorks to launch the new Mazda CX-7 SUV. The CX-7 anchors Mazda's presence in the emerging crossover segment of the automobile market. The campaign, named "Seven Days," ran from May 29 to June 26, 2006. Three objectives were established for the campaign:

1. Generate awareness of the New Mazda CX-7.

2. Create excitement surrounding the launch.

3. Encourage consumers to interact with the brand.

The target market was described as young professional males and females, college- or university-educated, household income of $100 000, located in urban markets nationally.

The media strategy featured a multimedia contest, with Mazda offering a secondary prize on each of the seven days and one grand "life changing" prize at the end of the contest: an adventure vacation to Sweden, Tuscany, Paris, Brazil, Kenya, or Australia. The prizes would act as a motivating call to action while allowing people to interact with the CX-7 brand via a virtual tour. Television promotional ads ran on Global TV nationally, and print ads ran in 10 CanWest daily newspapers including the *National Post*. These ads encouraged people to visit the website for details.

Campaign execution contained the following elements:

- Pre-promotion of the campaign, with TV spots on Global TV one week prior to launch

- Print ads in the *National Post* and 10 other daily newspapers
- Creation and hosting of a multimedia contest on the www.driving.ca and www.Canada.com contest websites
- Development of interactive online creative to drive traffic to the national contest website
- Inclusion of ad placements in Canada.com's bi-weekly newsletter (reached 290 000 subscribers)
- Headlining of the contest on Canada.com's daily headline newsletters
- Addition of a viral component encouraging consumers to refer a friend to the contest, and a chance to receive new offers from Mazda

The campaign generated tremendous awareness and created consumer excitement. Key results included the following:

- More than 7 million ad impressions delivered in one week
- More than 90 000 consumers entered the contest
- More than 30 000 unique consumers visited the contest website
- More than 7000 consumers opted in for additional mailings
- More than 1000 consumers referred a friend

This campaign strategy and execution shows how a carefully planned integrated marketing communications plan can produce effective results for an advertiser. It also shows how a media conglomerate like CanWest can put together an integrated campaign in-house, one that offers solutions across all media.

Source: Adapted from "Case study, interactive by example: Mazda," *Essential Interactive*, Volume 3, p. 13 n.d.

CanWest MediaWorks
www.canwestmediaworks.com

Measurement Units (IMU) in order to make the planning, buying, and creating of online ads more efficient.

The Internet Measurement Units (IMU), refers to the width and depth of an ad. The **rectangle** is a larger box-style ad (180 × 150 IMU) that offers more depth than a standard banner. A **big box** is a larger rectangle (300 × 250 IMU) that offers even greater width and depth to an ad. A **leaderboard** is an ad that stretches across the top of a webpage (728 × 90 IMU). A **skyscraper** is a tall, slim, oblong ad that appears at the side of a webpage (160 × 600 IMU). A larger ad such as the big box offers an opportunity to deliver a more complete message, even if the user doesn't click on it. Research

FIGURE **12.4**

Canadian online advertising revenue

Interactive Advertising Bureau of Canada

IAB Canada: Canadian Online Advertising Revenue, By Advertising Vehicle, as % of 2006 Total Revenue

2006

Email 2%

Classifieds / Directories 27%

Display 36%

Search 35%

Display
Search
Classifieds / Directories
Email

	2006	2005	Change
Display	$364M	$230M	+58%
Search	$353M	$197M	+79%
Classifieds/ Directories	$273M	$124M	+120%
Email	$20M	$11M	+82%
TOTAL	$1.01B	$562M	

Copyright © 2007 Interactive Advertising Bureau of Canada   4

does indicate that larger-size ads achieve higher scores for brand awareness and message association. Banner ads may be static in nature or include some kind of animation or movement to draw attention to the ad. Generally, response rates, or click rates, for **animated banners** are higher than for static banners.

The boom in high-speed internet service has fuelled the growth of rich media advertising. **Rich media** use multiple forms of information content and information processing and may include animation, sound, video and interactivity. These ads come in a variety of styles to grab the viewer's attention in different ways.

There are several inside-the-banner rich media options. An **expandable banner** employs multiple panels that are launched when the banner is clicked on. A **videostrip** shows a strip of video in the banner space but when clicked on expands to reveal the video and accompanying audio in a full-sized panel. A **push down banner** slides advertiser content out of the way to reveal additional content rather than covering it up.

There are also some outside-the-banner options. A **floating ad** moves within a transparent layer over the page and plays within a specific area of the page. A **window ad** downloads itself and plays instantly or when a new page is loading. A **wallpaper ad** is a large image that replaces the web page background.

ONLINE VIDEO

The massive influx of video content on the web (e.g., news, sports, amateur video content) was a 2006 phenomenon that had a profound impact on the internet. Advertisers are still just experimenting with the medium; in 2006, video advertising accounted for only about two percent of total online advertising revenue (U.S.).

From an advertiser's perspective, video ads are essentially the internet's version of a television commercial. The ad is delivered by a process called streaming media.

Streaming media involves continuous delivery of small packets of compressed data that are interpreted by a software player and displayed as full-motion video. The similarity to television advertising makes it attractive to traditional advertisers since the message will have a more emotional impact on viewers than other forms of online advertising that are more static, such as banner ads.

Execution-wise, streaming media is not as simple as running a television commercial online. A 30-second spot online is too long for the typical user, especially if the ad is interrupting something they are doing. The Internet Advertising Bureau suggests 10 seconds as a reasonable length for an online video ad. In terms of content, advertisers must resist the temptation to do online what they are doing offline. Internet users view the online medium as a form of entertainment. Therefore, messages delivered by online advertisers must contain an element of entertainment, or they won't be viewed.

Television shows are now streamed on network websites. Alliance Atlantis, for example, streams one of its flagship shows, *Holmes on Homes*, on the HGTV website. Refer to Figure 12.5 for an illustration. "Our users have indicated a strong affinity towards watching online video, so the streaming will provide premium content on demand," says senior vice-president Claude Galipeau. The *Globe and Mail* was the first advertiser on the show. The *Globe*'s ads appeared as an interruption (10-second video ads) in the online streaming of the show, along with banner ads.[8]

Online video ads are projected to grow significantly in the next few years. As more and more television networks provide shows on the internet, there will be more commercial breaks in the content. Just like television, there will be a selection of ads before, during, and after the show. **Pre-roll ads** refer to ads at the start of a video; **mid-roll ads** refer to ads that appear during the video; and **post-roll ads** appear after the video. On CTV.ca, all 44 minutes of shows such as *The O.C.*, *Smith*, and *Studio 60 on the Sunset*

Courtesy of The Holmes Group.

FIGURE 12.5

Popular TV shows are now streamed online and include short video commercials

Strip are available with five commercial breaks: one pre-roll, one post-roll, and three in the body of the show.[9]

SEARCH ADVERTISING

Harris Interactive
www.harrisinteractive.com

Search-engine marketing solves a basic need of connecting potential buyers to sellers but, until recently, it has only enjoyed a low profile in the advertising world. According to a Harris Interactive research study, 80 percent of internet traffic begins at a search engine.[10] Such a staggering figure points to a significant advertising opportunity.

With **search advertising**, an advertiser's listing is placed within or alongside search results in exchange for paying a fee each time someone clicks on your listing in those search results. This is also known as **pay-per-click advertising**. Most search engines, such as Google and Yahoo!, set advertisers against one another in auction-style bidding for the highest positions on search results pages. For example, Google offers a service called AdWords, which allows companies, for a small fee, to have a link to their website featured when a user searches for a particular word that the company has specified. To illustrate, if a user types in the word "tires" and Michelin has bought that word, an advertisement for Michelin appears on the screen.

Who appears at the top of a search advertising list depends on the bids for the search term. To demonstrate, at Yahoo!, the highest bidders always appear on top of search results pages. When the word "HDTV" was entered, an ad for HDTV at AOL appeared at the top of the list, followed by Hitachi Plasma HDTV, followed by Vikuiti Brighter LCD HDTV. The bids were $2.02, $2.01, and $2.00, respectively.[11]

SPONSORSHIPS

With a **sponsorship**, an advertiser commits to an extended relationship with another website. For example, a financial services company might sponsor the ROBtv.ca site or a beer company might choose to sponsor something on a sports site such as TSN.ca or thescore.ca. On thescore.ca, Burger King sponsors a regular feature called *King of the Court Cuts*, a segment that features highlights of all the exciting plays from a week's worth of NBA basketball. Burger King also sponsors a football contest called *King of Football*, a fantasy sports pool (pick the winners of games each week) where participants have a chance at winning a $20 000 grand prize. The Burger King logo and the "King" character are prominent on the web pages devoted to these sponsorships. Burger King is targeting the content based on the assumption that an audience comes to that website because they are interested in sports.

Sponsorships allow an advertiser to have a successful ad campaign without necessarily having to drive traffic to its website. Consumers trust the brands that they visit repeatedly for information on the web. Therefore, a second brand (a sponsor) may be perceived more positively through the sponsorship association. For an illustration of the sponsorship opportunities available at TSN refer to Figure 12.6.

EMAIL ADVERTISING

One of the most promising applications in online advertising doesn't use flashy graphics or oversized banners. **Permission-based email**, in which a user chooses to receive messages from a particular advertiser, is growing quickly. Other commonly used terms for permission-based email include *direct email* and *email marketing*. This form of advertising is relatively inexpensive, response rates are easy to measure, and it is targeted at people who want information about certain goods and services. See Figure 12.7 for an illustration.

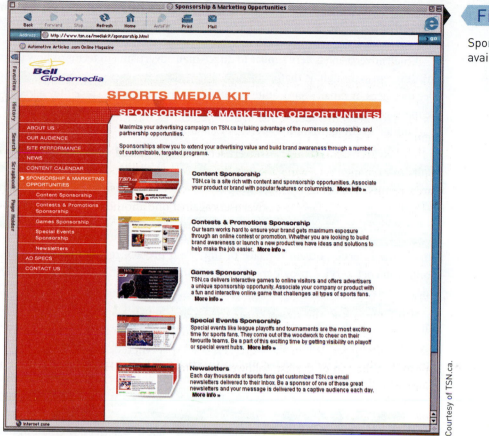

FIGURE **12.6**

Sponsorship opportunities available at TSN.ca

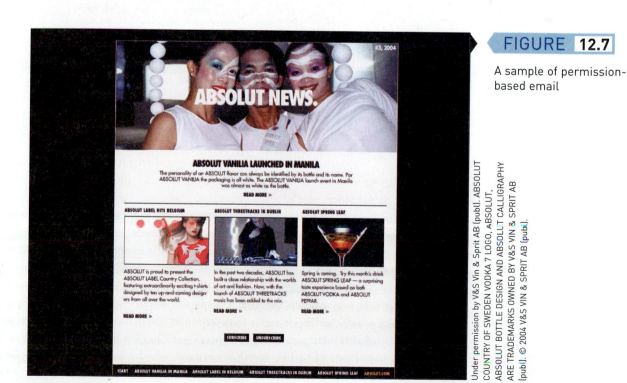

FIGURE **12.7**

A sample of permission-based email

An offshoot of email advertising is **sponsored email.** Many internet sites that mail information to subscribers now include a short message from a sponsor, along with a link to its website.

Email advertising is very similar to direct-mail advertising in terms of how it operates. The difference, though, is that email advertising generates higher response rates. Sending sales messages by email seems quite acceptable to internet users since they agree to accept the messages (i.e., users can subscribe and unsubscribe to email advertising as they wish).

Similar to direct mail, the success of an email ad campaign depends on the quality of the list. There are two kinds of lists: a rented email list and an in-house list. The **rented list** is usually obtained from a list broker. Typically, these lists include "opt-in" names and addresses. **Opt-in** means the people on the list have agreed to receive direct email.

Email advertisements sent to lists that are not opt-in are called *spam.* **Spam** refers to the inappropriate use of a mailing list. It is unsolicited "junk" email. Spam is a problem on the internet, but in the face of improved privacy regulations and spam filters (some internet service providers relegate spam to bulk or junk folders) means that today's inboxes are less cluttered.

Email advertising, done properly, can be very effective. The Interactive Advertising Bureau reports that Canada is one of the world's leaders in email marketing. Delivery rates of almost 93 percent, open rates of over 55 percent, and clickthrough rates of over 8 percent show just how effective email advertising can be. One of the keys to email success is relevance. Receivers will opt out if the content does not remain relevant to them.[12]

In the age of database marketing, the compilation of an in-house list is essential. Since all forms of advertising should invite people to visit a website, the site should include a section where people can sign up for email newsletters or email updates that could announce the introduction of new products. Online promotions such as contests provide another opportunity to secure email addresses. Sending email to customers and prospects that specifically request the mail will almost always work better than using a rented list.

Email also opens up an opportunity for viral marketing. **Viral marketing** refers to a situation in which the receiver of a message is encouraged to pass it on to friends. A research study in the United States reports that 89 percent of adult internet users share content with their friends via email. The goal of a viral campaign is to create content that people feel compelled to pass on. Usually such information is not the straight facts about a product but rather something that is risky or mischievous. Messages of this nature help generate buzz for the product.

WEBCASTING (WEBISODES)

A **webisode** involves the production of an extended commercial that includes entertainment value in the communications. Unlike television commercials, the webisode focuses more on creativity in order to engage users. While consumers are using digital video recorders to skip television ads they don't like, they are using the internet to tune in to commercials they want to see—an interesting phenomenon!

Schick Canada was one of the first companies to develop a webisode. Schick launched an eight-week webisode series to promote its Quattro razor. A digital personality named Pistol Pete Madigan engaged viewers with his wit and satirical style as he explored the human side of various men's issues (e.g., why he hates golf and why facial hair makes people look like they eat out of garbage cans). Schick's logo surrounds the program but the brand itself doesn't appear in some of the episodes. "When you do branded content on the internet, you build a relationship with your viewer. If you tip the scale too far in the direction of pure shill, people will click off," says David Sylvestre, creative director of Unplugged TV, the internet station that produced the webisodes.[13]

While the number of potential viewers of a webcast is much lower than for a conventional television ad, the fact that viewers are there for a reason indicates the benefit of showing commercials online. The behaviour of people watching a commercial on the web is much different than watching a television commercial. Further, if the webisode becomes popular the viral influence of online communications could take over—at least that's what the advertiser hopes for!

Unplugged TV
www.unpluggedtv.com

The Internet as an Advertising Medium

Internet advertising offers numerous advantages and disadvantages. Thus far, the internet has offered high expectations but, being a new medium, the lack of experience among advertisers and their agencies has been a problem. As time progresses and everyone gains more experience the true benefits of the internet will be realized.

ADVANTAGES OF ONLINE ADVERTISING

TARGETING CAPABILITY Since the internet is based on technology, advertisers have a new range of targeting capabilities. As discussed earlier, a person's browsing behaviour and personal preferences can be recorded by inserting cookies on a hard drive. Once one's preferences are known, an advertiser can target the individual with ads that are of potential interest. Significant database information is available to companies that want to pursue direct-marketing and advertising opportunities online. See Figure 12.8 for an illustration.

TRACKING AND ACCOUNTABILITY Advertisers can track how internet users interact with their brands while learning what they are interested in. Advertisers can get timely, detailed reports on the success of their campaign. Some email marketing campaign tools allow a company to watch for results in real time. Banner ads can be tracked the next day—with detailed numbers of impressions and clickthroughs. Many websites that sell advertising provide these detailed reports to clients online. Such measures gauge the effectiveness of the advertising investment. These measurements are difficult—if not impossible—to generate for traditional media.

TIMING The internet doesn't sleep—messages can be delivered 24 hours a day, 7 days a week, 365 days a year. As well, the content of a campaign can be changed at a moment's notice if need be. Technology allows for constant monitoring of a campaign for success or failure, so changes, updates, or cancellations can be made much more quickly than in any other medium.

Traditional Advertising → Online Advertising ← Direct Marketing

Traditional advertising through the mass media delivers messages to create awareness and interest in a product. Direct marketing sends out an offer and allows a customer to buy goods directly from the source. Online advertising does both if websites accommodate ecommerce opportunities.

> FIGURE **12.8**

Online advertising is the convergence of traditional advertising and direct marketing.

INTERACTIVITY AND ACTION Internet users like to be entertained along the way. That being the case, companies have an opportunity to interact with prospects and customers and develop more meaningful relationships with them. Users tend to return often to sites they enjoy. Therefore, appropriate interaction and the provision of information that makes a visit worthwhile can produce sufficient motivation for a prospect or customer to make an online purchase. No other medium can move a consumer from awareness to action as easily as the internet can. Specific software is available that allows organizations to pursue customer-relationship management objectives.

DISADVANTAGES OF ONLINE ADVERTISING

ACCEPTANCE OF ONLINE ADVERTISING While users indicate they do a lot of product research online, they remain skeptical of the adverting they see—it is viewed as more of an interruption or intrusion while they are doing other things. As the quality of online advertising improves and as the medium becomes more like television (e.g., the amount of video content available), the negative perceptions regarding commercialism will gradually change.

CONSUMER FRUSTRATION Consumers are starting to feel frustrated, even harassed, by the constant barrage of unsolicited emails and the presence of ads that were not requested, or arrive unexpectedly. Advertisers who persist in following these practices will ultimately suffer the wrath of frustrated consumers. Advertisers must adopt unique yet acceptable message strategies for the online universe if they are to be successful.

PRIVACY CONCERNS Consumers are very concerned about how information about them is collected and used by marketing and advertising organizations. While the internet has the capability of taking a consumer from awareness to action (purchase), the transfer of personal information and credit card information is the most widely cited reason for resisting online purchases. Consumers do perceive a loss of privacy since access to many sites involves complex registration procedures. With registration, customers give up information about themselves that can be used for marketing purposes at a later date.

Internet Advertising Rates and Buying Media Space

Several different advertising models are available. Since marketers and advertising agencies are accustomed to cost-per-thousand (CPM) comparisons before making critical media decisions, the CPM model is most popular online. Other pricing models include *pay-for-performance* and *flat fees*.

CPM MODEL

CPM is the price charged for displaying an ad 1000 times. The calculation for CPM is cost divided by impressions (number of impressions divided by 1000). For online advertising, an organization pays a rate for every 1000 impressions made. Therefore, if the total number of impressions was 1 000 000 and the CPM was $40.00, the total cost of the advertising campaign would be $40 000 (1 000 000 impressions/1000 × $40.00).

CPM rates vary based on the level of targeting desired by the advertiser, and they range anywhere from $10.00 to $100.00. The options include *run of site, run of category,* and *keyword targeting*. With reference to the rate card for OttawaCitizen.com shown in Figure 12.9, if the run-of-site rates are used, the placements of the ads are predetermined and are quoted based on the size of the ad. For example, a banner ad costs $13/M and a skyscraper ad costs $20/M. Note that there are additional charges for targeting requests (see the lower left corner of Figure 12.9). If targeting requests are applied, a 10-percent premium is charged for each request. Volume discounts may also be available based on the total dollar value of advertising purchased, but these are not included in the figure. To demonstrate, consider the following buying example:

EXAMPLE 1

Type of Ad:	Banner, ottawacitizen.com
Impressions Desired:	2 000 000
CPM:	$13.00
Cost Calculation:	(2 000 000/1 000) × $13 = $26 000

EXAMPLE 2

Type of Ad:	Skyscraper, ottawacitizen.com
Impressions Desired:	3 000 000
CPM:	$20.00
One target request:	+10%
Cost Calculation:	(3 000 000/1 000) × $20 × 1.10 = $66 000

CPM rate cards vary from one site to another, but rest assured the busier sites in terms of traffic charge a higher CPM for all of the options that are available. Popular sites such as Sympatico.msn.ca, Yahoo!, and various sports and media sites (TSN, Rogers Sportsnet, The *Globe and Mail*, to name a few) attract significant traffic and their CPMs are priced accordingly.

While these rates are the rates quoted, the reality of the situation is quite similar to offline advertising. CPM rates are negotiable and depend on factors such as length of the campaign, season, and relationship between client and vendor. Effective negotiation skills in the media-buying process could result in lower CPM rates.

PAY-FOR-PERFORMANCE MODEL

Advertisers must remember that the purpose of the banner is to stir initial interest so that the viewer clicks the ad for more information. Once clicked, the viewer sees the ad in its entirety, as in the case of a video ad or a link to the advertiser's website. Since clicking is the desired action, many advertisers feel they should pay on the basis of cost per click instead of CPM.

This system tends to devalue advertising and punish the website financially if the ad does not attract an audience. In the offline advertising world, the media are not responsible for an action being taken. That is left to the message! The job of the media is to offer access to an audience, not to share in the responsibility for the quality of the advertising itself.

The type of ad and the message content has an impact on clickthrough. For example, the cleverness of the message, along with a certain degree of targeting, can improve the clickthrough rate. Banners, for example, average about 0.5 percent, while rich media ads are in the 2.7-percent range. These figures may seem low, but if millions of internet users are exposed to the ad (impressions) the number of people who actually click for more information soon grows. Once a user clicks, the task is to convert a prospect into a buyer. Many campaigns are actually evaluated on the conversion rate.

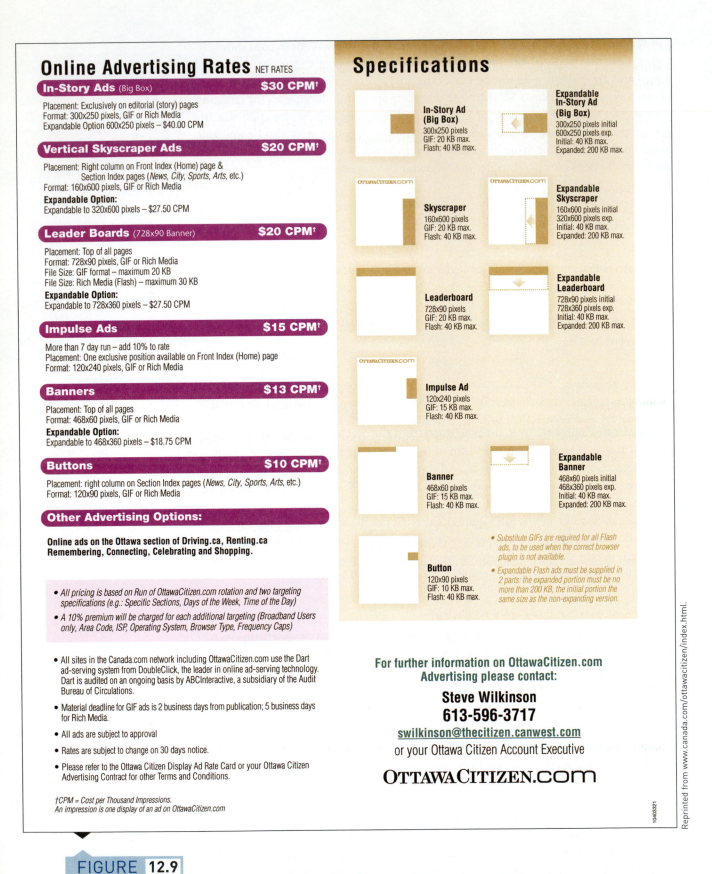

Online Advertising Rates NET RATES

In-Story Ads (Big Box) $30 CPM†
Placement: Exclusively on editorial (story) pages
Format: 300x250 pixels, GIF or Rich Media
Expandable Option 600x250 pixels – $40.00 CPM

Vertical Skyscraper Ads $20 CPM†
Placement: Right column on Front Index (Home) page &
        Section Index pages (News, City, Sports, Arts, etc.)
Format: 160x600 pixels, GIF or Rich Media
Expandable Option:
Expandable to 320x600 pixels – $27.50 CPM

Leader Boards (728x90 Banner) $20 CPM†
Placement: Top of all pages
Format: 728x90 pixels, GIF or Rich Media
File Size: GIF format – maximum 20 KB
File Size: Rich Media (Flash) – maximum 30 KB
Expandable Option:
Expandable to 728x360 pixels – $27.50 CPM

Impulse Ads $15 CPM†
More than 7 day run – add 10% to rate
Placement: One exclusive position available on Front Index (Home) page
Format: 120x240 pixels, GIF or Rich Media

Banners $13 CPM†
Placement: Top of all pages
Format: 468x60 pixels, GIF or Rich Media
Expandable Option:
Expandable to 468x360 pixels – $18.75 CPM

Buttons $10 CPM†
Placement: right column on Section Index pages (News, City, Sports, Arts, etc.)
Format: 120x90 pixels, GIF or Rich Media

Other Advertising Options:

Online ads on the Ottawa section of Driving.ca, Renting.ca
Remembering, Connecting, Celebrating and Shopping.

- *All pricing is based on Run of OttawaCitizen.com rotation and two targeting specifications (e.g.: Specific Sections, Days of the Week, Time of the Day)*
- *A 10% premium will be charged for each additional targeting (Broadband Users only, Area Code, ISP, Operating System, Browser Type, Frequency Caps)*

- All sites in the Canada.com network including OttawaCitizen.com use the Dart ad-serving system from DoubleClick, the leader in online ad-serving technology. Dart is audited on an ongoing basis by ABCInteractive, a subsidiary of the Audit Bureau of Circulations.
- Material deadline for GIF ads is 2 business days from publication; 5 business days for Rich Media.
- All ads are subject to approval
- Rates are subject to change on 30 days notice.
- Please refer to the Ottawa Citizen Display Ad Rate Card or your Ottawa Citizen Advertising Contract for other Terms and Conditions.

†CPM = Cost per Thousand Impressions.
An impression is one display of an ad on OttawaCitizen.com

Specifications

In-Story Ad (Big Box)
300x250 pixels
GIF: 20 KB max.
Flash: 40 KB max.

Expandable In-Story Ad (Big Box)
300x250 pixels initial
600x250 pixels exp.
Initial: 40 KB max.
Expanded: 200 KB max.

Skyscraper
160x600 pixels
GIF: 20 KB max.
Flash: 40 KB max.

Expandable Skyscraper
160x600 pixels initial
320x600 pixels exp.
Initial: 40 KB max.
Expanded: 200 KB max.

Leaderboard
728x90 pixels
GIF: 20 KB max.
Flash: 40 KB max.

Expandable Leaderboard
728x90 pixels initial
728x360 pixels exp.
Initial: 40 KB max.
Expanded: 200 KB max.

Impulse Ad
120x240 pixels
GIF: 15 KB max.
Flash: 40 KB max.

Banner
468x60 pixels
GIF: 15 KB max.
Flash: 40 KB max.

Expandable Banner
468x60 pixels initial
468x360 pixels exp.
Initial: 40 KB max.
Expanded: 200 KB max.

Button
120x90 pixels
GIF: 10 KB max.
Flash: 40 KB max.

- *Substitute GIFs are required for all Flash ads, to be used when the correct browser plugin is not available.*
- *Expandable Flash ads must be supplied in 2 parts: the expanded portion must be no more than 200 KB, the initial portion the same size as the non-expanding version.*

For further information on OttawaCitizen.com Advertising please contact:

Steve Wilkinson
613-596-3717
swilkinson@thecitizen.canwest.com
or your Ottawa Citizen Account Executive

OttawaCitizen.com

FIGURE 12.9

Online rate card for the
Ottawa Citizen

FLAT-FEE MODEL

Some websites charge a flat fee for advertising—typically, a set amount for the length of time the ad appears on the site. This practice is more common for sponsorships of contests or other special activities on a website. For example, a site such as TSN.ca might offer a flat rate sponsorship opportunity to an advertiser in combination with a CPM or pay-for-performance advertising package. Fee structures vary from one site to another. Lower traffic sites are more likely to use the flat-fee system.

Other Forms of Online Marketing Communications

There are other communications strategies available to marketers beyond advertising. Techniques referred to as podcasting and blogging are growing in popularity. Both options provide an organization the opportunity to deliver a more detailed and meaningful message. Corporate and brand websites also play an important role in the marketing communications mix.

PODCASTING

A **podcast** is a digital media file that is distributed over the internet for playback on portable media players and personal computers. The term podcast originates from the name of Apple's portable music player, the iPod. People can subscribe to podcasts they are interested in, and when new episodes become available they are automatically downloaded to the user's computer for listening or viewing (if video is included) whenever it is convenient.

Scotiabank was one of the first corporations in Canada to employ podcasting in its media mix. Their *MoneyClip* podcast series is the audio version of *MyVault News*, Scotiabank's digital newsletter. The podcasts feature straightforward advice and information to help people achieve their money-related goals. A host interviews a variety of experts on topics such as investing, retirement planning, home ownership and ways to save.[14]

Podcasts are developing to the point where some podcasters are offering advertising opportunities within the podcast. For example, the host can promote a sponsoring product during a podcast, or a pre-roll or post-roll ad (concepts presented earlier in the chapter) can be included with the podcast. From a message perspective, it is important that a podcast flow naturally—it shouldn't sound like it is being read from a prepared script. The more real and sincere it sounds, the more impact it will have on the listener.

BLOGGING

A **blog** is a website where journal entries are posted on a regular basis and displayed in reverse chronological order. Blogs provide commentary on news or particular subjects of interest such as politics, food, fashion, and so on. A typical blog includes text, images, and links to other blogs. Blogs are the property and works of everyday people who like to rant about things they like or don't like, and very often they will challenge the integrity of an organization in their blog—a situation beyond the control of an organization.

Anyone with a computer and internet connection can create a blog (be a blogger). To demonstrate, Michael Marx loves Barq's root beer (a Coca-Cola brand) and he keeps a blog dedicated to the brand (thebarqsman.com). He collects news about Barq's, commercials he likes, and posts musings on why he thinks Barq's is the best. The blog is written without the consent of Coca-Cola. But with so much good information being communicated about the brand, why would Coca-Cola object to it?[15]

Marketers and advertisers must find ways of employing blogs in the communications mix. A corporate blog, for example, can be an effective way to present relevant information in a positive manner. The blog provides an opportunity for the organization to be part of the discussion on matters that are very important to its well-being. It can be the human voice of the company!

Procter & Gamble has already benefited from blogs. When it launched Mr. Clean AutoDry, a car-washing product that dries spot-free, auto enthusiasts were trading notes about the product in auto blogs. To seed more discussion, P&G gave away AutoDry kits to bloggers, asking for their honest review. Some 80 percent gave the item a thumbs-up. Before the product had even reached the store shelves, brand awareness was 25 percent among consumers and 45 percent among car enthusiasts. Prominent retailers had no choice but to carry the product.[16]

COMPANY AND BRAND WEBSITES

Traditional forms of advertising can tell a story, but not necessarily the complete story. Therefore, traditional media combined with effective website content gives an advertiser ample opportunity to tell the whole story. Advertisers should include their website address in all forms of marketing communications.

To demonstrate how traditional media and websites can be combined, consider the nature of automobile advertising. Typically, automobile makers show unique and vivid visual images of their latest makes and models in television ads and glossy print ads. These ads project image but do little in terms of telling potential buyers about design and technical specifications. That task is best suited to the website.

Toyota Canada
www.toyota.ca

Toyota Canada overhauled its website in order to accommodate the needs of its visitors. Toyota's goal was to tap into the consumer's online information-gathering process. According to David Brinson, national manager for public relations and marketing, "Consumers now arrive at showrooms with an almost predestined vision of what they want. We have to provide them the best knowledge and information to help them make decisions." Toyota's design and communications strategy was structured to flow logically with the consumer's thought process when shopping. After the "Welcome to Toyota" introduction on the website, consumers move to model offerings, then to information areas such as safety and how to choose a colour, then to a car configuration page, and finally to a price quote and financing information.[17] Refer to the illustration in Figure 12.10 for details.

Organizations also establish microsites that serve unique purposes. A **microsite** is an individual webpage or series of pages that function as a supplement to a primary website. For example, Unilever has a corporate website in which all brands may have a page. However, for new product launches or high-profile brands, they will create a microsite with its own address. Such is the case of Axe deodorant.

Axe deodorant and body spray, a brand noted for its sexual benefits (at least that's what the target market is led to believe), uses its site to attract male customers. At **www.axe.ca** there is a sexy downloadable widget named Mindi to decorate desktops and extend the Axe experience from the site. "Multi-interfaced new dimensional intelligence" —Mindi—is new to the Axe site. When users download her, they get a video experience of her moving in to their desktops—she even unpacks her clothes, including sexy lingerie. When users turn on their computer Mindi greets them and offers a dating tip of the day. "It's a great way to engage consumers," says David Allard, Axe brand manager at Unilever.[18] For an illustration see Figure 12.11.

FIGURE 12.10

Toyota places high priority on web-based communications. Print ads create an image, and web-based communications provide details

FIGURE 12.11

The AXE website plays a key role in brand communications

Mobile Communications

Canadians have embraced cell phones to the point where they have become one of the fastest-growing consumer products ever. As of June 2006 some 17 million people (54 percent of the population) had a cell phone. "Cell phones have quickly proven to be an integral part of the personal and business lives of Canadians."[19] Cell phone penetration is highest among 18- to 34-year-olds (74 percent); almost as high among 35- to 54-year-olds (72 percent), while less than half of individuals in the 55-plus category own one.

Today, almost every cell phone sold can be outfitted with any or all of the following features: the ability to email and access the web, snap photographs or take videos, send and retrieve multimedia messages, download ring tones, and play music and games. Essentially, the cell phone is some combination of a personal computer, TV, and MP3 player. Opportunities for advertisers to communicate with consumers exist through text messaging, video messaging, and online video games and they can do so in a targeted manner. For additional insight into how Canadians are interacting with cell phones see Figure 12.12.

TEXT MESSAGING

Text messaging (also called **short message service** or SMS) is the transmission of text-only messages on wireless devices such as cell phones. Teens and young adults are attracted to text messaging because of its portability and low cost. To them, email is too slow—kids want instant messaging, whether using their cell phones or online chat services such as ICQ. While making voice calls remains the primary function of cell phones, the popularity of BlackBerry devices for email has allowed text messaging to emerge as a popular communications tool.[20]

The multi-purpose use of cell phones and other portable devices has yet to be fully explored by content providers, but to date the delivery of most content has been subscription based. Even though there is a threat of public backlash, if advertising takes hold on cell phones, consumers will gradually adapt to the practice, as they have done with the internet. It will be the younger generations of consumers that make or break the cell phone marketing-communications market.

Mobile phones have become the third information and entertainment screen for Canadian youth along with the TV and personal computers. A recent study conducted for Motorola Canada by Research Strategy Group revealed that people aged 15 to 34 spend 23 percent of their time using mobile phones; 37 percent watching TV, and 40 percent using a home computer. How people use their mobile phone is described below:

Function/Activity	Engaged in Activity (%)
Send and receive calls	98
Text messaging	61
Download ring tones	44
Play video games	32
Send and receive photos	22
Send and receive email	20
Access news, weather, and sports	14
Record and share video clips	7

Source: Adapted from "Canadian youth interacting with three screens," *Media in Canada*, October 20, 2005, www.mediaincanada.com. © Brunico Communications Ltd. Media in Canada is the trademark of Brunico Communications Ltd.

FIGURE 12.12

The small screen plays a key role in the lives of Canadians.

Marketers interested in reaching the youth market are looking seriously at text messaging. It is one of the latest weapons in the arsenal of marketing tactics used to reach youth. Advertisers are asking consumers to take time to text message and interact with their brands. Marketers now add "call-to-action" short codes to their marketing materials (such as outdoor posters, transit ads, and bottle caps). Cell phone users can punch in the codes in order to participate in contests, download free music, and receive ring tones or merchandise.

Molson Canada has used text messaging successfully as an marketing tactic, and they see it as an important CRM tool. Ross Buchanan, senior manager, relationship marketing, at Molson, says the brewer has "built everything off the short code we have ownership of: 665766, which spells out Molson." Molson implements SMS campaigns at most events of which it is a major sponsor. Canadian Rocks, for example, offers audiences at the Molson Amphitheatre a chance to upgrade to the best seats in the house. At the event, consumers type into their phones the Molson short code and a specific keyword promoted at the venue in order to be notified just before the headliner hits the stage. Refer to Figure 12.13 for an illustration. To develop a relationship with the customer, Molson sends a text message to all mobile users that responded to the promotion, asking if they'd like to receive ongoing communications about music. If they accept, they become a Molson Insider and receive special and exclusive information about events. Molson now has a database of one million names.[21]

All marketers must be careful how they use cell phones. If the messages are overly intrusive, their attempts could backfire. Too much commercialism is not a good thing among today's skeptical youth. It would also be dangerous for wireless carriers to open up their databases to commercial interests without having an opt-in from their customers. The risk of losing customers is a strong incentive for carriers to keep down the advertising noise.

FIGURE **12.13**

Molson builds customer relationships through text messaging

VIDEO MESSAGING

Broadcasters and other content providers see mobile as a rich content channel to promote television programs, films, and music. **Video messaging** is the next generation of cell phone communications. Using a subscription pricing model, consumers can download news and sports clips and selected television shows from major networks. The BlackBerry device is offering a television service called bbTV in partnership with Rogers Wireless and CanWest MediaWorks. The service offers 30- to 90-second audio and video content from Global TV programming and Rogers Sportsnet sports highlights. All downloads on bbTV begin and end with five-second ads. The service's first advertisers include Royal Bank, General Motors, Labatt, and McNeil Consumer Healthcare.

Whether or not consumers will enjoy watching video content on such a small screen is a question yet to be answered. Hugh Dow, president of M2 Universal, a media-buying agency, sees a bright future. He says, "We're living in a mobile generation now, where consumers are using a variety of ways to stay connected and receive information on the go. It is an important platform for reaching specific target markets."[22]

Marketers are excited about text messaging and video messaging due to the intimacy and immediacy of these forms of communication. Many cell phones are equipped with global positioning systems, so ads can be sent to consumers based on their location. The limiting factor so far is technology. Currently, there are only about one million phones on the market capable of playing video. However, industry experts are forecasting that as many as 18 million Canadians will own cell phones with video capability by the end of 2008.[23]

Video Game Advertising (Advergaming)

Advergaming refers to the integration of brands into video games, both games played online and games purchased directly by consumers. Integration of brands into games can generate positive brand awareness, higher brand preference ratings, and help achieve purchases. Video game advertising has initially been popular among male teenagers, as research indicates 49 percent of them visit game sites regularly. However, the profile of the typical gamer is changing. More females now play games online. The current split between male and female online gamers is 58 percent male and 42 percent female. Online gaming is also becoming the opiate of the middle class—80 percent of online gamers are from households with incomes between $35 000 and $75 000.[24] Knowing this profile, such traditional blue-chip advertisers as Procter & Gamble, Coca-Cola, Dell, Nokia, and Burger King have jumped into video game advertising.

Cadbury Adams used branded games to create awareness for some new flavours of Trident gum. Regular television and in-store advertising encouraged consumers to visit a game site to compete in a variety of adventure games. By playing the game, consumers could collect points towards weekly prizes such as MP3 players, and a grand prize of $10 000. The average user returned to the site 4 times and spent 40 minutes interacting with the brand.[25]

Social Network Media

The growth and development of social networks is changing the way in which marketers view their brands and customers. A **social network** connects people with different types of interests at one website. At the website, people become friends and form communities—in effect the community could be viewed as a potential target market. Refer to the illustration in Figure 12.14.

TYPES OF SOCIAL NETWORKS

Let's start the discussion of social networks by describing the various types of networks that exist. First there are **broad-reach sites** such as MySpace, YouTube, and Facebook. These sites offer an interactive, user-created network of friends, personal profiles, blogs, music, and videos. There are also **demographically focused sites** where communication is focused on issue-based interests shared by the community. The site www.care2.com, for example, deals with green living and activism. Finally, there are **specific topic sites** that focus on one subject. For example, Dogster is a dog lovers' site and Flixster is a site where members share film reviews and ratings. By far, broad-reach sites dominate the social networks, and their reach is significant: YouTube has 10.6 million unique visitors in Canada, Facebook has 8.8 million, and MySpace, 5.6 million.[26] Surprisingly, baby boomers are the largest group of visitors at MySpace and Facebook. Refer to Figure 12.15 for details.

Facebook
www.facebook.com

FIGURE **12.14**

Facebook is a popular social network destination for Canadians

Courtesy of www.facebook.com.

FIGURE **12.15**

Visitors to social network sites by age

Social network sites are visited by people of all ages, but, interestingly, baby boomers are the largest single group of visitors. This should be of interest to advertisers.

Ages	MySpace (%)	Facebook (%)	Xanga (%)	Total Internet (%)
12–17	11.9	14.0	20.3	9.6
18–24	18.1	34.0	15.5	11.3
25–34	16.7	8.6	11.0	14.5
35–54	40.6	33.5	35.6	38.5
55+	11.0	7.6	7.3	18.0
Unique Visitors (000)	55 778	14 782	8066	173 407

Source: Data from comScore Networks via *eMarketer* for August 2006.

SOCIAL NETWORK COMMUNICATIONS

Social networks have given real people real power. There is a shift in power from the brand marketer to the consumer marketer. This may sound rather strange, but social networks have given everyday people the opportunity to upload video content and much of it is brand-oriented content. It seems that anyone with a computer can get into the message-creation business!

User-generated messages delivered on social networks, or advertising messages created by amateur videographers, often carry more weight with consumers than marketer-generated content. **Consumer-generated content** refers to content created by consumers for consumers. It is done without external inducement and in many cases presents the brand effectively. A consumer-generated ad for the Apple mini iPod that appears on YouTube is one such example—check it out! Commercial news reports now cite bloggers as information sources—another sign of message legitimacy. This shift in power has been termed "brand democratization" by online communication experts.

To demonstrate the concept of brand democratization, consider the situation Apple faced when it launched its first-generation iPod. There was a problem with the life of the battery. Millions of disgruntled iPodders conferred on multiple websites, and Apple had no choice but to create a workaround to satisfy their unhappy customers. Who owns the brand? Is it Apple or is it the customer?

As marketing organizations move into the future, they are going to have to learn how to take advantage of brand democratization. The fact that consumers create content on their behalf should not be seen as a negative. There's an expression: "Any publicity is good publicity." Whether it is true or not is debatable, but, if consumers create and upload content and it is viewed by millions of people, there must be some benefit for the brand. The advent of consumer-generated content means that the consumers can participate in the marketing of the brand—they can create messages and even change the image of a brand. It sounds frightening, but essentially it is that ultimate form of engagement that so many marketers are searching for.

Initially, marketers were skeptical of the communications potential of these sites, but they have come to realize that tens of millions of people hang out there. These are people who are avoiding television commercials. Site owners and advertisers are trying to find ways to integrate branded content in order to take advantage of the word-of-mouth effects of networking sites. Positive word-of-mouth gives a brand momentum. There is nothing more powerful in the online world than when a customer uses a brand as a reference point in their profile, or when a person passes brand information along to a friend. Advertising opportunities also exist. At many social network sites the standard online advertising options discussed earlier in the chapter are available.

Are the advertisers buying in? Two key brands, Axe and Coca-Cola, certainly are. Axe has become the leading deodorant brand based on the promise that it helps men attract females. Axe recently implemented a promotion around a group called Gamekillers—people who get in the way of a seduction. The pitch is that Axe helps men stay cool in the face of Gamekillers. A page on MySpace was devoted to the topic, with message boards where people could trade complaints and tips about Gamekillers. The campaign enticed 250 000 people to take the Gamekillers quiz on the MySpace page.[27]

Coca-Cola went directly to YouTube with a crafty advertisement based on the popular PlayStation2 game, "Grand Theft Auto." The ad featured a video game character that spreads joy and happiness rather than the death and mayhem for which the game is well known. The ad was an online success, reaching 500 000 viewers in a one-month period. While the ad did not garner much mainstream media attention, it received rave reviews from bloggers and viewers.[28]

MEASURING THE IMPACT OF SOCIAL NETWORK COMMUNICATIONS

Unlike relatively traditional online advertising where clicks and conversion rates can be measured electronically, similar measurements do not exist in the social network environment. Advertisers have to look at a softer set of measurement tools to judge whether or not a communications effort was successful. For example, Volkswagen placed a new crop of finished commercials on YouTube and only a handful of people viewed them.

Then a user uploaded a grainy version of one of the commercials and it was viewed 1.7 million times.[29] If there is a lesson here, it might read as follows: sometimes things that are unplanned work best!

The viral nature of the internet generally, and social network sites specifically, is real. It doesn't take long for word-of-mouth (or is that word-of-mouse?) to spread on these sites. The viral component is a true indicator of communications success or failure. Dove created a 75-second video ad titled "Evolution" that used a time-lapse technique to show an imperfect woman being transformed into a billboard model through make-up, lighting, and digital editing. When the ad was posted on YouTube it was viewed by more than four million people. The Dove brand received significant publicity on TV talk shows such as *Ellen* and *Entertainment Tonight*. "This is better return on investment than we could ever have expected," said Alison Leung, Dove marketing manager for Unilever Canada.[30]

Marketers that realize the difference between offline communities and online communities will reap the benefits of online communications. To the online community the Dove message was highly acceptable—it caught their attention, it was fast-paced and innovative, and was discussed by millions of viewers—another measurement of success! The challenge for other advertisers is to figure out effective ways of integrating brands into the online community experience so that users respond to and interact with the brand in a positive manner

Unilever Canada
www.unilever.ca

SUMMARY

Companies are turning away from traditional advertising media such as television and newspapers and toward direct-response and interactive communications, and for good reason. Canadians are leaders in internet consumption, and as a medium it has surpassed outdoor, radio, and magazine advertising in terms of revenue.

The key elements of the internet are email and World Wide Web sites. Both are efficient ways to communicate information. Currently, the internet is widely used for information purposes, but advertisers are finding that online advertising, when combined with other media, produces substantial increases in brand awareness and brand sponsorship associations. Internet users tend to be younger, highly educated, and earn above-average incomes. These demographics make them an attractive target for advertisers.

Advertisers must tread carefully so as not to offend users. Unlike traditional media, the challenge for online advertisers is to create interesting interactive communications without alienating users. In the online world, marketing communications has to be entertaining as well as informative. To be successful, advertisers must adopt unique advertising messages that are acceptable to online users.

The online advertising industry is composed of sellers, buyers, and infrastructure companies. On the buying side are advertisers and advertising agencies. The selling side embraces a host of large independent websites along with advertising networks that represent a number of smaller websites. Web measurement is an important and controversial aspect of the internet. In this area, independent third-party companies such as Nielsen/NetRatings and comScore Media Metrix provide audited data that assists advertisers and agencies in planning advertising campaigns. Data compiled by these and other research organizations legitimize the internet as an advertising medium.

Interactive communications strategies can be tailored more directly to consumer preferences, a concept referred to as behavioural targeting. When this concept is applied, the ads that appear on screen are related to the consumer's previous surfing behaviour.

There is a variety of advertising alternatives to choose from. Among the options are display advertising, which includes banner and rich media in a variety of shapes, sizes, and degrees of sophistication. Other options include full-motion video, search advertising, sponsorships on other websites, email ads, and webisodes. Email advertising is popular since it is a cost-efficient way to reach prospects and current customers. Advertisers must be wary of consumers' frustration with spam, which is unwanted junk email. Online video ads are growing in popularity due to their similarity to television ads (users get a sense of familiarity based on their experience with traditional advertising media).

As an advertising medium, the internet offers targeting capability at a very reasonable cost and tracking capabilities that measure effectiveness of campaigns in a variety of ways (clicks, leads, and purchases). As well, the interactive nature of the medium provides an environment that fosters the building of solid relationships with customers. The fact that the internet is open 24/7 means an advertiser's message is always at hand. Some drawbacks of the internet include selective reach (higher-educated and higher-income groups are the main users), consumers' frustration with unwanted email and pop-up ads that appear on screens, and the perception among users that advertisers are invading their privacy.

Online advertising rates are typically quoted on a cost-per-thousand-impressions basis. Other options include cost-per-clickthrough and flat fees. Currently, the CPM pricing model is the model used most frequently by websites and online advertising networks.

Other forms of online communications include podcasts, blogs, and corporate and brand websites. Using any of these alternatives allows the advertiser to present information in a detailed and more meaningful manner. Advertising opportunities that are available through other online sources are also available in many podcasts and blogs.

Mobile media represent new opportunities to deliver advertising messages. Electronic devices such as cell phones and personal digital assistants are part of the daily lives of consumers. Text messaging is a relatively new medium, but it allows for consumers and brands to interact with each other, a definite step in developing brand loyalty. The next generation of cell phones will offer video capabilities, an even stronger way to deliver a message. Marketers are attracted to mobile media based on the immediacy and intimacy they offer.

Finally, video games are proving to be an effective means of reaching youth and young male adults. Both segments are spending more time playing games than they are watching television. Advertisers must capitalize on this trend and adjust their media budgets accordingly.

Online social networks such as MySpace and YouTube, among many others, represent unique advertising opportunities for the very near future. Currently, these sites feature user-generated content, some of which is composed of commercials generated by amateurs. Companies are placing their own commercials on social network sites, hoping that positive word-of-mouth (buzz) will generate views. The viral nature of the internet (users passing along information to friends) is another benefit for advertisers.

KEY TERMS

REVIEW QUESTIONS

1. What characteristics make the internet user different from users of traditional media?

2. Explain the concept of behavioural targeting as it applies to online communications.

3. Explain the following terms as they relate to advertising on the internet:

   a) click
   b) clickthrough rate
   c) ad network
   d) impression
   e) visit

4. What is search advertising, and how does it work?

5. What is banner advertising, and how does it work?

6. Identify and briefly explain the various types of banner ads.

7. What does "rich media" refer to? Briefly explain.

8. Briefly explain how an online advertising sponsorship works.

9. Briefly explain the following internet communications terms:

   a) permission-based email
   b) opt-in
   c) spam
   d) webisode
   e) podcast
   f) blog
   g) consumer-generated content

10. What does the term "advergaming" refer to?

11. Identify and briefly explain two advantages and two disadvantages of online advertising.

12. Briefly describe the different types of social media networks.

13. What is the CPM pricing model and how does it work? What factors influence the price charged in the CPM model?

14. If the CPM is $30.00 and the banner ad campaign achieves 1.5 million impressions, what is the total cost of the campaign?

15. If the total cost for a banner campaign was $30 000 and the impressions generated a total of 1.2 million, what is the CPM for the campaign?

16. How is a pay-for-performance advertising model different from the CPM model? What are the drawbacks for the web publisher if the pay-for-performance model is used?

DISCUSSION QUESTIONS

1. How important is interactive marketing communications now, and how important will it be in the future? Will it remain a complementary medium, or will it dominate the media mix? Describe and defend your opinion on this issue.

2. "Persistent invasions of consumer privacy will be the undoing of internet-based advertising." Is this statement true or false? Conduct some secondary research online to update the status of this issue. Report on your findings.

3. Visit the Yahoo! website or another portal website of your choosing and type a few keywords in the search box. Use general search terms such as finance, hockey, music, and movies. Do the ads on the search results page seem targeted in any way, and are they linked to the keyword? Report on your findings.

4. How important will mobile communications be in the future? Will consumers be accepting of advertising messages in this medium or will they perceive them to be a nuisance? Describe and defend your opinion on this issue.

5. Is email advertising an effective medium for traditional mainstream advertisers to employ? Research this issue and report on your findings.

6. Review how the pay-for-performance model for advertising on the internet works. What is your opinion on this model? Examine the situation from both the advertiser's and the website's perspective.

NOTES

1. Interactive Advertising Bureau, 2007, **www.iabcanada.com**.

2. Samantha Yaffe, "Are marketers undervaluing the internet?" *Strategy Media*, March 8, 2004, p. 1.

3. "Canadian internet use survey," *The Daily*, August 15, 2006, Statistics Canada, **www.statcan.ca**.

4. Tom Siebert, "Publicis acquires Digitas, moves to become dominant digital player," *Media Post Publications*, December 21, 2006, **www.mediapost.com**.

5. Louise Story, "Web advertising to be subject to stricter measurements," *Financial Post*, October 31, 2006, p. FP17.

6. "Get targeted," *Essential Interactive*, volume 3, p. 14.

7. Canadian Media Directors' Council, *Media Digest*, 2006–2007, p. 75.

8. "*Globe* to reach *Holmes on Homes* fans through online streaming," *Media in Canada*, October 16, 2006, **www.mediaincanada.com**.

9. Patti Summerfield, "Roll 'em," *Strategy*, January 2007, p. 29

10. Abbey Klaassen, "Ad age search marketing fact pack released," *Advertising Age*, November 5, 2006, **www.adage.com**.

11. "A sample search," Search Marketing Fact Pack, *Advertising Age*, **www.adage.com**.

12. "Driving email ROI," *Essential Interactive*, volume 3, p. 22.

13. Keith McArthur, "Webisodes are the new frontier of Internet ads," *Globe and Mail*, June 4, p. B1.

14. "The money clip podcast," **www.scotiabank.com**.

15. Tania Ralli, "Brand blogs capture the attention of some companies," *New York Times*, October 24, 2005, **www.nytimes.com**.

16. Kris Oser, "More marketers test blogs to build buzz," *Advertising Age*, September 13, 2004, pp. 3, 49.

17. Samson Okalow, "Marketers retool sites to exploit Web research boom," *Strategy*, May 3, 2004, p. 11.

18. "Axe's sexy widget," *Strategy*, October 2006, p. 9.

19. "Mobile revolution," *Mobile in Motion*, 2006, p. 4.

20. Chris Daniels, "The new frontier," *Essential Interactive*, Volume 2, p. 24.

21. "To text, and beyond," *Mobile in Motion*, 2006, p. 8.

22. "New in mobile," *Mobile in Motion*, 2006, p. 15.

23. *Ibid.*, p. 18.

24. Beth Snyder Buliki, "Who is today's gamer? You have No Idea," *Advertising Age*, May 14, 2007, p. 28.

25. Daniels, p. 26.

26. comScore Media Metrix Canada, Total Audience, April 2007.

27. Saul Hansell, "Joining the party, eager to make friends," *New York Times*, October 16, 2006, pp. C1, C8.

28. Ian Harvey, "Big business climbs aboard social media bandwagon," *The Globe and Mail*, September 21, 2006, p. B12.

29. Hansell, pp. C1, C8.

30. "The hard sell," *Globe and Mail*, November 21, 2006, p. B4.

Media Strategy and Execution:
UNIQUE MEDIA STRATEGIES YIELD GOOD RESULTS

Sears Capitalizes on Branded Content

At Christmas time, people are inundated with flyers and catalogues—it's a world of shopping right at one's finger tips. The media objective for Sears Christmas Wish Book was to break through the clutter.

MEDIA STRATEGY

A branded content strategy was recommended by ad agency Mediaedge:cia. Research findings indicated that viewers of the popular Canadian show *Corner Gas* were more likely to be catalogue shoppers. The show would be a perfect media vehicle if Sears could get beyond mere product placement. Once a deal was struck, the Sears Wish Book was successfully woven into the show's storyline.

MEDIA EXECUTION

Brent Butt, the writer and star of the show, was enthusiastic about including the Sears Christmas Wish Book in the show: "Sears was the perfect match for the program." At the beginning of the episode, four of the show's main characters reminisced about using the catalogue to shop when they were kids. Sears sponsored the program with billboards, and CTV included Sears in all pre-promotion for the episode—TV, newspaper, and radio spots were used to promote the show.

RESULTS

The pre-Christmas exposure for Sears and the Sears Wish Book catalogue resulted in strong sales for the season. That particular episode was the most watched episode of the season, attracting over two million viewers. See the illustration below.

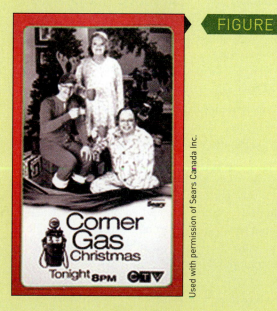

FIGURE 1

Used with permission of Sears Canada Inc.

BestBuy.ca Goes Interactive

Best Buy is committed to giving their customers a positive shopping experience, whether they buy in stores or online. Their product lines include consumer electronics, home office and entertainment products, and software.

MEDIA OBJECTIVE

In the electronics industry the "Daily Special" campaign format is popular. These campaigns are time-sensitive and encourage shoppers to purchase featured products during off hours (when stores are closed). The objective of the Best Buy campaign was to launch an Early Bird Offer and measure responses to a new twist on the Daily Special concept. Objectives were established for sales volume, conversion performance, and clickthrough performance.

MEDIA STRATEGY

The Early Bird campaign was targeted at early risers and offered customers different product and category discounts each day. Best Buy used Yahoo! Canada as their online advertising partner. Yahoo! offered rich media ads across their network and had the ability to target their audience by the time of day.

MEDIA EXECUTION

Ads were scheduled between 5 and 11 a.m. on weekdays. Rich media ads with a real-time countdown clock indicated the time sensitivity of the offer. Banner ads in different sizes provided message reach across Yahoo! Ads were placed to reach only Ontario and Quebec customers.

RESULTS

The campaign achieved a 200-percent conversion rate lift over past campaigns on Yahoo! Canada. Clickthrough rates were above the average for similar campaigns. Success was attributed to the flexibility of daypart targeting (Best Buy was at the right place at the right time with their offers), the sense of urgency communicated in the ads, and ad placements across the Yahoo! network. Daypart targeting is now a staple element of Best Buy's time-sensitive ad campaigns. See the illustration in Figure 2.

FIGURE 2

Source: Adapted from "Case study: Sears," *Strategy*, October 2006, p. 38; and "Case study: Interactive by example, Bestbuy.ca Day Part," *Essential Interactive*, Volume 3, p. 17.

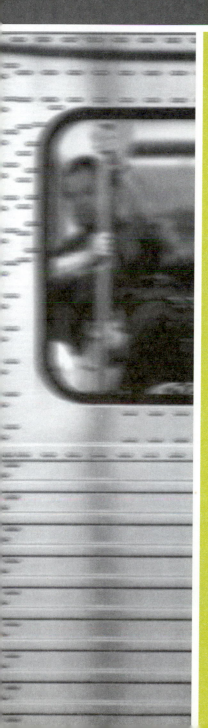

PART 5

Communicating the Message:
INTEGRATED MEDIA CHOICES

Part 5 looks at the various marketing and promotional choices that enhance the communications plan.

Chapter 13 introduces various sales promotion alternatives that are frequently used in integrated marketing communications campaigns. Discussion is divided between consumer promotions and trade promotions, with each area examined for its ability to achieve marketing and marketing communications objectives.

Chapter 14 describes the role of public relations, and event marketing and sponsorships in the integrated marketing communications mix. Various public relations techniques are introduced along with some principles for planning a public relations campaign. Event marketing and sponsorships now play a more prominent role in an organization's marketing communications mix. The strategic considerations for participating in an event, and the various benefits and drawbacks of such participation, are discussed in this chapter.

CHAPTER 13

Sales Promotion

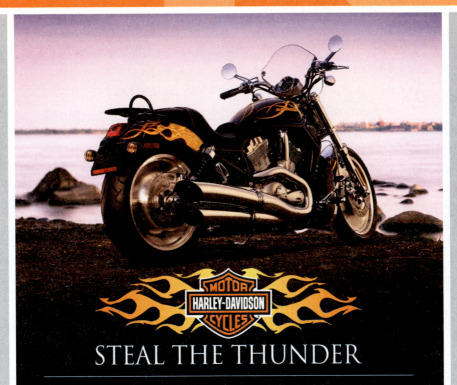

Courtesy of Larter Associates Inc.

After studying this chapter, you will be able to

1. Identify the roles of various consumer and trade promotion activities in the marketing communications process

2. Outline the nature of various consumer and trade promotion activities

3. Assess strategies for integrating sales promotions into the marketing communications mix

This chapter examines the various sales promotion activities that are often integrated into a marketing communications program or marketing program. In the context of marketing communications planning, the manager must evaluate the contribution that sales promotion activity will make to the achievement of overall objectives. Assuming sales promotions are a worthwhile strategy, decisions are made regarding the types of promotions to implement. For example, some promotions are good at achieving trial purchase, while other promotions are good at achieving multiple purchases or for building brand loyalty.

Initial discussion reviews the nature and intent of promotion activity in general. The various types of consumer promotion and trade promotion activities are presented, followed by a discussion of how sales promotions are integrated with other marketing communications strategies.

Sales Promotion

Sales promotion can be defined as activity that provides special incentives to bring about immediate response from consumers, distributors, and an organization's sales force; in other words, it encourages the decision to buy. Sales promotion plans are developed with three groups in mind. The *consumer,* or final user, must be motivated to take advantage of the promotion offer. The *distributor* must actively support the promotion to achieve its goals—greater volume of sales, higher profit margins, inventory movement, and more. Finally, the *sales force* must be motivated to sell the promotion to the trade at the wholesale and retail levels, in order to make the promotion work successfully for the firm.

Sales promotion activity can be subdivided into two broad categories: consumer promotions and trade promotions. **Consumer promotions** refer to those activities that are designed to stimulate consumer purchase, in effect to help pull the product through the distribution channel. Common types of consumer promotion activities include coupons, free sample offers, contests, premiums, cash-back offers, and a variety of frequent-buyer (loyalty) programs.

Trade promotions refer to those activities designed to encourage distributors to purchase additional volume and provide additional support to stimulate consumer purchase. In effect, trade promotions help push the product through the distribution channel. Common types of trade promotion activities include price discounts and allowances, co-operative advertising funds, and point-of-purchase display materials. Branded promotion merchandise or giveaway items that carry brand logos are a form of promotion that fits with either consumer promotion or trade promotion plans. Trade shows can also be a key component of an organization's consumer promotion or trade promotion plans.

SALES PROMOTION PLANNING

Promotion planning relies on input from the overall marketing plan—specifically, the marketing objectives and strategies. The sales promotion plan can be developed by the advertising agency, but more often a specialist agency does it. Regardless of who develops the plan, there is a direct relationship between advertising and sales promotion. Traditional thinking meant that the advertising agency created a national advertising campaign to position the product or service in the marketplace while the promotion plan complemented the advertising: it helped create demand for the product, encouraged trial purchase, and/or built loyalty through repeat purchase incentives. In today's environment, where planners consider an integrated marketing approach, sales promotions are not viewed as separate entities. They are planned at the same time to ensure that synergies are achieved across all forms of communications.

PROMOTION OBJECTIVES

Like other elements of the marketing mix, promotion activity must complement the total marketing effort. Thus, each element of the mix is assigned a goal based on what it is capable of contributing to the overall plans. As with other plans, promotion objectives should be realistically achievable, quantitative in nature (for measurement purposes), directed at a carefully defined target, and capable of being evaluated and modified when necessary.

It should be noted that the objectives for consumer promotions and trade promotions are quite different, but they complement each other when implemented. Objectives of consumer promotions focus on achieving *trial purchase* and *repeat or multiple purchases* and *building brand loyalty.* Trade promotions focus on *selling more volume* of merchandise and encouraging *merchandising support* among channel members that buy and resell products. These objectives are examined in detail in appropriate sections of this chapter.

PROMOTION STRATEGY

Promotion strategy focuses on the selection of the best promotion activity to meet the objectives. There are two basic types of promotion strategy: *pull* and *push.*

In a **pull strategy**, the organization creates demand by directing promotional efforts at consumers or final users of a product. Pull strategies tend to rely on a mixture of media advertising and consumer promotion activities. These activities cause consumers to search for the product in stores; by asking for the product, they can put pressure on the retailer to carry it. The promotion activities considered include coupons, samples, contests, and premiums.

In a **push strategy**, the organization creates demand for a product by directing promotional efforts at intermediaries, who in turn promote the product among consumers. Push strategies tend to rely on a mixture of personal selling and trade promotion techniques to create demand. These trade promotions include a variety of financial incentives referred to as listing allowances, performances, and co-operative advertising allowances. For a visual impression of the concept of pull and push promotion strategies refer to Figure 13.1.

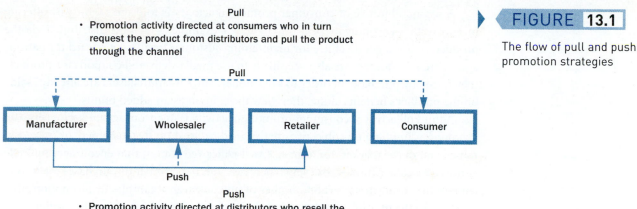

FIGURE 13.1

The flow of pull and push
promotion strategies

Most firms feel that attention must be given to both final users and channel members; thus, it is very common for firms to combine push and pull promotion strategies. Companies such as Kraft, Colgate-Palmolive, and Apple advertise their products heavily to end users while their sales force sells the products among business customers or channel members using a combination of trade promotion and personal selling. For a promotion to succeed, it must be advertised to create awareness; the promotional message must be integrated with long-term message strategies that focus on building a brand's image. Having a great promotional concept is just the start of a promotion plan.

Colgate-Palmolive
www.colgate.com

Consumer Promotion Planning

Consumer promotion is any activity that promotes extra brand sales by offering the consumer an incentive over and above the product's inherent benefits. It is designed to pull the product through the channel by encouraging consumers to take immediate purchase action. The most common objective of consumer promotion activity is to have the consumer make a *trial purchase*. In the case of a new product, the marketer is concerned that the initial trial and consumer acceptance of the product occur quickly. Even when a product is firmly established on the market, marketers will still attempt to secure trial purchase by non-users. See Figure 13.2 for an illustration of a trial purchase coupon.

FIGURE 13.2

A consumer promotion that
encourages trial purchase of
a new product

[handwritten margin notes: 1- trial, 2- protect loyalty, 3- multiple purchaser]

A second objective of consumer promotion activity is to *protect loyalty* by offering incentives that encourage repeat purchase. For example, a coupon distributed via the product itself is a good vehicle for maintaining customer loyalty—a reward for patronage. Current customers are also very likely to use media-delivered coupons for products they normally purchase, in order to save money. Since the purchasers are already "sold" on the product's benefits alone, they view the coupon as an added bonus.

A third objective of consumer promotion activity is to encourage *multiple purchases.* Promotions fulfilling this objective are designed to "load up the customer" or "take customers out of the market" for a time. A well-conceived contest that encourages multiple entries, or a cash refund whose value increases with the number of purchases made, or a coupon that stipulates a certain number of purchases, are examples of promotions that will achieve the multiple purchase objective. Refer to Figure 13.3 for an illustration.

Types of Consumer Promotion Activity

The major types of consumer promotion activities implemented in Canada include coupons, free sample distribution, contests such as sweepstakes or instant wins, cash rebates, premiums, frequent-buyer or loyalty programs, and delayed payment incentives. A survey conducted by NCH Promotional Services among packaged-goods companies (i.e., food, household goods, personal care products, pet food manufacturers) revealed that 77 percent of the manufacturers viewed coupons as their most important form of consumer promotion activity. Following in order of importance were sampling, contests, cash refunds, and premiums.

NCH Promotional Services
www.nchmarketing.com

COUPONS

Coupons are price-saving incentives offered to consumers to stimulate quicker purchase of a designated product. The array of products and services that use coupons is endless. Coupons are used to discount the price of movie and theatre tickets, to lower the price of restaurant meals, and to encourage purchase of a brand of breakfast cereal. Marketing organizations use coupons more frequently than any other type of consumer promotion. In 2004, the latest year that statistics are available, companies in the packaged-goods industry alone distributed a total of 2.9 billion coupons in Canada. A total of 100 million coupons for consumer-packaged-goods items were redeemed by consumers

FIGURE 13.3

A coupon offer (financial incentive) that encourages consumers to make multiple purchases

Courtesy of Nestlé Canada.

for a total savings on goods purchased of $118 million. The average value of a redeemed coupon is $1.19.[1] The most recent trends in coupon distribution and redemption among packaged-goods manufacturers are outlined in Figure 13.4.

OBJECTIVES OF COUPON PROGRAMS The traditional objectives associated with coupon promotions are to get non-brand users to make a trial purchase of a brand, to maintain current users, to speed up acceptance of a new product, and to encourage current customers to repurchase the brand (build loyalty). Coupons also help to attract users of competitive brands, encourage multiple purchases, and increase seasonal sales.

How effective are coupons in achieving these objectives? In a report on coupon usage issued by BBM Bureau of Measurement in 2005, it was found that 3.7 million Canadians (14 percent of the population) are frequent coupon users. Frequent coupon users are more likely to be female (61 percent) and are between the ages of 25 and 54 (58 percent). The average personal income of frequent coupon users is similar to the national average of $30 000.[2] Apparently, a prime target market enjoys taking advantage of coupon offers! The BBM Study also provided some interesting regional information. Quebec grocery shoppers, for example, use coupons more frequently than shoppers in other regions of Canada. Coupons are redeemed by all levels of society, regardless of factors such as age, income, and ethnic background.

Coupons are a resource that households refer to when planning shopping trips. For many, they are an ingrained part of shopping culture. Proof of a coupon's worth is demonstrated by companies such as Procter & Gamble, S.C. Johnson, General Mills, and Kraft, who continue to invest in traditional coupon programs each year. The fact that the number of coupons distributed each year in Canada continues to rise suggests the usefulness of this promotion technique.[3]

The stage the product has reached in its life cycle also has an impact on the objectives of a coupon promotion. When a product is in the introduction and growth stages, trial purchase is the marketer's main objective, so media-delivered coupons are popular. As the product moves into maturity and marketers become concerned with repeat purchase by current customers, they attempt to defend their consumer franchise by means of product-delivered coupons. If an objective is still to attract competitive-brand users (which is important, even at the mature stage), media-delivered coupons remain necessary. Coupons delivered in stores will encourage trial purchase and repeat purchase (brand loyalty). See Figure 13.5 for further insight into consumers and coupon usage.

METHODS OF COUPON DISTRIBUTION Coupons can be delivered to consumers in four different ways: by the product, by the media, in-store at the point of purchase, and electronically.

FIGURE 13.4

Coupons distributed and redeemed in Canada

Characteristic	2003	2004
Quantity Distributed	2.6 billion	2.93 billion
Quantity Redeemed	97 million	99 million
Average Face Value Coupons Distributed	$1.23	$1.55
Average Face Value Coupons Redeemed	$1.08	$1.19
Consumer Savings	$105 million	$118 million

Source: "Couponing takes off," press release, Resolve Corporation, February 2005.

FIGURE 13.5

The power of a coupon

> **Never underestimate the impact of a coupon offer. It is a tried-and-true promotion device that definitely achieves certain marketing objectives. Further, Canadian households use them frequently, as evidenced by the number of coupons distributed and redeemed annually. Here are a few important facts about coupons:**
>
> 1. The most common objective of a coupon offer is to increase product and brand usage. Getting trial purchase, encouraging brand switching, and inducing immediate purchase are less important.
> 2. In a fiercely competitive marketplace, coupons give consumers a reason to buy a national brand instead of a private-label brand.
> 3. Nine out of ten households use coupons: 70% of Canadian households have used coupons in the past month.
> 4. Coupons are used more frequently in households that have 3+ members and a household income of $30 000+. The use of coupons increases with age.
> 5. On average, 50% of consumers in the past three months were influenced by a coupon to buy a brand that they would not have bought without a coupon.
>
> Source: Wayne Mouland, NCH Promotional Services, "85% of consumers used coupons last year," press release, March 2001.

Product-delivered coupons appear in or on the package. One kind of product-delivered coupon, the *in-pack self-coupon*, is redeemable on the next purchase of the same product. The package is usually flagged somehow to draw attention to the coupon included inside the package. An *on-pack self-coupon* usually appears on the back or side panel of the package and is valid for a future purchase of the same product. An instantly redeemable coupon is valued when the product carrying the coupon is bought and the coupon is removed from the package. Another variation is the **cross-ruff** (or cross-coupon), an in-pack or on-pack coupon valid for the purchase of a different product. Such coupons also encourage the consumer to buy complementary products. For example, a cereal brand may carry coupons for a brand of orange juice, and vice versa, since they may have a similar target market. Refer to Figure 13.6 for an illustration.

FIGURE 13.6

A cross-coupon offer from Kellogg's cereal brands—free coupons for juice and tea

Courtesy of Dick Hemingway.

Media-delivered coupons are coupons distributed through a newspaper, magazine, co-operative direct-mail package, or by an online source. The Shop & Save envelope or the Val-Pak envelope received by households are examples of a co-operative direct-mail package; they are delivered numerous times each year and contain coupons for a range of non-competing products.

Savvy shoppers now look to online sources for valuable money-saving coupons. A consumer can select specific goods and services, survey the discounts offered, and then print the coupons off. Save.ca offers Canadian packaged-goods marketers the opportunity to provide coupons online. Many Canadian companies also offer online coupons at their brand websites. See the illustration in Figure 13.7.

Among media-delivered coupons, the **freestanding insert (FSI)** is the most popular method of placing coupons directly in the homes of consumers. A freestanding insert (FSI) is a preprinted advertisement in single- or multiple-page form that is inserted loose into newspapers. Distribution statistics reveal that 65 percent of all direct-to-consumer coupons are distributed by FSIs.[4] Free-standing inserts are marketed by distribution organizations that use such names as The Coupon Clipper, and Shop and Save.

The category of **in-store-delivered coupons** includes coupons distributed by in-store display centres and dispensing machines usually located near the store entrance, on the shelves via shelf pads (the consumer tears off a coupon that can be redeemed instantly), or by handout as the customer enters the store.

COUPON REDEMPTION BY MEDIA   The **redemption rate** is the number of coupons returned to the manufacturer expressed as a percentage of total distributed coupons. With reference to the figures that appear in Figure 13.8, there is clearly a consumer

FIGURE 13.7

Sample of an online-generated coupon

FIGURE 13.8

Average redemption rates
by method of delivery

Media	Range %	Average %
FSI	0.1–1.8	0.6
In-Store	1.2–32.7	9.8
In/On Pack	0.3–51.4	6.1
Direct Mail Addressed	1.9–22.6	6.5
Direct Mail Unaddressed	0.1–3.3	1.2
Magazine	0.1–7.0	0.8
Charity	0.5–28.5	16.9
Other	0.3–30.6	2.7
Internet	0.3–14.9	3.9

Source: Resolve Corporation, formerly NCH Promotional Services Ltd., 2003.

preference for in-store coupons. The statistical information in Figure 13.8 shows that in-store coupons (those that are instantly redeemable) have the highest average redemption rates (an average of 9.8 percent) among coupon offers.

The impact of delivering coupons by direct mail should not be underestimated. As the statistics in Figure 13.8 indicate, the average redemption rate for addressed direct mail is 6.5 percent and unaddressed direct mail 1.2 percent, compared to magazines at 0.8 percent. Since both media distribute coupons to generate trial purchases, it can be observed that direct mail does a better job than magazines. Redemption rates for newspaper and magazine coupons are relatively low compared with redemption rates for coupons distributed by other methods.

The method of delivery is only one factor that influences the rate of redemption for a coupon promotion. Other factors that play a major role are the face value of the coupon and the consumer's perception of the value of the discount offered by the coupon in relation to the price of the product. To save money in distributing paper coupons and to encourage more response from prospective and current customers, marketers are starting to communicate their offers online. The response rates achieved will provide input for future promotion plans.

COUPON COST AND REVENUE CALCULATIONS The costs of a coupon promotion should be monitored closely by the marketing organization. A variety of factors have an impact on the total costs of a coupon promotion: the method of distribution, which affects delivery costs and redemption costs; the printing costs; the handling costs for the retailer and clearing house (the latter being the agent responsible for redeeming coupons, paying retailers, and reporting redemption and cost information to the marketing organization); and the coupon's face value.

The marketer should weigh the costs of a coupon promotion against the potential revenues to ensure that a positive financial payout will result from the activity. The difference between revenues and costs would be the return on investment. The costs associated with a coupon offer include the monetary value of the coupon, distribution, printing, redemption, and handling fees. Retailers and a central clearing house such as Nielsen Promotional Services receive handling fees. Revenues can be estimated based on the value of the product sold by the manufacturer multiplied by the number of purchases generated by the coupon offer. Figure 13.9 illustrates in detail how to evaluate the financial payout of a coupon offer.

Coupon Promotion Plan	
Face Value of Coupon	$1.00
Handling Charge for Retailer	$0.15
Handling Charge for Clearing House	$0.05
Distribution Cost (direct mail)	$16.00/M
Distribution	3 million households
Printing Cost (digest-size ad with coupon)	$8.00/M
Redemption Rate	2.5%
Retail Price of Product (Manufacturer receives 65% of retail price when distributors' mark-ups are deducted)	$4.49

The cost and revenue calculations are as follows:

Costs	Cost Calculation	Total	Grand Total
Distribution	3 000 000 × $16/M	$48 000	
Printing	3 000 000 × $8/M	$24 000	
Coupon Redemption	3 000 000 × .025 × $1.20	$90 000	
Total Cost		**$162 000**	**$162 000**

Revenues	Revenue Calculation	Total	Grand Total
Per Unit of Revenue	$4.49 × .65	$2.92	
Total Revenue	3 000 000 × .025 × 0.80 × $2.92	**$175 200**	**$175 200**
Return on Investment			**$13 200**

Note: A misredemption rate of 20% is included above, hence the 0.80 factor in the revenue calculation.

FIGURE 13.9

Evaluating the financial impact of a coupon offer

The revenue calculation also considers the misredemption of coupons. A coupon is misredeemed if it was not used to purchase the product, but was sent to the clearing house anyway—this is a common occurrence in the industry. The illustration in Figure 13.9 considers a misredemption rate of 20 percent (80 percent are redeemed on an actual purchase).

FREE SAMPLES

A **free sample** is a free product distributed to potential users either in a small trial size or in its regular size. Sampling is considered to be the most effective method of generating trial purchase, as it eliminates a consumer's initial financial risk. Therefore, it is commonly practised when a company is introducing a new product or a line extension of an existing product (e.g., a new flavour if it is a food product). Unlike any other type of promotion, sampling is the only alternative that can convert a trial user to a regular user solely on the basis of product satisfaction.

The most frequently used method of sample distribution is in-store. There are several variations on in-store sampling: product demonstrations and sampling in stores, saleable sample sizes (small replica pack sizes of the actual product), and cross sampling. **Cross sampling** refers to an arrangement whereby one product carries a sample of another product (e.g., a regular-sized box of Cheerios cereal carries a small sample package of Lucky Charms cereal). The popularity of one brand is used to secure the trial usage of a less popular brand.

Other alternatives for delivering free samples include co-operative direct mail (provided the sample is small and light enough to be accommodated by the mailing envelope), home delivery by private organizations, event sampling, and, finally, by sample packs that are distributed to specific target markets. Several companies specialize in the distribution of samples in Canada. See Figure 13.10 for examples of product sample offers.

Sampling programs tend to be an expensive proposition for the marketing organization because of the product, packaging, and distribution costs. In spite of these costs, sample promotions rank second in popularity among marketers, so clearly the potential long-term benefits outweigh the short-term costs. Further, sampling combined with a coupon is the best way to gain trial and convert trial to immediate purchase. On the downside, a sample is the fastest and surest way to kill an inferior product.[5]

Companies are discovering new ways of delivering samples while at the same time generating positive publicity for the brand involved in the promotion. Some refer to it as on-site sampling; others call it experiential marketing. Regardless of what it is called, it involves potential customers interacting directly with the product. Nestlé used experiential marketing to help launch Coffee-Mate liquid. Over an eight-week period, street teams handed out over 800 000 cups of free coffee, flavoured with Coffee-Mate liquid. The program involved a tease, taste, and reveal approach; consumers were not told they were actually sampling Coffee-Mate until after they tried the product. Following the sample, consumers were given a $1.00 coupon towards their first purchase of Coffee-Mate liquid.[6]

Nestlé Canada
www.nestle.ca

FIGURE 13.10

A selection of free samples distributed directly to households and an inexpensive trial pack that can be purchased in stores (Cap'n Crunch)

Courtesy of Dick Hemingway.

Axe deodorant, a brand targeted directly at 18- to 24-year-old males, used on-site sampling to launch Axe Snake Peel, an occasional-use exfoliating shower scrub. Axe's advertising campaign centered on a secret brotherhood known as the Order of the Serpentine, which helps young men overcome the shame caused by questionable hook-ups—defined as a romantic encounter that ends in personal humiliation. In the ads, members of the order wore bright orange bathrobes embroidered with the logos for Axe and the Order of the Serpentine. For the sampling promotion, street teams were dressed in the same robes—a real attention getter! The street teams distributed 300 000 samples at ski events at Whistler, Blue Mountain, and Mount Tremblant. So popular was the promotion that the street teams were literally swarmed by spectators to get their hands on the product and to have their picture taken with the orange-robed street team members.[7]

Whistler Blackcomb
www.whistlerblackcomb

Television networks have found that there is value in sampling. Networks now offer streamed programming on the web as a means of creating interest for new shows. CBS for example, learned that 53 percent of online viewers became fans of their TV shows after getting interested online. "It's all about getting sampling," says CBS Corp. chief research officer David Poltrack. "We are now looking at dual distribution programming; over the air and on the internet."[8]

CONTESTS

Contests are designed and implemented to create temporary excitement about a product. The structure of a contest usually entails incentives for consumers to purchase; entrance often requires, for example, submission of a label or product symbol (or facsimile) and an entry form. Consumers are encouraged to enter as often as possible, resulting in multiple purchases by many consumers.

As a marketing vehicle, contests tend to attract the current users of a product but are less effective in inducing trial purchases than are coupons and samples. Consequently, contests are most appropriate in the mature stage of the product life cycle, when the aim is to retain current market share. *Sweepstakes* and *instant wins* are two major types of contests.

A **sweepstakes** contest is a chance promotion involving a giveaway of products and services of value to randomly selected participants who have submitted qualified entries. Prizes such as cash, cars, homes, and vacations are given away. Consumers enter contests by filling in an entry form, usually available at point-of-purchase or through print advertising, and submitting it along with a proof of purchase to a central location where a draw is held to determine winners. The odds of winning depend on the number of entries received. Usually, an independent organization selects the winners on behalf of the sponsor company.

Many brands now execute this type of contest online. Consumers are asked to visit a website to type in a PIN number they received in a package or on a package label. While entering the contest, the consumer may be asked to submit some personal information. This information is accumulated in a database for later use. In other words, the contest is a building block for developing a customer relationship management program. An example of a very successful online contest appears in Figure 13.11. The TSN/Wendy's "Kick for a Million" contest is TSN's most successful promotional campaign ever. In the second year of the contest there were 1.5 million entries. In the first year there were only 200 000 entries.[9] Why such an increase? When the promotion was launched for a second time in 2006, Game Cups were introduced at Wendy's restaurants. The objective of the Game Cup was two-fold, to provide customers with PIN numbers that could be registered online for bonus entries and to offer customers a chance at instant prizes. Moreover, in 2006 the value of the prizes to be won at the 20, 30 and

TSN and Wendy's collaborate on an online contest. Registration for TSN's Wendy's Kick for a Million contest occurs online

40 yard lines increased. Lastly, in the first year of the contest, the grand prize of $1 million was actually won when the winning entrant successfully kicked a 50-yard field goal—that creates excitement!

A **game (or instant win)** contest is a promotion vehicle that includes a number of predetermined, pre-seeded winning tickets in the overall fixed universe of tickets. Packages containing winning certificates are redeemed for prizes. Variations of this type of contest include collect-and-wins, match-and-wins, and small instant-wins combined with a grand prize contest. Restaurants such as McDonald's and Tim Hortons use this promotion vehicle frequently. McDonald's runs a game fashioned after the board game Monopoly, and Tim Hortons offers "Rrroll Up the Rim to Win" every spring.

Contests are governed by laws and regulations, and any company that runs one must publish the following information: how, where, and when to enter; who is eligible to enter the contest; the prize structure, value, and number of prizes; the odds of winning and the selection procedure; and conditions that must be met before a prize can be accepted (e.g., a skill-testing question must be answered).

A contest requires a significant investment in media advertising. In effect, the focal point of a brand's advertising switches temporarily from the product to the contest in an attempt to build excitement for the brand. To create awareness for the contest, a multimedia mix is frequently used (e.g., broadcast media to generate excitement and print media and online communications to communicate details). Point-of-purchase advertising is essential to draw attention to the promotion. Because of consumer involvement, contests are usually well received and supported by the retail trade; indeed, they are often launched with trade promotion programs to encourage feature pricing and maximize display activity at retail.

The success of a contest depends on the consumer's perception of the value and number of prizes to be awarded and of the odds of winning. Contest prizes should also match the image of the product (e.g., a quality product must offer quality prizes). In terms of attracting participation, automobiles generate the highest number of entries, but vacations and trips are the prizes most offered by sponsoring companies. When designing a contest, the marketer must consider the above factors and must either develop a high-value grand prize that will attract attention and create excitement or have prizes of less value awarded frequently to compensate for the disappointment factor associated with most contests ("I'll enter, but who ever wins?"). Many online contests now adopt the latter approach. In some cases prizes have been awarded on an hourly or daily basis. It keeps people visiting the website.

Tim Hortons runs one of the most popular and successful promotions in Canada—an instant-win promotion. For insight into its promotion activities, read the Advertising in Action vignette **Rrroll Up the Rim**.

CASH REFUNDS (REBATES)

A **cash refund**, or **rebate**, as it is often called, is a predetermined amount of money returned directly to the consumer by the manufacturer after the purchase has been made. It is a reward for buying a product within the promotion period. For packaged-goods companies, cash refunds are a useful promotion technique in the mature stage of the product life cycle; they effectively reinforce loyalty by tempting consumers to make multiple purchases.

The most common type of refund is the single-purchase refund, in which a consumer receives a portion of his or her money back for the purchase of a specified product. However, refunds are designed to achieve different objectives; hence, they can be offered in different formats. Refunds encourage consumers to make multiple purchases and stock their pantries. For example, the value of a refund may escalate with the number of items purchased; hence, the consumer is encouraged to make multiple purchases. An offer could be structured as follows: buy one and get $1.00 back; buy two and get $2.00 back; buy three and get $5.00 back.

In refund offers where multiple purchases are necessary, slippage generally occurs. Slippage happens when a consumer purchases a product intending to redeem a coupon, request a rebate, or send in for a premium, but fails to do so. Most advertisers project a certain degree of slippage in their promotions in order to forecast a promotion's cost and

Rrroll Up the Rim

How do you know when you have a successful promotion? Perhaps it's when the *Royal Canadian Air Farce* comedy troupe spoofs your idea on television. It's proof that you've worked your way into the cultural fabric of Canada. And that's what happened with the Tim Hortons "Roll Up the Rim" promotion. Like the call of the loon, "Rrroll up the rim to win" has hit the airwaves for 17 consecutive springs.

The promotion began in 1987 as a way to boost coffee sales during the summer, but it has evolved into a national obsession that draws customers to the doughnut shops year after year, win or lose. Customers are powerless to resist the temptation of winning something as small as a doughnut or muffin or as large as a colour television, bicycle, or automobile.

According to Ron Buist, director of marketing services at TDL Group (the corporate name for Tim Hortons), one of the keys to success is the KISS principle: "Keep it simple, and whenever possible, silly too. We want it to be fun, and most of all we want it to be easy to play." This promotion proves that a simple idea coupled with a memorable advertising slogan can generate a huge payoff for a company. The company won't discuss sales figures, but one Ontario franchisee says business climbs by 10 to 15 percent during the promotion.

It was a radio spot developed in 1993 featuring an actor with a thick Scottish accent rolling the letter R in the slogan that really got the ball rolling (pardon the pun). The ad drew a few complaints about how it was stereotyping Scots, but it also launched the slogan into the psyches of consumers. The Scottish accent has been dropped, but the rolling R remains in all forms of advertising.

The "Roll Up the Rim" promotion demonstrates the application of some important planning variables. To have a chance at being successful, a promotion contest should be easy to play, deliver a consistent theme, and include a catchy and memorable phrase. The advantage of having this kind of long-running promotion is self-evident. It becomes less of a promotion than a brand unto itself. "Roll Up the Rim" has become recognized as its own entity, much as a product would.

"Roll Up the Rim" is a well-known promotion, but each year it receives significant media advertising support to ensure success. A combination of television and radio advertising creates awareness and interest and drives traffic to the stores. Point-of-purchase material provides more details in the stores.

Sources: Adapted from Laura Pratt, "Roll Up the Rim major player for Tim Hortons," *Strategy*, May 22, 2000, p. 22; Liza Finlay, "Perpetual promos," *Marketing*, May 31, 1999, pp. 11–12; and John Heinzl, "Tim Hortons rrrolls up a winner," *Globe and Mail*, March 24, 1999, p. B29.

---

results. Slippage is a significant factor. In a survey of grocery shoppers, it was found that one-half of all refund participants sometimes neglect to submit a request for a refund even after they have bought the product with the intention of using the refund offer.[10]

Strategically, refund offers for packaged goods items should be advertised at point-of-purchase since it is the optimum time when consumers make brand purchase decisions. A common technique is to use **ad pads**, which are shelf pads with tearaway sheets containing details of the promotion offer. Rebates are now popular among a variety of durable goods. For example, manufacturers of computers and computer-related hardware offer rebate programs through distributors such as Staples Business Depot. Unlike packaged-goods rebates where there is a paper trail, consumers can apply for these rebates electronically—purchase information can be directly sent to the manufacturer or the manufacturer's agent handling the fulfillment portion of the promotion.

Rebates accomplish such objectives as the liquidation of inventory prior to the introduction of newer models, the generation of sales during traditionally weak periods, or at times when interest rates on loans are high. Rebate offers of $2000 or $3000 are

Staples Business Depot
www.staples.ca

quite common in the automobile industry when the economy takes a bit of a downward spin and new cars aren't selling. So ingrained have rebates become in the automobile industry, that consumers now postpone new car purchases while they wait for an attractive rebate offer.

PREMIUM OFFERS

A **premium** is an item offered free or at a bargain price to encourage consumers to buy a specific product. The goal of a premium offer is to provide added value to new and repeat purchasers. McDonald's and other fast-food restaurants consistently use premiums because they are effective with its primary target (families) and they reinforce the company's goal of offering value to consumers. Recently, fast-food restaurants have focused their premium efforts on characters from popular movies. McDonald's, for example, has a 10-year promotion agreement with Disney to distribute toy characters. It is part of its never-ending battle to be the preferred choice among young customers.

Premiums are usually offered to consumers in three ways: either as a mail-in (e.g., send in proofs of purchase and the item will be returned by mail), as an in-pack or on-pack promotion (e.g., an item is placed inside a package or attached to a package), or by a coupon offer distributed by in-store shelf talkers (small posters that hang from store shelves). Distributing premiums with a product is popular as it provides instant gratification. Cereal manufacturers are very active in premium promotion offers. Premiums with high perceived value have a direct impact at point-of-purchase as they encourage brand switching—attractive offers attract new customers, even if only on a temporary basis.

Beer manufacturers see premium offers as a vital tool for building business in the critical summer months. In recent years Labatt and Molson have been in a battle over which company offers the best value-added proposition to customers. To entice purchases the beer companies have offered t-shirts with appropriate brand logos, baseball caps with brand logos, extra bottles of beer, golf balls, and on and on it goes. Both companies found these promotions expensive, and, rather than create loyalty, they simply encouraged drinkers to switch brands constantly.[11]

To break out from the crowd, Lakeport Pilsener recently partnered with KFC by offering $4.00 vouchers redeemable for a KFC Mega Meal or Big Crunch Sandwich. This type of offer stimulates purchases of Lakeport Pilsener during the promotion period and drives a desirable target market to KFC restaurants. Both brands benefit. Refer to the illustration in Figure 13.12.

A well-thought-out premium offer helps achieve several marketing objectives. The premium can increase the quantity of brand purchases made by consumers, help retain current users, attract competitive users (as in the beer offer mentioned above), and provide a merchandising tool to encourage display activity in stores. A good premium offer enhances differentiation between competing products.

LOYALTY (FREQUENT-BUYER) PROGRAMS

Canadian retailers and various service industries such as airlines, credit cards, and hotels have made frequent-buyer or loyalty programs popular. A **loyalty program (frequent-buyer program)** offers consumers a small bonus, such as points or "play money," when they make a purchase. The bonus accumulates with each new purchase. The goal of such an offer is to encourage consumer loyalty, and that's what a program like Shoppers Drug

Courtesy of Dick Hemingway.

FIGURE **13.12**

Package-delivered premiums encourage buying decisions at point-of-purchase.

Mart's Optimum rewards program does. In this program, shoppers accumulate points that are redeemable on future purchases. The card is an integral component of Shoppers' new customer relationship management program. Shoppers can electronically cross-reference transaction data and work with its product suppliers to tailor offers to specific customers. Technology and the desire to manage customer relationships better is the fuel that drives loyalty programs.

Canadian Tire's program is, perhaps, the best-known and longest-running (over 50 years) frequent-buyer program in Canada. It rewards regular shoppers who pay for merchandise with cash or a Canadian Tire credit card with Canadian Tire "money." Canadian Tire now allows customers to collect virtual money on the company's house credit card, its website, and its affiliate MasterCard. Canadian Tire money captures the essence of a rewards program because customers really can purchase something for free.

Free rewards are a real incentive but people don't realize they may be paying for the privilege. Since loyalty programs add costs, customers may eventually tire of paying more for the goods they buy. The true benefit for the organization is the information it is collecting about customer purchase behaviour. The ability to mine such data is very useful as organizations move toward individualized marketing programs.

While rewards program are popular with consumers, so many companies offer them that they have actually become a part of the product. For example, hotel rewards programs such as Six Continents' Priority Club or Choice Hotels Choice Club are often duplicated by other competitors. In the airline industry today, offering a frequent-flyer program seems mandatory if an airline is to be on the consumer's consideration list.

DELAYED PAYMENT INCENTIVES

In a **delayed payment incentive** promotion, a consumer is granted a grace period during which he or she pays no interest or principal for the item purchased. Once the purchase is made from the retailer, a finance company assumes the agreement and charges interest if full payment is not made by the agreed-upon date.

Leon's Furniture pioneered the delayed payment concept in Canada with promotions called the "Don't Pay a Cent Event" and the "No Money Miracle." From Leon's perspective, this kind of incentive is but one part of an overall package that includes good value, good prices, and wide selection. This type of promotion is spreading to other retail markets. Home Depot, for example, offers an array of household repair and renovations services to its customers: interior and exterior renovations, electrical and plumbing upgrades, and shingle and window replacements, to name just a few. These types of services are expensive undertakings for consumers. To attract potential customers, Home Depot will offer six-month and one-year interest-free financing packages. Such an offer gives Home Depot a competitive edge over independent contractors who demand payment when such jobs are completed.

Leon's
www.leons.ca

COMBINATION OFFERS

To maximize the effectiveness of a promotion, marketers often combine the consumer promotion techniques discussed in this chapter. For example, it is quite common to combine a trial coupon offer with a premium or contest promotion. The coupon will get the initial purchase and the premium or contest will encourage repeat or multiple purchases. Melitta coffee effectively combines a coupon and contest in a sales promotion offer. See Figure 13.13 for details.

For a comparison of sampling and other promotion techniques that are best suited for achieving specific goals, see Figure 13.14.

Trade Promotion Planning

Trade promotion is promotional activity directed at distributors to push a product through the channel of distribution; it is designed to increase the volume purchased and encourage merchandising support for a manufacturer's product. For any new product, the objective of trade promotion activity is to *secure a listing* with distributors (wholesale and retail). A **listing** is defined as an agreement made by a wholesaler to distribute a manufacturer's product to the retailers it supplies. If, for example, the head office of Sobeys or A&P agrees to purchase a specific product, then it is available to all Sobeys and A&P retail stores. To secure a listing, manufacturers will offer distributors a combination of trade allowances and co-operative advertising allowances, which will cover the costs of the listing, of obtaining distribution, and possibly of selling the product at a special introductory price.

FIGURE 13.13

A combination offer: a coupon and contest offer encourages trial and repeat purchase

A second objective of trade promotions is to *build volume*, either on a seasonal basis or on a preplanned cyclical basis throughout the year. For example, it is quite common for a company to offer trade allowances and other merchandising programs quarterly for key products. The availability of trade allowances encourages retailers to purchase heavily during the promotion period to support the manufacturer's promotion, and to "load up" at the end of the promotion to improve profit margins on products that will be regularly priced at retail after the promotion period. Very often, large retailers will carry inventories that will tide them over from one promotion period to another—a situation that manufacturers should be concerned about, because incremental volume sold on deal, particularly at the end of a promotion period, will reduce the sale of

	Coupons	Sampling	Refunds	Contests	Premiums
Goals					
To generate trial on existing products	*	*			
To gain trial on new products	*	*			
To speed acceptance and first purchase of a new product by consumers	* *	* *	*		
To encourage multiple purchase of a new product and pantry loading	*		* *		*
To encourage repurchase among current users	*		*	*	*
To provide an extra tool to the sales force	*	*	*	*	*
To increase seasonal sales	*				
To help gain extra listings	*	*			
To help gain off-shelf product displays	*	*		* *	
To increase advertising effectiveness	*		*	* *	*
To add excitement and focus to in-store displays				*	
To focus brand advertising at specific target groups				*	*

Source: Wayne Mouland, NCH Promotional Services Ltd.

FIGURE 13.14

Consumer promotions best suited for achieving specific objectives

merchandise at regular prices. Short-term volume gains may not be to the manufacturer's advantage over a long period.

In the case of seasonal products, allowance programs are essential means of encouraging wholesalers and retailers to stock up before the season and to promote the product in the season. For example, sunscreen will be promoted in the spring, canning and preserving supplies in the late summer, baking supplies in the late fall before the holidays, and school supplies in the late summer.

A third objective is to  *secure merchandising support* from distributors. For many products sold through drug, grocery, hardware, or department stores, manufacturers will offer complete promotion programs to encourage display activity, feature pricing, and retail advertising support. Programs of this nature are often agreed to in a signed contract or promotion agreement, and the distributor is reimbursed only when the performance requirements of the agreement are met.

Types of Trade Promotion Activity

The most commonly used types of trade promotion activity are trade and performance allowances, co-operative advertising, retail in-ad coupons, dealer premiums, collateral material, dealer-display material, and trade shows.

TRADE ALLOWANCE

A **trade allowance** is a temporary price reduction designed to encourage larger purchases by distributors (wholesalers and retailers). Such price reductions may be offered in the form of a percentage reduction from list price, a predetermined dollar amount off list price, or as a free-goods offer (e.g., buy 10 cases, get 1 free). These allowances can be deducted from the invoice immediately, and in such cases are called *off-invoice allowances.* Or they can be offered on the basis of a *bill-back,* in which case the manufacturer keeps a record of the amount of merchandise shipped to distributors and, when the deal period is over, issues a cheque to reimburse the retailers for the allowances they have earned.

PERFORMANCE ALLOWANCE

A **performance allowance** is an additional discount (over and above a trade allowance) offered by manufacturers to encourage retailers to perform a specific merchandising function (e.g., display the product at retail, provide an advertising mention in a retail flyer, or offer a lower price at retail for a short period). Before paying the allowance, the manufacturer requires proof of performance from the retailer.

CO-OPERATIVE ADVERTISING ALLOWANCE

Co-operative advertising allowances are funds allocated to pay for a portion of a retailer's advertising. The weekly specials advertised by major supermarket chains, for example, are partially sponsored by the manufacturers whose products are part of the ads in any given week. In some cases, a manufacturer may agree to pay half of the retailer's cost of advertising (media and creative) if the retailer agrees to feature the manufacturer's product for a specified period. Frequently, the manufacturer provides advertising material that can be integrated into the retailer's own advertising.

To maximize the effectiveness of allowances offered to the trade, manufacturers combine the various allowances to develop a fully integrated promotion plan. The effective combination of all allowances can build short-term volume, possibly secure automatic distribution of a product to retail stores, encourage retail display activity, and obtain an ad in a weekly flyer at a reduced retail price for a specified period. Complete package plans combining the various allowances are attractive to retailers—the financial rewards are much greater, and the package facilitates the efficient use of advertising dollars to support the retailer's own advertising and merchandising activities.

To generate even more impact with trade customers and consumers, integrating trade promotions with consumer promotions and media advertising support is an effective combination. Such a multi-faceted approach gives retailers tangible reasons to get behind the promotion—a win-win situation for the manufacturer and the retailer.

RETAIL IN-AD COUPONS

A **retail in-ad coupon** is a coupon printed in a retailer's weekly advertising material, either in run-of-press newspaper advertising or in supplements inserted into a newspaper. These coupons are redeemable on national brands and are paid for by the manufacturers, not by the retailer. Such programs are the result of an agreement struck between the manufacturer's sales representative and the retailer's buyers. Usually, the funds to cover the cost of these coupons come out of the trade promotion budget, hence their inclusion as a trade promotion activity even though they are designed to encourage consumer response. This type of coupon program is appropriate for achieving the following promotion objectives: reducing trade inventories, building distribution levels, gaining trade support at store level, and ensuring that some of a brand's trade spending is passed on to the consumer in the form of a lower retail price.

DEALER PREMIUMS

A **dealer premium** is an additional incentive offered to a distributor by a manufacturer to encourage special purchase or to secure additional merchandising support from a retailer. Premiums are usually offered in the form of merchandise (e.g., a set of golf clubs, or other forms of sports- and leisure-oriented equipment and clothing); the value of the premium increases with the amount of product purchased by the retailer. Their use is often controversial. Some distributors forbid their buyers to accept premiums because they feel only the individual buyer, rather than the organization, benefits. Such a situation, often referred to as payola, may lead a buyer to make unnecessary purchases and ignore the objectives of the distributor. The other side of the argument is that the purchase of a manufacturer's products at a large savings (through allowances and premiums) offers direct, tangible benefit to the buying organization.

The extent of payola can be considerable (e.g., banknotes, liquor, airline tickets, and vacations). These practices are perceived by many to be unethical, and perhaps they should not occur. Nonetheless, some dealings do occur under the table, and students should be aware of it.

COLLATERAL MATERIAL

To facilitate the selling process, the sales force must provide considerable data in the form of **collateral materials** to customers (e.g., dealers, wholesalers, retailers, industrial companies). These materials include price lists, catalogues, sales brochures, pamphlets, specification sheets, product manuals, and audiovisual sales aids prepared by the manufacturer. Electronic brochures available through company websites are now very popular for communicating lengthy and complex information.

DEALER-DISPLAY MATERIAL (POINT-OF-PURCHASE)

Dealer-display material, or **point-of-purchase material**, consists of self-contained, custom-designed merchandising units, either permanent or temporary, that display a manufacturer's product. It includes posters, shelf talkers, channel strips (narrow strips containing a brief message attached to the channel face of a shelf), advertising pads or tear pads (tear-off sheets that explain the details of the promotion), and display shippers (shipping cases that convert to display bins or stands when opened). The use of such displays and materials is at the discretion of the retailers, whose space they occupy. The role of the manufacturer's sales representative is to convince the retailer of the merits of using the display. Retailers usually have an abundance of manufacturer's display material to choose from, so they can be selective.

TRADE SHOWS

Manufacturers often introduce new products or advertising campaigns to their dealer network and the public at large at trade shows. **Trade shows** are typically organized by an industry association each year to demonstrate the latest products of member manufacturers. There are, for example, toy shows, automobile shows, computer shows, and audio electronics shows. The unique benefit of a trade show is that it allows buyers and other decision-makers to come to a central location to secure the most recent product information from suppliers. For retailers and manufacturers, it is an important opportunity to develop a prospect list that the sales force can follow up on. Thus, participants compete for visitors' attention at the show and usually invest considerable sums to build unique and enticing display exhibits.

Home Depot sees great value in trade shows. According to Pat Wilkinson, director of marketing for Home Depot, "Trade shows are a key piece of a larger integrated marketing program. It is an interactive way of talking to customers outside the store." Enhancing the home in the age of cocooning is a trend that Home Depot is tapping into. Home Depot is also a large sponsor and advertiser on various decorating and home renovation shows on the HGTV network. Such shows are now quite popular, and they reach Home Depot's customers.[12]

BRANDED PROMOTION MERCHANDISE

The branded promotion merchandise industry is big business; in the United States it is an $18-billion market. **Branded promotion merchandise** is defined as useful or decorative products featuring an organization's logo or brand mark that are distributed to existing customers and prospects in appreciation for their business and their loyalty. As a promotional vehicle, branded promotion merchandise can be used in both consumer and trade programs. There are limitless ways to use them; some popular uses include business gifts, free goods at orientation programs, components of a corporate communications program or incentive program, and giveaways at trade shows.[13]

The value of branded promotion merchandise is somewhat underestimated by marketing organizations, as it is often viewed as an add-on activity. However, when properly integrated into a marketing communications plan, branded merchandise is effective in building brand awareness and loyalty among trade customers. A research study conducted by Promotion Resource Group found that 56 percent of branded merchandise recipients in a business-to-business situation rated branded promotion merchandise as the best method for building brand loyalty. It was rated ahead of traditional media such as television, radio, magazines, newspaper, and online advertising. These are items that buyers like to receive.

In terms of action, 73 percent of recipients said they were more likely to do business with the presenting company.[14] According to Jim Schroer, president and CEO of Carlson Marketing, "When you use promotional products where there is a company logo, theme, and brand message, you have an interactive experience, which is much more effective than advertising."[15] For additional insight into the usefulness of branded promotion merchandise, refer to Figure 13.15.

Carlson Marketing Canada
www.carlsoncanada.ca

Trends in Sales Promotion Planning

In marketing communications planning, the first strategic decision is to determine the relative importance of the various mix elements. The degree of importance has a direct impact on the amount of money that is allocated to any element. The same decision

Item	Ever Received (%)	Preferred or Favoured Item (%)	Still Have (%)
Clothing	47.6	28.0	83.7
Writing Instruments	61.2	15.0	77.8
Recognition Awards	11.7	14.0	58.3
Bags & Luggage	25.2	7.0	82.7
Sporting Goods	23.8	6.0	81.6

Source: Adapted from "Important trends in branded promotion merchandise—a survey of buyers and recipients," Promotion Resource Group, 2006.

FIGURE 13.15

Popular branded merchandise items and their staying power—the top five

procedure is used when allocating funds between consumer promotion and trade promotion. For some time there has been a trend toward more spending in trade promotions at the expense of advertising and consumer promotions. Several factors have played a role in creating this trend:

- *Media fragmentation* Consumers today have so many broadcast and print advertising options to choose from that the impact of any one option is not as significant as it used to be. For example, television networks have lost significant numbers of viewers to cable channels and the internet, and newspaper reading is now done online instead of using hard copy. If traditional forms of advertising are not as effective as they once were, advertisers have no alternative but to evaluate other forms of communication.

- *Demand for accountability* Organizations today prefer to invest in activities where return on investment can be measured. Managers realize that all forms of communication do help in one way or another, but if a certain activity can demonstrate measurable results then it will be the preferred option. Trade promotions do increase sales during the promotion period, so the results of this investment are tangible.

- *Buying-power concentration* There has been considerable consolidation in many retail markets (e.g., department stores, supermarkets, home and hardware chain stores). As a result, fewer outlets have much more power over the manufacturers that supply them with goods. For example, many manufacturers face considerable pressures to keep prices down from powerful retailers like Wal-Mart. In the grocery industry, one large chain, Loblaws and its various other banners, controls 40 percent of all food sales in Canada. Demand from such huge retailers forces manufacturers to spend more on trade promotions than they care to. The result is an imbalance between push strategies and pull strategies, a concept discussed earlier in the chapter.

Continued high-level spending on short-term activities such as trade promotion by manufacturers may inhibit the achievement of long-term marketing objectives for any given product. In fact, many manufacturers begrudge so much spending on trade promotions. These manufacturers estimate that more than a quarter of trade promotion spending goes directly to retailers' bottom lines rather than to actual in-store merchandising, temporary price reductions, or displays.[16]

It must be noted, however, that the large numbers of mature products that require only limited levels of advertising receive high levels of trade promotion support. Brand objectives are different in the mature stage of the product life cycle. This skews the overall spending average in favour of trade spending. In contrast, small numbers of new products that are in the introduction or early growth stage of the product life cycle will spend heavily on advertising and consumer promotion—their goal is to generate awareness and trial purchase.

Given these trends, it is essential that marketers maximize the effectiveness of their in-store promotions. The potential impact of a promotion plan calls for consumer and trade promotion plans to be carefully integrated. For more insight into this issue, see the Advertising in Action vignette **Value-Added Promotions Increase Sales**.

ADVERTISING IN ACTION

Value-Added Promotions Increase Sales

If the trend toward trade promotions continues, it can be forecast with reasonable accuracy that tactical in-store programs and trade marketing will unseat branding and advertising as the prime focus for many national brands. A frightening thought for many marketers!

The importance of in-store marketing is being driven by three main trends: corporations are being run by finance-oriented executives that are demanding accountability for every dollar spent; media fragmentation; and consolidation of retail distribution channels. In-store marketing budgets in Canada are growing dramatically because the trade is so concentrated here. Large retailers such as Wal-Mart, Canadian Tire, and Loblaws have incredible power over their suppliers. More importantly, however, they have the power to sell a lot of product, so manufacturers must exploit that potential.

Research indicates that retail shoppers do respond to in-store promotions. In fact, 72 percent of respondents in one research survey said they purchased a product due to a promotional offer. As well, 70 percent said they would try a new brand if the promotional offer is perceived as a good one.

Powerful retailers will support national brands, but will only do so if the manufacturer considers their goals as well as its own. From the retailer's perspective, the promotional activity must drive traffic to the stores and build incremental sales and profits.

With so much at stake in the soft drink and snack food product categories, PepsiCo has figured out the vital role and importance of in-store merchandising. The company sees in-store merchandising activities as a vital means of communicating with consumers at a critical time—decision time! PepsiCo has several primary brands that can be merchandised together— Pepsi-Cola products and Frito-Lay products being the most obvious combination. PepsiCo has been particularly successful at selling its ideas to retail partners when it pairs up Pepsi with complementary lines from their product portfolio. This is a strategy the company refers to as "power of one." PepsiCo believes that retailers are more likely to buy into a promotion when there are more players involved, because there is a potential to increase their sales.

A recent Super Bowl promotion involving Pepsi-Cola, Frito-Lay, and Gatorade incorporated miniature football stadium displays built out of Pepsi cases. The displays were a one-stop shopping destination for Super Bowl party planners! On the importance of such activities, Richard Burjaw, director of marketing for Pepsi-Cola, states, "When you get the customer to the point of sale, it always helps to close the sale with some reminders and some attention-grabbing in-store theatre."

Source: Adapted from Lisa D'Innocenzo, "Selling to the store," *Strategy*, February 9, 2004, pp. 1, 6.

Sales Promotion Integration with Marketing Communications

Sales promotion activity is not usually the focal point of a brand's marketing strategy. In most cases, it is used to supplement regular brand advertising. Regardless of the promotional direction the company or brand takes, it must ensure that the strategies employed are integrated with other marketing communications strategies so that synergies are created and objectives are achieved. Strategic decisions must be made on frequency of promotions, the relationship between the product and the promotion, the creative strategy, and the media strategy.

FREQUENCY OF PROMOTION ACTIVITY

How frequently an activity should be used depends on the type of activity and the consumer purchase cycle for that particular product. Once a year is usually adequate to generate excitement for a brand (a contest might be used in peak season to counter competitive activity or during a traditionally low season to stimulate incremental volume). In general, coupon activity can be implemented much more frequently than cash refunds, premium offers, and contests, and is less disruptive to the regular sales message. There is a risk that too much promotion can cheapen the image of a brand.

PROMOTION/PRODUCT RELATIONSHIPS

In the case of contests, sweepstakes, and premiums, the promotion offer must fit the product image and be attractive to the target market. In a contest situation, the prize must be of interest to the target market. For example, an all-expenses-paid vacation in Disneyland may be appropriate for a soup or cereal manufacturer, but inappropriate for the producer of an expensive gourmet coffee. If the target market is not interested, the promotion will fail. As well, the value of the prize must be factored into the equation. High perceived value encourages action by consumers, whereas low perceived value generates little interest.

CREATIVE STRATEGY

The marketer must consider that a promotion might be disruptive to the continuity of the regular sales message. It is possible that consumers not interested in the promotion will look elsewhere for product satisfaction. To avoid this potential problem, separate but integrated message strategies must be considered for promotion activity. Since a promotion is an added incentive, it temporarily becomes the unique selling point. It is logical, then, to integrate the offer into the regular sales message. The combination of a strong ongoing sales message with the added bonus of a promotion offer should help achieve both short-term and long-term objectives for the advertised product.

When assessing the relative effectiveness of a promotional advertisement (particularly a print advertisement), marketers typically analyze the response generated by the specific advertisement or campaign. In a coupon promotion, how many coupons were redeemed? For a contest, how many entries were received? For a premium offer, how many premiums were shipped? Such evaluations provide direction for the design of subsequent promotion-oriented advertisements.

The ideal promotion offer draws attention to the ad and conveys a message about the product. Also, a strong association between the promotional offer and the advertised product tends to increase advertising recall and persuasiveness.

Marketers should analyze their promotion planning efforts, giving consideration to the following questions:

- Does the promotion support the product image?
- Does the promotion distract the reader's attention from copy points that describe product qualities?
- Should the promotion offer be the most prominent feature of the ad, or should it be secondary to the product sales message?

MEDIA STRATEGY

Commitment to a sales promotion plan requires commitment to media advertising support. For any consumer promotion to have a chance, the target market must be made aware of the activity and the specific details of the promotion offer. Usually, a media mix is required to achieve the communications objectives of a promotion plan and the budget is spent in a concentrated period to generate high levels of awareness for the promotion.

BROADCAST MEDIA   To create awareness and encourage consumers to respond quickly is largely the responsibility of television and radio. High-impact advertising in a short period (a blitz campaign) is quite common. In the case of a contest or sweepstakes promotion, television and radio can create excitement and convey a sense of urgency (to get consumers to take advantage of the offer—*now*). As well, television and radio can direct consumers to websites where more detailed information about the promotion is available.

PRINT MEDIA   Various combinations of print media are used to create awareness, and, more importantly, to communicate essential details of the promotion offer. Consumers are conditioned to look for details at point of purchase, so this medium is a must for contests and other offers. For complex promotions such as contests, a well-balanced media mix is required. For a premium offer, free sample, or coupon, the marketer can be more selective.

ONLINE MEDIA   More and more brands promote online contests as a means of driving traffic to their website. As well, broadcast and print media encourage potential participants to visit the website for contest details and to register in the contest. Online communications helps to create excitement for a contest and provides a convenient means of communicating complex details such contest rules and regulations.

In addition to advertising the promotion to the consumer, the marketer must take appropriate action to notify the trade. As discussed earlier in this chapter, consumer promotion and trade promotion activity (the combination of pull and push) is often integrated into a complete plan to maximize impact on, and response from, both customer groups—consumers and distributors. Therefore, the marketing organization must provide the sales force with appropriate sales aids (promotion literature and display material) so that more effective presentations can be made to distributors. In terms of media, marketers can use selective direct mailings to all distributors, or place advertising in appropriate trade journals to reach wholesale and retail buyers. Such advertising should provide promotion details and encourage retailers to build inventories and participate in display activities to derive maximum benefit from the promotion.

For an applied illustration that integrates consumer and trade promotion strategies with other communications strategies, see the marketing communications plan that appears in Appendix II.

SUMMARY

The advertising manager must consider the impact that sales promotion activity will have on the achievement of marketing objectives, so a sales promotion plan is often developed concurrently with the advertising plan. Sales promotion activities are designed to encourage immediate purchase response by consumers and distributors. In comparison to media advertising, where the objective is to build an image, sales promotion encourages action immediately. There are two categories of sales promotion activity: consumer promotions and trade promotions.

Consumer promotions are designed to pull the product through the channel of distribution. Specific objectives are to achieve trial purchase by new users and to achieve repeat and multiple purchases by current users. The types of activities commonly used to achieve these objectives include coupons, cash refunds, samples, contests, premium offers, loyalty (frequent-buyer) promotions, and delayed payment incentives.

Each type of promotion is suited for certain objectives. Coupons, for example, are good at encouraging trial and repeat purchases, depending on the method of distribution. Samples are effective for trial purchase and are appropriate for use when launching a new product. Refunds, premiums, and contests are better suited for maintaining loyalty and are more commonly used by brands in the mature stage of the product life cycle.

Trade promotions are designed to help push the product through the channel of distribution. Specific marketing objectives are to secure listings and distribution, build volume on a preplanned cyclical basis, and achieve merchandising support from distributors. Trade promotion activities that help achieve these objectives include trade allowances, performance allowances, co-operative advertising, retail in-ad coupons, dealer premiums, point-of-purchase display materials, collateral materials, and trade shows. Branded promotion merchandise is a type of promotion that straddles both consumer and trade promotion. Small items emblazoned with brand logos that are given away are popular with recipients.

Sales promotion has traditionally been regarded as supplemental activity that supports regular product advertising, but the results are more effective when activities are planned and implemented as part of an integrated marketing communications effort. When planning promotions, the manager must guard against running them too frequently so as not to harm the image of the product. Promotions that are implemented should complement the existing image of the product. From a media-strategy perspective, a combination of broadcast, print, and online advertising is recommended as the means of creating awareness and communicating the details of the promotion offer.

KEY TERMS

REVIEW QUESTIONS

1. What are the objectives of consumer promotion and trade promotion activities?

2. Explain the difference between a pull promotion strategy and a push promotion strategy.

3. What types of coupon distribution are appropriate for the early stages of the product life cycle? For the later stages? What is the relationship between the method of coupon distribution and a promotion's objectives?

4. What are the major reasons that marketing firms use coupons?

5. What benefits come from a manufacturer's implementation of a free sample promotion offer?

6. What is experiential marketing, and what benefits does it provide the marketing organization?

7. What elements contribute to the success of a contest offer?

8. Briefly describe the following consumer promotion terms:

    a) Cross-ruff

    b) Redemption rate

    c) Instantly redeemable coupon

    d) Instant-win promotions

    e) Rebate

    f) Delayed payment incentive

    g) Slippage

9. What is the objective of a consumer premium offer, and when is the best time (i.e., stage in the product life cycle) to use a premium offer?

10. Briefly explain the nature of a loyalty (frequent-buyer) program.

11. What is the difference between a trade allowance and a performance allowance?

12. What role does co-operative advertising play in the development of a manufacturer's product?

13. Briefly describe the following trade promotion terms:

    a) Retail in-ad coupon

    b) Dealer premium

    c) Collateral material

    d) Branded promotion merchandise

DISCUSSION QUESTIONS

1. "Spending less advertising money directly with consumers, and more advertising money with the trade, will ultimately harm a brand's consumer franchise." Discuss this statement from the manufacturer's viewpoint.

2. The trends of marketing budget allocations and the merits of various consumer and trade promotion techniques have been presented in this chapter. If you were responsible for developing a promotion plan for a brand in the introduction stage of the product life cycle, what balance would you recommend between consumer promotion, media advertising, and trade promotion? Justify your position by using examples of your choice.

3. Conduct some secondary research on the Canadian coffee market (or another popular market of your choice) to determine what brands are the leaders in the market. Assume you are the brand manager for Maxwell House roasted coffee (or a popular brand in the other market you choose). What promotion strategies would you recommend to build brand loyalty, considering your market share and stage in the product life cycle? Be specific and justify your recommendations.

4. Conduct some secondary research on the role and importance of trade shows. Will trade shows play a more prominent role in the marketing mix and marketing communications mix in the future?

NOTES

1. "Coupons take off," Resolve Corporation, February 2005.

2. "BBM media snapshot: Canadians who frequently use coupons," *Media in Canada*, May 24, 2005, **www.mediaincanada.com**.

3. Steve Lohr, "Still holding value," *Financial Post*, September 5, 2006, p. FP10.

4. Wayne Mouland, "Those who use them, use them a lot," *Marketing*, February 10, 2003, p. 29.

5. "A special presentation on promotion fundamentals," NCH Promotional Services Ltd., 1998.

6. "Coffee-mate gets street smart," *Marketing*, February 23, 2004, p. 1.

7. Mike Mulligan, "Visibility cloaks," *Marketing*, June 26, 2006, p. 13.

8. Anne Becker, "CBS: Downloads spur sampling," *Broadcasting & Cable*, November 16, 2006, **www.broadcastingcable.com**.

9. "TSN's most successful contest gets more marketers in the game this year," *Media in Canada*, October 10, 2006, **www.mediaincanada.com**.

10. "A marketer's guide to promotion," NCH Promotional Services Ltd., 1996, p. 4.

11. John Heinzl, "You may be loyal, but it's costing you," *Globe and Mail*, January 31, 2003, p. B8.

12. Marina Strauss, "Home Depot takes show on the road," *Globe and Mail*, October 3, 2003, p. B10.

13. "Important trends in branded promotion merchandise: A survey of buyers and recipients," Promotion Resource Group, 2006, p. 2.

14. *Ibid.*, p. 1.

15. Willow Duttge, "Give it away now," *Advertising Age*, May 8, 2006, pp. 4, 87.

16. Jack Neff, "P&G trims fat off its $2B trade promotion system," *Advertising Age*, June 5, 2006, p. 8.

CHAPTER 14

Public Relations and Event Marketing and Sponsorships

WE SEE WHAT MOST DON'T

We see the heartbreaking effects of poverty, homelessness, abuse and addiction every day. And most importantly, we see the people who desperately need support and compassion. For us it's impossible to turn a blind eye to suffering. Last year in Canada, The Salvation Army served 2.5 million meals to the hungry, helped 10,000 people with addictions and provided one third of all shelter beds each night. This Christmas we ask you to open your eyes and your heart. And give.

SalvationArmy.ca ~ 1.800.SAL.ARMY

THE SALVATION ARMY

Giving Hope Today

Courtesy of The Salvation Army.

Learning Objectives

After studying this chapter, you will be able to

1. Identify the role of public relations and event marketing and sponsorships in achieving organizational objectives

2. Describe the various types of public relations activities

3. Identify the steps involved in the public relations planning process

4. Assess the usefulness of a variety of public relations tools

5. Evaluate public relations and event marketing and sponsorships as a communications medium

6. Identify the unique considerations involved in the planning and evaluation of event marketing programs

For many organizations, for quite a long time, public relations was an afterthought—something a company got involved with when it faced bad times. It was perceived as a reaction-oriented tactical vehicle for correcting problems that cropped up. Organizations now look at public relations differently. It is now a vital part of the communications mix due to the fragmentation of media and the variety of channels that are now available for people to consume.

Surprisingly, it wasn't until the 1990s, the era when integrated marketing communications took hold, that organizations recognized the true value of public relations. Public relations is now perceived more as a strategic tool that can be integrated with other forms of communications. It is another link in the chain that helps an organization achieve its objectives.

For some organizations, particularly those in the not-for-profit sector, public relations may be the lead component of the marketing communications mix. For charitable organizations or cause-oriented organizations in which fundraising is an objective, public relations plays a key role in creating awareness and understanding of issues related to the charity or cause.

Event marketing and sponsorships have gradually increased in importance over the past few decades. At one time the decision to participate in an event was at the whim of a senior company executive—and the events selected were sexy and interesting to them. Now, event marketing is a very sophisticated activity and, because of its target-marketing capability, companies are integrating events and sponsorships with other marketing communications programs.

This chapter examines the increasingly important role that public relations and event marketing and sponsorships can play in an organization. In-depth discussion about developing policies and procedures, strategies, and plans for public relations and event marketing are presented in this chapter.

Defining Public Relations

Public relations consists of a variety of activities and communications that organizations undertake to monitor, evaluate, and influence the attitudes, opinions, and behaviours of groups or individuals who constitute their publics. The word "public" is a crucial aspect of the definition. An organization's publics are varied and include shareholders, employees, suppliers, the government, distributors (wholesalers and retailers), and consumers. The word "relations" is important, for it signifies the organization is involved in a relationship with these publics, and that relationship should be a positive one. For the relationship to be positive, the nature of communications between the organization and the various publics should be open, honest, and forthcoming.

Prior to examining public relations in detail, students should clearly understand the basic differences between advertising and public relations. While each form of communication approaches a situation from a different perspective, they do work together to build a strong and positive image for a company or brand.

Public relations is distinguished from advertising in two ways:

1. While advertising is primarily concerned with product image, public relations concerns itself more frequently with corporate image. For example, it spreads good news about an organization or helps remedy a problem situation that suddenly arises. In the latter situation, an organization is often at the mercy of the media, for the media determine what information is communicated to the public.

2. Advertising is controlled and paid for by a sponsor, whereas public relations is a form of communications controlled by the media and not paid for directly by the company that the media story concerns. The media determine the amount and content of the message, constrained only by the known facts of the situation presented. Organizations, however, can and often do include paid advertising as part of their public relations activity.

At the product level, **publicity** is used to help market goods and services. Publicity is one aspect of public relations; it is the communication of newsworthy information designed to familiarize the public with the features or advantages of a product, service, or idea. Typically, publicity attends the launching of a new product, the opening of a new store, a technological breakthrough, or the achievement of some milestone. To demonstrate, it was just a few years ago that the fast-food restaurant industry was under fire from consumers and public health advocates for not offering healthier, low-fat items. Pizza Hut responded by introducing the Fit 'n Delicious Pizza. The focal point of the public relations program was a media tour featuring well-respected nutritionist Jackie Nugent. Publicity generated from the tour resulted in a cover story in the Money section of *USA Today* and countless other news reports in local newspapers and television stations.[1]

Since publicity is usually not paid for by the sponsor, the sponsor accepts whatever media coverage it receives. A good report about a company can make a company credible with the public. It can be more convincing than advertising, as there is an implied endorsement by the media.

The Publics

Public relations has to be sensitive to two different publics: internal and external. **Internal publics** involve those whom the organization communicates with regularly.

These parties are close to the day-to-day operations of the organization and include employees, distributors, suppliers, shareholders, and regular customers. Employees, for example, must be educated about an organization's policies and procedures, and they should know about the direction a company is heading, in order to help the company prosper. Internal communications in the form of email, bulletin boards, newsletters, posters, and displays are means of keeping employees tuned in.

External publics are not close to the organization and are usually communicated with infrequently. They include the media, governments (all levels), prospective shareholders, the financial community, and community groups. Communicating externally involves the use of an intermediary—the press. Both the broadcast and print media have considerable influence on public opinion, so the smart organization calls upon their services to promote their cause. The press can positively or negatively influence an organization's reputation. Given such power, it is in the best interests of an organization to develop positive media relations.

The Role of Public Relations

The role of public relations is varied but generally falls into six key areas: corporate public relations, reputation management, generating publicity, developing sound relationships with the media, developing positive relationships with the community, and fundraising (as undertaken by not-for-profit organizations).

CORPORATE PUBLIC RELATIONS

As suggested earlier, public relations can play a vital role in building and protecting the image of a company. A smart company today takes a proactive stance and communicates the good things it is doing loudly and clearly. For example, a company may communicate with its publics in the form of corporate advertising. Corporate advertising may communicate to the public what the company is doing in terms of social responsibility, or show how it helps resolve customers' problems.

A company may also be active in the area of **issue management.** Communications in this realm informs the public about where a company stands on an issue that is important to its various publics. For example, a company's stance on environmental issues may be of utmost importance. Is the company taking a proactive stance on protecting the environment? If it is, then a loud and clear message should be sent to the public.

These kinds of messages can be delivered to the public by paid advertising or through public relations. If a company chooses to advertise, it will do so through corporate advertising. Corporate advertising is a form of paid communication that undertakes the task of creating a positive attitude and goodwill toward a company. Corporate advertising does not sell a product but, since the objective is to enhance the image of a company, there could be some long-term and indirect effect on sales. The direct influence of corporate advertising is difficult to measure. Figure 14.1 shows an example of corporate advertising.

REPUTATION MANAGEMENT

Public relations is also a vital form of communication for a company during a crisis. It simply makes good business sense to invest in a program that will protect a reputation that takes years to build and only seconds to lose. How a company manages its public relations during a crisis often influences the final outcome in the public's mind. For

FIGURE 14.1

An example of
corporate advertising

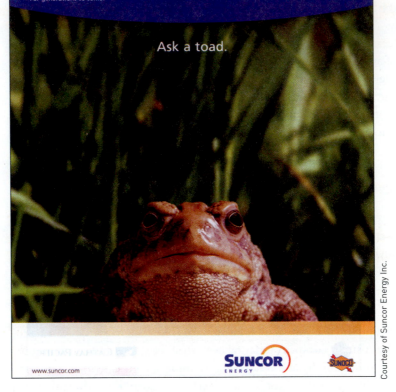

Can a reclaimed oil sands mine make good habitat?

It's a fact – oil sands mining disturbs land. But not forever. Ensuring that native plants and animals can thrive on our reclaimed lands is a top priority for Suncor Energy. Case in point: our reclamation ponds are choice real estate for the Canadian Toad, a species that may be at risk in Alberta. Paying close attention to the details – even toads – is one part of Suncor's commitment to stakeholders. Our aim is to develop energy resources in a way that supports the well-being of the environment, economic prosperity and quality of life. For generations to come.

Ask a toad.

www.suncor.com

SUNCOR ENERGY

Courtesy of Suncor Energy Inc.

instance, a drug manufacturer may face an angry public when a drug it markets is linked to certain unexpected health problems. A company must also face the music when its spokesperson (possibly a celebrity endorser) is caught doing something wrong. When the press gets hold of these types of stories and informs the public, a company has to be instantly ready to go into crisis-management mode.

Labatt Brewing Company encountered such a situation when its advertising spokesperson for Alexander Keith's beer was brought up on child-pornography charges. The popular actor who played an outlandish Scotsman and brand cheerleader in the commercials was largely responsible for the success of Keith's beer and its rise to become the leading specialty beer in Canada. Labatt took a proactive stance and immediately dropped the campaign. In a somewhat ironic stand for a market-driven company, Labatt expected consumers to separate the beer from the advertising.[2] Time will tell!

When an organization faces a delicate situation, the most critical element is leadership. Crises breed fear and confusion, and stakeholders want assurances that someone is in control. A strong leader, willing to be visible on all issues, is essential. When the existing leadership is compromised or tainted by scandal, the best approach is to bring in new leadership with a strong reputation and a commitment to transparency.[3] For some additional tips on how an organization should handle a crisis situation, refer to Figure 14.2.

An organization's leader must be trained to handle the barrage of reporters when he or she is placed in the media spotlight—glaring lights and reporter scrums can be

> How well an organization manages a crisis situation has a direct impact on how the public perceives the outcome. Here are some vital tips to ensure effective communications with the public:

ONE INDIVIDUAL MUST ASSUME A LEADERSHIP ROLE

People want strong leadership and a sense that decision makers are in charge and have a plan.

PEOPLE NEED MORE THAN INFORMATION

They need moral support, a human touch, and a single face with which to identify their hopes for recovery. The 9/11 recovery plan in New York, for example, was led by mayor Rudolf Giuliani.

PEOPLE NEED A CONSISTENT MESSAGE

A strong leader will provide consistency and amplify the essence of the message when necessary. A consistent approach to messaging offers reassurance.

TIMING IS EVERYTHING

Once the issue has been contained, advise the public that you are open for business again. The message must offer reassurance and provide proof that appropriate actions have been taken.

Source: Adapted from David Weiner, "The SARS crisis: lessons learned," a public relations advertising feature, *Marketing*, 2003.

FIGURE 14.2

PR tips for handling crisis situations

intimidating. Leaders must be prepared to act quickly and show that they have control of the situation. Company presidents and high-level executives must also meet the demands of a more sophisticated and more demanding consumer audience or suffer the consequences of their wrath.

PRODUCT PUBLICITY

A primary objective of public relations is to generate news about a product or service that a company is marketing. **Publicity** is news about a person, product, or service that appears in the print or broadcast media. Essentially, publicity must be newsworthy; what may seem like news to a company may not be news to the media. Opportunities to communicate newsworthy information include the launch of a new product, revealing new information based on research evidence (e.g., a discovery), securing a significant contract that will generate new jobs, and achieving significant sales and profit results.

Newsworthy information is usually communicated by a press release or press conference. These are the major tools of the trade and are discussed in detail in the next section. Information is carefully prepared and distributed to the media in such a way that editors are tempted to run all or parts of the story. The preparation of such information is the responsibility of a public relations firm. Similar to advertising, public relations is a highly specialized field, and practitioners require experience and expertise to implement a plan properly. Public relations practitioners have established contacts with media editors over the years, and they rely on their relationships with editors to get their clients' information into the news.

Here's an example to demonstrate how publicity works. Perrier implemented a public relations campaign when it launched its new one-litre plastic bottle. Objectives of the campaign were awareness and trial of the new product in key markets. Perrier employed a celebrity in the form of Ted Allen, star of *Queer Eye for the Straight Guy*, to promote the bottle. Recognizing that plastic isn't exactly news, the PR agency developed a message focusing on how the new bottle could be consumed in new situations, such as a park and a swimming pool. New recipes, summer entertaining tips, and two planned events provided a timely news hook to emphasize the lightweight, unbreakable bottle. Product samples were distributed at the events. The campaign garnered 35 broadcast interviews, more than 100 newspaper placements, and a 400-percent increase in website hits. The total print and broadcast impressions was in the 30-million range. Not bad for a plastic bottle![4]

PRODUCT PLACEMENT AND BRANDED CONTENT

Product placement is the insertion of brand logos or branded merchandise into movies and television shows. Branded content involves building a branded product right into the script. Both options are excellent ways of generating buzz for a product. Industry experts agree that BMW sparked the trend toward placements when its new Z3 Roadster appeared in the James Bond film *Golden Eye*. The latest Bond film, *Casino Royale*, starring Daniel Craig as the new Bond, prominently features a Sony laptop computer in several crucial scenes.

BMW
www.bmw.com

Product placement and **branded content** have morphed into a media strategy more so than a public relations strategy. This topic was discussed in Chapter 7. Nonetheless, product placement does generate all kinds of publicity for brand names when the press starts talking and writing about it. In *Talladega Nights: The Ballad of Ricky Bobby*, a movie staring Will Ferrell, the Wonder Bread logo appeared clearly and in focus for 11 minutes and 32 seconds. The brand was mentioned by the actor on two occasions. Wonder Bread was the main corporate sponsor for Mr. Ferrell's character. It is estimated that Wonder Bread achieved the equivalent of $4.3 million of advertising exposure by being in the film.[5]

Wonder Bread
www.wonderbread.com

Measuring the impact of product placement is difficult, but some market research shows that if a product is placed appropriately, consumers will remember the brand and associate it with the TV show in which it was placed. Using *American Idol* as an example, 64 percent of respondents to a survey recalled the Coca-Cola brand and 39 percent recalled the Ford brand after viewing the show. Coca-Cola appears on the desk of the *Idol* judges. Does such recall translate into sales? Another study found 52 percent of respondents would buy a product after being exposed to a television commercial but only 23 percent would respond from a branded entertainment experience.[6]

BUZZ MARKETING (WORD-OF-MOUTH)

Buzz marketing describes activities that companies undertake to generate personal recommendations for a branded product. Such activity is growing in popularity based on the belief that independent referrals have more impact on consumers than traditional forms of communications. There is a sense among consumers receiving the message that it is more believable. Product seeding is a form of buzz marketing.

Product seeding involves giving a product free to trendsetters who, in turn, influence others to become aware of the product and hopefully purchase the product. Trendsetters create buzz by chatting up the product whenever the opportunity arises. Matchstick, an agency that specializes in product seeding campaigns, offers a simple methodology to prospective clients. "We seed products with influential consumers," says Patrick Thoburn, co-founder. Nike uses the seeding strategy by handing out free shoes to hip kids.[7] The Gap (through Matchstick) recruits women who shop at the Gap and love the brand to become brand ambassadors. An ambassador's role is to go out and chat up the Gap's new clothing lines to their friends. Calculating a return on the investment is difficult to measure, however. The Gap, for example, will never know if an ambassador's friend will ever visit the Gap, let alone buy a specific product.

The Gap
www.gap.com

For more insight into strategies for generating brand buzz, read the Advertising in Action vignette **Igniting the Buzz**.

MEDIA RELATIONS

Generating publicity is the responsibility of a media relations expert. Media relations specialists are employed by public relations companies, and their primary responsibility is to develop unique and effective relationships with the media that cover the particular industry in which they specialize (e.g., financial information, computer hardware and

ADVERTISING IN ACTION

Igniting the Buzz

One of the latest trends in marketing is buzz marketing. Loosely defined, buzz involves using the power of word-of-mouth communications to create excitement and awareness, and stimulate sales of a product. Some refer to it as guerilla marketing, while others call it stealth marketing. Regardless of the name, it refers to unconventional ways of spreading news about a product.

Gatorade teamed up with The Running Room (a retailer that specializes in running equipment and apparel) to generate buzz for a new Gatorade product, Propel—a low-calorie, vitamin-supplement drink mix that helps keep the body hydrated. The Running Room operates running clinics for its clients that attract 50 000 participants annually. At the clinics, and during the runs that are part of the clinics, there's lots of chatting among participants. The clinics provided Propel an opportunity to directly reach "influencers" who were part of their target market (active men and women between 25 and 35 years of age). When one runner says to another: "This [Propel] will help you stay hydrated," it has so much more meaning than the same message delivered by a television commercial. There is simply more credibility to such an endorsement.

The Vespa motor scooter created some real buzz through a little street theatre. Here's the situation. You are sitting at a restaurant patio and a delivery guy pulls up on a Vespa scooter. He leaves the Vespa to do his thing and five minutes later a pretty girl comes by and asks, "Is that your Vespa?" You shake your head no and she says, "That's too bad. I'd really like a ride on it." The girl asks everyone on the patio about the scooter. Finally, the delivery guy comes back and the girl asks him for a ride. He obliges, hands her an extra helmet, and the two ride off together.

Did the street theatre work for Vespa? According to Glen Hunt of Dentsu Advertising, who was the creative mastermind behind it all, it did work. Hunt says, "Eighty percent of the time, the actors would ride off to applause. Talk about buzz!" The agency was actually reluctant to talk to the media about the campaign for fear it would ruin the stunt's surprise element with the crowd. They hit every patio in Toronto, all summer long.

Buzz marketing offers several advantages. The biggest advantage is the low cost—it's much less expensive than an ad campaign. If the seeding works, it will attract the attention of the media, and next thing you know there's a story in the newspaper! With consumers spending less time with the media, public relations and buzz are taking on a new role in building and protecting a brand.

continued

On the other side of the coin, the spreading of buzz cannot be controlled. It will spread but it cannot be moulded, directed, or stopped. It grows, gains momentum, and eventually fades if it is not refuelled. Buzz only lasts so long!

Do buzz marketing and word-of-mouth communications really work? Well, we know these methods are gaining in popularity, but some marketing managers remain skeptical about their effectiveness. At the same time, these managers know that finding innovative ways of breaking through the clutter of competitive activity is essential for success.

Source: Adapted from "Propel runs with it," *Strategy*, June 2006, p. 30; Pia Musngi, "Vespa creates buzz in the streets," *Media in Canada*, September 15, 2005, www.mediaincanada.com; and Karl Moore, "Gotta get that buzz," *Marketing*, July 5, 2004, p. 9.

Vespa Canada
www.vespacanada.com

software, automobiles, retailing). Their role is to get industry analysts on board, to the point where they will communicate favourable information about a company or brand.

The relationship between a media specialist and a reporter is one that develops over time. It is predicated on characteristics such as respect, honesty, accuracy, and professionalism. Reputation for fair play is crucial; once a reputation is lost, a PR practitioner cannot function effectively. In this regard, a specialist has to treat all media outlets fairly. Showing favouritism to one media outlet over another on a breaking story of high media value could backfire on the specialist and his or her client in the long run. The media do not forget!

COMMUNITY RELATIONS AND PUBLIC AFFAIRS

In an era of social responsibility, companies are placing high value on programs that foster a good public image in the communities in which they operate. Many companies encourage their employees to give back to the community; some even provide a few hours of work time each week to get involved. Community relations officers of large organizations arrange community events and often provide funds or other resources to sponsor community events and teams. It's all part of being a good corporate citizen.

Tim Hortons is an excellent example of a community-minded company. The phrase "We never forget where we came from" is often used in its advertising. In a public relations sense, the company gives meaning to this phrase through numerous community sponsorships that include funding the Timbits Minor Sports program (hockey and soccer), supplying jerseys to league teams, and providing free ice skating for families in hundreds of communities during the holidays. Tim Hortons also sends thousands of underprivileged kids to camp every year through the Tim Hortons Children's Foundation. The annual Camp Day promotion (an in-store fundraising promotion) raises more than $6.6 million, and in-store coin boxes raise another $4.5 million annually to support camp activities.[8]

Public affairs involves programs and strategies to deal with governments. As indicated earlier, governments (federal, provincial, and local) establish laws and regulations that dictate how companies conduct business. It is quite common for a company to hire another company that specializes in lobbying. Lobbying involves activities and practices that are designed to influence government policy decisions. Naturally, a company or an industry wants government policy to conform to what's best for business. Needless to say, governments have to balance economic well-being with social and environmental well-being, and therein lies the conflict among business, governments, and special-interest groups (e.g., groups that attack companies on the basis of their handling of environmental issues).

446

FUNDRAISING

Public relations can play a key role in the marketing mix in the not-for-profit market sector. Fundraising, for example, relies heavily on public relations. A national organization like the United Way or Salvation Army faces a huge challenge each year. Some people perceive the organization to be a big "money hole" and wonder where all of the donations go. To change this perception, public relations is used to educate the public about how the funds are used in order to predispose people to give, to solicit commitment, and to make people feel good about giving. The goal of fundraising campaigns for the United Way or the Salvation Army is to create a positive image and secure support by sending a message to the public that clearly states what the organization is all about. Refer to Figure 14.3 for an illustration.

WE SEE WHAT MOST DON'T

We see the heartbreaking effects of poverty, homelessness, abuse and addiction every day. And most importantly, we see the people who desperately need support and compassion. For us it's impossible to turn a blind eye to suffering. Last year in Canada, The Salvation Army served 2.5 million meals to the hungry, helped 10,000 people with addictions and provided one third of all shelter beds each night. This Christmas we ask you to open your eyes and your heart. And give.

 Giving Hope Today

SalvationArmy.ca ~ 1.800.SAL.ARMY

Courtesy of The Salvation Army.

FIGURE 14.3

A public service announcement with an emotional message encourages understanding and helps raise funds for the Salvation Army

Public Relations Planning

Public relations should be as closely linked to a company's bottom line as a financial plan or a marketing plan. Strategic communications planning should be based on the business challenges that lie ahead, marketing needs and strategies, and corporate vision. Any plan that is based on these characteristics must now include a comprehensive public relations program.

The nature of a public relations plan is dictated by the situation at hand. Will it be a proactive plan that can be carefully set out in advance and implemented with precision, or will it be a reactive plan that is being undertaken only because of some unforeseen circumstance occurring? A public relations plan usually involves five steps: situation analysis, establishing objectives, devising a strategy, executing the plan, and evaluation. Essentially, the process is very similar to developing an advertising plan, though the tools used are very different.

SITUATION ANALYSIS

Before any plan can be devised, a situation analysis is conducted to reveal the true nature of the problem to be resolved or the opportunity to be pursued. Clarification is crucial because a good communications strategy has to be focused if it is to be successful. For example, specific plans may be needed to resolve a crisis situation, to launch a new product, or to announce company expansion plans or financial results.

ESTABLISHING OBJECTIVES

Public relations objectives must relate specifically to the achievement of marketing objectives. Typically, marketing objectives relate to achieving specific sales, profit, and market-share goals. Objectives for launching new products are stated in terms of generating awareness and trial purchase among the target audience over a period of time. For established products, marketing objectives are stated in terms of increasing use among current users.

Regardless of the situation or desired outcome, public relations objectives tend to be similar to advertising objectives, for the two disciplines work hand in hand toward a common goal. While not adopted universally, there is a new school of thought about public relations and advertising: PR first, advertising second. PR plants the seed, while advertising harvests the crop. Such thinking is based on the premise that advertising can't start the fire; it can only fan the fire after it's been started. To get something out of nothing, you need the validity that third-party endorsements bring.[9]

Richard Branson, founder of everything operating under the Virgin brand name, firmly believes in such a philosophy. Branson is well known for his action-packed stunts at new product launches. When launching Virgin Mobile in Canada he descended from the skies by means of a high-wire to crush the competition in the Virgin Mobile "emergency services" monster truck. The big-wheeled truck rolled over three cars to demonstrate—with his usual flamboyance—his intention to crush the competition. His promise to Canadians was to free customers chained to long-term contracts, hidden fees, and high rates. An extensive advertising campaign mapping out Virgin Mobile's benefits followed the launch. See the picture in Figure 14.4.

Virgin Mobile
www.virginmobile.ca

Courtesy of Todd Korol/Reuters/Landov.

FIGURE 14.4

Virgin Mobile launches in Canada with a typical Richard Branson publicity stunt

When a new product is being launched, the objectives of both public relations and advertising are focused on creating awareness. For both of these disciplines, stating objectives in terms of awareness is valid for the key role of both in positively affecting attitudes and causing consumers to act. As marketing campaigns become more integrated and seamless, however, the effectiveness of the various components of the marketing mix and marketing communications mix becomes more difficult to measure.

Realistic expectations of public relations should be stated in terms of what it can influence. Therefore, objectives such as building recognition, creating a positive image, introducing new products, and building store traffic fall within the realm of a public relations plan.

Publicity objectives can be more sharply focused and be quantitative in nature. Publicity objectives should take into account the media through which the message will be transmitted and the target audience reached by the media. No matter how targeted an audience might be or might not be (in marketing terms), chances are they will be reached by the mass media (e.g., in a news story on television or a story in a general interest magazine or daily newspaper). If so, gross audience objectives (in terms of impressions) can be established.

To demonstrate the concept of gross impressions, consider the case of Smirnoff vodka when it launched a new package and label design in an attempt to attract younger drinkers. A half-page article about the introduction and a picture of the new package design appeared in the *Toronto Star* (the result of a sound public relations plan). The *Star*'s weekday circulation is 440 000 copies. That figure represents the potential minimum number of impressions the Smirnoff article will achieve. Undoubtedly, a similar article appeared in many other newspapers across Canada.

DEVELOPING THE PUBLIC RELATIONS STRATEGY

Similar to a marketing strategy or an advertising strategy, a public relations strategy considers a common set of variables that includes the target market, geographic location, seasonal considerations, and timing. As well, a decision must be made on the most efficient and effective way to reach consumers and cause them to act. A specific task is assigned to public relations (and other communications disciplines) so that the combined efforts are mutually reinforcing and so that all audiences receive the same message.

Strategy deals primarily with how the plan will be implemented. In the case of a new product introduction, for example, public relations may be the initial contact point for consumers and trade customers. The role of public relations is to reach those parties who have the power to influence behaviour, including industry analysts, key media, and consumers classified as innovators and early adopters. The strategic role of public relations should be examined in terms of how well it can do the following:

- Design the timetable so that the message will reach opinion leaders (analysts, trade audiences, and influential media) well in advance of the public.

- Maximize the news value of new product introductions, new advertising campaigns, and event sponsorships.

- Time PR events to reinforce advertising and sales promotion campaigns and/or maintain high visibility between campaigns.

- Reach important secondary markets, defined geographically, psychographically, and ethnically, that might not be targeted by advertising and sales promotions.[10]

Strategically, the PR message has to be different from the advertising message. With public relations it's about information and education rather than unique selling points and fancy slogans. Therefore, any claim made in a press release must be substantiated with factual information (e.g., citing consumer research data that confirms a claim or point of view, or explaining an issue thoroughly and accurately). For publicity-oriented programs, product news can be dramatized easily. Without drama and fanfare, the press release will wind up in some editor's recycling box.

A company may employ a **borrowed-interest strategy** in order to spark interest among editors. A borrowed-interest strategy promotes a newsworthy activity that is related to the product. An example of a borrowed-interest strategy could be when a company or brand participates in or sponsors an event, or if a brand is going to launch a big sales promotion activity to stimulate sales. An Olympic sponsorship involving significant sums of money is certainly a newsworthy activity for companies such as Bell, Coca-Cola, and McDonald's. In fact, Bell invested $200 million in the 2010 Vancouver Winter Olympics to become the exclusive telecommunications supplier. That's news, big news! Bell Canada sees this investment as a way of increasing market share in Western Canada, where it is considered an upstart telecommunications provider. According to Linda Oglov, vice president of Olympic partnership with Bell in Vancouver, "This is the cornerstone of Bell's expansion in the West."[11]

2010 Vancouver Winter Olympics
www.vancouver2010.com

EXECUTING THE PLAN

Executing the plan involves the specific actions and activities that will be used to achieve objectives. In other words, the directives provided in the strategy section of the plan are translated into action plans. The plan will specify what activities will occur, who will perform them, when they will occur, and at what cost. The timing and costs of all activities should be integrated into the marketing plan. The importance of executing details cannot be overemphasized. All things being equal, it is how the information is presented that could differentiate one brand from another. It can make a difference!

To get the message out, public relations has many more options than advertising does. The PR arsenal includes press releases, press conferences, press kits, audiovisual materials, websites, and blogs. These tools are discussed in more detail in the next section of the chapter.

EVALUATING EFFECTIVENESS

Like other forms of communication, public relations activities are evaluated through a variety of research methods that can be either qualitative or quantitative in nature. In some way, results achieved should be compared to the objectives that were originally established for the program. If, for example, the objective of a campaign was to alter the public's perception about a company (e.g., the problem dealt with building a better image), a focus group could be used before and after the campaign is implemented. Shifts in attitudes and opinions in the post-campaign group would determine the relative effectiveness of the campaign. Alternatively, a company could conduct a public opinion poll before and after the campaign.

A company likes to know how much exposure was actually received as a result of its public relations activities. This is referred to as **content analysis**. Organizations that keep track of content do exist. They record what is being reported, where, to how many people, over what period of time, in which media, and how the coverage changes over time.

The Canadian Public Relations Society has unveiled a new tool called the Media Relations Rating Point System (MRP) that considers criteria such as type of media, whether a photograph was published in colour or black and white, whether a spokesperson was quoted, the tone of the article (was it positive or negative?), along with audited reach numbers from a single data source in News Canada.[12] Executives who approve PR budgets know intuitively that PR works, but there is pressure to show some kind of return on investment. The new MRP system offers a solution to the ROI situation. For more insight into the ratings system refer to Figure 14.5.

The Tools of the Trade

The tools available to execute public relations programs are diverse. There are those that are used routinely to communicate newsworthy information and those that are used periodically or on special occasions only. This section discusses those vehicles that are used routinely. See Figure 14.6 for information about some unique and periodically used vehicles.

PRESS RELEASES

A **press release** (news release) is a document containing all of the essential elements of the story (who, what, when, where, and why). The release is written in a format that

FIGURE **14.5**

An illustration of a media relations ratings system

Measuring pubalic relations activity is difficult. This illustration is intended to demonstrate a standardized means of tracking the effectiveness of public relations programs.

The Canadian Public Relations Society (CPRS) recommends that an organization look at the **tone of the message** that appears in the media and then measure the message against a **predetermined list of criteria**. If meaningful criteria have been established, the results can be measured.

The CPRS recommends a **10-point rating system**. A **maximum of 5 points** is awarded for the **tone** of the piece: positive = 5 points; neutral = 3 points; negative = 0 points. In addition, one point is awarded for each **criterion** that is met (to a maximum of five criteria).

For this illustration, assume a story was reported in two different newspapers and one TV news report. Measuring the articles and report revealed the following results:

	Newspaper 1	Newspaper 2	TV News Report
TONE			
Positive	—	5	5
Neutral	3	—	—
Negative	—	—	—
CRITERIA			
Company/Brand Mention	1	1	1
Photo Included (or Video)	—	1	1
Spokesperson Quote	1	1	—
Prominence/Position	—	1	—
Key Message Delivered	1	1	1
Total Score	**6**	**10**	**8**

Analysis: The article in Newspaper 2 delivered better results. It delivered exactly what the organization was looking for. For more complete details about this measurement system refer to the CPRS website, **www.cprs.ca**.

communicates key details early. Editors make quick decisions on what to go with and what to discard. Copies of the release are mailed to a list of preferred editors (e.g., established and reliable contacts based on past relationships), and it can also be distributed by a national newswire service. News releases are distributed at news conferences or sent to the media directly by mail, fax, and email. It is now common for companies to post their press releases on their websites. A sample press release appears in Figure 14.7.

PRESS CONFERENCES

A **press conference** is a gathering of news reporters invited to witness the release of important information about a company or product. Because the conference is time-consuming for the media representatives, it is usually reserved for only the most important announcements. A crisis situation, for example, is usually handled by a press

> **Here are some tactical suggestions for getting the media and the public to take notice of a brand or company.**
>
> **AWARDS**
>
> Brand-sponsored awards that support brand positioning and leadership (e.g., Purina dog food sponsors annual awards for dogs that are heroes).
>
> **CAUSE-RELATED MARKETING**
>
> Corporate or brand support of causes based on the interests of customers (e.g., Tim Hortons financially supports little league hockey across Canada).
>
> **CEOS**
>
> The top executive should be the company's most effective media spokesperson (e.g., Bill Gates at Microsoft; Steve Jobs at Apple).
>
> **BRANDED MERCHANDISE**
>
> Select merchandise that will positively communicate a brand message (e.g., golf shirts, bomber jackets, key chains)
>
> **PLANT TOURS**
>
> Make the factory a popular tourist attraction (e.g., virtually every tourist to Smiths Falls, Ontario, visits the Hershey chocolate factory. A free sample is provided at the end of the tour).
>
> **ROAD SHOWS**
>
> The brand hits the road using a decorated vehicle as a means of attracting attention. Product samples may be given away at each stop (e.g., Shoppers Drug Mart launched their Optimum loyalty card using a Hummer, and Sunlight detergent used a set of vans resembling sunlight boxes for their "Go Ahead. Get Dirty" campaign).
>
> **SURVEYS**
>
> The results of surveys are a proven way of achieving positive media exposure. Data derived from marketing research should be used for publicity purposes.
>
> **TRADE SHOWS**
>
> Shows are the ideal launching pad for new products. Be where your customers are (e.g., Comdex shows display the latest gadgetry in computers and telecommunications).

FIGURE 14.6

Some unique and innovative public relations tools

conference. A **press kit** is usually distributed at a conference. The press kit includes a schedule of conference events; a list of company participants, including biographical information; a press release; photographs; copies of speeches; videos; and any other relevant information. Video news releases—stories prepared by a company for use by television stations—are somewhat controversial. Critics see them as propaganda and object when stations don't mention their origin. Nonetheless, if the shoe fits, the media will wear it—a good video can save the station time and money.

PUBLICATIONS

A publication or **house organ** is a document that outlines news and events about the organization and its employees. It can be distributed internally to employees or externally to suppliers, distributors, shareholders, and alumni. A house organ can be published in the form of a newsletter, booklet, brochure, newspaper, or magazine. The objective of the house organ is to generate goodwill and build positive public opinion

FIGURE 14.7

Molson announces the launch of a new can by press release

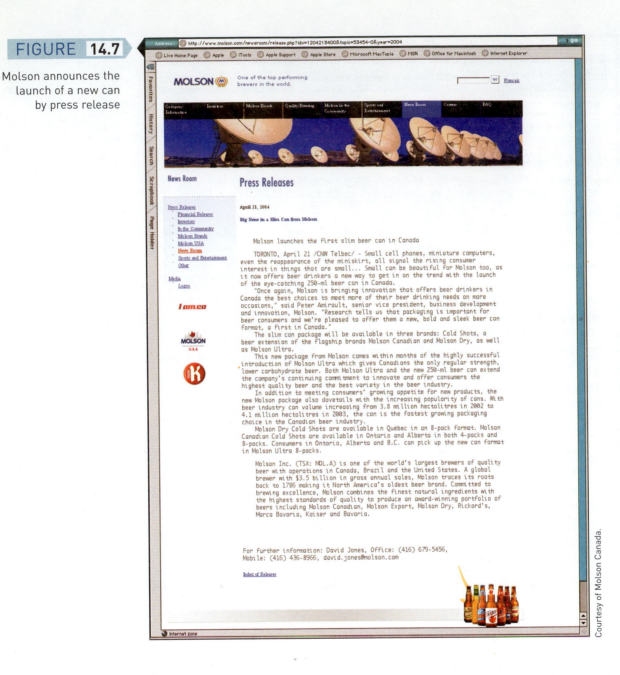

about the organization. Most colleges and universities have an alumni publication that is well received by former students. They like to know what's going on at their alma mater. An annual report is a vital publication for publicly held companies. It is a statement of the company's health and wealth and is used to attract new investors and build corporate image. The content of annual reports along with other relevant information about a company is now readily available at most company websites.

POSTERS AND DISPLAYS

Posters and displays are a common form of internal employee communications. They communicate vital information regarding safety, security, employee benefits, and special events. Displays and exhibits are a portable and mobile form of communication. An exhibit typically provides a history of an organization, product displays and information, and future plans (e.g., plant expansion, new product innovations). Exhibits are appropriate for shopping malls and colleges and universities. At colleges and universities, an exhibit staffed with company representatives is a useful vehicle for distributing recruitment information to graduating students.

Internally, **bulletin boards** are a useful vehicle for keeping employees informed about news and events. For example, social events are commonly announced on boards in central locations (staff lounges, cafeterias, and common areas). **Email** is now a quick and convenient way to communicate important information to employees as are **electronic signs** that are strategically located throughout a building.

WEBSITES

Corporate and brand websites are now an integral element of marketing communications. Since the purpose of the website is to communicate information about a company, it can be an effective public relations tool. Visitors to a website quickly form an impression about a company based on the experience they have at the site. Therefore, the site must load quickly and be easy to navigate. Providing some kind of entertainment or interactive activity also enhances the visit. The website provides an opportunity to inform the public of an organization's latest happenings. Content can vary from financial information to product information to games and contests. It is now quite common to post all press releases about a company on the corporate website. See the illustration in Figure 14.8 for details.

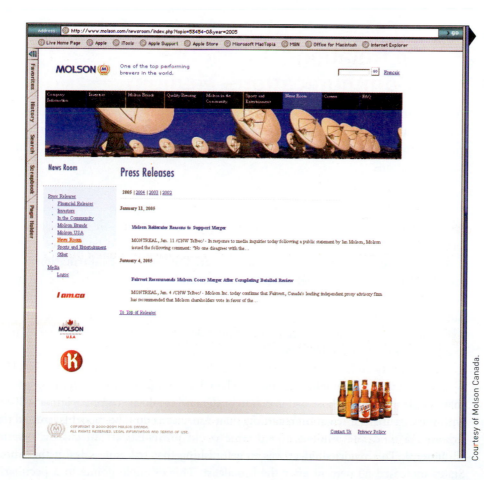

FIGURE 14.8

Companies publish press releases at their websites

BLOGS

As described in Chapter 12, a blog is a personally owned, frequently updated publication of personal thoughts on a website. But companies are now finding ways to use blogs—for example, as a tool to present current information to employees and other stakeholders.

The popularity of blogs has changed the nature of public relations. Today, the consumer-generated content of a blog has just as much weight as information presented by corporations and traditional media outlets. "Consumers are in control, and consumers are the media. It's paradigm shift that's going to change PR forever."[13] PR practitioners are going to have to adjust to this change—they must be more like journalists, and post professional-quality material on blogs.

Since there is no control over the content of a personal blog, the information posted about an organization can be positive or negative. And bad news travels fast! In February 2007 a New York City TV station broadcast a video of dozens of rats running around a local KFC/Taco Bell restaurant. As it turns out, there are few things that will spread more quickly on the web, and with more negative repercussions, than a video of rats running rampant in a fast-food outlet. By mid-day, and before corporate owner Yum could post a response on its own website, more than 100 blogs had either linked to or posted the story and footage of the incident. A search on Google news for "rats and KFC" yielded 443 stories—what Yum thought was a local story quickly became an international news story. Yum should have acted more quickly, shown more concern, and outlined their program to correct the situation on a blog.[14]

Public Relations as a Communications Medium

Public relations is only one element in the integrated communications mix, but it can play a key role in specific situations. Those responsible for corporate and brand communications should be aware of the basic benefits and drawbacks of public relations communications.

ADVANTAGES OF PUBLIC RELATIONS

Public relations is often perceived negatively by the consumer—it is associated with terms such as "spin" and "propaganda." In reality, nothing could be further from the truth. Public relations done properly can be a **credible source of information**. Simply stated, when the message is delivered by an independent third party, such as a journalist or broadcaster, the message is delivered more persuasively than any form of advertising. Further, articles appearing in the media are perceived as being more objective than advertisements. If a company can win favourable press coverage, its message is more likely to be absorbed and believed.[15]

Third-party endorsements by trusted media personalities can **drive up sales**. Here is an illustration to dramatize the point. The CBS news program *60 Minutes* reported that people in France, whose diet is rich in butter and cream and who consume red wine with meals, suffer far fewer heart attacks than Americans do. The report suggested that drinking a moderate amount of red wine could prevent heart attacks by lowering cholesterol. This reported effect was so astonishing that red wine sales in the United States increased 50 percent after the broadcast. This example points to a peculiarity about public relations: no matter how many millions of dollars are spent on ads, nothing sells a product as well as free publicity, especially something that discusses health claims.[16]

Public relations provides assistance in **building relationships** with consumers and other publics. In today's competitive environment, the product alone cannot build consumer confidence. Public relations can help build rapport through an ongoing dialogue with consumers. It is a relationship-building tool that can make a difference—it can separate one brand from the rest of the pack. Such a benefit is important, given the rising costs of communicating via media advertising, the fragmentation of the media, and the clutter of commercial messages in all forms of media.

DISADVANTAGES OF PUBLIC RELATIONS

One of the biggest drawbacks of public relations is the **lack of control** of the company. Through press releases and press conferences, the company does its best to communicate factual information and hopes that it will be presented accurately by the media. Since the media are pressed for time and space, all materials received from companies and selected for use are edited. If only some of the facts are communicated, the story could be misrepresented or presented in a less than desirable manner. Despite this possibility, there are those who believe that any publicity is good publicity!

Catching the eyes and ears of editors is crucial to the success of any public relations program. That is a challenge, considering the enormous amounts of material that flow into media outlets each day. Consequently, the cost of preparing and delivering information may go to **waste**. The senior management of an organization must recognize the waste factor and be prepared to absorb the costs associated with it. Simply stated, what is important to the company and its management group may not be perceived as important by the media. End of story!

Event Marketing and Sponsorships

Event marketing and sponsorships are fast becoming important elements of the marketing communications mix. **Event marketing** is the process, planned by a sponsoring organization, of integrating a variety of communication elements to support an event theme. For example, Nike plans and executes road races in large urban markets and supports the event with advertising, public relations, and sales promotion activities to achieve runner participation and buzz for the event. To make these events successful, Nike must invest in other forms of communication to generate awareness and encourage participation.

Event sponsorship is the financial support of an event (e.g., an auto race, a theatrical performance, a marathon road race) by a sponsor in return for advertising privileges associated with the event. Bell Canada made a significant financial commitment to be an exclusive telecommunications sponsor of the 2010 Vancouver Winter Olympics. Bell is giving the organizing committee $200 million: $90 million in cash; $60 million in telecommunications equipment; and $50 million in games-related marketing. Is such a large investment a good investment? According to Michael Sabia, CEO of Bell, "Just a one-percent increase in market share will generate $300 million worth of improved shareholder value. It is the perfect platform to enhance Bell's brand as the leading national provider of communications services."[17]

According to IEG Consulting, a Chicago-based sponsorship measurement firm, the North American sponsorship market is valued at $11.1 billion, and it is a growing market.[18]

Factors including the fragmentation of traditional media and the penetration of new media alternatives such as cell phones means companies are placing less emphasis on television advertising. Some funds are being shifted to activities that generate interaction with customers—event marketing and sponsorships are two of those activities.

From the $11.1-billion sponsorship pie, sports sponsorships dominate, with approximately $7.8 billion in revenues, or 70 percent of all event sponsorship revenue. Other sponsorship revenues are divided between arts and cultural events, entertainment events, and cause-related events. IEG is forecasting a reshuffling of sponsorship investment in the coming years. They project a decline in sports investment and modest increases in spending in other sponsorship areas.[19]

SPORTS SPONSORSHIP

On an ongoing basis, the most popular of the sports are auto racing, golf, tennis, and running. Each of these sports attracts an elite group of sponsor companies. In golf, for example, Mercedes and Buick are closely associated with professional golf tournaments, and Cadillac is a featured sponsor for the entire Senior PGA tournament schedule.

In Canada, sports sponsorships are dominated by some of our largest manufacturers, service companies, and retailers. The automobile industry is well represented by companies such as General Motors and Ford, the brewing industry by Molson and Labatt, and the financial industry by RBC Financial Group, BMO Financial Group, Visa, and MasterCard. Labatt has been a long-time sponsor of hockey, football, and baseball in Canada. Over the years it has sponsored National Hockey League broadcasts and the Canadian Adult Recreational Hockey Association. The company has supported the Canadian Football League since its inception and is a long-time sponsor of the Hamilton Tiger Cats and Winnipeg Blue Bombers. Labatt is also synonymous with baseball through its association with the Toronto Blue Jays.

How effective is the investment in sports sponsorship? A recent survey among North American marketing executives indicates that events deliver the greatest return on investment over other customary tools, including advertising. A full 82 percent of these executives perceive event marketing to be a strategic and efficient business tool.[20] Considering Bell Canada's investment in the 2010 Vancouver Winter Olympics, described above, Bell fully expects a handsome return on its investment.

A key indicator of success is the effect the association with a sponsored event has on consumers' awareness of a brand or company. Having a company's name splashed all over the media in a positive way is always a good thing, and being associated with a big-time event can improve employee morale. Bell Canada has been a long-time sponsor of the Bell Canadian Open (a PGA tour event) but has recently bowed out, citing the need to streamline its sponsorship portfolio.[21] Such a move suggests the strategic nature of event marketing and sponsorship decisions.

LEVELS OF SPORTS SPONSORSHIPS An organization's involvement in sports sponsorship does not have to be extravagant. The degree of involvement and financial commitment depends on the organization's marketing objectives and its overall strategy. Sports sponsorship can be subdivided into classifications from global events to local events. See Figure 14.9 for a table showing different levels of sports sponsorship.

To illustrate, Visa associates itself with national and international events—a reflection of the card's status around the world. In contrast, Tim Hortons takes more of a grass-roots approach to sponsorships, preferring to sponsor local sports programs across Canada. The company's Timbits sponsorship program, offered through local franchisees,

Toronto Blue Jays
bluejays.mlb.com

$ **GLOBAL**
Olympic Games

INTERNATIONAL
U.S. Open (Golf),
Tour de France,
British Grand Prix

NATIONAL
Canada Summer Games,
Canadian Curling Championship

REGIONAL
Ontario Summer Games, OHL,
Western Jr. Hockey League

$

LOCAL
Minor sports programs, road races for charitable causes

Costs associated with sponsorship increase at each level.

provides jerseys for community-based soccer and hockey leagues. The sponsorship program fits nicely with the target audience the company is trying to reach.

The grandest of sports sponsorships is the Olympic Games. The Olympics present an attractive but expensive opportunity for corporate sponsors. Financial support of the Canadian Olympic Association (COA) gives a company the right to run advertising and sales promotion programs in the years and months preceding the Games. Many leading companies such as Bell Canada, General Motors, and Visa renew their commitment to the Olympics each time around because they see great value in participation. Independent research studies show a positive correlation between Olympic sponsors and the public's perception of them: 78 percent of those surveyed said they feel very positive toward companies that are official sponsors of the Olympic Games. Further, 67 percent said that Olympic sponsors are companies they can trust.[22]

AMBUSH MARKETING   A recent phenomenon associated with sports-event marketing is the practice of ambush marketing. **Ambush marketing** is a promotional strategy used by non-sponsors to capitalize on the popularity or prestige of an event by giving the false impression that they are the sponsors. Such a strategy works because people are often confused about who the real sponsors are. Ambush marketing is undeniably as effective as it is damaging, attracting consumers at the expense of the true sponsors, all the while undermining an event's integrity and, most importantly, its ability to attract future sponsors.

Labatt Breweries of Canada walked away from its long-running sponsorship of the Olympic Games due in part to the ambush efforts of arch-rival Molson. While Labatt was sponsoring the Games, Molson was sponsoring Olympics-bound teams or athletes, and that type of association lessened the impact of Labatt's exclusive advertising deal. In the 2002 Olympic Winter Games in Salt Lake City, Labatt was the official games sponsor, but was overshadowed when Molson gave $1 million to the Canadian Hockey Association to sponsor the men's and women's Olympic hockey teams. Molson reaped a marketing windfall when both hockey teams won gold. Both companies ran ads around the winter games, so it was difficult for consumers to judge who was the "official" Olympic sponsor.[23]

VENUE MARKETING AND SPONSORSHIPS   An offshoot of sports sponsorship is **venue marketing**, or **venue sponsorship**. Here, a company or brand is linked to a physical site such as a stadium, arena, or theatre. For example, GM Place (home of the Vancouver Canucks), the Bell Centre (Montreal Canadiens), and the Air Canada Centre (Maple Leafs and Raptors). These companies agree that such sponsorships offer huge opportunities for building or improving their image at a reasonable cost and with minimal risk. Exposure via television broadcasts of games and mentions in the print and broadcast media when the results of games are reported are so frequent that the corporate name is soon closely linked with the building. Refer to the illustration in Figure 14.10

To an outsider, the costs of venue marketing are considerable: the Bank of Nova Scotia recently announced a $20-million fifteen-year deal to tie its name to the home of the Ottawa Senators. The arena is now called Scotiabank Place. Scotiabank has significantly increased its marketing budget in recent years and believes sponsorship marketing delivers "more bang for the buck."[24] For more insight into sports sponsorships and venue sponsorships, see the Advertising in Action vignette **Brand Exposure Counts**.

ATHLETE SPONSORSHIPS   Rather than sponsoring an event, some companies find that sponsoring a star athlete can pay dividends. Companies will search for an athlete whose image and reputation is a close match to their own.

FIGURE 14.10

Linking a brand name to a venue increases brand exposure and helps build brand image

Courtesy of Dick Hemingway.

ADVERTISING IN ACTION

Brand Exposure Counts

How many times have you heard Ron MacLean introduce *Hockey Night in Canada* broadcasts on a Saturday night as coming "live from the Air Canada Centre in Toronto"? This type of announcement at any arena where a game is being broadcast demonstrates the benefit of investing in naming rights. However, the cost of naming rights for a building is substantial.

BMO Bank of Montreal recently struck a deal with Maple Leaf Sports and Entertainment to have its name directly associated with a new soccer stadium built in Toronto. The stadium houses the new Toronto FC soccer franchise, starting in 2007. The stadium is known as BMO Field. The cost? A cool $30 million for 10 years, or $3 million a year! Is it worth it?

BMO says it is. They are actually following their rivals in pursuing venue marketing: there is also the TD Banknorth Garden, where the Boston Bruins play, and the RBC Centura Centre, where the Carolina Hurricanes play. Scotiabank now has its name on the arena where the Ottawa Senators play.

Securing naming rights will increase brand awareness. According to TD Bank, the corporation gets about 250 000 print and broadcast brand mentions a year from the hockey and basketball games played in their arena. Banks are generally well-known entities already, so why are they investing significant sums in venue sponsorship? In the case of RBC and TD, both are attempting to increase brand awareness in the United States as they expand their operations there. Another thought is that banks are seen as being hugely profitable, and they want to give something back to the community.

BMO is a well-known bank in Canada, so brand awareness is not that much of an issue. BMO's connection with soccer offers other benefits. The deal is attractive because soccer has national reach yet is a sport that is not as commercialized as hockey, football, and basketball. As well, the connection will be strong within some of Canada's ethnic groups. The bank stands to reach hundreds of thousands of people entering Canada who have not been exposed to Canadian bank brands.

In justifying the investment, BMO CEO Tony Comper says, "Soccer is hugely popular, particularly among many of Canada's cultural communities. BMO is going to be part of the excitement of the world's most popular sport at Canada's newest sports venue."

Source: Adapted from Duncan Mavin, "National soccer teams to play at BMO field," *Financial Post*, September 21, 2006, p. FP3.

The key to working with an athlete is the celebrity endorsement it brings. Both Reebok and Gatorade were quick to sign Sidney Crosby to a lucrative endorsement deal. Crosby is considered by many experts to be the heir apparent to Wayne Gretzky, hockey's all-time leading scorer. Crosby is the centrepiece of Reebok's hockey equipment campaign, which uses the slogan, "I am what I am." When Crosby is interviewed by the media he is always seen wearing Reebok clothing and equipment. As part of the deal, Crosby will participate in numerous corporate functions during the life of the deal.[25]

There are risks associated with star sponsorships. Should the star engage in unbecoming activity, a sponsoring brand or company could suffer from negative publicity generated by the press. As a form of protection for the sponsor, ethics clauses are built into contractual arrangements with the stars.

ENTERTAINMENT SPONSORSHIP

Corporations invest huge amounts of money to sponsor concerts and secure endorsements from high-profile personalities in the hope that the celebrity–company relationships will pay off in the long run. Companies such as Molson, Coca-Cola, and PepsiCo, which are interested in targeting youth and young adult segments, use entertainment sponsorship as a vehicle for developing pop-music and youth-lifestyle marketing strategies.

In Quebec, for example, Budweiser beer is synonymous with rock music. The brand's rock strategy dates back to 1989 when it sponsored a Rolling Stones concert. Flush with success, Budweiser staked out the "rock music for the young" positioning in the early 1990s, capitalizing on its distinctive brand equity elements (fun, rock music, and partying). Rock became the heart and soul of the brand, and anchored a full range of integrated marketing communications programs including advertising, promotions, sponsorships, events, and point-of-sale advertising. Over the years, the campaigns used slogans such as "Bud = King of Rock" and "Rock Attitude." Between 1994 and 2004 Budweiser rose to become the best-selling beer in Quebec.[26]

According to Nicolas Dubé, creative director at Palm Publicité Marketing, "Bud owns rock music in Quebec because we are always knocking on the same door. Unlike the rest of Canada, where Bud's target market relates heavily to sports and male bonding activities, Quebecers relate very well to rock.[27]

Festivals (film, comedy, and music) offer opportunities to reach a cross-section of adult target audiences. At festivals as popular as the Toronto International Film Festival there are waiting lists for top-level sponsorships. It seems that companies are eager to align themselves with the movie stars who attend these types of events. Among the sponsors are Bell Canada, Cineplex Entertainment, Motorola, Visa, and Federal Express. The very popular Montreal International Jazz Festival attracts sponsors such as General Motors, TD Canada Trust, Loto Quebec, and Bell. Do festivals produce an audience, and is the investment worthwhile? The Just for Laughs Comedy Festival in Montreal reaches more than 1.7 million people each summer, mostly over the age of 30.[28] With such reach, the festival has little problem attracting sponsors.

CULTURAL AND ARTS SPONSORSHIP

Arts and cultural event opportunities embrace dance, film, literature, music, painting, sculpture, and theatre. What separates cultural events from sports and entertainment events is audience size. Depending on the sponsor, this can be an advantage or a disadvantage. A company such as Molson prefers the mass-audience reach of a sporting event, whereas Mercedes-Benz or BMW may prefer to reach a more selective and upscale audience through an arts event. Perhaps only 2500 people attend a particular cultural event, but those people most likely fit the demographic and psychographic profile of the target market. Typically, their education level would be above average, as would their income. Such an audience profile would be a good match for promoting a new luxury car.

The primary benefit that companies gain from sponsoring the arts is goodwill from the public. Most firms view this type of investment as part of their corporate citizenship objectives (e.g., they are perceived as a good, contributing member of society). BMO Financial Group, for example, is a long-standing sponsor of numerous cultural events and organizations that include the Governor General's Literary Awards, the Stratford Festival, the Toronto Symphony Orchestra, the National Business Book Award, and the National Ballet School.

Bell Canada, a long-time sponsor of the Stratford Festival, enhanced its presence at the event through unique signage in the lobby of two theatre venues. Two giant-sized plasma screens looped information about the festival, as well as sponsorship recognition. Bell has always invested in the communities it serves and has a varied sponsorship portfolio, which includes major cultural and sporting events that enable it to be present in the community throughout the year. See figures 14.11 and 14.12 for details.

Montreal International Jazz Festival
www.montrealjazzfest.com

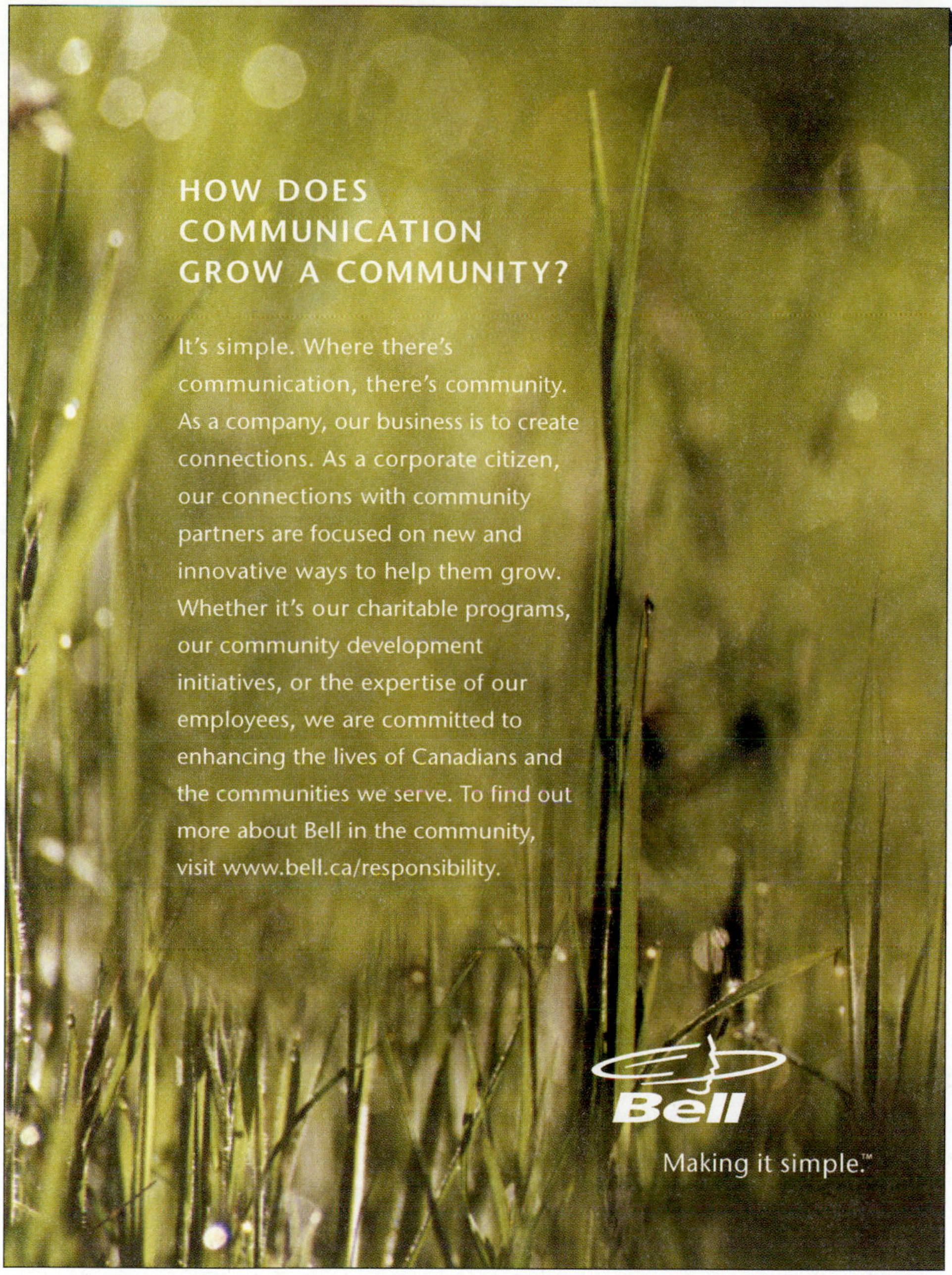

Courtesy of Bell Canada.

FIGURE 14.11

A corporate ad that communicates Bell's commitment to the community

CAUSE MARKETING SPONSORSHIPS

Cause marketing involves a partnership between a company and a non-profit entity for mutual benefit. The relationship between the parties has a significant meaning to consumers. This meaning, when associated with a brand or company, can have a positive effect on the consumer's perception of the brand. Such is the benefit that CIBC derives from its ongoing title sponsorship of the Canadian Breast Cancer Foundation CIBC Run for the Cure, in which the overall goal is to raise funds to help find a cure for breast cancer. Other sponsors of this cause include Kimberly-Clark Worldwide, Air Canada, and the Ford Motor Company of Canada.

Canadian Breast Cancer Foundation
www.cbcf.org

FIGURE **14.12**

A selection of sponsorships
from Bell Canada

SPORTS

- Bell and the Air Canada Grand Prix (Formula 1 auto racing)
- Bell Challenge Cup (Pee Wee hockey challenge)
- Bell and the Molson Indy (CART auto racing)
- Bell Classic (women's charitable golf fundraiser)
- The Bell Canadian Open (men's professional golf)
- Bell Raptorball (grassroots basketball programs)
- Toronto Maple Leafs (telecommunications sponsor at the Air Canada Centre)
- Ottawa Senators (telecommunications sponsor)
- Toronto Rock Lacrosse (telecommunications sponsor)
- Ottawa Rebels Lacrosse (telecommunications sponsor)
- Canadian Olympic Team

CULTURE

- Bell Encourages Young People to Participate in Expo-Sciences (cross-Canada science exposition)
- Stratford Festival (major sponsor and communications partner)
- Shaw Festival (major sponsor and communications partner)
- Toronto Word on the Street Festival (major sponsor and communications partner)
- Toronto International Film Festival (major sponsor and communications partner)
- Vancouver International Film Festival (major sponsor and communications partner)
- Sprockets—Toronto International Film Festival for Children (major sponsor and communications partner)
- Bell Mobility and the Santa Claus Parade in Toronto
- Just For Laughs Festival, Montreal

Source: Adapted from the Bell Canada website: www.bell.ca.

There are other ways for a company to associate with a worthy cause. For example, the pink ribbon is a recognizable emblem representing efforts to eradicate breast cancer. Brands carrying this emblem donate a portion of their sales to the cause. This type of campaign raises funds for the charity and helps a company give back to society while building their charitable reputation.[29]

In today's competitive business world, marketing executives are searching for new ways to connect with consumers emotionally. Not-for-profit organizations are proving to be good business partners to achieve this goal. BMO Financial Group, for example, makes a significant investment in civic and community causes to help build vibrant, safe, and tolerant communities. BMO sponsors the United Way, a Take Our Kids to Work program, and Fashion Cares, a program to help fight against AIDS and HIV. BMO also makes financial contributions to hospitals and various foundations. BMO donates in the neighbourhood of $40 million annually to causes and charitable organizations.[30]

Strategic Considerations for Event Marketing

Advertisers cannot approach event marketing and sponsorships in a haphazard way. Their primary reason for entering into sponsorships is to create a favourable impression with their customers and target groups. To accomplish this, the fit between the event and the sponsor must be a good one. For instance, Nike sponsors national and international track and field events as well as community-based events such as fun runs. Much of the company's success has been based on event sponsorship and the distribution of merchandise that bears Nike's trademark logo—the swoosh. Generally, event sponsorship is a vehicle for enhancing the reputation of a company and the customer's awareness of a brand. The most effective sponsors adhere to the following principles when considering participation in event marketing.

- *Select events offering exclusivity* The need for companies to be differentiated within events they sponsor calls for exclusivity, meaning that direct competitors are blocked from sponsorship. Also, a concern among sponsors is the clutter of lower-level sponsors in non-competing categories that reduce the overall impact of the primary sponsor.

- *Use sponsorships to complement other promotional activity* The role that advertising and promotion will play in the sponsorship must be determined first. Sponsorship of the proper event will complement a company's other promotional activity. For example, Adidas determined that a sponsorship arrangement with the NBA would be fruitful. Their 11-year global merchandising deal will make Adidas the official uniform and apparel provider for the league. The Adidas logo will appear on all NBA apparel. The deal with the NBA is a strategic move that will close the gap between arch-rival Nike and Adidas. Adidas has a similar deal with the National Football League.[31]

- *Choose the target carefully* Events reach specific targets. For example, while rock concerts attract youth, symphonies tend to reach audiences that are older, urban, and upscale. As suggested earlier, it is the fit, or matching of targets, that is crucial. Do the demographics of the event audience match as closely as possible the demographics of the target market?

- *Select an event with an image that sells* The sponsor must capitalize on the image of the event and perhaps the prestige or status associated with it. As discussed earlier in the chapter, Bell Canada sees great business potential now that it is the exclusive telecommunications supplier to the 2010 Vancouver Winter Olympics. The Olympics has the kind of cachet that will make it the cornerstone of a multimedia promotion campaign in the years preceding the games.

- *Establish selection criteria* In addition to using the criteria cited above, companies evaluating potential events for sponsorship should consider the long-term benefit such sponsorship offers compared to the costs in the short term. For example, being associated with an event that is ongoing, popular, and successful is wise, as there is less risk for the sponsor. Before committing financial resources to an event, a company should also consider whether it is likely to receive communications exposure through unpaid media sources and whether it will be able to administer the event efficiently. Events that receive substantial media exposure are very attractive. High levels of exposure offset any real or opportunity costs. An organization should establish firm objectives in terms of awareness and association scores, image improvement, and sales, so that proper evaluation of the activity can be undertaken.

Measuring the Benefits of Event Marketing and Sponsorship

One reason many companies are reluctant to enter into sponsorship programs is that results are difficult to measure. Large sums of money are spent at one time for a benefit that may be short-lived. The basic appeal of event marketing is that it provides an opportunity to communicate with consumers in an environment in which they are already emotionally involved. Beyond this, companies conduct marketing research to determine the impact that sponsorship association has. The following indicators, many of which are obtained from research, are used to measure the benefits of sponsorship.

1. *Awareness* How much awareness of the event within the target group is there, and how well do people recall the brand or product name that sponsored the event? If the event is promoted properly, the lead sponsor's name should be top-of-mind with both attendees and television viewers of an event.

2. *Image* What change in image and what increase in the consumer perception of leadership or credibility results from the sponsorship? Market research before and after event participation may be necessary to identify this benefit. As indicated earlier in the chapter, sponsors who are associated with the Olympic Games received excellent scores on image and leadership in post-event marketing research.

3. *New clients* How many new clients were generated as a result of the company's sponsoring an event? It is important to include current and prospective customers in the event. For example, inviting customers to view the event from a **luxury box** and to have them enjoy the trappings associated with the box goes a long way in solidifying business relationships.

4. *Sales* Do increases in sales or market share occur during post-event periods? Participating in an event isn't like dropping a coupon; the actual impact may be longer-term. In fact, the real sales benefit may take years to materialize, as it takes time for a sponsor to become closely associated with an event.

5. *Specific target reach* Do the events deliver constituency? Carefully selected events reach specific targets that are difficult to reach by conventional communications. For example, preteens and teens are difficult to reach through conventional media but can be reached effectively through sponsorship of rock concerts and music tours.

6. *Media coverage* What value was derived from editorial coverage? Did the sponsorship result in free publicity for the sponsor? The industry benchmark for sports sponsorship is currently 4:1, meaning $4 in exposure (e.g., free air time) for every $1 spent on sponsorship and its marketing support. Assuming an organization invests in a service to track exposure, it can measure spending equivalencies between free media exposure and comparable advertising.

For sponsorships to be successful, there must be sound business reasons for participating, and the activity must be carefully and seamlessly integrated with corporate marketing and marketing communications plans. For every dollar spent on securing the sponsorship rights, an additional investment of $2 to $3 is needed to promote the association with the event. The organization must leverage the use of its website, incorporate the sponsorship into public relations campaigns, and run thematic promotions to get all customer groups (trade and consumers) involved. The various forms of marketing communications must complement each other.

Event Marketing and Sponsorship as a Communications Medium

When assessing whether to be involved with event marketing and sponsorships, an organization weighs the pros and cons of the activity in the context of how well it fits with other marketing and marketing communications strategies. There are numerous advantages and disadvantages of event marketing.

ADVANTAGES OF EVENT MARKETING AND SPONSORSHIP

The primary advantage of event marketing is *target marketing*. Participating in the right event allows an organization to reach its target audience directly and in an environment where the target is receptive to messages (e.g., an auto race where sponsorships are part of the ambience of the event). Sponsorships can also provide *face-to-face access* to current and prospective customers. For example, if a financial services company holds an investment seminar with an open invitation to the public, it will have access to new clients in a non-competitive environment; at such an event, the message is delivered to a large group at one time. Finally, participation in the right events and sponsorships enhances a company's *public image*. Whether it's involvement with huge events such as the Olympics, or just supporting local community events, the effect on image is the same. As cited earlier in the chapter, companies that are perceived to be doing good things are liked better and trusted more.

DISADVANTAGES OF EVENT MARKETING AND SPONSORSHIP

The most prominent disadvantage to events and sponsorships is *cost*. Any event on a national or international scale involves significant financial commitment, and to enjoy the benefits of such events, the commitment is necessary for an extended period. Opting in and out of big events leaves a confusing image with the public. As indicated earlier in the chapter, successful events must be supported with additional spending on advertising and promotion. One complaint commonly raised by event participants is the *clutter* of advertising and signage at events. If there are too many sponsors, the message being delivered by an individual sponsor is diluted; hence, the investment is questionable. As well, the presence of *ambush marketing tactics* by competitors is diluting the product category exclusivity aspect of event participation. Finally, accurately *measuring the effectiveness* of the event or sponsorship in producing sound business results is difficult. It would be nice to know what the return on investment is, but there are so many variables that ultimately contribute to sales and market share performance that the impact of events and sponsorship cannot be isolated.

SUMMARY

Public relations refers to the communications that a firm has with its various publics. Controlled by the media, it is a form of communication for which the organization does not pay, but it is based on information supplied by the organization. Public relations plays a role in developing an organization's image and is an important means of communication in times of crisis.

Two diverse groups are important to an organization, and public relations programs communicate with both of them. Internal publics include employees, distributors, suppliers, shareholders, and regular customers. External publics include the media, governments, prospective shareholders, the financial community, and community groups. Organizations communicate with the various publics through press releases, press conferences, publications, posters and displays, websites, and blogs. Any form of online communications now plays an important role in building corporate and brand image.

Public relations play a key role in several areas, including corporate advertising, reputation management, publicity generation, buzz marketing, media relations, community relations and public affairs, and fundraising. A public relations campaign is planned much like any other communications plan. It starts with a situation analysis and then firm objectives and strategies are devised. Once the plan is implemented, research procedures are undertaken to track the effectiveness of the campaign.

Event marketing and sponsorship programs are now an important element of a firm's promotion mix, particularly among large Canadian corporations. Sponsorship is popular in three areas: sports, entertainment, and cultural events. Sports attract the lion's share of sponsorship dollars. Many companies now see value in sponsoring athletes in order to benefit from their celebrity, or in attaching their corporate name to sports venues in order to increase brand exposure.

Unlike other types of promotion, events and sponsorships have an indirect impact on product or company performance. The benefits derived from this activity include goodwill and increased awareness, as opposed to measurable increases in sales or market share.

Organizations must carefully consider certain criteria before jumping into event marketing. They should look for events that offer exclusivity; that complement other marketing communications strategies; that closely match their target market's profile; and that deliver high levels of media exposure. If the right events are selected and the association with the event is leveraged through advertising and promotion, the organization should enjoy high levels of awareness, an improved image, and stronger sales. The latter will likely occur in the long term.

KEY TERMS

ambush marketing 459
borrowed-interest strategy 450
branded content 444
cause marketing 463
content analysis 451
corporate advertising 441
event marketing 457
event sponsorship 457

house organ 453
lobbying 446
media relations 445
press conference 452
press kit 453
press release 451
product placement 444
product seeding 444

public affairs 446
public relations 440
publicity 440
situation analysis 448
venue marketing
   (venue sponsorship) 460

REVIEW QUESTIONS

1. What is the difference between public relations and publicity?

2. Identify and briefly explain the role of public relations in the following areas:

   a) Reputation management
   b) Publicity generation
   c) Media relations
   d) Product seeding
   e) Buzz marketing
   f) Community relations
   g) Fundraising

3. What is lobbying, and why is it necessary for organizations to engage in such a practice?

4. What are the key elements of a public relations strategy?

5. What is a borrowed-interest strategy, and how does it apply to public relations?

6. What is a press kit, and what role does it serve?

7. What is a house organ, and what role does it play in an organization?

8. Identify the basic advantages and disadvantages of using public relations campaigns as a means of communication.

9. What is the difference between event marketing and event sponsorship?

10. Briefly explain the following event marketing terms:
    a) Ambush marketing
    b) Venue marketing

11. Identify and briefly explain the essential factors an organization should review when deciding to participate in event marketing.

12. What are the primary benefits an organization gains when it invests in event marketing?

DISCUSSION QUESTIONS

1. "Public relations now plays a more important role in the communications mix of business organizations today." Discuss the merits of this statement and provide examples to justify your opinion.

2. Assume you are a public relations consultant and Coca-Cola has approached you for advice. They want your recommendation for a celebrity spokesperson to endorse Powerade (a sports beverage), along with a public relations recommendation to announce the signing of the celebrity. Develop a brief plan of action. Be as specific as you can. Provide justification for the celebrity you recommend.

3. Visit the websites of the following companies (use other companies if you wish). Evaluate each site as a vehicle for public relations activity. Does the site provide worthwhile information that will create goodwill for the company? Explain.

   a) The Body Shop www.the-body-shop.com
   b) Apple www.apple.com
   c) BMW www.bmw.com

4. If you were the marketing communications manager for any one of the following products, what events would you sponsor? What benefits would you derive from these sponsorships? Be specific.

   a) Budweiser beer
   b) Gillette personal care products
   c) Hallmark cards
   d) Michelin tires
   e) American Express traveller's cheques

5. It seems that measuring the effectiveness or return on investment of event marketing and sponsorships is difficult. If so, is it justifiable for companies to invest significant sums of money in event marketing (global, international, and national events)? Do the benefits outweigh the costs? What is your opinion?

6. Is cause marketing a worthwhile endeavour for corporate Canada to invest in? How does a company benefit by being involved in cause-related marketing activities? Explain.

NOTES

1. Pizza Hut case study, Ogilvy PR, **www.ogilvypr.com**.

2. Oliver Moore, "Beer icon's the buzz of bars," *Globe and Mail*, February 17, 2006, p. A12.

3. Linda Smith, "When the trust begins to rust," *Marketing*, March 1, 2004, p. 12.

4. Public Relations Success Stories, "Delivering a message from a new bottle," Cone Public Relations, **www.coneinc.com**.

5. Rich Thomaselli, "Movie gives Wonder Bread exposure worth $4.3 million," *Advertising Age*, August 7, 2006, **www.adage.com**.

6. Rebecca Harris, "Brand watchers," *Marketing*, May 15, 2006, p. 6.

7. Emily Mathieu, "Nokia seeds bloggers with free camera phones," *Financial Post*, June 30, 2006, p. FP7.

8. **www.timhortons.com**.

9. Jack Trout and Steve Rivken, *The New Positioning* (New York: McGraw-Hill, 1996), p. 147.

10. Thomas L. Harris, *Value-Added Public Relations* (Chicago: NTP Publications, 1998) pp. 243–244.

11. Eve Lazarus, "Creative games management," *Marketing*, May 9, 2005, **www.marketingmag.ca**.

12. Paul-Mark Rendon, "Telltale metrics," *Marketing*, July 31–August 7, 2006, p. 17.

13. Kevin Newcomb, "MWW debuts blog marketing practice," **www.clickz.com/news/print.php/3454471**.

14. Kate MacArthur, "Taco hell: Rodent video signals new era in PR crises," *Advertising Age*, February 26, 2007, pp. 1, 46.

15. Regis Mckenna, *Relationship Marketing* (Reading, Mass: Addison-Wesley Publishing, 2001), p. 5.

16. Kevin Goldman, "Winemakers look for more publicity," *Wall Street Journal*, September 29, 1994, p. 353.

17. "Vancouver 2010 selects Bell Canada as premier national partner," press release, Bell Canada Enterprises, November 18, 2004.

18. "Sponsorship spending to see biggest rise in five years," IEG Inc., **www.sponsorship.com**.

19. "Where dollars go," IEG Inc., **www.sponsorship.com**.

20. "Event marketing tops list of marketing tactics for ROI," based on research from the George P. Johnson Company and MPI Foundation, Meeting Professionals International, **www.mpiweb.org**.

21. Andy Holloway, "One hole golf could do without," *Canadian Business*, August 2006, p. 17.

22. David Shiffman and Scott Neslund, "Calculating Olympic impact," *Marketing*, October 30, 2000, p. 48.

23. Paul Brent, "Olympics deals not 'exclusive' enough," *Financial Post*, April 5, 2004, p. FP4.

24. Keith McArthur, "Scotiabank Place? Oh don't you mean the Corel Centre?" *Globe and Mail*, January 12, 2006, **www.globeandmail.com**.

25. Robert Thompson, "The next one sets record off the ice," *National Post*, March 9, 2005, p. A3.

26. CASSIES 2005 Cases, **www.cassies.ca**.

27. Lucy Saddleton, "Cast in rock: Quebec Bud effort targets rockers where they drink," *Strategy*, April 5, 2004, p. 16.

28. Brendan Christie, "Join the party," *Strategy*, April 5, 2004, p. 15.

29. Kate MacNamara, "Too much pink you think," *National Post*, December 16, 2006, p. FW3.

30. BMO Financial Group, **www.bmo.com**.

31. Rich Thomaselli, "Adidas signs 11-year, $400 million deal with NBA," *Advertising Age*, April 11, 2006, **www.adage.com**.

Below-the-Line Marketing and Marketing Communications

A landscape of increasingly fragmented media, consisting of text messaging, internet, and viral marketing along with traditional staples of television, radio, and print advertising, makes it harder for brands to break through the clutter. Consequently, marketers are looking at promotions, event marketing, and public relations as a means of connecting with their customers.

In the past, marketers perceived promotions and event marketing as activities that would influence sales volume in the short term, and the exact role that public relations could play in building a brand was somewhat of a mystery. That way of thinking is changing—marketers are now devising sophisticated promotions and involving themselves with the softer side of communications to build brands and brand awareness in the consumer's mind over the long term. Businesses are looking for integrated solutions to their marketing problems, and that means opportunities in sales promotion, event marketing and sponsorships, and public relations are rising.

To illustrate how marketers are shifting their priorities, consider the following marketing communications strategies.

Kraft Canada

Packaged goods marketing organization Kraft Canada is constantly running sales promotions for its various product lines, but it has never run one bigger and perhaps more effective than its recent "Every Pack Wins Crayola" promotion. The back-to-school promotion saw Kraft give away more than 500 000 Crayola products when consumers claimed their prizes online through the YTV website.

The Crayola promotion involved 12 different product lines and resulted in huge product displays in Canada's largest supermarket chains (see Figure 1).

According to Carol Giles, director of customer marketing services at Kraft, "The back-to-school

FIGURE 1

Courtesy of Tannen Maury/Bloomberg News/Landor.

promotion delivered the highest online redemption rate in Kraft history. Combining the strength of two recognized and established brands in the back-to-school market, this unique program aimed to further increase awareness and to reward customers quickly and easily with every purchase."

The promotion was a genuine hit with moms. They saw the incredible value in it. The promotion ran from July to December 2003 and was communicated through television ads, *What's Cooking* magazine, *Not for Adults* magazine, in-store displays, and Kraft's website. So successful was the promotion that Kraft planned to repeat it in 2004 and also planned to double the number of Crayola prizes.

Molson Breweries of Canada

What's a new product launch without a party? "A party can bring a brand to life," says Justine Rae, manager of events and promotions at Molson Sports and Entertainment. Rae managed the spring 2003 launch of Molson's Brazilian import, A Marca Bavaria. A launch party can play a role in communicating the essence of the brand and where the brand is going to be positioned. It also gives the brand an opportunity to interact with consumers and key influencers. How a brand is reflected at a party is all in the details!

In this day and age it's not good enough to just show people a good time—anyone can do that—it's about creating a brand experience. For A Marca Bavaria, that meant reflecting adventure, sensuality, and fun—qualities that are associated with Brazil and, in Molson's view, beer. Molson opted for a "Passport to Adventure" theme and invitations were designed in the form of boarding cards.

"Authenticity is a big part of the brand," Rae says. "We actually spoke to people in Brazil to make sure we were targeting and representing things in a positive light." Lush green plants, a feisty Samba band, spicy foods, Brazilian dancers, and plenty of free beer helped "transport" guests from snowy Toronto to tropical Brazil—if only for a few hours.

"If guests are impressed by the event, they'll carry your message to the masses and ignite a buzz among the brand's target audience. It's essential to get the support of key influencers." In Molson's case, that meant bar and restaurant staff and owners, the media, and trendsetters who drive tastes and trends in industries such as fashion and music.

L'Oréal Canada

L'Oréal brand Garnier Fructis sponsored the eighth annual World Ski & Snowboard Festival in Whistler, B.C., in April 2003. The event drew 260 000 resort visits over 10 days.

Garnier Fructis chose this event because Whistler/Blackcomb is the mecca of the board/free-skier movement. These people have the same spirit as Garnier Fructis—free spirit, accessibility, and irreverence. It is now an Olympic sport. "It's all about catching the wave at the right time and surfing it for a good number of years."

Involvement with this kind of event does seem out of character for an established company like L'Oréal, but Garnier Fructis desires universal appeal with consumers. It wants to get out with the people, it wants to be more grassroots, and it wants its communications to have a bit of an edge. Garnier wants to be perceived as a street-fighting type of brand.

To maximize exposure at the event the brand set up the Style Zone. "We set up chairs with kids from the mountain who knew the scene and a bit about hair styling. Not professionals, just average kids. The kids learned about the brand's attributes in Garnier Fructis 101. They got consumers styled up—2000 of them in total, mostly kids between 18 and 24 years old, the primary target market for the brand."

Sales results are hard to measure, but L'Oréal is very happy about reaching its target in their environment—an environment that was a mixture of sports, music, and the right venue.

Unilever Canada

Unilever wanted to launch a new Lever 2000 body wash with a splash, but with the Lever 2000 brand not having much marketing support in recent years the company had to find something unique that would resonate with consumers. How about a shower in the streets!

The objective of the Lever 2000 Pure Rain Body Wash was to generate awareness and offer trial sizes as incentives for a sale. The brand was targeted at people 18 to 35 years old.

Experiential marketing in the form of a street-level sampling program was the centrepiece of the launch. Consumers in high-traffic locations in Toronto, Montreal, and Calgary bumped into merchandisers

FIGURE   2

LEVER 2000 is a registered trademark owned by Unilever Canada Inc. and is used with permission.

called the Shower Heads on the streets. In a one-week blitz, the Shower Heads, wearing shower caps and even portable shower stalls, handed out 59-mL–sized samples. See Figure 2 for an illustration.

To create additional buzz, transit shelters in Toronto and Calgary were disguised as large, communal showers, complete with showerheads and water droplets on glass panels. Exterior shelter posters showed a nude male reaching for a towel. Inside, there was a poster of a mirror and wash basin.

Radio played a key role in generating buzz. In Calgary, listeners to Power 107 qualified to win a trip to the rainforests of Belize by taking cordless phones into the shower, on air, and singing songs—a very high degree of customer involvement to say the least!

About 170 000 samples were distributed in one week, and over a four-week period more than 1.2 million impressions were generated by transit-shelter advertising. The launch was a huge success! According to ACNielsen, the brand took the lead position in the category of Refreshing Body Washes, and it has become the fifth-largest body wash in the country.

Unilever successfully tapped in to something good. A recent study from the United States revealed that experiential marketing events are more influential than either television advertising or direct mail in influencing how people make their purchase decisions. By location, consumers show a preference for such events at shopping malls, in stores, and other public events.

Source: Adapted from Fawzia Sheikh, "Casting off the one-off," *Marketing*, May 10, 2004, pp. 15–16; Michelle Warren, "Life of the party," *Marketing*, July 28–August 4, 2003, p. 2; Sara Minogue, "Fructis aims for free skiers," *Strategy*, June 2, 2003, p. 18; and Unilever Canada's Shower Heads Promotion, 2002 Promotion Awards, *Marketing*, 2002.

CASE 1: CADBURY SCHWEPPES ACCELERADE
COMMUNICATIONS BRIEF

Company Profile

Cadbury Schweppes is a multinational confectionary and beverage company. It recently acquired Accelerade from PacificHealth Laboratories for $4 million plus royalties (see Figure 1). Accelerade gives Cadbury an entry into one of the fastest-growing beverage categories: sports drinks.

The Cadbury Schweppes product portfolio is vast and contains many popular brands. The confectionary division includes Trident, Dentyne, Bubblicious, Cadbury Dairy Milk, Mr. Big, Hall's, and Mentos. The beverage division includes Canada Dry, Dr. Pepper, 7Up, A&W Root Beer, Schweppes, Sunkist, Hawaiian Punch, and Mott's.

In Canada, Cadbury Schweppes operates as two separate companies: Cadbury Beverages Canada; and Cadbury Adams Canada Inc. Both are based in Toronto.

Market Profile

The North American beverage market is divided into many product categories that are growing at different rates. The top seven product categories and their latest annual growth rates are as follows:

Product Category	Growth, 2006 vs. 2005 (%)
Carbonated Soft Drinks	-1.5
Bottled Water	+10.0
Fruit Beverages	-2.4
Sports Drinks	+12.0
Ready-to-Drink Tea	+26.0
Energy Drinks	+49.0
Ready-to-Drink Coffee	+10.0

- Carbonated soft drinks remain the dominant product category, accounting for 60 percent of all beverages sold.
- Over the past five years, carbonated soft drinks have been losing ground to bottled water, fruit beverages, sports drinks, and energy drinks. In response, Coca-Cola and PepsiCo have modified their product portfolio and placed more emphasis on growing product categories. Cadbury Schweppes has divested their European soft drinks business.

- The energy drink market in the United States is estimated to be worth US$5.0 billion at retail (2006). The Canadian market is not as developed as the American market and is estimated to be worth C$450 million at retail (2006).
- Sports drinks were initially niche products reserved for athletes, but in more recent times they have moved into the mainstream as refreshing beverage alternatives.
- The gradual shift away from soft drinks toward juices, water, and sports drinks reflects consumers' healthier lifestyles. The health and wellness trend is definitely influencing beverage choices.

Competitor Profile

The beverage market is dominated by two companies: Coca-Cola and PepsiCo. Cadbury Schweppes is a third competitor, but their overall market share is much lower than Coke and Pepsi.

- Primary brands in the Coca-Cola portfolio cover most product categories and include Coca-Cola and Diet Coke, Minute Maid fruit juices, Powerade, Dasani, Full Throttle, and Rock Star.
- Primary brands in the PepsiCo portfolio cover most product categories and include Pepsi-Cola and Diet Pepsi, Mountain Dew, Tropicana fruit juices, Gatorade, Aquafina, Mountain Dew Amp, and SoBe Adrenaline Rush.
- The sports drink market in Canada (and elsewhere) is dominated by Gatorade. Estimated market shares are as follows:

Brand	Market Share (%)
Gatorade (Pepsi)	80
Powerade (Coca-Cola)	15
Other and Private Label	5
Total	**100**

- Gatorade is scientifically formulated and proven to quench thirst, replace fluids and electrolytes, and provide carbohydrate energy to enhance athletic performance.
- Gatorade is famous for its presence on football fields. It is common for players to shower the head coach with Gatorade after winning a big game.
- Gatorade has extended its relationship with sports into hockey and basketball. Gatorade and other Pepsi beverages are exclusive suppliers to the NHL (all 30 teams), and NHLPA. This contract agreement plays a key role in gaining brand exposure in Canada.
- Gatorade's key spokesperson is hockey star Sidney Crosby (Pittsburgh Penguins). Crosby appears in all forms of advertising (see the Gatorade website: **www.gatorade.ca**.). All advertising for Gatorade revolves around the tagline "Is it in you?"
- Gatorade has evolved into more of a mainstream refreshment beverage consumed by non-athletes and children.
- Powerade offers the same benefits as Gatorade, but even with the marketing resources of Coca-Cola, the brand has not made much of an impact on the market. It is the official sports drink of NASCAR, the U.S. Olympic team, FIFA, and the Arena Football League. The brand does not have a similar presence in Canada. The home of the Brampton Battalion (Ontario Hockey League) is called the Powerade Centre.
- Powerade's key spokesperson is basketball star LeBron James of the Cleveland Cavaliers.

Brand Profile—Accelerade

Sports drinks rehydrate and replenish the carbohydrates (in the form of sugars, sucrose and glucose) and electrolytes (sodium and potassium salts) depleted during vigorous exercise.

Courtesy of Dick Hemingway.

FIGURE 1

Cadbury Schweppes recently acquired Accelerade

Accelerade's differential advantage is that it's "a protein-enhanced sports drink that allows athletes to get the most out of their workout. It provides a 4:1 carbohydrate to protein ratio that is clinically proven to enhance endurance by 29 percent over ordinary sports drinks."

Accelerade is available in four flavours: Fruit Punch, Mountain Berry, Citrus Grapefruit, and Peach Mango. It is anticipated that Accelerade will be priced slightly higher than Gatorade, the higher price being justified based on superior benefits offered by the brand.

Positioning Strategy

There is an opportunity for Accelerade to position itself as a legitimate sports drink. Workout enthusiasts swear by it:

> Accelerade will be positioned as the preferred sports drinks for everyday athletes, extreme athletes, and endurance athletes wanting to maximize their performance level.

Key-Benefit Statement

Accelerade promises superior endurance for athletes.

Support-Claims Statement

Accelerade will increase endurance by 29 percent, speed muscle recovery for 40-percent greater endurance during a second workout, and hydrate 15 percent better than traditional sports drinks. Endurance athletes have been using the product in powder form for years. The new liquid format offers convenience to users.

More specific information about the product and the science behind it are available at the website: **www.accelerade.com**.

Problem

Accelerade is entering a rapidly growing market dominated by one brand. It is a David versus Goliath type of challenge. Accelerade must carve out its niche in the market by attracting hard-core athletes and athletically inclined individuals who are serious about fitness, and who work out regularly.

Challenge

Your immediate challenge is to devise a new marketing communications plan to introduce Accelerade to the Canadian market. The plan will be a launch campaign, but it must cover one calendar year.

Prior to developing the plan, you should research the sports drink market further to update facts and figures where necessary. Any information you uncover should be included in the background section of your plan.

It is your responsibility to provide a clear **description of the target market** that Accelerade will pursue. The target-market profile will influence the direction of your creative and media recommendations. You must also establish solid **marketing objectives** for the launch year (e.g., sales volume, market share, distribution).

As you proceed through the plan, you must include appropriate objectives, strategies, and execution details for all components of the marketing communications mix you are recommending.

Budget

The budget for the campaign is **$2.5 million**. Should you wish to increase the budget you must provide proper justification.

It is recommended that you refer to the various plan models in the textbook for guidance in developing your plan. You should confirm with your instructor the expectations for execution details in the creative and media sections of the plan.

Source: Kenneth Hein, "Cadbury's objective: Make Gatorade sweat," www.brandweek.com, April 9, 2007; David Jones, "Cadbury looks to fruit, sports drinks for growth," Reuters, March 2007, www.reuters.com; "PepsiCo, NHL, and NHLPA sign multi-year deal," press release, June 19, 2006, www.nhlpa.com; Gatorade, www.wikipedia.org; Powerade, www.wikipedia.org.

CASE 2: SATURN VUE GREEN LINE

COMMUNICATIONS BRIEF

Market Profile

- Unit sales of all automotive vehicles in Canada average about 1.5 to 1.6 million per year (2005–2006). Cars account for 54 percent of the market and trucks 46 percent.
- Domestic models made by General Motors, Ford, and DaimlerChrysler are losing market share to foreign models, particularly Japanese models.
- By market segment, the compact and sub-compact segment is the largest, accounting for 55 percent of all unit car sales in Canada. A majority of Canadians are looking for economical vehicles.

Company	*Market Share (%)
General Motors	23.8
DaimlerChrysler	13.9
Ford	13.5
Toyota	12.1
Honda	10.1
All Other	26.6
Total	**100.0**

*Canadian market shares as of March 2007.

- Concern for the environment by consumers and governments is increasing the demand for fuel-efficient automobiles. All companies are introducing hybrid technology. Toyota is the leader in product offerings in the hybrid segment of the market.
- While consumers are interested in hybrid automobiles, hybrids are more expensive than traditional models. Prospective customers must evaluate cost increases in the short term against fuel savings in the long term. Acceptance of hybrids as reflected by the numbers of vehicles sold has been lower than expected by manufacturers.
- The sports utility vehicle segment is extremely competitive and is losing market share to a newer generation of vehicles called crossovers. Consumers are showing preference for a smaller, more stylish type of utility vehicle.

Product Profile

The Saturn VUE and Saturn VUE Green Line compete in the compact segment of the sports utility vehicle market (see Figure 2). The Saturn VUE Green Line offers many unique selling points:

- It has the lowest mileage ratings of any SUV on the market—8.8L/100 km in the city and 6.7L/100 km on the highway.
- It is an affordable vehicle, priced in the $28 000 to $32 000 range.
- It delivers a 20-percent improvement in fuel economy compared to the standard VUE model.
- It is a functional, stylish, and affordable automobile offering hybrid technology to more Canadians than ever before.

Competitor Profile

In the "green" segment of the SUV market, the Saturn VUE competes with the Toyota RAV-4, the Honda CR-V, and the Ford Escape. These competitors have similar-size engines, similar technology, and comparable gas mileage ratings.

Advertising plays a key role in differentiating each brand. The Ford Escape offers an environmental message. In one television commercial, a family driving the Escape is shown in a lush green forest mingling with a family of deer. The commercial ends with the tagline, "Built for life in Canada," a line used in all Ford advertising.

The Toyota RAV-4 is positioned as an intelligent choice for consumers who think fast, never quit, and like to push things to the limits. The RAV-4 gets you there! The tagline, "Toyota, moving forward," appears in all RAV-4 ads.

FIGURE 2
The Saturn VUE

The Honda CR-V focuses on bold design, roominess (for a small vehicle), and safety. The tagline, "Be prepared," summarizes their message strategy—this is a vehicle that won't let you down.

All competitors employ a battery of media that includes television, magazines, newspapers, outdoor, and online communications. The media mixes do vary from one competitor to another.

Positioning Strategy

Saturn VUE Green Line will be positioned as an economical yet stylish hybrid sports utility vehicle that will appeal primarily to environmentally conscious families with children.

Key-Benefit Statement

The Saturn VUE Green Line is an affordable hybrid SUV with the lowest entry price and the best fuel efficiency ratings in its class.

Support-Claims Statement

Saturn offers the lowest entry price of any hybrid sports utility vehicle. Independent tests confirm that Saturn VUE Green Line has the best fuel efficiency ratings among all hybrid SUVs.

Current Creative Strategy

Saturn employs a universal tagline for all of its models: "Like always. Like never before." This tagline communicates Saturn's attention to quality and reliability while constantly improving the driving experience for its customers.

The Green Line was launched with a unique tagline: "Going green without going broke." This phrase captured the essence of the brand's positioning strategy and communicated the unique selling points of the vehicle—that a consumer could be environmentally conscious at an affordable price.

Target-Market Profile

In general terms, some research studies reveal that hybrid owners tend to have higher education and incomes, are older than the average car buyer, and tend to drive their cars less (perhaps due to their concern for the environment).

The Saturn VUE Green Line wants to attract the following customer:

- 35-plus years of age; parents with children
- family income $70 000-plus
- reside in major urban areas across Canada
- environmentally conscious
- engage in family travel and recreational pursuits

Problem

While awareness of the Saturn VUE is high among Canadian drivers, awareness of the Green Line model remains low. The Green Line model needs a new marketing communications campaign that is distinct from those of other Saturn vehicles. A new message and media strategy is needed to break through the clutter of advertising in the sport utility segment of the market.

Challenge

The immediate challenge is to create a marketing communications plan that will create awareness and interest in the Saturn VUE Green Line. The ultimate goal is to drive traffic to Saturn dealers for a test drive and then a purchase. The sales objective for the year is 2000 units.

Prior to embarking upon this challenge, you must conduct the necessary online research to familiarize yourself with the Canadian automobile market, the external trends that are influencing sales in the market, and to evaluate what competitors are doing in terms of marketing communications. All of this information will be included in the background section of your plan.

Once you have assessed the market situation, you should then review the positioning strategy and target-market profile and determine if any changes are necessary. As you proceed with the plan, you must incorporate specific objectives, strategies, and execution details for the various sections of the plan. For certain, advertising (creative and media) will play a significant role, but your recommendations may also include other components of the marketing communications mix. It is your plan!

Budget

The budget for the campaign is **$4.0 million** for a one-year plan cycle. The start and end dates of the plan year are left to your discretion based on your knowledge of the automobile market (e.g., January 1 to December 31 or October 1 to September 30, etc.).

For the purposes of this plan you are concerned only with the Canadian market, and you should employ only Canadian media. It is recommended that you refer to the various planning models in the textbook for guidance in developing your marketing communications plan. You should also confirm with your instructor the expectations for execution details in the creative and media sections of the plan.

CASE STUDY 3: MR. LUBE

COMMUNICATIONS BRIEF

The Company

Mr. Lube opened its first store in 1976 and introduced a new concept to the Canadian market—the drive-through oil change. Currently there are 92 stores operating in Canada, 59 of which are franchise-operated and 32 of which are corporate units. The franchises are geographically dispersed, but penetration is much lower in Eastern Canada. The company is committed to providing a franchise system that offers a range of premium vehicle maintenance services in a clean, efficient, and first-class manner.

Province	No. of Outlets
British Columbia	18
Alberta	18
Saskatchewan	4
Manitoba	4
Ontario	43
Quebec	3
New Brunswick	1
Nova Scotia	1
Total	**92**

A new ownership group recently acquired Mr. Lube. They have developed a "Fast-Forward" strategic plan that calls for considerable growth (30 new outlets) over the next three years. The goal is to expand the overall automotive maintenance market and gain a larger share of the market.

Market and Competitor Profile

The size of the automotive maintenance market generally and the oil-change market specifically is unknown. However, given the fact that every car owner in Canada should be changing their oil two or three times a year, the market is huge.

The market is divided between quick oil change service providers and independent automotive repair shops. Automotive dealers also provide this service. Current market shares in the industry are as follows:

Provider	Market Share (%)
Mr. Lube	41
Pennzoil	14
Jiffy Lube	10
All Other and Independents	35
Total	**100**

New-car dealers also offer oil changes, and that takes potential new business away from Mr. Lube. There is a perception among new-car buyers that oil changes must be done by the dealer in order to protect new-car warranties. However, this is not in fact true. Mr. Lube can service new cars for basic automotive services without affecting warranties. Mr. Lube has to alter this perception held by consumers.

Jiffy Lube is a direct competitor, offering a similar list of automotive services. Their marketing communications stress fast, efficient, 10-minute service. A limiting factor for Jiffy Lube is low penetration. Currently, there are only 36 outlets across Canada.

Product Profile

- Mr. Lube specializes in fast oil changes and a variety of related automotive services. The standard oil change takes about 15 minutes and includes washing windshields, checking tire pressure, oiling door hinges, a free cup of coffee, and a copy of the daily newspaper to read. Mr. Lube offers quality Castrol motor oil.
- Additional services include a fuel system service, transmission fluid service, differential fluid service, cooling system fluid change, and cabin air filter service. All services are provided at recommended intervals.
- Mr. Lube also sells batteries, provides light bulb replacements, and rotates tires.
- No appointment is necessary.
- The company maintains a database of all manufacturers' recommendations, which guarantees the right type of services for all makes and models.
- Services offered by Mr. Lube are personalized; customers get a feeling of engagement when visiting a Mr. Lube location, a feeling that someone cares about their car.

Target-Market Profile

All car owners require routine automotive maintenance for their vehicle, therefore, demographics and psychographics are not a factor. Anyone owning a car is a potential customer. Time (or lack of time) is often an issue for customers contemplating an oil change. Geography is also a factor, as Mr. Lube locations are concentrated in Ontario, Alberta, and British Columbia. Penetration is much lower in all other regions.

Marketing Communications Strategy

- In markets where Mr. Lube currently operates, the stores are recognizable from the street based on the attractiveness of their blue and yellow colour scheme. External signage is highly recognizable and effective (see Figure 3).
- Some national and local advertising has been implemented, but awareness of the brand name and what it stands for remains relatively low.
- Past advertising employed the slogan: "Doing it right. Before your eyes." This slogan captures the essence of the services offered but it is not one that is easily remembered. The company believes it is time to retire this slogan and move in a new direction. A new image is needed for the brand.

Problem

The decisions to get an oil change and where to get an oil change are low-involvement decisions for consumers. Mr. Lube wants to increase the profile of the oil-change business by presenting a new image to consumers. The company also wants to alter the perceptions that

Courtesy of Dick Hemingway.

A Mr. Lube location

exist among consumers about where oil changes can occur. The services offered by Mr. Lube do not void new-car warranties. Altering this perception creates significant opportunity to attract new customers.

Advertising Objectives

- To increase the awareness level of Mr. Lube and the services it provides
- To present a new and more exciting image of the company
- To alter consumer perceptions regarding warranty specifications and oil-change choices
- To encourage a trial visit and increase traffic at all outlets

Positioning Strategy

Mr. Lube offers quick, convenient, and personalized automotive services that address all of the routine maintenance needs of Canadian car owners.

Creative Objectives

Message content must focus on the unique strengths of the services offered by Mr. Lube:

- Quick and convenient service (no appointment needed)
- Personalized service (relax with a coffee and newspaper)
- All services are provided according to manufacturer's specifications

Challenge

Your immediate challenge is to devise a new marketing communications plan that will address the key issues described above. The new campaign will cover a one-year period.

Prior to developing the campaign, you must conduct appropriate research to familiarize yourself with current market and competitive conditions. Any information you collect should be included in the background section of your plan.

When developing the plan, you must include appropriate objectives, strategies, and execution details for all advertising recommendations (creative and media) and for any other marketing communications activities you recommend.

Budget

The budget for the campaign is **$2.0 million**.

It is recommended that you refer to the various plan models in the textbook for guidance in developing your plan. You should also confirm with your instructor the expectations for execution details in the creative and media sections of the plan.

Source: Eve Lazarus, "Changing oil," Marketing, April 16, 2007, www.marketingmag.ca; www.cfa.ca/franchisedetail.aspx?item=Mr.+Lube+Canada; www.mrlube.com.

SCHICK QUATTRO RAZOR

Marketing Background

MARKET SIZE AND GROWTH

The men's grooming market embraces shaving products, skin care products, hair care products, and fragrances. Combined, these categories represent US$8 billion in sales annually. The Canadian grooming market is estimated to be C$800 million.

The grooming market is growing at a rate of more than 10 percent annually. Such significant growth is attributed to attitude changes among men who pay more attention to grooming, new product introductions, and intense competition between large and resourceful companies in all product categories. Continuous technical innovation is a key factor sustaining growth in this market.

AC Nielsen data indicate the Canadian razor market to be worth C$291 million (2007) at retail. With wholesale and retail margins deducted, the value of the razor market at point of manufacture is estimated to be C$204 million.

The razor market is growing at an average annual rate of more than 2.5 percent. It is much more established than the other product categories in the male grooming market. At this rate of growth, the market is forecast to be worth C$298 million in 2008.

MARKET SEGMENTS

The razor market is divided between reusable razors and blades, and disposable razors. The reusable segment can be further segmented on the basis of price: regular- or competitively priced razors and premium-priced razors.

Gillette is the dominant leader in the reusable segment, and Bic is the leader in the disposable segment. Both Gillette and Schick are currently investing considerable financial resources in reusable razors with expensive replacement blades. Price does not seem to be an issue in this segment. Male consumers seem willing to pay the price for each product improvement that comes along.

EXTERNAL ENVIRONMENTS INFLUENCING THE RAZOR MARKET

Health and Wellness There is a growing desire today for men to look and feel healthy.

Demographic Trends Young men and aging baby boomers are concerned with the looking-glass self as well as their own self-image. The goal of older men is to look and feel young. Young urban males, referred to as "metrosexuals," who dress well and are socially active, are influencing change by making purchases in all grooming categories.

Societal Attitudes General taboos are breaking down; that is, impeccable grooming habits associated with the gay community now transcend all lifestyles.

Media Influences Images portrayed in "lad magazines" such as *Maxim*, *Stuff*, and *UMM* promote the ideal body image for young males today. The lads are out to impress the lassies.

MARKET SHARE

Since Energizer purchased the Schick brands from Pfizer in 2002, the battle between Gillette and Schick has intensified. Schick has become much more aggressive, from a product development and marketing perspective.

Since the launch of the Schick Quattro in 2004, Schick has managed to increases its market share from 14 percent to 18 percent in Canada. They have captured some market share from Gillette and all other brands.

Brand	Market Share 2003	Market Share 2007
Gillette	76	73
Schick	14	18
Bic/Revlon/all Other	10	9
Total	**100**	**100**

Schick's market share comprises five brands: Xtreme3 and Xtreme3 Comfort Plus (disposable razors), Protector, ST Slim Twin for Men, and Quattro. Quattro was launched in 2004 and has achieved a 9% market share.

CONSUMER DATA

Contemporary males of all ages are searching for innovative products that improve appearance. A genuine desire to look and feel better is shaping the male grooming market today.

- Males tend to be brand loyal; once they find the right brand they stick with it.
- Males prefer basic items that offer tangible benefits; they shun products they perceive as pampering.
- Males' interests now extend well beyond shaving; skin care products are becoming more popular with males of all ages.
- Women frequently purchase grooming products for their male spouse or mate.
- Price is not an issue in the purchase decision; quality and performance are important influencers. Men are willing to pay for technology that offers a more comfortable shave.
- Men spend 51 minutes a day grooming; women spend 55 minutes.

COMPETITOR ANALYSIS

The razor market is dominated by Gillette brands. Schick, other brands, and private label brands are distant followers.

- Gillette's market share is split between four key brands: Gillette Sensor 3, Gillette Mach 3 Turbo, Gillette M3Power, and the new Gillette Fusion. The Fusion brand also includes a shaving gel that was launched at the same time as the new razor (2006).
- Razor sales are extremely important to Gillette: 40 percent of Gillette's sales revenue and 70 percent of Gillette's operating profit are generated from razor and blade sales.
- Gillette is a resourceful brand; its key strengths are in technology, product innovation, and marketing.
- The Gillette brand name has an enviable image and reputation among males. It is a well-known, male heritage brand.
- Gillette is now owned by Procter & Gamble, so conceivably there are even more resources available for marketing and marketing communications. Gillette invests significant sums of money in marketing activity and appears to be getting a better return for its investment.

COMPETITOR ACTIVITY ASSESSMENT

All Gillette brands are marketed by similar means. Each brand receives considerable marketing support, as Gillette's goal is to build and protect market share.

Product   Gillette promises a clean, close, and comfortable shave. The Mach 3 Turbo offers a closer shave with fewer strokes and less irritation. The M3Power is battery-operated and promises a close, comfortable shave.

Gillette Fusion incorporates multiple innovations—not just more blades. By spacing the blades 30-percent closer together than before, Gillette says it has created a new "shaving surface" that reduces irritation. An enhanced "Lubrastrip" infused with vitamin E and aloe refines the shaving experience further. The razor has five blades on the front and a precision trimmer blade on the back to trim sideburns, shave under the nose, and shape facial hair.

Technological advancements keep Gillette in the forefront of razor product development. Male consumers perceive Gillette brands to be reliable.

Price   The Sensor 3 is competitively priced; the Mach 3 Turbo is premium-priced (about 15-percent more). The M3Power razor and Fusion razor are higher in price. The additional benefits offered by the M3Power and Fusion razors justify the higher price.

Distribution   All Gillette brands have extensive retail distribution in drug, grocery, and mass merchandise stores. Gillette's financial resources allow for significant spending with channel customers to ensure that distribution is maintained.

Marketing Communications   Gillette brands have significant media advertising support to create awareness and interest. As well, sales promotions are implemented annually across all company brands to generate seasonal interest and to stimulate purchasing patterns. Trial coupons, product sampling, and contests are important elements of Gillette's marketing communications mix.

The Gillette brand has always been associated with sports. Recently, Gillette has focused on sports sponsorships and is the official sponsor of NASCAR in the shaving products, alkaline battery, and oral care categories.

Gillette summarizes its positioning strategy in all of its marketing communications with the famous slogan: "The Best a Man Can Get."

BRAND ACTIVITY ASSESSMENT—SCHICK QUATTRO

Product   The Schick Quattro offers four-blade titanium technology and design that guarantees a close comfortable shave. While the Quattro has one less blade than the Gillette Fusion, the impact on the shave is negligible. Three options are available: Quattro, Quattro Power, and Quattro Midnight.

Price   The Quattro is priced higher than Gillette Mach 3 and but lower than the Gillette M3Power or the Gillette Fusion. Offering a quality product at a better price is desirable for building the brand in the short term.

Distribution   Quattro has achieved excellent distribution in supermarkets, drug stores, and mass merchandisers such as Wal-Mart. Various consumer and trade promotion activities have produced excellent display activity at point-of-purchase.

Marketing Communications   Since the launch of the Quattro, the budget for marketing communications has been about $2.5 million annually. Television and print advertising account for the lion's share of the budget and support the brand nationally. Selective use of outdoor advertising has added reach and frequency in key urban markets. Promotional activities, including trial coupons, sampling programs, and contests, have contributed to the brand's success.

Marketing Plan

MARKETING OBJECTIVES

1. To increase market share for Schick Quattro from 9 percent to 10 percent in 2008.
2. To generate sales revenue of $20 800 000 for Schick Quattro (at point of manufacture) in 2008.
3. To continue to position Schick Quattro as a razor that provides a superior shave to any competing product on the market.

TARGET-MARKET PROFILE

Razor products appeal to all males, but since older males exhibit a high degree of brand loyalty (Gillette's dominant position in the market), Quattro will give priority to younger males whose loyalties have yet to be established.

Primary Target Market   Since brand loyalty is an issue in this market, priority will be given to younger males who are in the process of forming brand relationships. However, all males between the ages of 16 and 49 years are potential targets due to attitude and lifestyle considerations. Across all ages, the penchant for good grooming has increased significantly in recent years

Demographics

- Primary: males 16 to 29 years old
- Secondary and post-secondary education
- Students, newly employed graduates, career-minded
- Income is not that important

Psychographics

- Time-pressed daily routines
- Socially active; friends and significant others
- Recreational orientation with an interest in sports viewing and participation
- Very concerned with appearance and health; a strong desire to look and feel good

Geographics

- Across Canada, but metropolitan markets will be given priority

Behaviour Response   These males are looking for products that are reliable, easy to use, and offer superior performance. Price is not a significant issue in the purchase decision.

Secondary Target   A secondary target comprising males between the ages of 30 and 49 years will also be targeted. While this age group tends to be more loyal and have an established regimen for purchasing shaving products, they are nonetheless interested in innovative products that will improve their self-image. Their psychographic and geographic profile is similar to that of the primary target.

PRODUCT STRATEGY

Schick Quattro has numerous unique selling points; hence there are numerous benefits for potential users.

- ***Blades and Head*** Four precisely synchronized blades and head allow for optimal contact over the contours of a man's face. There are two conditioning strips containing aloe and vitamin E.

- *Handle Design*   An ergonomic design with a comfortable, slip-resistant handle (textured rubber grips) offers enhanced precision and control.
- *Blade Changing*   When the blade "clicks" in, a successful blade change has been made.
- *Convertible Stand*   With a futuristic look, the stand allows the razor to air-dry upright, or store securely for travel.
- *Packaging*   A highly advanced (futuristic-looking) package design draws attention to the revolutionary nature of the Quattro. Blade refills will be available in packages of four or eight.

PRICE STRATEGY

The Schick Quattro will be competitively priced with the Gillette Mach 3 model at $11.99, and be priced below both the M3Power model and the Gillette Fusion model. The advantage of Quattro's four-blade system will be communicated by advertising and other forms of marketing communications. The goal is to generate high perceived value for the Quattro. The price strategy complements the competitive positioning strategy that Quattro is adopting.

DISTRIBUTION STRATEGY

The Quattro razor has excellent distribution in drug, grocery, and mass-merchandising stores across Canada. To ensure that distribution is retained at a high level and to ensure ongoing merchandising support at point-of-purchase, there will be a significant investment in consumer promotion and trade promotion activities.

POSITIONING STRATEGY

Schick Quattro is positioned as a distinctive and competitive alternative to the Gillette Fusion razor (and other Gillette models). Schick offers a technologically advanced four-blade system that provides optimal contact over the contours of the face, resulting in the best possible shave.

Marketing Communications Strategy

BUDGET

The budget for 2008 is **$3.0 million** for all marketing communications activity. The budget represents 14.4 percent of forecast revenues for the year and reflects the position of a growing brand in a highly competitive market.

ADVERTISING OBJECTIVES

1. To achieve a 75-percent awareness level among the primary target market, described as males 16 to 29 years old.
2. To encourage trial purchase by members of the primary and secondary target markets.
3. To position Schick Quattro as a product that offers customers equal or better performance than the Gillette Fusion razor.

Creative Plan

CREATIVE OBJECTIVES

1. To communicate that Schick Quattro offers a close, comfortable, and smooth shave.
2. To communicate that the four-blade system (precisely synchronized blades with two conditioning strips) provides enhanced performance compared to any other razor.

KEY-BENEFIT STATEMENT

The Schick Quattro razor offers an incredibly close, smooth shave.

SUPPORT-CLAIMS STATEMENT

Numerous tests have been conducted using proper marketing research methods to evaluate and determine the performance level of the Schick Quattro. Tests confirm the Quattro offers men the best shave possible. As well, the four-blade synchronized system offers technology that is equal to anything offered by competing brands.

CREATIVE STRATEGY

This is almost a David-versus-Goliath battle. Therefore, advertising will not incorporate direct comparisons with the Gillette Mach 3. Since the Schick Quattro offers equal or better performance, clear, direct, and precise claims will be made in all forms of advertising. The ads will tempt males to compare the Schick Quattro with any Gillette product.

Image   By showing how effectively the product performs, the consumer will see how easy the product is to use and how reliable it is at providing the key benefit: a close, comfortable shave. The goal is to communicate in such a manner that Schick Quattro is quickly perceived as a serious alternative to any Gillette product.

Theme   The four-blade synchronized system separates Schick Quattro from all other brands. Therefore, advertising messages will focus on blade technology and the benefits it offers.

Tone and Style   All messages will be straightforward, positive, and easy to understand. By showing the razor in action and the satisfaction of the user after shaving (perhaps when he is with a significant other), the choice will be obvious to the consumer.

Appeal Techniques   Precise appeal techniques will be determined by the ad agency. The benefits offered by Schick Quattro stand alone: a superior shaving experience will be communicated positively and convincingly in order to stimulate interest and to invite comparison. Any comparison made with Gillette product will be implied rather than made directly.

Slogan   The current tagline, "The power of 4 for an incredibly close, smooth shave," captures the essence of the brand's positioning strategy. This tagline will be retained in all forms of marketing communications.

CREATIVE EXECUTION

All advertising and other forms of marketing communications will deliver the same style of message. It is anticipated that the campaign will embrace 30-second television spots, four-colour magazine advertisements, outdoor posters, online banners, and a website. Other integrated marketing activities will include trial coupons, a contest, product seeding, and an interactive component.

Media Plan

BUDGET

From the total budget of **$3.0 million**, a sum of $2.2 million is allocated to media advertising. The media plan will cover the period January 1, 2008, to December 31, 2008.

MEDIA OBJECTIVES

Who   The primary target market is males, 16 to 29 years old, interested in appearance and health (a desire to look and feel good), living in metropolitan markets across Canada. A secondary target market embraces males, 30 to 49 years old.

What   The message for the Schick Quattro will focus on the benefits offered by the four-blade synchronized shaving system. Such innovation offers males an incredibly close, comfortable shave.

When   Ads will be placed throughout the year, with a heavier schedule in February and March (hockey), and August and September (back-to-school months).

Where   The placement of ads will be national in scope, with additional coverage in key urban markets. The budget available will determine the extent of key-market coverage.

How   Since this is a very competitive market with two brands (Fusion and Quattro) vying for attention, reach and frequency will be given equal attention. Continuity issues will be addressed by alternating media and by retaining a media presence at different spending levels throughout the year. An interactive component will be introduced to engage consumers with the brand.

MEDIA STRATEGY

Target-Market Strategy   A profile-matching strategy will be employed to reach both the primary and secondary target markets. The primary target market is difficult to reach since they multi-task when using the media. The primary target spends more time online than the secondary target. It is recommended that a stronger online presence be included in the media plan. A shotgun strategy is also recommended to improve overall brand awareness and to reach members of the secondary target.

Market Coverage   Schick Quattro is available all across Canada, so there is a need to employ media that reach a national audience. Key urban markets such as Toronto, Montreal, Vancouver, Ottawa-Gatineau, Edmonton, and Calgary will receive additional coverage. Reaching young urban males remains a priority. The degree of key-market coverage will depend on how far the budget can be stretched while still generating the desired impact on the target audience.

Timing   Ads will be scheduled throughout the year using a pulsing strategy. The multi-media campaign will use different media at different times of the year as a means of extending reach and frequency. Higher spending levels are recommended during February and March, when the hockey season is in full swing (to reach sports-minded males), and August and September, a period when young people get back into more rigid schedules and routines (back-to-school months).

Reach/Frequency/Continuity   Since brand awareness and trial purchases are immediate objectives, selecting media that maximize reach and frequency will be a priority. Reach will be stressed throughout the entire year, with various media being employed at different times to reach the same target market in different ways. Flights of advertising will be planned to ensure message continuity and maximum impact regardless of the media being employed at any given time.

Media Selection Rationale   A combination of television, magazines, outdoor posters, and online communications is recommended.

a) ***Television*** The quickest and most dramatic way to demonstrate the tangible benefits of the Schick Quattro is through television. Since television is a multi-sense medium, the demonstration can be more dramatic. While television is a mass medium and males in this age category are watching less television than they used to, television is still the best medium for reaching a large audience. A combination of conventional networks (to reach the mass audience) and sports cable networks (to reach a more targeted audience) will be employed. Further, our primary competitor is a heavy user of television, so there must be an attempt to mute the impact of their message in this medium.

b) ***Magazines*** Using magazines provides Schick an opportunity to reach the primary and secondary targets effectively and efficiently. For the younger half of the primary target, titles such as *Maxim* and its clones offer potential. For the older half of the target market, general interest magazines offer effective reach.

c) ***Outdoor Posters*** The target market is time-pressed and on-the-go. Therefore, outdoor posters are an ideal medium for reaching the target while they are travelling around town. The habitual nature of one's travel patterns, either to and from school or to and from work, means the Schick Quattro message will be seen repeatedly through the course of a week. Outdoor posters offer effective reach and frequency among males in the target market and are an ideal medium for emphasizing the brand name and showing what the package looks like. Outdoor advertising enhances reach in key urban markets.

d) ***Online Advertising*** Banner advertising and sponsorships on sports sites are a natural choice since sports-oriented males in both the primary and secondary target markets visit these sites frequently.

e) ***Website*** A dedicated website (**www.schickquatttro.ca**) provides an opportunity to tell a more complete story about Schick Quattro. The product benefits can be explained in more detail, some entertainment value can be offered, and the target consumer can interact more directly with the brand.

Media Rejection Rationale Radio was not recommended because the product and package would not be visible. The futuristic design of the product and package are essential elements for achieving awareness and brand recognition objectives. Newspapers were not recommended due to the black-and-white nature of the medium. As well, the primary customer is not a consistent reader of newspapers.

MEDIA EXECUTION

For a summary of the media expenditures by medium and time of year, refer to the Exhibits Section at the end of this plan. The budget has been effectively allocated between media advertising, sales promotion and public relations activities.

Sales Promotion Plan

CONSUMER PROMOTION OBJECTIVES

1. To generate awareness and interest for the Schick Quattro among the primary target market.
2. To encourage first-time purchases of the Quattro shaving system.

TRADE PROMOTION OBJECTIVES

1. To maintain key account listings across Canada.
2. To stimulate merchandising support (retail product advertising, special prices, and display activity) at planned intervals throughout the year.

SALES PROMOTION STRATEGY

Given the competitive nature of the retail market and the control retailers have over the sale of razor products, equal attention must be given to pull and push strategies. To encourage trial purchases, coupons will be distributed through magazines, and contest incentives will be communicated through in-store advertising.

To protect product listings and encourage merchandising support, adequate funds will be allocated to trade promotions. Funds will also be allocated for the production of point-of-purchase materials that can be used at shelf locations and on displays.

SALES PROMOTION EXECUTION

Coupons   A trial coupon ($2.00 value) will be issued in three waves in *Maxim* and *Maclean's* magazines. This combination reaches the primary and secondary targets nationally.

Contests   A contest offer will be communicated through in-store advertising (shelf pads and display cards). In combination with trade promotion funds, this promotion will increase sales volume in the short term and create some excitement at point-of-purchase.

Contest prizes will be the following:

- Grand prize: Toyota Prius automobile
- Second prize: one of three Sony flat screen high-definition televisions
- Third prize: one of ten Apple iPods

An online contest will be communicated in conjunction with Rogers Sportsnet. Schick Quattro will be the sponsor of a Fantasy League Soccer Contest called Premiership Predictor. Prizes will be issued weekly, with weekly winners qualifying for a grand prize.

Trade Allowances   Sufficient funds will be allocated to protect listings in key accounts, increase sales volume, and secure periodic merchandising support throughout the year. A sum of $500 000 is earmarked for trade promotion spending for the year.

Point-of-Purchase Material   Funds will be allocated for shelf pads, posters and sundry other point-of-purchase materials that are appropriate for in-store product displays. A budget of $25 000 will be established for this activity.

For a summary of all sales promotion activities, their timing, and costs, refer to the Exhibits section of this plan.

Public Relations Plan

PUBLIC RELATIONS OBJECTIVES

- To generate awareness, interest, and trial usage among the younger portion of the primary target market

PUBLIC RELATIONS STRATEGY

- To employ a group of influencers to help spread the message about the Schick Quattro razor

PUBLIC RELATIONS EXECUTION

To generate some buzz about the Schick Quattro, a **product seeding** campaign will be implemented among all major Junior "A" hockey teams across Canada. Junior teams consist of players between the ages of 16 and 20 years. A shaving kit comprising a case, the Schick Quattro shaving system, and two sets of replacement blades, will be given to each player on all junior teams.

The cost of the initial seeding promotion is estimated to be $55 200. See the Exhibits section for details.

Exhibits: Media Execution and Other Marketing Communications Execution

EXHIBIT 1 **Television Advertising**
All TV spots are 30 seconds in length.

Network	# of Spots	Cost/Spot	Total Cost
CTV—Prime Time	36	$16 000	$576 000
TVA—Prime Time	24	$4 000	$96 000
Rogers Sportsnet	30	$5 000	$150 000
Total	**90**		**$822 000**

EXHIBIT 2 **Magazine Advertising**
All magazine ads are one-page, four-colour.

Magazine	Frequency	Cost/Page	Total Cost
Maclean's	8	$30 000	$240 000
Maxim	6	$26 500	$159 000
UMM	4	$7 400	$29 600
Famous	4	$16 800	$67 200
Le Magazine Famous	4	$8 600	$34 400
Total	**26**		**$530 200**

EXHIBIT 3 **Outdoor Advertising**
Outdoor ads are horizontal posters (CBS Outdoor).

Market	GRPs	Rate (4 weeks)	Weeks	Total Cost
Toronto	25	$98 600	8	$197 200
Montreal	25	$74 100	8	$148 200
Vancouver	25	$74 600	4	$74 600
Edmonton	25	$19 200	4	$19 200
Calgary	25	$21 400	4	$21 400
Ottawa-Gatineau	25	$38 100	4	$38 100
Halifax	25	$6 700	4	$6 700
Total				**$505 400**

EXHIBIT 4 **Online Advertising**

Ads are leader boards on TSN.ca and Rogers Sportsnet.ca. (ads directly link to the Schick Quattro website).

Site	Impressions/Month	CPM	Cost/Month	# of Months	Total Cost
TSN	1 500 000	$30	$45 000	5	$225 000
Sportsnet	1 300 000	$20	$26 000	5	$130 000
Total					**$355 000**

EXHIBIT 5 **Media Expenditures by Market**

National media comprises network television, national magazines, and online advertising. Key-market media is outdoor advertising.

Market	$ Expenditure	% of Total	% of Key Markets
National Media	$1 707 200	77.1	
Key Markets	$505 400	22.9	
Total	**$2 212 600**	**100.0**	
Key Markets			
Toronto	$197 200		39.0
Montreal	$148 200		29.3
Vancouver	$74 600		14.8
Edmonton	$19 200		3.8
Calgary	$21 400		4.2
Ottawa-Gatineau	$38 100		7.5
Halifax	$6 700		1.4
Total	**$505 400**		**100.0**

EXHIBIT 6 **Expenditures by Medium**

Medium	Expenditure	% of Total
Television	$822 000	37.1
Magazines	$530 200	24.0
Outdoor	$505 400	22.9
Online	$355 000	16.0
Total	**$2 212 600**	**100.0**

EXHIBIT 7 **Media and Marketing Communications Expenditures by Month**
Expenditures include all activities except trade promotions.

Month	Expenditure	% of Total
January	$165 900	6.6
February	$221 120	8.8
March	$379 200	15.2
April	$213 400	8.5
May	$94 900	3.7
June	$94 720	3.7
July	$96 900	3.8
August	$429 400	17.1
September	$379 920	15.8
October	$204 600	8.2
November	$101 900	4.0
December	$114 000	4.6
Total	**$2 495 960**	**100.0**

EXHIBIT 8 **Consumer Promotions—Coupons**

Magazine	Circulation	Frequency	Redemption (%)	Total Cost
Maclean's	371 500	3	2	$49 038
Maxim	115 000	2	2	$10 120
Total	**486 500**			**$59 158**

An on-page coupon with a face value of $2.00 will appear in 3 issues of *Maclean's* and 2 issues of *Maxim*. A handling fee of $0.20 must be added to the face value of the coupon.

Costs are calculated as follows:

Circulation × frequency × redemption rate × face value and handling fees = cost of coupon offer

Maclean's × 371 500 × 3 × .02 × $2.20 = $49 038
Maxim × 115 000 × 2 × .02 × $2.20 = $10 120

EXHIBIT 9 **Consumer Promotions—Contests**

Prize	# Winners	Prize Cost	Total Cost
Grand Prize (Car)	1	$35 000	$35 000
TV	5	$2500	$12 500
iPod	10	$250	$2 500
Related Contest Promotion Costs			
Shelf Pads (in-store)			$15 000
Posters (in-store)			$10 000
Total Cost			**$75 000**

EXHIBIT 10 **Total Sales Promotion Expenditures (Including Trade Promotion)**

Activity	Cost
Coupon Offers	$59 160
Contest	$75 000
Trade Promotions	$500 000
Total	**$634 160**

EXHIBIT 11 **Public Relations—Product Seeding Campaign**

Activity	Cost
Product Seeding—Junior "A" Hockey 46 teams x 30 units x $40.00	$55 200

EXHIBIT 12 **Sponsorship Costs—Television and Online**

Sponsorship Activity	Cost
Rogers Sportsnet TV "NHL Hits of the Week" (Wednesdays)	$54 000
Rogers Sportsnet.ca "NHL Hits of the Week"	$18 000
Rogers sportsnet.ca—Schick Quattro "Premiership Predictor" Contest	$40 000
"Premier Predictor" Prizes	$10 000
Total	**$122 000**

EXHIBIT 13 **Total Marketing Communications Budget**

Activity	Expenditure	% of Total
Media Advertising	$2 212 600	73.2
Sales Promotion	$634 160	21.0
Public Relations	$55 200	1.8
Sponsorships	$122 000	4.0
Total	**$3 023 960**	**100.0**

EXHIBIT 14 **Plan Budget vs. Actual Budget**

Budget	Budget $
Estimated Budget (Based on Activities)	$3 023 960
Plan Budget	$3 000 000
Expenditure Over Budget	($23 960)

Sales and marketing communications budgets will be reviewed quarterly. Adjustments to the budget will be made when necessary.

EXHIBIT 15 **Blocking Chart**

Activity	Jan	Feb	Mar	Apr	May	Jun	Jul	Aug	Sep	Oct	Nov	Dec
Television												
CTV		6	6	6				6	6	6		
TVA	4		4		4			4	4			4
Sportsnet	5	5	5							5	5	5
Magazines												
Maclean's	1	1		1		1		1	1	1		1
Maxim	1		1		1		1		1		1	
UMM		1		1				1				1
Famous	1			1			1			1		
Le Magazine Famous	1			1			1			1		
Outdoor												
Toronto			← →						← →			
5 Other Markets								← →				
Online												
Sportsnet.ca	← →										← →	
TSN.ca					← →							
Quattro website	←											→

Continued

Consumer Promotion	Jan	Feb	Mar	Apr	May	Jun	Jul	Aug	Sep	Oct	Nov	Dec
Ad + Coupons		←→				←→			←→			
Contest								←→				
Public Relations												
Product Seeding									←→			
Sponsorships												
Sportsnet TV	←——————→										←———→	
Sportsnet.ca	←——————→										←———→	
Sportsnet.ca contest	←——————→										←———→	

Notes:

Television—Figures indicate the number of spots on each network (prime time).

Magazines—Figures indicate one insertion in each month scheduled (*Maclean's* is a weekly magazine).

Outdoor—eight-week flight in Toronto and Montreal; four-week flight in Vancouver, Edmonton, Calgary, Ottawa-Gatineau, and Halifax.

Online—Ads placed for 1.5 million impressions on TSN and 1.3 million impressions on Sportsnet each month.

Consumer Promotion—Coupons distributed in three waves in two magazines: *Maclean's* and *Maxim*. The contest will start in August (in-store ads).

Product Seeding—Sample packs will be distributed to Junior "A" teams in September.

Sponsorships—The TV, internet sponsorships, and an online contest coincide with the regular NHL season and the Premier League Soccer season.

Website—The Schick Quattro website (schickquattro.ca) is maintained by a separate budget.

This marketing communications plan was compiled for illustration purposes. It is designed to show the relationship between various components of marketing communications and how they interact with each other to achieve marketing and marketing communications objectives. The plan also shows the direct relationships between objectives, strategies, and execution for the various sub-plans within.

The following is a summary of relevant advertising regulations and information about Advertising Standards Canada, an organization responsible for administering regulations in Canada.

Advertising Standards Canada

Advertising Standards Canada is a national industry association committed to ensuring the integrity and viability of advertising through self-regulation. Membership in the organization consists of advertisers, advertising agencies, media organizations, and suppliers to the advertising industry.

ASC administers the *Canadian Code of Advertising Standards*, the principal instrument of self-regulation. The *Code* sets the standards for acceptable advertising and is regularly updated to ensure it remains vital, current, and relevant. It contains 14 clauses (see below) that set the criteria for acceptable advertising and is also supplemented with interpretation guidelines on the application of the *Code*'s clauses.

Through regional councils, consumer complaints about advertising are accepted, reviewed, and adjudicated. ASC is also responsible for some other self-regulating codes and provides commercial clearance services for food, non-alcoholic beverages, cosmetics, and tobacco products. It also administers guidelines for advertising directed to children.

The primary codes and guidelines administered by ASC include the *Canadian Code of Advertising Standards*, *Gender Portrayal Guidelines*, and *The Broadcast Code for Advertising to Children*.

The Complaint Process

Consumers who witness advertising that is contrary to the *Canadian Code of Advertising Standards* must lodge a complaint in writing (emailed complaints are accepted) with one of the national or regional Consumer Response Councils. Complaints can be submitted by letter or by filling in a form that is available at the ASC website. All written complaints are acknowledged and reviewed, and if there appears to be a violation, the advertiser will be contacted.

The critical factor in determining whether an advertisement should be reviewed is not the number of complaints received. The fundamental issue is only whether an advertisement appears to contravene the *Code*.

If there is an infraction of the *Code*, the advertiser in question is notified. The advertiser can respond to the complaint. If a violation has occurred, the advertiser is asked to amend the advertisement or withdraw it. Once the advertiser has taken either of these steps, the complaint is closed and the complainant is informed in writing of the corrective action. If the complaint is not sustained, the Council will explain why to the complainant. Occasionally, an advertiser refuses to take corrective action. In this case, the Council will advise broadcasters and publishers carrying the ad. Usually, the media drop the ad in question.

Each year ASC publishes one or more reports on consumers' complaints about advertising. The purpose of these complaint reports is to serve, for the benefit of the advertising industry and the interested public, as a guide for the interpretation of the *Code* as applied to advertising issues that concerned the public.

Canadian Code of Advertising Standards

The *Code* was first published in 1963. It is periodically reviewed and updated when necessary. The *Code* sets the criteria for acceptable advertising and forms the basis upon which advertising is evaluated in response to consumer or trade complaints. It is endorsed by all members of ASC.

For the purpose of the *Code*:

Advertising is defined as any message (the content of which is controlled directly or indirectly by the advertiser) expressed in any language and communicated in any medium to Canadians with the intent to influence their choice, opinion, or behaviour.

Advertising also includes advocacy advertising, political advertising, and election advertising. **Advocacy advertising** is advertising that represents information or a point of view bearing on a publicly recognized controversial issue. **Political advertising** is advertising by any part of local, provincial, or federal governments, or concerning policies, practices, or programs of such governments, as distinct from election advertising. **Election advertising** refers to advertising by political parties, a political or government policy or issue, an electoral candidate, or any other matter before the electorate.

Scope of the *Code*

Authority applies only to the content of advertisements and does not prohibit the promotion of legal products or services or their portrayal in circumstances of normal use. The context and content of the advertisement; the audience actually, or likely to be, or intended to be, reached by the advertisement; and the medium/media used to deliver the advertisement are relevant factors in assessing its conformity with the *Code*.

The provisions of the *Code* should be adhered to both in letter and in spirit. Advertisers and their representatives must substantiate their advertised claims promptly when requested to do so by any one or more of the Councils. The *Canadian Code of Advertising Standards* includes 14 clauses. These clauses cover the following areas:

- Accuracy and Clarity
- Disguised Advertising Techniques
- Price Claims
- Bait and Switch
- Guarantees
- Comparative Advertising
- Testimonials
- Professional or Scientific Claims
- Imitation
- Safety
- Superstition and Fears
- Advertising to Children
- Advertising to Minors
- Unacceptable Depictions or Portrayals

For complete text of the *Code,* visit the Advertising Standards Canada website at **www.adstandards.com**.

Gender Portrayal Guidelines

Advertising Standards Canada has established firm guidelines for the portrayal of men and women in advertisements. The guidelines are updated periodically to reflect changes in the social and professional roles of men and women in Canadian society. The current guidelines are not intended to be a "how-to" guide for portraying men and women, but they do provide direction in those areas, which, based on previous consumer complaints, appear to be the most problematic. The guidelines are as follows:

1. *Authority* Advertising should strive to provide an equal representation of men and women in roles of authority in actual advertising presentations, including announcers, voice-overs, experts, and on-camera authorities.
2. *Decision-Making* Women and men should be portrayed equally as single decision-makers for all purchases including big-ticket items. In joint decision-making processes, men and women should be shown as equal participants, whether in the workplace or at home.
3. *Sexuality* Advertising should avoid the inappropriate use or exploitation of both women and men.
4. *Violence* Neither sex should be portrayed as exerting domination over the other by means of overt or implied threats, or actual force.
5. *Diversity* Advertising should portray both women and men in the full spectrum of diversity and as equally competent in a wide range of activities both inside and outside the home.
6. *Language* Advertising should avoid language that misrepresents, offends, or excludes women or men.

The *Broadcast Code for Advertising to Children*

Children's advertising is defined as paid commercial messages directed to persons less than 12 years of age. Key elements of the *Code* are as follows:

- Messages cannot be subliminal (e.g., they cannot be below the threshold of normal awareness).
- Characteristics such as performance, speed, and size cannot be exaggerated.
- Ads should not encourage children to buy, or ask their parents to buy, a product or service.
- Direct-response techniques that invite the audience to purchase products or services by mail or telephone are prohibited.
- The same commercial message or more than one commercial message promoting the same product cannot be aired more than once during a half-hour children's program.
- The use of puppets, persons, and characters well known to children as endorsers to promote products is to be avoided.
- Prices must be clear and complete. Accessories that seem to be part of the product but must be purchased at extra cost must be clearly stated and shown.
- Commercial messages shall not make comparisons with a competitor's product or service when the effect is to diminish the value of other products or services.
- There will be no portrayal of unsafe situations except for specific safety messages (e.g., using flames or fire or showing extreme recreational activities).
- Advertising cannot imply that owning or using a product makes the child superior, or that without it a child will be open to ridicule or contempt.
- Where measurable claims are made regarding performance, safety, speed, durability, etc., the advertiser must be prepared on request to provide evidence supporting such claims.

For more complete details of gender portrayal guidelines, the broadcast code for advertising to children, and other industry regulations, visit the ASC website at **www.adstandards.com**.

Other Codes and Guidelines

The following are other codes and guidelines administered by Advertising Standards Canada.

- Guide to Food Labelling and Advertising
- Advertising Code of Standards for Cosmetics, Toiletries, and Fragrances
- Guidelines for the Use of Comparative Advertising in Food Commercials
- Guidelines for the Use of Research and Survey Data in Comparative Food Commercials
- Guiding Principles for Environmental Labelling and Advertising
- Trade Dispute Procedure

Where to Write

You may obtain a free copy of the *Canadian Code of Advertising Standards* by writing to ASC in either Toronto or Montreal:

Standards Division
Advertising Standards Canada

175 Bloor Street East
South Tower, Suite 1801
Toronto, ON   M4W 3R8
Tel: (416) 961-6311
Fax: (416) 961-7904
Email: **info@adstandards.com**
Website: **www.adstandards.com**

Les normes canadiennes de la publicité

4823 rue Sherbrooke ouest, Bureau 130
Montreal, QC   H3Z 1G7
Tel: (514) 931-8060
Fax: (514) 931-2797
Email: **info@normespub.cpm**
Website: **www.normespub.com**

REGIONAL COUNCILS

British Columbia Consumer Response Council
bccouncil@adstandards.com

Alberta Consumer Response Council
albertacouncil@adstandards.com

Atlantic Consumer Response Council
atlanticcouncil@adstandards.com

Account director The senior member of the account management group in an advertising agency, responsible for the agency's performance in handling client accounts.

Account executive The liaison between the agency and client; coordinates the agency's services for the benefit of the client and represents the agency's point of view to the client.

Account shifting Moving an advertising account from one agency to another.

Account supervisor A mid-manager in an agency who manages the activities of a group of account executives; generally takes a longer-term perspective on product advertising assignments.

Ad network A specialist company that represents a host of websites and serves as a sales force for participating publishers. This term could apply to other media as well.

Ad-tiles Ad messages affixed to the floor of retail stores. Also called floor advertising.

Advergaming The integration of brands into video games, games played online, or in games purchased directly by consumers.

Advertising A paid form of marketing communication designed to stimulate a positive response from a defined target market.

Advertising manager Generally, the individual in the client organization responsible for advertising planning and implementation.

Advertising plan An annual planning document that outlines the advertising activities (creative and media) for the forthcoming year. The plan includes discussion of objectives, strategies, and tactics for both creative and media plans.

Advertising research Any form of research providing information useful in the preparation or evaluation of creative, of media alternatives, and of media usage.

Advertising share A brand's media expenditure, expressed as a percentage of total product-category media expenditures.

Advocacy advertising Advertising that communicates a company's stand on a particular issue (usually one that will affect a company's operations).

Affiliates Independent stations that carry network programming.

Agate line A non-standardized unit of space measurement in a newspaper equal to one column wide and one-quarter-inch deep.

Agency commission Compensation that a medium pays an agency for placing advertising with the medium. Agencies use a commission system, a fee system, or a combination of both.

Agency of record (AOR) A central agency, often used by multiple-product advertisers that use more than one advertising agency, responsible for media negotiation and placement.

Aided recall A research situation where respondents are provided with certain information to stimulate thought.

AM (amplitude modulation) Refers to the height at which radio waves are transmitted.

Ambush marketing A promotional strategy used by non-sponsors to capitalize on the status and prestige of an event by giving a false impression that they are the sponsors.

Animated banners An internet banner ad that spins or has some form of action.

Animated commercials A commercial technique involving the use of hand-drawn cartoons or stylized figures and settings.

Answerprint Final post-production stage of a television commercial, where film, sound, special effects, and opticals are combined and printed (final copy of an advertisement for distribution to television stations).

Appeal The creative angle taken to motivate a consumer to purchase a particular product or service.

Approach The initial contact with a prospect in a personal-selling situation.

Art director The individual responsible for the visuals in an advertisement (illustrations in a print ad and storyboards in a broadcast ad).

Assortment media strategy A media strategy where media dollars are distributed more equitably among several media types.

Attitude An individual's feelings, favourable or unfavourable, toward an advertised product.

Audience flow In radio, the change in audience demographics based on the time of day.

Audience fragmentation The splintering of an audience across a greater number of channels (consumers have more channels to choose from).

Backlit poster A luminous sign containing advertising graphics printed on translucent polyvinyl material.

Balance   The relationship between the left side and the right side of a print advertisement. Equal weight (left versus right) refers to formal balance, and unequal weight is informal balance.

Banner (internet)   On the internet, an ad that stretches across the page in a narrow band. The viewer clicks on the ad for more information. Banner ads are now available in a variety of shapes and sizes.

Banners (outdoor)   In outdoor advertising, large-size vinyl-painted ads that are framed and mounted on the outside of a building.

Behaviour-response segmentation   Dividing buyers into groups according to their occasions for using the product, the benefits they require in a product, the frequency with which they use it, and their degree of brand loyalty.

Billboard   (1) A common name associated with outdoor poster advertising. (2) In television, a sponsoring announcement at the beginning, end, or break of a television program.

Bleed (bleed page or bleed ad)   A situation where the coloured background of an advertisement extends to the edge of the page so that there is no margin.

Blitz schedule   A schedule characterized by heavy media spending in a short space of time (saturation), with spending tapering off over an extended period of time.

Blocking chart   A visual document usually one or two pages in length that outlines all of the details of a media execution.

Body copy   Informative or persuasive prose that elaborates on the central theme of an advertisement.

Bounce back   Advertisements and offers distributed in monthly charge account statements or with the delivery of goods purchased by direct mail.

Brand Development Index (BDI)   The percentage of a brand's sales in a region in relation to the population of the region.

Brand manager   An individual assigned responsibility for the development and implementation of marketing programs for a specific brand or group of brands.

Branded content   The inclusion of information about a branded product in the script of a television show or movie.

Build-up schedule   A schedule characterized by low initial media weight that gradually builds to an intensive campaign.

Bus murals   Painted advertising on the side of a bus or the tail of a bus.

Business-to-business advertising   Advertising of finished products and services that is directed at other businesses that can use the advertised items to advantage.

Button(s)   On the internet, an ad in the shape of a small square or circle.

Buzz marketing   Activities that generate personal recommendations for a branded product.

Call centre   A central operation from which a company operates its inbound and outbound telemarketing programs.

Car cards   Print ads in racks above the windows in buses and subway cars. Also called interior overhead cards.

Cash refund   A predetermined amount of money returned directly to a consumer by a manufacturer after a purchase has been made.

Catalogues   Reference publications, usually annual, distributed by large retail chains and other direct-marketing organizations.

Category manager   An individual who is assigned responsibility for developing and implementing marketing programs for products grouped into the category (e.g., all laundry detergent products).

CD-ROM   A computer-based multimedia sales presentation platform.

Circulation   The average number of copies of a publication sold by subscription, through retail outlets, or distributed free to predetermined recipients.

Circulation list   A magazine subscription list that targets potential customers by interest or activity.

Clicks   A form of advertising measurement on the internet. It is a count of every time a visitor clicks on a banner ad.

Clickthrough rate   A ratio that indicates the success of an advertiser in attracting visitors to click on its ad. The formula is clicks divided by ad impressions.

Closing   In a personal-selling situation, asking for the order. If the buyer says no, the close is referred to as a trial close.

Cluster   The grouping of commercials in a block of time during a program break or between programs.

Clutter   (1) In broadcast advertising, the clustering of commercials together in a short space of time. (2) In print advertising, the extent to which a publication's pages are fragmented into small blocks of advertising.

CNU (Canadian newspaper unit)   A standardized newspaper format that divides a 13-inch-wide broadsheet into 6 columns and a 10¼-inch-wide tabloid into 5 columns. Each unit has a depth of 30 modular agate lines. A broadsheet contains 60 CNUs; a tabloid has 30 CNUs.

Combination rates   Rates used for selling advertising time on independent radio stations controlled by one owner.

Comparative advertising A form of advertising where a brand is compared with a competitive brand on the basis of similar attributes that are judged to be important to the target market.

Compiled list A direct-mail list that is prepared from government, census, telephone, warranty, and other publication information.

Comprehensive A mechanical art layout that has all copy and illustrations pasted precisely into place (often referred to as camera-ready artwork).

Concentrated media strategy A media strategy in which a majority of media dollars are allocated to one primary medium.

Concept shop A store within a store that allows a company to showcase its full range of products in a certain area.

Consumer advertising Persuasive communications designed to elicit a purchase response from consumers.

Consumer behaviour The acts of individuals in obtaining and using goods and services; the decision processes that precede and determine these acts.

Consumer promotion Promotion activity directed at consumers and designed to encourage quicker purchase response.

Content analysis A process of recording exposure actually received as a result of public relations activities.

Contest A consumer promotion technique that involves the awarding of cash or merchandise prizes to consumers when they purchase a specified product.

Continuity The length of time required to ensure impact on a target market through a particular medium.

Continuity discount A discount based on the purchase of a minimum number of designated spots over an extended period of time (usually 52 weeks).

Controlled circulation Publications that are distributed free to individuals who fall within a specific demographic segment or geographic area.

Cookie An electronic identification tag sent from a web server to a browser to track a person's browsing patterns.

Co-operative advertising The sharing of advertising costs and materials by suppliers and retailers or by several retailers.

Co-operative direct mail Mailings containing specific offers from non-competing products (e.g., coupons, samples, subscription offers).

Copywriter The individual responsible for developing the headline, body copy, and signature in a print advertisement or the script in a broadcast ad.

Corporate advertising Advertising designed to convey a favourable image of a company to its various publics.

Coupons Price-off incentives offered to consumers to stimulate quicker purchase of a designated product. (Coupons are usually product-delivered or media-delivered.)

Coverage The percentage of individuals reached by a publication in a specific geographic area.

CPM (cost per thousand) Cost of delivering a message to 1000 individuals.

Creative boutique An advertising agency that specializes in the development of creative concepts and executions.

Creative brief A document prepared by the client for the agency that outlines all relevant information pertaining to a new creative development assignment.

Creative concept The central theme, or basic sales message, that an advertisement communicates through verbal and visual devices.

Creative department The department in an advertising agency that provides creative services such as copy and art.

Creative execution A more precise definition of creative strategy (i.e., tactical considerations regarding the best way to present products for maximum impact, such as celebrity spokespersons, dramatizations, and use of colour).

Creative objectives Clearly worded statements that outline the basic content of an advertising message (i.e., brand name and benefits that are of high interest to potential buyers).

Creative research Evaluating and measuring the impact of an advertising message on a target market.

Creative strategy Clearly worded statements that provide direction regarding how the message will be presented. Such statements usually consider appeal techniques, tone, style, and theme.

Cross-coupon (cross-ruff) One product carrying a coupon offer for another product (often done by complementary products, such as coffee and biscuits).

Cross-marketing A strategy in which two independent organizations share facilities and/or resources to market their goods to similar customers.

Cross-sampling One product carrying a free sample of another product.

Custom-designed research Primary research that focuses on resolving a specific problem or obtaining specific information.

Customer relationship management A practice designed to attract, cultivate, and maximize the return from each customer a company does business with.

DAR (day-after recall) Research conducted the day following the respondent's exposure to a commercial message to determine the degree of recognition and recall of the advertisement, the brand, and the selling message.

Data mining The analysis of information that establishes relationships between pieces of information so that more effective marketing and communications strategies can be identified and implemented.

Database marketing A system for analyzing data contained in a database concerning customers and prospects, for the purpose of identifying new target markets and opportunities and preparing marketing and communications plans targeted to the customers most likely to buy.

Daypart A block of time during the day, in a station or network's daily programming schedule, used to distinguish viewing and listening patterns.

Dealer premium An additional incentive (usually merchandise) offered to a distributor by a manufacturer to encourage special purchase or to secure additional merchandising support from a retailer.

Delayed payment incentive The granting of a grace period during which no interest or principal is paid on a purchased item.

Demographic segmentation The process of dividing a large market into smaller segments on the basis of various combinations of age, sex, income, occupation, education, race, and religion.

Department maker (POP) An elaborate, often permanent merchandise display unit (store-within-a-store concept).

Dialogue copy Messages delivered from someone's point of view.

Direct advertising A form of media advertising that communicates messages directly to marketing prospects.

Direct mail A form of direct advertising that uses the postal service as the vehicle for delivering the message.

Direct marketing A marketing system, controlled by the marketer, whereby products are developed, then promoted to a variety of end users through a variety of media options, and then distributed to the customer.

Direct-response advertising Advertising through any medium (mail, television, telephone, or fax) designed to generate a response that is measurable.

Direct-response print A response-oriented message delivered to prospects by magazine or newspaper advertisements.

Direct-response television (DRTV) Television advertising that has two distinct formats: the 30-, 60-, or 120-second spot, and the 30-minute infomercial.

Direct segmentation Targeting customers on an individual basis.

Display advertising Advertising that appears anywhere in a newspaper, excluding the classified section.

Display cards (POP) Small advertisements located at point-of-purchase (shelf talkers, tear-off ad pads, counter posters) that are designed to encourage impulse purchases.

Display shipper (POP) A shipping carton containing a pre-determined amount of merchandise that, when assembled, will form a temporary display at point-of-purchase.

Door cards In subway cars, ads positioned on both sides of the exit doors.

Double targeting Devising a single marketing strategy for both genders or an individual strategy for each of the genders.

Double truck In newspaper advertising, an ad that covers an entire two-page spread.

Efficiency The relative cost effectiveness of a particular medium, based on CPM.

Electronic coupons Discounts offered at point-of-purchase after a transaction has been made.

Email A means of communication on the internet. It is a cost-effective way for companies to communicate with customers and prospects.

Endorsement A form of advertising that uses a celebrity (e.g., rock star, television personality, sports star) to present the product message.

End-product advertising Advertising by a firm that makes part of a finished product (e.g., Kodak advertises the benefits of processing film on Kodak paper).

Engagement The degree of involvement a person has with the media when they are using it.

Even schedule The purchase of media time and space in a uniform manner over an extended period of time.

Event marketing The process, planned by a sponsoring organization, of integrating a variety of communication elements behind an event theme.

Event sponsorship The financial support of an event by a sponsor in return for advertising privileges associated with the event.

Event-oriented advertising Retail advertising that revolves around a central theme that a target market will find appealing, such as an annual midnight-madness sale.

Execution (tactics) Action plans that outline specific details of implementation.

Exterior bus poster A poster-type advertisement appended to the side or rear section of a bus.

Eye-camera test A test whereby a hidden camera records eye movement to gauge the point of immediate contact in an advertisement, how a reader scans the ad, and the amount of time spent reading.

Fade An optical effect in a television commercial, whereby one scene gradually disappears and another gradually appears.

Family life cycle The stages an individual progresses through during a lifetime (bachelor stage to solitary survivor).

Feature sheet A sheet, commonly used in radio personality announcements, that provides the station with the key benefit and the slogan for the product advertised. The DJ develops the specific message wording from the sheet.

Flexform advertising An advertisement that does not conform to normal shapes (an odd-shaped ad designed to stand out from traditional square advertising spaces in a newspaper).

Flexibility The ability to modify media spending plans throughout the media spending (planning) period.

Flights (or flighting) Refers to the purchase of media time in periodic waves of advertising, separated by periods of total inactivity.

Flow The reader's eye movement (e.g., from left to right and from top to bottom) when reading an advertisement.

FM (frequency modulation) The speed at which waves travel, in thousands of cycles per second (kilohertz).

Format A term that, in the context of radio, describes the nature of the programming done by an individual station.

Fragmentation A situation where a television or radio station audience has numerous stations to choose from.

Freelancer A self-employed, independent creative specialist (e.g., a graphic artist, a copywriter, or an art director).

Free-standing insert (FSI) Preprinted ads that are inserted loose into newspapers.

Frequency The average number of times an audience is exposed to an advertising message over a period of time, usually a week. Also called average frequency.

Frequency discount A discount based on a minimum number of spots purchased over a specified period of time.

Frequent-buyer program A promotion strategy that provides consumers with a small bonus, such as points or play money, when a purchase is made. These incentives are intended to encourage loyalty toward a product or company.

Fulfillment costs The costs to receive and fill orders received by direct-marketing techniques.

Full-service agency An advertising agency that provides a complete range of services to the client (i.e., creative and media planning, marketing research, sales promotion, and, possibly, public relations).

Game (instant win) A promotion that includes a number of predetermined, pre-seeded winning tickets.

Gatefold A printed magazine advertisement that consists of a series of folded pages, with the folded pages conforming to the publication's page size.

Geographic segmentation The process of dividing a large geographic market into geographic units (e.g., Canada is divided into the Maritimes, Quebec, Ontario, the Prairies, and British Columbia).

Geomapping A database management technique that targets an audience based on demographic, psychographic, and behavioural data.

Grid card A broadcasting price schedule that quotes different price levels, depending on certain criteria such as demand for time, frequency of advertising, volume of advertising, and time of year.

Grocery cart advertising Advertising (small posters) appended to the ends of shopping carts, which are visible to approaching shoppers in supermarkets.

Group head (or associate media director) The member of the media department who carries an administrative workload and is responsible for the management of the department.

GRP (gross rating points) An aggregate of total ratings in a schedule, as determined by reach multiplied by frequency, usually in a weekly period, against a target audience.

Guaranteed position A specific position for an advertisement, with a premium rate charged for such positioning.

Gutter The blank space on the inside page margins in a bound publication, or the blank space between two facing pages in a newspaper.

Hiatus The period of time between advertising flights.

Hierarchy-of-effects model Various theories concerning how advertising influences the behavioural stages an individual passes through prior to making a purchase decision.

Hit Any connection to an internet site.

Homepage The initial page of an advertiser's website on the internet. A viewer who clicks on certain buttons on the homepage will get more detailed information about that website.

Hooker (or tag) The local dealer's name added to national advertisements in newspapers.

Horizontal co-operative advertising The sharing of advertising costs by a group of retailers.

Horizontal publications Publications appealing to people who occupy the same level of responsibility in a business.

Horizontal rotation The placement of radio commercials based on the day of the week.

Horizontal split A situation in the layout of a print advertisement where the page is divided across the middle, with an illustration in one half and copy in the other.

House list An internal customer list.

House organ A document that outlines news and events about an organization and its employees.

Impressions (1) In online advertising, the number of times a banner image is downloaded to a page being viewed by a visitor. (2) The total audience reached by a media plan. Often referred to as "total exposures," impressions are calculated by multiplying the number of people who receive a message (reach) by the number of times they receive it (frequency).

Inbound telemarketing The reception of calls by the order desk, or customer inquiry and direct-response calls generated from toll-free telephone numbers.

Industrial advertising Advertising of products that are used to produce and distribute other products.

Infomercial A long commercial (e.g., 10 to 30 minutes in length) that presents in detail the benefits of a product or service.

In-house agency An organizational structure used in a manufacturer's or retailer's operation that handles its own advertising function; creative is developed by staff copywriters and artists; media time and space are purchased by in-house specialists; external agencies are used only as needed.

Insert A preprinted advertisement (e.g., a leaflet, a reply card) that is specially placed in a newspaper or magazine.

Insert layout The inclusion of a secondary visual (an insert) in a print layout.

Insertion order A statement of specifications for an advertisement sent by an advertising agency to print media, including insertion dates, size, position, and rates.

Institutional advertising Advertising designed to create a favourable image of a store or product in the minds of potential and current customers.

Integrated marketing communications (IMC) The coordination of all forms of marketing communications into a unified program that maximizes the impact on consumers and other types of customers.

Interlock The synchronizing of sound and picture for a television commercial through the use of a special editor's projector.

Internet A network of computers linked together to act as one.

Interstitial An ad that pops onto a computer screen during a browsing period. Often referred to as a pop-up.

Key-benefit statement A statement of the basic selling idea, service, or benefit that an advertiser promises a consumer.

Key-market media plan Purchasing media time on the basis of market priorities (i.e., on a market-by-market basis).

Kiosks Interactive computers in stand-alone cabinets usually located in stores. The kiosk is interactive and communicates information about company products.

Layout The design and orderly formation of the various elements of an advertisement, within specified dimensions. A layout integrates all copy elements with the illustration to create a complete message.

Lifestyle advertising A form of advertising that attempts to associate a product with the lifestyle of a certain market segment.

Line rate The newspaper advertising rate charged for one modular agate line.

List broker A company specializing in finding or developing lists for direct-marketing purposes. They find prospects based on descriptions provided by marketing organizations.

Live-action commercials Advertisements that use real-life situations with real people.

Lobbying Activities and practices designed to influence policy decisions of governments.

Local-spot advertising Purchase of advertising time on a station by local market advertisers.

Long copy A copy-dominant advertisement that makes little or no use of illustration.

Long-form DRTV Extended commercials lasting from 30 to 60 minutes (also called infomercials).

Long list In the agency selection process, a listing of the advertising agencies that could potentially meet the advertising needs of a client.

Make good A rerun of an advertisement at the publisher's expense, to compensate for an error in or substandard printing of the original insertion.

MAL (modular agate line) A standardized unit of space equal to one column wide and one-quarter-inch deep. Broadsheet column widths are $2\frac{1}{16}$ inches; tabloids $1\frac{15}{16}$ inch.

Market discount (transit) A discount based on the purchase of a predetermined list of markets.

Market segmentation The process of dividing a large market into smaller homogeneous markets (segments) according to common needs and/or similar lifestyles.

Marketing communications plan A single document that provides details for all of the components of a communications plan (e.g., advertising, sales promotion, events, public relations, internet, and so on).

Marketing control The process of measuring and evaluating the results of marketing strategies and plans, and taking corrective action to ensure objectives are achieved.

Marketing objectives Statements identifying what a product will accomplish over a one-year period of time.

Marketing plan An annual planning document for a product, service, or company that includes background analysis (of the market, the product, and the competition) and objectives, strategies, and tactics for the forthcoming year.

Marketing planning Planning activities that relate to the achievement of marketing objectives.

Marketing research The systematic gathering, recording, and analyzing of data to resolve a marketing problem.

Marketing strategies The process of identifying target markets and satisfying those targets with a blend of marketing-mix elements.

Marketing tactics Detailed activity plans that contribute to the achievement of marketing objectives.

Media billings The total dollar-volume of advertising handled by an agency in one year.

Media brief A document prepared by a client for an agency that outlines relevant background information pertaining to the development of a new media strategy and plan.

Media buyer A media specialist who is familiar with the competitive claims of the various media alternatives. The media buyer's primary function is to purchase media time and space for clients as efficiently as possible.

Media convergence The consolidation of ownership of a variety of media outlets by relatively few companies.

Media delivery A method of coupon distribution using various print media alternatives, including newspapers, magazines, and co-operative direct mail.

Media director The most senior media position in an advertising agency; responsible for the management of the media department and accountable for media planning and placement for all clients.

Media mix The combination of media used in a media schedule.

Media objectives Clearly worded statements that outline exactly what a media plan should accomplish (e.g., who, what, when, where, and how).

Media placement The actual purchase of media time and space once a media plan has been approved.

Media planner A media specialist who assesses the strengths, weaknesses, costs, and communications potential of various media in order to develop a media plan.

Media planning Preparation of a plan that documents how the client's money will be spent to achieve advertising objectives.

Media relations In public relations, a company's ability to develop a good relationship with the media that cover their particular industry.

Media strategy Strategic recommendations showing how media objectives will be achieved.

Media supervisor A senior-level media specialist who supervises the activities of media planners and buyers.

Media-buying service An advertising agency that specializes in media planning and placement.

Merge/purge The process of purchasing lists, combining them, and then stripping them of duplicate names.

Mission statement A statement of purpose for an organization that usually reflects the organization's operating philosophy.

Mixed interlock The addition of sound effects and music to the interlock.

Mixed tape The finished radio commercial tape containing the spoken words, music, and special effects.

Modular agate line (MAL) A standardized unit of space measurement in a newspaper equal to one column wide and 1/4-inch deep. A modular agate line is wider than an agate line.

Modular display rack (POP) A permanent display unit, provided by a manufacturer, to display a certain line of merchandise.

Motives Conditions that prompt action to satisfy a need (the action elicited by marketing and advertising activity).

Multiple illustration In a print advertisement layout, the use of many individual illustrations in sequence.

Narrative copy Messages presented in the third person.

Narrowcasting Specialized programming designed to attract a narrowly defined target market (a special age or interest group).

National advertising (or general advertising) Advertising of a trademarked product or service wherever that product or service is available.

Needs A state of deprivation—the absence of something useful.

Network advertising Advertising that comes from one central source and is broadcast across the entire network of stations.

Noise Competitive advertising messages aimed at a specific target market.

Objection(s) An obstacle that a salesperson must confront and resolve if a sales transaction is to be completed.

Objectives Statements outlining what is to be accomplished in a plan (corporate, marketing, or advertising plan).

Omnibus study (syndicated service) Research data collected by, or available to, participants in a common study. (The Print Measurement Bureau databank, for example, provides such studies.)

Online advertising The placement of electronic communication on a website, in email, or over personal communications devices connected to the internet.

Opinion-measure testing A form of research yielding information about the effect of a commercial message on consumers' brand-name recall, their interest in a brand, and their purchase intentions.

Optimizer A software program that searches a media database(s) to identify media combinations that increase target reach or reduce the cost of buying it.

Outbound telemarketing Telephone calls and faxes a company makes to a customer to develop new accounts, generate sales leads, and even close a sale.

Outdoor advertising Advertising that is directed at vehicular or pedestrian traffic (e.g., posters or billboards, backlit posters, transit-shelter advertising, and mall posters).

Pace (television) Designing message content so that it falls within the time parameters of the commercial—usually 15, 30, or 60 seconds.

Package plans Discounted rate plans that combine prime-time spots with fringe time and daytime spots.

Pass-along reader (secondary reader) A person who reads a magazine after having received it secondhand.

Perception How individuals receive and interpret messages (three levels have been defined: selective exposure, selective perception, and selective retention).

Performance allowance An additional trade discount (beyond a trade allowance) used to encourage retailers to perform a specific merchandising function.

Permission-based email A situation where an individual agrees to accept email advertising and marketing offers.

Personal selling A personalized form of communication that involves a seller presenting the features and benefits of a product or service to a buyer for the purpose of making a sale.

Personality announcement In radio, a situation where the disc jockey presents a commercial message in his or her own style.

Planning The process of anticipating the future business environment and determining the courses of action to take in that environment.

Point-of-purchase (POP) advertising Advertising or display materials located in a retail environment to build traffic, advertise a product, and encourage impulse purchasing.

Pop-up coupon A coupon printed on heavier paper stock and stitched into a popular consumer magazine. (It is usually positioned directly before an advertisement for the couponed product.)

Portal page When an internet banner ad is clicked on, the visitor is linked to the advertiser's website or special webpage that gives more information about the company or product.

Position charge An additional cost for requesting a particular location in a medium.

Positioning The place a brand occupies in the minds of consumers; in other words, the selling concept that motivates purchase.

Poster A picture-dominant advertisement that uses a minimum of copy.

Post-testing The evaluation and measurement of a message's effectiveness during or after the message has run.

Pre-approach An information-gathering exercise to qualify customers.

Pre-emption A situation in which a special program replaces regular programming. Advertisers of the regularly scheduled programs are rescheduled for comparable time slots at a later date.

Preferred position Requesting a specific position in a medium.

Premium An item offered free, or at a low price, to encourage consumers to buy a specific product (offered to consumers in four different forms).

Premium rates In radio, an extra charge the advertiser pays for sponsoring a special program.

Press conference The gathering of news reporters invited to witness the release of important information about a company or product.

Press release A document containing all essential elements of a story (who, what, when, where, and why).

Pre-testing Evaluating commercial messages or advertisements, prior to final production, to determine the strengths and weaknesses of the communications.

Primary reader A person qualifying as a reader who receives the publication initially.

Primary research Refers to data observed, recorded, and collected on a first-time basis with a view to resolving a specific problem.

Prime/fringe/daytime (television) In television, the basic dayparts sold—prime time normally runs from 7:00 to 11:00 p.m.; fringe time usually from 4:30 to 6:30 p.m. and 11:00 p.m. to sign-off; daytime from sign-on until 4:30 p.m.

Product advertising Advertising that informs customers about the benefits of a particular brand.

Product delivery A method of coupon distribution using coupons inside or on a package.

Product life cycle The path a product follows from its introduction to its eventual withdrawal from the market (a four-stage process).

Product manager (brand manager) A manager in the client organization who is assigned responsibility for carrying out the marketing planning (four Ps) for a product or a group of products.

Product placement The visible placement of branded products in television shows and commercial movies.

Product Seeding Giving a product free to trendsetters who, in turn, influence others to become aware of the product, and hopefully purchase it.

Profile-matching strategy Matching the demographic profile of a product's target market with a specific medium that has a compatible profile.

Promotional advertising Advertising designed to accomplish a single task—to get consumers to take action immediately.

Prospecting A systematic procedure for developing sales leads.

Psychographic segmentation Market segmentation based on the activities, interests, and opinions (the lifestyles) of consumers.

Public affairs In public relations, the development of programs and strategies to deal with governments.

Public relations The firm's communications with its various publics (shareholders, employees, suppliers, governments).

Publicity The communication of newsworthy information about a product, service, or idea.

Publisher's statement A statement of circulation data issued by a publisher to the Audit Bureau of Circulations. The statement, used in ABC's compilation of circulation data, is unaudited at the time of issue but is subject to audit by the ABC.

Pull strategy Creating demand for a product by directing promotional efforts at consumers or final users of the product.

Pulsing (or pulse media schedule) Refers to the grouping of advertisements in flights over a predetermined period of time.

Pupillometer A device that measures the pupil dilation (enlargement) of a person's eye when the person is reading.

Push strategy Creating demand for a product by directing promotional efforts at intermediaries, who in turn promote the product among consumers.

Qualitative research Data collected from a small sample size; usually the initial step in assessing target-market feedback for an idea or concept.

Quantitative research Data collected from a much larger sample size that quantifies respondents' feelings, attitudes, and opinions.

Ratings Audience estimates expressed as a percentage of a population in a defined geographic area.

Reach The total audience (number of people reached) potentially exposed, one or more times, to an advertiser's message over a period of time (a week).

Reach plan (total audience plan) A plan that involves rotating a radio commercial through the various dayparts so that the same message can reach different groups of people.

Readers per copy The average number of people who read a single issue of a publication.

Recall testing A test that measures an advertisement's impact by asking respondents to recall specific elements (e.g., the selling message) of the advertisement.

Recency A media advertising model that suggests advertising works best by reminding consumers of a product when they are ready to buy.

Recognition tests Tests that measure a target audience's awareness of a brand, of its copy points, or of the advertisement itself after the audience has been exposed to the message.

Redemption rate Refers to the number of coupons actually redeemed. The rate of redemption for a specific coupon offer equals the number of coupons redeemed divided by the number of coupons distributed.

Reference group (or peer groups) A group of people with a common interest who have an influence on the individual member's attitudes and behaviour. It is a group to which a person thinks they belong.

Refund (rebate) A predetermined amount of money returned directly to a consumer by a manufacturer after specified purchases have been made.

Related recall The percentage of a test commercial audience who claim to remember a test commercial and can provide, as verification, some description of the commercial.

Relationship marketing Marketing strategies designed to reach customers on a one-to-one basis. These strategies are based on the collection of useful information from internal and external databases.

Reply card (business reply card) A type of mail that enables the recipient of direct-mail advertising to respond without paying postage (encourages response).

Repositioning Changing the place a product occupies, relative to competitive products, in the consumer's mind.

Residual The additional payments granted to actors or models for appearing in a commercial over an extended period of time. Individuals are paid for each time the advertisement appears onscreen (during a 13-week cycle).

Response list A list of proven mail-order buyers.

Retail advertising Advertising by a retail store (the advertising of a store name, image, and location, and the re-advertising of branded merchandise carried by the retailer).

Retail in-ad coupon A coupon printed in a retailer's weekly advertising, either via run of press or supplements inserted in a newspaper.

Rich media Internet media that allow for greater use of interaction with animation, audio and video, and advanced tracking and measurement capabilities.

Rich-media banners Banner ads that engage a viewer by means of a contest, game, or request for information.

Rifle strategy A strategy that involves using a specific medium that effectively reaches a target market defined by a common characteristic.

Roadblocking Buying up space at the same time on many stations and programs so that the viewers can barely avoid seeing the commercial.

ROP (run of paper or run of press) The placing of advertisements anywhere within the regular printed pages of a newspaper.

ROP colour A colour process printed in a newspaper during the regular press run.

ROS (run of schedule) A discount offered to advertisers who allow the television or radio station to schedule the commercial at its own discretion.

Rotation plan A selection of radio time slots, specified by the advertiser and based on time of day (vertical rotation) and day of week (horizontal rotation).

Rough art The drawing of an advertisement, done to actual size and with the various elements (i.e., headline, copy, illustration, and signature) included to show relative size and position.

Rough cut The best film takes (as shot on location or in a studio) spliced together to form the video portion of a television commercial.

Sales presentation A persuasive delivery and demonstration of a product's benefits in a personal-selling situation.

Sales promotion Activity designed to generate prompt response from consumers, distributors, and the field sales force.

Sample Free distribution of a product to potential new users.

Satellite paper A publication whose typesetting signal is sent to distant printing facilities via satellite for regional or expanded national distribution.

Script A document used in the production of television and radio commercials. In the case of television, the script describes the video presentation on one side, the audio on the other. In the case of radio, the audio presentation, sound effects, and music are described in the script.

Search advertising An advertiser's listing placed within or alongside search results in exchange for paying a fee each time someone clicks on the listing in a search situation.

Seasonal discounts (television) Discounts offered to advertisers in traditionally slow seasons. (Television viewership drops in the summer, so additional summer discounts are offered.)

Seasonal schedule A schedule whereby media spending is heavier in the preseason (to create awareness) and tapers off during the season of usage.

Secondary research The compiling and publishing of data by disinterested sources; the data are used by companies for purposes other than resolving a specific problem.

Selective media plan (rifle strategy) A plan for reaching a specific target market via a specific-interest medium.

Selective-spot advertising During a network show, some commercial time is not allocated and is left to regional or local stations to sell. Advertisers can purchase this time on a station-by-station basis.

Self-concept An individual's understanding of him- or herself. (In advertising, four categories of consumer self-concept are significant: real self, self-image, looking-glass self, and ideal self.)

Short-form DRTV Short direct-response television commercials lasting from 15 to 120 seconds.

Short rate A charge incurred by an advertiser who does not meet a contractual estimate of advertising time or space.

Shortlist A brief list of the advertising agencies that a prospective client is interested in hiring; the agencies are invited to make a business presentation to the client (to win an account).

Shotgun strategy A strategy involving the use of mass media to reach a more loosely defined (i.e., more general) target market.

Showing In outdoor advertising, the purchase of multiple panels in a geographic market to maximize reach.

Signature The part of an ad that closes the selling message. It usually contains the brand name, logo, and slogan. It is often called a tagline.

Simulcasting A situation in which an episode of a U.S. network program is scheduled to appear on a Canadian station at the same time. Cable companies must carry the Canadian signal, and, therefore, viewers are exposed to Canadian advertising.

Situation analysis The compilation of internal and external data to assist in resolving a problem.

Skip schedule The purchase of media time and space on an alternating basis (every other week, month, etc.); use of alternate media types.

Skyscrapers Tall, skinny, oblong ads that appear on the side of a webpage.

Slippage When a consumer collects proofs of purchase for a refund offer but neglects to follow through and submit a request for the refund.

Social classes Hierarchically ordered groups whose members share similar values, interests, and beliefs.

Social network website A website that connects people with different interests in a social environment. Such a network may also have a specific focus or topic of interest.

Social responsibility marketing In conducting business, a firm considers the best interests of consumers and society.

Solo direct mail Individually prepared and distributed direct-mail offers. Also called selective direct mail.

Spam Inappropriate use of a mailing list or other communications facility as if it were a broadcast medium. Also referred to as junk email.

Specialty advertising A form of advertising that uses items, often clothing or small gifts, to communicate an advertiser's name, logo, and brief message.

Spectacular A non-standardized outdoor advertising unit constructed according to the customized specifications of the advertiser (often with protruding components, to attract attention).

Split run A situation in which an advertiser splits the full circulation of a newspaper to test two different advertisements—half the circulation contains one ad; the other half contains another ad. It is commonly used to test the effectiveness of different advertising layouts.

Split 30s Two 15-second commercials for the same product, one appearing at the start and one at the end of a commercial cluster.

Spot television The purchase of local broadcast time on a station-by-station basis (sometimes called selective spot).

Stair risers Ads that appear on the sides of steps in subways.

Starch readership test A post-test recognition procedure that measures readers' recall of an advertisement (noted), their ability to identify the sponsor (associated), and whether they read more than half of the written material (read most).

Statement stuffers (bounce backs) Advertisements that are distributed by monthly charge account statements.

Station posters Advertisements located on platforms and entrance and exit areas of subway and light rail transit systems.

Storyboard A set of graphic renderings in a television-frame format, accompanied by appropriate copy, depicting what a finished commercial will look like.

Strategic alliance A relationship between two or more companies who decide to work co-operatively to achieve common goals.

Strategic planning The process of determining objectives and identifying strategies and tactics that will contribute to the achievement of objectives.

Strategies Statements that outline how objectives will be achieved.

Subculture Subgroups of a larger culture that have distinctive lifestyles, yet maintain important features of the dominant culture.

Subheadline (subhead) A smaller headline that amplifies the main point of a headline.

Super A print message superimposed on a television frame.

Superboard (bigboard) In outdoor advertising, a much larger outdoor poster that is more expensive to produce.

Superbus A bus completely covered so that it displays an advertising message.

Supplements Prepaid and preprinted advertisements inserted into the folds of newspapers (commonly used by large department store chains).

Support-claims statement A statement describing the principal characteristics of a product or service that substantiate the promises made about the product in the key-benefit statement.

Sweepstakes A chance promotion involving a giveaway of products or services of value to randomly selected participants.

SWOT analysis An evaluation of a brand's (company's) strengths, weaknesses, opportunities, and threats.

Tagline An alternative expression for the signature portion of an advertisement. Usually includes the brand name, a distinctive logo, and a slogan.

Target market (or target audience) A specific group of individuals at whom an advertising message is directed.

Tearsheet A page supplied to an advertiser by a newspaper that carries the advertiser's insertion; the tearsheet verifies that the advertisement ran as scheduled.

Telemarketing (and telefaxing) Advertising that uses telecommunications to promote the products and services of a business.

Testimonial A form of advertising in which a credible source, usually a typical consumer, presents the product message.

Text messaging The transmission of text-only messages on wireless devices such as cell phones and personal digital assistants.

Thumbnail sketches Small, experimental sketches of a variety of design concepts.

Tipping Gluing items into the seam (gutter) of a magazine (e.g., recipe pamphlets or small catalogues).

Torture test An advertising technique whereby a product is exposed to extremely harsh punishment in a commercial to substantiate a claim.

Total paid circulation In print, the total of all classes of a publication's distribution for which the ultimate purchasers have paid (single-copy sales plus subscription sales).

Trade advertising Advertising by manufacturers directed at channel members to secure distribution of the advertised product.

Trade allowance A temporary price reduction intended to encourage larger purchases by distributors.

Trade promotions Promotion activity directed at distributors and designed to encourage volume purchases and merchandising support for a manufacturer's product.

Trade show An event that allows a company to showcase its products to a captive audience. Buyers visit trade shows to seek new information; hence, the show is a means for a company to generate leads.

Transient rate The base rate, or open rate, charged to casual advertisers in a newspaper; it is the maximum rate charged.

Transit cards (or car cards) Print advertisements contained in racks above the windows of public-transit vehicles.

Trial close A failed attempt at closing a sale.

Triples Three transit ads placed side by side, giving advertisers more impact capability.

Unaided recall A research situation where respondents are provided no information to encourage thought.

Unity (print) The blending of all elements in a print advertisement to create a complete impression.

Unity (television) The visual and aural flow of a broadcast commercial, from the customer's perspective.

USP The unique selling points of a particular brand.

Venue marketing The linking of a brand name to a physical site such as an arena, stadium, or theatre.

Vertical co-operative advertising The sharing of advertising costs between a supplier and a retailer.

Vertical publications Publications that reach people with different jobs in the same industry.

Vertical rotation The placement of radio commercials based on the time of day.

Vertical split A type of print advertisement layout in which copy dominates one side and illustration the other—left and right sides are divided by an imaginary line down the middle of the page.

Viral marketing A situation where the receiver of an electronic message is encouraged to pass it on to friends.

Virtual advertising The insertion of electronic images such as signs, logos, and packages into live or taped programs.

Visit A sequence of hits made by one user at an internet site.

Voice-over Spoken copy or dialogue delivered by an announcer who is heard but not seen.

Volume discount A discount that is based on the dollar volume purchased over a 52-week period.

Web browser A software program that allows the user to navigate the World Wide Web.

Website A company's location on the internet. A website provides a company the opportunity to communicate information about itself, including words, graphics, video clips, and audio clips.

White space The part of an advertisement that is not occupied by any elements.

Wild postings Ads that appear on the sides of hoardings at construction sites (often in downtown areas).

Wipe An optical effect in a television commercial that involves one scene pushing the other away.

World Wide Web The collection of websites on the internet.

Zapping The practice of switching channels by means of a remote control device to avoid commercial messages.

Zipping A method of reducing commercial viewing that involves fast-forwarding them or eliminating them with a PVR.

Index

516   INDEX